D1561499

Augustine and Tradition

AUGUSTINE AND TRADITION

INFLUENCES, CONTEXTS, LEGACY

Essays in Honor of J. Patout Burns

·

Edited by

DAVID G. HUNTER AND JONATHAN P. YATES

WILLIAM B. EERDMANS PUBLISHING COMPANY
GRAND RAPIDS, MICHIGAN

Wm. B. Eerdmans Publishing Co.
4035 Park East Court SE, Grand Rapids, Michigan 49546
www.eerdmans.com

27 26 25 24 23 22 21   1 2 3 4 5 6 7

ISBN 978-0-8028-7699-7

Library of Congress Cataloging-in-Publication Data

Names: Hunter, David G., editor. | Yates, Jonathan, 1969– editor.
Title: Augustine and tradition : influences, contexts, legacy ; essays in honor of
   J. Patout Burns / edited by David G. Hunter and Jonathan P. Yates.
Description: Grand Rapids, Michigan : Wm. B. Eerdmans Publishing Co., 2021.
   | Includes bibliographical references and index. | Summary: "An analysis of
   Augustine's life and writings in the context of other traditions—those preceding
   him and contemporary with him—as a way of better understanding his signifi-
   cance in religious and cultural heritage"—Provided by publisher.
Identifiers: LCCN 2021021561 | ISBN 9780802876997
Subjects: LCSH: Augustine, of Hippo, Saint, 354-430. | LCGFT: Essays.
Classification: LCC BR65.A9 A8625 2021 | DDC 270.2092—dc23
LC record available at https://lccn.loc.gov/2021021561

Contents

I

AUGUSTINE AND THE NORTH AFRICAN TRADITION

CONTENTS

II

AUGUSTINE AND THE PHILOSOPHICAL
AND LITERARY TRADITION

III

AUGUSTINE AND THE GREEK PATRISTIC TRADITION

IV

AUGUSTINE AND HIS LATIN
CONTEMPORARIES/SUCCESSORS

Contents

Acknowledgments

The editors gratefully acknowledge the Cottrill-Rolfes Chair of Catholic Studies at the University of Kentucky for providing a subvention that made possible the publication of this volume. At Boston College Mr. Austin J. Holmes and Mr. Jordan Parro, PhD students in theology, provided valuable editorial assistance in the final phases of its preparation.

The editors also wish to acknowledge that the late Professor Maureen Tilley, who collaborated closely with Professor J. Patout Burns on studies of early Christianity in North Africa, would have been a very willing contributor to this volume if her untimely death had not intervened. Her presence is deeply missed.

INTRODUCTION

The present volume took its first steps toward becoming reality over the course of one particular morning. It was Sunday, November 20, 2016, and we (Jonathan and David) had just finished breakfast at David's hotel in San Antonio, Texas. We were both in Texas for the Annual Meeting of the American Academy of Religion and the Society of Biblical Literature. The weather was particularly nice, so we decided to take in the Riverwalk, which had not yet become busy. As we were walking, we stopped on a landing of one of the many staircases that connect the two levels of the area and began to discuss in earnest whether or not something like this collection might actually be feasible. It was not our first discussion of this project, yet we both recognized that the time had come either to commit to the project or to let it go—regardless of its merit, much less of the considerable merits and contributions of its honoree, J. Patout Burns. By the end of 2016, the arrangements had been made and the project was underway.

Our original plan was to have the volume literally in hand in time to honor Patout on the occasion of his eightieth birthday, which would be celebrated in October of 2019. While that proved impossible for several reasons, we persevered, convinced that, whenever we finally handed Patout his copy, the investments of all involved would be well compensated. As we began to plan the volume's contents, we quickly recognized that Patout's wide-ranging and long-running contributions both to systematic theology and to historical theology would make finding the necessary common ground for a single volume a challenge. In the end, we decided that Augustine of Hippo should be the focus. Not only do both of us have expertise in this area of study (one that continues to attract historians, theologians, philosophers, and ethicists from all over the world), but it is argu-ably the area that Patout himself knows best, his aforementioned expansiveness notwithstanding.

The title we settled on is *Augustine and Tradition: Influences, Contexts, Legacy*. While we never lost sight of the goal to add to current scholarship on Augustine himself, we determined that it would be useful to examine Augustine's relation-ship to the traditions that preceded him and to some of his most important Christian contemporaries. These would necessarily include literary, theological, and philosophical traditions, as well as scripture and liturgy. We also wanted it, as Patout's own research and writing have frequently done, to begin with the Christian traditions of North Africa and the Mediterranean world, as well as those representatives of Greco-Roman culture who exerted the most influence on Augustine. The unifying theme of this volume is contained in the follow-ing questions: To what extent did Augustine's thought, teaching, or exegesis converge with or diverge from the traditions of his day? How did the cultural traditions of late antiquity shape him and how did he shape them?

Choosing appropriate contributors to this volume proved to be a challenge, albeit a gratifying one. While we considered it desirable that contributors have some direct connection to Patout either as friends, colleagues, or former stu-dents, it was also essential that they be experts in the areas that had to be cov-ered, which ranged widely across the cultural fields of late antiquity. Fortunately, Patout's range has been equally wide, and we were able to invite a spectrum of scholars, junior and senior, to write on the required topics. As the table of contents shows, we were able to recruit experts in North African liturgy and martyrology (Andrew McGowan and William Tabbernee) as well as scriptural interpretation (Michael Cameron); essays on the North African writers Ter-tullian and Optatus of Milevis also appear (Geoffrey Dunn and Alden Bass). Augustine's relation to prior philosophical traditions naturally looms large in a volume such as this, and several chapters are devoted to Neoplatonic and other philosophical influences (John Peter Kenney, Thomas Clemmons, and James Wetzel) as well as to the classical Latin literary tradition (Dennis Trout). Lastly, we were fortunate to enlist studies on several Greek patristic theologians, Origen and the Cappadocians (Joseph Trigg and Mark DelCogliano), and a variety of Augustine's Latin predecessors and contemporaries, Marius Victorinus (Stephen Cooper), Ambrosiaster (Theodore de Bruyn), and Ambrose (John C. Cavadini). The collection is rounded out with a chapter on Augustine's *Nachleben* in the ninth-century theological controversies on predestination (Brian Matz).

Introduction

In the interest of informing the readers of this book about its honoree, some attention to the course of Patout's education and intellectual development is in order. His intellectual formation took place in a variety of contexts and has undergone considerable evolution over the course of his life. Like St. Augustine himself, Patout responded to new situations and new challenges with an intellectual flexibility that has enabled him to remain open to varied approaches to historical and theological research. This brief biography will sketch some of the main stages in this development.

JESUIT

Patout's initial postsecondary education took place as part of his formation as a priest in the Society of Jesus (Jesuits). It began in 1957 at St. Charles College in Grand Coteau, Louisiana, with language studies—the focus was on Latin, but his program included Greek and French as well. The Jesuit novices read Cicero, Vergil, Ovid, Horace, and some of the historians, primarily to gain facility in both written and spoken Latin. Graduate studies in philosophy followed at Assumption Hall, Spring Hill College, in Mobile, Alabama. Following the curriculum of the Gregorian University in Rome with variations introduced by the interest of some of the professors, these studies remained largely within the scholastic system.

At this juncture Patout came under the influence of the Jesuit philosopher Arnold Benedetto, SJ, who introduced him to what would become his most satisfying work: the reading and interpretation of philosophical and theological systems through the analysis of primary texts. Under the tutelage of Benedetto, Patout began to study the writings of Francisco Suárez, SJ, who died in 1617. Suárez was the first to use prose exposition—as opposed to the medieval *quaestio* method—an approach that proved enormously influential as a way of interpreting scholasticism. This led to Patout's first academic publication.[1] Other philosophical studies at this time included the sixteenth-century controversy *de auxiliis* (how God moves creatures into action) between Bañez and Molina. Attention to the question of the divine assistance in conversion and the problem of willing the good presaged Patout's later examination of this issue in the writings of Augustine.

---

1. "Action in Suárez," *New Scholasticism* 38 (1964): 453–72. In 1990 the title of the journal was changed to *American Catholic Philosophical Quarterly*.

Toward the end of his philosophical studies (1963–1964), Patout began to read contemporary Catholic existential philosophy. Of even greater influence, however, was Joseph Maréchal's *Le point de départ de la métaphysique*, a work that Patout examined in a seminar that year. This would result in two articles: one finished when he was teaching at Spring Hill College during the third year of "regency" as a Jesuit scholastic, the other written during his first year of theological studies at Regis College in Toronto.[2] The influence of Benedetto during these years was profound. As Patout himself has described it, "Benedetto's guidance and example were foundational for me as a scholar and a teacher. He taught me to attend to systems of thought as integrated wholes and opened the way into intellectual history."[3] As Patout moved on to his studies at Regis College, he continued to work in this manner and to apply the methods that he had learned under Benedetto.

In Toronto, Patout worked primarily under Frederick Crowe, SJ, whose technique in teaching was to track the historical development of Christian doctrines as they became dogmas. At this point Patout began to read the work of Bernard Lonergan, SJ, including his articles on operative grace that were based on his dissertation. Lonergan's work on grace showed how Aquinas's explanation of God's operation in human beings changed over the course of his writing career. Lonergan was also able to interpret Thomas's final position by highlighting the developments within his understanding of human freedom of choice, the forms of divine assistance necessary, and the ways in which divine providence ruled the material universe. Patout later received permission from Lonergan to prepare an edition of the *Gratia Operans* articles that could be published in book form. This volume appeared in 1971.[4]

At the same time, Fred Crowe decided to offer a course on the history of grace, and Patout entered his class especially interested to read Augustine as a source of Aquinas's teaching on grace. Reading Augustine under the influence of Lonergan and Crowe meant looking for development and, by extension, working against the reigning assumption that Augustine had not changed but had only become clearer and more explicit in expressing his fundamental insights.

2. "Maréchal's Approach to the Existence of God," *New Scholasticism* 43 (1968): 72–90; "Spiritual Dynamism in Maréchal," *The Thomist* 32 (1968): 528–39.

3. Private communication to the editors.

4. Bernard Lonergan, *Grace and Freedom: Operative Grace in the Thought of St. Thomas Aquinas*, ed. J. Patout Burns (New York: Herder, 1971).

Patout discovered a change in Augustine's explanation of the operative grace of conversion and the beginning of faith by comparing *Ad Simplicianum* to the works against Pelagius. As he proceeded from Toronto to Yale to pursue doctoral studies, this issue became central to his doctoral dissertation.

In his application to Yale to work with Jaroslav Pelikan, Patout proposed a fuller study of the grace of conversion in Augustine. It proved to be a thesis that could be controlled, even though it meant reading everything that could be dated with any certainty in Augustine—that is, everything except the preached works. After courses with Hans Frei, David Kelsey, George Lindbeck, and of course Pelikan, Patout graduated in December 1974, although the dissertation was not ready for publication for another three years. While he had applied to Yale with the intention of becoming a systematic theologian—in the model of Fred Crowe, with an interest in the Holy Spirit and the church—he left Yale considerably more committed to historical theology.

PROFESSOR

From 1974 to 1980 Patout served as assistant professor and then associate professor of historical theology at the Jesuit School of Theology in Chicago. These years saw the publication of his dissertation-based book, *The Development of Augustine's Doctrine of Operative Grace*,[5] as well as two collections of primary source readings that have continued to serve as textbooks. A volume on the Holy Spirit, with Gerald Fagin, SJ, was published by Michael Glazier and later reprinted by Wipf & Stock.[6] Another anthology, *Theological Anthropology*, has been in use since 1981, and Burns is now preparing a second edition for the Fortress series Ad Fontes.[7]

After a brief tenure at Loyola University in Chicago, during which time he served as chair of the Department of Theology (1980–1985), Patout's academic life took a different turn. Leaving the Society of Jesus, for the next fifteen years Patout taught in secular universities: first in the Department of Religion at the University of Florida (1986–1990) and then in an endowed chair at Washington

---

5. Paris: Études Augustiniennes, 1980.

6. J. Patout Burns and Gerald M. Fagin, *The Holy Spirit*, Message of the Fathers of the Church 3 (Wilmington, DE: Glazier, 1984; repr., Eugene, OR: Wipf & Stock, 2002).

7. *Theological Anthropology*, Sources of Early Christian Thought (Philadelphia: Fortress, 1981).

University in St. Louis (1990–1999). These new contexts provided the opportunity to adopt new perspectives and to learn new methods in the study of religion. In a faculty seminar he was introduced to the work of Mary Douglas by Dennis Owen and Sheldon (Shaya) Isenberg. Douglas's system of analysis of a culture on the basis of its coherence (group) and its internal differentiation of membership (grid) provided a way to identify a tendency to give more or less efficacy to certain rituals that affect, in their turn, other aspects of the culture.

Utilizing the insights of Douglas to interpret the rich information contained in the surviving correspondence of Cyprian of Carthage, together with the excellent work of Graeme Clarke that sets those documents in their historical context, Patout came to see that Douglas's method might provide clues that would help answer the question of why Cyprian's baptismal theology failed to carry the day in third-century Christianity. His application of Douglas's social anthropology to North African sacramental theology eventually led to a monograph on Cyprian and his legacy.[8]

But a new project soon appeared on the horizon. Robin Jensen (soon to be Patout's partner in life as well as in scholarship) initiated a proposal to the National Endowment for the Humanities for a multidisciplinary study of Christianity in North Africa that would attempt to coordinate literary with archeological evidence. Its objective was to demonstrate the interaction between religious practice and doctrine. The proposal included two archaeologists (Graeme Clarke and Susan Stevens), an epigrapher (William Tabbernee), an art historian (Robin Jensen), and two historical theologians (Maureen Tilley and Patout himself). All six participated in an initial trip to Tunisia in the summer of 1996; later Robin Jensen, Maureen Tilley, and Patout participated in another conference on North African Christianity in Algeria in 2001. Other scholars joined them in semiannual sessions at annual meetings of the North American Patristics Society and the Society of Biblical Literature to study particular topics. A little more than a decade later, the group committed the results of these studies to Patout and Robin Jensen to produce a manuscript for publication. The volume was published in 2014.[9]

In 1999 Patout moved from Washington University to an endowed chair in Catholic studies at Vanderbilt University Divinity School. As the North Africa project began to show promise, Patout submitted a proposal to the Luce Foun-

8. *Cyprian the Bishop* (London: Routledge, 2002).
9. J. Patout Burns Jr. and Robin M. Jensen, *Christianity in Roman Africa: The Development of Its Practices and Beliefs* (Grand Rapids: Eerdmans, 2014).

dation for a study of the theology that Augustine preached in his sermons, his commentaries on the Psalms, and his expositions of the Johannine literature. His objective was twofold: to compare and contrast his preached theology with the controversial theology that we find in his treatises against, for example, the Donatists and the Pelagians, and to attend to the role of practices in shaping doctrine. Augustine's sermons contain more evidence of actual church practice than what is revealed by his expository or controversial treatises. This research contributed to the Roman Africa project as well as to his own project on preaching. The latter study, which is currently in preparation for Eerdmans, builds on and provides much greater specificity for the practices and doctrines that it covers than did the North Africa book.

Emeritus

In 2011 Patout retired from Vanderbilt as emeritus professor, but he has remained active both as a teacher and a researcher. In 2015 Robin Jensen was appointed to the Department of Theology of the University of Notre Dame as Patrick O'Brien Professor of Theology, and Patout was offered a courtesy appointment as Guest Professor of Theology. He occasionally participates in seminars, regularly consults with doctoral students, and sometimes serves on dissertation committees. As noted above, he maintains several active research projects related to North African Christianity and Augustine's preached theology. Having contributed to several historical and theological fields over the last half century, including more than four decades of teaching at notable universities, Patout shows few signs of slowing down. He remains a model and inspiration for readers and scholars of Augustine all over the world. This collection of essays is but a small token of thanks and admiration to this distinguished scholar, colleague, and friend.

Abbreviations

For the abbreviations of patristic works, we have followed the system of the *SBL Handbook of Style*, 2nd ed. The exception is the works of Augustine, which are abbreviated according to the system of the *Augustinus-Lexikon*.

ACW	Ancient Christian Writers
ANF	*Ante-Nicene Fathers*
AttA	*Augustine through the Ages: An Encyclopedia*. Edited by Allan D. Fitzgerald. Grand Rapids: Eerdmans, 1999
AugLex	*Augustinus-Lexikon*. Edited by Cornelius Mayer et al. 5 vols. Basle: Schwabe, 1986–
AugStud	*Augustinian Studies*
BA	Bibliothèque Augustinienne
BETL	Bibliotheca Ephemeridum Theologicarum Lovaniensium
CCCM	Corpus Christianorum: Continuatio mediaevalis. Turnhout: Brepols, 1969–
CCSL	Corpus Christianorum: Series Latina. Turnhout: Brepols, 1953–
ColAug	Collectanea Augustiniana
CPG	*Clavis Patrum Graecorum*. Edited by Maurice Geerard. 5 vols. Turnhout: Brepols, 1974–1987
CPL	*Clavis Patrum Latinorum*. Edited by Eligius Dekkers. 2nd ed. Steenbrugis: Abbatia Sancti Petri, 1961
CSEL	Corpus Scriptorum Ecclesiasticorum Latinorum
ECF	Early Church Fathers

Abbreviations

FC	Fathers of the Church
HTR	*Harvard Theological Review*
IPM	Instrumenta Patristica et Mediaevalia
JECS	*Journal of Early Christian Studies*
JLA	*Journal of Late Antiquity*
JTS	*Journal of Theological Studies*
LAHR	Late Antique History and Religion
LCL	Loeb Classical Library
MA	*Miscellanea Agostiniana.* Edited by Germain Morin and Antonio Casamassa. 2 vols. Rome: Tipografia Poliglotta Vaticana, 1930–1931
NPNF¹	*Nicene and Post-Nicene Fathers,* Series 1
NPNF²	*Nicene and Post-Nicene Fathers,* Series 2
OECS	Oxford Early Christian Studies
PatrMS	Patristic Monograph Series
PG	Patrologia Graeca. Edited by Jacques-Paul Migne. 162 vols. Paris, 1857–1886
PL	Patrologia Latina. Edited by Jacques-Paul Migne. 217 vols. Paris, 1844–1864
RBén	*Revue bénédictine*
REAug	*Revue des études augustiniennes et patristiques*
RechAug	*Recherches Augustiniennes*
SAQ	Sammlung ausgewählter Kirchen- und dogmen-geschichtlicher Quellenschriften
SC	Sources chrétiennes
SEAug	Studia Ephemeridis Augustinianum
SHCT	Studies in the History of Christian Traditions
StPatr	*Studia Patristica*
TTH	Translated Texts for Historians
VC	*Vigiliae Christianae*
VCSup	Supplements to Vigiliae Christianae
WGRW	Writings from the Graeco-Roman World
WS	*Wiener Studien*
WSA	The Works of Saint Augustine: A Translation for the 21st Century. Hyde Park, NY: New City, 1990–

PART I

·

Augustine and the North African Tradition

Chapter 1

Augustine's Rhetorical Reading of Genesis in *Confessiones* 11–12

Michael Cameron

Introduction:
The Puzzle of Scripture's Function in *Confessiones*

Augustine dapples *Confessiones* (*conf.*) with so many scripture quotations, fragments, allusions, evocations, and echoes—more than 1,500 by one count[1]—that he can seem to muffle his own voice. Augustine tells us that, at the time of writing, scripture was his constant waking companion; practically speaking, so must it be for readers who wish to enter the depths of his book. Yet they must not merely note the citations as tools of proof, walls of defense, or types of allegory. Scripture is existentially vital, even visceral to Augustine in *Confessiones*; he clings to it as a drowning man clutches driftwood, not merely quoting it but digesting and transforming it into his personal idiom in a way that invites the reader to do the same. Grasping scripture's function in this work therefore calls for something different and more comprehensive than making lists, something that will make sense of Augustine's experience and strategy in using it the way he does.

Two big questions arise from scripture's appearance in *Confessiones*. First, how does Augustine come to understand the texts so as to frame and advance

---

I mark here my deep gratitude to Patout Burns, for his superb scholarship, with its analytical depth and ambidextrous facility in history and theology, and for his model of writing clarity, important since graduate school when I discovered *The Development of Augustine's Doctrine of Operative Grace*. Later I came to know Patout's personal generosity and wisdom, and have benefited often from his kindness and good advice over many years.

1. A. Solignac, "Loci Sacrae Scripturae," BA 14:667–79.

his story? This is a *hermeneutical* question. Second, how does he present the texts so as to teach and persuade readers toward his ends? This is a *rhetorical* question. The two questions can be distinguished but not separated; each deeply implicates the other. Getting a handle on Augustine's use of scripture in *Confessiones* will require broad examination from different angles.

I limit this chapter to investigating books 11–12, which form something of a unity for their intense focus on a single text, Gen. 1:1: "In the beginning God made heaven and earth." The chapter imports a template from recent scholarship called "hermeneutical rhetoric" as a tool to explore a fresh approach to Augustine's reading of this text in these two books.

Setting Context for Scripture's Function in Confessiones

The heavy use of scripture in *Confessiones* calls for framing within the context of Augustine's purpose for writing and awareness of his audience. This emerges briefly at the start of book 11's examination of reasons for writing as Augustine turns from autobiographical storytelling to his close reading of Genesis: "I do it to arouse my own loving devotion towards you, and that of my readers."[2] Thomas F. Martin, drawing on the work of Pierre Hadot, discerns a pedagogy in *Confessiones* in Augustine's construction of "spiritual exercises."[3] Annemaré Kotzé, following Erich Feldmann and others, speaks broadly of Augustine's purpose to produce a "protreptic" that aims "to change both the worldview and the conduct of the addressee."[4] Knowing scripture—that is, learning to surrender to its formative grace and power—is the modus operandi of this change (i.e., conversion). Hence *Confessiones* not only cites the Bible but also models ways of reading it. Each citation trains apprentices to read alongside Augustine as he

2. *Conf.* 11.1.1 (BA 14:270; trans. Boulding, *Confessions*, WSA I/1, 284): "cur ergo tibi tot rerum narrationes digero? non utique ut per me noueris ea, sed affectum meum excito in te et eorum, qui haec legunt."

3. Thomas F. Martin, OSA, "Augustine's *Confessiones* as Pedagogy: Exercises in Transformation," in *Augustine and Liberal Education*, ed. Kim Paffenroth and Kevin L. Hughes (Aldershot, UK: Ashgate, 2000), 25–51.

4. Kotzé often links protreptic with paraenetic, which "presupposes a shared worldview" and therefore "aims only at improving the conduct of its audience." She often combines these adjectivally as "protreptic-paraenetic." Annemaré Kotzé, *Augustine's "Confessiones": Communicative Purpose and Audience* (Leiden: Brill, 2004), 58; in relation to books 11–13, see 169–70, 181–96. See also her article "The Puzzle of the Last Four Books of *Confessiones*: An Illegitimate Issue?," *VC* 60 (2006): 65–79, and Erich Feldmann, "*Confessiones*," *AugLex* 1:1134–93.

tells his story and stages performative scripture readings for them to imitate. Augustine uses biblical fragments as small hermeneutical footbridges over which readers may carry their stories into Augustine's biblically inspired story, and thus cross over into scripture for themselves.

The scriptural fragments appear as part of a story he tells about his developing relationship to the Bible itself, a long twisting journey that eventually arrives at the perspective from which *Confessiones* is written. He stumbles out of the gate onto that rocky road, first rejecting the Bible, then distorting it, before reorienting to it, accepting it, and finally embracing and savoring it. In so doing Augustine imitates the unforgettable text that had wooed him to seek wisdom as an older adolescent, Cicero's *Hortensius,* a book that had changed his young feelings and prayers to God. That encounter leads to a first experimental reading of the Bible that ends badly and sets off a decade's downward spiral. But when Ambrose reverses and expands his thinking about scripture, it sets the stage for Augustine's biblically induced embrace of Nicene Christianity. Thereafter Augustine immerses himself in biblical texts, especially the Psalms, and he passes through the gates of the new "world of the text" that scripture opens up.[5] He invites readers to enter that world with him, offering in the final three books of *Confessiones* to immerse readers in the book of Genesis and to take a sustained look into his life and thinking beneath scripture's load-bearing sky-dome.[6] There is revealed the full perspective from which *Confessiones* has

5. For Augustine in *Confessiones* the Bible is more than a book; it is a way of seeing, an ethos, a total environment that yields life, correction, mercy, and nourishment. He pictures himself living in and from scripture like a forager in a teeming forest (*conf.* 11.2.3). To convey this totality, I borrow the concept of "the world of the text" from the hermeneutical approach of Paul Ricoeur. He writes, "To speak of the world of the text is to emphasize that trait of every literary work by which it opens up a horizon of possible experience, a world in which it would be possible to dwell. A text is not an entity closed in upon itself; it is the projection of a new universe, different from the one in which we live. Appropriating a work through reading it is to unfold the implicit horizon of the world which embraces the action, the personages, the events of the story told." Paul Ricoeur, "Life: A Story in Search of a Narrator," trans. J. N. Kraay and A. J. Scholten, in *A Ricoeur Reader: Reflection and Imagination,* ed. M. J. Valdés (Toronto: University of Toronto Press, 1991), 431.

6. The metaphor Augustine uses to describe scripture's all-embracing authority is *firmamentum,* taken from the description of the creation of sky in Gen. 1:7–8 (*conf.* 13.15.16). Sarah Ruden comments that "a *firmamentum* in Latin is a support or prop, mainly one used in building, so that a cunning author could riff on and on about physical and spiritual support" (Augustine, *Confessions,* trans. Sarah Ruden [New York: Modern Library, 2017], xxix–xxx.) Is-

been written, which has merged genres of protreptic, spiritual exercises, and Christian storytelling with rhetorically appropriated biblical fragments. This embeds the scriptural subplot of his individual turn to God within the larger story of the cosmic turn to God told in scripture, "from the beginning when you made heaven and earth to that everlasting reign when we shall be with you in your holy city."[7]

Scripture Reading for Self-Understanding

What sort of scriptural "world" does Augustine arrive at in the latter books of *Confessiones*? Augustine himself writes of the dual structure of *Confessiones* in his retrospective *Retractationes* (*retr.*), where he says that the first part, books 1–10, comes "from my own life," and the second part, books 11–13, "from sacred Scripture."[8] Older scholarship tended to prioritize part 1's vivid narrative, even if that turns part 2 into a dry and virtually unintelligible addendum that goes off the exegetical rails. Recent scholarship reverses this view, positing books 11–13 as the work's climax and books 1–10 as an extended narrative introduction. In this perspective, Augustine's story moves from pagan literature to holy scripture[9] and emerges into the world opened up by scripture as "the outcome of the journey" toward self-understanding.[10]

abelle Bochet uses the word as a master image for her magisterial study of Augustine's interpretative practice, *"Le firmament de l'Écriture": L'herméneutique augustinienne* (Paris: Études Augustiniennes, 2004). Jacques Ollier uses it for his study focused on *Confessiones*, referred to below, titled *Firmamentum narrat: La théorie augustinienne des "Confessiones"* (Paris: Collège des Bernadins, 2011).

7. *Conf.* 11.2.3 (BA 14:276; trans. Boulding, 286): "ab usque principio, in quo fecisti caelum et terram usque ad regnum tecum perpetuum sanctae ciuitatis tuae." Cf. Marie-Anne Vannier, *"Creatio," "Conversio," "Formatio" chez S. Augustin*, Paradosis 31 (Fribourg: Éditions Universitaires, 1991), 123–37.

8. *Retr.* 2.6[5].1 (BA 12:461): "de me ... de sanctis scripturis." Kotzé, following Marjorie O'Rourke Boyle, argues for translating *de* as "(deriving) from" rather than the more usual "about" (*Augustine's "Confessiones,"* 22–23).

9. Leo C. Ferrari, "From Pagan Literature to the Pages of the Holy Scriptures: Augustine's *Confessiones* as Exemplary Propaedeutic," in *Kerygma und Logos: Festschrift für C. Andresen*, ed. A. M. Ritter (Göttingen: Vandenhoeck & Ruprecht, 1979), 173–82.

10. Isabelle Bochet, "Interprétation scripturaire et compréhension de soi: Du *De doctrina christiana* aux *Confessiones* de Saint Augustin," in *Comprendre et interpréter: Le paradigm herméneutique de la raison*, ed. Jean Greisch (Paris: Beauchêsne, 1993), 29. Bochet's phrase is "l'aboutissement de l'itinéraire." Translations from this work are mine.

At the beginning of book 11 Augustine shifts gears. Declining to continue his narrative into his immediate postbaptismal story, Augustine focuses instead on the marvels of reading scripture as the one thing he considers still worth telling about his life. But the perspective achieved narratively with this "arrival" has been operative all through *Confessiones*; the same spiritually remade man who plumbs the depths of Genesis in part 2 also fashions the narrative of part 1. Thus there exists "a direct relation between the two parts": part 1's confession of sin and praise depends on part 2's perspective looking out from within scripture's world, "for the only one who can gain access to such a confession is the self that allows itself to be instructed and judged by Scripture."[11] This tightly wound circular unity means that the "place of arrival is at the same time a point of departure. For the reading of scripture is *the very mainspring of the work* [emphasis added]: indeed, it is what makes possible the new self-comprehension that Augustine presents in the *Confessiones*."[12] In testimony to this circularity, many note that Augustine's wonderstruck praise in the opening line of *Confessiones* ("Great are you, O Lord, and exceedingly worthy of praise" (a composite of Ps 47:2 [48:1], 95[96]:4, and 144[145]:3) reappears at the beginning of book 11. The difference is his later explicit inclusion of his reading community. The Psalms mosaic in book 1 launches Augustine's individualized story, whereas book 11 hopes that "together we may declare" its words—that is, to co-inhabit the Psalms within a shared space of soul.[13] Books 11 and 12 train readers to offer the same full-throated confession of love and praise for God that moved Augustine to write in the first place. In so doing, he hopes, readers will commence writing their own editions of *Confessiones*.

The Fundamental Role of Rhetoric

Augustine's concern for his audience draws our attention to strategies of communication in *Confessiones*; the mosaic of scriptural texts-within-texts is one of these. It is easy to overlook the importance of such rhetorical strategies in Augustine, either by reducing them to abstract principles (e.g., from book 4 of *De doctrina christiana*) or by demoting them as mere decoration, manipulative

---

11. Bochet, "Interprétation scripturaire," 32.

12. Bochet, "Interprétation scripturaire," 28; the italicized phrase translates Bochet's "au principe même de l'ouvrage."

13. *Conf.* 11.1.1 (BA 14:270): "ut dicamus omnes: magnus dominus et laudabilis ualde."

"performance," or even outright deception. Recent studies, however, have begun to attend to the substantive role played by rhetoric in ancient exegesis and theology.[14] Jean Doignon has observed, "A new movement seems to be dawning which consists of envisioning, using a much wider angle than that of figures [of style], the impact of rhetoric upon apologetic, exegesis, and even Christian theology; we reach toward clarifying the ways and means of these fields of knowledge by means of the schemas of *inuentio* and *dispositio*."[15] *Inuentio* and *dispositio* represent the first two of five parts or stages in classical rhetorical composition: invention (*inuentio*), arrangement (*dispositio*), style (*elocutio*), memory (*memoria*), and delivery (*actio*).

Jacques Ollier reads the latter books of *Confessiones* through the lens of Isabelle Bochet's insight into Augustine's exegesis for self-understanding in order to analyze the specific role of rhetorical arrangement, *dispositio*. Augustine writes to train his audience, says Ollier, not merely to impress with style, but in order "to form an ideal reader" who is capable of doing biblical exegesis of the primordial days (of creation), and "thereby to interpret himself."[16] Books 11 and 12 prepare readers to follow Augustine's way of reading scripture about to take center stage in book 13. Ollier notes that Augustine's series of precise moves shows a "progression of rhetorical argumentation that establishes the reader in a movement that constrains him or her to move from one point to another." This "curvature [*courbure*] of Augustinian thought" defines his approach, writes Ollier, just as it also embodies "the very definition of rhetoric."[17]

Complementing Ollier, I propose to use the first rhetorical element, *inuentio*, as a window into Augustine's exegetical strategy. I use the adjectival form "inventional" to refer to dynamics that draw on *inuentio* as the principal element of rhetorical composition. *Inuentio* does not, however, refer to creating material de novo; it is rather hitting upon the right material to speak about. That is, *inuentio* means "discovery" in the sense of "finding" (*inuenire*) the subject matter of discourse. For ancient rhetors, *inuentio* "literally means a 'coming upon,' a discovery

14. For example, see Brian Gronewoller, "God the Author: Augustine's Early Incorporation of the Rhetorical Concept of *oeconomia* into His Scriptural Hermeneutic," *AugStud* 47, no. 1 (2016), 65–77, and the literature he cites in note 2.

15. Quoted in Ollier, *Firmamentum narrat*, 22. Doignon was writing in 1979. Translations from this work are mine.

16. Ollier, *Firmamentum narrat*, 29: "à constituer un lecteur ideal . . . par là de s'interpreter lui-même."

17. Ollier, *Firmamentum narrat*, 308.

of that which is there, or already there, to be discovered. The term has little to do with originality or with creation *ex nihilo*."[18] That is to say, the inventional enterprise focuses on retrieval by a process of imitation. Yet this imitative *inuentio* produces "not conspicuous likeness of the original, but rather what is understood and revalued in the original."[19] I contend that Augustine's elaboration of Gen. 1:1 in *Confessiones* 11–12 reflects just this sort of imitative inventional understanding and reevaluation that intertwines hermeneutics and rhetoric.

HERMENEUTICAL RHETORIC

For conceptual help I turn to promising recent scholarship in contemporary rhetorical studies. The work of Michael Leff has helped revive the discipline of rhetoric from its post-Enlightenment desuetude and academic marginalization.[20] Leff's close analysis of ancient and modern rhetorical pieces opposes "weak," utilitarian views that reduce rhetoric to "a sheerly instrumental calculus" that has "evacuated the text as a site of rhetorical action."[21] His "strong case" for rhetoric reconstructs it "not as ornamentation, nor as an instrument for disseminating truths gained through other means, but as the very medium in which social knowledge is generated."[22] In other words, "strong" rhetoric deals with substance and not merely with style, with content as well as form. Leff's insights emerge not from the instabilities of postmodern theory but from close, disciplined analysis of ancient oratory, especially in works of Cicero. In pragmatic Ciceronian fashion, Leff uses a case-study approach that avoids mere "mechanical" applications of abstract rules for rhetorical production and emphasizes appropriate accommodation to each audience's circumstances. Cicero, translating the Greek

---

18. Rita Copeland, *Rhetoric, Hermeneutics, and Translation in the Middle Ages: Academic Traditions and Vernacular Texts* (Cambridge: Cambridge University Press, 1991), 151.

19. Copeland, *Rhetoric*, 151.

20. A curated collection of Leff's essays has appeared: Antonio de Velasco, John Angus Campbell, and David Henry, eds., *Rethinking Rhetorical Theory, Criticism, and Pedagogy: The Living Art of Michael C. Leff* (East Lansing: Michigan State University Press, 2016).

21. Stephen Howard Browne, "Michael Leff and the Return of the Rhetorical Text," *Rhetoric & Public Affairs* 13, no. 4 (2010): 681.

22. Michael Leff, "Cicero's *Pro Murena* and the Strong Case for Rhetoric," *Rhetoric & Public Affairs* 1, no. 1 (1998): 63.

6666

tradition of Isocrates, called this "decorum."[23] As Cicero refused to separate form and content, practice and theory, Leff works to catch theoretical perspectives in the act of rising organically out of real rhetorical moments, often describing rhetoric using life-force words like "metabolism" and "circulation."

In a seminal study of 1997, Leff develops a Ciceronian approach that he calls "hermeneutical rhetoric" in order to show "how interpretative processes become inventional resources."[24] For his case study, Leff uses the Gettysburg Address of Abraham Lincoln for the way it "copies and reinvents" Thomas Jefferson's nation-defining sentence in the Declaration of Independence, "all men are created equal."[25] Leff shows how Lincoln's "strong" rhetoric refuses to see Jefferson's "equality" as a fixed entity. This idea does not remain true by simple repetition; for Lincoln, the meaning of equality develops in and through history in ways that past ages did not necessarily foresee or intend. In this way, this "canonical" American statement, "all men are created equal," expresses not a self-evident fact merely to be acknowledged but an ideal to be continually made true in new contexts. To adapt Augustine's parallel characterization of scripture in *Confessiones*, it "grows."[26] Paradoxically, the old maintains itself by newness.[27] For Leff, Lincoln's decorum-based recomposition of a sentence written by a slaveholder to include enslaved people

---

23. Decorum refers literally to the "fittingness" of discourse—that is, its appropriateness to particular subjects, circumstances, and audiences in a way that links form and content. The classic exposition of decorum appears in Cicero's *De oratore* 69–74 and 122–25. See Michael Leff, "Decorum and Rhetorical Interpretation: The Latin Humanistic Tradition and Contemporary Critical Theory," *Vichiana* Ser. 3, vol. 1 (1990): 107–26; reprinted in *Rethinking Rhetorical Theory*, 163–84 (n. 20 supra).

24. Michael Leff, "Hermeneutical Rhetoric," in *Rhetoric and Hermeneutics in Our Time: A Reader*, ed. Walter Jost and Michael J. Hyde (New Haven: Yale University Press, 1997), 198. This essay is reprinted in *Rethinking Rhetorical Theory*, 307–29.

25. Leff, "Hermeneutical Rhetoric," 204–12.

26. *Conf.* 3.5.9 (BA 13:376): "quae [i.e., scriptura] cresceret cum paruulis."

27. Leff, "Hermeneutical Rhetoric," 209. It is safe to say that neither Jefferson nor Lincoln intended or foresaw the use of the Declaration made by a Black man, Martin Luther King Jr., before the Lincoln Memorial at the 1963 March on Washington. In his address popularly known as the "I Have a Dream" speech, King's focus was equal opportunity in jobs and housing for African Americans. He appealed to the canonical status of Jefferson's line "all men are created equal," calling it the nation's "creed." King makes a hermeneutical-rhetorical move, however, that distinguishes him epistemologically from both Jefferson and Lincoln. Addressing the circumstances of Black people who have been excluded from justice and equality by systemic racism, he likens this sentence to an undelivered promise, "a bounced check," calling on America to "live out its true meaning."

is "a hermeneutic tour-de-force."[28] Because its "circulation of influence between past and present allows Lincoln to change American tradition without destroying it," Leff concludes, "it illustrates what I have called a hermeneutical rhetoric."[29]

Though Leff's final exposition focuses on Lincoln, his original model for "hermeneutical rhetoric" was Augustine.[30] An unpublished conference address of 1993, titled "Knowing What to Take Out of Egypt: Notes Toward Hermeneutical Rhetoric," invokes Augustine's well-known use of the story of Israel "plundering" Egypt to portray Christianity's adaptation of pagan wisdom in *De doctrina christiana*.[31] But Augustine's influence goes beyond the title of the talk. Leff shows how Augustine's framework for Christian rhetoric derives recognizably from Cicero, even though "scriptural interpretation replaces Ciceronian invention as the ground for rhetorical argument." Augustine had not merely "skimmed the preceptive surface" of Cicero's *De oratore*. Rather, showing a "profound understanding of Cicero," even though his source of wisdom has shifted to the Bible, Augustine preserves Cicero's union of wisdom and eloquence. He further follows Cicero's pattern of finding eloquent models to *develop* rather than disembodied precepts to *parrot*. Augustine also commends the practice of accommodative decorum "in its full, complex Ciceronian resonance, as [a] flexible principle that guides rhetorical practice." In so doing he "captures something of Cicero's spirit and turns it to productive use within the metabolism of his own Christian rhetoric." Yet Leff adds—and this is important for understanding Augustine's hermeneutical rhetoric in reading Moses in *Confessiones*, to be discussed below—"Augustine's purpose is not to understand Cicero; rather his understanding of Cicero serves his own rhetorical purposes. In other words, *we have here a paradigm for hermeneutical rhetoric*."[32] While attaching the proviso that Augustine's

28. Leff, "Hermeneutical Rhetoric," 208.

29. Leff, "Hermeneutical Rhetoric," 212.

30. The point for Leff is not that the rhetorical practices of Augustine and Lincoln were identical. Rather, they shared a recognizably Ciceronian rhetorical tradition that unites form and content, diagnoses the needs of audiences in specific situations, speaks from within rhetorical guidelines rather than following rules, allows accommodative "decorum" to develop content circumstantially, and brings new truth from old words for new times.

31. *Doctr. chr.* 2.40.60 (BA 11/2:226). The rest of this paragraph draws on this unpublished address, the text of which was graciously communicated to me by Professor Antonio de Velasco of the University of Memphis, one of the editors of the collection of Leff's essays, *Rethinking Rhetorical Theory* (n. 20 *supra*). I thank Professor de Velasco for his generous help.

32. Emphasis added. Leff's comments might easily be transposed to speak of Lincoln's Ciceronian reading of Jefferson.

interpretative purpose was broader than simply to understand Moses, I wish to use the paradigm of hermeneutical rhetoric to examine Augustine's reading of Gen. 1:1 in *Confessiones* 11 and 12.

Four summary areas link Leff's paradigm of Ciceronian hermeneutical rhetoric to Augustine's "inventional" exegesis of Moses:[33] (1) the view of theory and practice; (2) the relation between *imitatio* and *inuentio*; (3) declaration as fact and as norm; and (4) care for the reading community, which embraces Augustine's detours into the issues of authorial intention and interpretative diversity.

Theory and Practice

Augustine's rhetorical practice in *Confessiones* 11–13 is suppler and more suggestive than theoretical abstractions can describe. Augustine reads Genesis not by importing abstract criteria from without; rather, meaning emerges as the biblical text's lexical depths interact with his purposes for writing *Confessiones*. For this reason, I suggest that understanding Augustine's reading of the Bible in *Confessiones* requires patiently sifting through episodes of his actual practice. As with his exegetical homilies, the best strategy is to watch what Augustine actually does with the texts.

The "Ciceronian resonance" of decorum appears in Augustine's desire to shape interpretative acts that accommodate his reading audience. Augustine aims to stir love, to lead to self-understanding, and to train readers to sustain themselves in the new scriptural world; each of these aspects affects his reading of Gen. 1:1. "In the beginning God made heaven and earth" is not a mere statement of fact, and simple reassertion will not do; one must ask, seek, and knock in order to receive, find (*inuenire*), and open its implications.[34] Augustine's questions emerge quickly. Having accepted the statement of Moses *that* God created, Augustine queries analytically: "Let me listen and understand how (*quomodo*) you 'made heaven and earth.'"[35] This *quomodo* question marks a shift of epistemological perspective. As Lincoln's perspective on equality during the Civil War's

33. "Moses" here and throughout the chapter stands for the author Augustine assumed was the historical Moses.

34. E.g., *conf.* 12.1.1 (BA 14:344), invoking Matt. 7:7–8 in the context of investigating Gen. 1:1: "multa satagit cor meum, domine, in hac inopia uitae meae pulsatum uerbis sanctae scripturae tuae . . . petite, et accipietis; quaerite, et inuenietis; pulsate, et aperietur uobis. omnis enim, qui petit, accipit et quaerens inueniet et pulsanti aperietur."

35. *Conf.* 11.3.5 (BA 14:278; trans. is my own): "audiam et intellegam, quomodo in principio fecisti caelum et terram."

break with slavery shifts from Jefferson's perspective during the Revolutionary War's break with England, so Augustine repositions himself epistemologically in relation to creation as compared to Moses. The ancient lawgiver's statement about creation's beginning, a seemingly self-contained declaration of faith, now becomes more: it mutates to be a premise and a platform for finding wider and greater realities to which it points. Laboring to discover these leads to creating spiritual exercises that enlarge the capacity of readers to understand scripture.

Augustine makes a series of logical inferences that generate fresh conclusions and new questions, which are themselves followed by new premises and further extensions of logic. The exegetical *inuentio* slowly builds up a structure of understanding that grows with each new question and answer. The resulting framework makes Gen. 1:1 say more than the flat assertion that creation happened. And new insights remove blockages to understanding that might impede readers who wish to enter and remain in the new scriptural world. Augustine's procedure, therefore, not only answers his challengers; it also doubles as a set of training exercises for those who ask, seek, and knock at scripture's door.

Relation between Imitatio *and* Inuentio

Augustine reads Gen. 1:1 to gain access to the reality mediated by its words—that is, to the subject matter of creation. He draws this out by acts of rhetorical *imitatio* that sift the text for its embedded implications, and builds a presentation that ministers to the audience reading *Confessiones*.[36] Augustine follows the counsel given by Seneca that a declaimer should "bring to light only what he has made of" the model being used, in order to reshape its meaning and re-present his understanding in a new discourse. That new discourse, says Seneca, resembles its source only "as a child resembles his father, and not as a picture resembles its original; for a picture is a lifeless thing."[37] Augustine similarly draws Moses's

---

36. This differs from the hierarchical "neoplatonic process of imitation" that interests Brian Stock as he pursues the metaphor of Augustine "reading" himself as a text in *Confessiones*. For Stock, philosophy informed Augustine that "men and women are ceaselessly engaged in mimetic interplay with the persons they want to be," and this is a catalyst for conversion. *Augustine the Reader: Meditation, Self-Knowledge, and the Ethics of Interpretation* (Cambridge, MA: Belknap, 1996), 35.

37. Seneca, *Ep.* 84.8–9: "This is what our mind should do: it should hide away all the materials by which it has been aided, and bring to light only what it has made of them. . . . I would have you [make it be like the model] as a child resembles his father, and not as a

meaning from Gen. 1:1 to create not a "conspicuous likeness" but a discourse based on what he has "understood and revalued" in it. The ancients understood that such imitations are "the products of inventional force" that, as such, "inhere in both original and the new."[38]

Augustine predicates his work of *imitatio* on the creative act of *inuentio*. He reads Gen. 1:1 not merely to explain the intention of Moses but in order to "understand and revalue" his words—that is, in order to enter the world that the text opens up and to persuade readers to follow and remain with him there. It is characteristic of Augustine's way of reading scripture to combine past and present so as to make the text a medium for the reading community's self-understanding; it becomes not only a destination but also a point of departure for the community's own adventure in biblical understanding and conversion.[39]

Fact and Norm

Another way to view Augustine's hermeneutical rhetoric is to see the declaration "In the beginning God made heaven and earth" as both *statement of fact* and *declaration of norm*. As fact, it is a plain-sense description of creation's inception; as norm, it authorizes exegetical *inuentio*. Eternally true in itself *beyond time* as fact, as norm the saying of Moses establishes itself *in time* by incremental, experiential

---

picture resembles its original; for a picture is a lifeless thing." ("hoc faciat animus noster: omnia, quibus est adiutus, abscondat, ipsum tantum ostendat, quod effecit.... similem esse te uolo quomodo filium, non quomodo imaginem imago res mortua est.") Quoted with text and translation in Copeland, *Rhetoric, Hermeneutics, and Translation*, 27. Copeland comments, "The relationship between model and copy, like that of lineage, is *predicated on the act of invention*; the model, or ancestor, discovers and posits the ground for future invention" (27; emphasis added).

38. The clips come from Copeland's comments on this passage in Seneca; *Rhetoric, Hermeneutics, and Translation*, 27.

39. The opening lines of *De doctrina christiana* declare that the first task of interpreting the Bible is to determine "a way of discovering the matters that need to be understood" (1.1.1 [BA 11/2:76; trans. is my own]: "modus inueniendi quae intellegendi sunt"). In her comments on this passage, Rita Copeland virtually describes Leff's program of hermeneutical rhetoric: "The role of invention in [Augustine's] system is to provide the terms for the exegetical act itself. Here invention assumes the value and identity of hermeneutical action.... [If] hermeneutics could take on the function and character of rhetoric, it is also the case that rhetoric, and specifically rhetorical invention, could be redefined as a hermeneutical procedure." *Rhetoric, Hermeneutics, and Translation*, 154.

proofs among generations of readers who feel the text's force and live its truth. In other words, readers "perform" the text in countless individual circumstances that grow the text's meaning; this "history of effects" (*Wirkungsgeschichte*, in the famous language of Hans-Georg Gadamer) carves that growth into the consciousness that grounds the community's confession of sin and praise. Moses's statement cannot be fully understood in static isolation, hallowed in a book or on a plaque. The pressure of historical circumstance must extrude fuller latent meaning; we might say that as a statement addressed to different audiences and circumstances, it demands renewal and reinvention *precisely in order to remain true.*

For example, already by Augustine's time Christianity's reading of Gen. 1:1 had been shaped by controversy with groups that opposed the church's Jewish-biblical legacy of realism about creation, which was denied by, for example, Marcionites, Gnostics, and Manichaeans. Indeed, problematic readings still pressed the community of Augustine's time, as his own Manichaean story showed. But even before that, the church itself had been conceived in a complex, equivocal relationship between the revelation of Christ, the writing of Moses, and the claims of Moses's spiritual progeny, the synagogue. The "Old Testament" mediated to Christians both an identification with and otherness from the Jewish reading community. Christ's descent from Jewish flesh represented a *continuum,* but his descent from heaven represented a *nouum,* an irruption of utter newness that transcended and altered the ancient Jewish way, even as it confirmed and fulfilled it. The resulting dislocation within the biblical tradition portended a profound reconfiguration of language that was centuries in the making.[40] This history of these effects on the understanding of creation is etched in the Nicene-Constantinopolitan Creed of 381, where the church's insistence on retaining both old and new is made visible: Gen. 1:1 was a fact and an affirmation but also a norm and a guide to further understanding.

Augustine's inventional pirouette from fact to norm appears in book 11's "creative equivocation"[41] concerning the word "beginning," which generates an *inuentio* that embraces the entire revelation story. He acknowledges the simplest meaning of *principium* as "launch point." But the event of creation was unprece-

40. Rowan Williams, *The Wound of Knowledge* (Eugene, OR: Wipf & Stock, 2000), 1: "Christian faith has its beginnings in an experience of profound contradictoriness, an experience which so questioned the religious categories of the time that the resulting reorganization of religious language was a centuries-long task."

41. The phrase comes from Leff, "Hermeneutical Rhetoric," 210, who examines Lincoln's similar move in the Gettysburg Address that plays on shades of meaning in the word "dedicate."

dented and unrepeatable; it would not do merely to understand it as the first in a series. How did God create without a tool that was not itself already created? The text says that God spoke creation into existence. But since language itself had not been created, Augustine reasons, "You are evidently inviting us to understand that the word in question is that Word who is God, God with you who are God. He is uttered eternally, and through him are eternally uttered all things."[42] This Word "is 'the Beginning' in that he also speaks to us."[43] On hearing him, we "surrender ourselves once more to him from whom we came. . . . In this Beginning you made heaven and earth, O God. You made them in your Word, your Son, your Power, your Wisdom, your Truth."[44] Augustine's play on *principium* passes from small-*w* "word" in Genesis to capital-*W* "Word" in Christ, using step-by-step inferences that lead from temporality to logic to scripture. This reveals the pedagogy of Augustine's "inventional" approach. He does not look simply to reproduce the meaning of Moses, but using "strong" hermeneutical rhetoric, he reconfigures it. Augustine's reading of Moses is thus—to use Leff's words that describe the practice of Cicero—"constituted . . . by rhetorical action."[45]

Authorial Intention, Interpretative Diversity, Community Formation

After a brief poetic interlude praising scripture that both recaps his argument thus far and anticipates its development,[46] the rest of book 12 stages a sort of legal drama wherein Augustine defends his reading of Gen. 1:1 against the charge that he has violated the intention of Moses. Fellow Catholics who disagree with his reading, whom he calls "the naysayers" (*contradictores*), are the plaintiffs; God is judge, and readers of *Confessiones* are conscripted as members of the jury. He defends his exegetical *inuentio* by explaining his premises and

42. *Conf.* 11.7.9 (BA 14:286): "uocas itaque nos ad intellegendum uerbum, deum apud te deum, quod sempiterne dicuntur omnia."

43. *Conf.* 11.8.10 (BA 14:288; trans. Boulding, 291): "ipsum est uerbum tuum quod et principium est, quia et loquitur nobis." *Principium* linguistically weds Gen. 1:1 and John 1:1 to John 8:25; Augustine's Old Latin text reads Christ's statement, "(I am) the Beginning," as an answer to his adversaries' question about his identity, "Who are you?" For a review of the issues surrounding this text cluster, see James J. O'Donnell, *Augustine: Confessions*, vol. 3, *Commentary, Books 8–13* (Oxford: Clarendon, 1992), 268–70.

44. *Conf.* 11.8.10 and 9.11 (BA 14:288; trans. Boulding, 291–92): "reddentes nos, unde sumus. . . . in hoc principio deus, fecisti caelum et terram in uerbo tuo, in filio tuo, in uirtute tua, in sapientia tua, in ueritate tua."

45. Leff, "Cicero's *Pro Murena*," 83.

46. *Conf.* 12.14.17.

conclusions and by exploring the underlying hermeneutical issues. While answering questions about the reading process, Augustine simultaneously trains
aspiring readers to think with the Bible in a way that secures their place in
the "world" opened up by the text. Augustine presents three interlocking de-
fenses of his inventional exegesis of Gen. 1:1: the first explains his expansive
construction of the biblical author's intention; the second treats the problem
of diverse interpretations that can both confuse and engender disagreement;
the third concerns the character, strength, and nourishment of the reading
community. The remainder of the chapter reviews each of these aspects in turn,
examines their components, and sets them in the context of the aim of *Confessiones* to train audiences to read scripture rightly. Along the way I highlight
the links between Augustine and Lincoln in their shared Ciceronian tradition
of hermeneutical rhetoric.

Authorial Intention

Lincoln and Augustine faced comparable originalist complaints that their readings had deviated from authority based on authorial intention, as it were, "behind
the text." Senator Stephen Douglas had attacked Lincoln on grounds that at the
time the Declaration of Independence was signed, slavery was legal in all thirteen
colonies and many of its signers, including Jefferson, were enslavers.[47] Therefore,
declared Douglas, "all men are created equal" plainly and literally referred only
to white men. "The signers never dreamed of the Negro," he said, charging that
the "monstrous heresy" of Lincoln's "Chicago doctrine" threatened American
democracy. Lincoln defended his "inventional" reading of the Declaration with
a textualist argument that focused on words as the sheath and shaper of authorial
intention.[48] "Equal," Lincoln asserted, is what the Fathers "said, and this they
meant." Conceding that the Declaration's signers could not change the social
condition of slaves by fiat, Lincoln declared that they manifestly intended to
announce a "maxim"—that is, a norm—by which to measure and direct the character of the American community through time.[49] The originalist accusation of

47. Stephen Douglas, "Opening Speech in the Galesburg Debate, October 7, 1858," in
Created Equal? The Complete Lincoln Douglas Debates of 1858, ed. Paul M. Angle (Chicago:
University of Chicago Press, 1958), 294; quoted in Leff, "Hermeneutical Rhetoric," 207–8.

48. Abraham Lincoln, "Speech on the Dred Scott Decision, Springfield, Illinois, June 27,
1857," in *Abraham Lincoln: Speeches and Writings*, ed. Don Fehrenbacher (New York: Library
of America, 1989), 1:398; quoted in Leff, "Hermeneutical Rhetoric," 208–9.

49. Lincoln said, "They meant simply to declare the right [of equality], so that enforce-

the *contradictores* against Augustine similarly insists that his readings were not in the mind of Moses, who thought of creation only as a starting point. Augustine likewise portrays Gen. 1:1 as a maxim or principle, not merely a statement of fact, that was meant to guide the investigations of faith. Using a textualist argument similar to Lincoln's, Augustine suggests the text's *words* contain multiple resonances and implications that demand close attention in order to arrive at the fullest understanding of their truth. Augustine thus distinguishes between Gen. 1:1 as a fact that describes creation's inception and Gen. 1:1 as a norm that opens a gate to the "world of the text."

Augustine summarizes the claim of the *contradictores*: "Moses did not mean what you say; he meant what I say."[50] Augustine affirms the opponents' hermeneutical priority of finding the biblical author's intention, which is unassailably authoritative and when found should be "taken as paramount."[51] But actual cases show how difficult it is to specify exactly that authorial intention. Augustine twice says that he does not know precisely what Moses had in mind in Gen. 1:1.[52] Human weakness, the vagaries of language, and the priorities of different readers make such judgments risky. But Augustine does know certainly that salvation cannot depend on readers locating elusive authorial intention.

Nevertheless, whatever the precise thoughts of Moses in this or that text, Augustine contends, we do know *something* of his broad intention from scripture's blanket dual command to love God and neighbor (Deut. 6:5; Lev. 19:18; Matt. 22:37–40).[53] Moses not only received and wrote down these commands but was

---

ment of it might follow as fast as circumstances should permit. They meant to set up a standard maxim for a free society, which should be familiar to all, and revered by all; constantly looked to, constantly labored for, even though never perfectly attained; constantly approximated, and thereby constantly spreading and deepening its influence, and augmenting the happiness and value of life to all people of all colors everywhere." Quoted in Leff, "Hermeneutical Rhetoric," 208–9.

50. *Conf.* 12.25.34 (BA 14:398; trans. Boulding, 333): "non hoc sensit Moyses, quod tu dicis, sed hoc sensit, quod ego dico." Cf. 12.15.17 (BA 14:368), where Augustine phrases the complaint as misconstruing the intention of God's Spirit expressed "through" Moses: "non" inquiunt "hoc uoluit in his uerbis intellegi spiritus dei, qui per Moysen famulum eius ista conscripsit, non hoc uoluit intellegi, quod tu dicis, sed aliud, quod nos dicimus."

51. *Conf.* 12.32.43 (BA 14:420; trans. Boulding, 341): "sit igitur illa quam cogitauit ceteris excelsior."

52. *Conf.* 12.24.33, 12.32.41.

53. *Conf.* 12.25.35 (BA 14:402–4): "propter quae duo praecepta caritatis sensisse Moysen, quidquid in illis libris sensit . . . crediderimus."

himself subject to them. Knowing that Moses was imbued with love's concern for breadth and harmony, what prevents us from believing that he was aware of all the many possible true constructions of his words in imitation of the graciously accommodating God who spoke to him? After all, God carefully fit the sacred writings to the minds of many people through (*per*) Moses.[54]

Augustine's idea of how truth emerges in time differs from Lincoln's but also relates to it. For Lincoln, history was not only a documentary record; it was a dynamic force rolling through time toward truth's fullness, "projected forward into the future from motives uncovered through reflective reading of the past."[55] Lincoln's diachronically oriented, Romantic view of history saw truth revealed, as it were, "horizontally"—that is, gradually blossoming in time from seeds expectantly planted in the past, creating an organic bond of participation between past and future communities. Lincoln thus could discriminate between the Declaration as empirical description and ideal principle, between indelible fact and moral norm, while tightly interweaving past intent and present circumstance.[56] Augustine's synchronic, Platonic outlook envisioned supereminent Truth, majestically immutable and transcendent, sharing itself "vertically" through truth-speaking individuals whose pronouncements "participate" in it. Yet Truth was mediated in time by historically situated persons, events, and words that mixed truth in the vagaries of time in ways that require hermeneutical work. Truth is thus embedded in salvation history, which the Spirit guides inexorably in real time toward eschatological fulfillment. The paradigm is christological. By the time of the writing of *Confessiones*, a fuller perception of Christ's incarnation had reorganized Augustine's sense of history's agency in mediating spiritual reality and truth; it came "sacramentally."[57] Augustine's sense of participation in truth, therefore, also had a horizontal dimension. Both Lincoln and Augustine understand time as a dimension of truth that allows canonical texts to grow and change. Their mechanisms of "participation" are different, but their respective readings merge communities of past and present in similar ways.

54. *Conf.* 12.31.42 (BA 14:418): "cur non illa omnia uidisse credatur per quem deus unus sacras litteras uera et diuersa uisuris multorum sensibus temperauit?"

55. Leff, "Hermeneutical Rhetoric," 208, quoting David Zarefsky, *Lincoln, Douglas, and Slavery in the Crucible of Debate* (Chicago: University of Chicago Press, 1990), 164.

56. Leff, "Hermeneutical Rhetoric," 208; Zarefsky, *Lincoln, Douglas, and Slavery*, 152.

57. For more on this, see my *Christ Meets Me Everywhere: Augustine's Early Figurative Exegesis*, Studies in Historical Theology (New York: Oxford University Press, 2012), 199.

Interpretative Diversity

Multiple possibilities for meaning from texts present challenges to conceiving how they relate to authorial intention. To address this, Augustine stages a dialogue and asks the *contradictores* a question that reframes their accusation: Do they mean to say that everything Augustine said was untrue? No, they reply, they disagree only about authorial intention.[58] This answer (obviously ventriloquized by Augustine) represents a crucial concession in the debate that allows Augustine to introduce truth-speaking, apart from authorial intention, as a criterion for judging inventional exegesis. Augustine rhetorically takes inventory of everything true that can be drawn from the words of the passage, ten times repeating the phrase "it is true that."[59] These syncopated repetitions build rhetorical momentum for Augustine's argument that because all true statements participate in Truth, his true statements do.

Augustine makes a clarifying distinction: "I perceive that two sorts of disagreement can arise when something gets asserted by truth-telling messengers using signs. One occurs in a dispute about the truth involved in the matter, and the other in disagreement about the intention of the one who makes the assertion."[60] Augustine pulls these issues apart in order to judge them separately. The *contradictores*, he thinks, unhelpfully collapse questions about the intention of Moses into the ultimate subject matter and truth-reference of his words. Focusing on the words of Moses, one can find a plethora of true meanings. Augustine's textualism counters the originalism of the naysayers.

Interpretative diversity is cause for astonishment, Augustine reflects; and yet we think nothing of similar phenomena in the ordinary workings of nature, of language, and of the human community. The tiny mouth of a mountain spring sends streams gushing in many directions.[61] Likewise, we know language expresses truth variously; every person with a quick flash of insight still "hauls his discovery through the meandering channels of his own discourse, which are somewhat longer."[62] Similarly, we know communities routinely accommodate

58. *Conf.* 12.15.18–12.16.19.
59. *Conf.* 12.19.28.
60. *Conf.* 12.23.32 (BA 14:396; trans. is my own): "duo uideo dissensionum genera oboriri posse, cum aliquid a nuntiis ueracibus per signa nuntiatur, unum, si de ueritate rerum, alterum, si de ipsius qui enuntiat uoluntate dissensio est."
61. *Conf.* 12.27.37.
62. *Conf.* 12.27.37 (BA 14:406; trans. Boulding, 335): "per longiores loquellarum anfrac-

messages to the varying capacity of its members. Scripture accommodates vastly different capacities of its readers, and many possibilities for meaning occur to the minds of its advanced readers.[63]

The problem, Augustine argues, lies not in interpretative diversity per se but in how we handle it. Conjuring an image of himself as Moses, he imagines approaching the awesome task of writing scripture.[64] What does he wish to achieve and what strategies does he use? Augustine-as-Moses wishes for such eloquence and skill of accommodative decorum that his very few words welcome the simple, challenge the learned, and anticipate every true meaning that readers might think of. At the very least, Augustine-as-Moses would hew to his own command to love one's neighbor. He cannot imagine Moses being so miserly as to refuse to his readers the benefits that he, Augustine, would give. This thought experiment undergirds the plausibility of multiple meanings in the mind of Moses.

While not a full-blown declamation, the Augustine-as-Moses fantasy makes two moves that recall *imitatio*: it sifts the original model for essential subject matter, and it takes up the concern to address one's own audience. It was precisely the task of *imitatio* among ancient declaimers to project themselves into the words of a model discourse in order to revalue and restate its most meaningful elements for constructing new compositions. Retrieving another's words was not a matter of passive replicating or obsequious aping but one of engaging and reconstituting them in ways that merged with new circumstances. Augustine lifts the cover on the working pistons of the engine that drives his process of *imitatio*: "I collect and combine, and so I discover."[65] This process puts Moses and the *Confessiones* reading community into genuine dialogue, mediated by the hermeneutical rhetoric of Augustine, who in turn can ground and defend his inventional exegesis.

Lincoln draws new truth from Jefferson's majestic vision of equality while conscious of future fulfillment that neither he nor Jefferson has witnessed. But Lincoln anticipates that fulfillment by taking steps that prepare future reading

---

tus trahat." Cf. *cat. rud.* 2.3 (BA 11/1:48; trans. is my own), where Augustine describes frustration with translating his own flashes of insight into coherent speech "because often this understanding bathes the mind in something like a flashflood of light, while bringing this understanding to expression is a slow, long-drawn-out and far different process" ("maxime quia ille intellectus quasi rapida coruscatione perfundit animum, illa autem locutio tarda et longa est, longeque dissimilis").

63. *Conf.* 12.28.39–12.29.40.

64. *Conf.* 12.26.36.

65. *Conf.* 12.15.18 (BA 14:370; trans. is my own): "colligo atque coniungo et inuenio."

communities for the changed reality. Lincoln reads the Declaration of Independence in the new situation of the Civil War in a way that retrains readers to live in a reinvented American social community without slavery. The Jeffersonian text brought America to birth; Lincoln would bring it to maturity by adapting it to a new circumstance. That adaptation, argues Leff, draws on hermeneutical rhetoric's "capacity for stable innovation—for building community through tradition without becoming mired in a staid traditionalism."[66] Augustine similarly proposes a reading of Gen. 1:1 that carries a depth of meaning that only future ages and new communities will discover (*inuenire*). In short, Lincoln and Augustine both use hermeneutical rhetoric to reach through their respective canonical words into the "world of the text" that had opened up, and there find measures of new truth to reshape their reading communities and to prepare future communities to find still more.

Community Formation

Neither Augustine reading Moses nor Lincoln reading Jefferson pursue abstract hermeneutical theory. They work out arguments in concrete situations as positioned responses, framed within heated controversies and designed to do partisan work.[67] In short, both immerse themselves in their particular reading communities and circumstances. This is the drive behind their common attention to Ciceronian "decorum," the dimension of discourse that accommodates meaning to concrete audiences and circumstances. The hermeneutical rhetoric of both Lincoln and Augustine presupposes reading communities that are each "a locus of deliberating subjects who change themselves and one another by renewing and revaluing moments in their history."[68] Both Augustine and Lincoln devise rhetorical ways to renew tradition by reframing, revaluing, and reinventing their communities' canonical words.

Augustine's discussions of authorial intention and interpretative diversity in book 12 address two potential stumbling blocks for aspiring readers of scripture: how to understand a text's controlling source of meaning, and how deal with disagreements among interpreters. Up to this point, these discussions might seem like interesting and useful detours that, nevertheless, delay arrival at the promised

66. Leff, "Hermeneutical Rhetoric," 203.
67. Leff, "Hermeneutical Rhetoric," 209.
68. Leff, "Hermeneutical Rhetoric," 204.

destination in the world opened up by scripture. But Augustine's ultimate concern becomes clear as he frames them both within a third all-embracing reality: the community of readers, along with the responsibility to shape its character.

For Augustine, a reader enters the world opened up by scripture not as an individual but with a reading community; right reading depends not only on one's personal ingenuity and integrity but also on the quality of a person's reading community. The dynamics are reciprocal: right reading feeds a community; a good community determines good reading; bad reading malforms a community; a disintegrating community reads badly. While membership in the reading community does not require lockstep agreement about individual interpretations, it does require care for the quality of communal relationships—that is, for the practice of love. Augustine's detours into authorial intention and interpretative diversity now reveal themselves as remedial exercises in developing what might be called "hermeneutical love," a form of scripture's command for unconditional love of neighbor as applied to the work of reading. Working through these problems suggests that the Spirit purposefully embedded problem passages in scripture in order to offer practical resources to the community to develop this love. Guided and guarded by the practice of accommodative love, reading communities can hold an expansive view of authorial intention along with a robust sense of interpretative diversity.

Augustine might have simply laid out readings of Gen. 1:1 on "the beginning," on time, and on "the heaven of heavens" and left it at that. But his inventional exegesis aimed to stir love in his readers by creating spiritual exercises generated by hermeneutical rhetoric that would promote the health of the reading community. Amidst the unavoidable diversity of interpretations, and the possible confusion, dissent, or even opprobrium they might engender, Augustine models a way of reading with generosity, humility, and charity. A strong community gathered around the text hears a call, not to generate biblical position papers that only reveal correct answers from the back of the holy Book, so to speak, but to give counsel and training in how to read with love.

Thus at the beginning of his discussion Augustine praises the divine law of love on which all the Law and Prophets depend (12.18.27; cf. Matt. 22:40). After weighing the evidence for the proliferating interpretative diversity in readings of Gen. 1:1,[69] Augustine takes up a position that sees interpretative judgment

---

69. As Solignac points out, Augustine's discussion concerns the problem of diverse possible meanings in scripture, not the multiplicity of its literal sense, or polysemy; see his *note*

primarily as an act of love. He acknowledges the clash of ideas in the work of interpretation but then alters the question to refer to persons instead of ideas: "I repeat, what does it matter to me if what I think the author thought is different from what someone else thinks he thought?"[70] This subtle shift introduces the theme of the community of interpreters where, while conversing about the texts, people can and do disagree. Augustine avers that love, undaunted by disagreements (which are not unexpected), intuitively looks for commonality. He observes that both he and the *contradictores* seek the intention of Moses, and both think that whatever Moses meant was true. Hence they already form a reading community; and this is a fact with implications for hermeneutics that must be explored. A community of love does not object when people see different meanings that divine Truth nevertheless shows to be true, even if Moses did not intend them. This suggests that divine approval operates across a range of possible true readings and that, since they all come from the one source of gracious Truth, we can be sure that divine grace operates within each person who accepts these readings. The upshot is that every such graced person is worthy of love in the reading community.[71]

Augustine asserts (and models) his desire to be counted as a member of the graced reading community—that is, among "those who feed on your truth in the wide pastures of charity"—so that he may "be united with them in you and in you find my delight in company with them."[72] But virtuous readers commit to the understanding of a text not because it is theirs but because it is true; while, by contrast, those "infatuated" with a view "not because it is true but because it is theirs," and so jealously make truth their private property, by definition excommunicate themselves from that company.[73] The reason is that they mislocate the root of right reading; it lies not in the community itself but beyond it and

---

complémentaire 25, "Diversité des interprétations de l'Écriture" (BA 14:611). This point seems to have been misperceived by Bertrand de Margerie, SJ, "Does Augustine's Moses Stand for Multiplicity in Unity?," in *An Introduction to the History of Exegesis*, vol. 3, *Saint Augustine*, trans. Pierre Fontnouvelle (Petersham, MA: Saint Bede's, 1983), 47–88.

70. *Conf.* 12.18.27 (BA 14:384; trans. Boulding, 327): "quid, inquam, mihi obest, si aliud ego sensero, quam sensit alius enim sensisse, qui scripsit?"

71. *Conf.* 12.20.29–12.21.30.

72. *Conf.* 12.23.32 (BA 14:396; trans. Boulding, 332): "coniungar autem illis, domine, in te et delecter cum eis in te, qui ueritate tua pascuntur in latitudine caritatis."

73. *Conf.* 12.25.34 (BA 14:400–402): "sed amant suam non quia uera est, sed quia sua est . . . [quisquis] sibi proprie uindicat et suum uult esse quod omnium est a communi propellitur."

above it, "in the immutable Truth which towers above our minds."[74] Differences over the meaning of a text actually create a precious opportunity for community members to practice the love that the texts themselves are most concerned with. This love is glaringly absent in people who vaunt their views and exclude others—ironically so, since they contradict the very texts they claim to know better than anyone! Augustine therefore welcomes interpretative diversity as purposeful and salutary, while praying for the reading community's "harmony" (*concordia*) and for its open agreement that, whatever the Lawgiver intended, "he had in mind what you revealed to him to be the best of all meanings in the light of truth, and with respect to the profit it would yield."[75]

The final sections of book 12 grandly synthesize Augustine's three themes of authorial intention, interpretative diversity, and the reading community. Addressing the *contradictores* who had disagreed so disagreeably with him and with each other, he asks: What happens when a second plausible reading emerges?

> I think that I will be answering in a more religious spirit if I say, "Why not both, if both are true?" And if there is a third possibility, and a fourth, and if someone else sees an entirely different meaning in these words, why should we not think that [Moses] was aware of all of them since it was through him that the one God carefully tempered [*temperauit*] his sacred writings to meet the minds of many people who would see different things in them, and all true?[76]

Augustine posits his inventional exegesis as a mediation between the authorial intention of Moses and the truth-reference of his words.[77] Augustine reveals his conviction that Moses, knowing that truth continually breaks forth from God's word, intentionally licensed the "inventional" readings of future generations, including Augustine's:

74. *Conf.* 12.25.35 (BA 14:402): "in ipsa quae supra mentes nostras est inconmutabili ueritate."
75. *Conf.* 12.30.41 (BA 14:418; trans. Boulding, 340): "ita honoremus, ut hoc eum te reuelante, cum haec scriberet, adtende credamus, quod in eis maxime et luce ueritatis et fruge utilitatis excellit."
76. *Conf.* 12.31.42 (BA 14:418; trans. Boulding, 340): "religiosius me arbitror dicere: cur non utrumque potius, si utrumque uerum est, et si quid tertium et si quid quartum et si quid omnino aliud uerum quispiam in his uerbis uidet, cur non illa omnia uidisse credatur, per quem deus unus sacras litteras uera et diuersa uisuris multorum sensibus temperauit?"
77. Recalling the distinction made in *conf.* 12.23.32; see n. 60 *supra*.

I am convinced that when he wrote those words, what he meant and what he thought was all the truth we have been able to find [*inuenire*] there, and whatever truth we have not been able to find, or have not found yet, but which is nonetheless there to be found [*inueniri*].[78]

For Augustine, in other words, Moses intended not only to convey a clear factual claim about the beginning of creation but also to issue an invitation to develop "inventional" readings that would reveal the breadth of his intention to make his statement a channel of deeper truth.

Augustine clinches his claim by threading his three concerns into an observation about the text's divine provenance—a claim that notably appears at the end, not the beginning, of his argument, deriving the theological appeal from reason rather than faith. Whatever Moses was thinking, it is inconceivable that God's Spirit should have been unaware of any possible true meaning of Gen. 1:1. Even if Moses had intended only one of these (authorial intention), the abundance of plausible true meanings (interpretative diversity) signals that the Spirit intended all of them to feed future readers (community formation). Therefore, whatever meaning one settles on (interpretative diversity), whether Moses intended it or not (authorial intention), we know that God has ensured that it would feed and never mislead the community (community formation).

The close of book 12 opens the door to book 13, where Augustine pursues one, and only one, line of interpretation for the seven-day creation story of Genesis. Whether or not the meaning he finds matches Moses's intended meaning, Augustine writes, he hopes that at least it will be a true one. If it is, then readers can be sure that it renders "what your Truth intends to reveal to me through the words of Moses"—note the textualist emphasis—"since it was your Truth who communicated to him whatever he intended."[79] Book 12's final sentence lands elegantly upon a pinpoint, the word *uoluit* ("he intended"), which artfully suggests a tantalizing ambiguity about authorial intention. Grammatically *uoluit* might refer either to the intention of the divine Spirit or to the intention of Moses, but hermeneutically in all likelihood it refers to both.

78. *Conf.* 12.31.42 (BA 14:420; trans. Boulding, 340): "sensit ille omnino in his uerbis atque cogitauit, cum ea scriberet, quidquid hic ueri potuimus inuenire et quidquid nos non potuimus aut nondum potuimus et tamen in eis inueniri potest."

79. *Conf.* 12.32.43 (BA 14:422; trans. is my own): "quod mihi per eius uerba tua ueritas dicere uoluit, quae illi quoque dixit quod uoluit."

CONCLUSION

Lincoln thought that Jefferson's statement about equality could not be left to languish in its late eighteenth-century cage; such ferocious social implications cannot be tamed. Augustine thinks similarly about the ancient declaration of Moses. In order to release the power of these statements, Lincoln and Augustine draw on ancient Ciceronian rhetorical practices that allow a process of retrieving from ancient words a "circulation of influence"[80] whereby new meaning is released that accommodates and strengthens new reading communities.

The hermeneutical rhetoric in books 11 and 12 of *Confessiones* Christianizes ancient *imitatio* by pursuing exegetical *inuentio* on the basis of communal *caritas*. Augustine pursues his penetrating investigation of Gen. 1:1 in order to train and fortify his reading community—which includes Moses, all naysayers, yea-sayers, and aspiring readers of both the Bible and *Confessiones* of all times and places. Augustine perceives readers of scripture as a single interactive body whose living "circulation of influence" enables them, as he describes it in a work written soon after *Confessiones*, to "indwell one another" across time and space "through the bond of love," by whose dynamic *inuentio* "things that had been old become new."[81]

---

80. Leff, "Hermeneutical Rhetoric," 212.

81. *Cat. rud.* 12.17: "So strong is the feeling of common passion that, when our hearers are moved by us as we speak, and we by them as they learn, we indwell one another. . . . And this is all the truer the deeper our friendship is, because the measure that we are 'in' them through the bond of love is also the measure in which things that had been old become new for us." ("tantum enim ualet animi compatientis affectus ut, cum illi afficiuntur nobis loquentibus et nos illis discentibus, habitemus inuicem. . . . et tanto magis, quanto sunt amiciores, quia per amoris uinculum in quantum in illis sumus, in tantum et nobis noua fiunt quae uetera fuerunt" [BA 11/1:110; trans. is my own].)

Chapter 2

AUGUSTINE AND THE NORTH AFRICAN LITURGICAL READING TRADITION

Andrew McGowan

INTRODUCTION

Augustine the Liturgist

It is easy to forget how much of Augustine's immense body of writing is liturgical. The number of *Sermones* (*s.*) is well known, but the *Enarrationes in Psalmos* (*en. Ps.*) is his largest single work, if considered as a unit. If those sermons on the Psalms are liberated from being considered a "commentary," and added to the homiletic corpus along with the sets of sermons on the Gospel of John (*In Iohannis euangelium tractatus* [*Io. eu. tr.*]) and Epistles of John (*In epistulam Iohannis ad Parthos* [*ep. Io. tr.*]), the discourses connected with sacramental performance dominate Augustine's corpus.

Liturgy provides the necessary context for Augustine's work, and his sermons also provide much of what we know about that liturgy. The plentiful references he makes to worship are a considerable, if necessarily unsystematic, source for reconstructing how liturgy worked in Augustine's Hippo. To these literary clues we can add local conciliar decrees, some comments in other contemporary authors,

This essay is offered as a token of thanks to J. Patout Burns for wise and weighty insight on so many matters Christian and African, and with warm memories of visiting Hippo and some of the other venues at which Augustine preached together in 2012. I also wish to thank Paul F. Bradshaw for conversations and encouragement that led to my first foray into this topic some years ago.

archaeological evidence, and the sermons themselves to reconstruct a sense of Augustine's liturgy that is hard to match for the Western church of the fourth and fifth centuries.[1]

The same material means that there is considerable evidence for how scripture was read—and interpreted—in the liturgy of Hippo. Augustine's work as preacher has a particular value for considering the forms of reading practice, especially but not exclusively of the scriptures. After considering previous scholarship and offering some parameters for the shape and scope of reading practices in the liturgy of Hippo, I offer a brief survey of evidence for patterns and practices across the liturgical year.

Studying Augustine's Liturgy: Scholarship and Method

Consideration of the specific places, texts, and practices of early Christian liturgy is properly connected both with how such instances came to be and with how they relate to what came after. Each of these processes, however, has some attendant pitfalls. In the case of early Christian liturgy, Jewish practice and belief in particular can readily be treated as a sort of immediate backdrop to understanding Christian practice, but are thereby reified. Despite the best efforts of numerous recent scholars,[2] there continues to be an appetite for accounts of early Christian worship that interpret even modern liturgy by tracing it to real or supposed Jewish roots, at the cost of that sort of supersessionism that treats late ancient Judaism as a single system, implicitly incapable of innovation after the time of Jesus.

This danger may seem a bit remote from interpreting the liturgy of Augustine's time. In matters of reading, however, the danger still lurks. This can take form in assumptions about inherited synagogal practice and the significance of the course readings that played a part in the liturgy of Hippo. There have been

1. John Chrysostom provides a sort of Eastern analogue, and the work done by Wendy Mayer and Pauline Allen explores his homiletical output for social-historical and, to some extent, liturgical purposes; see, e.g., Wendy Mayer and Pauline Allen, *John Chrysostom*, ECF (London: Routledge, 2000).

2. See, e.g., Paul F. Bradshaw, *The Search for the Origins of Christian Worship: Sources and Methods for the Study of Early Liturgy* (London: SPCK, 2002); Paul F. Bradshaw and Lawrence A. Hoffman, *The Making of Jewish and Christian Worship*, Two Liturgical Traditions 1 (Notre Dame, IN: University of Notre Dame Press, 1991).

suggestions—including those underlying the reform of liturgical readings in many Christian denominations and the various forms of "Common Lectionary"—that course readings through particular books had been characteristic of Jewish liturgical practice and were thus "inherited" by Christian communities.

The idea of a synagogal course reading carried across into early Christian practice is fraught with problems, including the assumption that the form of the earliest Christian gatherings—and their reading practices in particular—was synagogal in origin or inspiration. The hypothesis weakens when assumptions of immutability are taken away from consideration of early Jewish practice. While there were later patterns of course reading in synagogues, they were not universal or uniform.[3] Church and synagogue may have influenced each other; but as so often, this story needs to be rewritten less as one of liturgical parent and child and more of sibling rivalry, of two dynamic traditions competing and responding.

A second issue of method concerns the aftermath of Augustine's practice. The study of early liturgy is often driven teleologically, as a quest for practices that shed light on later and more familiar ones. Thus, at times, scholars have been inclined to read back the terms and practices of later periods into evidence for which they are inappropriate. This must be said to apply to the common idea of a "lectionary" at Hippo.

A lectionary implies a developed and fixed scheme of readings, even if an incomplete one. Readings in the fourth-century liturgy of Hippo are, as we shall see, best understood as a combination of course readings, traditional associations between texts and feasts or observances, and choices made by the bishop. This is not a lectionary at all, even if it can be related to the emergence of lectionaries. The pattern is better seen not merely as one of readings, which prejudices the issue, but as a reading culture, a *habitus*. Attention solely to the "lections" risks yielding a distorted and incomplete sense of how reading practices worked.

A more adequate approach to Augustine's readings, to which this study can only be a small contribution, must set the evidence in closer relation to other ancient reading practices.[4] We may be misled by thinking of these ancient liturgical performances in terms shaped by the very limited role played by public reading in

---

3. Lee I. Levine, *Ancient Synagogue: The First Thousand Years*, 2nd ed. (New Haven: Yale University Press, 2005), 567–70.

4. See, for instance, William A. Johnson, "Toward a Sociology of Reading in Classical Antiquity," *American Journal of Philology* 121 (2000): 593–627, and Johnson, *Readers and Reading Culture in the High Roman Empire: A Study of Elite Communities* (New York: Oxford University Press, 2010).

the modern world, when most ancient "reading" was communal, and most ancient "readers" were hearers. Reading associated with ancient scholastic and sympotic cultures, most obviously, is highly relevant to how Augustine's readings were perceived.[5] Synagogal practices are also relevant, not so much as progenitor of Christian lections, but as another part of this wider world of communal reading.[6]

The purpose of reading scripture—and other texts—was not so much to fulfill a liturgical rubric as it was to provide both edification and a basis for instruction. And, as Augustine's preaching demonstrates, the acts of reading and learned commentary are intertwined, which renders the liturgy of the church at Hippo an exemplary but not unique instance of a Christian reading and interpretive culture. Liturgical reading remained close to other ancient practices of discourse, art, and education, even while exhibiting forms of repetition and tradition that might point ahead to the emergence of lectionaries and to the increasingly unique significance of the liturgical setting.

Studying Augustine's Liturgy and "Lectionary"

Numerous studies have addressed the wider context of liturgical practice in Augustine's Hippo. For the eucharistic liturgy as a whole, the venerable analysis of "The African Rite" by W. C. Bishop, an extended study of Augustine's writings as a source for liturgical history more generally by P. W. Roetzer, and the shorter account from Klaus Gamber on the Eucharist are noteworthy.[7] Patout Burns and Robin Jensen's *Christianity in Roman Africa* now stands as the most useful synthetic description of Augustine's liturgy for many purposes and is especially notable for its consideration of literary and archaeological evidence together, as well as of historical developments in African liturgical life from earlier periods.[8]

---

5. While somewhat earlier, the focus of Brian J. Wright, *Communal Reading in the Time of Jesus: A Window into Early Christian Reading Practices* (Minneapolis: Fortress, 2017), remains instructive.

6. See esp. the important discussion in Alistair Stewart-Sykes, *From Prophecy to Preaching: A Search for the Origins of the Christian Homily*, VCSup 59 (Leiden: Brill, 2001).

7. W. C. Bishop, "The African Rite," *JTS* 13 (1912): 250–77; P. Wunibald Roetzer, *Die heiligen Augustinus Schriften als liturgie-geschichtliche Quelle: Eine liturgie-geschichtliche Studie* (Munich: Hueber, 1930); and Klaus Gamber, "Ordo Missae Africanae: Der nordafrikanische Messritus zur Zeit des hl. Augustinus," *Römische Quartalschrift für christliche Altertumskunde und für Kirchengeschichte* 64 (1969): 139–53.

8. J. Patout Burns Jr. and Robin M. Jensen, *Christianity in Roman Africa: The Development of Its Practices and Beliefs* (Grand Rapids: Eerdmans, 2014); cf. Robin Margaret Jensen and

G. G. Willis's book *St Augustine's Lectionary*, published in 1962, remains the most thorough study on Augustine's liturgical readings in English,[9] although scholars have been properly critical at a number of points. Willis's method for reviewing Augustine's homiletic material in search of a "lectionary" was to include only explicit references by Augustine. While commendable, this quest for the fixed pattern reflected in his book's title helped to embed a circularity of method. In the end even Willis agreed that "lectionary" could not properly describe liturgical readings at Hippo.

Other studies have added to and amended Willis's picture for more specific periods or feasts, such as Easter and saints' days,[10] but have sometimes been even less circumspect about ideas such as a lectionary or *ordines* of readings. These have focused on issues such as Augustine's use of particular biblical books, on the liturgical year, on specific feasts and seasons,[11] or on the extent of readings.[12] The discovery of additional sermons has led to advances, but also to critical questions about the reliability of the manuscript tradition of the sermons, and of what can be inferred from titles and texts as received.[13]

J. Patout Burns, "The Eucharistic Liturgy in Hippo's Basilica Major at the Time of Augustine," *AttA*, 335–38.

9. Geoffrey G. Willis, *St Augustine's Lectionary* (London: SPCK, 1962).

10. Poque describes Willis's work as "décevant"; see Suzanne Poque, "Les lectures liturgiques de l'octave pascale à Hippone d'après les Traités de S. Augustin sur la première épître de S. Jean," *RBén* 74 (1964): 217–41, here 220. See also Guy Lapointe, *La célébration des martyrs en Afrique d'après les sermons de saint Augustin* (Montréal: Communauté chrétienne, 1972).

11. Jean-Paul Bouhot, "La lecture liturgique des Epîtres Catholiques d'après les sermons d'Augustin," in *La Lecture liturgique des Épîtres catholiques dans l'Église ancienne*, ed. Christian-Bernard Amphoux and Jean-Paul Bouhot (Lausanne: Zèbre, 1996), 269–81; Victor Saxer, ed., *Saint Augustin: L'année liturgique; Sermons choisis* (Paris: Desclée de Brouwer, 1980); Poque, "Les lectures liturgiques"; also Suzanne Poque, ed., *Sermons pour la Pâque*, SC 116 (Paris: Cerf, 1966); Anton Zwinggi, "Die Perikopenordnungen der Osterwoche in Hippo und die Chronologie der Predigten des hl. Augustinus," *Augustiniana* 20 (1970): 5–34; Lapointe, *La célébration des martyrs*.

12. Martijn Schrama, "*Prima Lectio Quae Recitata Est*: The Liturgical Pericope in Light of Saint Augustine's Sermons," *Augustiniana* 45, no. 1–2 (1995): 141–75.

13. Martin Klöckener, "Die Bedeutung der neu entdeckten Augustinus-Predigten (Sermones Dolbeau) für die liturgiegeschichtliche Forschung," in *Augustin Prédicateur (395–411): Actes du Colloque International de Chantilly (5–7 septembre 1996)*, ed. Goulven Madec (Paris: Études Augustiniennes, 1998), 129–70; Hubertus R. Drobner, "The Transmission of Augustine's Sermons: A Critical Assessment," in *Tractatio Scripturarum: Ministerio Sermonis*, vol. 2, *Philological, Exegetical, Rhetorical and Theological Studies on Augustine's Sermons*, ed. Anthony Dupont, Gert Partoens, and Mathijs Lamberigts, IPM 65 (Turnhout: Brepols, 2012), 97–116.

Only quite recently has a more comprehensive account of readings than that of Willis been published: Michael Margoni-Kögler's very substantial *Die Periko-pen im Gottesdienst bei Augustinus*.[14] Margoni-Kögler steps away somewhat from assumptions about a "lectionary" to the more diffuse notion of *Schriftlesung*. His book reviews the data painstakingly and considers cases of possible reading both more broadly than Willis and with the benefit of the subsequent scholarship. This major work is now the indispensable starting point for considering liturgical readings at Hippo.

Yet reading practice in Augustine's liturgy spills beyond the boundaries of lections, or of whether or not a text was liturgically "read." Even a superficial reader of Augustine's homiletical works knows well that his exegetical method is highly intertextual, rather than based on exposition of a sole text on its own terms. The often thick interpolation of other texts, as well as his assumption that they can and must be read in the light of each other (meaning, of course, in the light of Christ), is characteristic of Augustine's hermeneutics. Yet it is also relevant to recasting assumptions about liturgical reading at Hippo. That is to say, more texts were arguably being "read" or heard and discussed in Augustine's liturgy than those that were assigned to lectors. And, as we shall see, the agents of reading and the texts themselves are a more diverse collection than is often assumed.

THE LITURGY AND READING AT HIPPO

Liturgical Context

Since the bulk of the homiletic material seems likely to have been delivered in the context of the Eucharist, the liturgical setting for most of these discourses (or at least its first part) is a reasonable starting point.

---

14. Michael Margoni-Kögler, *Die Perikopen im Gottesdienst bei Augustinus: Ein Beitrag zur Erforschung der liturgischen Schriftlesung in der frühen Kirche* (Vienna: Verlag der Öster-reichischen Akademie der Wissenschaften, 2010). Some of his conclusions are available in English: Margoni-Kögler, "North African Liturgical Readings: The Augustinian Legacy and Some Western Parallels," in *Liturgies in East and West: Ecumenical Relevance of Early Liturgical Development; Acts of the International Symposium Vindobonense I, Vienna, November 17–20, 2007*, ed. Hans-Jürgen Feulner, Österreichische Studien zur Liturgiewissenschaft und Sakramententheologie 6 (Zürich: LIT, 2013), 261–74. Also useful is Michael Margoni-Kögler, "Lectio," *AugLex* 3:914–23.

The Eucharist at Hippo began without any entrance ritual per se. Clergy of course came in, as the people did, apparently through the main doors, and not necessarily as a distinct group, let alone in a procession. The text most often quoted in support of something like a "procession"—namely, *De ciuitate dei* (*ciu.*) 22.8—depicts Augustine, along with some laypeople who had brought him news, simply coming to see something that had just happened inside the church: "We went in [*procedimus*] to the people, the church was full, it sounded with voices of praise."[15] When clergy reached the apse where they were to be seated, the bishop or presbyter greeted the people (*s.* 229A.3) to call the service to order. Readings followed immediately. When the lector rose, it was the congregation rather than the leader who offered a greeting: "Peace be with you."[16]

Lections could be specific to a feast or season or chosen by the preacher for other reasons. There were also course readings through certain books, although this has at times been exaggerated or romanticized, as already noted. Even when it was customary to read from a particular book, there is no reason to think that this led to a rigorously governed course reading, with sections allocated to particular days. Whatever earlier patterns may actually have been, and whatever their origins, Augustine's sermons suggest course readings were not a general or default practice; they were fairly specific, and sometimes seasonal.[17] They are as much a version of the principle of episcopal discretion, extended over time, as of some supposed substrate of custom. Without much earlier evidence to bring to bear on the question, it is difficult to judge whether the mixture of course reading, discretionary reading, and seasonal or festal tradition attested in Augustine's writings was tending toward or away from course readings. Nevertheless, these elements provide a structure for that *habitus* of the church at Hippo, even as other elements beyond these forms of choice are necessary to provide a fuller picture.

Old Testament

The first reading, by a designated lector, was sometimes (but not always) from the Old Testament.[18] Some assume that the church at Rome, whose practice

---

15. *Ciu.* 22.8 (LCL 417:246–47, trans. adapted from Green): "procedimus ad populum, plena erat ecclesia, personabat uocibus gaudiorum."

16. *Ep.* 43.8.21 (CSEL 34/2:102) and 53.1.3 (CSEL 34/2:154). Willis, *St Augustine's Lectionary*, 3, suggests the greeting is from the bishop, but the texts suggest otherwise.

17. The most specific study is Anton Zwinggi, "Die fortlaufende Schriftlesung im Gottesdienst bei Augustinus," *Archiv für Liturgiewissenschaft* 12 (1970): 85–129.

18. Burns and Jensen, *Christianity in Roman Africa*, 268n218.

eventually prevailed in the West, departed from an old and widespread norm by omitting the Old Testament from the establishment of the eventual pattern of readings at the Eucharist. This assumption is sometimes connected with the synagogal fallacy discussed above. Old Testament readings disappeared in some places, but we cannot readily access the variety of local reading customs. The idea that readings had ever conformed to a schema of canonical subcategories such as "law, prophets, apostle, Gospel" (cf. *s.* 341),[19] or began from an Old Testament core and expanded, is dubious at best.[20] When an Old Testament reading was clearly offered at Hippo, there is sometimes no corresponding clarity that a New Testament reading, other than the Gospel (which is certainly an established feature), was used too;[21] on more festive days, both prior readings may have been more likely.[22]

There may have been seasonal associations for reading certain books of the Old Testament, as there certainly were for some of the New Testament (cf. *infra*). In Lent there may be traces of a course reading, or something more like a discretionary but not exhaustive progression, through the patriarchal story in Genesis attested in readings.[23] Otherwise, Old Testament readings seem to have been chosen from time to time across books and genres, although the historical books seem less in evidence than the prophets and wisdom literature.[24] The principle of discretion exercised by the preacher is fundamental to understanding the overall pattern or practice, here and otherwise.

Psalms

The use of a psalm was a more consistent feature than readings from other parts of the Old Testament. In fact, to start with the canonical status of Jewish scriptures in general might not be particularly illuminating of early Christian practices of reading or psalmody. The liturgical psalm was not simply a "reading" but a song, sometimes incorporating a congregational response (see, e.g., *en. Ps.* 119.1) or

---

19. *Pace* Bishop, "African Rite," 254.

20. Andrew B. McGowan, *Ancient Christian Worship: Early Church Practices in Social, Historical, and Theological Perspective* (Grand Rapids: Baker Academic, 2014), 81–86.

21. Lapointe, *La célébration des martyrs*, 93–94.

22. Dupont suggests feast days are the main factor; see Anthony Dupont, *Preacher of Grace: A Critical Reappraisal of Augustine's Doctrine of Grace in His "Sermones ad Populum" on Liturgical Feasts and During the Donatist Controversy*, SHCT 177 (Leiden: Brill, 2014), 7.

23. Bishop, "African Rite," 263; Margoni-Kögler, *Die Perikopen*, 85 and 609.

24. Bishop, "African Rite," 264; Gamber, "Ordo Missae Africanae," 144.

other forms of sung participation (e.g., *s.* 176.1; see also *infra*). This different presentation did not make it any less likely that Augustine would comment on the psalm than he did on other texts, as the *Enarrationes in Psalmos* make plain.

One curious incident on which Augustine comments illustrates how this performance might have worked:

> We had prepared a short psalm for our consideration today, and indicated to the reader that this was the psalm to be sung. But at the last minute he apparently became flustered and read this one instead. We have deemed it preferable to see in the reader's mistake a sign of the will of God and to follow that, rather than to do our own will by sticking to our original plan. If, therefore, it turns out that we have detained you for a long time on account of the length of this psalm, you must not blame us but believe that God has willed us to work in such a way as to be fruitful.[25]

Another such mistake is recorded in Sermon 352, where although there is no reference to a different psalm having been chosen, Augustine indicates that he had not selected Ps. 51 but that the cantor had been inspired to do so. Clearly the preacher had discretion to choose the psalm, rather than it being set by some existing scheme. This was done in advance because it had to be prepared by the cantor, but even that preparation underlines the fact that there was no established pattern. The liturgical performance of the psalm and its preparation may also mean that other cases of mistaken or misplaced readings were less likely to unfold without correction.

There was obviously a developed role of cantor, whether or not it was referred to by that name.[26] The performance was not solely that of the cantor, however, since the assembly took part, at least in some cases. One interesting consequence of the congregational participation in "reading" psalmody appears

---

25. *En. Ps.* 138.1 (CCSL 40:1990; trans. adapted from Boulding, *Expositions of the Psalms*, WSA III/20, 257): "psalmum nobis breuem paraueramus, quem mandaueramus cantari a lectore; sed ad horam, quantum uidetur, perturbatus, alterum pro altero legit. maluimus nos in errore lectoris sequi uoluntatem dei, quam nostram in nostro proposito. si ergo uos in eius prolixitate aliquamdiu tenuerimus, nobis non imputetis; sed credatis deum nos non infructuose laborare uoluisse."

26. Christopher Page, *The Christian West and Its Singers: The First Thousand Years* (New Haven: Yale University Press, 2010), 99–101 and 544n17.

in Augustine's discussion of accuracy of translation and grammar in *De doctrina christiana* (*doctr. chr.*):

> There is also that mistake we cannot now remove from the mouths of our psalm-singing congregations, "But on him my sanctification shall flourish" (*floriet*; Ps. 132:18), which in no way detracts from the sense; still, the better educated listener would prefer it to be corrected, and *florebit* substituted for *floriet*; and the only thing that stops such a correction being made is the habit the singers have got into.[27]

The "singers" here are not specialists who could perhaps have been corrected but the people whose preferred or learned forms of the text (*cantantium populorum*) seem to lie beyond Augustine's capacity for liturgical pedagogy. Thus, not all scriptural or reading practice was the passive absorption of the trained lector's or cantor's performance, nor was it derived from codices alone. In Hippo, the people—along with their communal memory—had some custody of the text.[28]

Epistle

The use of New Testament readings other than the Gospel is clear and common but does not quite amount to a set liturgical "Epistle." As noted, Old Testament and New Testament readings often seem to be alternatives, but at times there are both. Overall, a basic threefold pattern is discernable—first reading, psalm, and Gospel—though this is sometimes expanded into a fourfold shape when both Old Testament and Epistle or Acts readings, or even noncanonical texts such as martyrs' acts and recent miracle stories (cf. *infra*),[29] are included.

These readings seem to be chosen according to the same three basic patterns identified. There are high days, both saints' festivals and feasts in the liturgical cal-

---

27. *Doctr. chr.* 2.13.20 (CCSL 32:45–46; trans. adapted from Hill, *Teaching Christianity*, WSA I/11, 139): "illud etiam, quod iam auferre non possumus de ore cantantium populorum: super ipsum autem floriet sanctificatio mea, nihil profecto sententiae detrahit, auditor tamen peritior mallet hoc corrigi, ut non floriet, sed florebit diceretur; nec quicquam impedit correctionem, nisi consuetudo cantantium."

28. See further Page, *Christian West and Its Singers*, 204–5.

29. For more on Augustine's relationship to the Western martyriological tradition, please see the chapter by Tabbernee in this volume.

endar, such as those associated with nativity and passion, where particular readings seem now to be customary (cf. *infra*). There are times when a course reading is taking place, although the evidence for customary reading of the Epistles in course is scant, with the famous exception of those from 1 John, which actually seems to reflect discretionary rather than customary practice. Last and most importantly, the discretion of bishop or preacher was as important here as otherwise, although it is difficult to tell how and when one system or practice is in use rather than another.

The most famous and indeed influential example of course reading in the Augustinian homiletic corpus—itself a combination of seasonal and course-based patterns—is that of the Acts of the Apostles during Easter (s. 227.1). This seems to have been established and expected by Augustine's time (s. 315.1), although that does not mean that there were set lections for each day. This case is connected to that other well-known course reading, the lections from 1 John. At the beginning of *In epistulam Iohannis ad Parthos*, Augustine indicates that he has stopped a set of addresses on the Johannine Gospel—some of which we have in the longer and better-known *In Iohannis euangelium tractatus*—because only the resurrection narratives could be read in Easter week.

> Your Holiness recalls that we are accustomed to preach on the Gospel according to John while observing the order of the text. But now the solemnity of the holy days has intervened, when every year in the church certain passages from the gospel have to be read, which means that others cannot be. The sequential order that we had embarked on, then, has had to be set aside for a short while but not abandoned.[30]

While this "custom" of preaching on John is curious (perhaps a pattern or practice that year, rather than something more traditional), this is one of the clearest statements we have both for the fact of set readings and for their seasonal or festal limitation.

While the extended nature of both sets of Johannine sermons has led some to imagine these as given at different gatherings,[31] the references to eucharistic

---

30. *Ep. Io. tr.* prologue (PL 35:1977; trans. Ramsey, *Homilies on the First Epistle of John*, WSA I/14, 20): "meminit sanctitas uestra euangelium secundum iohannem ex ordine lectionum nos solere tractare. sed quia nunc interposita est solemnitas sanctorum dierum quibus certas ex euangelio lectiones oportet in ecclesia recitari quae ita sunt annuae ut aliae esse non possint, ordo ille quem susceperamus necessitate paululum intermissus est, non amissus."

31. E.g., Ramsey, WSA I/14, 10.

lections in the addresses on the Epistle encourage the view that these were also offered at the Eucharist, the greater length perhaps related to the catechetical and mystagogical practices of the Lent-Easter complex.[32]

Gospel

The reading of the Gospel was, like the psalm, a stable feature of the eucharistic liturgy. There is no sign that it was accompanied by any specific ritual, although deacons read (*s.* 382.3), though perhaps not always. Specific lections were associated with particular feasts, and sometimes sets of Gospels within a season were associated by genre or content rather than as sections of one work, as in the case of the resurrection accounts in Easter week.

Augustine's citation of Matthew more than other Gospels is not surprising, although the sermon texts do not always make it easy to tell which version of a story or saying in the synoptic tradition had been read. The assumptions of earlier editors, whose bias toward Matthew might be even greater, have not made the question easier.[33] Augustine's tendency to intertextuality also shifts the question a little; when a sermon text seems to include elements of different synoptic versions, there might be different explanations, but we may have to consider it as part of a "reading" practice that spilled beyond the limits of formal lections.[34]

There were, presumably, books (codices) of the scriptural works for liturgical use, perhaps with the Gospels bound together, as in later practice. There may also have been books that gathered the liturgical readings for the martyr cult, along with the *passiones* or *acta* (cf. *infra*); this is one factor that might help explain the curiosity of a conflated Gospel text for the celebration of St. Cyprian in Carthage, where the texts of Mark 8:34–5 and John 12:25 seem to have been combined:

> We heard it just now, when the holy gospel was read: "Whoever wishes," he said, "to follow me, let him deny himself." This might seem rather obscure, so the heavenly teacher added some more, and said, "Whoever loves his soul will lose it, and whoever loses it for my sake will find it."[35]

32. See Poque, "Les lectures liturgiques," which discusses this in detail.

33. Margoni-Kögler, *Die Perikopen*, 244, 281.

34. See Hill, *Sermons 51–94*, WSA III/3, 181–82.

35. *S.* 313D.1 (*MA* 1:532; trans. Hill, *Sermons 306–340A*, WSA III/9, 105): "modo audiuimus, cum sanctum euangelium legeretur: qui uult me, inquit, sequi, neget seipsum. quasi obscurum uideretur, addidit adhuc caelestis magister, et dicit: qui amat animam suam, perdet

Sermons for St. Vincent's Day reflect a less striking conflation—something akin to a textual variant—when parts of Matt. 10 apparently served as a traditional Gospel, but the version of the story about fearing those who kill the body from Luke 12:4 is cited (*s.* 277; cf. *ss.* 276 and 277A). This may again suggest something like a martyrial "lectionary"—that is, an artifact rather than a complete pattern of lections—in which a particular version of the text was preserved.

The sermon seems typically to have followed the Gospel, delivered from the bishop's chair in the apse. The surviving sermons indicate the address could have lasted anywhere from a few minutes to an hour or more. In one case Augustine (*s.* 31) refers to having a book of scripture in his hand, perhaps implying it was unusual to do so.[36] The text was, however, in some sense present in the sermon.

Beyond Scripture: Martyrs and Miracles

Reading the Martyrs

If the idea of a lectionary at Hippo is problematic, there was certainly a calendar, and readings associated with particular days are one of the exceptions or additions to a foundation of discretionary reading practices. Among the clearest elements of this calendar are the feasts of martyrs and some other saints. Some scriptural readings seem to have become traditional, such as the use of Prov. 31 for the Scillitan Martyrs (*s.* 31). But the prominent use of (mostly) non-scriptural martyriological *acta* as liturgical readings on their feast days at Hippo reveals the mistake of imagining any emergent *ordo* of readings primarily as a means of addressing or arranging scripture itself.[37] These other readings seem usually to have taken the place in which either an Old Testament or a New Testament reading would otherwise be used, rather than being a supplement or an otherwise lesser element.

Augustine's extant sermons give a useful picture of liturgical use of martyr texts, but they also indicate his active interest in them—not just a tradition of

---

eam; et qui perdiderit eam propter me, inueniet eam." Cf. 313C. See further Margoni-Kögler, *Die Perikopen*, 164.

36. Burns and Jensen, *Christianity in Roman Africa*, 247.

37. Burns and Jensen, *Christianity in Roman Africa*, 268n225; Lapointe, *La célébration des martyrs*.

reading them.[38] A sermon for the Feast of St. Fructuosus and His Companions (*s*. 273), for instance, has Augustine take as his text an utterance of the martyr Eulogius from the *acta*.[39] Five of six extant sermons in honor of St. Vincent of Saragossa (*ss*. 274–77A) allude directly to *acta* no longer extant. The three surviving sermons for St. Perpetua and St. Felicitas (*ss*. 280–82) all make significant reference to the *Passio*.

The curious prominence of the Maccabean martyrs in North Africa illustrates the relationship between martyr acts, canon, and calendar in a surprising way. There are three extant sermons (*ss*. 300–301A), the same number as for the popular Perpetua and Felicity. This feast, on August 1, was accompanied by the reading of the account of seven martyr-brothers from 2 Macc. 7, which is treated precisely as a set of *acta*. In this case, the question of canon is raised by Augustine, at least rhetorically, as an objection to the reading rather than as a justification for it. Augustine's technique is to invoke hypothetical Jewish observers who wonder how these men could be considered Christian martyrs. His answer implies that it is the brothers' actions and faith that makes them genuine martyrs (cf. *s*. 300.6); but, strikingly, this also implies that it is the genre of martyr *acta*—more than the authority of canonical scripture, which might have seemed a more obvious defense—that drives the liturgical use of this story. There are other cases—for example, the feasts of St. Stephen and of John the Baptist—where a canonical text again serves this dual function, and hence where the people may have received the story as much or more in terms of the martyrial genre than simply as scripture.

The reading of some martyr acts and not others may also have been determined by prosaic issues such as the extent of an ecclesial library. In the case of St. Lawrence, who was celebrated on August 10, for which day there are at least five sermons,[40] Augustine makes no reference to *acta* despite saying that "on this festival sacred readings have resounded. We have heard and we have sung, and we have listened carefully to the Gospel reading."[41] While he does allude to Lawrence's

---

38. For more details, see Margoni-Kögler, *Die Perikopen*, 143–70; Lapointe, *La célébration des martyrs*, 104–16.

39. *S*. 273.3 (PL 38:1249): "ego non colo Fructuosum, sed deum colo, quem colit et Fructuosus."

40. Hill suggests that *s*. 302 is a composite made up of two sermons dedicated to St. Lawrence. See *Sermons 273–305A*, WSA III/8, 312–13.

41. *S*. 302.1 (PL 38:1385; trans. is my own): "huic sollemnitati sanctae lectiones congruae sonuerunt. audiuimus et cantauimus, et euangelicam lectionem intentissime accepimus."

story here, this seems an appeal to general knowledge rather than to anything actually read. These *acta* were well known to Ambrose, hardly far away in space or time, but they may not have been widely or anciently distributed in the West.[42] This may mean there simply was no copy of the *acta*, or, at least, no generally accepted version of them, at either Hippo or Carthage. To complicate matters, two of Augustine's sermons, one from Carthage and another from an uncertain location, imply a reading on St. Lawrence's Day from Cyprian's *Ad Fortunatum*, much of which was a catena of biblical texts, but which had exhortation to martyrdom as its overall theme.[43] It may be that this treatise represents yet another non- or, at best, quasi-scriptural liturgical reading at Carthage, if also not at Hippo.

This reading of martyr acts may not have been a widespread practice outside Africa. The endorsements pronounced at synods and councils in Hippo and Carthage during the 390s suggest a measure of defensiveness, or at least of desire to establish clear boundaries for this quasi-scriptural practice, rather than a recent and very local origin.[44] However, to exaggerate the African peculiarity of the custom might fall into a trap of assuming some universal pattern of reading from which this was a deviation, or to which it was an addition.

There is every reason to assume that communal reading at eucharistic assemblies had actually been the, or at least an, original context for the generation of martyriological *acta*.[45] This could represent the maintenance of an old tradition, and one that might once have been widespread, although there may have been a surge in composition or elaboration of these texts for liturgical purposes in the later third and fourth centuries.[46] While the liturgical elements in some of the most important martyr *acta* do not themselves require a eucharistic context, they certainly encourage it.[47] So the absence of these works in

42. Lapointe, *La célébration des martyrs*, 100.

43. These are *s.* 303 and *s.* 305A; Hill (WSA III/8, 316n1) notes doubts about both the authorship and the integrity of *s.* 303, but the association between St. Lawrence and the reading of *Ad Fortunatum* would be even stronger if the source were not Augustine.

44. See the excerpts from the *acta* in Lawrence J. Johnson, *Worship in the Early Church: An Anthology of Historical Sources* (Collegeville, MN: Liturgical Press, 2009), 2:4–8.

45. McGowan, *Ancient Christian Worship*, 245–46; see also Candida R. Moss, *The Other Christs: Imitating Jesus in Ancient Christian Ideologies of Martyrdom* (New York: Oxford University Press, 2010), 13–15.

46. Éric Rebillard, *The Early Martyr Narratives: Neither Authentic Accounts nor Forgeries* (Philadelphia: University of Pennsylvania Press, 2020), 27 and 31–32.

47. Candida R. Moss, *Ancient Christian Martyrdom: Diverse Practices, Theologies, and Traditions* (New Haven: Yale University Press, 2012), 140–41.

the liturgies of other centers might mean they were omitted, as different assumptions about the canon and the purposes of scripture and of reading came to the fore, rather than having been added to the African rite only recently or idiosyncratically.

Miracles

A further set of extrabiblical readings commonly used at Hippo is that of *libelli miraculorum*, accounts of wonders performed in association with martyr cults in particular. These are not quite comparable to the martyriological *acta* in that they seem to be a separate category of texts, read in addition to scripture rather than in place of it, and for specific reasons and occasions.

Augustine discusses the background in *De ciuitate dei*:

> For the canon of sacred scripture, which has rightly been brought to a close, causes the earlier miracles to be recited everywhere and to stick in everyone's memory. But these recent miracles are barely known to all the residents of the city or district where they are performed. All too often they are known only to a very few, and the rest have no knowledge of them at all, especially if the city is a large one. And when they are told to other persons in other places—despite the fact that they are reported by Christian believers to Christian believers—there is no sufficient authority to back them up and ensure that they are believed without doubt or difficulty.[48]

A number of his sermons refer to the *libellus miraculorum* associated with the intervention of St. Stephen, especially in the cure of a blind man that features in that discussion. Augustine refers more than once to this book and its apparent reading in church:

---

48. *Ciu.* 22.8 (PL 48:816; trans. adapted from Babcock, *City of God (Books 11–22)*, WSA I/7, 509; the translation "no authority with the weight of Scripture" for "non tanta ea commendat auctoritas" overinterprets): "canon quippe sacrarum litterarum, quem definitum esse oportebat. illa facit ubique recitari et memoriae cunctorum inhaerere populorum; haec autem ubicumque fiunt, ibi sciuntur uix a tota ipsa ciuitate uel quocumque commanentium loco. nam plerumque etiam ibi paucissimi sciunt ignorantibus ceteris, maxime si magna sit ciuitas; et quando alibi aliis que narrantur, non tanta ea commendat auctoritas, ut sine difficultate uel dubitatione credantur, quamuis christianis fidelibus a fidelibus indicentur."

Tired out though I am, and scarcely able to speak, accept ungrudgingly a few words from me. After all, we also have the booklet about the favors God has granted through his holy martyr, so let us listen to that too even more willingly.[49]

Another sermon (s. 319) indicates that the St. Stephen miracles book was to have been read, but was omitted because of the heat of that day. A different *libellus* is referred to in Sermon 286, a sermon on St. Gervase and St. Protase. A set of brief sermons extending from Easter Day through Easter week (ss. 320–24) refer to a miracle that had taken place on the Sunday; Sermon 322 is itself actually the *libellus*, perhaps not quite a sermon but a witness to the effect of the martyr cult.

This type of work and its reading do not represent quite the same tradition as the martyr *acta*, even if some affinity with these as well as with scripture (at least in Augustine's eyes, as the discussion in *De ciuitate dei* indicates) is evident. Rather, the *libelli* seem to be an evolving genre, allowed for in part by the precedent of the martyr texts, but also a limited analogue to scripture itself.[50] In Augustine's case, as elsewhere, the *libelli* seem to be intended for public reading in church and not just for personal edification.[51] They add to the sense that the reading practices of Hippo would be poorly understood merely by attending to canonical scripture; but, as we shall see further, their character also reflects some of what Augustine and his contemporaries sought in their concern about the limits of scripture.

Beyond the Canon

There were other exceptions to the much-emphasized limit of scripture. Augustine indicates that the question of canonical writings was not completely settled everywhere in practice, even in the act of suggesting otherwise. While his clarity on this subject in a letter to the presbyter Quintian allows us to believe that the Christians at Hippo were kept on a strictly canonical diet except as already noted, Augustine also implies that other African locales provided exceptions:

49. S. 94 (PL 38:580; trans. Hill, WSA III/3, 478): "a me autem fatigato et uix loquente, pauca libenter accipite. habemus enim et libellum de beneficiis dei per sanctum martyrem datis, pariter libentius audiamus."
50. Yvette Duval, "Sur la genèse des *libelli miraculorum*," *REAug* 52, no. 1 (2006): 97–112.
51. Duval, "Sur la genèse des *libelli miraculorum*."

As for you, do not first throw the church into a scandal by reading to the people writings that the canon of the church has not accepted. After all, heretics, and especially the Manichees, often use these writings to throw the minds of the unlearned into confusion, and I hear that they like to hide out in your territory.[52]

Augustine goes on to refer to a junior reader named Privation, whose status is apparently being negotiated between local bishops:

> I wonder whether he can be counted as a lector who has only once read the scriptures, and those non-canonical ones [*etiam non canonicas*]. For, if he is a lector in the church for this reason, then those scriptures are, of course, ecclesiastical. But if those scriptures are not ecclesiastical, whoever reads them, even in church, is not a lector of the church.[53]

On the one hand, the way Augustine calls these unnamed writings "not ecclesiastical" by way of casting a shadow on their value seems to exclude martyr *acta* and *libelli miraculorum*. On the other hand, there is little reason to think that Manichaean works are at issue, since that would have generated an even higher level of rhetorical response. It is more likely that these were either Old Testament pseudepigrapha[54] or popular Christian works like the Shepherd of Hermas. We have seen that exceptions to canonical status were allowed for specific genres, but the quasi-scriptural pretensions of other works were precisely what disqualified them for Augustine. A solid *libellus* was better than a dubious Gospel.

---

52. *Ep.* 64.3 (CSEL 34/2:230–31; trans. Teske, *Letters 1–99*, WSA II/1, 254): "uos ipsi prius nolite in scandalum mittere ecclesiam, legendo in populis scripturas quas canon ecclesiasticus non recepit! his enim haeretici et maxime manichaei solent imperitas mentes euertere, quos in campo uestro libenter latitare audio."

53. *Ep.* 64.3 (CSEL 34/2:231; trans. Teske, WSA II/1, 254): "miror enim utrum iam potest lector deputari, qui non nisi semel scripturas etiam non canonicas legit. si enim propterea iam ille lector ecclesiasticus, profecto et illa scriptura ecclesiastica est; si autem illa scriptura ecclesiastica non est, quisquis eam quamuis in ecclesia legerit, ecclesiasticus lector non est."

54. Monceaux points out that the African councils of this period do not mention Baruch or Lamentations, which could make them "Old Testament Pseudepigrapha," but he also suggests these were implied as part of Jeremiah; Paul Monceaux, *Histoire littéraire de l'Afrique chrétienne depuis les origines jusqu'à l'invasion arabe*, vol. 5, *Saint Optat et les premiers écrivains donatistes* (Paris: Leroux, 1905), 231–32.

All this means that liturgical reading at Hippo was not bound by the limits of canon as typically defined, even if canonical scripture was of course overwhelmingly its largest part. Such reading, canonical or not, was clearly shaped by the community and rule of faith, of which the canon was both measure and reflection. Scripture itself, however, is not quite the heart of liturgical reading; it speaks, however—with unique quantity and force, certainly for Augustine and perhaps for his hearers—to the heart, the history to which contemporary miracles and historic martyrdoms also attested, and hence to the same divine purpose. This *habitus* of reading then encompasses not only the mixture of customary, discretionary, and course readings, but also the threefold structure of lections at the typical liturgy. The library from which these come turns out not merely to be scripture but to include martyriological and miracle texts, which illustrates that the reading culture was not yet determined merely by the question of how to read scripture itself, but by the more basic question of just how and what to read at all.

Seasons

Christmas[55]

There does not seem to have been an Advent season as such, or even any less formal liturgical preparation for Christmas at Hippo: extant sermons from close before and after Christmas show little sense of "season." The readings at Christmas, however, show clear patterns and also variations that have stumped or misled scholars looking for a supposed lectionary. Assumptions about uniform development and the supposed presence or absence of Old Testament readings as a norm at one point or other have interfered with attempts to provide an accurate picture.[56]

There may be two patterns at Christmas, at least of the Gospel readings: while Luke 2 is unsurprisingly well-attested, Augustine may also have used the Matthean story (cf. s. 370); likewise, he preaches a number of times on John 1. This variety could reflect two liturgies or stations, as well as the usual discretion being exercised by an episcopal preacher, or even some more general development over time toward a preference for a particular Gospel. Isaiah 7 seems likely to

55. See Margoni-Kögler, *Die Perikopen,* 49–77.
56. Margoni-Kögler, *Die Perikopen,* 67–70.

have been read at least on one occasion (*s.* 370),[57] as were Pss. 18, 84, and 95.[58] Epistles from Rom. 5 (*s.* 185) and Phil. 2 (*s.* 196A) may have been read as well.

There are two or three sermons for the Kalends of January, which focus on warning against pagan observances (*ss.* 197–98A). To call this Circumcision or even an Octave of Christmas is misleading.[59] While at least one sermon (*s.* 196A) concerns the circumcision of Jesus and seems to be from close to Christmas, it does not address the Kalends and does not support the existence of any "feast." Epiphany sermons do look back to Christmas, and the stories told in the Gospels on the two days are often compared. The use of Matt. 2 seems clear, but other readings are only implicitly present.

Lent

Sermons from the beginning of Lent focus on admonition to fasting, and those during Lent reflect catechetical and liturgical preparations for Easter baptisms. Homilies for catechumens may have been given at separate gatherings. Some portions of the *In Iohannis euangelium tractatus* were given in Lent (e.g., 7–12), as were some of the *Enarrationes in Psalmos* (e.g., 95, 128–33).[60]

Three sermons from the beginning of Lent (*ss.* 205–7) make repeated reference to Isa. 58 (perhaps vv. 3–7) and Luke 6:37–38. Another (*s.* 195) addresses the story of the man healed at the pool of Bethsaida (John 5:1–18). A sermon on the bread of life discourse in John 6 (*s.* 132) focuses on the catechumens and hence may be closer to Easter, but this is not clear. Another (*s.* 136) treats John 9, along with some interesting commentary about reading:

> We have heard the reading of the Gospel which we usually do. But it's good to be reminded of it; it's good to restore the youth of our memories from our elderly forgetfulness. In any case, this most familiar of readings has given us as much pleasure as if it were brand-new.[61]

---

57. On this sermon, see Margoni-Kögler, *Die Perikopen*, 49n136.

58. Ps. 84 being most explicit; cf. *s.* 189.

59. Willis, *St Augustine's Lectionary*, 22 and 61.

60. Anne-Marie La Bonnardiere, *Recherches de chronologie augustinienne* (Paris: Études Augustiniennes, 1965), 52. In *St Augustine's Lectionary*, 23–24, Willis gives Lenten readings from *In Iohannis euangelium tractatus*.

61. *S.* 136 (PL 38:750; trans. Hill, *Sermons 94A–147A*, WSA III/4, 354): "audiuimus lectionem sancti euangelii, quam solemus: sed bonum est commoneri; bonum est ab obliuionis ueterno memoriam renouare. denique uetustissima lectio, quasi noua, nos delectauit."

All this Johannine material could be added to the *In Iohannis euangelium trac-tatus*, which at least overlap with Lent, in order to suggest a seasonal association, yet we should hesitate to label this a course reading as such. It may be that, like the possible Genesis readings noted *supra*, some Johannine passages are becoming traditional for the season.

There are also sermons associated with the "Tradition" of the Creed and with its "Rendition," the latter of which was also the occasion for instruction on the Lord's Prayer.[62] Most scholars put the *traditio* on the Saturday that fell fifteen days before Easter, and place the *redditio* a week later, but the *traditio* could just as well have been a further week earlier.[63] Preaching on these occasions was geared to those liturgical texts, but the Matthean account of the Lord's Prayer may have been the liturgical Gospel on the day that the focus was on prayer.

It is anachronistic to speak of a Holy Week as such at Hippo circa 400, and while there are elements of a *Triduum*,[64] Augustine's forty days of fasting give way directly to fifty days of celebration.[65] The rituals and observances of the week are hard to reconstruct, but there was clearly some intensification of preparation. One year Ps. 21 (22) was read or sung on Wednesday;[66] in a discourse on the same psalm, Augustine says of it that "the passion of Christ was quite obviously read as the gospel."[67] This may be from that same Wednesday *statio* and may even be from the same year; indeed, it could be a *quasi-euangelium* from a non-eucharistic event. The Johannine footwashing story was read at some point shortly before Easter, presumably on Thursday.[68]

Augustine had inherited a tradition of reading the passion story from the Gospel of Matthew on Friday, one example of the tendency for readings to become traditional on feasts or in specific seasons more quickly than they did otherwise. Yet this same example shows the flexibility still attached to these practices. In a sermon for Easter Tuesday (*s.* 232), Augustine refers back to the unease expressed by the people when he had once changed the Friday custom: "Once upon a time I wanted the passion to be read according to all the evangelists on successive

62. On the catechetical and ritual processes, see Burns and Jensen, *Christianity in Roman Africa*, 201–4.
63. P. Verbraken, "Les sermons CCXV et LVI de Saint Augustin," *RBén* 68 (1958): 5–40, cited by Poque, *Sermons pour la Pâque*, 26.
64. See *ep.* 54 (CSEL 34/2:158–168); Poque, *Sermons pour la Pâque*, 71–72.
65. See *s.* 252 (PL 38:1171–79).
66. *Ep. Io. tr.* 2.2 (PL 35:1989–90); this took place at the first "station," presumably of that day.
67. *En. Ps.* 21.2.2 (CCSL 38:123): "passio Christi tam euidenter quasi euangelium recitatur."
68. See *s.* 119.1 (PL 38:673).

years. It happened; people didn't hear what they were used to and were upset."[69] Once again the community seems to have been as much the keeper of emergent customary lections as were the clergy.

The surviving sermons for Friday (*ss.* 218–18C) may obliquely refer to Augustine's interest in the other passion narratives, in that they seem more focused on the Johannine account than on Matthew's. Sermon 218, an exposition that refers to details of the John text—clearly not to those of Matthew—could belong to the year Augustine upset local tradition.

Easter

As we have seen, Augustine interrupts his sequence of homilies on John's Gospel at Easter because there was a set of expected readings (*ep. Io. tr.* prol.). This is another place where we can see both the general absence of a "lectionary" and the emergence of seasonal (not just festal or occasional) associations of certain readings and times.

At the vigil, the main and perhaps the only celebration at Easter (cf. *infra*), a significant series of Old Testament readings was involved, interspersed with prayer and psalms or canticles.[70] Augustine's plentiful scriptural quotations and allusions in sermons related to the vigil may include readings other than those cited, but they are too numerous to be clear. Some of the likely elements are the Gen. 1 creation story, the canticle of Exod. 15, Isa. 2, the Prayer of Azariah (from the LXX of Dan. 3), and Ps. 41. That these clear elements, apart from the Gospel, are all from the Old Testament is not coincidental. The shape of the vigil seems to be a discursive movement through salvation history, to which the Gospel is the response rather than just the culmination of a series. This also has some implications for the Easter Gospels, which will be treated below.

It is clear that Matt. 28 was the Easter Gospel, and Augustine names it first when referring in sermons to lists of the resurrection narratives that are read through the week. In such lists he consistently says Matthew was read on the first day (*s.* 232; cf. *infra*), which must mean at the vigil. Willis had assumed that the second Gospel in Augustine's lists, which varies but is always another synoptic account, was that of a second celebration on Easter morning, but this seems

---

69. *S.* 232 (PL 38:1108; trans. Hill, *Sermons 230–272B*, WSA III/7, 25): "uolueram aliquando, ut per singulos annos secundum omnes euangelistas etiam passio legeretur. factum est; non audierunt homines quod consueuerant, et perturbati sunt."

70. *S.* 223A (*MA* 1:11–17); see further Margoni-Kögler, *Die Perikopen*, 100–110.

unlikely.[71] John 1, which is not found in Augustine's lists, was also clearly read at some point (*ss.* 225 and 226; cf. *ss.* 119, 120, and 121).

The catalog of sermons in Augustine's library given by Possidius mentions twenty-three items from the vigil, but none (other) from Easter day.[72] This is one reason to consider the possibility that the distinction between the vigil and a morning service—and, hence, between different supposed Gospels—may be illusory. Preaching may have happened at different points of a complex observance; a number of sermons are addressed to the newly baptized, but perhaps closer to the offertory than to the Gospel.[73] The use of John 1, which in sermons seems more closely associated with mystagogy of the *infantes* than with the vigil readings, may have been part of a baptismal rite rather than the Gospel of a second Eucharist.

One of those Easter instructions to the newly baptized (*s.* 277) refers to the course reading of the Acts of the Apostles, as noted *supra*. Two different readings from Acts are attested on the Sunday after Easter (cf. *infra*), which again suggests that there was no lectionary for specific days but rather a flexible course reading. Psalm 117 was also used in this latter portion of the celebration (*s.* 225).

Easter Week

The Gospel readings in Easter week provide some challenges. Augustine explicitly refers to a series of Gospels for the week, beginning with Matthew, in a number of sermons (*ss.* 232, 235, 247, and 239):

> Yesterday evening the story of the Savior's resurrection was read from the Gospel, but it was read from the Gospel according to Matthew. Today, however, as you heard the lector proclaiming it, the Lord's resurrection was chanted as the evangelist Luke wrote about it.[74]

71. See C. Lambot, "Les sermons de Saint Augustin pour les fêtes de Paques: tradition manuscrite," in *Mélanges en l'honneur de Monseigneur Michel Andrieu*, Revue des Sciences Religieuses, Volume Hors Série (Strasbourg: Palais Universitaire, 1956), 263–78.

72. Possidius, *Indiculum* 174 (*MA* 2:205); see Poque, *Sermons pour la Pâque*, 74 and 78.

73. Cf., e.g., *s.* 272 (PL 38:1246–48), which was preached during Pentecost, when the *infantes* have the eucharistic offerings that are already on the altar pointed out to them.

74. *S.* 235 (PL 38:1117–18): "hesterno die, id est nocte, lecta est ex euangelio resurrectio saluatoris, lecta autem ex euangelio secundum Matthaeum. hodie uero, sicut audistis pronuntiare lectorem, recitata est nobis domini resurrectio, sicut Lucas euangelista conscripsit." The emendations by Hill, who claims that the better reading is "based on a faulty historical understanding of earlier liturgical practice," may redound on the translator here. Cf. WSA III/7, 41.

Except for routinely beginning with Matthew, the lists are variable. It was clearly customary (as Augustine himself noted in the discussion of his Good Friday faux pas) to read different accounts on the days of Easter week. However, the reported resurrection narratives, following the Matthean at the vigil, are not consistent. The patterns are something like this:

s. 232	Matthew, Mark, Luke
s. 247	Matthew, Luke, Mark, John, (Luke?)
s. 235	Matthew, Luke
s. 239	[ ], Luke, Mark

Suzanne Poque sought to establish four *ordines* by correlating tractates of the *In epistulam Iohannis ad Parthos* in some manuscripts with the Gospel references in them.[75] In reality, these are all manifestations of a consistent rubric that all the accounts ought to be read, not of different lectionaries at different times. If some development can be sought, the pattern agreeing with the canonical order of the Gospels might be later. And since Augustine does explain the practice of reading them in these terms (*s.* 235.1), it could be logical to see a movement in that direction during his episcopate.

Two of the sermons in the *In epistulam Iohannis ad Parthos* given around this time mention Gospel readings from Matt. 5–6. In the manuscript tradition, Matt. 7 is for Saturday of the week, but since Augustine had explained the origin of the tractates on the Epistle by saying that only the Resurrection Gospels could be read that week, this remains unclear.[76]

Sunday after Easter

The Sunday after Easter was the completion of an extended *sacramentum* for the newly baptized (*s.* 260) and the feast of the Twenty Martyrs who were patrons of the church at Hippo (*ss.* 257 and 148). John 20:24–31 (and possibly the verses

75. Poque claims the existence of an "*ordo Hipponensis*" in order to provide (dubious) gravitas to what seems likely still to have been a fluid, if not completely amorphous, pattern of readings. For the Gospels of the four "systems" that could be reconstructed, see Poque, "Les lectures liturgiques," 239; for other readings, see Poque, *Sermons pour la Pâque*. The whole enterprise of working from the manuscript tradition on these issues has been questioned pointedly by Drobner, "Transmission of Augustine's Sermons."

76. For the manuscript tradition of the titles on the Tractates, see M. Comeau, "Sur la transmission des sermons de Saint Augustin," *Revue des études latines* 10 (1932): 408–22. For a more critical view, see once again Drobner, "Transmission of Augustine's Sermons."

immediately preceding) was read at one gathering (s. 259); this seems more like a fixed practice than those readings for the previous week. Augustine's citation of Acts 4:20 in Sermon 260E indicates how far the course reading had advanced one year; another year the story in Acts 5:1–11 is cited (s. 148), which could indicate a long reading or, more probably, just a flexible system. Psalm 115 (116) was used more than once; although it resonates with the reading from the Acts of the Apostles in Augustine's translation, it is also fitting for the Twenty Martyrs observance and is used elsewhere in connection with martyrs.[77] At the later assembly, Ps. 117 (118), used on Easter Day, reappears (s. 258, s. 260D).

Ascension and Pentecost

Readings for Ascension are difficult to identify. Unsurprisingly, Acts 1 seems to feature; others are implied and somewhat varied. The simplest explanation is, again, that the readings were not fixed.[78] There may also have been various assemblies, and some of Augustine's surviving sermons may have been preached at Carthage.[79]

Augustine's sermons for Pentecost have recurrent themes. There was an assembly early at the *Memoria Theognis*, where part of Tob. 2 was read (s. 272B), perhaps along with Rom. 7. The expected story from Acts was also read (s. 378). The Gospel may have been Matt. 9 or a parallel, since the saying about wineskins also repeatedly appears.[80]

CONCLUSION

The reading practices of Augustine's liturgy are complex, and neither arbitrary nor formless. To speak of a "lectionary" at Augustine's Hippo is certainly fanciful, to the point that it should simply be avoided. In fact, the reading culture combines some customary lections for times and seasons—course readings as well as specific readings for days—with considerable exercise of episcopal choice, again both in courses through books and in specific lections. Of these, discretion is the

---

77. Poque, *Sermons pour la Pâque*, 110n1.
78. Margoni-Kögler, *Die Perikopen*, 126–30.
79. Saxer, *Saint Augustin*, 20–21.
80. M. Hoondert, "Les sermons de saint Augustin pour le jour de la Pentecôte," *Augustiniana* 46, no. 3/4 (1996): 291–310; Margoni-Kögler, *Die Perikopen*, 133–39.

most important factor overall, although customary associations—of which congregations seem to have been custodians as much as bishops were—are stronger at certain points.

Gospel and psalmody, rather than scripture in some general sense, are the consistent markers or representatives of how the canonical literature shaped liturgy. While in theory Augustine upheld clear boundaries of canonical authority, he both accepted and added to the exceptions—not from so-called apocrypha but from the *passiones* and *libelli*. These connected the Christians at Hippo with divine power derived not only from ancient prophetic words but also from recent and local deeds. He also pursued a number of course readings that worked well for his expository agenda; some of these were clearly traditional, others less so. Together these factors comprise a culture of liturgical reading, driven not just by the bishop but also by the community. This is not solely an approach to reading scripture, but also marks and celebrates sacred time.

From a more diachronic perspective, Augustine's sermons could also be seen to reflect a church calling its liturgical readings into a state of order, toward fixed associations of lections with feasts and with periods of the church's year. Yet that process had much further to go. As a preacher, however, Augustine seems less concerned with issues of structure and order in the external shape of lections than with seeking a shape within the lections themselves, a structure that is shaped more by Gospel than by canon or lection. From this perspective, the famous example of the wrong psalm being read is not so remarkable. Augustine expected to encounter Christ in any psalm and, for that matter, in every passage of scripture. But these signs referred to what or whom North African Christians encountered also in the martyrs, in miracles, and in the sacramental life within which all of his preaching activity was grounded.

Chapter 3

Augustine and Tertullian

Geoffrey D. Dunn

Introduction

Augustine's supposed antipathy toward Tertullian is known well enough, although the connection often merits no more than a footnote in modern studies.[1] The most explicit statement by Augustine about Tertullian is found in *De haeresibus* (*haer.*), and what modern comment there is about that passage focuses on who the "Tertullianists" were, what their relationship with Tertullian was, and what Augustine's source for this information could have been. While important and explored in some detail *infra*, there is a broader, typically African Christian connection between the two, not only throughout Augustine's writings, but also embedded in this text itself. Patout Burns and Robin Jensen have noticed this link in their magnum opus, observing that "Augustine drew upon both of these predecessors [Tertullian and Cyprian] to develop a theology characteristic of Western Christianity."[2]

Burns and Jensen also offer a suggestion that could be applied to the passage in *De haeresibus* regarding why scholars have concentrated more on some parts

1. Peter Brown, *Augustine of Hippo: A Biography*, new ed. (Berkeley: University of California Press, 2000), e.g., has no reference to Tertullian in his index. Major exceptions include Gustave Bardy, "Saint Augustin et Tertullien," *L'année théologique augustinienne* 13 (1953): 145–50, and K. Greschat, "Theologische Traditionen Nordafrikas vor Augustin (Tertullian, Cyprian)," in *Augustin Handbuch*, ed. Volker Drecoll (Tübingen: Mohr Siebeck, 2007), 92–98.

2. J. Patout Burns Jr. and Robin M. Jensen, *Christianity in Roman Africa: The Development of Its Practices and Beliefs* (Grand Rapids: Eerdmans, 2014), xlvi.

of the passage and less on others. They remark that, in contrast to the Greeks, "these Latins worried about the adequacy of human organizations and ministers to mediate the divine life."[3] Thus, scholars are attracted to insights into church life and practice in North Africa, and particularly to questions of schism and the boundaries used to separate groups of Christians, including alleged or perceived states of holiness. In other words, the theological aspects behind Augustine's reception of Tertullian have been less carefully considered.

In this chapter I shall argue that even *De haeresibus* points us beyond questions of the Tertullianists' identity and of ecclesiological fences in coming to an understanding of the relationship between Tertullian and Augustine, even if Augustine did not acknowledge the full extent of that relationship.[4] This chapter aims to explore that connection in *De haeresibus* and will do so particularly regarding remarriage and theological anthropology (the nature of the soul).

AUGUSTINE'S *DE HAERESIBUS*

We may begin by examining Augustine's explicit statement about Tertullian in *De haeresibus*, firstly in light of what has interested most commentators (schism) and secondly in light of the other details that he acknowledges clearly about his attitude toward Tertullian (heresy):

> The Tertullianists are named after Tertullian, whose many eloquently written works are still read. These people were gradually dying out toward our time, but were able to survive in their last remaining members in Carthage. When I was present there a few years ago, as I think you too remember, they were completely gone. The remaining few entered the Catholic Church and handed over their basilica, which is now quite famous, to the Catholic Church. Tertullian, then, as his writings indicate, says that the soul is certainly immortal, but he argues that it is a body. He holds not only that the soul is a body, but also that God himself is. He is not said to have become a heretic on these grounds. For we can suppose that he called the divine nature and substance a body, but not the sort of body with some parts that we can or must think of as larger and other

3. Burns and Jensen, *Christianity in Roman Africa*, xlvi–xlvii.
4. Cf. Burns and Jensen, *Christianity in Roman Africa*, xlvii: "Yet he [Augustine] never explicitly cited his predecessors against one another."

parts that we can or must think of as smaller. Such bodies we call bodies in the proper sense. And yet, he held something of that sort regarding the soul. But he could, as I said, be thought to say that God is a body, because he is not nothing, because he is not emptiness, because he is not a quality of body or of soul, but is whole everywhere and not divided by any stretches of space, remaining without any change in his nature and substance. Hence, Tertullian did not become a heretic on those grounds, but because he joined the Cataphrygians, whom he had earlier attacked, and began to condemn second marriages as immoral, contrary to apostolic teaching. Afterward, he withdrew from them and founded his own small congregations. He also said that the worst souls were turned into demons after death.[5]

De haeresibus was a work requested from Augustine late in 427 CE by Quodvultdeus, the Carthaginian deacon who would succeed Aurelius as bishop of Carthage before the Vandals captured the city in 439 CE and exiled him to Italy.[6] Quodvultdeus wanted not only a summary of heresies but also a refuta-

5. *Haer.* 86 (CCSL 46:338–39; trans. Teske, *Arianism and Other Heresies*, WSA I/18, 54–55): "tertullianistae a tertulliano, cuius multa leguntur opuscula eloquentissime scripta, usque ad nostrum tempus paulatim deficientes, in extremis reliquiis durare potuerunt in urbe carthaginensi. me autem ibi posito ante aliquot annos, quod etiam te meminisse arbitror, omni ex parte consumpti sunt. paucissimi enim qui remanserant in catholicam transierunt, suam que basilicam, quae nunc etiam notissima est, catholicae tradiderunt. tertullianus ergo, sicut scripta eius indicant, animam dicit immortalem quidem, sed eam corpus esse contendit, neque hanc tantum, sed ipsum etiam deum. nec tamen hinc haereticus dicitur factus. posset enim quoquo modo putari ipsam naturam substantiam que diuinam corpus uocare, non tale corpus cuius partes aliae maiores, aliae minores ualeant uel debeant cogitari, qualia sunt omnia quae proprie dicimus corpora, quamuis de anima tale aliquid sentiat. sed potuit, ut dixi, propterea putari corpus deum dicere, quia non est nihil, non est inanitas, non est corporis uel animae qualitas, sed ubique totus, et per locorum spatia nulla partitus, in sua tamen natura atque substantia incommutabiliter permanet. non ergo ideo est tertullianus factus haereticus, sed quia transiens ad cataphrygas, quos ante destruxerat, coepit etiam secundas nuptias contra apostolicam doctrinam tamquam stupra damnare, et postmodum etiam ab ipsis diuisus sua conuenticula propagauit. dicit sane ipse animas hominum pessimas post mortem in daemones uerti." I am here omitting any reference to *Praedestinatus*, since that seems to have relied directly on Augustine's work.

6. *Epp.* 221, 222, 223, and 224 (CSEL 57:442–46, 446–49, 449–51, 451–54). On Quodvultdeus, see Daniel Van Slyke, *Quodvultdeus of Carthage: The Apocalyptic Theology of a Roman African in Exile*, Early Christian Studies 5 (Strathfield, NSW: St Pauls Publications, 2003), and

tion of them. It is this second section that remained incomplete at the time of Augustine's death. As his replies to Quodvultdeus indicate, the major sources of information on which Augustine drew were Epiphanius of Salamis (an epitome) (1–57), Philaster of Brescia (58–80), Eusebius, and Jerome, with the latter two providing information on more recent heresies.[7] It is possible that Augustine could have been influenced in writing about the Tertullianists by Jerome, from whom he derived his comments about the Helvidians in section 84, although little of what Augustine writes about Tertullian matches what is in Jerome's *De uiris illustribus* (*Vir. ill.*).[8] Yet, given that immediately after his comments on the Tertullianists he wrote about Abeloim and the Pelagians,[9] where his information was firsthand, it is more than likely that Augustine was writing about the Tertullianists from some degree of personal knowledge. Indeed, he wrote about what he knew of them in Carthage on the basis of his visits there; and it should not be surprising that Augustine, the African, knew more about them than did Jerome.

If Augustine's source for material on the Tertullianists was personal rather than derivative and was hastily put together because he felt providing an original contribution was beyond him, then any criticism of Augustine's uncritical use of sources for earlier parts of *De haeresibus* would not apply to what he writes about the Tertullianists. Given that Quodvultdeus was Carthaginian, the information Augustine supplied ought not to have been entirely unknown to the deacon. It is certainly possible that Augustine's information was based on locally accepted hearsay, but, given his association with Carthage over many decades, it would be surprising if Augustine had never bothered to confirm its veracity.

Quodvultdeus, *Quodvultdeus of Carthage: The Creedal Homilies; Conversion in Fifth-Century North Africa*, trans. Thomas Macy Finn, ACW 60 (New York: Newman, 2004).

7. Roland J. Teske, "*Haeresibus, De*," *AttA*, 412–13. See also Sydney Sadowski, "A Critical Look and Evaluation of Augustine's *De haeresibus*," *Augustinianum* 55 (2015): 466–67.

8. Jerome, *Vir. ill.* 53 (Ernest Cushing Richardson, ed., *Hieronymus: Liber de uiris inlustribus; Gennadius: Liber de uiris inlustribus*, Texte und Untersuchungen 84 [Leipzig: Hinrichs, 1896], 31–32).

9. *Haer.* 87–88 (CCSL 46:337–42). In *haer.* 83 (CCSL 46:337), Augustine explicitly notes that, henceforth, he will be discussing heresies that he encountered personally.

Augustine and Tertullian the Schismatic/Heretic: The Tertullianists

Augustine was unequivocal about Tertullian; the man, though eloquent, was a heretic, belonging to the Cataphrygians—even though he eventually left them and formed his own sect. Tertullian's label of "heretic" was not because of his beliefs about the nature of the soul but rather because of his schismatic actions, his departure from the church, and his beliefs about second marriage.[10] What has drawn recent attention are the statements concerning Tertullian as a schismatic. Despite the confidence with which they are expressed, Augustine's assertions in this regard have been challenged in some recent scholarship.

Just as he did with the evidence in Jerome about Tertullian's biography, Timothy Barnes dismisses the biographical accuracy provided by Augustine: "On the matters in question, neither Jerome . . . nor Augustine and 'Praedestinatus' . . . possessed any authentic information."[11] Barnes argues that the Tertullianists could well have been simply the name by which the Montanists (or Cataphrygians or followers of the New Prophecy that first appeared early in the second century in Phrygia in Africa) were later known.[12] Douglas Powell argues that, whatever else Tertullian's Montanism was, it was not schismatic.[13] It was more a local adaptation of what existed in Phrygia and an *ecclesiola in ecclesia*. He also argues not only that Tertullian did not split from the church, but that there is also no evidence that he later split from his Montanist sect within the church.[14] Powell suggests that when the Montanists were expelled from the church in Rome and went their own way, the Montanists in Africa remained part of the

10. While Augustine certainly distinguished schism from heresy and did so in ways familiar to modern Christians, it is still interesting to note how closely he links schism with heresy here.

11. Timothy David Barnes, *Tertullian: A Historical and Literary Study*, rev. ed. (Oxford: Clarendon, 1985), 57.

12. Barnes, *Tertullian*, 258–59. See J. M. Fuller, "Tertullianus," in *A Dictionary of Early Christian Biography and Literature*, ed. H. Wace and W. C. Piercy (London: John Murray, 1911), 940, who also claims that Tertullian became head of the Montanists in Africa, an idea not followed by Barnes. On Montanism, see Christine Trevett, *Montanism: Gender, Authority and the New Prophecy* (Cambridge: Cambridge University Press, 1996), 2, 69, 75, and 225, who agrees that Tertullian was never schismatic but part of an *ecclesiola in ecclesia*.

13. This is also my own view: cf. Geoffrey D. Dunn, *Tertullian*, ECF (London: Routledge, 2004), 6–7.

14. Douglas Powell, "Tertullianists and Cataphrygians," *VC* 29 (1975): 33–54.

church and were known as Tertullianists ("continuing Montanists," as it were), and that Augustine could have been somewhat confused.[15]

David Rankin entertains the possibility that Augustine's comments were inference-based—that is, that, given their name, the Tertullianists could have been established by Tertullian himself, without that necessarily being the case.[16] William Tabbernee, agreeing that Tertullian and the Montanists in the early third century never left the church, posits the idea that perhaps sometime in the middle of the third century a group of African Christians did separate from the church, naming itself after Tertullian, whose views (Montanist and other) they admired.[17] David Wilhite also dismisses the reliability of Augustine's testimony about Tertullian founding the Tertullianists,[18] although he is inclined to accept the argument of L. J. van der Lof that Tertullian did not belong to a group within the church but simply belonged to the church itself.[19]

This amounts to a rereading of Augustine in the light of a rereading of Tertullian's biography and the latter's comments about his admittedly tempestuous relationship with fellow Christians. The growing scholarly consensus, though it admits of nuance, is that Augustine knew of Tertullianists but that he merely assumed that they were founded by Tertullian and that, therefore, the assumption

15. Powell, "Tertullianists and Cataphrygians," 53. Cf. J. Massingberd Ford, "Was Montanism a Jewish Christian Heresy?," *Journal of Ecclesiastical History* 17 (1966): 145–58.

16. David Rankin, *Tertullian and the Church* (Cambridge: Cambridge University Press, 1995), 41–51. On 45, Rankin attempts to distinguish Cataphrygianism, the original form, from New Prophecy, its African form.

17. William Tabbernee, *Montanist Inscriptions and Testimonia: Epigraphic Sources Illustrating the History of Montanism*, PatrMS 16 (Macon, GA: Mercer University Press, 1997), 476. See also Tabbernee, *Fake Prophecy and Polluted Sacraments: Ecclesiastical and Imperial Reactions to Montanism*, VCSup 84 (Leiden: Brill, 2007), 129–32 and 268–69; and Tabbernee, *Prophets and Gravestones: An Imaginative History of Montanists and Other Early Christians* (Peabody, MA: Hendrickson, 2009), 245n5.

18. David E. Wilhite, *Tertullian the African: An Anthropological Reading of Tertullian's Context and Identities*, Millennium Studies 14 (Berlin: de Gruyter, 2007), 25n134.

19. L. J. van der Lof, "The Plebs of the Psychici: Are the Psychici of De Monogamia Fellow-Catholics of Tertullian?," in *Eulogia: Mélanges offerts à Antoon A. R. Bastiaensen à l'occasion de son soixante-cinquième anniversaire*, ed. G. J. Bartelink, A. Hilhorst, and C. H. Kneepkens (Steenbrugge: Abbey of St Peter, 1991), 353–63; David E. Wilhite, "Identity, Psychology, and the *Psychici*: Tertullian's 'Bishop of Bishops,'" *Interdisciplinary Journal of Research on Religion* 5 (2009): 6n12; and Wilhite, "Perpetua of History in Recent Questions," *JECS* 25 (2017): 307–19, esp. 312, which is contra Christoph Markschies's support for *ecclesiola in ecclesia*.

continues, he not only defected from the church into the Montanists but then defected from the Montanists in order to form his own group.[20]

This leaves several questions unaddressed. That the Tertullianists had had their own basilica in Carthage should not be all that surprising, but Augustine's comment that it was now a famous one (*quae nunc etiam notissima est*) compels one to ask whether it was one that we know today from the archaeological record.[21] The other point of interest that Augustine raises is his claim that, before he had joined them, Tertullian had demolished the Cataphrygians (*quos ante destruxerat*). On what basis Augustine reached such a conclusion is hard to determine, unless he simply assumed that, if Tertullian had been orthodox before he became schismatic, then, by definition, he must originally have been critical of a schismatic group like the Montanists.

AUGUSTINE AND TERTULLIAN THE HERETIC: SECOND MARRIAGE

As noted *supra*, Augustine claimed in *De haeresibus* that Tertullian was condemned as a heretic because, in joining the Cataphrygians, he rejected second marriage (i.e., the remarriage of a widow or widower, not remarriage after divorce) as debauchery. Tertullian's views on this topic are well known. Writing to his wife, Tertullian urged her not to remarry after his death,[22] since abstinence is good, although, given feminine weakness, he understood that she might choose to remarry and urged her to ensure that she married a Christian.[23] Sometime later, writing to a Christian widower, Tertullian still recognized the permissibility of a second marriage,[24] but urged him even more insistently not to remarry, since this would simply be giving in to the temptation to fornicate by giving the act legal protection.[25] In his even later *De monogamia*, Tertullian declared that the Paraclete had revealed opposition to someone's remarriage after the death

---

20. Perhaps on the further inference that the two labels of Cataphrygians and Tertullianists must refer to distinct groups.

21. See Liliane Ennabli, *Carthage: Une métropole chrétienne du IVᵉ à la fin du VIIᵉ siècle*, Études d'Antiquités africaines (Paris: CNRS, 1997), 36.

22. *Ux.* 1.7.3 (CCSL 1:381). Regarding Tertullian's faulty logic, see Dunn, *Tertullian*, 54.

23. *Ux.* 2.1.2–4 (CCSL 1:383–84).

24. *Cast.* 8.1 (CCSL 2:1026).

25. *Cast.* 8.2–9.5 (CCSL 1:1026–28).

of their spouse, in opposition to the widely held teaching of the church, which allowed it.[26] The remainder of the pamphlet was intended to demonstrate that this recent revelation was foreshadowed in the scriptures. William Le Saint states that in these three works we could witness Tertullian's changing opinion on re-marriage and his split from the church.[27] While one would certainly disagree with him on the second point, it is clear that we have here more than just rhe-torical gymnastics from Tertullian; his attitude clearly hardened over time.[28]

While it is quite clear from *De bono uiduitatis* (*b. uid.*) that he held widow-hood in high esteem and advised Christian widows not to remarry, following 1 Cor. 7:39–40,[29] Augustine maintained that second marriages were not con-demned and were even commendable,[30] except for those widows who had un-dertaken a vow of widowhood,[31] and, even in the latter case, a second marriage remained legitimate. Augustine included an explicit criticism of Tertullian when he wrote that not even Tertullian and the Cataphrygians or Novatianists con-demned first marriages.[32] Tertullian's "noisy, mindless puffing" (*buccis sonantinus, non sapientibus*) is held to be responsible for the growth of the Cataphrygians and Novatianists, and his rejection of second marriage is labeled as the activity of a "foul mouth" (*maledico dente*).[33]

While he stated that one of the reasons why Tertullian was condemned as a heretic was his position on second marriage, there are two brief points we can make about Augustine's reactions. The first is that Augustine was singling out

26. *Mon.* 2 (CCSL 2:1229–30).

27. Tertullian, *Treatises on Marriage and Remarriage: To His Wife; An Exhortation to Chas-tity; Monogamy*, trans. William P. Le Saint, ACW 13 (New York: Newman, 1951), 5.

28. See Paul Mattei, "La place du *De monogamia* dans l'évolution théologique et spiritu-elle de Tertullien," *StPatr* 18, no. 3 (1989): 319–28; and Geoffrey D. Dunn, "Tertullian," in *The Early Christian World*, 2nd ed., ed. Philip F. Esler (London: Routledge, 2017), 959–75, esp. 962 and 970–71.

29. *B. uid.* 12.15 (CSEL 41:320–22). The remarriage of widows and widowers is not con-sidered in *b. coniug.* (CSEL 41:187–231).

30. *B. uid.* 4.5–5.7 (CSEL 41:308–12). On this treatise see Geoffrey D. Dunn, "The Ele-ments of Ascetical Widowhood: Augustine's *De bono viduitatis* and *Epistula* 130," in *Prayer and Spirituality in the Early Church*, vol. 4, *The Spiritual Life*, ed. Wendy Mayer, Pauline Allen, and Lawrence Cross (Strathfield: St Pauls Publications, 2006), 247–56.

31. *B. uid.* 11.14 (CSEL 41:320).

32. *B. uid.* 5.7 (CSEL 41:310–12).

33. *B. uid.* 4.6 (CSEL 41:309–10).

Tertullian's view in *De monogamia*, rather than his earlier pamphlets. The second is that, even though it was for this reason that Tertullian was condemned, Augustine did not have as much to say about it as he did about the nature of the soul, a position for which he did not condemn Tertullian.

AUGUSTINE AND TERTULLIAN THE NONHERETIC: THE NATURE OF THE SOUL[34]

Augustine makes the following observations about Tertullian's understanding of the soul (*anima*) in *De haeresibus*: the soul is immortal (*immortalis*), and it is a type of body (*corpus*), just as God is a type of body. But, whereas Tertullian is said not to have made the mistake of equating God's body with the fleshly body, since it is true that the nature (*natura*) or substance (*substantia*) of God is a reality and not "not real" (*non est nihil, non est inanitus*), to some extent he did equate the fleshly body with the soul as body. While Augustine was prepared to give Tertullian some leeway in his definition of body with regard to God, he was less inclined to do so with regard to his definition of body with regard to soul.[35]

How accurate is Augustine's understanding of Tertullian's position? In a recent article, Eliezer Gonzalez argues that early North African Christianity had a more subtle and complex understanding of the afterlife beyond simplistic notions of "resurrection of the flesh" or "immortality of the soul." In other words, we should not approach early Christian theological anthropology through Cartesian dualism of a body/soul distinction.[36] Tertullian certainly was dualistic, but his definitions of body and soul were different from those proposed in the seventeenth century. Indeed, as Eric Osborn points out, Tertullian could write about

34. The corporeality of the soul has long interested Patout Burns. See his *Theological Anthropology*, Sources of Early Christian Thought (Philadelphia: Fortress, 1981).

35. Jérôme Lagouanère, "Augustine, lecteur critique du *De anima* de Tertullien," in *Tertullianus Afer: Tertullien et la littérature chrétienne d'Afrique*, ed. Jérôme Lagouanère and Sabine Fialon, IPM 70 (Turnhout: Brepols, 2015), 231–58. On 233, Lagouanère correctly observes that Augustine devoted most of his attention in this chapter of *De haeresibus* to his views on the soul.

36. Eliezer Gonzalez, "Anthropologies of Continuity: The Body and Soul in Tertullian, Perpetua, and Early Christianity," *JECS* 21 (2013): 480–82. See also Gonzalez, *The Fate of the Dead in Early Third Century North African Christianity: Passion of Perpetua and Felicitas and Tertullian*, Studien und Texte zu Antike und Christentum 83 (Tübingen: Mohr Siebeck, 2014); and Dale B. Martin, *The Corinthian Body* (New Haven: Yale University Press, 1995), 6.

body and soul, flesh and spirit, flesh and soul, or spirit and body.[37] Tertullian also asserted the simplicity of the soul, such that spirit and mind are functions of the soul rather than elements of it,[38] and he rejected the idea of the transmigration of the soul from one body to another.[39]

One of Tertullian's prime concerns was about the origin of the soul; he is regarded as a firm advocate of traducianism—the belief that all souls were transmitted by the parents at the moment of conception of the flesh and, therefore, not created directly by God (and therefore are not preexistent), that every soul exists potentially in Adam (such that every soul needs cleansing through sacramental initiation),[40] and that the soul is generated in the womb at the same time as the flesh is, such that there is no time when one exists without the other (and therefore cannot be infused into a fully formed body at birth),[41] and is, therefore, not eternally preexistent as Plato taught,[42] even though, once created, it is immortal (against Soranus).[43] All of this means that the flesh and the soul are transmitted to a new individual through his or her parents.[44] As Jerónimo Leal points out, for Tertullian, traducianism was primarily a means of explaining the transmission of original sin.[45] The question of the implications of parental or divine origin of the soul was not his main interest. Thus, Tertullian can insist that God is involved in this process as the ultimate origin of the soul.[46] The difficulty in holding both the view that all souls exist in Adam and thus are created by God and the view that each soul is generated parentally is, for later interpreters,

37. Eric Osborn, *Tertullian: First Theologian of the West* (Cambridge: Cambridge University Press, 1997), 214. See also Jonathan Barnes, "*Anima Christiana*," in *Body and Soul in Ancient Philosophy*, ed. D. Frede and B. Reis (Berlin: de Gruyter, 2009), 447–64.

38. *An.* 10–21 (CCSL 2:794–814).

39. *An.* 28–32 (CCSL 2:824–32).

40. *An.* 40.1 (CCSL 2:843).

41. *An.* 25–27 (CCSL 2:818–24).

42. *An.* 4.1 (CCSL 2:786).

43. *An.* 54–58 (CCSL 2:861–69).

44. *An.* 27.8–9 (CCSL 2:824). See Taylor G. Petrey, "Semen Stains: Seminal Procreation and the Patrilineal Genealogy of Salvation in Tertullian," *JECS* 22 (2014): 343–72.

45. Jerónimo Leal, *La antropología de Tertuliano: Estudio de los tratados polémicos de los años 207–212 d.C.*, SEAug 76 (Rome: Institutum Patristicum Augustinianum, 2001), 126.

46. Cf. *An.* 3.4–4.1 (CCSL 2:785–86); 11 (CCSL 2:796–97); and 22.2 (CCSL 2:814), where Tertullian says that souls have their origin in the breath of God, not matter. For criticism of aspects of the alternative to traducianism, see Edmund Hill, *Being Human: A Biblical Perspective*, Introducing Catholic Theology (London: Geoffrey Chapman, 1984), 31–36.

a weakness in Tertullian's position. Perhaps it is also a warning not to read Tertullian too simplistically as a traducian, and especially with a preconceived notion of what traducianism is. It could be that we need to reevaluate the complexity of Tertullian's theological anthropology.[47]

Most importantly for our purposes, Tertullian held—following the Stoics but against the Platonists—that the soul was corporeal.[48] In saying that the soul is a body, he did not mean that it has flesh; it is a spiritual body, just as God is a spiritual body (or both body and spirit).[49] It has existence and reality but not materiality and physicality. A soul that is not corporeal is nonexistent, a nothing. While on more than one occasion he did express his binary components of the human person as body and soul (*substantiae corporis animaeque*),[50] it is

47. For his own summary on the nature of the soul, see *An.* 22.2 (CCSL 2:814–15). For the most detailed analysis of *An.*, see J. H. Waszink, *Quinti Septimi Florentis Tertulliani De Anima*, rev. ed., VCSup 100 (Leiden: Brill, 2010). See also Petr Kitzler, "Tertullian's Concept of the Soul and His Corporealistic Ontology," in Lagouanère and Fialon, *Tertullianus Afer*, 43–62; cf. 56: "Strictly speaking, Tertullian contradicts himself at this point [*An.* 8.4], since he declared the soul to be a body *sui generis*, which means that it must not share the qualities of other bodies."

48. *An.* 5–7 (CCSL 2:786–90). The importance of Luke 16:19–31 in the development of Tertullian's arguments cannot be overstated, especially with attributing both bodily functions and the possibility of experiencing reward and punishment and of being detained in Hades to Lazarus's soul and the souls of the patriarchs, which are corporeal in the particular sense with which Tertullian used the word.

49. *An.* 5 (CCSL 2:786–87); and *Prax.* 7.7–9 (CCSL 2:1166–67): "spiritus enim corpus sui generis in sua effigie." On the latter, see Ernest Evans, *Tertullian's Treatise against Praxeas: The Text Edited, with an Introduction, Translation, and Commentary* (London: SPCK, 1948), 236.

50. *An.* 27.1 (CCSL 2:822). See also *Res.* 32.8 (CCSL 2:962–63) and 35.3 (CCSL 2:967): "ego corpus humanum non aliud intellegam quam omnem istam struem carnis." Here he clearly states the equivalence of body and flesh when speaking about the material element of a person, distinguishing this use of "body" from when it is used in reference to the soul in 35.5 (CCSL 2:967): "animae corpus." It follows that he clearly distinguished body as flesh and body as soul ("distinguitur corpus ab anima, et relinquitur intellegi corpus id, quod in promptu est, caro scilicet"). The problem arises with his extension or change of meaning of *corpus* with regard to the soul as well. The point to be made is that, while the physical body (the flesh) is material, the spiritual body (the soul) is nonmaterial but is still somehow corporeal (in the sense that it is real and not fictitious). Gonzalez, "Anthropologies of Continuity," 485, incorrectly claims that "by corporeal, he [Tertullian] means that it is *material* and bodily, though subtle" (emphasis added), which is not what is found in *An.* 7 or *Res.* 17 (CCSL 2:941), the two passages offered in support. In the latter, at 17.2, Tertullian does indeed say that the soul is corporeal ("animam corporalem . . . habentem proprium genus [substantiae] solidi-

clear that Tertullian used the word "body" in at least two ways: to refer to the physical element (the flesh, as opposed to the spiritual element, the soul) in the human person,[51] and to refer to the reality (and this is what he meant by corporeality) of the spiritual element (which is not necessary to prove for the physical element because it is visible). On this second level both the spiritual element and the physical element of the human person are bodies,[52] and so Tertullian's binary elements are better referred to as soul and flesh rather than soul and body.[53] This might well have been the reason that his pamphlet on the resurrection of Christ is titled *De carne Christi* and not *De corpore Christi*.[54] Of course, in all of this one must keep in mind the unity of the physical body (flesh) and the spiritual body (soul) in the one human person, even though the soul is superior to the flesh.[55]

Perhaps it is Tertullian's inconsistency in applying terminology that caused Osborn to offer the unhelpful claim that between *Apologeticum* and *De anima*

---

tatis." However, the fact that he goes on to say that the soul still ought to be joined with the flesh (17.3: "non qua sentire quid sine carne non possit, sed qua necesse est illam etiam cum carne sentire"), indicates that the soul is both corporeal and *nonmaterial*. See Petr Kitzler, "*Nihil enim anima si non corpus*: Tertullian und die Körperlichkeit der Seele," *WS* 122 (2009): 145–69; Kitzler, "*Ex uno homine tota haec animarum redundantia*: Ursprung, Entstehung und Weitgergabe der individuellen Seele nach Tertullian," *VC* 64 (2010): 353–81; and Kitzler, "Tertullian's Concept of the Soul."

51. Leal, *La antropología de Tertuliano*, 40: "En Tertuliano, *corpus*, tiene un primer sentido de componente material del hombre, como se puede ver en algunos pasajes." See also Leal, "La salvación en el tratado *de anima* de Tertuliano," in *Pagani e cristiani alla ricerca della salvessa (secoli I–III): XXXIV Incontro di studiosi dell'antichità cristiana, Roma, 5–7 maggio 2005*, SEAug 96 (Rome: Institutum Patristicum Augustinianum, 2006), 505–11.

52. Leal, *La antropología de Tertuliano*, 41: "Hay, además, un *corpus animae* y un *corpus carnis*."

53. See *An.* 37.5 (CCSL 2:840): "societatem carnis atque animae." Rather unhelpfully (and seemingly too much influenced by Cartesian dualism), P. Holmes, *ANF* 3:218, translated this as "the conjunction of the body and the soul." The same lack of attention to any distinction between *carnis* and *corpus* is found in the translation of Edwin Quain in *Tertullian, Apologetical Works, and Minucius Felix, "Octavius,"* trans. Rudolph Arbesmann, Sister Emily Joseph Daly, and Edwin A. Quain, FC 10 (Washington, DC: Catholic University of America Press, 1950), 267.

54. On which see Ernest Evans, *Tertullian's Treatise on the Incarnation: The Text Edited with an Introduction, Translation, and Commentary* (London: SPCK, 1956).

55. *An.* 40.2 (CCSL 2:843). Cf. Peter Brown, *The Body and Society: Men, Women, and Sexual Renunciation in Early Christianity* (New York: Columbia University Press, 1988), 77.

Tertullian changed his mind, as well as the unhelpful phrasing when writing that Tertullian argued first for an incorporeal soul and then later for a physical soul.[56] As Leal states, for Tertullian, despite his affinity with Stoicism, there is a great deal of difference between matter and body, for the soul has substance but not materiality.[57] It would be fair to say that Augustine similarly did not appreciate Tertullian's lack of consistency with his use of the term "body," or, at least, found the idea of something being corporeal but nonmaterial difficult to accept.

In his discussions of Tertullian's views on the soul in *De haeresibus*, was Augustine confused by Tertullian's multiple meanings for *corpus*, or did he reject Tertullian's definition of corporeality? An answer to this question is necessary for assessing the accuracy of Augustine's comments about Tertullian's view. It seems that Augustine understood but rejected Tertullian's reference to the soul as corporeal, since he took Tertullian's definition of corporeality as unacceptable. What is significant, though, is Augustine's statement that Tertullian was not condemned as a heretic for his supposedly erroneous views on the nature of the soul.

How do Augustine's comments on Tertullian's view on the soul in *De haeresibus* compare with other statements on this issue elsewhere in Augustine's vast oeuvre? In *De quantitate animae* (*an. quant.*), an early composition in the form of a Socratic dialogue, Augustine argued that a body must have dimension, which seems to be something equivalent to materiality,[58] but the soul, which can grasp incorporeal (or theoretical) things, must be incorporeal and immaterial and, therefore, ought not have a body.[59] In another early work, *De immortalitate animae* (*imm. an.*), Augustine stated that, though the soul animates the body, it can never become a body.[60] His comments are directed against unnamed opinions held by others, among whom Tertullian must be included.

In the lengthy *Epistula* (*ep.*) 147 to Paulina, written about 413 or 414 CE and about whether the fleshly eyes can see God, Augustine deals with those unnamed

---

56. Osborn, *Tertullian*, 214–15. In fact, in *Apol.* 48.4 (CCSL 1:166); *Test. an.* 4.1 (CCSL 1:178); and *Marc.* 4.34.12 (CCSL 1:638), Tertullian argued, as he would in *An.* 7.1–4 (CCSL 2:790), for a corporeal but nonmaterial soul.

57. Leal, *La antropología Tertuliano*, 43–44: "Tertuliano . . . afirma que la diferencia del corporalismo estoico con el tertulianeo consiste en que para éste hay una gran diferencia entre *matreria y cuerpo*, mientras que para aquellos la diferencia es solo de grado: para Teretuliano el alma es de una *sustancia* (Stoff) tal, que no admite confusion con la *materialidad* (Materie)."

58. *An. quant.* 4.6 (CSEL 89:137–39).

59. *An. quant.* 13.22 (CSEL 89:157–58).

60. *Imm. an.* 15.24 (CSEL 89:125–27).

individuals who believe that God "is nothing but a body, supposing that whatever is not a body is not a substance at all."[61] It is obvious that he means to criticize Tertullian as well as those of similar views, and to do so "in every way."[62]

In *De Genesi ad litteram* (*Gen. litt.*), composed more than a decade before *De haeresibus*, we find Augustine offering an earlier criticism of Tertullian's understanding of the soul.[63] While Petr Kitzler reads Augustine as having some sympathy for Tertullian—despite ultimately rejecting his position—that sympathy is difficult to find in Augustine's comments.[64] For Augustine, every body must be passible, and God is certainly not passible. As Jérôme Lagouanère states, for Augustine, there is an assimilation between substance and body and suffering, a view that presents problems for Tertullian's idea of corporeality.[65] God has no body; likewise the soul must not be a body.[66] Augustine could tolerate no definition of body that omitted materiality.[67] Augustine here also questioned the notion of traducianism in light of how Eve came to be, arguing that the scriptural evidence does not permit one to decide for or against either traducianism or creationism,[68] although he did have sympathy for traducianism insofar as it made the notion of original sin easier to understand.[69] Tertullian had clearly advocated traducianism when discussing Eve's origin (from Adam).[70]

Augustine wrote *Epistula* 166 to Jerome at about the same time as *De Genesi ad litteram* was completed (ca. 415 CE). Tertullian is not named in the letter but is certainly the object of criticism when the soul is discussed. Augustine was troubled by this topic because it raised questions regarding a complex of doctrines such as original sin, the fate of unbaptized people after death, free will, grace, and predestination.[71] In *Epistula* 166, Augustine asserts that, although it is

61. *Ep.* 147.21.49 (CSEL 44:324; trans. Teske, *Letters 100–155*, WSA II/2, 345): "omnino corpus esse praesumunt, putantes quidquid corpus non est, nullam prorsus esse substantiam."

62. *Ep.* 147.21.49 (CSEL 44:324; trans. Teske, WSA II/2, 345): "omni modo."

63. *Gen. litt.* 10.25.41 (CSEL 28/1:328).

64. Kitzler, "Tertullian's Concept of the Soul," 60.

65. See Lagouanère, "Augustin," 254: "Or, Augustin, en insistant sur l'assimilation de la substance au corps, et donc au pâtir, souligne l'une des difficultés majeures du corporalisme tertullianien."

66. *Gen. litt.* 10.24.40 (CSEL 28/1:327–28). See also 7.12.18–7.21.31 (CSEL 28/1:211–19).

67. See Lagouanère, "Augustin," 251–52.

68. *Gen. litt.* 10.1.1–10.10.17 (CSEL 28/1:295–307). See Lagouanère, "Augustin," 234–36.

69. *Gen. litt.* 10.23.39 (CSEL 28/1:326–27).

70. *An.* 36.4 (CCSL 2:839). Cf. Lagouanère, "Augustin," 236–38.

71. *Ep.* 166.2.3 (CSEL 44:548–50).

difficult for some to believe, the soul is incorporeal.[72] Yet the fact that Tertullian called the soul corporeal because he wanted to assert its existence and reality was something Augustine could accept. He claimed that he did not want to quibble with words, but then proceeded to do so to the extent that he made it clear what he favored:

> If every substance or essence or that which in some way exists in itself, whatever it might more suitably be called, is a body, then the soul is a body. Likewise, if one wants to call only that nature incorporeal that is supremely immutable and is whole everywhere, then the soul is a body because it is not something of that sort. But if a body is only that which stands still or is moved through an area of space with some length, breadth and depth so that it occupies a larger place with a larger part of itself and a smaller place with a smaller part and is smaller in a part than in the whole, then the soul is not a body.[73]

Augustine's ambivalence on the origin of the soul, in terms of traducianism or creationism, is also evident in *Epistula* 190, a missive written to Optatus of Milevis in 418 CE. He was firm, however, that the soul is a spirit and not a body (as well as being firm against the idea of transmigration of souls).[74] While Augustine points out that Optatus's creationist position makes it difficult to prove the necessity of infant baptism, he also points to problems with the traducian position, which he identified with Tertullian. Augustine's understanding of Tertullian here is that the latter taught that all souls derived from the soul of the first man (thus explaining the transmission of original sin). The problem with this view is that Tertullian believed that the soul was not spirit (*spiritus*) but body (*corpus*) and that God was only body (*nisi corpus*).[75] Augustine writes that nothing could be more perverse (*peruersius*) than Tertullian's position. But this was because

72. *Ep.* 166.2.4 (CSEL 44:550–53).

73. *Ep.* 166.2.4 (CSEL 44:550–51; Teske, *Letters 156–210*, WSA II/3, 80): "si corpus est omnis substantia uel essential uel si quid aptius nuncupatur id, quod aliquot modo est in se ipso, corpus est anima. item si eam solam incorpoream placet appellare naturam, quae summe incommutabilis et ubique tota est, corpus est anima, quoniam tale aliquid ipsa non est. nisi quod per loci spatium aliqua longitudine, latitudine, altitudine ita sistitur uel mouetur, ut maiore sui parte maiorem locum occupet et breuiore breuiorem minusque sit in parte quam in toto, non est corpus anima."

74. *Ep.* 190.1.4 (CSEL 44:140).

75. *Ep.* 190.4.14 (CSEL 44:148–49).

Augustine misunderstood, rejected, oversimplified, or, at least, had not come to realize that Tertullian held that a body could be corporeal and nonmaterial.

We find something in *Confessiones* (*conf.*), which Kitzler believes reflects Augustine's rejection of Tertullian, even though the Carthaginian author is nowhere mentioned in the relevant passage.[76] Augustine notes that as he struggled with the Manichaean notion of good and evil as two infinite opposing powers, he came to the conclusion that God could not be responsible for the creation of evil, since evil could not be a substance and God (and mind for that matter) could not be a bodily substance.[77] This seems to Kitzler to be what Tertullian had taught, and *Confessiones* suggests that on this question Augustine would later come to see Tertullian's point of view as being too similar to that of the Manichaeans.[78]

Augustine did not want to be definitive about the origin of the soul, but he certainly did have problems with what he saw as Tertullian's traducianism. Perhaps it was Augustine's lack of certainty on the question that, in *De haeresibus*, stopped him from labeling Tertullian's unacceptable views as heretical.

CONCLUSION

This chapter has examined the reception of Tertullian by Augustine through the lens of *De haeresibus*. Just as the topic of whether Augustine or the Donatists better reflected the African tradition found in Cyprian has become important for contemporary scholarly research,[79] the topic of Tertullian's reception among later African Christians—including the Donatists—now clearly needs more scholarly attention. While there are differences between them, Tertullian and Cy-

---

76. Kitzler, "Tertullian's Concept of the Soul," 59.

77. *Conf.* 5.10.20 (CCSL 27:69).

78. See D. L. Paulsen, "Early Christian Belief in a Corporeal Deity: Origen and Augustine as Reluctant Witnesses," *HTR* 83, no. 2 (1990): 105–16; and C. W. Griffin and D. L. Paulsen, "Augustine and the Corporeality of God," *HTR* 95 (2002): 97–118.

79. See, e.g., J. Patout Burns, "Appropriating Augustine Appropriating Cyprian," *AugStud* 36 (2005): 113–30; Geoffrey D. Dunn, "The Reception of the Martyrdom of Cyprian of Carthage in Early Christian Literature," in *Martyrdom and Persecution in Late Antique Christianity: Festschrift Boudewijn Dehandschutter*, ed. J. Leemans, BETL 241 (Leuven: Peeters, 2010), 76; and Matthew Alan Gaumer, "Dealing with the Donatist Church: Augustine of Hippo's Nuanced Claim to the Authority of Cyprian of Carthage," in *Cyprian of Carthage: Studies in His Life, Language, and Thought*, ed. Henk Bakker, Paul van Geest, and Hans van Loon, LAHR 3 (Leuven: Peeters, 2010), 181–201.

prian do represent a continuum of theological development,[80] and the problems Augustine had with Cyprian would resonate with those he had with Tertullian.[81] However, the fact that Tertullian was not a bishop or a martyr and that he did not have to deal with issues like the validity of baptism performed in schism means that his ideas might not have been promoted explicitly by the Donatists and, thus, that Augustine did not have to deal with them as extensively.

In any case, Augustine had little good to say about Tertullian in *De haeresibus*, clearly labeling him a heretic. The latter's hard-line attitudes, attractive to many in Africa who thought like the Donatists, sat uncomfortably with Augustine. It was not only Tertullian's supposed schismatic Cataphrygianism that merited his condemnation, but also his theological and disciplinary aberrations on the possibility of remarriage after the death of one's spouse that sealed the fate of his reputation. At the same time, Tertullian's views on the nature of the soul, particularly its origin and corporeality, although criticized more extensively in *De haeresibus*, did not contribute to his condemnation. This was possibly because Augustine did not want to take a definitive stand on these questions. Tertullian's belief in the corporeality of the soul (i.e., its reality but immateriality) was misunderstood or rejected or deliberately misrepresented in Augustine's other writings. Perhaps Tertullian's distinctions between body and flesh and the relationship between flesh and soul as two bodies within the body need a fresh examination in our post-Cartesian world.

80. See, e.g., Cahal B. Daly, *Tertullian the Puritan and His Influence* (Dublin: Four Courts, 1993).

81. An initial foray into the use of Tertullian in the Donatist controversy is Elena Zocca, "Tertullien et le donatisme: quelques remarques," in Lagouanère and Fialon, *Tertullianus Afer*, 63–104. On the relationship between Tertullian and Cyprian, see Laetitia Ciccolini, "*Tertullianus magister*: Tertullien lu par Cyprien de Carthage," in Lagouanère and Fialon, *Tertullianus Afer*, 141–66.

Chapter 4

AUGUSTINE AND THE NORTH AFRICAN
MARTYRIOLOGICAL TRADITION

William Tabbernee

INTRODUCTION

On display at the Bardo National Museum in Tunis is a large rectangular pave-
ment mosaic dating from the sixth or seventh century CE. The mosaic was discovered in 1902 in the ruins of the Chapel of the Monastery of Saint-Étienne and
consists of seven "medallions," each recording the name of a martyr. While some
of the letters are now missing, the accuracy of the restored text seems assured
(fig. 1).[1] The central medallion commemorates St. Stephen, Christianity's first
martyr, whose relics were brought to North Africa around 418 CE. He is flanked
by Saints Speratus, Felicitas, and Perpetua to his left and to his right by Saints
Sirica, Saturus, and Saturinus—all, apart perhaps from St. Sirica,[2] early martyrs
of North Africa.

One of my most treasured memories is that of examining the Stephen mosaic
in the Bardo Museum with Professor Patout Burns. It was the summer of 1996
and we, along with other colleagues, had recently commenced what would turn
out to be an almost twenty-year-long collaboration concerning the practice of
Christianity in Roman North Africa. Among other topics, we were keen to discover, particularly from archaeological material, all that we could about the way

1. See William Tabbernee, *Montanist Inscriptions and Testimonia: Epigraphic Sources Illustrating the History of Montanism*, PatrMS 16 (Washington, DC: Catholic University of America
Press, 1997), 112–14.
2. Tabbernee, *Montanist Inscriptions*, 113.

St. Stephen and North African Martyrs Mosaic, Bardo National Museum, Tunis
(Photo by Robin Jensen)

martyrs were commemorated, venerated, and integrated into the daily lives of ordinary Christians.[3]

This chapter examines Augustine's sermons about martyrs, both North African and others, including the way he employed written documents such as the Acts of the Martyrs to instruct, inspire, and, where applicable, correct the beliefs and practices of his audiences.[4] I argue that, even when Augustine had little specific knowledge about particular local martyrs on whose feast day he was delivering a sermon, he was so well acquainted with the wider martyriological tradition that he could easily draw on common martyriological themes to elucidate the exegetical lessons he wanted his listeners to take from the readings of the day.

For Augustine, the *whole* Western martyriological tradition, not just that of North Africa, was critical for illustrating homiletically how martyrs exemplified the faith for all Christians to imitate even though few if any of them would be called on to die for that faith. Gervasius and Protasius, patron saints of Milan whose relics were discovered in 386 while Augustine was still a catechumen residing in that city, were prime examples of the wider but relevant martyriological tradition. The example par excellence, of course, was St. Stephen, Christianity's protomartyr.

The translation to North Africa of Stephen's relics, and those of Gervasius and Protasius, provided the basis for a new approach to Augustine's preaching at martyrs' shrines, where he utilized his sermons on these and other "true" martyrs as opportunities for consolidating ecclesiastical authority on behalf of the Catholic/Caecilianist community against Donatists, Pelagians, and others deemed schismatics or heretics.[5]

---

3. Much of what we discovered is incorporated in the volume publishing the results of our work; see J. Patout Burns Jr. and Robin M. Jensen, in collaboration with Graeme W. Clarke, Susan T. Stevens, William Tabbernee, and Maureen A. Tilley, *Christianity in Roman Africa: The Development of Its Practices and Beliefs* (Grand Rapids: Eerdmans, 2014), esp. 113–20, 134–46, 519–51.

4. On the separation between Caecilianists and Donatists in North Africa, see Burns and Jensen, *Christianity in Roman Africa*, 47–51, 54–57, 398–401.

5. For a helpful survey of earlier scholarship on Augustine's sermons on martyrs, see

The Acts of the Martyrs (*Acta Martyrum*)

On July 22, most likely in the year 397,[6] moments before Augustine is about to enter the pulpit, probably of the Caecilianist cathedral in Carthage,[7] he is told that this is the feast day of the martyrs of Maxula. Augustine didn't have "the slightest idea either of where Maxula was or who the martyrs were"—at least according to the context speculatively provided by the English translator of the recently discovered longer version of the sermon preached on that occasion (*Sermones* [*s.*] 283augm.).[8]

The readings for the day included Rom. 7:7–9. From the content of the preserved text of the sermon, it is clear that Augustine had intended to deliver a fairly traditional homily on this text. Much of the extant sermon still emphasizes the importance of divine law for enabling Christians to recognize sin and to know that they should not lust: *Non concupisces* (*s.* 283augm.2–3; cf. Rom. 7:7; Exod. 17:20). Augustine, however, quickly adjusted his original sermon so that it would fit the occasion. He adroitly paired Rom. 7:7 with the Vetus Latina text of part of Jer. 17:16: *Et diem hominum non concupiui, tu scis* ("And the day of men I have not lusted after, you know"). Having explained that being afraid to die is to lust after life, Augustine tells his hearers that Jer. 17:16 was "the watchword of martyrs; they did not lust after the day of men, in case they should fail to reach the day of God. They didn't lust after the day so soon to end, in order to reach the day that has no end."[9]

Anthony Dupont, *Preacher of Grace: A Critical Reappraisal of Augustine's Doctrine of Grace in His "Sermones ad Populum" on Liturgical Feasts and during the Donatist Controversy*, SHCT 177 (Leiden: Brill, 2014), 137–42. For Augustine as preacher, see Shari Boodts and Anthony Dupont, "Augustine of Hippo," in *Preaching in the Patristic Era: Sermons, Preachers, and Audiences in the Latin West*, ed. Anthony Dupont, Shari Boodts, Gert Partoens, and Johan Leemans, New History of the Sermon 6 (Leiden: Brill, 2018), 177–97.

6. Dating Augustine's sermons is notoriously difficult; see, e.g., Hubertus R. Drobner, "The Chronology of Augustine's *Sermones ad populum*," *AugStud* 31 (2000): 211–18; 34 (2003): 49–66; 35 (2004): 43–53; Daniel E. Doyle, "Introduction to Augustine's Preaching," in *Essential Sermons*, trans. Edmund Hill, ed. Boniface Ramsey, WSA III (Hyde Park, NY: New City, 2007), 21–22. The dates given in this chapter are based on those provided or suggested in the relevant volumes of WSA III/1–11. All dates, however, should be considered provisional rather than definitive; see Boodts and Dupont, "Augustine of Hippo," 181–84.

7. The basilica is not identified, but it was most likely the Basilica Restituta where Augustine, when in Carthage, normally preached at the invitation of Aurelius, who served as bishop from ca. 391 to 429. See, e.g., *ss.* 19, 29, 90, 112, and 277.

8. Edmund Hill in *Newly Discovered Sermons*, WSA III/11, 251n5.

9. *S.* 283augm.3 (François Dolbeau, *Vingt-six sermons au peuple d'Afrique*, 2nd ed., Collection des études augustiniennes, Série antiquité 147 [Paris: Études Augustiniennes, 2009], 197;

The reference to martyrs here is sufficiently generic to have been applicable to the martyrs of Maxula, even if Augustine knew little about them. The same may be said about the sermon's (apparently) hastily composed opening two sentences:

> Let us by all means admire the courage of the holy martyrs in their sufferings, but in such a way that we proclaim the grace of God. They themselves, after all, certainly did not wish to be praised in themselves, but in the one to whom it is said, "In the Lord shall my soul be praised."[10]

By the time Augustine was halfway through his homily, he seems to have forgotten that multiple martyrs were being celebrated that day. He tells his hearers, "Reflect, brothers and sisters, upon the day of the martyr; it's right that we should spend some time drawing encouragement from his patience."[11] The patience of martyrs-to-be during their trial and suffering was, according to Augustine, just one of the many virtues to be imitated by contemporary Christians (cf. *infra*) and would readily have come to Augustine's mind as he was trying to figure out what to say about the Maxultian martyrs.

That Augustine may have been ignorant of the specific details of these martyrs is not particularly surprising. Once, when preaching on the martyrdom of St. Stephen, Augustine expressed relief that, unlike for many martyrs, there *was* material available for Stephen that could be read out on his feast day (*s.* 315.1; cf. Acts 7:54–60).

Besides biblical accounts, there were also extracanonical documents on which Augustine could, and did, draw for information about at least some of the more famous martyrs. These documents, the acts of the martyrs (*acta martyrum*),[12] comprise not only edited versions of the official records (*acta*) of the

---

trans. Hill, WSA III/11, 246): "haec uox in martyribus fuit: non concupierunt diem hominum, ne non peruenirent ad diem dei. non concupierunt diem cum breui fine, ut peruenirent ad diem sine fine."

10. *S.* 283augm.1 (Dolbeau, *Vingt-six sermons*, 196; trans. Hill, WSA III/11, 245): "fortitudinem sanctorum martyrum sic in eorum passione miremur, ut gratiam domini praedicemus. neque enim et illi in seipsis laudari uoluerunt, sed in illo cui dicitur: in domino laudabitur anima mea."

11. *S.* 283augm.4 (Dolbeau, *Vingt-six sermons*, 198; trans. Hill, WSA III/11, 247): "considerate, fratres, diem martyris; bonum est, ut in ipsius patientiae exhortatione uersemur."

12. The most recently published collection of such martyr acts is Éric Rebillard, ed., *Greek and Latin Narratives about the Ancient Martyrs* (Oxford: Oxford University Press, 2017).

interrogation and sentencing of the martyrs but also more extensive accounts of their sufferings (*passiones*). Occasionally, as in the case of the Carthaginian martyrs Perpetua and Felicitas, both kinds of *acta martyrum* were created over time. *Acta martyrum* frequently contain spurious hagiographical material, but they—especially the *passiones*—were written not primarily to provide accurate historical accounts but to make pastoral, theological, or ecclesiastical claims.

By Augustine's time, it had become customary in North African churches on martyrs' feast days for a lector to read aloud before the sermon the relevant *acta* or *passio*. This practice applied not only to the *acta martyrum* of North African martyrs but also to those from elsewhere in the Latin West. For example, the liturgical calendar of Hippo Regius included the feast day of Fructuosus, bishop of Tarragona (Spain), as well as that of one of Augustine's predecessors, Theogenes. Theogenes was executed during the Valerian persecution—possibly on January 26, 258, or, more likely, on that same calendar day in 259. If so, then the martyrdoms of Theogenes and Fructuosus occurred at almost the same time.

Probably on January 21, 396, and most likely at the shrine dedicated to St. Theogenes at Hippo (see *s.* 272B.2),[13] Augustine preached a sermon on the feast day of Fructuosus and his companions. The sermon was preceded by the reading of the *Passio sanctorum martyrum Fructuosi Episcopi, Auguri et Eulogi Diaconorum*,[14] to which Augustine refers during his homily:

> Blessed are the saints in whose memory we are celebrating the day on which they suffered; they have received an eternal crown, immortality without end, in exchange for temporal well-being; in these solemn celebrations they have left us lessons of encouragement. When we hear how the martyrs suffered, we rejoice and glorify God in them. . . . You heard the interrogations of the persecutors, you heard the replies of the confessors, when the *passion* of these saints was being read.[15]

---

13. As with the dates, especially the year, the specific location for a sermon is often only a supposition.

14. Text and trans. in Rebillard, *Greek and Latin Narratives*, 253–63.

15. *S.* 273.2 (PL 38:1248–49; trans. Hill, *Sermons 273–305A*, WSA III/8, 17–18, modified): "beati sancti, in quorum memoriis celebramus diem passionis illorum: illi acceperunt pro temporali salute aeternam coronam, sine fine immortalitatem; nobis dimiserunt in istis solemnitatibus exhortationem. quando audimus quomodo passi sunt martyres; gaudemus et glorificamus in illis deum: nec dolemus quia mortui sunt. etenim si mortui pro Christo non essent, numquid usque hodie uiuerent? quare non faceret confessio, quod factura fuerat

As January 21 was also the feast day of the thirteen-year-old martyr Agnes who died in 304, Augustine mentions her as well:

> Blessed are those whose *passion* has been related; blessed too is Saint Agnes, who also suffered on this same day; a virgin who was what she was called. Agnes means "lamb" in Latin, "chaste" in Greek. She was what she was called; she was deservedly rewarded with a martyr's crown.[16]

That Augustine had access to a written account of Agnes's martyrdom is unlikely. A Latin *passio* was indeed produced for this martyr, but perhaps not until after Augustine's time. It is not known whether a *passio* existed about Theogenes.

On January 23, 404, the day after the feast day of another popular Spanish martyr, St. Vincent of Caesaraugusta (Saragossa), who, like Agnes, had died in 304, Augustine, preaching at Carthage's cathedral, reminds the congregation, "Yesterday we heard the praises of a true martyr: what torments he endured; how hideous they were, how various, how continuous!"[17] That the public reading had been part or all of the *passio* is confirmed by Augustine's additional comment, which also gives a sense of the drama and the emotions generated by such *passiones*: "We saw it all, we were actually present. That account of his passion spoke to our hearts; we were enthralled."[18] Three versions of *acta martyrum* relating to Vincent have survived. The one used by Augustine was probably the so-called *passio breuior*.[19]

---

aegritudo? audistis persequentium interrogationes, audistis confitentium responsiones, cum sanctorum passio legeretur."

16. *S.* 273.6 (PL 38:1250; trans. Hill, WSA III/8, 20, modified): "beati quorum passio recitata est. beata Agnes sancta, cuius passionis hodiernus est dies. uirgo quae quod uocabatur, erat. Agnes latine agnam significat; graece, castam. erat quod uocabatur: merito coronabatur."

17. *S.* 359B.13 (Dolbeau, *Vingt-six sermons*, 337; trans. Hill, WSA III/11, 344): "hesterna die martyris ueri laudes audiuimus: quae tormenta pertulit, quam ingentia, quam multa, quam densa!"

18. *S.* 359B.20 (Dolbeau, *Vingt-six sermons*, 341; trans. Hill, WSA III/11, 348); "vidimus, interfuimus. lectio illa cum corde nostro locuta est: delectati sumus."

19. See Louis de Lacger, "Saint Vincent de Saragosse," *Revue d'histoire de l'Église de France* 13, no. 60 (1927): 325–27. For the text, see "Acta S. Vincentii Martyris, Archidiaconi Caesaugustani, Qui Passus est Valentiae in Hispania, et Relatio Translationis Eiusdem," *Analecta Bollandiana* 1 (1882): 260–62.

AUGUSTINE AND THE NORTH AFRICAN MARTYRIOLOGICAL TRADITION

Namphano and His Companions

In 389 or 390 CE, Augustine received a letter (*Epistula* [*ep.*] 16) from Maximus of Madaura, a venerable grammarian with whom Augustine had most likely studied as a boy (cf. *Confessiones* [*conf.*] 2.3.5). Maximus complains to Augustine that Christians venerated martyrs more than gods and visited martyrs' tombs in droves. He also pokes fun at the names of a few of the martyrs, including one called Namphano (see *ep.* 16.2), which sounds like *Nymph*ano. Joining in the fun, Augustine retorts that some of the gods also have funny names, such as Cloacina—derived from "sewer" or "toilet" (*ep.* 17.2).

Maximus refers to Namphano as *archimartyris*. This designation led earlier historians to assume that Namphano was the very first North African martyr, speculating that he died before 180 CE.[20] However, Maximus does not call Namphano "protomartyr" (i.e., first martyr) but "archmartyr" (chief martyr), probably signifying no more than that Namphano was the most important member of a group of martyrs. Augustine states that there is *also* a Catholic Christian church in Madaura whose members categorically do not worship any deceased person (cf. *ep.* 17.5). Therefore, it seems best to conclude that the Madauran martyrs were Donatists who died in the fourth century CE, rather than (proto-)Catholics who died in the second.[21] Consequently, martyrs from a town called Scilli or Scillium remain the earliest-known North African Christian martyrs.

The Scillitan Martyrs

Just as Namphano appears to have been chief among the Madauran martyrs, a man named Speratus was the preeminent member of a group of Christians executed in Carthage on July 17, 180 CE. At least six of these martyrs came from Scilli, which was somewhere close enough to Carthage for them to have been tried by the gov-

---

20. E.g., Roderic L. Mullen, *The Expansion of Christianity: A Gazetteer of Its First Three Centuries*, VCSup 69 (Leiden: Brill, 2004), 316.

21. Jane Merdinger, "Roman North Africa," in *Early Christianity in Contexts: An Exploration across Cultures and Continents*, ed. William Tabbernee (Grand Rapids: Baker Academic, 2014), 234.

ernor in his own offices (*Acta martyrum Scillitanorum* [*Act. Scill.*] 1),[22] rather than while he was conducting assizes elsewhere in Africa Proconsularis. Speratus was probably at least a lector within the Scillitan Christian community, as he had (canonical?) books and Pauline epistles in his possession (*Act. Scill.* 12). The extant *Acta martyrum Scillitanorum* is a minimally edited transcript of the final day of the trial of the Scillitans before P. Vigellius Saturninus, governor of Africa Proconsularis. When the martyrs' sentence of beheading was announced (*Act. Scill.* 14), six additional Christians were named (*Act. Scill.* 16). These other martyrs may have been Carthaginians.[23] Whether a longer, more complete Christian version of the whole proceedings, including the trial of the other six martyrs, ever existed is unknown. Augustine employed the version that has come down to us.

Among the surviving sermons of Augustine, four were preached on July 17, the feast day of the Scillitan Martyrs (*ss.* 37, 299D, 299E, 299F). The *Act. Scill.* was read as part of the service on at least one of these occasions, as Augustine refers back to what Donata, one of the martyrs, had said during her trial (*s.* 299E.2; cf. *Act. Scill.* 9). By Augustine's time, the cult of the Scillitan Martyrs was well established in Carthage. Relics of these martyrs were housed in a basilica known formally as the Basilica of Celerina and the Scillitani (Victor of Vita, *Historia persecutionis Africae Provinciae* 1.9) and informally as the Celerina or the Scillitanorum.[24]

Perpetua and Her Co-martyrs

Tertullian's *Ad martyras* was written around 197 CE to an unnamed group of imprisoned Carthaginian "martyrs-designate," encouraging them to remain firm in their faith. The earliest indisputably Carthaginian martyrs whose names we know are Iucundus, Saturninus, Artaxius, and Quintus (*Passio sanctarum Perpetuae*

22. Text and trans. in Rebillard, *Greek and Latin Narratives*, 351–59.

23. William Tabbernee, "Scillitan Martyrs," in *The New Westminster Dictionary of Church History*, ed. Robert Benedetto and James O. Duke (Louisville: Westminster John Knox, 2008), 1:598.

24. William Tabbernee, "Montanism and the Cult of the Martyrs in Roman North Africa: Reassessing the Literary and Epigraphic Evidence," in *Text and the Material World: Essays in Honour of Graeme Clarke*, ed. Elizabeth Minchin and Heather Jackson, Studies in Mediterranean Archaeology and Literature 185 (Uppsala: Astrom Editions, 2017), 305. Celerina was probably not an otherwise unknown Carthaginian martyr but a wealthy fourth-century donor of the basilica that honored the Scillitan Martyrs: see *The Letters of St. Cyprian of Carthage*, trans. Graeme W. Clarke, vol. 1, ACW 43 (New York: Newman, 1984), 190–91.

et Felicitatis [*Pass. Perp.*] 11.9). They died in 203, if not earlier. Soon thereafter, a local persecution claimed the lives of Revocatus, Felicitas, a second Saturninus, Secundulus, Vibia Perpetua, and Saturus (*Pass. Perp.* 2.1, 4.5, and 19.1–21.11). Their arrest, imprisonment, visions, contests with wild beasts, and ultimate deaths in the amphitheater of Carthage are recounted in the almost contemporary *Passio Perpetuae* and radically revised, fourth-century *Acta brevia Perpetuae et Felicitatis*.[25] A memorial plaque installed above the crypt in the Basilica Maiorum at Carthage during the sixth century testified that the relics of Perpetua and her co-martyrs were enshrined there.[26] Although the *year* in which Perpetua and the others died remains slightly uncertain,[27] the calendar *day* (March 7) is confirmed by the reference to the emperor Geta's birthday (*Pass. Perp.* 7.9 and 16.3) and the (partially reconstructed) fourth line of the martyrs' commemorative plaque: *Felicit(as), Per[pe]t(ua), pas(si) n[on(as) Mart(ias)].*[28]

Augustine preached annually (*s.* 280.1) on the feast day of Perpetua and Felicitas, but only four of the sermons are extant (*ss.* 280, 281, 282, and 394).[29] A fifth sermon also refers extensively to Perpetua and Felicitas (*s.* 159A.11]) but was probably preached on July 15, 397, the feast day of the Carthaginian deacon Catulinus and his companions, who died around 303, during the Diocletianic persecution. Catulinus's fellow martyrs were Ianuarius, Florentinus, Iulia, and Iusta. Catulinus's relics were enshrined at the Basilica Faustus in Carthage, presumably the sermon's venue. The four other sermons on Perpetua and Felicitas were probably delivered in Augustine's own cathedral, the Basilica Pacis in Hippo; the years of their delivery are unknown.

For far too long scholarly interpretations of the way in which Augustine utilized the *Passio Perpetuae et Felicitatis* were influenced by the theory that at least the introduction and conclusion of the *passio* were written by an editor who, if

25. Text and trans. of both in Rebillard, *Greek and Latin Narratives*, 295–349. See also Petr Kitzler, *From "Passio Perpetuae" to "Acta Perpetuae": Recontextualizing a Martyr Story in the Literature of the Early Church*, Arbeiten zur Kirchengeschichte 127 (Berlin: de Gruyter, 2015).

26. Tabbernee, *Montanist Inscriptions*, 105–17.

27. Timothy D. Barnes, *Early Christian Hagiography and Roman History*, 2nd ed. (Tübingen: Mohr Siebeck, 2016), 305, for example, argues for 204 rather than the traditionally assumed 203.

28. Tabbernee, "Montanism and the Cult of the Martyrs," 299.

29. Two of these (cf. *ss.* 280.1 and 282.2) explicitly note that the *passio* had already been read out to the congregation beforehand.

not Tertullian himself, was equally favorably disposed toward the New Prophecy movement—that is, Montanism.[30] Proponents of this theory argue that in these sermons Augustine purposefully subverted the "Montanistic" elements of the *passio*.[31] Such alleged "Montanistic" elements include an emphasis on dreams, visions, and prophesying (*Pass. Perp.* 1.3–4) and the ability of confessors to access God immediately (*Pass. Perp.* 4.1–2). Opponents argue that everything in the *passio* itself, including the introduction and conclusion, could have been composed by a Christian not influenced by the New Prophecy and that the so-called Montanistic elements are simply normative characteristics of North African Catholic Christianity.[32]

Whether "Montanistic" or not, the impact of the *passio*'s introduction and conclusion on Augustine has been grossly overestimated. Indeed, the version of the *passio* to which Augustine had access (at least originally) may not even have contained these elements as produced in modern editions. Only one extant manuscript contains the prologue and the last part of the conclusion.[33] It has usually been taken for granted that these are integral to the very first edition of the *passio* and that they give the *passio* its "Montanistic" overtones because they contain an appeal to have new prophesies, new visions, and new deeds of heroism recognized and valued as much as those of old (*Pass. Perp.* 1.1–6, 21.11b). However, to assume that certain portions were original and edited out later—either to shorten the *passio* to a more suitable length for public reading in church on the martyrs' feast days or to delete the *passio*'s "Montanistic" content—seems less plausible than to propose that they were added to the original version.[34] If so, the

30. On the New Prophecy/Montanism, see William Tabbernee, *Fake Prophecy and Polluted Sacraments: Ecclesiastical and Imperial Reactions to Montanism*, VCSup 84 (Leiden: Brill, 2007); Christine Trevett, "Montanism," in *The Early Christian World*, 2nd ed., ed. Philip F. Esler (London: Routledge, 2017), 867–84.

31. Rex C. Butler, *The New Prophecy and "New Visions": Evidence of Montanism in the Passion of Perpetua and Felicitas*, PatrMS 18 (Washington, DC: Catholic University of America Press, 2006), 106–10.

32. Maureen A. Tilley, "The Passion of Perpetua and Felicity," in *Searching the Scriptures: A Feminist Commentary*, ed. Elisabeth Schüssler Fiorenza (New York: Crossroad, 1994), 2:832–36; Christoph Markschies, "The *Passio Perpetuae et Felicitatis* and Montanism?," in *Perpetua's Passions: Multidisciplinary Approaches to the "Passio Perpetuae et Felicitatis,"* ed. Jan N. Bremmer and Marco Formisano (Oxford: Oxford University Press, 2012), 286–87.

33. Codex Casiensis (Monte Casino) MS 204. See Thomas J. Heffernan, *The Passion of Perpetua and Felicity* (Oxford: Oxford University Press, 2012), 371–72 and 374–81.

34. That there were, in fact, additions to the original version even within the text of the

passio that Augustine knew may only have consisted of *Pass. Perp.* 2.1–21.11a. In his extant comments on Perpetua and Felicitas, Augustine never cites nor refers to anything beyond what we find in 2.1 to 21.11a.

The reason for this additional material seems to be less of a claim of legitimacy for the Montanist "New Prophecy" than an attempt to officially sanction the *Pass. Perp.* for public reading in church.[35] Such approval was given by ecclesiastical councils held at Hippo in 393 and Carthage in 397 CE. It is likely, therefore, that the previously assumed "Montanist" prologue and conclusion were written not in the early third century but toward the end of the fourth. If so, by Augustine's time, at least two versions of the Latin *passio*—as well as a Greek rendition and the derived Latin *acta*—were circulating in North Africa.[36]

Whether or not Augustine also ended up seeing a copy of the *passio* with a new introduction and expanded conclusion is unknown, but, even if he did, it may be assumed that he understood the additions to argue the case for the liturgical canonicity of the *passio*—not for the legitimacy of Montanism. Consequently, none of Augustine's sermons on Perpetua and Felicitas should be taken as denouncing their (or the *passio*'s editor's) "Montanism." As far as Augustine was concerned, Perpetua and Felicitas (and their *passio* [and *acta*]) were completely "Catholic," and he utilized the record of their martyrdom in the same way as he utilized all other *acta martyrum*: to emphasize the martyrs' virtues in order to inspire and motivate his audience to pursue such virtues in their own lives.

Cyprian

Although Perpetua and Felicitas may have been the most famous of the early North African martyrs, Cyprian, the bishop of Carthage who was martyred on September 14, 258, was the most esteemed. His feast day was celebrated throughout North Africa. Augustine preached sermons on Cyprian's heavenly "birthday" in Hippo (*s.* 310) as well as in Carthage. There, Cyprian was commemorated

---

document seems clear from *Pass. Perp.* 15.7, which relates (as a completed action) that one of the (Christian) sisters brought up (*educauit*) the baby girl Felicitas delivered in prison.

35. Joseph Farrell, "The Canonization of Perpetua," in Bremmer and Formisano, *Perpetua's Passions*, 304–5.

36. Heffernan, *Passion of Perpetua*, 427–30 and 445–55. There is no evidence that Augustine utilized the Greek *passio*, but, contrary to earlier scholarly opinion, the recently discovered longer version of his *s.* 282 shows that Augustine knew and was linguistically influenced by a version of the *acta*. See Bremmer and Formisano, *Perpetua's Passions*, 5.

especially at the Mensa Cypriani and the Memoria Cypriani, basilicas built over the traditional sites of Cyprian's execution and burial respectively. The Memoria was also referred to as the Mappalia, so named after the road next to which it was situated. Subsequently it was called "St. Cyprian's" (and eventually "St. Monica's").[37]

Augustine preached at least fifteen times in Carthage on the occasion of Cyprian's feast day, frequently first at the Mappalia during the evening vigil (ss. 308A, 311, 312, 313C, 313F; en. Ps. 32.2.9) and then the following morning at the Mensa (ss. 305A, 309, 310, 313A, 313B, 313E; en. Ps. 32.2.9). Sermones 313D and 313E could have been preached at either location. Augustine also preached at the Mensa on at least one other occasion when it wasn't the feast day of St. Cyprian (en. Ps. 80.4.23), and he also frequently mentioned Cyprian in sermons preached on the feast day of other martyrs (e.g., s. 313G.3)

Augustine had an ambivalent attitude not only to Cyprian himself but also to the Carthaginian basilicas where Cyprian was commemorated. It was probably at the Memoria/Mappalia where he left his mother behind when, against her wishes, he sailed away to Rome (conf. 5.8.15). It was also at the Mappalia that abuses at martyrs' shrines were (or at least had been) most evident. Although in 404 CE he thanked Carthaginian Christians for their obedience to Aurelius in discontinuing the inappropriate singing, dancing, and drinking (s. 359B.5), the very next year, during a sermon preached at the Mappalia on the feast day of St. Cyprian, Augustine reminded some of the same people that such practices would never again be tolerated: "What we celebrate here is the holy festival of martyrs. So there is no dance here."[38]

Augustine's ambivalence about Cyprian himself stemmed not only from the fact that Augustine disapproved of Cyprian's endorsement of the rebaptism of heretics or schismatics[39] but also from the fact that Cyprian had become a problematic role model for Caecilianists/Catholics. Both groups appealed to Cyprian's legacy to legitimate their respective claims to being the "true Church." Consequently, Augustine's early sermons on Cyprian primarily highlight Cyprian's virtues as a martyr rather than his example as a bishop or as a teacher/ theologian. For example, Sermon 311 begins: "It is the passion of the most blessed

---

37. Burns and Jensen, Christianity in Roman Africa, 145–46.

38. S. 311.6 (PL 38:1416; trans. Hill, WSA III/9, 73): "sed celebratur hic sanctitas et solemnitas martyrum; non hic saltatur."

39. Merdinger, "Roman North Africa," 241.

martyr Cyprian that has made this day into a feast for us. . . . But the right way to celebrate the festival of the martyrs should be imitating their virtues."[40]

Only gradually did Augustine figure out how he could utilize the tradition about Cyprian in his fight against the Donatists with a clear conscience. The solution was to emphasize Cyprian's teaching on the unity of the church itself, rather than the means by which Cyprian sought to restore that unity—that is, through allowing the rebaptism of heretics and schismatics. A sermon preached on Cyprian's feast day, probably in 410, starts out by praising Cyprian as "a trustworthy and trustful martyr" but immediately adds that "he won God's favor by a twin grace, by the way he was a bishop and the way he was a martyr. As *bishop* he defended and held onto *unity*; as *martyr* he taught and gave an example of the confession of *faith*."[41] Augustine then contrasts Cyprian's faith with that of heretics and Cyprian's example as a bishop and martyr with that of the Donatists:

> The heretics, though, and the Donatists, *who falsely boast that Cyprian belongs to them*, should pay attention to the way he exercised his office of bishop, and they wouldn't break away; to the way he went to his martyrdom, and they wouldn't throw themselves [over cliffs?]. The heretic breaking away in heresy, the Donatist jumping deliberately to his death, is certainly not Christ's disciple; certainly not one of Cyprian's comrades.[42]

The cliff-jumping Donatists were the so-called Circumcellions (cf. *s.* 313E.5, 7). Augustine doesn't identify the heretics, but presumably he had the Pelagians in mind. As with Augustine's use of Cyprian against Donatists, in combatting Pelagians, Augustine highlights Cyprian's emphasis on the unity of the church.[43] Even more so than in his anti-Donatist polemics, Augustine,

40. *S.* 311.1 (PL 38:1414; trans. Hill, WSA III/9, 71): "istum nobis festum diem passio beatissimi Cypriani martyris fecit: cuius nos uictoriae celebritas in istum locum deuotissimos congregauit. sed celebratio solemnitatis martyrum, imitatio debet esse uirtutum."

41. *S.* 313E.1 (*MA* 1:536; trans. Hill, WSA III/9, 109, modified and emphases added): "gemina ergo gratia commendatur deo, episcopatu et martyrio. episcopatus eius defendit et tenuit unitatem; martyrium eius docuit et impleuit confessionem."

42. *S.* 313E.2 (*MA* 1:537; trans. Hill, WSA III/9, 110, emphases added): "haeretici autem et donatistae, qui se ad Cyprianum falso iactant pertinere, si episcopatum eius attenderent, non se separarent; si martyrium, non se praecipitarent. non est omnino discipulus Christi, non est comes Cypriani, haereticus in haeresi separatus, aut donatista in morte praecipitatus."

43. See Jonathan Yates, "Augustine's Appropriation of Cyprian the Martyr-Bishop against the Pelagians," in *More Than a Memory: The Discourse of Martyrdom and the Construction of*

in other sermons in which he specifically refers to Pelagius and/or those who agreed with Pelagius's views on the capacity of human beings to live moral lives by their own volition, points to the humanity of the martyrs and especially to the grace of God in enabling the martyrs to endure what otherwise they could not have endured.[44] Even though some heretics and schismatics had died for their own particular cause, according to Augustine, they were neither Christians nor martyrs (ss. 138.2, 313E.7).

Sermon 309 was preached at the Mensa on Cyprian's feast day in an unknown year. Augustine commences by acknowledging the obligation he owes and which he joyfully discharges: "Such a happy and religious occasion as this, on which we are celebrating the martyr's passion, requires me to pay the debt of the sermon I owe to your ears and hearts."[45] He then narrates Cyprian's exile, arrest, and trial in considerable detail, suggesting that the account of Cyprian's martyrdom, the *Acta proconsularia Sancti Cypriani* (*Act. procon.*), was not read out to the wor-shipers—at least not on this occasion. Augustine's summary, however, shows that he was very familiar with this document. The *Acta proconsularia*, based on the official transcript of Cyprian's trial, was produced soon after Cyprian's mar-tyrdom. A more hagiographical document, the *Vita et passio Cypriani* (*V. Cypr.*), was composed well after Augustine's time.[46]

Other North African Martyrs

Less than a year after Cyprian's death, a riot broke out in Carthage that resulted in the arrest and execution of some Carthaginian clergy and other Christians, including catechumens.[47] The account of their martyrdom, the *Passio sanctorum*

Christian Identity in the History of Christianity, ed. Johan Leemans with Jürgen Mettepennin-gen (Leuven: Peeters, 2005), 121.

44. *Ss.* 229.5, 6, 8–10; 335B.5; and 348A.1, 8, 9, 13. See also Anthony Dupont, Gratia *in Au-gustine's "Sermones ad Populum" during the Pelagian Controversy: Do Different Contexts Furnish Different Insights?*, BSCH 59 (Leiden: Brill, 2012), which also includes an overview of the Pelagian controversy.

45. *S.* 309.1 (PL 38:1410; trans. Hill, WSA III/9, 63): "sermonem a nobis debitum au-ribus et cordibus uestris exigit tam grata et religiosa solemnitas, qua passionem beati martyris celebramus."

46. Text and trans. of both *Act. procon.* and *V. Cypr.* in Rebillard, *Greek and Latin Narra-tives*, 197–251.

47. See Barnes, *Early Christian Hagiography*, 86–92.

Montani et Lucii,[48] was modeled in part on the *Passio sanctarum Perpetuae et Felicitatis.* The same may be said about the *Passio sanctorum Mariani et Iacobi* (*Pass. Mar. Iac.*).[49] One of Augustine's extant sermons (*s.* 284) was preached at Carthage, probably in 397, on the anniversary of the martyrdom of Marianus, a lector, and James, a deacon, who were executed near Cirta, Numidia, on May 6, 259. Augustine clearly knew this *passio*: the focal point of his sermon was on Marianus's mother, Mary, whom both the *passio* (13.1–3) and Augustine compare favorably to Mary the mother of Christ. Augustine rhetorically addresses the martyr's mother: "Yes, you, too, Mary are holy [*sancta*], not your namesake's equal of course in merit but her equal in desire. Blessed are you also. She gave birth to the Prince of martyrs, you gave birth to a martyr of the Prince."[50]

In his concluding remarks, Augustine brings the attention of his listeners back to the saints whom they are honoring: "By the grace of the Lord, then, imitate your fellow servants . . . imitate Marianus and James. They were only human, they were fellow servants of yours; born just like you, but crowned [with the martyr's crown] by the one who was not born in that way."[51]

There is no surviving evidence that Augustine ever preached about the martyr Montanus and his companions. It would be surprising, however, if he had not done so, as the cult of this Carthaginian martyr became very popular in Numidia.[52] Similarly, there are no extant sermons by Augustine about Maximilianus, a young Christian who was executed at Theveste, Numidia, on March 12, 259, for refusing military service (*Acta Maximiliani* 1.1 and 3.1).[53] Fortunately, there *is* surviving evidence that, in addition to those discussed *supra*, Augustine preached on the feast day of, or otherwise referred to, a great many North African martyrs. The following are illustrative, not exhaustive, examples.

The Eight Martyrs and the Twenty Martyrs of Hippo

In addition to Theogenes, two groups of Christians were martyred at Hippo Regius, and Augustine referred to each collectively. Neither the names nor the

48. Text and trans. in Rebillard, *Greek and Latin Narratives*, 265–93.
49. Text and trans. in Rebillard, *Greek and Latin Narratives*, 175–95.
50. *S.* 284.2 (PL 38:1288; trans. Hill, WSA III/8, 87).
51. *S.* 284.6 (PL 38:1293; trans. Hill, WSA III/8, 93, modified).
52. Tabbernee "Montanism and the Cult of the Martyrs," 307–9.
53. Text in Herbert Musurillo, ed. and trans., *The Acts of the Christian Martyrs* (Oxford: Clarendon, 1972), 245–49.

date of execution for "the Eight Martyrs" is now known, but their local fame was such that, during 425–426 CE, Augustine had a basilica built on the outskirts of Hippo to honor their memory (s. 356.10). Presumably, this basilica either replaced or covered an earlier shrine. Augustine also briefly mentions these martyrs in Sermon 313G.3.

A little more is known about "the Twenty Martyrs." A list of their names existed in antiquity and was read out before Augustine preached Sermon 325. However, Augustine himself only mentions that the list commenced with Bishop Fidentius, included Valeriana, and concluded with Victoria (s. 325.1). The names of the other seventeen martyrs remain unknown. All twenty died on or about November 15, probably in 304. A chapel was erected to their memory at Hippo in the fourth century. Presumably Augustine preached sermons 325 and 326 there on their feast day.

Sermon 326 quotes some of the interchange between the martyrs and a Roman official, indicating that there was an *acta martyrum* regarding the Twenty Martyrs extant in Augustine's day. The sermon itself, probably preached before 400, shows that excesses at martyrs' shrines were still a major concern:

> The solemn feast of these blessed martyrs has brought us a happier day than usual. What makes us happy is that the martyrs have passed over from this land of labor and toil to the territory of peace and quiet; but they earned this not by dancing but by praying; not by drinking but by fasting; not by being quarrelsome but by their endurance.[54]

Leontius

The Basilica Leontiana at Hippo Regius was built by another of Augustine's episcopal predecessors, Leontius, martyred during the Diocletianic persecution, perhaps as early as 303 CE. In 395, while still a presbyter, Augustine wrote to his friend Alypius, bishop of Thagaste, complaining of the banquets held within the walls of the basilica on the feast day of an unnamed martyr. The martyr is undoubtedly Leontius (cf. *ep.* 29.10). In the days leading up to this feasting, Au-

---

54. S. 326.1 (PL 38:1449; trans. Hill, WSA III/9, 165, modified): "solemnitas beatissimorum martyrum laetiorem nobis reddidit diem. laetamur, quia de terra laboris ad regionem quietis martyres transierunt: sed hoc non saltando, sed orando; non potando, sed ieiunando; non rixando, sed tolerando meruerunt."

gustine preached against the practice, but the only surviving sermon preached at the Basilica Leontiana that mentions Leontius (*s.* 362) was delivered on May 4, Ascension Day, most likely in 411 but possibly in 422. In either case, Ascension Day also fell on the anniversary of the interment of Leontius's bones in the basilica—which was probably also his feast day and not a separate festival.

Crispina

On December 5, 304, a matron named Crispina was tried before Annius Annulinus, proconsul of Africa Proconsularis, at Theveste and beheaded the same day (*Passio sanctae Crispinae* 1.1–4.3).[55] A shrine, presumably with her relics, was erected at Theveste soon thereafter, eventually becoming an extensive and popular pilgrimage site. In the fifth century, the complex consisted of a martyrium, a basilica, a monastery, and a hostel.[56]

Crispina's cult spread to Hippo Regius, where she had a shrine dedicated to her, and also to Carthage, where she was celebrated, along with other martyrs, on her feast day. Augustine preached a number of sermons that included remarks about Crispina (cf. *ss.* 286.2, 313G.3, 354.5; *en. Ps.* 120.13; 137.3, 7, 14, 17). Occasionally, he added personal details not contained in Crispina's *passio*, presupposing the existence of a more extensive oral or written tradition.

The Martyrs of Utica

Perhaps as many as three hundred Christians were put to death around the year 258 at Massa Candida, just outside Utica, a town thirty-five kilometers from Carthage. According to the liturgical calendar of Carthage, their feast day was August 18, and that of their bishop, Quadratus, was August 20. Augustine, however, in a sermon on Quadratus that was probably preached at Hippo in 397, mentions that their respective feast days were four days apart (*s.* 306C.1), a detail that may indicate a difference in the calendars of Hippo and Carthage. Augustine preached on the feast days of the Massa Candida Martyrs and that of Quadratus not only in Hippo (*ss.* 306, 306C, 306D; *en. Ps.* 49.9) but also in Utica (*ss.* 306B, 306E, 335E; *en. Ps.* 144) and probably Carthage (*s.* 306A).

---

55. Text and trans. in Musurillo, *Acts of the Christian Martyrs*, 302–9.
56. Burns and Jensen, *Christianity in Roman Africa*, 114–15, 524–25, and figs. 98–100.

Augustine and the Broader Western Martyriological Tradition

Since at least the time of Cyprian, there had been strong ecclesiastical relations between Carthage and Rome, including similar patterns of ministry, liturgy, and the veneration of saints. Each bishopric had its own favorite local martyrs, such as Perpetua and Felicitas in Carthage, and Agatha, Lucia, Agnes, and Cecilia in Rome. However, (at least) by the time of Gregory the Great, who was pope from 590 to 604, Felicitas and Perpetua (in that order) had been incorporated into the canon of the Roman Mass. Immediately following the apostles and male martyrs such as John the Baptist and St. Stephen, they headed the list of female martyrs on whom the faithful called to pray for them.[57]

Even though John the Baptist, Stephen, Perpetua, and Felicitas themselves had had no direct historical association with Rome, they had universal appeal as the earliest martyrs about whom significant details were known. Their prayers were assumed to have been especially efficacious on behalf of the faithful. The Roman view of these male and female "protomartyrs" was undoubtedly shared in North Africa. Carthaginian Christians celebrated two feast days associated with John the Baptist: June 24 commemorated his actual birthday and December 27 his beheading by Herod. Like the Maccabees, whose feast day was August 1, John the Baptist was considered a Christian martyr before Christ (s. 380.8; cf. 300.1–3, 6).

Augustine preached numerous sermons on the feast days of the apostles, especially Peter and Paul (e.g., ss. 295–99C), each of whom, by the time of Augustine, had a basilica named after him in Carthage.[58] After St. Stephen's relics were brought to North Africa, Stephen became the region's most popular nonlocal martyr/saint. Nonetheless, a number of other foreign-born martyr/saints remained or became very popular—including Laurence, Gervasius, and Protasius, to name just three.

Laurence

St. Laurence was a deacon in Rome under Sixtus II, who was pope in 257–258. Both deacon and pope were martyred in 258, but Laurence's more gruesome

---

57. Farrell, "Canonization of Perpetua," 318.
58. See Burns and Jensen, *Christianity in Roman Africa*, 135.

death captured the imagination of many later Christians. Not one of Augustine's six extant sermons on St. Laurence (*ss.* 302–5, 305A; *In Iohannis euangelium tractatus* [*Io. eu. tr.*] 27.12) alludes to a *passio*. This may well be because none of the known versions of it were written until after 430, the year of Augustine's death. Augustine invariably told the martyr's story in his own words during sermons on Laurence's feast day (August 10):

> Saint Laurence was an archdeacon. The treasures of the Church were demanded of him by the persecutor, as the tradition states. Which is why he suffered such dreadful torments, it is quite horrifying to hear about them. Placed on a gridiron, he was scorched all over his body, tortured with the most excruciating pain by fire. Yet he overcame these bodily afflictions with the sturdy strength of his charity, helped by the one who had made him like that.[59]

The tradition about Laurence that Augustine retells was most likely passed on to him by his mentor, Ambrose of Milan. Ambrose referred to Laurence in his own writings (e.g., *De officiis ministrorum* 1.41 and 2.28). He even composed a hymn (*Apostolorum supparem*) on Laurence's martyrdom to be sung on Laurence's feast days. Reverberations of Ambrose's hymn are discernible in Augustine's *ss.* 302 and 305A. The influence of Ambrose's employment of the Western martyriological tradition on Augustine's own knowledge and use of that tradition should not be underestimated.

Gervasius and Protasius

Another of Ambrose's hymns on martyrs, *Grates tibi, Jesu, nouas,* offers a grateful song of thanks to Jesus by the author for having been chosen to unearth the bones of Gervasius and Protasius, years after the location of the graves of these early Milanese martyrs had been lost. The fortuitous discovery of the skeletons of Gervasius, and the miraculous healing of a blind man who touched the relics during their transfer to the Basilica Ambrosiana in 386, served to consolidate Ambrose's ecclesiastical authority over against the Homoians in the city. Almost

---

59. *S.* 302.8 (PL Suppl. 1:104; trans. Hill, WSA III/8, 304): "sanctus Laurentius archidiaconus fuit. opes ecclesiae de illo a persecutore quaerebantur, sicut traditur; unde tam multa passus est, quae horrent audiri. impositus craticulae, omnibus membris adustus est, poenis atrocissimis flammarum excruciatus est: uincens tamen omnes corporis molestias magno robore caritatis, adiuuante illo qui talem fecerat."

forty years later, it also provided a model for Augustine's homiletic utilization of relics in combating heretics and schismatics in North Africa.

Sometime before 425 CE, a memorial shrine housing relics of Gervasius and Protasius was established on an estate called Victoriana, about thirty kilometers from Hippo, where a young man was healed not only of demon possession but also of the blindness caused by the exorcism (*De ciuitate dei* [*ciu.*] 22.8). Augustine presumably preached Sermon 286 there, on June 19, 425:

> So today, brothers and sisters, we are celebrating the memorial shrine [*memoria*] set up in this place in honor of Saints Protasius and Gervasius, the martyrs of Milan. Not the day when it was set up here, but the day we are celebrating today is the day of the discovery of the death of these saints, precious in the sight of the Lord, by bishop Ambrose, that man of God. Of that glorious occasion for the martyrs I was myself also a witness. I was in Milan, I know about the miracles that occurred. . . . A blind man, known to the whole city, had his sight restored; . . . God doesn't grant health to everyone through the martyrs; but to all who imitate the martyrs, he does promise immortality.[60]

As early as about 401, Augustine had recounted the same story (*conf.* 9.17.16), which he repeats or alludes to frequently in other works in order to make a particular point. For example, in his *Ad catholicos fratres* (*cath. fr.*), written around 401–405, Augustine denies the charge—apparently made by Donatists—that Caecilianists claim that theirs is the "true church" because of miracles such as those at the shrine of Gervasius and Protasius. Augustine's response was that

60. S. 286.4–5 (PL 38:1299–300; trans. Hill, WSA III/8, 103, modified): "celebramus ergo hodierno die, fratres, memoriam in hoc loco positam sanctorum Protasii et Geruasii, Mediolanensium martyrum. non eum diem quo hic posita est, sed eum diem hodie celebramus, quando inuenta est pretiosa in conspectu domini mors sanctorum eius per Ambrosium episcopum, hominem dei: cuius tunc tantae gloriae martyrum etiam ego testis fui. ibi eram, Mediolani eram, facta miracula noui, attestante deo pretiosis mortibus sanctorum suorum: ut per illa miracula iam non solum in conspectu domini, sed etiam in conspectus hominum esset mors illa pretiosa. caecus notissimus uniuersae ciuitati illuminatus est, cucurrit, adduci se fecit, sine duce reuersus est. nondum audiuimus quod obierit: forte adhuc uiuit. in ipsa eorum basilica, ubi sunt eorum corpora, totam uitam suam seruiturum se esse deuouit. nos illum gauisi sumus uidentem, reliquimus seruientem. non cessat deus attestari: et nouit quomodo ipsa miracula sua debeat commendare. nouit agere, ut magnificentur: nouit agere, ne uilescant. non omnibus donat per martyres sanitatem: sed omnibus promittit imitatoribus martyrum immortalitatem."

miracles like these do not prove that the church in which they occur is Catholic, but that the miracles are proven authentic because they occur within the Catholic Church.[61] At that stage of his thinking about martyrs, shrines, and relics, Augustine didn't expect that miraculous occurrences such as that he had personally witnessed in Milan fifteen years earlier would also occur in North Africa (cf. *ep.* 78.3). A quarter of a century later, Augustine's mind about this completely changed.

St. Stephen

In 415 news spread that the tomb of St. Stephen had been found in a cave at Carphargamala, a Byzantine settlement near Jerusalem. The relics were taken to Jerusalem and eventually to Constantinople. Small bags containing dust and earth that had touched the bones ("secondary relics"), and perhaps even some bone fragments, were brought to North Africa in 416 from the Holy Land by Orosius, a presbyter from Portugal. During the following decade, St. Stephen's relics were distributed to a number of Christian communities, including Uzalis, Carthage, and Hippo Regius.

In a sermon preached in 425 CE at the deposition of some of St. Stephen's relics in a chapel built in or near Augustine's Basilica Pacis, Augustine compares the discovery of these relics with that of Gervasius and Protasius:

> Your Holinesses are waiting to hear what has been enshrined in this place today. They are the relics of the first and most blessed martyr, Stephen. You heard, when the account of his passion was read . . . , how he commended his spirit to the Lord, how also at the end he knelt down and prayed for those who were stoning him. From that day to these times his body lay hidden. Recently, however, it came to light, as the bodies of the martyrs usually do come to light, by a revelation of God, when it so pleased the Creator. In this way some years ago, when I was a young man living in Milan, the bodies of the martyrs Gervasius and Protasius came to light. . . . The truth [about the location of Stephen's bones] was revealed to the man who pointed out the things that were discovered. The place, you see, was indicated by preceding signs and it was discovered to be just as it had been revealed in them. Many people received relics from there, because that was God's will and they came as far as here. So both this place and this day is being commended to your Graces' devotion;

61. *Cath. fr.* 19.50 (CSEL 52:298).

each is to be celebrated to the honor of God, whom Stephen confessed. After all, we haven't built an altar in this place to Stephen, but an altar to God from Stephen's relics.[62]

The many miracles connected with the relics of Stephen at such "altars" are described by Augustine in some of his other sermons on the protomartyr (e.g., *ss.* 321–24; cf. *ciu.* 22.8).[63]

Although he had previously denied that Catholics based their claim to legitimacy on miracles performed at martyrs' shrines, Augustine later argued that the possession of the relics of St. Stephen by Caecilianist/Catholic communities in North Africa—along with the miracles that occur at the shrines (cf. *s.* 323.4)—are proof that Catholics comprise the "true church." *Mater Ecclesia*, Mother Church, which had endowed St. Stephen with martyrdom (cf. *s.* 317.6), was now visibly present at Augustine's church in Hippo (and in similar North African Caecilianist communities) through the enshrined sacred dust that had touched Stephen's bones (cf. *s.* 317.1).

From Ambrose's use of the relics of Gervasius and Protasius in his battle against the Homoians, Augustine understood and grasped the opportunity afforded him by the fortuitous presence of his friend Orosius in the Holy Land at

62. S. 318.1–2 (PL 38:1437–38; trans. Hill, WSA III/9, 147, modified): "exspectat sanctitas uestra scire quid hodie in isto loco positum sit. reliquiae sunt primi et beatissimi martyris Stephani. audistis, cum passionis eius lectio legeretur de libro canonico Actuum Apostolorum, quemadmodum lapidatus sit a iudaeis, quemadmodum domino commendauerit spiritum suum, quemadmodum etiam in extremo genibus fixis orauerit pro lapidatoribus suis. huius corpus ex illo usque ad ista tempora latuit; nuper autem apparuit, sicut solent apparere sanctorum corpora martyrum, reuelatione dei, quando placuit creatori. sic ante aliquot annos, nobis iuuenibus apud Mediolanum constitutis, apparuerunt corpora sanctorum martyrum Geruasii et Protasii. scitis quod Geruasius et Protasius longe posterius passi sunt, quam beatissimus Stephanus. quare ergo illorum prius, et huius postea? nemo disputet: uoluntas dei fidem quaerit, non quaestionem. uerum autem reuelatum fuit ei, qui res ipsas inuentas monstrauit. praecedentibus enim signis locus demonstratus est; et quomodo fuerat reuelatum, sic et inuentum est. multi inde reliquias acceperunt, quia deus uoluit, et huc uenerunt. commendatur ergo caritati uestrae et locus et dies: utrumque celebrandum in honorem dei, quem confessus est Stephanus. nos enim in isto loco non aram fecimus Stephano, sed de reliquiis Stephani aram deo."

63. These four sermons were preached in Hippo in 426 on four consecutive days starting on Easter Sunday. See also Anthony Dupont, "Imitatio Christi, Imitatio Stephani: Augustine's Thinking on Martyrdom; The Case Study of Augustine's Sermons on the Protomartyr Stephanus," *Augustiniana* 56, no. 1 (2006): 29–61.

the very time of the discovery of St. Stephen's relics. In the second century, the Roman presbyter Gaius had "trumped" the claims to legitimacy of the local Montanist leader Proclus by pointing out that it was the "Catholics," not the "Montanists," who possessed the "trophies"[64] of Saints Peter and Paul.[65] Augustine held a similar winning card against the Donatists when preaching on the feast day of St. Stephen (i.e., December 26): it was the North African Caecilianists, not the Donatists, who possessed the relics of St. Stephen. These relics provided physical testimony to the continuity of the true faith from the Holy Land to the (Caecilianist, not Donatist) churches in North Africa.

MAJOR PASTORAL THEMES IN AUGUSTINE'S USE OF THE NORTH
AFRICAN AND WESTERN MARTYRIOLOGICAL TRADITION

As noted, Augustine believed that he had a moral duty, a debt to both God and the martyrs to keep their memory alive by preaching about them on their feast days and on other relevant occasions. He did not discharge this debt merely to combat Donatists and Pelagians when the occasion demanded it, but rather as a consistent homiletic program by which to inspire, instruct, and, where necessary, correct and encourage his hearers.

Pastoral Instruction

Augustine's sermons on the martyrs gave him the opportunity to educate his hearers on a wide variety of theological topics ranging from Christology (e.g., *ss.* 273.1 and 276.1) to ecclesiology (e.g., *ss.* 22.4, 37.1, 280.6, and 299A.7). The primary focus of these sermons, however, was pastoral instruction. Taking his cue from whatever virtue, or virtues, he deemed appropriate from the combination of biblical texts prescribed for the day and relevant *acta martyrum*, Augustine expounded on these virtues and invariably exhorted the catechumens and the faithful to imitate the martyrs by exhibiting the same virtues in their own Christian life. Typical are statements such as the following from a sermon on the Scillitan

64. Memorial shrines, including relics.

65. Eusebius, *Hist. eccl.* 2.25.7 (text and trans. Lake, LCL 153:181–83). See William Tabbernee, "'Our Trophies Are Better Than Your Trophies': The Appeal to Tombs and Reliquaries in Montanist-Orthodox Relations," *StPatr* 31 (1997): 206–17.

Martyrs: "May the holy martyrs pray for us that we should not only celebrate their feasts, but also imitate their virtues."[66]

Among the virtues repeatedly highlighted by Augustine are *courage* (e.g., *ss.* 283augm.1, 285.1, and 299A.1), especially in overcoming fear (e.g., *s.* 318.2 and 335.1); *patience* (e.g., *ss.* 277A.2, 283augm.4, 284.3, and 397.4), particularly in suffering—even if one's suffering is due to illness and not a call to martyrdom (e.g., *ss.* 286.7, 328.8, and 335D.3); *endurance*, including endurance of pain (e.g., *s.* 283augm.3); and especially *obedience*. Obedience is owed not only to God directly but also to the bishop as God's representative (e.g., *s.* 359B.4–8, 12, 23).

For Augustine, martyrs such as Perpetua also demonstrate that there are times when *dis*obedience is a virtue. Perpetua's refusal to accede to her father's pleas for her to save herself by sacrificing to the gods (*Pass. Perp.* 3.1–4, 5.1–6) demonstrated that, depending on the circumstances, it is not only permissible but imperative to disobey one's parents. Although such disobedience may appear to run counter to the biblical command to honor one's father and mother (Exod. 20:12; cf. Eph. 6:2–3), it is totally consistent with Jesus's mandate (Luke 14:26) that to be a disciple requires one to hate one's father and mother and even life itself (*s.* 159A.6).

"Hating one's life," for Augustine, means exercising the virtue of *self-denial*. Martyrs viewed their lives as superfluous (e.g., *s.* 62.14) and feared for their souls rather than their bodies (e.g., *s.* 65.7–8), although this did not mean that voluntary martyrdom was permissible (e.g., *s.* 313E.5). Unlike the Donatist Circumcellions, Caecilianist martyrs did not take their own lives by jumping off cliffs or other means. Although Christians should be ready to give up their lives for God, for most of Augustine's listeners, self-denial meant detachment from temporal goods (e.g., *ss.* 299D.5 and 345.7).

According to Augustine, Christians could (and should) also imitate the martyrs by exemplifying the triple virtues of faith, hope, and love (cf. 1 Cor. 13:13). Martyrs professed *faith* through their lives as well as, ultimately, through their deaths (e.g., *ss.* 51.8 and 394.1). They lived and died with the *hope* of being resurrected (e.g., *s.* 229H.3) to eternal life (e.g., *s.* 302.7) in the kingdom of heaven (e.g., *s.* 105A.1). Martyrs suffered as witnesses for truth (e.g., *s.* 328.2) and justice

---

66. S. 299F.4 (PL Suppl. 2:791; trans. Hill, WSA III/8, 273): "orent pro nobis martyres sancti ut non solum eorum sollemnia <celebremus>, uerum etiam eorum mores imitemur." Cf. *ss.* 64.1, 284.6, 325.1, and 351.11.

(e.g., *s*. 159.8) out of *love* (e.g., *s*. 229J.3)—without which their martyrdom would have been meaningless (e.g., *ss*. 138.2 and 169.15). Augustine's congregants can strengthen their own love by loving and imitating the martyrs (e.g., *s*. 295.8).

Pastoral Correction

Pastoral instruction included pointing out beliefs or practices that needed to be corrected and changed. Augustine's main concern relating to martyrs was the manner in which some people behaved at martyrs' shrines. Dancing or getting drunk on saints' feast days was no way to honor the martyrs and their sufferings (e.g., *ss*. 198.9 and 335A.3; cf. *ep*. 22.2–6 and 29.1.11). Nor, however, was praying to them. While praising martyrs is a means of praising God (e.g., *s*. 302.12), praying to martyrs is an insult to God (e.g., *s*. 159.1). Martyrs are not gods and should not be treated as if they were (e.g., *ss*. 198.46 and 273.7). Christians must worship the God of the martyrs, not the martyrs themselves (e.g., *s*. 335H.2); instead of praying to the martyrs, people should ask the martyrs to pray for them (e.g., *s*. 198.12).

Augustine also wanted to stop his congregants from referring to Donatists as having martyrs. Even though some Donatists (and other schismatics or heretics) had died for their cause,[67] they were not in fact martyrs. Only those who belonged to the (true) church and who were put to death for the right cause can be called martyrs. The cause, not the punishment (or the suffering), is what makes a martyr a martyr: *non poena sed causa* (e.g., *ss*. 53A.13; 306.2; 325.2; 327.1, 2; 335.2; and 359B.17).[68]

Pastoral Encouragement

Augustine recognized that for his listeners to be able actually to exhibit the Christian virtues he highlighted in his sermons, they needed encouragement. Encouragement was also required to help Christians correct their beliefs and, especially, change their behavior. Augustine provides this encouragement by emphasizing

67. On Donatist *acta martyrum*, see Maureen A. Tilley, ed., *Donatist Martyr Stories*, TTH 24 (Liverpool: Liverpool University Press, 1997).

68. Wojciech Lazewski, "La Sentenza Agostiniana Martyrem Facit Non Poena Sed Causa" (PhD diss., Pontificia Universitas Lateranensis, 1987); Adam Ployd, "*Non poena sed causa*: Augustine's Anti-Donatist Rhetoric of Martyrdom," *AugStud* 49, no. 1 (2018): 25–44.

two recurring themes in his homilies: the devil has been and will continue to be defeated; and human weakness has been and will continue to be overcome.

In almost every one of his sermons on the martyrs, Augustine mentions directly or alludes to the defeat of Satan/the devil (e.g., *ss.* 32.26, 273.6, and 275.1–2), that ancient, cunning snake/demon (e.g., *ss.* 64A.3 and 359B.15) whose head was trampled on by Perpetua (*ss.* 280.1, 4, and 281.2; cf. *Pass. Perp.* 4.7). By imitating the martyrs, Christians, when tempted, can likewise trample the devil underfoot.

For Augustine, human weakness is neither an excuse for not defeating the devil nor an impediment in the battle against him. Just when it seems that martyrs are about to be conquered by the devil, the devil is conquered by Christ acting through the martyrs (e.g., *ss.* 32.26 and 281.1). Although Augustine has frequently been criticized for his apparent negative attitude to women martyrs such as Perpetua and Felicitas,[69] this criticism is unwarranted. In fact, a close reading of his sermons on these and other female martyrs demonstrates that Augustine had an extremely high regard for them in that they overcame what he—and everyone else in his day and age—perceived to be the burden of being "the weaker sex." For example, in a sermon on the feast day of St. Eulalia, preached most likely at Hippo on December 10 of about 410, Augustine explains:

> This Saint Eulalia, you see, from the province of Spain, a holy and valiant woman, who by her love overcame the weakness of her sex like Saint Crispina, was like the blessed Cyprian, like many other holy martyrs, like the Eight, like the Twenty, and all their companions.[70]

Clearly, Perpetua and Felicitas (e.g., *s.* 286.2) weren't the only women martyrs singled out for the "weakness of their sex." However, in overcoming this "weakness," women martyrs are to be considered not only the equivalent of male martyrs (*ss.* 280.1, 299E.1, 305A.2) but superior to them because they have overcome

69. For example, Brent D. Shaw, "The Passion of Perpetua," *Past and Present* 139 (1993): 36–37; Joyce E. Salisbury, *Perpetua's Passion: The Death and Memory of a Young Roman Woman* (New York: Routledge, 1997), 172–76; Hanne Sigismund-Nielsen, "Vibia Perpetua—an Indecent Woman," in Bremmer and Formisano, *Perpetua's Passions*, 104 and 116–17; Heffernan, *Passion of Perpetua*, 365.

70. S. 313G.3 (*MA* 1:595; trans. Hill, WSA III/8, 124, modified): "ista enim sancta Eulalia, de prouincia Spania, sancta et fortis femina, quae per affectum uicit sexum, sicut sancta Crispina, sicut beatus Cyprianus, sicut alii multi martyres sancti, sicut octo, sicut uiginti, et omnes eorum socii."

an additional obstacle. In preaching about Perpetua and Felicitas—on a feast day named after them rather than their male companions—Augustine points out:

> In this company of outstanding glory there were also men who were martyrs, men who on the same day were victorious by means of their most strenuous passions; and yet they have not graced this same day with their names. This has not happened because the women were preferred to men on the basis of the excellence of their morals, but because—and it was a greater miracle—female weakness defended the most terrible enemy and male strength fought for perpetual felicity.[71]

Conclusion

Perpetua, Felicitas, and all the other famous (or not-so-famous) martyrs about whom Augustine preached served as object lessons. The North African/Western martyriological tradition furnished Augustine with innumerable examples of virtues to imitate, practices to avoid, and beliefs to rethink. Possession of relics of St. Stephen also solidified the claim that only the Caecilianists/Catholics comprised the true church and that, consequently, only Caecilianists/Catholics had true martyrs. Even if schismatics and heretics suffered what they considered "martyrdom," it is "not the punishment but the cause which makes the martyr." Only the Caecilianist/Catholic martyrs or those whom the Donatists and others venerated in common with the Caecilianists/Catholics were true martyrs precisely because they died for the right cause. It was only the true martyrs who, despite their own human weakness, defeated the devil, and only they who provided true encouragement to Augustine's listeners that they could do the same, even in circumstances where they were unlikely to have to suffer martyrdom themselves.

When he preached at Carthage on the feast day of the martyrs of Maxula in 397 CE, Augustine may not have known very much, or anything, about these particular martyrs—but he knew enough about the North African/Western martyriological tradition as a whole so as to render specifics about the Maxultians

---

71. *S.* 282auct.6(3) (Isabella Schiller, Dorothea Weber, and Clemens Weidmann, "Sechs neue Augustinuspredigten: Teil 1 mit Edition dreier Sermones," *WS* 121 [2008]: 264; trans. Sigismund-Nielsen, "Vibia Perpetua," 103).

irrelevant. By drawing on that broader martyriological tradition, he could, and did, exhort his listeners to imitate the Maxultians and all other martyrs:

> Bestir yourselves, Christian hearts! Join up, be a soldier for God; with him no hard service can be in vain, with him no danger can be fruitless. By dying in battle, you see, the soldier of the world loses his reward, whereas it's precisely by dying that the soldier of Christ finds his.[72]

---

72. S. 283augm.4 (Dolbeau, *Vingt-six sermons*, 198; trans. Hill, WSA III/11, 247): "expergiscimini, corda christiana; militate deo apud quem non potest labor irritus, apud quem non potest esse infructuosum periculum. miles enim saeculi in pugna morte perdet praemium, miles Christi morte inuenit praemium."

Chapter 5

AUGUSTINE AND OPTATUS OF MILEVIS

Alden Bass

INTRODUCTION

In 393 CE, some two years after being ordained a presbyter in Hippo, Augustine was tasked by his patron Aurelius of Carthage with the reunification of the African church. For nearly a century, the church had been divided between two factions, the Donatists and Caecilianists.[1] Over the past half century, the Donatist party had flourished and now threatened to completely overtake the Caecilianists. Aurelius had inherited the smaller Caecilianist party, which, despite imperial support, had fallen into disarray under a series of do-nothing primates; ecclesiastical reform was his first priority. Augustine's intellectual and rhetorical abilities, recognized by Donatists and Caecilianists alike, qualified him to take the lead in reconciling the parties. Yet, as a relatively new Christian recently returned from Italy, he was unfamiliar with the theological controversies of North Africa. In the numerous letters, sermons, and treatises he would write against the Donatists over the next twenty-five years, Augustine would rely heavily on the anti-Donatist apology of a Caecilianist bishop from western Numidia, Optatus

---

1. For historical background on the schism and the issues surrounding it, see the essays in Richard Miles, ed., *The Donatist Schism: Controversy and Contexts* (Liverpool: Liverpool University Press, 2016). Although, strictly speaking, it cannot be shown that Aurelius acted alone in tasking Augustine, É. Rebillard ("Augustine in Controversy with the Donatists before 411," in Miles, *Donatist Schism*, 297–316, esp. 302 and 305) asserts that the *Psalmus contra partem Donati* and *Contra epistolam Parmeniani* were both written at the behest of the senior bishops. If correct, it follows that the anti-Donatist campaign was not begun on Augustine's initiative but was more of a concerted effort by Caecilianist leadership.

of Milevis. With its carefully sourced account of the schism's history and articulation of the essential points of disagreement between the factions, Optatus's treatise was an invaluable primer for Augustine. As Paul Monceaux declared nearly a century ago, "In sum, the bishop of Hippo perfected the war machine; but this machine was designed, created, and set in motion by Optatus of Milevis, who in this area is the precursor to the master Augustine."[2]

"Precursor" is a common description for Optatus, whom the "master" is thought to have quickly surpassed.[3] Yves Congar represents the consensus: "Optatus was an initiator. Augustine took him first as a guide; but he gradually completed the dossier, corrected and extended the narrative, and worked out the questions of exegesis and doctrine."[4] At the same time, Augustine's voluminous anti-Donatist corpus and his tremendous influence on later theology belies the unoriginality of his polemic. "The same arguments recur again and again," Robert Eno writes, "the historical facts concerning the origins of the schism are constantly rehearsed. . . . Were [the Donatists] really such dunces?"[5]

In three decades, Augustine did not deviate significantly from the course adopted from his Milevan predecessor. Mature works such as his presentation at the Conference of Carthage in 411 CE cite the same biblical texts and repeat the same basic arguments—in some cases nearly verbatim. On at least one issue, the use of coercion, Augustine actually grew closer to Optatus later in life. Augustine's engagement with *On the Donatist Schism* (*Schis.*) in the formative years of his

2. Paul Monceaux, *Histoire littéraire de l'afrique Chrétienne depuis les origines jusqu'à l'invasion arabe*, vol. 5, *Saint Optat et les premiers écrivains donatistes* (Paris: Leroux, 1920), 306 (trans. is my own).

3. Few works have given sustained attention to Augustine's debt to Optatus. Short treatments can be found in the following: Antoon A. R. Bastiaensen, "Augustin et ses prédécesseurs latins chrétiens," in *Augustiniana Traiectina: Communications présentées au Colloque International d'Utrecht 13–14 novembre 1986*, ed. J. den Boeft and J. van Oort (Paris: Études Augustiniennes, 1987), 46–47; Mark Edwards, "Augustine and His Christian Predecessors," in *A Companion to Augustine*, ed. Mark Vessey (Hoboken, NJ: Wiley-Blackwell, 2012), 217; and H.-J. Sieben, "Optatus episcopus Mileutanus," *AugLex* 4:319–22.

4. Yves Congar, "Optat de Milev," BA 28:721–22 (trans. is my own).

5. Robert Eno, "Some Nuances of Donatist Ecclesiology," *REAug* 18 (1972): 46. For more on Augustine's misunderstanding of his opponents, see Jesse A. Hoover, *The Donatist Church in an Apocalyptic Age* (Oxford: Oxford University Press, 2018), 26–34. Augustine's failure on this count is puzzling. Some biographers have suggested that Augustine held his Donatist opponents in contempt as the party of the lower class and unworthy of serious intellectual engagement. See, e.g., Peter Brown, *Augustine of Hippo: A Biography*, new ed. (Berkley: University of California Press, 2000), 217, and Rebecca West, *St. Augustine* (New York: Appleton, 1933), 140.

early priesthood profoundly shaped him, to the extent that he was unwilling (or unable) to hear his opponents on their own terms. Many of Optatus's misreadings, exaggerations, and intentional obfuscations—the products of his position as an embattled minority bishop—crept into Augustine's writings, coloring and ultimately compromising his effectiveness as a polemicist. In the end, he was no more successful in persuading the Donatists than Optatus had been.

OPTATUS, CAECILIANIST APOLOGIST

Augustine valued Optatus as a theologian and a churchman, counting him among Latin luminaries such as Cyprian, Lactantius, and Hilary, the "good and faithful men among our brothers" who through their education and rhetorical training brought "a load of gold, silver, and garments from Egypt" in defense of the church.[6] Augustine referred to Optatus's teaching as "the tradition of the universal church."[7] In *Ad catholicos fratres* (*cath. fr.*) 29.50, he praised Optatus as a champion of the faith alongside his mentor Ambrose. Yet, while Augustine went on to eulogize Ambrose at length, he said nothing more about Optatus.

Little is known about Optatus today, and it seems that he was unremarkable even in his own time. Mirielle Labrousse calls his presence in Augustine's corpus "ghostly."[8] There is no indication that Augustine ever had contact with the elderly bishop, who died a few years after Augustine returned to Africa in 388 CE. If he heard tales of Optatus's holiness or ministry during his visits to Milevis in the 390s, or from his friend Severus, who served the Caecilianist parish there, he never mentioned them.

Nevertheless, we know that Optatus was descended from a patrician Roman family—perhaps a military family—in the environs of Milevis, part of the Latinized "four cities" of upper Numidia.[9] He renounced his classical education

---

6. *Doctr. chr.* 2.40.61 (CCSL 32:73; trans. is my own). See Jean Doignon, "'Nous bons hommes de foi': Cyprien, Lactance, Victorin, Optat, Hilaire (*De doctr. Christ.* 2,40,61)," *Latomus* 22 (1963): 795–805. Fulgentius of Ruspe included him with Ambrose and Augustine in *Ad Monimum* 2.13, 15 (CCSL 91:49).

7. *Bapt.* 1.8.9 (BA 29:115; trans. is my own). Here, with reference to his teaching on the baptism of heretics.

8. Mirielle Labrousse, "Le baptême des hérétiques d'après Cyprien, Optat et Augustin: influences et divergences," *REAug* 42 (1996): 225. She concludes her essay by suggesting that Augustine intentionally occluded Optatus so as not to alienate Donatist readers.

9. For more on the biography of Optatus, see Monceaux, *Histoire littéraire*, 5:241–95; André

when he became a Christian, as part of the post-Constantinian influx. Sometime in the early 360s he was named bishop of Milevis. His career resembles that of other North African Christian literati such as Cyprian, Augustine, and his fellow Milevan, Faustus, whose path differed only in becoming a Manichaean bishop. Though his work was read outside Africa by the likes of Jerome, Ambrosiaster, and Innocent I, Optatus is remembered mainly for his contribution to the African controversy.[10] Brent Shaw dubs him "the sectarian terrier of his age."[11]

Optatus wrote only one work in his lifetime, an apology for the Caecilianist party in seven books known variously as *Against Parmenian, Against the Donatists*, and *On the Donatist Schism*.[12] Parmenian, to whom the polemic was addressed, was the Donatist primate and successor of Donatus of Carthage. Parmenian had returned to Africa around 361 CE, after being released from exile by the emperor Julian. Parmenian's arrival heralded a period of revival and expansion for the Donatists. He recovered the basilicas that had been seized, ritually purified them with a salt ceremony, and reinstalled Donatist clergy. He initiated a series of liturgical reforms, taking a harder line than his predecessors on issues such as rebaptism and public penance. He wrote Christian songs promoting Donatist themes, which proved popular with a broad audience. These actions dramatized the separatism encouraged by the Donatist leadership and effectively reestablished the Donatists as a distinct communion after over a decade of exclusive Caecilianist rule. His efforts were further rewarded with the conversion of a number of Caecilianists priests and nuns, who were reinitiated as Donatists.

In the early 360s Parmenian wrote an encyclical celebrating the Donatists' return to power and recovery of their basilicas.[13] Using Cyprian's favorite clus-

---

Mandouze, "Optatus," in *Prosopographie chrétienne du Bas-Empire: 1, Prosopographie de l'Afrique chrétienne (303–533)* (Paris: CNRS, 1982), 795–97; Mirielle Labrousse, "Optat de Milève (Saint)," in *Dictionnaire de Spiritualité* (Paris: Beauchesne, 1982), 11:824–30; Clementina Mazzucco, *Ottato di Milevi in un secolo di studi: Problemi e prospettive* (Bologna: Pátron Editrice, 1993).

10. For a more detailed accounting of Optatus's reception, see Alden Bass, "Scripture in Optatus of Milevis," in *The Bible in Christian North Africa, Part I: Commencement to the "Confessiones" of Augustine (ca. 180 to 400 CE)*, ed. Jonathan Yates and Anthony Dupont, Handbooks of the Bible and Its Reception 4.1 (Berlin: de Gruyter, 2020), 189–212, esp. 189.

11. Brent D. Shaw, *Sacred Violence: African Christians and Sectarian Hatred in the Age of Augustine* (Cambridge: Cambridge University Press, 2011), 148.

12. See CSEL 26. Mirielle Labrousse, *Optat de Milève: Traité contre les Donatistes*, SC 412–13 (Paris: Cerf, 1996). English translation in Optatus, *Against the Donatists*, trans. Mark Edwards, TTH 27 (Liverpool: Liverpool University Press, 1997).

13. As demonstrated by David E. Wilhite, "True Church or True Basilica? The Song of Songs and Parmenian's Ecclesiology Revisited," *JECS* 22 (2014): 399–436.

ter of images from Song of Sol. 4:12, "the bride, the enclosed garden, the sealed fountain," Parmenian explained how the Donatist church alone could rightfully claim the six *dotes*, or endowments, of the true catholic church. Now lost, the treatise was widely read—Optatus complained that it was "in the hands and mouths of many."[14] Optatus responded in the early 360s with a treatise of six books; nearly twenty years later, sometime in the early 380s, the argument was expanded in a seventh book.[15] Optatus offered a historical account of the origin and rise of the Donatist faction based on documentary evidence that blamed the Donatists for originally breaking communion. The *dotes*, he countered, are found among the Caecilianists. He also defended the use of imperial force against the Donatists during the "persecutions" of 317 and 347 CE, suggesting that their own violence and irrationality were the cause of the repressions. Optatus decried Parmenian's separatist practices and called for the Donatists to be reconciled to the Caecilianists. All Parmenian had to do, he said, was confess his error in order to be received into "the pious bosom of Mother Church."[16] Coming from a minor bishop stationed in western Numidia, such an offer to the most powerful clergyman in the African church must have seemed laughable.

AUGUSTINE ASSUMES THE TORCH

Though the Donatists were no less a menace in his day, Augustine did not share Optatus's beleaguered position.[17] Possidius reported that Augustine returned to Africa just as "the catholic church in Africa began to lift its head, having for a long time lain prostrate."[18] His ordination in 391 CE coincided with a decisive turnover in leadership for both parties. After decades of ineffective rule by the bishops Restitutus and Genethlius, the Caecilianists elected the very capable Aurelius, armed with his program of reform. On the other side, Primian succeeded

14. *Schis.* 1.4.4 (SC 412:178; trans. Edwards, 4).

15. On the dating and composition of the text, see Labrousse, "Introduction," SC 412:12–18.

16. *Schis.* 7.2.1 (SC 413:216; trans. Edwards, 137).

17. See Geoffrey G. Willis, *Saint Augustine and the Donatist Controversy* (London: SPCK, 1950), 1–35; W. H. C. Frend, *The Donatist Church: A Movement of Protest in Roman North Africa* (Oxford: Oxford University Press, 2000), 227–43. On the political and legal context of this period, see Erika T. Hermanowicz, *Possidius of Calama: A Study of the North African Episcopate in the Age of Augustine* (Oxford: Oxford University Press, 2008), 97–155.

18. *Vita Aug.* 7 (H. T. Weiskotten, ed. and trans., *Sancti Augustini Vita scripta a Possidio Episcopo* [Oxford: Oxford University Press, 1919], 52–54).

Parmenian as head of the Donatist faction around 390. A volatile and divisive leader, he reversed many of the gains made by his predecessor. The Donatist position was further compromised by political scandal. In the late 380s, the *comes Africae*, a Donatist Christian named Gildo, allied with Optatus of Thamugadi to unify the African church by force; their efforts were cut short by Gildo's execution after a failed coup in 398. The Donatist association with the Gildonian revolt convinced the emperor Honorius that decisive action was required for the good of the empire. Urged on by the Caecilianist representatives at the court, he issued an Edict of Union in 405 ordering the Donatists to yield their basilicas and cease meeting. This legislation marked a turning point in the controversy and emboldened Augustine in his efforts to bring about real unity between the communions, a confidence that Optatus never enjoyed.

When Aurelius tapped Augustine to spearhead the unification effort, he had surprising little knowledge of Donatist theology or practice. His hometown of Thagaste had at one time been a Donatist stronghold (cf. *Epistula* [*ep.*] 93.5.17), and at least some of his family remained in their communion (cf. *ep.* 52). He would have encountered Donatists throughout his early life, such as his classmate Vincentius (cf. *ep.* 93.1.1). Perhaps because of his general disaffection with Christianity in his youth or because of some specific prejudice against the Donatists, Augustine never bothered to familiarize himself until his commission at the Council of Hippo in 393 CE. According to Possidius, after that time evangelizing the Donatists became his constant concern, a problem he worked on "day and night."[19] Rather than undertaking a personal investigation, however, he turned to Optatus's treatise to understand his adversaries. In later years he would read their writings himself and personally interview Donatist leaders, who corrected him on several important points.[20] But by that time the die had been cast.

Augustine undertook serious study of Optatus's work in the winter of 393 CE in preparation for writing the *Psalmus contra partem Donati* (*ps. c. Don.*), a popular song of 297 lines.[21] In order to reach ordinary people, whom he believed had been

19. *Vita Aug.* 9 (trans. Weiskotten, 58–59).

20. The early phase of the controversy is well documented in Rebillard, "Augustine in Controversy with the Donatists before 411." On the development of Augustine's anti-Donatist polemic in his letters, see Gavril Andreicut, "The Church's Unity and Authority: Augustine's Effort to Convert the Donatists" (PhD diss., Marquette University, 2010), 138–65.

21. Allusions in his Galatians commentary make it clear that Augustine had read Optatus before 393 CE. See Eric Plumer, *Augustine's Commentary on Galatians: Introduction, Text, Translation, and Notes*, OECS (Oxford: Oxford University Press, 2003), 68–70.

deceived by devious bishops and imprisoned by custom, he composed a catchy song following an alphabetical pattern calculated to convince the Donatist faithful of the strength of the Caecilianist position. It was also easily memorized. In structure and content, *Psalmus contra partem Donati* is essentially *On the Donatist Schism* set to meter—Geert Van Reyn has called it "Optatus for dummies."[22] The song had little effect on its intended audience, but the rhymed design of the song indelibly impressed Optatus's text on Augustine's mind. Traces of the work can still be heard in an impromptu sermon to the Donatists of Caesarea nearly thirty years later.[23]

The Shared Patrimony of Cyprian's Ecclesiology

Optatus's influence on Augustine is difficult to distinguish from that of the broader African tradition, which had been distilled in the work of the martyr-bishop Cyprian of Carthage. Cyprian's experience of persecution and ecclesiastical schism prefigured the controversy between Caecilianists and Donatists, each of whom claimed to be his true heir.[24] The fundamental question for Cyprian, indeed the governing issue for all African theology, concerned the boundaries of the Christian community, outside of which there was no salvation. Early in his pastorate, he defined the ecclesial community by their sanctity, a people set apart from the world by their access to life-giving sacraments. Later, after the

22. Geert Van Reyn, "Hippo's Got Talent: Augustine's *Psalmus contra partem Donati* as a Pop(ular) Song," in *The Uniquely African Controversy: Interdisciplinary Studies on Donatist Christianity*, ed. Anthony Dupont, Matthew Gaumer, and Mathijs Lamberigts (Leuven: Peeters 2015), 261. Monceaux observed that Optatus was "sa source unique." *Histoire littéraire de l'afrique Chrétienne depuis les origines jusqu'à l'invasion arabe*, vol. 7, *Saint Augustin et le Donatisme* (Paris: Leroux, 1923), 82–83. For a brilliant treatment of the function of the *ps. c. Don.* in the controversy, see Shaw, *Sacred Violence*, 441–89.

23. E.g., Augustine opens the *s. Caes. eccl.* (BA 32:416–45) with a reflection on *pax Christi* citing John 14:27 (cf. *ps. c. Don.* 5), the same verse with which Optatus begins *Schis*. In the same context Augustine also quotes Eph. 2:14 (cf. *Schis*. 4.2.30) and 1 Cor. 1:13 (cf. *Schis*. 2.5.2, 5.6.2). In *s. Caes. eccl.* 2, he calls Emeritus "our brother," giving the same justification from Isa. 66:5 as did Optatus (cf. *Schis*. 1.3.1). He goes on to recite the Optatine arguments against schismatic sacraments (*s. Caes. eccl.* 3) and the evidence exonerating Caecilian (*s. Caes. eccl.* 7).

24. *Bapt*. 3.3.5 (BA 29:184). For more on Cyprian's influence on the fourth-century controversy, see J. Patout Burns Jr., *Cyprian the Bishop* (New York: Routledge, 2002), 166–76. Also Vasilije Vranić, "Augustine and the Donatist Claims to Cyprianic Ecclesiological Legacy," *Philotheos* 7 (2007): 232–40.

controversy over the readmittance of lapsed Christians, Cyprian came to see the bishops as representatives of ecclesial sanctity, themselves unified as a network of saints promoting and preserving the holiness of the body. These issues defined the Donatist-Caecilianist division; each faction developed different aspects of Cyprian's ecclesiology, with Parmenian highlighting holiness and separatism and Optatus emphasizing unity and the toleration of sinners.[25]

Augustine's early reception of the Cyprianic tradition was mediated through Optatus.[26] He read some Cyprian early in his priesthood, but not extensively. As he notes in *Retractationes* (*retr.*) 1.20.3, he initially attributed rebaptism to Donatus of Carthage, not realizing that Cyprian had ardently defended the practice. He critically engaged Cyprian around 400 CE in the treatise *On Baptism* (*bapt.*), yet as late as 408 Augustine incorrectly maintained that Cyprian had recanted his views on rebaptism later in life (*ep.* 93.10.38 and *Contra Cresconium Donatistam* [*Cresc.*] 2.31.39). The African tradition that he had received via Optatus distorted Augustine's understanding of the African saint.

Optatus has been read as an "innovator," breaking with the Cyprianic tradition in his contest with the Donatists.[27] Insofar as the Donatists venerated the bishop—Cyprian's writings were treated like scripture—Optatus may have intentionally distanced himself. Cyprian receives only two passing mentions in *On the Donatist Schism* (cf. 1.10.5 and 1.19.3). And it is certainly the case that Optatus had begun to adopt certain Roman traditions such as Petrine primacy, the rejection of rebaptism, and (arguably) a more European biblical text. Nevertheless, his debt to Cyprian, particularly in his theology of the church and the bishops, is unmistakable.[28]

25. Labrousse, "Introduction," SC 412:117–21. J. P. Burns, "Establishing Unity in Diversity," *Perspectives in Religious Studies* 32 (2005): 381–99. Geoffrey D. Dunn, "Optatus and Parmenian on the Authority of Cyprian," in Dupont, Gaumer, and Lamberigts, *Uniquely African Controversy*, 179–96. See also, H. Koch, "La sopravvivenza di Cipriano nell'antica letteratura cristiana: Cipriano ed Ottato," *Ricerche Religiose* 7 (1931): 321–35.

26. Robert Eno makes this case in "The Significance of the Lists of Roman Bishops in the Anti-Donatist Polemic," *VC* 47 (1993): 158–69. Matthew Alan Gaumer notes that Augustine did not receive Cyprian directly from Optatus, which is correct; Optatus was, however, one of the first mediators of the Cyprian tradition. See *Augustine's Cyprian: Authority in Roman Africa* (Leiden: Brill, 2016), 60–63.

27. James Alexander, "Donatism," in *The Early Christian World*, ed. Philip F. Esler (New York: Routledge, 2000), 2:964.

28. Robert Eno argues for strong continuity in "The Work of Optatus as a Turning Point in the African Ecclesiology," *The Thomist* 37 (1973): 668–85. Jane Merdinger casts him as "a

Mater Ecclesia

One common ecclesiological image derived from Cyprian was *Mater Ecclesia*, a recurring motif in African Christian art and architecture. "One source, one mother who is prolific in offspring, generation after generation," Cyprian wrote, "of her womb we are born, of her milk we are fed, of her Spirit our souls draw life breath."[29] From this maternal metaphor Optatus developed his primary insight regarding the schism. Caecilianists and Donatists are brothers born from the same "sacramental womb," he reasoned, and as sons of the same mother they are inalienably joined. The "bonds of sacred kinship between us and you cannot be completely broken."[30] Though genetic ties cannot be dissolved, they can be strained by bad behavior. Donatist leaders had brought "dissension between us and our brothers."[31] These bishops had "deserted their catholic mother" and were now "cut off from the root of mother church."[32]

Optatus departed from the Cyprianic tradition in extending the maternal embrace of the church to schismatics.[33] Cyprian had made no practical distinction between schismatics and heretics, locating both Novatianists and Marcionites outside the safety of the church.[34] The Donatists followed him in maintaining

---

traditional African churchman taking his cue from Cyprian" in *Rome and the African Church in the Time of Augustine* (New Haven: Yale University Press, 1997), 59. Bradley Daugherty likewise recognizes the Cyprianic shape of his work in "The Bishops of North Africa: Rethinking Practice and Belief in Late Antiquity" (PhD diss., Vanderbilt University, 2015), 136–69.

29. *Unit. eccl.* 5 (CCSL 3:253; *De Lapsis and De Ecclesiae Catholicae Unitate*, trans. M. Bévenot [Oxford: Clarendon, 1971], 67): "unum tamen caput est et origo una, et una mater fecunditatis successibus copiosa; illius fetu nascimur, illius lacte nutrimur, spiritu eius animamur." For a full theological and aesthetic analysis of *mater ecclesia*, see B. Peper, "The Development of *Mater Ecclesia* in North African Ecclesiology" (PhD diss., Vanderbilt University, 2011).

30. *Schis.* 4.2.4 (SC 413:82; trans. Edwards, 85).

31. *Schis.* 1.2.1 (SC 412:174; trans. Edwards, 2).

32. *Schis.* 1.11.1 (SC 412:196; trans. Edwards, 11).

33. *Schis.* 1.11.1 (SC 412:196). Maureen Tilley, "When Schism Becomes Heresy in Late Antiquity: Developing Doctrinal Deviance in the Wounded Body of Christ," *JECS* 15 (2007): 1–21; also Gerald Bonner, "*Dic Christi Veritas Ubi Nunc Habitas*: Ideas of Schism and Heresy in Post-Nicene Age," in *The Limits of Ancient Christianity: Essays on Late Antique Thought and Culture in Honor of R. A. Markus*, ed. William Klingshirn and Mark Vessey (Ann Arbor: University of Michigan Press, 1999), 63–79.

34. *Ep.* 73.7–8. See also Geoffrey D. Dunn, "Heresy and Schism in Cyprian of Carthage," *JTS* 55 (2004): 551–74.

that Africa was divided into *duas ecclesias*, each holding an exclusive claim to the sacraments. The Caecilianists, they believed, were born from a "false mother" and were not actually sons, only cuckoos in the ecclesial nest (cf. Cyprian, *Ep.* 73.24.3). Optatus protested that the one church was actually still unified, though in *duas partes*.[35] "We are all Christians," book 1 begins, "dearest brothers" who hold "a single faith."[36] Unlike heresy, schism was not a substantial conflict over doctrine or practice. "Between you and us there is one and same manner of church life, the same shared scriptural readings, the same faith, the same sacraments of the faith, the same mysteries."[37] Schism was simply unresolved misunderstanding. Parmenian was his *carissimus frater* no matter how vociferously the Donatist bishop objected. "If you disdain to hear with goodwill this name of brother which I frequently pronounce," Optatus wrote, "let it be distasteful to you, but to me it is imperative."[38] He justified himself by quoting Isa. 66:5: "Those who decline to be called your brothers, say to them nevertheless, 'You are our brothers.'"[39]

Optatus's fraternal welcome of his rivals inspired Augustine's pastoral approach to the schism. At the beginning of his first anti-Donatist work, the *Psalmus contra partem Donati* (cf. *supra*), he appealed to Donatists as *fratres*, an address he would use in all of his communication. He assured his opponents at the Conference of Carthage of 411 CE that the language was used not merely "to soften their animosity" but rather out of "a recognized brotherhood and the community that creates one and the same heredity."[40] Like Optatus, he stressed their similarities: "We have the same baptism. . . . We have both customarily read the gospels. . . . We have both customarily celebrated the holidays of the martyrs. . . . We both always observed the festival of Easter."[41] The *Psalmus contra partem Donati* concludes with a dramatic personification of Mother Church called into a courtroom

---

35. *Schis.* 2.13.3 (SC 412:266).

36. *Schis.* 1.1.1 (SC 412:172; trans. is my own).

37. *Schis.* 5.1.11 (SC 413:116; trans. Edwards, 98); cf. 3.9.4, 4.2.3.

38. *Schis.* 4.2.4 (SC 413:82; trans. Edwards, 85).

39. *Schis.* 1.3.1 (SC 412:176; trans. Edwards, 2, modified). Luigi Vitturi accepts Optatus's approach as sincere in *La fraternità ecclesiale in Ottato di Milevi: "La dote della sposa"* (Padova: Edizioni Messaggero, 2015), 113–32. Shaw, *Sacred Violence*, 63–65, takes a more cynical view.

40. *Gest. conl. Carth.* 3.242 (SC 224:1178; trans. is my own).

41. *En. Ps.* 54.19 (CCSL 39:671; cited by Shaw, *Sacred Violence*, 64): "baptismum habebamus utrique . . . euangelium utrique legebamus . . . festa martyrum celebrabamus . . . Paschae solemnitatem frequentabamus." Cf. *ep.* 108.1.3–2.5.

to plead as a family witness that her feuding children be reconciled.[42] The theme echoes through his works, down to his sermon to Emeritus in 418 CE: "Why do we who adore the same Father not acknowledge one Mother?"[43]

Wall or Cornerstone

A second Cyprianic ecclesiological analogy—that of the "walled garden" from Song of Sol. 4:12—demonstrates the way Optatus was willing to modify the tradition. The Donatists used this image to justify their practice of separatism; the wall protected the family from the contamination of the world and preserved *unitas*. Optatus transformed the protective wall into a supportive foundation stone. Applying the prophecy of Ezek. 13, a central text in *On the Donatist Schism*, he averred that the Donatist bishops were "false prophets" who "[built] a ruinous wall" and then cried "Peace, peace."[44] These schismatic wall-builders divided the people of God, literally separating husband and wife, parents and children (cf. *Schis.* 3.10). Incorporating the Pauline language of Eph. 2, he argued that God desires not a dividing wall but a house built on the cornerstone of Christ: "One wall cannot have the cornerstone which is Christ, who, receiving the two peoples in himself, one from the Gentiles, the other from the Jews, joins both walls in the bond of peace."[45] Optatus's reading of Song of Sol. 4:12 through Eph. 2 captured Augustine's imagination. He used the cornerstone language in at least thirty-seven sermons and five works.[46] Unlike the wall, which separates, the cornerstone joins together in love. "'For [Christ] is our peace, who has made both one'—not Donatus, who has made the one into two."[47] True peace could only come when the wall of hostility was torn down and the dissenting bishops were either won over by persuasion or removed by other means.

42. *Ps. c. Don.* 270 (BA 28:188).

43. *S. Caes. eccl.* 5 (BA 32:432; trans. is my own): "qui ergo adoramus unum patrem, quare non agnoscimus unam matrem?"

44. *Schis.* 1.2.1 (SC 412:174); 3.10.4 (SC 413:66).

45. *Schis.* 3.10.4 (SC 413:66–68; trans. is my own): "nec lapidum habere angularem unus paries potest. qui lapis est Christus duos in se suscipiens populos, unum de gentibus, alterum de Iudaeis, qui nodo pacis iungit utrumque parietem."

46. See William Rader, *The Church and Racial Hostility: A History of Interpretation of Ephesians 2:11–22*, Beiträge zur Geschichte der biblischen Exegese 20 (Tübingen: Mohr Siebeck, 1978), 46–51.

47. *C. litt. Pet.* 2.71.158 (BA 30:416; trans. is my own): "ipse est enim pax nostra, qui fecit utraque unum, non Donatus, qui fecit de uno duo."

IGNORANT BROTHERS

Optatus's first priority was to establish that it was the party of Donatus that had broken unity and not the Caecilianists. To accomplish this he would use the "irresistible proof" of documentary evidence.[48] He assumed that Parmenian, who was not a native of Africa, had been "poorly instructed," having trusted "false reports" invented by mendacious bishops.[49] "I see that you are as yet ignorant that the schism at Carthage was created by your own leaders," he wrote.[50]

At least during the early years of his campaign, Augustine followed Optatus in believing that an accurate presentation of the schism's origin would convince his opponents of their error. His first anti-Donatist works are characterized by a mild tone of laying out the facts. In one of his earliest letters, he entreated the Donatist Maximinus, "Let us deal with the facts; let us deal with reason; let us deal with the authorities of the divine scriptures."[51] He presumed his hearers to be both reasonable and open to correction. "You who delight in peace, judge what is true," repeated the refrain of the *Psalmus contra partem Donati*. With the benefit of the doubt he wrote to Crispinus of Calama, "You are accustomed to toss about false statements about past events, perhaps not because you want to lie, but because you are mistaken."[52] These "mistakes" could be cleared up by consulting Optatus's factual account, as he declares at the beginning of *Contra epistolam Parmeniani* (*c. ep. Parm.*): "Anyone who wishes can read the story and the documents which are as numerous as they are convincing given by a catholic bishop of venerable memory, Optatus of Milevis."[53]

Optatus made use of a dossier of materials chronicling the early days of the schism—local court records, church proceedings, and imperial bureaucratic reports—which was later appended to *On the Donatist Schism*.[54] The Donatists had their own dossier, but even they appealed to Optatus's collection in some cases,

48. *Schis.* 1.5.4 (SC 412:182; trans. Edwards, 5).

49. *Schis.* 1.5.2 (SC 412:180; trans. Edwards, 4).

50. *Schis.* 1.10.5 (SC 412:194; trans. Edwards, 10): "sed uideo te adhuc ignorare schisma apud Carthaginem a uestris principibus factum."

51. *Ep.* 23.7 1 (CSEL 34/1:72; trans. Teske, *Letters 1–99*, WSA II/1, 65): "re agamus, ratione agamus, diuinarum scripturarum auctoritatibus agamus."

52. *Ep.* 51.1 (CSEL 34/2:145; trans. Teske, WSA II/1, 198): "soletis de praeteritis rebus gestis, qui uultis, falsa iactare forte non mentiendi studio sed errore."

53. *C. ep. Parm.* 1.3.5 (BA 28:218; trans. is my own): "legant qui uolunt quae narret et quibus documentis quam multa persuadeat uenerabilis memoriae Mileuitanus episcopus catholicae communionis Optatus."

54. Cf. *schis.* 1.14.2. Cf., e.g., 1.14–27; 2.3–4, 15–19; 3.3–4, etc. Edwards does not believe

much to Augustine's amusement (cf. *Breuiculus conlationis cum Donatistis* [*breuic.*] 3.20.38 and *ep.* 141.9). In Augustine's hands, the dossier became well thumbed.[55] Augustine, or one of his fellow councilors, actually had a reference copy of Optatus on hand at the Conference of Carthage in 411 CE (*breuic.* 3.20.38). Throughout his career Augustine continued to expand the Caecilianist dossier, filling in gaps and bringing it up to date. He acquired a copy of the proceedings of the Numidian conference at Cirta, which had been utilized by Optatus, but which were not included in his appended dossier (cf. *Cresc.* 3.27.30). Augustine also collected more recent materials, such as the conciliar letter of the Maximianist synod of Carbussa (cf. *en. Ps.* 36[2].20) and the minutes of the Primianist Council (cf. *Gesta cum Emerito Donatistarum episcopo* [*Emer.*] 10–11). Optatus's dossier was not accepted uncritically—he adjusted the date of the Cirta conference, for instance—but he trusted the documents.[56]

Along with the dossier, Augustine accepted Optatus's interpretation of events. Optatus blamed the original division on three villains: a wealthy matron named Lucilla who had been rebuked by Caecilian and sought revenge; a pair of disgruntled presbyters, Bostrus and Caelestius, who hoped to profit from Caecilian's fall; and the ambitious Donatus, who wanted nothing less than to rule Carthage. Optatus's presentation became a set piece in Augustine's anti-Donatist repertoire, sometimes followed word for word.[57] This narrative first appears in *Psalmus contra partem Donati*, then again (now recited from memory) in his debate with Fortunius in 397 CE (cf. *ep.* 43.2). He delivered the same in a sermon around 403 (cf. *en. Ps.* 36.18–23) and in a polemical treatise around 405 (cf. *c. ep. Parm.* 1.4.6–9, 1.5.10, 1.6.11). Augustine recited virtually the same story at the Conference of Carthage of 411, which would become the official Roman version after being ratified by the tribune Marcellinus (*breuic.* 3.25.43).

---

he compiled the dossier himself (Optatus, *Against the Donatists*, xxvi–xxix). See also Louis Duchesne, "Le dossier du Donatisme," *Mélanges de l'école française de Rome* 10 (1890): 589–650.

55. *Ep.* 51.2 (CSEL 34/2:145; trans. Teske, WSA II/1, 199): "We have the proconsular acts in our hands."

56. *Cresc.* 3.27.30 (BA 31:324–26). The authenticity of some of Optatus's documents has been challenged. T. D. Barnes questions the accuracy of the "protocol of Cirta" in "The Beginnings of Donatism," *JTS*, n.s., 26 (1975): 13–22. Klaus Martin Girardet argues that the Donatist appeal in *Schis.* 1.22 was likely forged; see "Konstantin d. Gr. und das Keichskonzil von Arles (314): Historisches Problem und methodologische Aspekte," in *Oecumenica et Patristica: Festschrift für Wilhelm Schneemelcher zum 75. Geburtstag*, ed. Damaskinos Papendreou, Wolfgang Bienert, and Knut Schäferdiek (Stuttgart: Kohlhammer, 1989), 151–74. Other faked documents pertaining to the schism were circulating, such as the forgery of the Donatist Ingentius.

57. E.g., the language of *c. ep. Parm.* 1.3.5 closely follows *Schis.* 1.18.

Optatus's account was imperfect and contentious. The vindictive matron, greedy clerics, and the arrogant bishop were stock rhetorical figures; the truth was certainly exaggerated, if not completely fabricated in some cases.[58] Optatus was unaware of some major events, such as the Synod of Arles in 315 CE (cf. *ep.* 43.2.4, 53.2.5; *c. ep. Parm.* 1.6.1). Other points may have been intentionally overlooked, such as the murder of the interim bishop during the investigation of Caecilian (cf. *ep.* 44.4.8) and the significance of the African council that condemned Caecilian, which had been attended by seventy bishops (cf. *ep.* 43.2.3). When exposed to these facts in his debate with Fortunius in 397, Augustine expressed surprise and disbelief. He was further taken aback that Donatists were in communion with transmarine churches and that Donatus of Carthage had attended the (eastern) Council of Serdica in 343 (cf. *ep.* 44.3.6). Nevertheless, these revelations did little to alter the narrative originally constructed by Optatus.[59]

Estranged Brothers

While Optatus was trying to wrest control of the historical narrative, he also sought to reconfigure the authority of the episcopal office to favor the Caecilianists. Charismatic Donatist bishops such as Donatus and Parmenian wielded great spiritual, and in some cases temporal, power. They were revered by the people. In the Donatists' view, the local bishops embodied ecclesial unity, who had the dual responsibility of (a) promoting holiness in the church through teaching the law and administering the sacraments and (b) guarding the purity of the church by means of ecclesiastical discipline. They were enabled by the "power of the keys," the spiritual authority to bind and loose sin (Matt. 16:19). Following

58. E.g., much attention has been given to the story of Lucilla. See Robert Wiśniewski, "Lucilla and the Bone: Remarks on an Early Testimony to the Cult of Relics," *JLA* 4 (2011): 157–61; and Jennifer Eyl, "Optatus's Account of Lucilla in *Against the Donatists*, or, Women Are Good to Undermine With," in *A Most Reliable Witness: Essays in Honor of Ross Shepard Kraemer*, ed. Susan Ashbrook Harvey et al., Brown Judaic Studies 358 (Atlanta: SBL Press, 2015), 155–64. On other questionable interpretations, see Timothy D. Barnes, *Early Christian Hagiography and Roman History*, Tria Corda 5 (Tübingen: Mohr Siebeck, 2010), 135–36.

59. Matteo Dalvit has shown how Optatus's mischaracterizations were knowingly perpetuated by Augustine; see "The Catholic Construction of Donatist Key Figures: A Critical Reading of Augustine and Optatus," in Dupont, Gaumer, and Lamberigts, *Uniquely African Controversy*, 237–50.

Cyprian, the Donatists held that their authority to perform these tasks derived from the holiness of the bishop as well as the integrity of the episcopal college, which passed down "the keys."

Optatus believed that the separatist bishops had exceeded their mandate; by enforcing high moral and cultic standards, they had obstructed Christian unity, quite literally. Donatists refused to sell Caecilianists' bread, to greet them in the street, or to bury them in their cemeteries. Donatist bishops ritually purified Caecilianists' basilicas as if they were pagan temples and exorcised and rebaptized any Caecilianist who wished to join their community. Taken together, Optatus's arguments abstracted spiritual power from the particular and embodied African bishops to a universal and intangible heavenly authority mediated through the Roman see, the see with whom the Caecilianists had exclusive communion.

Optatus began by undermining the sanctity of the Donatist leaders. Documents such as the Protocol of Cirta "proved" that Numidian Donatists were guilty of acquisitiveness, hypocrisy, murder, and even the arch-sin of *traditio*. Their separation from the Caecilianists was motivated not by theological conviction, Optatus charged, but by a desire to enhance their status so that the people would "speak well of you, swear by your names," and "respect your persons instead of God."[60] At the head was Donatus of Carthage, whose aspiration to be "a great man," a "prince of Carthage," and to elevate himself above the emperor made him the epitome of sinful pride.[61] Optatus went so far as to identify Donatus as the "prince of Tyre" from Ezek. 28, a title traditionally ascribed to Satan. Augustine thought this interpretation was flawed (*en. Ps.* 47.6), yet he echoed the sentiment that Donatus and his bishops were driven by diabolical *superbia*.[62]

Sinners Should Be Tolerated

Far more effective than Optatus's ad hominem attacks was his subtler work of redefining the role of the bishop and the nature of the church in a post-Constantinian world.[63] Fundamentally, Optatus challenged the assumption that

---

60. *Schis.* 2.21.6 (SC 412:288; trans. Edwards, 51): "bene nominant et per uos iurant et personas uestras iam pro deo habere noscuntur."

61. *Schis.* 3.3.11–15 (SC 413:26–29; trans. Edwards, 64–65).

62. See É. Lamirande, "Vanité et orguiel des Donatistes," BA 32:735–36.

63. A brief summary of his ecclesiology can be found in Walter Simonis, *Ecclesia visibilis et invisibilis: Untersuchungen zur Ekklesiologie und Sakramentenlehre in der afrikanischen Tradition von Cyprian bis Augustinus* (Frankfurt: Knecht, 1970), 43–49.

the unity of the church necessitated the expulsion of sinners. Citing the parable of the wheat and weeds (Matt. 13:24–30), he argued that good and evil coexist in the church until the day of judgment. "In one field diverse seeds spring up, just as in the church the host of souls is not homogeneous . . . and so we have agreed to lead you back and receive you into unity, because it is not granted to us either to separate or reject those, though they be sinners, who were born with us in the same field."[64] Unlike his rivals, who read the weedy field as the world, Optatus understood both wheat and weeds to be in the church. Just as Christ retained Peter, the disciple who denied him, so Christian bishops should tolerate the weeds, even those who were deniers and *traditores*.[65]

Augustine espoused Optatus's ecclesiology, agreeing that the toleration of sinners was the *quaestio magna* in Africa.[66] He would later use the term *corpus permixtum* to describe the church as a blended family of saints and sinners (*breuic.* 3.20; *Contra Donatistas* [*c. Don.*] 9.12), but the concept is already present in *Psalmus contra partem Donati*.[67] Augustine was reluctant to use Peter as an example, though he did speak of the apostles' toleration of Judas (*Cresc.* 2.19.24 and *Io. eu. tr.* 50.10–11). He also made frequent use of the parable of the wheat and weeds, much later calling it his trusty weapon in the struggle against the Donatists.[68] His language echoed Optatus's: "In this way, after all, in this world, in which the Catholic Church is spread through all the nations, this world that the Lord calls his field, we tolerate [the wicked]."[69]

64. *Schis.* 7.2.5–6 (SC 413:218; trans. Edwards, 138): "et in uno agro nascuntur diuersa semina, sicut in ecclesia non est similis turba animarum . . . ideo uos adductos recipere in unitate consensimus quia nobis non licet uel separare uel repellere, quamuis peccatores in uno agro nobiscum natos."

65. *Schis.* 7.3.7 (SC 413:224)

66. *Retr.* 2.43 (CSEL 36:151).

67. *Ps. c. Don.* 8–19 (BA 28:150–52). See R. A. Markus, *Saeculum: History and Society in the Theology of St. Augustine* (Cambridge: Cambridge University Press, 1970), 122–32. Ironically, Optatus's contemporary Tyconius, a Donatist theologian, was an even greater influence on Augustine's ecclesiology.

68. *Gest. Pel.* 12.27 (CSEL 42:80). Some instances of the parable's use: *ps. c. Don.* 146, 178–79, 199, 213–14, 260 (BA 28:170, 174, 178, 180, 186); see also *ep.* 53.3.6 (CSEL 34/2:154); *c. ep. Parm.* 1.14.21 (BA 28:260–62); *bapt.* 4.9.13 (BA 29:266); *Cresc.* 2.36.45 (BA 31:256); *ep.* 23.6 (CSEL 34/1:70); *s.* 252.5 (PL 38:1174); *en. Ps.* 21(2).1 (CSEL 38:121); *c. lit. Petil* 2.26.61 (BA 30:304); *ep.* 108.7 (CSEL 34/2:619). The list could be expanded.

69. *Ep.* 105.5.16 (CSEL 34/2:609; trans. Hill, *Letters 100–155*, WSA II/2, 63). J. S. Alexander notes the similarities of language in "The Donatist Case at the Conference of Carthage of A.D. 411" (PhD diss., University of St. Andrews, 1970), 64.

Judgment Should Be Deferred

As Jesse Hoover has ably demonstrated, Donatist separatism was driven, at least in part, by an apocalyptic eschatology.[70] Bishops had been entrusted to purge the ecclesial body of sin before the Lord's return so that the church could be presented to Christ as a pure bride "without spot or wrinkle" (Eph. 5:27 RSV). The Matthean parables of the dragnet and of the wheat and the weeds supported this position. In both parables, "angels" are sent out by Christ to "gather out of his kingdom all causes of sin and all evildoers" and to "separate the evil from the righteous" (Matt. 13:41, 49 NRSV modified). According to Donatist interpreters, the bishops were the discriminating angels. Optatus objected. The angels are angels, and Christ alone can separate good from evil; so "let us acknowledge that we are human," he continued, and tolerate sinners in the church until the day of judgment.[71] The judgment of the Donatists was premature and usurped the place of the Righteous Judge.

Like Optatus, Augustine ignored the apocalyptic assumptions of his opponents: "the harvest is the end of the world, not the era of Donatus."[72] Turning the parable against them, he wrote, "Your imagination that you are separating yourselves, before the time of the harvest, from the tares which are mixed with the wheat, proves only that you are tares."[73] Expelling the wicked does not preserve the unity of the church but destroys it (cf. *en. Ps.* 131.13). Any kind of final judgment in the present is tantamount to blasphemy, because God alone knows the heart.[74] The bishop ought rather to await patiently the righteous judgment of God, as Augustine explained at length in the Conference of Carthage of 411 CE (cf. *breuic.* 3.10.19). Deferring the separation of sinners until the second advent diminished the disciplinary power of the Donatist bishops.

---

70. Hoover, *Donatist Church*, 1–24.

   . 71. *Schis.* 7.2.6 (SC 413:218; trans. Edwards, 139).

72. *C. litt. Pet.* 3.2.3 (BA 30:586). Augustine would revisit this theme often: *c. ep. Parm.* 3.3.19 and 5.26 (BA 28:440, 460); *Cresc.* 3.81.93 (BA 31:458); *breuic.* 3.8.10 (BA 32:154); *en. Ps.* 8.1 (CSEL 38:49); 25(2).5 (CSEL 38: 144); 36(1).11 (CSEL 38:345); *Io. eu. tr.* 27.11 (PL 35:1620–21); *ep.* 93.9.33 (CSEL 34/2:479); *ciu.* 20.9 (CSEL 40/2:427); and *s.* 259.2 (PL 38:1197).

73. *Ep.* 76.2 (CSEL 34/2:329; trans. Teske, WSA II/1, 298).

74. Cf. *Schis.* 4.3.1 (SC 413:85; trans. Edwards, 85). Both Optatus and Augustine conflated public and private sin.

Catholicity Comes through Communion . . .

Optatus further diminished the power of local bishops by shifting the definition of "catholicity." Africans had long understood *catholicos* as moral and ritual integrity: the catholic church obeyed the whole law, and its leaders possessed the fullness of the sacraments (cf. *breuic.* 3.3.3 and *ep.* 93.7.23). Optatus ostensibly accepted this Cyprianic understanding of the church (cf. *Schis.* 2.1.2). He rejected, however, the Donatists' sectarian zeal, which had cut them off not only from the Caecilianists in Africa but also from all the churches contaminated by communion with Caecilian's bishops. He alleged that the Donatists restricted the work of the Spirit to "a tiny portion of Africa, in the corner of a little region."[75] Optatus countered that catholicity is manifest through communion with the whole church which is *"in toto terrarium orbe diffusa."*[76] He mounted a biblical case for ubiquity, using a half dozen psalms, such as 2:8: "I shall give you the nations as your inheritance and the ends of the earth as your possession."[77]

Optatus's geographical definition of catholicity became a standard Caecilianist argument. Augustine used some form of the phrase *"ecclesia toto orbe diffusa"* in nearly every anti-Donatist work.[78] Optatus's *testimonia* from the Psalter formed the core of his case, which he enhanced with references to even more psalms,[79] to Gen. 12 and the Abrahamic covenant that was directed at "all families of the earth" (cf. *c. ep. Parm.* 1.2.2 and 1.4.6), and to New Testament texts such as Rom. 1:5, "the promise shown to all nations" (cf. *ep.* 49.2 and *ep.* 53.3.6).[80] In his debates, he pressed Donatist leaders to show proof of their communion with the transmarine churches (cf. *ep.* 44.3.5). In his writings he mocked them relentlessly for their narrow provincialism, as had Optatus, who thought it indecent to limit the church to North Africa.

---

75. *Schis.* 2.1.3 (SC 412:236; trans. Edwards, 29): "ergo ut in particula Africae, in angulo paruae regionis apud uos esse possit."

76. *Schis.* 2.2.1 (SC 412:244). On Optatus's misreading of the Donatist position, see Eno, "Some Nuances," 46–50.

77. *Schis.* 2.1.7 (SC 412:238–40). Cf. Pss. 71:8; 49:1; 96:1; 102:15. Cf. *cath. fr.* 8.20–22 (BA 28:552–60).

78. E.g., *ps. c. Don.* 203–4 (BA 28:178); *Cresc.* 2.36.45 (BA 31:254); *ep.* 93.10.44 (CSEL 34:487). Further references can be found in Daniel E. Doyle, "Spread throughout the World: Hints on Augustine's Understanding of Petrine Ministry," *JECS* 13, no. 2 (2005): 233–46.

79. E.g., 22:28 in *ep.* 51.5 (CSEL 34/2:148) and 72:8 in *ep.* 66.1 (CSEL 34/2:235).

80. Some or all of these biblical references appear in, e.g., *ep.* 23.2, 4; *agon.* 29.31; *en. Ps.* 21; and *s.* 2.30.

... with Rome

Against their claims of visible, sacramental unity in Africa, Optatus offered two specific tests of catholicity—communion (1) with the biblical "seven churches of Asia" and (2) with Rome, maintained by the "exchange of official letters."[81] A central symbol of the church's unity was the *cathedra*, the first of the church's endowments and the center of spiritual authority. As David Wilhite has argued, Parmenian likely understood the *cathedra* as the primatial seat of Cyprian in Carthage, reacquired by the Donatists after Julian's restoration.[82] Since Caecilianist access to the throne of Cyprian had been cut off, Optatus turned to Rome. Rome was "the first episcopal see," and therefore temporally prior to Carthage.[83] Rome was also elevated by its association with the "head of all the apostles," Peter, who is "preferred to all the apostles."[84] According to Matt. 16:19, Peter received the "keys of the kingdom" from Jesus and, thus, Peter alone can "vouchsafe them to others."[85] Peter's *cathedra*—not the African primate's—is the *origo* of sacramental power, which is handed down through apostolic succession. He provided a catalog of Roman bishops in *On the Donatist Schism* 2.3.2–3, challenging Parmenian to find any Donatist bishops in the list. Communion with the Roman church became the keystone of Optatine catholicity, as Peter's see was the symbol of the united church.

Using an interpretation of Matt. 16:18 attributed to Ambrose, Augustine added that Peter was the "rock" on which the church was founded in *Psalmus contra partem Donati* 229–40.[86] He later qualified this interpretation, but the primacy of the Petrine see was central in his early polemics, such as the lost *Against the Letter of Donatus* described in *Retractiones* 1.20.1. In *Epistula* 53.1.2 he provided Generosus of Cirta a genealogy of Roman bishops copied almost verbatim from Optatus, urging him to show this list to the Donatists of Cirta to prove that none

81. *Schis.* 2.2.3–4 (SC 412:246; trans. Edwards, 33); cf. *Schis.* 4.3.3; Aug. *ep.* 53.1.2; *Cresc.* 2.37.46.

82. Wilhite, "True Church or True Basilica," 413–15.

83. *Schis.* 2.2.2 (SC 413:244; trans. Edwards, 32).

84. *Schis.* 7.3.4 (SC 413:222; trans. is my own). On Optatus's commitment to Roman primacy, see Merdinger, *Rome and the African Church*, 50–60, and Eno, "Work of Optatus."

85. *Schis.* 7.3.3 (SC 413:222; trans. Edwards, 139).

86. See Yves Congar, "L'interpretation de Mat., XVI, 18," BA 28:716–17n8. On the relation between Optatine catholicity and the Roman bishop, see Doyle, "Spread throughout the World," 233–46.

of them were on it.[87] Episcopal succession guaranteed the purity of Rome, and communion with Rome guaranteed the purity of her clients.

Christ Alone Can Sanctify

Holiness depends on right relations rather than personal righteousness. Yet even this attenuated sanctity is relativized. Traditionally, African clergy who had sinned publicly could not administer the sacraments until they had been reconciled through penance or rebaptism lest their sin contaminate the church. Like sin, grace must be physically transmitted; God's spirit of holiness passes through the priest into the sacramental matter of water, oil, or wine; Donatists called their priests "Givers" (*Schis.* 5.4.7). Because of this, Optatus had to justify how a guilty bishop could still impart holiness. Breaking down the sacrament into three elements—the faith of the believer, the sanctity of the minister, and the ritual itself—he reduced the role of the priest from the medium of God's Spirit to an administrator of the rite. The name of the Trinity, not the bishop, imparts grace, he argued. Christ himself performs the baptism, a view he supported by citing John 1:33.[88] In order to loosen their hold on the people, Optatus transformed the bishop into a bureaucrat, whose power derived from his ministerial office rather than his embodied holiness.

Augustine, like Optatus, minimized the role of the bishop in the sacramental process. Although he significantly expanded Optatus's arguments in the seven books of *On Baptism*, he still relied heavily on *On the Donatist Schism*, as Labrousse has shown.[89] Bishops "are not holy in themselves."[90] Baptism is the operation of Christ, and any sacrament performed in his name is valid.[91] Together with the faith of the candidate, the rite confers an indelible and unrepeatable sign

---

87. *Cresc.* 2.37.46. Both Augustine's textual and his theological dependence on Optatus is discussed in Eno, "Significance of the Lists," 164–67.

88. *Schis.* 5.2, 4–5, 7; cf. Aug. *ep.* 51.5. See also T. Sagi-Bunič, "Controversia de Baptismate inter Parmenianum et S. Optatum Milevitanum," *Laurentianum* 3 (1962): 167–209.

89. Labrousse, "Le baptême des hérétiques," 223–42. In the conclusion to his study on Augustine's theology of the clergy, Rémi Crespin writes, "On rencontre, en effet, sous la plume d'Optat de Milev des expressions toutes proches de celles d'Augustin, sur ces mêmes sujets: sainteté et consistance propres des *sacramenta*, vertu sanctificatrice du *nomen*, garantie de la validité du baptême attachée à la conformité des *verba* avec celles de l'institution." See his *Ministère et Sainteté: Pastorale du clergé et solution de la crise donastiste dans la vie et la doctrine de saint Augustin* (Paris: Études Augustiniennes, 1965), 282.

90. *Bapt.* 4.18.25 (BA 29:296–98).

91. *Bapt.* 5.4.4 (BA 29:328–30).

that cannot be lost, even if given by a schismatic or heretical priest.[92] Optatus was too steeped in Cyprianic thinking to admit the baptism of heretics (whom he believed polluted the church), but his logic led Augustine to that conclusion. Nevertheless, though the sacraments of nonconformists are valid, they are not effective or "fruitful." The end of the sacrament is charity, and the sacraments can have effect only in communion with the catholic church.[93] As long as the Donatists remain estranged from their "catholic" brothers in schism, their sacraments would be ineffective.[94] Sacraments are useless without brotherly love.

INCORRIGIBLE SONS

Augustine's doctrine of charity as the bond of unity is among his most sublime contributions to the Christian tradition. Charity became key not only in discriminating effective sacraments but in defining the bounds of the church (cf. *bapt.* 1.8.10). The theme is developed in his sermons on 1 John (i.e., *In epistulam Iohannis ad Parthos tractatus decem* [*ep. Io. tr.*]), but it derived from Paul's response to ecclesial divisions in 1 Corinthians, which was first applied to the schism by Optatus, who offered charitable toleration as an alternative to the ritual reintegration practiced by the Donatists. Citing 1 Cor. 13:4-5, Optatus asserted that "charity can cover a multitude of sins";[95] past sins such as betrayal should be "buried for the good of unity."[96] Optatus had introduced 1 Cor. 13 in his third book to disqualify the Donatist martyrs from the time of Macarius: "If I . . . give my body to the flames, and have not charity within me, I am nothing" (*Schis.* 3.8.10). Giovanni Cecconi has shown how the discourse of charity became the primary Caecilianist strategy for confronting the Donatist martyr-ethic that developed in the aftermath of the Macarian persecution.[97] At that time, Donatist bishops had refused imperial funds

92. *Bapt.* 6.1.2 (BA 29:404–6); cf. *c. ep. Parm.* 2.13.29.
93. *Bapt.* 1.8.10 (BA 29:82); *un. bapt.* 13.22 (BA 31:710).
94. *Bapt.* 1.7.9 (BA 29:78–79); cf. *Io. eu. tr.* 13.16.
95. Optatus attributes this phrase to Paul, though it actually comes from 1 Pet. 4:8.
96. *Schis.* 7.3.4 (SC 413:222; trans. Edwards, 140).
97. Giovanni A. Cecconi, "Elemosina e propaganda. Un analisi della 'Macariana persecutio,'" *REAug* 31 (1990): 42–66; on Augustine's reception of Optatus, see Michael Gaddis, *There Is No Crime for Those Who Have Christ: Religious Violence in the Christian Roman Empire* (Berkley: University of California Press, 2005), 131–37; on the shared biblical arguments, see Jonathan P. Yates, "The Use of the Bible in the North African Martyriological Polemics in

sent by Constans in the belief that Christian charity (like grace) can be transmitted only through ordained ministers. Their rejection of the imperial agents Paul and Macarius sparked the persecution that produced the martyrs Donatus and Marculus. Optatus countered that their refusal to welcome the agents was a sign that they lacked charity and proved that they deserved the persecution.

Not only were they lacking charity, the Donatists bore an active hatred against the Caecilianists. Optatus recounted stories of the Circumcellions, mobs of peasants associated with the Donatists who attacked Caecilianist priests and property.[98] Their violence was irrational; *furor* and *insania* characterized them, marking them as potential threats to imperial order.[99] Their insanity was linked to superstitious practices—*nefas* in *On the Donatist Schism* 6.1.2 and *uana et praua superstitio* in 3.8.7—terms applied to those who exceeded the imperially defined bounds of reasonable religion. Such "barbarous peoples" were incompatible with Roman civilization.[100] Augustine maintained Optatus's accusations of irrationality and violence among the Donatists, whom he also called *insanus*.[101] Remaining outside the unity of the church compromised their ability to discern and speak truth, even when confronted with obvious facts (cf. *en. Ps.* 57.5–6).

Beneath the language of charity and fraternity in Optatus and Augustine lay a dark truth: in an invisible church held together by charity, the most serious violation is the rupture of brotherhood. Schism is "one of the worst kinds of evil,"[102] a crime far worse than the betrayal of scripture and worthy of the harshest pun-

Late Antiquity," in *Martyrdom and Persection in Late Antique Christianity: Festschrift Boudewijn Dehandschutter*, ed. Johan Leemans, BETL 241 (Leuven: Peeters, 2010), 418.

98. Optatus's reports of Donatist violence have been challenged. See Peter I. Kaufman, "Donatism Revisited: Moderates and Militants in Late Antique North Africa," *JLA* 2 (2009): 131–42. Also Cécile Barreteau-Revel, "'Faire l'unité dans l'église d'Afrique du Nord: La réintegration des donatistes à la transition des IVe et Ve siècles,'" in *Les Pères de l'Église et les dissidents: Dissidence, exclusion, et réintegration.dans les communautés chrétiennes des six premiers siècles*, ed. Pascal-Grégoire Delage (La Rochelle: Caritas Patrum, 2010), 236–37; and Shaw, *Sacred Violence*, 700–704, who called the violence "fictive."

99. Cf. *Schis.* 2.5.3, 3.4.3, 6.1.2, etc. Optatus may have included reasonableness in his definition of catholicity, though the text is unclear. In *Schis.* 2.1.4 the term "catholic" is defined not only as *diffusa* but also as *rationabilis* (2.1.4 [SC 412:238]). In his apparatus, Ziwsa emended *rationalibus* to *non nationalibus* (CSEL 26:33n14), the reading accepted by Edwards (29n2). O. R. Vassall-Phillips retained *rationabilis*, "according to reason," which he thought was meant to contrast heresy. *The Work of St. Optatus* (London: Longmans, Green, 1917), 59n3.

100. *Schis.* 3.3.5 (SC 413:22); cf. Aug. *ciu.*19.24.2 (CSEL 40/2:400).

101. Shaw, *Sacred Violence*, 57–60.

102. *Schis.* 1.13.1 (SC 412:200; trans. is my own): "in africa duo mala et pessima admissa esse constat, unum in traditione, alterum in schismate."

ishment. While attempting to maintain that schismatics, unlike heretics, remained "brothers," Optatus treated the Donatists as if they were heretics outside the church (cf. *Schis.* 4.5.6). Augustine made explicit what Optatus only sensed: the consistent refusal of unity eventually becomes heresy (cf. *Cresc.* 2.7.9 and *haer.* 69.1–2). Anyone in schism manifests that they are destitute of charity (cf. *De unico baptismo contra Petilianum ad Constantinum* [*un. bapt.*] 15.25). The Caecilianist position was foolproof: either tolerate us in unity or be guilty of the intolerable sin.

The significance of Augustine's schism-to-heresy argument was more than a theological clarification. Theodosius made heresy a punishable offense under Roman law (*Codex Theodosianus* 16.6.4), and, after a petition by the Caecilianists in 399 CE, Honorius applied the antiheresy laws to Donatists; further Caecilianists' lobbying resulted in Donatism being formally declared a heresy in 405. Optatus himself had classified Parmenian with the heretics Arius and Photius because of rebaptism, but he recognized that rebaptism was a deviant practice rather than a false belief. Augustine considered rebaptism both an inherently uncharitable practice and a heretical act warranting judicial punishment (*ep.* 66.1).[103] Believing that real change comes through education and reformation of the heart (*ep.* 93), he initially resisted state prosecution of the schism.[104] Increasing frustration with his failure to win hearts and minds through his preaching and writings led him to reconsider this position. In 402 he threatened the Donatist bishop Crispinus with a hefty fine (*ep.* 66.1), and by 405 Augustine fully condoned state intervention (*c. ep. Parm.* 1.8–13). In order to strengthen his case, Augustine subtly modified Optatus's reports of violence, substituting *Circumcelliones* with *Donatistae* in his letter to Boniface, thereby implicating the whole faction.[105]

What set Optatus apart from the earlier African tradition was his faith in Rome as a guarantor of order and meaning. When Optatus spoke of the catholic church spread through the "whole world," he meant the civilized Roman world.[106] The church was subordinate to the empire: "For the republic is not in the church,

---

103. Augustine was also under pressure from more aggressive fellow bishops who did not share his faith in persuasion. Hermanowicz fills in the details of the anti-Donatist lobby at the imperial court for whom Augustine served as a sort of theological consultant (*Possidius of Calama*, 97–130, 156–87).

104. As he himself noted in *retr.* 2.5 (CSEL 36:137); cf. *ep.* 34.1 (CSEL 34/2:23). See John R. Bowlin, "Augustine on Justifying Coercion," *Annual of the Society of Christian Ethics* 17 (1997): 49–70; and Peter Brown, "Religious Coercion in the Later Roman Empire: The Case of North Africa," *History* 48 (1963): 283–305.

105. As observed by Hoover, *Donatist Church*, 47.

106. *Schis.* 3.2.7 (SC 413:16).

but the church is in the republic, i.e. the Roman Empire."[107] Magistrates not only restrained evil, but they were God's means of unifying the church—"agents of unity."[108] Macarius, originally sent to Africa to distribute funds to the poor, enjoined the "uniform and universal worship of the one God in the church."[109] Behind Optatus's invitation to *pax* in his treatise lay an anxiety over the *pax deorum* that guaranteed the prosperity of the empire; he equated the *tempore bono pacis* with the Constantinian settlement.[110] Optatus was convinced that only a Christian emperor such as Constantine or Constans could unite the separated sons of *Mater Ecclesia*.[111] Augustine retained Optatus's positive assessment of the empire, at least until the turn of the century.[112] While his confidence in the empire certainly waned after Alaric's conquest, his collaboration in the prosecution of the Donatists stemmed from this belief that the church and empire shared responsibility for *pax, unitas,* and *concordia*.

Optatus himself made no recourse to state coercion. Against Parmenian's accusations, he vigorously denied that the Caecilianists had colluded with the state in the repressions of 317 or 347 CE (cf. *Schis.* 3.2.1). Still, he defended the actions of the imperial agents, whom he called "ministers of God's will."[113] The same word, *operarius*, is used both of clergy and of Roman officials.[114] The fact that they killed was no obstacle for Optatus.[115] He recited a litany of Old Testament figures such as Moses, Phineas, and Elijah who executed scores of disobedient

107. *Schis.* 3.3.5 (SC 413:22; trans. is my own): "non enim respublica est in ecclesia, sed ecclesia in republica, id est in imperio romano."

108. *Schis.* 3.1.1 (SC 413:8).

109. *Schis.* 3.8.5 (SC 413:58; trans. Edwards, 76): "contra sub Macario commonebantur omnes ut deus unus pariter in ecclesia ab omnibus rogaretur."

110. *Schis.* 7.1.4 (SC 413:194).

111. *Schis.* 2.15.2.

112. Lohse argues that Augustine accepted Optatus's positive assessment of the state, at least until the turn of the century. B. Lohse, "Augustins Wandlung in seiner Beurteilung des Staates," *StPatr* 6 (1962): 470–75.

113. *Schis.* 7.6.6 (SC 413:240).

114. *Schis.* 1.6.2 (SC 412:184) and 5.5.9 (SC 413:138).

115. For their part, the Donatists asserted that their suffering vindicated their claim to be the true church (*Schis.* 2.14.1 [SC 412:268]). The "true brother" was revealed through the persecution of the "false brother," just as in the storied biblical brothers Cain and Abel, Isaac and Ishmael, and Jacob and Esau. Persecuting authorities are "evil" (*Schis.* 3.5.1), and men such as Macarius should be excommunicated (*Schis.* 7.6.1 [SC 413:238]).

people.[116] The rebellion of Korah offered a particularly clear example of the judicial execution of schismatics (cf. *ep.* 53.3.6).

Augustine never went so far as Optatus, who celebrated Donatist deaths as a sign of God's justice; he lobbied against capital punishment, even in his later years. Yet Augustine came to see physical *correptio* as inevitable. Chastened by the "pedagogy of fear," the Donatists would acknowledge the truth of the Caecilianist position and join them, at which point "perfect love will drive out fear."[117] Augustine used many of the same Old Testament examples as Optatus to justify coercion. The Donatists objected that such violence had ended with the gospel age: Jesus commanded Peter to "put away the sword" (*Schis.* 3.7.8) and killing was forbidden to Christians (*ep.* 44.4.9). When Fortunius challenged Augustine to justify coercion using the New Testament, he uncharacteristically had no reply (*ep.* 44.4.9).[118] Though Augustine never stopped using Optatus's language of brotherhood, he came more and more to see the Donatists as rude children who sometimes needed to be beaten until they came to their senses (*ep.* 185.6.21).

CONCLUSION

Optatus's influence on Augustine is most evident in his early writings before 405 CE. His close reading of *On the Donatist Schism* in 393 CE and distillation of the work in his *Psalmus contra partem Donati* set a template that he would follow throughout his anti-Donatist campaign. More than any particular doctrine, Augustine adopted Optatus's ecclesiology and followed Optatus in his pastoral approach to the controversy, appealing to the Donatists as misinformed brothers with the same *Mater*. Like Optatus, he built a case exonerating Caecilian of the charges of *traditio* using archival documents, and then appealed to those same

---

116. *Schis.* 3.6–7 (SC 413:48–56). For more on his biblical arguments, see P. Marone, "'Et modo Deo placuit quod passos vos esse dicitis': Ottato e la violenza in nome di Dio," in *Cristianesimo e violenza: Gli autori cristiani di fronte a testi biblici "scomodi"; XLIV Incontro di Studiosi dell'Antichità Cristiana, Roma 5–7 maggio 2016* (Rome: Institutum Patristicum Augustinianum, 2018), 285–93.

117. *Ep.* 185.6.22 (CSEL 57:21); cf. 1 John 4:8.

118. He eventually concocted several justifications for coercion: Jesus forcefully expelling the moneychangers from the temple; Saul being blinded by the heavenly light; and, most famously, the phrase *"compelle intrare"* that occurs in the parable of the wedding banquet as found in Luke 14:16–24 (cf. *ep.* 185.6.22–24 [CSEL 57:20–23]).

documents to prove that Donatus of Carthage was responsible for the schism and to show the hypocrisy of Donatist claims to sanctity. Optatus's distinction between schism and heresy, though imperfectly developed, became in Augustine's writings a key insight for understanding sacramental action and the role of the minister. More importantly, Optatus's metaphor of the estranged brothers helped him develop the concept of *caritas* as the bond of ecclesial unity, one of Augustine's greatest contributions to Christian theology. Finally, Optatus's justification for state violence against the Donatists, initially rejected by Augustine, in later years became the nucleus for his own justification for compulsion. One wonders how differently Augustine's efforts to correct the Donatists and to reconcile the parties would have looked had he started with the open dialogues he had with Fortunius or Proculeianus rather than with the polemic of Optatus.[119]

.

119. In the mid to late 390s, some years after studying Optatus and writing his early anti-Donatist tracts, Augustine sought personal engagements with Donatist leaders, including Maximin of Sinitum and the rival bishop in his own city, Proculeianus (see *ep.* 23 [CSEL 34/1:23–27] and *ep.* 34 [CSEL 34/1:63–73]). While Augustine (and most Donatist bishops) perceived these as adversarial contests, at least one meeting, the conversation with Fortunius of Tubursi in 397 CE documented in *ep.* 44 (CSEL 34/2:109–21), turned into a listening session for Augustine. He complimented the elderly bishop's "sound judgement and feelings" (*ep.* 44.6.13 [CSEL 34/2:121]). For more on these exchanges, see Frend, *Donatist Church,* 249, as well as *supra.*

PART II

·

Augustine and the Philosophical and Literary Tradition

Chapter 6

Augustine and the Platonists

John Peter Kenney

Introduction

In our lives as scholars, we learn from friends who kindle in us the light of knowledge.[1] It was Patout Burns—through his scholarship and conversation—who taught me a transformative scholarly lesson: to read Augustine. By that I mean to read him as Patout has: carefully, closely, and attentively, alert to the twists of his thinking and the chronological turns of his developing thought. That insight brought with it a subtle resistance to those approaches to Augustine whose principal method is the appraisal of his thought through the lens of contemporary theology or philosophy. The use of Augustine in that fashion may indeed be a worthy task, but it ought first to be grounded in the recovery of his thought as articulated in its own terms.

One stumbling block for some readers of Augustine is his fundamental commitment to scriptural exegesis. This is especially true for philosophers interested in tracing and estimating his reliance on classical philosophy. Yet it must be recognized that from the time of his ordination in 391 CE the primary foundation of Augustine's thought was scriptural. The Bible dominated both his thinking and his practice. Indeed, the scriptures came to saturate his discourse, as any page of the *Confessiones* attests, and its conceptions become solvents for his own

1. *Conf.* 4.8.13–4.9.14 (J. J. O'Donnell, *Augustine: Confessions*, vol. 1, *Introduction and Text* [Oxford: Clarendon, 1992], 38–39; ET Augustine, *Confessions*, trans. Henry Chadwick [Oxford: Oxford University Press, 1991], 60–61).

ideas. This scriptural consciousness moved him away from traditional forms of philosophical dialectic of the sort attested in the Cassiciacum dialogues toward the development of a scriptural dialectic that opened the soul to the presence of God. To read the works of Augustine written after 391 CE is to discover treatises that are explicitly or implicitly exegetical. For that reason, it is impossible to regard Augustine as a Platonic philosopher in the traditional sense, for whom the categories and methods of philosophical dialectic were normative. His was a Christian philosophy in which scriptural contemplation became a dispositive means for the ascent of the soul.[2] To read Augustine, then, requires following him through that transformation from discursive philosophy into scriptural contemplation.

This chapter is thus an exercise in Augustinian originalism. Having been asked to write on Augustine and Platonism for this volume, I propose to look again at Platonism's definitive estimation by Augustine in *Confessiones* (*conf.*), with some reference to its recapitulation in the *De ciuitate dei* (*ciu.*). It must be admitted that the topic of Augustine and Platonism remains perennially exigent in large measure because of the emphasis Augustine placed on Platonism in the conversion narrative of *Confessiones*. My goal in this essay is to push beyond the surface tale that Augustine tells and to probe the significance and limitations of Platonism that is embedded in the text. I will begin by reviewing the reading of Augustine's account of Platonism in *Confessiones* 7 that I have articulated in several earlier projects.[3] Then I will offer a revised interpretation, one that emerges from a tighter and more focused textual analysis of Augustine's criticism of Plotinian Platonism.

THE GOLD OF THE EGYPTIANS

When Augustine introduces his readers to Platonism in *Confessiones*, he likens it to the gold that the Israelites took as spoils from the Egyptians.[4] That well-worn image turns on the value of that gold in contrast to its use in the making of idols.

---

2. John Peter Kenney, "Faith and Reason," in *The Cambridge Companion to Augustine*, ed. Eleonore Stump and David Meconi (Cambridge: Cambridge University Press, 2014), 275–91.

3. John Peter Kenney, *The Mysticism of Saint Augustine: Rereading the "Confessions"* (New York: Routledge, 2005) and *Contemplation and Classical Christianity: A Study in Augustine* (Oxford: Oxford University Press, 2013).

4. Cf. Exod. 3:22; 11:2; and *conf.* 7.9.15 (O'Donnell, 1:81). This apologetic image has a long history that includes Philo, Irenaeus, Clement, and Origen, just to name a few. Cf. Pier Franco Beatrice, "The Treasure of the Egyptians," *StPatr* 39 (2006): 159–83.

Platonism was golden, even if its use could be idolatrous. What was that inherent value? The narrative of *Confessiones* supplies a certain measure of conceptual suspense in that regard, following the spiritual wanderings of its protagonist among various sorts of materialism. Chief among these was Manichaeanism, whose dualistic philosophy postulated two cosmic energies in conflict: Light/Goodness and Darkness/Evil. This amounted to an attenuated materialism in Augustine's estimation, and that was the root of his spiritual confusion: "When I wanted to think of my God, I knew of no way of doing so except as a physical mass. Nor did I think anything existed which is not material. That was the principal and almost sole cause of my inevitable error."[5]

Thereafter, at the end of *Confessiones* 5, we find him slipping into moderate skepticism precisely because of his inability to break from a materialist understanding of God and the conceptual *aporiae* that follow from it. With respect to the Manichaeans, he says: "If I had been able to conceive of spiritual substance, at once all their imagined inventions would have collapsed and my mind would have rejected them. But I could not."[6] That inability to conceptualize nonmaterial existence is prominently marked off as the core failure of his long quest for religious truth. In saying this, he underscores by anticipation the philosophy that will supply that lack: Platonism.

The same is true of his descriptions of his failure to resolve the problem of evil. When he abandoned Manichaeanism, he was at an impasse. He had come to believe that God, the maker of souls and bodies, was immune to pollution or change and completely immutable.[7] Even so, he still had no answer to why evil existed. He imagined that the physical universe was a vast mass that the immutable God enveloped and permeated. But that reflection failed to explain why evil was to be found in a world made by that permeating and good God.[8] This failure was not just conceptual but moral. His materialism was, he insists, rooted in his fixation on the material things of this world and the pleasures that

5. *Conf.* 5.10.19 (O'Donnell, 1:54–55; trans. Chadwick, 84–85): "et quoniam cum de deo meo cogitare uellem, cogitare nisi moles corporum non noueram (neque enim uidebatur mihi esse quicquam quod tale non esset), ea maxima et prope sola causa erat ineuitabilis erroris mei."

6. *Conf.* 5.14.25 (O'Donnell, 1:57; trans. Chadwick, 89): "quod si possem spiritalem substantiam cogitare, statim machinamenta illa omnia soluerentur et abicerentur ex animo meo: sed non poteram."

7. *Conf.* 7.3.4 (O'Donnell, 1:74–75).

8. *Conf.* 7.5.7 (O'Donnell, 1:76–77).

accrue from them. These external things had captured his moral self and, with it, his intellect.[9] The moral dimension of materialism brought with it the profound risk that his soul would be captured by the very evil that he was seeking to understand and to explain. His moral materialism and his philosophical materialism were thus interwoven in ways that left him enchained. He feared—in a striking claim—that "I might myself become the evil I was investigating."[10]

It was Christ who delivered him from the chains of materialism through the books of the Platonists. That divine intervention is repeatedly iterated.[11] The *libri Platonicorum* were, therefore, sanctioned instruments chosen by the divine physician for their medicinal value. They were the necessary antidote to materialism that the previous sections of the text had been foreshadowing. On this reading, the value of Platonism can be understood to be conceptual. It supplied the previously unknown idea of spiritual existence, of a level of reality distinct from the physical cosmos defined in spatial and temporal terms. In that sense Platonism offered Augustine a major conceptual advance. But the text of *Confessiones* makes clear that Platonism catalyzed something far beyond the notional grasp of a novel idea.[12] Those books were brought before him by divine providence, and through them he was admonished to return into himself. It is only with divine guidance that the eye of his soul could see the immutable light of a transcendent God. That God was disclosed as the God of Exod. 3:14, the One who is reality itself. This knowledge was immediate and infallible. Augustine maintains that the Platonic books had brought him to the certain understanding that nonspatial and immaterial reality exists. He says he was more certain of this than of his own existence.

On this reading, therefore, the Platonists' books served a precisely articulated cognitive function. They were the divinely chosen vehicle for apodictic insight into the nature of God, the long-awaited conversionary moment that utterly changed Augustine's thinking. From the certainty of this cognition subsidiary

9. *Conf.* 7.7.11 (O'Donnell, 1:79–80), a text that juxtaposes the internal and the external in a fashion that foreshadows the famous "Late have I loved you" passage of 10.27.38 (cf. O'Donnell, 1:134).

10. *Conf.* 7.3.4 (O'Donnell, 1:74–75; trans. Chadwick, 113): "non tenebam explicatam et enodatam causam mali. quaecumque tamen esset, sic eam quaerendam uidebam, ut non per illam constringerer deum incommutabilem mutabilem credere, ne ipse fierem quod quaerebam."

11. *Conf.* 7.7.11, 7.9.13, 7.10.16 (O'Donnell, 1:79–80, 80–81, 81–82).

12. *Conf.* 7.10.16 (O'Donnell, 1:81–82).

insights followed, including the impoverished ontological status of the fallen soul and the nonbeing of evil.[13] Immediately after the ascension narrative of *Confessiones* 7.10.16, the fruits of that instance of transcendental contemplation are assayed in reference to evil.[14] The success of this Platonist moment was, therefore, essential to Augustine's conversion narrative, for the problem of the existence of evil had now been dissolved. For this reason, interpretations that regard the ascension narrative of 7.10.16 as a failure miss its role as the cognitive lynchpin of his rejection of materialism and the catalyst of his acceptance of a transcendent God.[15] The gold of the Egyptians was insight into the eternal, the transcendent, and the divine.

Augustine offers a second ascension narrative at 7.17.23, and it underscores this same theme of cognitive insight through contemplation. It is unclear whether this account records a separate instance of contemplative knowledge or just an appraisal of the same ascension in a different light. Nonetheless, the inner ascent of the soul leads once again to momentary knowledge of the divine: "so in the flash of a trembling glance it attained to that which is."[16] In this iteration, the focus is less on its cognitive success than on its brevity and the violent force of its cessation. What impedes the soul's contemplative state is its *pondus*, its moral weight. He tells us that his soul was freighted down by his *consuetudo carnalis*, primarily his sexual habit. That is no surprise, since his readers have by this point been apprised of his vagrant sexuality in numerous prior passages.[17] Here we learn that the soul is caught up to God by the beauty of the divine, but then instantly ripped away by its moral ballast. Though the reality of a transcendent God is no longer in doubt, the means for associating with God are unavailable. The soul's path to stable communion with God is blocked.

This narrative, with its enjambment of psychic ascension on high and immediate descent into materiality, sets the stage for the principal anti-Platonist polemic of *Confessiones*.[18] Puffed up with knowledge of the transcendent derived

---

13. *Conf.* 7.12.18, 7.13.19 (O'Donnell, 1:82–83, 83).

14. *Conf.* 7.11.17–7.13.19 (O'Donnell, 1:82–83).

15. Pierre Courcelle, *Recherches sur les Confessions de Saint Augustin* (Paris: de Boccard, 1950), 157–67, and *Les Confessions de Saint Augustin dans la tradition littéraire: Antecédénts et posterité* (Paris: Études Augustiniennes, 1963), 17–88.

16. *Conf.* 7.17.23 (O'Donnell, 1:84–85; trans. Chadwick, 127–28): "et peruenit ad id quod est in ictu trepidantis aspectus."

17. E.g., *conf.* 2.2.2–3, 2.3.6–8, 3.1.1, 3.3.5, 4.2.2 (O'Donnell, 1:16, 17–18, 23, 24, 33).

18. *Conf.* 7.20.26–7.21.27 (O'Donnell, 1:86–87).

from his reading of Platonism, Augustine characterizes himself at this stage as full of presumption. Yet divine providence had provided for just this developmental sequence, since his soul was now in a state to recognize the need for scriptural wisdom in order to achieve salvation:

> I was puffed up with knowledge. Where was the charity which builds on the foundation of humility which is Jesus Christ? When would the Platonist books have taught me that? I believe that you wanted me to encounter them before I came to study your scriptures. Your intention was that the manner in which I was affected by them should be implanted in my memory, so that when later I had been made docile by your gentle fingers, I would learn to discern and distinguish the difference between presumption and confession, between those who see what the goal is but not how to get there and those who see the way which leads to the home of bliss, not merely as an end to be perceived but as a realm to live in.[19]

What Platonism provided, therefore, was knowledge of transcendence. What it did not secure was a means for stable and continuing association of the soul with God through contemplation. On this reading, then, the gold of the Egyptians was knowledge of a transcendent God, precious because it was both novel and transformative. But it was not sufficient for the soul's salvation. To the extent that pagan Platonism promised more than knowledge, it was misguided, inflated, and presumptuous. Platonism was a path to knowledge of God, but not to salvation.

This reading of the mixed value of Platonism in *Confessiones* 7 has much to recommend it. It contrasts with interpretations of the theological narrative that treat these prebaptismal ascensions as failures, while regarding the postbaptismal "vision at Ostia" as a success.[20] But that approach neglects the anti-Manichaean

---

19. *Conf.* 7.20.26 (O'Donnell, 1:86; trans. Chadwick, 129–30): "insuper et inflabar scientia. ubi enim erat illa aedificans caritas a fundamento humilitatis, quod est Christus Iesus? aut quando illi libri me docerent eam? in quos me propterea, priusquam scripturas tuas considerarem, credo uoluisti incurrere, ut imprimeretur memoriae meae quomodo ex eis affectus essem et, cum postea in libris tuis mansuefactus essem et curantibus digitis tuis contrectarentur uulnera mea, discernerem atque distinguerem quid interesset inter praesumptionem et confessionem, inter uidentes quo eundum sit nec uidentes qua, et uiam ducentem ad beatificam patriam non tantum cernendam sed et habitandam."

20. Cf. Kenney, *Mysticism of Saint Augustine*, 1–14, for a detailed discussion of these alternative readings.

and, more broadly, anti-materialist force of the *libri Platonicorum*. Those books were brought to his attention by Christ, the physician of souls, and reading them catalyzed the first cognitive stage of his conversion. What they did not secure was the transcendence of the soul, its stable and continuous association with divine wisdom. Cognitively necessary but soteriologically insufficient, Platonism in *Confessiones* 7 had proven nonetheless to be Egyptian gold.

"A Glimpse of the Homeland"

The more I have continued to study *Confessiones,* the less certain I am that this "Egyptian gold" reading fully captures its depiction of Platonism. That is in part because of the abrupt and dismissive force found in Augustine's rejection of Platonism in *Confessiones* 7. And then there is the overarching importance of Christ and the efficacy of his assistance iterated throughout Augustine's account of his reception of Platonism. This Christian dimension permeates the entire depiction of that encounter, so that it becomes evident that Augustine is not so much presenting an exegesis of the *libri Platonicorum* as offering a thoroughly Christian reinterpretation of them. We might now reflect on these suspicions, not in the interest of rejecting the "Egyptian gold" reading but, rather, in the interest of deepening it.

Despite his praise for Platonism and the conversionary insight that it offered, Augustine is quite harsh and even personal in his rejection of it.[21] The regnant theme of this critique is the pride of the Platonists, which emerges from the philosophy found in their works. For Augustine, you become what you read. Earlier, as we saw, he had worried that his soul might become evil by its reflections on primordial evil in Manichaeanism. Now with Platonism the problem is a haughtiness founded on philosophical knowledge and a moral danger that follows from that misplaced confidence. He says that he, too, succumbed to this. He was proud of the certainty of his new knowledge: that God is infinite and not diffused through space; that God truly exists and is always the same; that God is immutable and the source of all other beings. He says he, too, was now puffed up with knowledge. But without charity and the humility of Christ, he was in danger of losing his way. As we saw in the quotation from 7.10.26 *supra,* the presumption of the Platonists was rooted in the false belief that philosophy could draw the

---

21. *Conf.* 7.20.26–7.21.27 (O'Donnell, 1:86–87).

soul to God. The discovery of the *libri Platonicorum* was, therefore, intended by Christ to teach a moral lesson beyond metaphysical insight.

It was precisely this pride that was behind the sequencing of Augustine's discovering Platonism. It was, he says, God's intention that he would read those pride-inducing works before he studied the scriptures, the better to be shown the inadequacy of Platonism and the futility of his own presumption. That is how he first introduces Platonism:

> First you wanted to show me how you "resist the proud and give grace to the humble," and with what mercy you have shown humanity the way of humility in that your "Word was made flesh and dwelt among" men. Through a man puffed up with monstrous pride, you brought under my eye some books of the Platonists, translated from Greek into Latin.[22]

There follows an extensive comparative inventory of Platonism and Nicene Christianity, one that concedes the positive but limited value of Platonism.[23] The substance of that review is captured in a quote from Simplicianus, the spiritual mentor of Ambrose, who congratulated Augustine for reading the Platonists instead of the other pagan philosophers because "in all the Platonist books God and his Word keep slipping in."[24] But what Augustine did not find in Platonism was the incarnation of Christ. This he repeats over and over, with texts drawn from John 1:1–16, Phil. 2:6–11, Rom. 5:6, and Rom. 8:32. Using Matt. 11: 29 and Rom. 1:21–3, he concludes with a harsh description of the Platonists:

> But those who, like actors, wear the high boots of a supposedly more sublime teaching do not hear him who says "Learn of me, that I am meek and humble in heart, and you shall find rest for your souls." Even if they know "God, they do not glorify him as God or give thanks, but are lost in their own thoughts

---

22. *Conf.* 7.9.13 (O'Donnell, 1:80; trans. Chadwick, 121): "et primo uolens ostendere mihi quam resistas superbis, humilibus autem des gratiam, et quanta misericordia tua demonstrata sit hominibus uia humilitatis, quod uerbum tuum caro factum est et habitauit inter homines, procurasti mihi per quendam hominem immanissimo typho turgidum quosdam platonicorum libros ex graeca lingua in latinam uersos."

23. *Conf.* 7.9.13–14 (O'Donnell, 1:80–81).

24. *Conf.* 8.2.3 (O'Donnell, 1:89; trans. Chadwick, 135): "in istis autem omnibus modis insinuari deum et eius uerbum."

and their foolish heart is obscured; professing themselves to be wise, they have become fools."[25]

Pride in their supposedly sublime teaching has misdirected Platonists in two respects: having become lost in their speculations, they trust in the autonomy of their own wisdom, and, as a result, they fail to recover a proper relationship with God. Later the exact cause of these failures is more fully diagnosed. Augustine maintains that all the truth of the Platonist books is contained in the epistles of Paul along with the crucial concept of divine grace. Any truth that philosophers have discovered has come from God, but that point of origination is something they persist in ignoring.[26]

The problem of Platonism goes deeper, then, than just soteriology. It fails in its central claim of providing true knowledge of the divine, understood in its own terms—that is, participatory knowledge of being itself. It has a speculative grasp of God, one that is important for its initial insight into the nature of the divine, but one that nevertheless leaves the soul at a spiritual distance from the God that it seeks. Because it cannot cure the soul from sin, especially from the original sin that is the source of its estrangement from God, Platonism cannot offer the soul immediate knowledge of God. It falls short, then, both as a form of cognition and as a soteriology. If contemplative knowledge was, for the school of Plotinus, rooted in the soul's immediate participation in the One, then epistemology and soteriology are conjoined. The central problem of Platonism for Augustine was, therefore, that it failed to offer the type of contemplative knowledge that allows the soul to achieve stable, immediate, and eternal association with the divine. Its failure went deep, for its claims to be a path to both contemplative knowledge and salvation are simultaneously impeached—at least from Augustine's standpoint. This observation thus presses the account of Platonism beyond the "Egyptian gold" reading into a darker, more powerful indictment. Augustine concludes *Confessiones* 7 with a striking description of the mere glimpse of the divine that Platonism provides and, in consequence, its danger for the soul:

25. *Conf.* 7.9.14 (O'Donnell, 1:81; trans. Chadwick, 122): "qui autem cothurno tamquam doctrinae sublimioris elati non audiunt dicentem, 'discite a me quoniam mitis sum et humilis corde, et inuenietis requiem animabus uestris,' etsi cognoscunt deum, non sicut deum glorificant aut gratias agunt, sed euanescunt in cogitationibus suis et obscuratur insipiens cor eorum; dicentes se esse sapientes stulti facti sunt."

26. *Conf.* 7.21.27 (O'Donnell, 1:86–87).

It is one thing from a wooded summit to catch a glimpse of a homeland of peace and not to find the way to it, but vainly to attempt the journey along an impractical route surrounded by the ambushes and assaults of deserters with their chief, "the lion and the dragon." It is another thing to hold on to the way that leads there, defended by the protection of the heavenly emperor.[27]

The perilous path of Platonism is one that begins and ends with a distanced appraisal of the transcendent homeland. It can promise neither secure knowledge nor salvation to the peregrine soul. Platonists are, in Augustine's polemical account, lost in metaphysical theories and forced to settle at best for a vision of God from afar. Why he believes this must now be examined further.

The Impasse of Interiority

The core of this Augustinian critique of Platonism rests on what might be called the impasse of interiority. If transcendence was the key insight that transformed Augustine's understanding of God, it was the turn into the self that offered the path to its realization. In this respect Augustine is a particularly salient example of the immense change in the vector of human religiosity in late antiquity, as spatial representations of the divine were discarded and the practice of sacrifice to the celestial gods came slowly to an end.[28] One no longer went up into the heavens to locate the divine, but went into the self in order to leave behind the levels of consciousness attached to space, time, and the material cosmos. That turn into the self may include introspection, but it was not reducible to it, since reflecting on the inner states of the embodied self was to tarry at the level of this lower world. The goal was to go within and to pass beyond this ontological zone entirely.

The Platonism of the school of Plotinus was in the vanguard of that great shift, one that tightly conjoined transcendence with interiority. When Augustine encountered the conception of divine transcendence in the books of the

27. *Conf.* 7.21.27 (O'Donnell, 1:87; trans. Chadwick, 131–32): "et aliud est de siluestri cacumine uidere patriam pacis et iter ad eam non inuenire et frustra conari per inuia circum obsidentibus et insidiantibus fugitiuis desertoribus cum principe suo leone et dracone, et aliud tenere uiam illuc ducentem cura caelestis imperatoris munitam."

28. Guy Strousma, *The End of Sacrifice: Religious Transformations in Late Antiquity* (Chicago: University of Chicago Press, 2008), 56–83.

Platonists, he also grasped that it brought with it the notion of the soul's inner transcendence, its ascension through levels of consciousness. Only by purifying itself and deepening its own latent connection to the divine reality could it achieve complete and stable knowledge of God. Through interior contemplation the Plotinian soul could reach profound enlightenment, reaching at its apex a unitive consciousness of the One that transcends all finite modes of knowledge.[29] It is precisely this interior reorientation, this reversion of the soul to the transcendent, that Augustine denies to Platonism in *Confessiones* 7. He rejects the central doctrine of the school of Plotinus, that the soul has an inherent capacity to discover its transcendent existence, at once achieving knowledge of its true nature and recovering its latent divinity.

The *Confessiones* is an extended autobiographical rejection of this representation of human nature and of the soul's capacity for transcendence. His argument culminating in book 7, Augustine insists that he did not find in his soul a means of self-transcendence. He regards that as a universal judgment, true not only of himself but of humanity in general. And so, Platonism was fundamentally and culpably wrong. It offered only distanced knowledge of the transcendent and was misguided in its representation of the soul's capacity for interior self-transcendence. For the human soul needs the power of interior contemplation to be conferred on it from without, from the transcendent God himself. This was the impasse of interiority for Augustine. To know God fully and deeply the soul requires a power it does not possess. The interior path to the transcendent God is blocked by the moral detritus of the fall. For this reason, his account of contemplation, catalyzed by his initial reading of the Platonist books, makes abundantly clear that the power of Christ was necessary in order for the interior turn to be successful: "By the Platonic books I was admonished to return into myself. With you as my guide I entered into my innermost citadel and was given the power to do so because you had become my helper." The text goes on to underscore the divine source of this higher knowledge: "When I first came to know you, you raised me up to make me see that what I saw was Being, and that I who saw am not yet being."[30] This recognition of the absolute reality of God is possible

---

29. *Ennead* VI 9.4.3 (*Plotini Opera*, 3 vols., ed. Paul Henry and Hans-Rudolf Schwyzer [Oxford: Oxford University Press, 1964–1982]).

30. *Conf.* 7.10.16 (O'Donnell, 1:81–82; trans. Chadwick, 123): "et inde admonitus redire ad memet ipsum, intraui in intima mea duce te, et potui, quoniam factus es adiutor meus. . . . et

only through the power vested in the soul by Christ. That divine intervention is necessary for immediate knowledge of God. But it is also sufficient, for nothing else is needed beyond Christ the mediator.

It is here that the specifically incarnational character of Augustine's account becomes evident. As we saw when discussing Augustine's comparative inventory of Platonist and Christian doctrines,[31] it was the salience of the incarnation that was underscored. The force of that critical lacuna is now obvious. Without the incarnation itself, the power that the soul required to break through the moral debris of the fall and into the depth of divine transcendence is inaccessible. Interior contemplation can only be achieved by humbly recognizing the poverty of the soul and its need for a mediator. Augustine takes stock of this point in an extended meditation on Pauline and Johannine themes.

> I sought a way to obtain strength enough to enjoy you; but I did not find it until I embraced "the mediator between God and man, the man Jesus Christ," "who is above all things, God blessed forever." He called and said: "I am the way and the truth and the life." The food which I was too weak to accept he mingled with flesh, in that "The Word was made flesh," so that our infant condition might come to suck from your wisdom by which you created all things. To possess my God, the humble Jesus, I was not yet humble enough. I did not know what his weakness was meant to teach.[32]

His weakness was meant to teach humility, a defining characteristic of the incarnation for Augustine just as it was for Paul. And though made weak in his assumption of the human condition, Christ is nonetheless strong in his divinity. It is the mediator of 1 Tim. 2:5 whose strength allows Augustine's soul to achieve interior ascension. It is the incarnate Christ of John 1:14 and 14:6 who alone is

---

cum te primum cognoui, tu adsumpsisti me ut uiderem esse quod uiderem, et nondum me esse qui uiderem."

31. Cf. *supra* where *conf.* 7.9.13–14 (O'Donnell, 1:80–81) is discussed.

32. *Conf.* 7.18.24 (O'Donnell, 1:85; trans. Chadwick, 128): "et quaerebam uiam comparandi roboris quod esset idoneum ad fruendum te, nec inueniebam donec amplecterer mediatorem dei et hominum, hominem Christum Iesum, qui est super omnia deus benedictus in saecula, uocantem et dicentem, 'ego sum uia et ueritas et uita,' et cibum, cui capiendo inualidus eram, miscentem carni, quoniam uerbum caro factum est ut infantiae nostrae lactesceret sapientia tua, per quam creasti omnia. non enim tenebam deum meum Iesum, humilis humilem, nec cuius rei magistra esset eius infirmitas noueram."

the way, the truth, and the life. What the soul had lacked the incarnate power of Christ supplied to his soul, but only when he was humble enough to admit that spiritual deficit. What he sought in his intellectual pride through Platonic philosophy had now been secured by embracing Christ the mediator. The passage then expands that insight in explicitly incarnational terms:

> Your Word, eternal truth, higher than the superior parts of your creation, raises those submissive to him to himself. In the inferior parts he built for himself a humble house of clay. By this he detaches from themselves those who are willing to be made his subjects and carries them across to himself, healing their swelling and nourishing their love. They are no longer to place confidence in themselves, but rather to become weak. They see at their feet divinity become weak by his sharing in our "coat of skin." In their weariness they fall prostrate before this divine weakness which rises and lifts them up.[33]

The eternal truth of the divine Word is transcendent of creation, but on that basis he paradoxically took on human weakness to serve as a mediator, descending into the lower world of space and time and dwelling there. The Word nourishes fallen souls and heals their tumescent pride by drawing them out of their self-orientation toward himself. Recognizing their inherent spiritual poverty, they no longer place their confidence in themselves. Moreover, in a striking claim, Augustine emphasizes that the central vector of Platonist metaphysics has thereby been revised. While souls participate in the transcendent Word, the Word in its incarnation also shares in the human condition. Its descending participation into our "coat of skin"—a vivid image from Gen. 3:21—is a supreme act of self-abnegation. Here the text recapitulates Augustine's earlier quotation of Phil. 2:6–11 (cf. *conf.* 7.9.14), where the kenosis of Christ was identified as a critical lacuna in Platonism. Now we can see the importance of that fact. The Word has humbled himself in order to assume human nature. In consequence, fallen souls, exhausted by their failure to ascend, bow down before the humility of this

---

33. *Conf.* 7.18.24 (O'Donnell, 1:85; trans. Chadwick, 128): "uerbum enim tuum, aeterna ueritas, superioribus creaturae tuae partibus supereminens subditos erigit ad se ipsam, in inferioribus autem aedificauit sibi humilem domum de limo nostro, per quam subdendos deprimeret a seipsis et ad se traiceret, sanans tumorem et nutriens amorem, ne fiducia sui progrederentur longius, sed potius infirmarentur, uidentes ante pedes suos infirmam diuinitatem ex participatione tunicae pelliciae nostrae, et lassi prosternerentur in eam, illa autem surgens leuaret eos."

self-sacrifice. It is, then, in humility that they can ascend through the strength extended by the incarnate Word. But it was precisely this that was absent in the Platonist books. Only through the incarnate Word can the impasse of interiority be broken and the soul's immediate knowledge of God be achieved.

This assertion challenges the Platonism of Plotinus directly. For Plotinus, the soul's capacity to recover a latent connection with its undescended self secured its link to transcendence. The embodied soul could thereby become more real, sloughing off the moral failures of life in the body and the confusions inherent in temporal existence here below. In doing so, the rising soul could become the true reality it had once been before its embodiment and thus engage in the higher intellection of *nous*. That noetic level brought it into participation with the intelligibles, taking on their eternity, their stability, their very nature as being. In this interior ascent of the soul, knower and known are united, and the soul rediscovers its eternal nature.[34] Augustine clearly recognized these fundamental claims by Plotinus and his school. Because epistemology and soteriology are tightly conjoined in this Platonism, interior contemplation is the means to reach both immediate knowledge of the divine and eternal communion with the One. In rejecting the autosoteriology of Plotinus, Augustine was therefore also denying that Platonists could achieve immediate contemplative knowledge of the One. In asserting the possibility of the soul's immediate contemplative presence with the One, the Platonists were mistaken.

In *Confessiones* 7 Augustine forcefully rejects the Platonist claim that the soul can achieve both immediate knowledge of the divine and salvation through philosophy. It must be admitted that he had not always been so hostile. Indeed, in some of his early works (i.e., those from the late 380s and early 390s), he had suggested that Platonists may well be right about this in exceptional cases.[35] But in *Confessiones* he writes as a recently ordained Catholic bishop, someone whose estimation of the depravity of our fallen human nature had deepened. While Platonists in the circle of Plotinus may have believed that "the philosopher is his own savior," to use Porphyry's phrase,[36] Augustine was now convinced of the universal necessity for divine mediation by the incarnate Christ. As for the Platonist assertion of immediate knowledge of the divine, that was just their pride speaking. Platonists had indeed discovered the transcendent nature of the

34. Cf. Kenney, *Mysticism of Saint Augustine*, part 1.
35. Cf. Kenney, *Contemplation and Classical Christianity*, 67–69.
36. Kenney, *Mysticism of Saint Augustine*, 53.

divine, but their knowledge was distant, not intimate. They only stand on the wooded summit that philosophy offers and look off to the transcendent world in the distance. These insights gleaned from his reading of St. Paul had a visceral impact on him: he was left trembling.[37]

"Your Voice from on High"

How shall we come to terms with this claim that the incarnate Word was the necessary guide for the soul? What exactly did Augustine mean by this claim in the context of his ascension narratives? Answers can be found by looking closely at the role that scripture plays in the narrative, both before and within those contemplative texts. For that is what separates him from the Platonists, whose school, after all, he did not join. Instead, he became a catechumen under the instruction of Ambrose.[38] From him Augustine learned to make the reading of the Christian scriptures the center of his own meditative practice.

Thus far we have followed the theme of transcendence and the undoubted impact that the Platonist books had on his development. But, in order to complete Augustine's treatment of Platonism, we need to reflect on the ways in which scripture served both a conversionary and a sustaining role in Augustine's new religion.

The central books of *Confessiones* tell the story of Augustine's gradual reversal of his Manichaean attitude toward the Bible and his halting acceptance of its spiritual value. Because he had no conception of divine transcendence, he had been confined to literal readings of the Old Testament, whose contents seemed open to rational and moral criticism. But when he heard passages interpreted "spiritually," he realized that an alternative hermeneutic might make these texts more defensible, even if he remained ignorant of spiritual substance.[39] This shifting attitude toward biblical interpretation was not an isolated change but was bound up with his larger struggles with materialism.

He gives a considerable amount of attention and detail to the sequence of this transition. Indeed, he claims to have first discovered that Catholics did not re-

---

37. *Conf.* 7.21.27 (O'Donnell, 1:86–87).

38. For Augustine's references to Ambrose, see *conf.* 5.13.23–5.14.24 and 6.3.3–6.4.6 (O'Donnell, 1:56–57 and 59–61).

39. *Conf.* 5.14.24 (O'Donnell, 1:57).

gard the God of the Bible as having a body. But he still had no notion of spiritual substance.[40] Even after discerning from the preaching of Ambrose the method of reading the scriptures spiritually and of "removing the mystic veil," he did not come to understand divine transcendence; nor did he come to believe.[41] This halting development was, he later realizes, God's intention. He spells this out in a remarkable passage that offers some telling insights on his mature assessment of Platonism:

> For if I had first been formed in mind by your holy books, and if you had made me know your sweetness by familiarity with them, and then I had thereafter met those volumes, perhaps they would have snatched me away from the solid foundation of piety. Or if I had remained firm in the conviction which I had imbibed to my soul's health, I might have supposed that the ideas could be gained from those books by someone who had read only them.[42]

Had he first read the scriptures without the insight of transcendence and subsequently discovered the Platonist books, then they might have seemed entirely compelling. Alternatively, he might have remained a Christian but surmised that Platonism had a similar theology. Instead, the actual sequence he experienced brought him first to the recognition of transcendence in Platonism and then to the study of scripture, though he was now furnished with the ability to recognize the depth of their spiritual meaning. In this respect, *Confessiones* 7 underscores the full force of this confluence. Both ascension narratives are catalyzed and sustained by the very element that the Platonic books had been shown to lack in the comparative inventory of 7.9.13–14: the incarnate Word. For it is Christ who is the guide of the soul, opening its deep interior vistas.

He recounts that he turned then to the reading of scripture: "With avid intensity I seized the sacred writings of your Spirit and especially Paul."[43] Now

---

40. *Conf.* 6.3.4 (O'Donnell, 1:60).

41. *Conf.* 6.4.6 (O'Donnell, 1:61; trans. Chadwick, 94): "cum ea quae ad litteram peruersitatem docere uidebantur, remoto mystico uelamento, spiritaliter aperiret."

42. *Conf.* 7.20.26 (O'Donnell, 1:86; trans. Chadwick, 130): "nam si primo sanctis tuis litteris informatus essem et in earum familiaritate obdulcuisses mihi, et post in illa uolumina incidissem, fortasse aut abripuissent me a solidamento pietatis, aut si in affectu quem salubrem inbiberam perstitissem, putarem etiam ex illis libris eum posse concipi, si eos solos quisque didicisset."

43. *Conf.* 7.21.27 (O'Donnell, 1:86–87; trans. Chadwick, 130–31): "itaque auidissime arripui uenerabilem stilum spiritus tui, et prae ceteris apostolum Paulum."

these texts could be properly understood according to the spiritual exegesis of Ambrose and the transcendent metaphysics of the Platonists. That had been the intent behind the providential sequencing of their discovery. And it was as he read scripture that he realized that the presence of Christ had been behind those early ascents. Their very success had served the divine intention by securing the certainty of transcendence as well as underscoring the necessity of grace.

One way to look at the embedded scriptural references that suffuse Augustine's conclusion on interior ascension at 7.18.24 (cf. *supra*) is to treat them as retrospective interpretation, as Christian reflection on this prebaptismal ascent of the soul catalyzed by his reading of Platonism. The account is the product of Christian recognition about what had actually occurred. For it was the divine Word that had lifted him up, a fact that was now clear to him as the Word continued speaking to his innermost self through scripture. Those sacred texts reproved and healed him, conferring on his soul a new moral lucidity and a power to pivot beyond earthly existence. He was no longer in danger of being confined to a merely material life as he had feared in his latter days as a Manichaean. But a new danger had now emerged in his false spiritual pride, puffed up by the certainty of his transcendental experiences. But, by reading the scriptures after his contemplative experiences of transcendence, he came to discern the real source of those ascensions in Christ. In this respect, the scriptural aspect of these accounts underscores precisely what the Platonists had failed to recognize: the power of the divine Word speaking into the depth of the contemplative soul and thereby transfiguring it.

On Augustine's account, contemplative knowledge of God comes through faith that has been formed by the scriptures. That is what the Platonists and the other mutually contradictory schools of philosophy lack:

> So since we were too weak to discover the truth by pure reasoning and therefore needed the authority of the sacred writings, I now began to believe that you would never have conferred such pre-eminent authority on the scripture, now diffused through all lands, unless you had willed that it would be a means of coming to faith in you and a means of seeking to know you.[44]

44. *Conf.* 6.5.8 (O'Donnell, 1:61–62; trans. Chadwick, 96): "ideoque cum essemus infirmi ad inueniendam liquida ratione ueritatem et ob hoc nobis opus esset auctoritate sanctarum litterarum, iam credere coeperam nullo modo te fuisse tributurum tam excellentem illi scripturae per omnes iam terras auctoritatem, nisi et per ipsam tibi credi et per ipsam te quaeri uoluisses."

Scripture has, therefore, an essential epistemic function, one that is necessary because of the inability of *liquida ratio*, pure reasoning, to reach truth. Moreover, scripture directs the soul away from the false pride in its own cognitive resources and onto the path of humility by which it can believe in and seek God. Submission to the tutelage of scripture was therefore an essential turning point in the pilgrimage of his soul, an ironic but salutary result of his encounter with Platonism. *Confessiones* 7 concludes by pressing this point against the Platonists, and it does so by emphasizing the insufficiency of Platonism in comparison to the theology of St. Paul:

> I began to read and found that all the truth I had read in the Platonists was stated there with the commendation of your grace, so that he who sees should not boast as if he had not received both what he sees and also the power to see. For what has he which he has not received? Moreover, he is not only admonished to see you, who remains ever the same, but also healed to make it possible for him to hold on to you. So also the person who from a distance cannot yet see, nevertheless walks along the path by which he may come and see and hold you.[45]

This, then, is the regnant image of Platonic philosophy in *Confessiones* 7: vision from afar. Platonists were just spectators looking out at the transcendent. Theirs was a worthy and profound insight about God; and their transcendental monotheism was spiritually transformative for Augustine. But their claim to immediate knowledge of God, achieved by the natural powers of the undescended soul, was fundamentally misguided.

"NONE COME CLOSER TO US THAN THESE"

One question that emerges from this analysis of Platonism in *Confessiones* 7 is how it relates to the other extensive assessment that Augustine presented in *De*

---

45. *Conf.* 7.21. 27 (O'Donnell, 1:87; trans. Chadwick, 130–31): "et coepi et inueni, quidquid illac uerum legeram, hac cum commendatione gratiae tuae dici, ut qui uidet non sic glorietur, quasi non acceperit non solum id quod uidet, sed etiam ut uideat (quid enim habet quod non accepit?) et ut te, qui es semper idem, non solum admoneatur ut uideat, sed etiam sanetur ut teneat, et qui de longinquo uidere non potest, uiam tamen ambulet qua ueniat et uideat et teneat."

ciuitate dei. This judgment was influenced both by the immediate context of that project in the aftermath of the fall of Rome and by Augustine's increased knowledge of the diversity of later pagan Platonism. But the main points of his treatment were generally the same. Yet again, he has both praise and blame to accord to Platonism. Here is his initial positive view: "If therefore Plato said that the wise person imitates and knows and loves this God, and that whoever participates in him is happy, what use is there to examine other philosophies? None come closer to us than these."[46] The reason for this claim is familiar: the Platonists stand out above all other philosophers because of their rejection of materialism: "Therefore we see that these philosophers have been justly preferred to the others since they discerned that nothing material is God and for that reason they transcended everything material in searching for God."[47]

We need now to look carefully at why exactly the Platonists deserve such fulsome praise in this later work. As in the *Confessiones*, the struggle against materialism makes the Platonists natural allies of Augustine's Nicene theology. He regards them as fellow proponents of a transcendent God who is the author of all things, the illuminator of truth, and the one who bestows happiness. The Platonists are therefore worthy of respect because of their commitment to an ultimate, transcendent God. In praising them in contrast to other philosophies, Augustine explains that their superiority is rooted in their philosophical monotheism:

> They have so understood God that they have discovered him to be the cause of being, the principle of understanding, the rule of life. These three might be thought to pertain: first to what is natural, second to what is rational, and third to what is moral. For if man was thus created, then through that which is superior within him he might touch that which exceeds all, that is, the one, true, supremely good God, without which no nature exists, no teaching instructs, no experience gains. God should be sought, where for us all things are connected. He should be discerned, where for us all things are discerned. He should be loved, where for us all things are morally right.[48]

46. *Ciu.* 8.5 (CCSL 47:221; trans. is my own): "si ergo Plato dei huius imitatorem cognitorem amatorem dixit esse sapientem, cuius participatione sit beatus, quid opus est excutere ceteros? nulli nobis quam isti propius accesserunt."

47. *Ciu.* 8.6 (CCSL 47:222–23; trans. is my own): "uiderunt ergo isti philosophi, quos ceteris non inmerito fama atque gloria praelatos uidemus, nullum corpus esse deum, et ideo cuncta corpora transcenderunt quaerentes deum."

48. *Ciu.* 8.4 (CCSL 47:220; trans. is my own): "aliquid tale de deo sentiunt, ut in illo

Augustine regards these three features of Platonic theology as elements of the core teachings of the school. As such, the doctrines of Platonism merit respect and approbation. They constitute a parallel form of transcendental monotheism to Nicene Christianity, one that forcibly rejected the materialism that remained both a powerful philosophical current and a common aspect of late antique culture. By virtue of this teaching, Plato and his followers deserve, in Augustine's opinion, their preeminence over other pagan philosophers. This "well-deserved fame and glory" applies to their thinking in metaphysics, logic, and moral philosophy.[49] Indeed, the Platonists recognize that the real goal of philosophy is the enjoyment of God: "This true and highest good Plato called God. A philosopher is a lover of God since philosophy aims at the happy life, and whoever will love God will be happy by delighting in him."[50] He then offers this summary of Platonist teaching:

> Every one of these philosophers therefore understands God as the supreme and true being, the author of created things, the light of knowledge, the good of all actions, the source of our being, the beginning of nature, the truth of doctrine, and the happiness of life.[51]

Notice that the congruence of Platonism with Augustine's Christianity comes at the level of notional commitments. The Platonists have achieved a cognitive grasp of God, one that had proven critical in his own spiritual development. Indeed, their theoretical understanding of God exceeds that of the other pagan schools.

---

inueniatur et causa subsistendi et ratio intellegendi et ordo uiuendi; quorum trium unum ad naturalem, alterum ad rationalem, tertium ad moralem partem intellegitur pertinere. si enim homo ita creatus est, ut per id, quod in eo praecellit, adtingat illud, quod cuncta praecellit, id est unum uerum optimum deum, sine quo nulla natura subsistit, nulla doctrina instruit, nullus usus expedit: ipse quaeratur, ubi nobis serta sunt omnia; ipse cernatur, ubi nobis certa sunt omnia; ipse diligatur, ubi nobis recta sunt omnia."

49. *Ciu.* 8.6 (CCSL 47:222).

50. *Ciu.* 8.8 (CCSL 47:225; trans. is my own): "ipsum autem uerum ac summum bonum plato dicit deum, unde uult esse philosophum amatorem dei, ut, quoniam philosophia ad beatam uitam tendit, fruens deo sit beatus qui deum amauerit."

51. *Ciu.* 8.9 (CCSL 47:225; trans. is my own): "quicumque igitur philosophi de deo summo et uero ista senserunt, quod et rerum creatarum sit effector et lumen cognoscendarum et bonum agendarum, quod ab illo nobis sit et principium naturae et ueritas doctrinae et felicitas uitae."

In this "late" consideration of Platonism, Augustine returns to Rom. 1:18–32, St. Paul's assessment of pagan philosophy.[52] Philosophical knowledge of God was, in fact, revealed knowledge, even if the Platonists were unaware of it. Yet, while offering some acquaintance with God, their knowledge did not lead to glorification of or gratitude toward God. Philosophy did not forestall the wise from becoming foolish, for they pursued false practices and became proud of their reputation for wisdom. By contrast, Christians can find the one true God without philosophy by pursuing their own faith, where they will also find the grace by which they can be united with God. In light of this Pauline approach to philosophy, Augustine is precise about his positive judgment of the Platonists: the reputation of the Platonists among pagan philosophers is in proportion to the superiority of their understanding of God as creator of heaven and earth.

Yet, for Augustine, that conceptual superiority again yields the paradox of Platonism. Platonists are monotheists and are well aware that true knowledge and happiness are possible only when the soul is united with God. Nonetheless (and paradoxically), the Platonists countenance or actively pursue polytheism:

> Now we selected the Platonists as being deservedly the best known of all the philosophers, because they have been able to realize that the soul of man, though immortal and rational (or intellectual), cannot attain happiness except by participation in the light of God, the creator of the soul and of the whole world. They also assert that no one can attain this life of blessedness, the object of all mankind's desire, unless he has adhered, with the purity of chaste love, to that unique and supreme Good, which is the changeless God. And yet those philosophers themselves have either yielded to the futile errors of people in general or, in the Apostle's words, "have dwindled into futility in their thinking," in that they have supposed (or are willing that it should be supposed) that many gods are to be worshipped.[53]

---

52. *Ciu.* 8.10 (CCSL 47:226.).

53. *Ciu.* 10.1 (CCSL 47:271–72; ET Augustine, *Concerning the City of God against the Pagans*, trans. Henry Bettenson [London: Penguin, 2003], 371): "elegimus enim Platonicos omnium philosophorum merito nobilissimos, propterea quia sapere potuerunt licet inmortalem ac rationalem uel intellectualem hominis animam nisi participato lumine illius dei, a quo et ipsa et mundus factus est, beatam esse non posse; ita illud, quod omnes homines appetunt, id est uitam beatam, quemquam isti assecuturum negant, qui non illi uni optimo, quod est incommutabilis deus, puritate casti amoris adhaeserit. sed quia ipsi quoque siue cedentes uanitati

Romans 1:18–23 is once again his key to coming to grips with Platonism. The virtue of Platonists is their conceptual understanding of the one God. Their failure is their confusion regarding how to achieve contemplative knowledge of God. In their mistaken estimation of the power of philosophy and their practice of polytheism, the Platonists have diffused the force of their monotheistic insight and, as a result, have lost their way. They do not know how to complete their undoubted notional understanding of God with full participation of the intellectual soul in God. Yet, according to Augustine, that is the shared goal of both Platonism and Christianity: "For our good, that final good, about which the philosophers dispute, is nothing else but to cleave to him whose spiritual embrace, if one may so express it, fills the intellectual soul and makes it fertile with true virtues."[54] Christians are commanded, he says, to love God with their whole heart, soul, and strength, and, through grace, are given the ability to do so.

In contrast to *Confessiones,* when he wrote *De ciuitate dei,* Augustine had a much clearer grasp of the role of theurgy in Platonism and especially the practices of the school of Iamblichus and his followers. In *De ciuitate dei* 10 he concentrates his attack on what he regards as the inconsistencies of Porphyry. While Porphyry believes that theurgy can put the spiritual element of the soul into the proper condition to see the gods, it cannot take the soul any further. That is because the higher, intellectual soul is not purified by theurgy and so is unable to see God and apprehend true realities.[55] Therefore, theurgy may be a useful preparation for genuine philosophical contemplation, but it cannot offer the soul what it truly desires. Here Augustine offers a "good Platonist / bad Platonist" critique, pitting Plotinus against Porphyry. Plotinus is depicted as recognizing that only contemplation of the One brings happiness. From this it follows that the cultivation of *theoria* is superior to theurgy.

> For this vision of God is a vision of such beauty and altogether deserving of such a love, that Plotinus says without hesitation that anyone who fails to

---

errori que populorum siue, ut ait apostolus, euanescentes in cogitationibus suis multos deos colendos ita putauerunt uel putari uoluerunt, ut quidam eorum etiam daemonibus diuinos honores sacrorum et sacrificiorum deferendos esse censerent."

54. *Ciu.* 10.3 (CCSL 47:275; trans. Bettenson, 375–76): "bonum enim nostrum, de cuius fine inter philosophos magna contentio est, nullum est aliud quam illi cohaerere, cuius unius anima intellectualis incorporeo, si dici potest, amplexu ueris impletur fecundatur que uirtutibus."

55. *Ciu.* 10.2, 10.9 (CCSL 47:274, 281–83).

achieve it is altogether unfortunate, no matter how richly endowed he may be with other kinds of goods.[56]

Despite this recognition of the power of contemplation, Augustine rejects Platonist claims of achieving it on the same grounds as he did in *Confessiones* 7.

We return now to Augustine's core criticism of Platonism. Since contemplative knowledge is also salvation, the Platonists claim to achieve both, even if they might disagree about the intermediate means for its accomplishment. Yet in this they are mistaken, having failed to find the true mediator who alone can purify the soul. Augustine notes that even Porphyry recognized that the faults and ignorance of the soul can only be purified by a mediator: "That can only be done through the *patrikos nous*, that is, the Mind or intellect of the Father, which is acquainted with the Father's will. But you do not believe that this is what Christ is."[57]

Thus, the Platonists have an intuitive grasp of much that Augustine's Nicene Christianity teaches, but they overestimate their own epistemic and soteriological capacities:

> You Platonists have here some kind of an intuition of the goal to which we must strive, however dimly seen through the obscurities of a subtle imagination. And yet you refuse to recognize the Incarnation of the unchanging Son of God, which brings us salvation, so that we can arrive at those realities in which we believe, and which we can in some small measure comprehend. Thus you see, to some extent, though from far off and with clouded vision, the country in which we must find our home; but you do not keep to the road along which we must travel.[58]

---

56. *Ciu.* 10.16 (CCSL 47:289; trans. Bettenson, 394 [modified]): "illa namque uisio dei tantae pulchritudinis uiso est et tanto amore dignissima, ut sine hac quibuslibet aliis bonis praeditum atque abundantem non dubitet plotinus infelicissimum dicere."

57. *Ciu.* 10.28 (CCSL 47:303, trans. Bettenson, 412–13): "ignorantiam certe et propter eam multa uitia per nullas teletas purgari dicis, sed per solum πατρικὸν νοῦν, id est paternam mentem siue intellectum, qui paternae est conscius uoluntatis. hunc autem Christum esse non credis."

58. *Ciu.* 10.29 (CCSL 47:304; trans. Bettenson, 414): "ubi, etsi uerbis indisciplinatis utimini, uidetis tamen qualitercumque et quasi per quaedam tenuis imaginationis umbracula, quo nitendum sit; sed incarnationem incommutabilis filii dei, qua saluamur, ut ad illa, quae credimus uel ex quantulacumque parte intellegimus, uenire possimus, non uultis agnoscere.

Here we find reiterated the same imagery for the cognitive and soteriological capacity of Platonism that Augustine articulated in *Confessiones* 7. What Platonism offers is a theoretical understanding of the transcendent God. But it fails in its claims to offer immediate contemplative knowledge of God and to secure the salvation of the soul. Platonists may, in their pride, claim to advance a more sublime teaching, but only the humility of the incarnate Christ can fulfill that deepest human longing.

Conclusion: Ecclesial Wisdom

It is crucial that these texts describing Augustine's understanding of Platonism be read in their proper context. They describe a major fault line that was opening in the intellectual and religious culture of late antiquity, one that has remained with us in various ways ever since. There are several crucial aspects that follow from Augustine's qualified rejection of Platonism, and they warrant brief consideration. They cluster around what might be called the ecclesial turn in late antique thought, the shift toward a new communal path to wisdom rivaling pagan philosophy. That path was the practice of Christianity as understood by Augustine and other Nicene thinkers. As we have seen, Augustine's appreciation of the theoretical superiority of Platonism to other forms of philosophy was genuine and, at a critical moment in his life, conversionary. But Augustine was never a member of a Platonic school, never studied under a Platonist teacher, never devoted himself to the sustained practice of dialectic, and never wrote commentaries on the Platonic texts.[59] After his ordination, he gradually shifted his writing from the Ciceronian style of the early Cassiciacum dialogues to scripturally grounded reflection. In the *Reconsiderations* (*retr.*) he makes this point explicitly, contrasting his initial philosophical language with his mature discourse rooted in the language of the church.[60] The path to wisdom was now to be found in the church's books, not in the books of the Platonists, and it was their guidance for his soul that he sought. Paradoxically, it was to the scriptures that the Platonist

---

itaque uidetis utcumque, etsi de longinquo, etsi acie caligante, patriam in qua manendum est, sed uiam qua eundum est non tenetis."

59. O'Donnell, *Confessions*, 2:416.
60. *Retr.* 1.3.2 (CCSL 57:13).

books had directed him, and it was the deeper meanings of the scriptures that he now sought to discern. That scriptural dialectic became the center of his practice throughout his life as a bishop, preacher, and exegete. This is not to say that he no longer valued Platonism or that he did not continue to read those Platonist works. The lengthy discussions of Platonism in *De ciuitate dei* 8 and 10 indicate clearly that he continued to do both. But he had found a new path distinctive in its practice and intellectual norms, an ecclesial path to wisdom.

One need look no further than Augustine's biographical excursus on Monica in *Confessiones* 9 to see the larger significance of his new ecclesial philosophy.[61] According to that book's ascension narrative, Monica achieves communion with eternal wisdom in that moment at Ostia. She succeeds in reaching divine wisdom itself, though she is no philosopher. Her preparation had been a Christian life, schooled by the scriptures, prayer, and the sacraments. It is the power of Christ that drew her soul into the eternal wisdom at that "moment of understanding" (*momentum intellegentiae*).[62] Her contemplative ascent was the fruition of a life lived outside the domain of philosophy as prescribed by the Platonist schools; instead, she pursued it in the school of Christ. That ecclesial dimension, so clearly exhibited in the life of Monica, is the key to understanding Augustine's mature account of contemplative knowledge. Patout Burns has expressed this point succinctly:

> That beatifying knowledge of God for which humans were created could be briefly glimpsed by the learned in mystical ascent. In the life of the church, Augustine intimated, Christ offered even the unlearned a privileged opportunity to recognize and experience the heavenly beatitude that was the goal of human life. In his preaching, he invited his hearers to discern anticipations of the blessed life in communal experiences. These glimpses of life's goal—somewhat like the one Augustine shared with his mother in Ostia—confirmed that Christ accompanied his people on this more humble path.[63]

---

61. For more detailed discussions of Monica at Ostia, see Kenney, *Mysticism of Saint Augustine*, chap. 8; Kenney, *Contemplation and Classical Christianity*, chap. 5; and Gillian Clark, *Monica: An Ordinary Saint* (Oxford: Oxford University Press, 2015).

62. *Conf.* 9.10.25 (O'Donnell, 1:114; trans. Chadwick, 172).

63. J. Patout Burns, "Augustine's Ecclesial Mysticism," in *The Wiley-Blackwell Companion to Christian Mysticism*, ed. Julia A. Lamm (London: Wiley-Blackwell, 2013), 203.

It was to this broad, communal path, accessible not just to a philosophical elite, that Augustine turned in his pursuit of divine wisdom. In doing so, he put aside the "supposedly more sublime teaching" of the Platonists, retaining their understanding of the metaphysical architecture of reality, but rejecting their claims to participatory knowledge of God. While the Platonists recognized that souls "are renewed to be wise by participation in wisdom abiding in them," they failed to find the only power by which they could achieve that end.[64] That is the incarnate Christ, present in his church, who alone can lift souls up to the divine wisdom.[65]

64. *Conf.* 7.9.14 (O'Donnell, 1:80–81; trans. Chadwick, 122): "et quia participatione manentis in se sapientiae renovantur ut sapientes sint."

65. *Conf.* 7.18.24 (O'Donnell, 1:85). I would like to express my thanks to Austin Holmes, a graduate student in the Department of Theology at Boston College, for his assistance in the editing of this chapter.

Chapter 7

AUGUSTINE AND PORPHYRY

Thomas Clemmons

INTRODUCTION

Porphyry's importance for and among fourth- and fifth-century Christian writers is immense. Augustine says, "Porphyry was the most learned of the philosophers, although the most fierce enemy of the Christians."[1] When many Christians of the fourth and fifth centuries write about Platonism on the ground—that is, intellectual paganism—they are often writing about Porphyry. When Augustine writes his *De ciuitate dei* (*ciu.*), he repeatedly refers to Porphyry. When Christians engage and incorporate pagan oracles, they often draw from Porphyry. From Lactantius through Cyril of Alexandria, Porphyry, as much as or more than any other thinker, represents intellectual pagan piety.

To convey the importance of Augustine's complex engagement with Porphyry, I proceed by several sections. In the first section, I provide an overview of Porphyry, especially the implications of his philosophy and theology as they relate to Augustine. From this I turn to Augustine's first explicit reference to Porphyry in *De consensu euangelistarum* (*cons. eu.*) and his more extensive response in *Epistula* (*ep.*) 102. Next, I address Augustine's sermons against the philosophers concerning the resurrection (*Sermones* [*ss.*] 240–42). Building on this foundation, I examine Porphyry's place in *De ciuitate dei*, especially books 10 and 19.[2]

---

1. *Ciu.* 19.22 (CCSL 48:690; trans. Babcock, *City of God (Books 11–22)*, WSA I/7, 380): "doctissimus philosophorum, quamuis Christianorum acerrimus inimicus." Cf. *s.* 241.7 (PL 38:1137–38).

2. In this essay I have proceeded in a manner that, I hope, pays suitable tribute to my

Porphyry's Life and Writings

Around 234 CE, Porphyry was born in Tyre, a coastal city of Syria. He appears to have become familiar with Christianity at a young age.[3] In his youth, Porphyry traveled to Athens to study rhetoric with the great rhetor and philologist Longinus. Porphyry's writings such as *Homeric Questions* and the brief tract *De antro nympharum* were likely the fruit of his study with Longinus. In addition, Porphyry's understanding of Homer as *the* theologian and of the importance of oracles draws from Longinus's commitment to traditional pagan religion and culture.[4]

Along with his advanced technical training, Porphyry, more so than his predecessors, evidences a turn to the "theological." Porphyry overtly concerns himself with interpreting the pagan oracles, such as the writings of Homer, as theological texts revealed by the gods. Consonant with this project, it is Porphyry who appears to have introduced the language of theosophy into the Greek intellectual tradition.[5]

In his thirties, after his studies with Longinus, Porphyry went to Rome to study with Plotinus (ca. 263 CE).[6] After Plotinus's death, Porphyry may have

---

teacher, J. Patout Burns, in both method and substance. I use a diachronic approach to Augustine's works, including his *epp.*, *ss.*, and both minor and major writings; identify his engagement, integration, and critique of Porphyry; and note the development or refinement of Augustine's thought through his responses to Porphyry. Such a contextually thorough and attentive approach to reading Augustine and his sources is one of the many debts that Augustinian scholarship owes to Patout.

3. Modern attempts to reconstruct Porphyry's life vary in detail, as do the ancient sources. See, e.g., Andrew Smith, "Porphyrian Studies since 1913," in *Aufstieg und Niedergang der römischen Welt* 36.2:719–73, part 2, *Principat*, 36.2, ed. H. Temporini and W. Haase (New York: de Gruyter, 1987), 719–73, and Mark Edwards, "Porphyry and the Christians," in *Studies on Porphyry*, ed. George Karamanolis and Anne Sheppard (London: Institute of Classical Studies, 2007), 111–26.

4. See Richard Lamberton, *Homer the Theologian: Neoplatonist Allegorical Reading and the Growth of the Epic Tradition* (Berkeley: University of California Press, 1986).

5. See Andrew Smith, "Porphyry and the 'Platonic Theology,'" in *Proclus et la Théologie Platonicienne*, ed. Carlos Steel and Alain Philippe Segonds (Leuven: Leuven University Press, 2000), 177–88. For his use of theosophy, see *Philosophy from Oracles*, fr. 323, in Andrew Smith, *Porphyrius: Fragmenta* (Leipzig: Teubner, 1993).

6. Plotinus certainly influenced Porphyry. However, both the chronology of Porphyry's works and claims that Plotinus's rational philosophy cured Porphyry of superstitious mysticism are disputed. See J. Bidez, *Vie de Porphyre* (Gand: Van Goethem, 1913), and, contra Bidez, see Pier Franco Beatrice, "*Quosdam Platonicorum Libros*," *VC* 43 (1989): 248–81, as well as

returned to the eastern Roman Empire, where likely he died around 304 CE. In this later period he is thought to have composed numerous works, including two of his more influential writings: *De regressu animae* and *Aduersus Christianos.*

The latter work highlights Porphyry's meticulous and extensive critique of Christianity. Wilken has proposed that Porphyry wrote the *Aduersus Christianos* at the behest of the emperor Diocletian.[7] Porphyry might even have composed his work as part of the propaganda campaign that Diocletian put forward in support of his official persecution of Christians. The evidence for this claim is inconclusive. Nevertheless, Porphyry's connection with the Diocletian persecution as well as his anti-Christian writings are likely why he, more than other philosophers, is known in the fourth and fifth centuries as a prominent, vocal enemy of Christianity. Porphyry was not simply a philosophical critic; he was a strident adversary of Christianity and possibly even part of the brain trust behind the brutal Diocletian persecution.[8]

PORPHYRY AND CHRISTIANITY

Porphyry's criticisms of Christianity differed from other opponents of Christianity such as Celsus. He does not merely pillory Christ as a magician or a huckster; on the contrary, Porphyry rebukes pagan critics of Christianity who had simply sought to slander Christ. According to Porphyry, when pagans consulted their own oracles, they were compelled to praise Christ. Drawing from an oracle and parts of the Gospels, Porphyry claims that Christ was a wise man who ascended to become a hero or lower *daimon.*[9] Christ, therefore, deserves piety not as God, as the Christians believe, but as a hero.

Porphyry does not hold that Christ is a higher *daimon* (such as Apollo), deserving a broader piety. Rather, Christ is a local hero. Porphyry asserts that this

---

John J. O'Meara, "Porphyry's *Philosophy from Oracles* in Eusebius' *Praeparatio Evangelica* and Augustine's *Dialogues* of Cassiciacum," *RechAug* 6 (1969): 103–39.

7. Robert Louis Wilken, *The Christians as the Romans Saw Them*, 2nd ed. (New Haven: Yale University Press, 2003), 126–63, esp. 148–59, and Henry Chadwick, *The Sentences of Sextus*, Texts and Studies 5 (Cambridge: Cambridge University Press, 1959), 66.

8. *Pace* Wilken, see Andrew Smith, "Philosophical Objections to Christianity on the Eve of the Great Persecution," in *The Great Persecution*, ed. D. Vincent Twomey and Mark Humphries (Dublin: Four Courts, 2009), 33–48, esp. 33–38.

9. *Cons. eu.* 1.15.23 (CSEL 43:22); cf. *ciu.* 19.22 (CCSL 47:690).

was in fact what Christ thought of himself. Christ saw himself as a soul being purified in order to make a higher ascent. The problem with Christianity, Porphyry avers, is not Christ but Christ's disciples. The disciples' errors consist in their naive exaltation of Christ as God and in their hubris to spread the name of Christ throughout the world. For Porphyry, Christ deserves local piety; Christ does not merit worldwide adulation and adoration, which should be reserved for the noetic deities.[10]

In this claim, we see a positive dimension of Porphyry's theology. Local cults devoted to certain lower "divine" figures merit only local piety. To confuse a lower *daimon*, Christ, with the high God of Platonism, the One, is to worship the "bodily" and not pursue the release of the true intellect in contemplation of the One. The expansion of this logic (though in a slightly different form) is witnessed in the anti-Christian tract by the emperor Julian the Apostate, *Against the Galileans*. The title of the work reveals Julian's attempt to localize Christ as a Galilean—hence, limited to the region of Galilee—and to critique the Christian movement, which extols Christ as the high God.

As is evident from his criticism of Christians as worshiping the body, Porphyry abhors the Christian claim of the resurrection of the body. For Porphyry, even if this is taken to be a spiritual body, the condition of "bodily" resurrection cannot be the final state of perfection. True perfection—that is, the highest ascent of the intellectual soul—is bodiless pure intellect.[11]

Because the highest aim of the soul is intellectual union with the One, we might suppose Porphyry to have a negative view of religion, oracles, and public piety. However, Porphyry's view is more nuanced. He both criticizes the common public religious cult of sacrifices and argues for its usefulness. Porphyry holds that such sacrifices may be helpful as civic piety, though they might appeal to lower, even evil, *daimones*. Hence, public cultic piety has a positive place for Porphyry. The enfleshed soul should not boldly scorn its current condition. To reject the local, public cult is to consider oneself above one's current condition

10. At *ciu.* 10.21 (CCSL 47:295; trans. Babcock, *City of God (Books 1–10)*, WSA I/6, 328–29), Augustine criticizes the term "hero" as applied to those "souls of the dead marked by some special merit."

11. For two possible readings of this phrase and a discussion of its implications, see Michael Chase, "'*Omne Corpus Fugiendum*?' Augustine and Porphyry on the Body and the Postmortem Destiny of the Soul," Χώρα 2 (2004): 37–58. See also Eric Dubreucq, "La Chair, la Grâce et l'Esprit: Métempsycose et Résurrection de Porphyre à Saint Augustin," *Archives de Philosophie* 60, no. 1 (1997): 25–45, esp. 31–35.

and the reverence due to local justice. For Porphyry, this does not mean that the public cult leads to spiritual or intellectual purification. Spiritual purification is aided by theurgy, other mystical practices, and virtue.[12] The loftiest purification of the soul is engendered only through philosophical, intellectual advancement. Therefore, even while Porphyry places greater emphasis on the philosophical and intellectual advancement of the soul and, beneath this, the theurgic rituals and spiritual purification, the public cult is an important part of piety for the lower soul in the flesh. The Christian is thus indicted as a usurper who both foolishly rejects due piety at each level and strangely claims to universalize and localize the process of purgation for the "intellectual" soul.

These two verbs, to universalize and to localize, depict two central aspects of Porphyry's criticism of Christianity. Christianity "universalizes" in that it claims that Christ and the Christian liturgy alone purify the whole soul, including the spiritual and intellectual. For Porphyry, cults are local and therefore vary. Different cults, Egyptian, Babylonian, or Greek, lead by different means to the purgation of the soul in the physical body; some can even lead to the purgation of the spiritual soul. However, these rites do not advance the soul to the loftiest intellectual ends. That Christianity posits one solution for all humanity and for the entire human (or soul) is, for Porphyry, utterly absurd.

Christianity "localizes" in that it claims that the highest and complete purgation of the soul occurs in a particular context: the church. For Porphyry, such mediation, which is implied by localization, is not needed for the purgation of the intellectual soul. The intellect adheres to the One; it needs no localized mediation. The One is utterly transcendent, receiving neither hymns nor worship (as even the noetic gods do). Christians distort the One with their claim to worship the highest God as present in a particular, localized place.[13]

Thus, Porphyry was not simply a critic of Christianity. Rather, he was an adversary who articulated a complex system that confronted many of Christianity's central claims. For example, Porphyry was a thinker who was always concerned with the salvation of the soul.[14] Regarding the soul's salvation, he also shared with Christians an understanding of the importance of prophecy and mediation

12. Concerning theurgy, see Crystal Addey, *Divination and Theurgy in Neoplatonism: Oracles of the Gods* (Burlington, VT: Ashgate, 2014), 24–40; cf. *ciu.* 10.9–11 (CCSL 47:281–86).

13. *Ciu.* 10.19 (CCSL 47:293–94).

14. Andrew Smith writes, "One word which dominates his thought is σωτηρία, the salvation of the soul." *Porphyry's Place in the Neoplatonic Tradition: A Study in Post-Plotinian Neoplatonism* (The Hague: Martinus Nijhoff, 1974), 145.

in the ascent of the soul to God. It is not surprising that such a thinker would attract the attention of Christians, all the more so as he aimed criticism directly at Christianity.

Like Eusebius and Jerome, Augustine took up the task of replying to Porphyry. Augustine differed from his predecessors in that his engagement with Porphyry was not exclusively negative. From his initial reading of Porphyry, to his first explicit citation, to the last book of *De ciuitate dei,* Augustine was drawn to return and respond to the philosopher. His own thinking sharpened through his prolonged exchange with Porphyry, who continued to hold enormous sway. In *De ciuitate dei* Augustine addressed Porphyry and his enduring influence:

> But what am I doing? I know that it is pointless to speak to a dead man, but that applies only to you. There are also people who hold you in high regard and feel real affection for you, either due to some sort of love of wisdom or due to their curiosity about those arts which you should never have studied; and in rebuking you, I am speaking to them.[15]

DE CONSENSU EUANGELISTARUM

The first explicit reference to Porphyry in Augustine's works is found in *De consensu euangelistarum,* composed around 404 CE.[16] The first book of this work, which explicitly references Porphyry, is an extended defense of the veracity of the Gospels against "pagan" criticisms.[17] While the entire first book is not directed against Porphyry explicitly, the criticisms to which Augustine responds are remarkably similar to those we know were made by Porphyry.[18] Porphyry's objections to Christianity focus on the Gospels: they were not

---

15. *Ciu.* 10.29 (CCSL 47:304–5; trans. Babcock, WSA I/6, 339): "sed quid faciam? scio me frustra loqui mortuo, sed quantum ad te adtinet; quantum autem ad eos, qui te magnipendunt et te uel qualicumque amore sapientiae uel curiositate atrium, quas non debuisti discere, diligunt, quos potius in tua compellatione alloquor, fortasse non frustra."

16. Pierre-Marie Hombert, *Nouvelles recherches de chronologie augustinienne* (Paris: Études Augustiniennes, 2000), 33–37.

17. *Cons. eu.* 1.7.10 (CSEL 43:10–11).

18. See Wilken, *Christians as the Romans Saw Them,* 137–60. For the claim that *cons. eu.* was not written against Porphyry, see Gillian Clark, "Acerrimus inimicus? Porphyry and the City of God," in *Le Traité de Porphyre Contre les Chrétiens,* ed. Sébastian Morlet (Paris: Études Augustiniennes, 2011), 395–406.

written by those who knew Jesus; they include things that could not have been witnessed by their authors, such as the birth of Christ; and they do not precisely agree with one another. Augustine counters the first and second of these objections by noting that two of the Gospels, John and Matthew, were written by those who knew Christ closely, who investigated the testimony of those close to him such as the Virgin Mary, and who were his disciples. In addition, the two other Gospels, Luke and Mark, were composed by those who learned directly from Christ's disciples. These evangelists point to the depth of witness and instruction. The Gospels are accounts not simply of eyewitnesses, but also of those who were instructed, believed, and understood who Christ was.[19]

Regarding the third objection that the Gospels differ in their content, Augustine explains that the Gospels vary only insofar as they emphasize different dimensions. Mark and Matthew highlight the kingship of Christ and how Christ's deeds relate to the present life. Luke accentuates that Christ is the true priest who offers himself to and for humanity. These three Gospels emphasize the true humanity of Christ and what Christ did in "an earthly manner by means of human flesh."[20] The Gospel of John, on the other hand, is primarily concerned with the true divinity of Christ, who is equal to the Father.

Augustine's reply outlined an understanding of Christ that expands beyond the limits placed on Christ by Porphyry. As noted, Porphyry understands Christ to be a virtuous hero who ascends after his death as lower *daimon* to a higher spiritual level. His position is so well known that "Porphyrianism" was employed by defenders of Nicaea, such as Athanasius and Constantine, as a label for an interpretation of Christ that insists that he was merely human.[21] Augustine's response highlights how each evangelist points beyond the depiction of Christ as a virtuous hero. While John's accentuates Christ's divinity, the other Gospels extend the mission of Christ to the whole of humanity.

The universality of Christ's mission, which indicates the divinity of Christ, is perhaps the most prominent theme in *De consensu euangelistarum*. Augustine repeatedly emphasizes that the Christian faith and teaching concerning Christ has spread to the whole world.[22] Christ was not simply a local "wise man." Christ,

---

19. *Cons. eu.* 1.1.2–1.2.3 (CSEL 43:2–4).

20. *Cons. eu.* 1.4.7 (CSEL 43:6–7; trans. Paffenroth, *New Testament I and II*, WSA I/15–16, 141): "quas Christus per humanum carnem temporaliter gessit."

21. Constantine, in time, condemned Porphyry's writings. Cf. Smith, "Philosophical Objections," 36–39.

22. *Cons. eu.* 1.14.21 (CSEL 43:19–21).

Augustine states, is truly God become flesh for all humanity. That Christianity has spread throughout the world is consonant with the Christian claims concerning Christ drawn from the Gospels.

Moreover, those who argue that Christ's disciples distorted who Christ claimed to be are confronted by the prophecies of the Old Testament concerning Christ.[23] Porphyry, understanding the importance of prophetic claims for Christianity, produced an extensive critique of Christian prophecy. The philosopher did not reject all prophecy. Rather, Porphyry was exclusively concerned to disprove that there is prophecy concerning Christ because Christ cannot be who the Gospels say he is. In response, Augustine highlights the universality of what Christ offers in the incarnation and the prophetic preparation that secures this interpretation. Both prophecy and the universality of Christianity realize the divinity of Christ and the mission of Christ for humanity.[24]

Thus, in De consensu euangelistarum Augustine uses Porphyry as an example of the praise pagans give to Christ. He is also aware of the attempt to separate Christ both from the Old Testament, the prophets, and Israel on the one hand, and from the disciples and the church on the other. Through this re-narration, Christ becomes a pagan wise man who supports the pagan system of daimones, intelligible gods, and the high God. Augustine's rejoinder outlines the inconsistencies of the pagan system, in both narrative and practice.[25] He also stresses, as noted above, the importance of Christ as foretold by Israel and proclaimed universally by the church born from Christ in these "Christian times." It is through Christ that the human is able to unite to wisdom and return to God. Augustine articulates the dependence of this union and ascent on the incarnation, passion, and resurrection of Christ. Through faith in the visible and temporal mediation of Christ (a mediation that is carried forward in the church), the human is brought to truth and eternity.[26] Interestingly, these very emphases draw the criticisms that Augustine was compelled to address in Epistula 102.

---

23. Cons. eu. 1.15.23 (CSEL 43:22) and 1.16.24 (CSEL 43:22–23).

24. Cons. eu. 1.11.17 (CSEL 43:16–17) and 1.35.54 (CSEL 43:60–61). For Porphyry's claims, see Jerome's Commentary on Daniel prologue (CCSL 75A:771–72).

25. Cons. eu. 1.32.50 (CSEL 43:54–55); 1.27.42 (CSEL 43:41–42); and 1.34.52 (CSEL 43:57–58); Cf. 1.19.27–1.25.38 (CSEL 43:25–37), which includes many of the points and examples Augustine will employ in books 4–8 of ciu.

26. Cons. eu. 1.26.40–41 (CSEL 43:39–41); 1.31.47 (CSEL 43:47–51); especially 1.33.51 (CSEL43:55–57) and 1.35.53 (CSEL 43:58–60).

EPISTULA 102

Some four years after he composed the first book of *De consensu euangelistarum*, Augustine received a letter from Deogratias, a priest in Carthage, seeking aid in answering six questions attributed to Porphyry. The questions were particularly pointed and touched on issues central to pagan criticism of Christianity. Several of the questions put forth objections that Augustine had not treated in depth in his prior writings. The letter eventually became known—even by Augustine himself in his *Retractationes* (*retr.*)—as an independent tractate called *Quaestiones expositae contra paganos numero sex* (*qu. c. pag.*).

The first question, *de resurrectione*, asks which corresponds to the promised resurrection, that of Lazarus or Christ?[27] The objection runs as follows:

> If it is the resurrection of Christ how can this resurrection of one who was born without a father correspond to the resurrection of those who were born with a human father? But if it is the resurrection of Lazarus . . . the resurrection of Lazarus was from a body that was not yet decaying, from that body still called "Lazarus," while our resurrection will be drawn after many ages from an unidentifiable matter. Second, if the state after the resurrection will be blessed, with no injury to the body and no necessity from hunger, why is it that Christ ate and showed his wounds? But if he did this on account of unbelief, it was a pretense; if, however, he revealed what was true, then wounds we have received will be present in the resurrection.[28]

27. This chapter discusses only the first three questions. The fourth question treats Christianity's teaching that eternal damnation results from temporal sin (Porphyry quotes Matt. 7:2, "With the measure you use, it will be measured out to you," as proof of Christianity's inconsistencies on this point); the fifth concerns why Solomon said that "God does not have a son" (allegedly a scriptural citation that, in fact, is not in the Bible, as Augustine notes); and the sixth, which Augustine regards as a general pagan derision of Christian scripture, discusses the implausibility of Jonah's story and the meaninglessness of the gourd plant that sprouts over him.

28. *Ep.* 102.2 (CCSL 31B:9; trans. Teske, *Letters 100–155*, WSA II/2, 22, slightly modified): "'si Christi,' inquiunt, 'quomodo potest haec conuenire resurrectioni natorum ex semine eius, qui nulla seminis condicione natus est? si autem Lazari resurrectio conuenire asseritur, ne haec quidem congruere uidetur, si quidem Lazari resurrectio facta sit de corpore nondum tabescente, de eo corpore quo Lazarus dicebatur; nostra autem multis saeculis post ex confuso eruetur. deinde si post resurrectionem status beatus futurus est nulla corporis iniuria,

The question displays Porphyry's strident critique of the Christian conception of the resurrection of the body. That bliss or beatitude could be bodily in any sense is utterly absurd for Porphyry. Augustine does not yet quote Porphyry's famous phrase "omne corpus fugiendum" as he will a few years later.[29] Rather, he replies that the paradigm of the future resurrection is based on Christ, whose humanity and death were real, even though he was born of a virgin. Concerning the general restoration of the body, Augustine states plainly that it is not impossible for God to restore and alter the body, even following the complete decay of the body following death. Porphyry seems to have misplaced the agent causing the resurrection of the body. It is not a product of natural growth or the shedding of one heavier body for a lighter spiritual one through the agency of the ascending soul. Instead, God, the same high God who made the heavens, the earth, and all the marvels of nature, causes the resurrection of the body. Surely a philosopher does not reject God's omnipotence?[30]

In the second part of the question, Augustine perceives the desire to mock Christianity as inconsistent: Christ both ate after the resurrection and says food is not necessary. Augustine counters that the resurrected body will not need food, but through its new perfection might partake of it. Indeed, Augustine turns the question back on Porphyry. If the resurrected body was limited so that it could not partake of food, even if one desired, would it not be something less than "an imperfect felicity" (*imperfecta felicitas*)?[31] Porphyry has only focused on the body in need, not on the body made perfect.

Regarding the "wounds" of Christ, Augustine corrects Porphyry's inattentive observation. They are not called "wounds" (*uulnera*) but "scars" (*cicatrices*). The distinction is important. Wounds may endure against one's will and reveal the weakness of the flesh. However, Christ's scars remained because he willed to show the certainty of the plan of salvation and that one body did not rise in the place of another. Christ's scars point to the wounds he had received for humanity; that is, they show that "the very same body rose that they had seen

---

nulla necessitate famis, quid sibi uult cibatum fuisse Christum et uulnera monstrauisse? sed si propter incredulum fecit, finxit; si autem uerum ostendit, ergo in resurrectione accepta futura sunt uulnera.'"

29. That Augustine does not quote the Porphyrian *sententia* raises doubts that he knew it when he wrote *ep.* 102.

30. Victor Yudin argues that Porphyry rejects the omnipotence of God. "Porphyry against the Resurrection in Augustine," *StPatr* 50 (2011): 301–7.

31. *Ep.* 102.6 (CCSL 31B:11–12; trans. Teske, WSA II/2, 24). Cf. *s.* 241 (PL 38:1133–38).

crucified."[32] They are like the scars of a brave soldier who desires for the scars to remain even though they could have been wholly removed.

For Augustine the resurrected body possesses continuity with one's body in this mortal life. Resurrection is not a departure or unshackling from the prison that is the body. It is a perfection of the body, a more "superior" body, which is able to enjoy a perfect blessedness and beatitude. What is also evident, especially in light of his critique of Porphyry in *De consensu euangelistarum*, is that the resurrected body depends on the resurrection of Christ. The resurrection of the body is not part of a natural progression as it is for Porphyry, where the soul sheds its lower "*uehiculum*" for a loftier, more subtle "body" or vehicle. Rather, the resurrection of the body is a restoration of the body incorporated into the work and person of Christ.

The second question, *De tempore christianae religionis*, is much more complicated when compared to Augustine's response to Porphyry in *De consensu euangelistarum*. As discussed, an important aspect of Augustine's argument in that text is his emphasis on the *Christiana tempora*, a phrase that traces all the way back to *De uera religione* (*uera rel.*; ca. 390 CE). In *De consensu euangelistarum* Augustine argued for the divinity of Christ in part through the singular significance of the historical dispensation of God's mercy in time, which culminated in the incarnation. The prophets all point to the incarnation, and the church is drawn from the effects of the incarnation to include the whole world. This very singularity, so dependent on the incarnation in history, is the focus of Porphyry's second objection. Porphyry's acute question is as follows:

> If Christ says that he is the way of salvation, grace, and truth, he locates in himself alone the return of souls who believe in him. What did people do for so many ages before Christ? To leave aside the times before the kingdom of Latium, let us take the beginning of humanity from Latium itself. . . . For many centuries Rome itself was without the Christian law for a long stretch of time. What was done concerning countless such souls who were without any sin at all, since the one in whom they could have believed had not yet offered his coming to human beings? The world along with Rome was fervent in the rites of the temples. Why did he who is called the savior absent himself for so many centuries? . . . What happened to Roman or Latin souls which were deprived of the grace of Christ's coming?[33]

---

32. *Ep.* 102.7 (CCSL 31B:12; trans. Teske, WSA II/2, 24): "non aliud pro alio, sed hoc, quod crucifixum uiderant, resurrexisse monstraret."

33. *Ep.* 102.8 (CCSL 31B:13; trans. Teske, WSA II/2, 24–25): "'si Christus,' inquiunt, 'salutis

Porphyry's criticism focuses on the temporal locatedness of Christianity as well as the implication, which Augustine will discuss in *De ciuitate dei*, that there can be no single or universal way for the return of the soul. Porphyry, as witnessed in his *Philosophy from Oracles*, but also in this quote drawn from the *Contra Christianos*, rejects the claims of singularity and universality while arguing for the function of local piety and theurgic rites.[34]

To this end, Augustine's initial retort notes the obvious. All religious rites and ceremonies are localized and initiated in certain times. Does not the Roman religion have a beginning, before which other rites and religious practices existed? Would Porphyry deem the Roman religion invalid because it has a *terminus a quo*? Certainly not. Hence the Roman rites, if valid and beneficial, were so because the worship itself was valid and beneficial. If these religious practices were useless, they must be abandoned. Moreover, if these rites and practices were beneficial initially, not only is Porphyry's criticism moved onto those who lived before the Roman religion was established, but also, Augustine deduces, these rites ought not to have undergone any changes or novelties in the passing of time. Augustine does not simply observe that Porphyry is dancing around the need to assess whether or not the Christian religion is valid and beneficial; he also demands that Porphyry attend to his own principle. If the efficacy of a religion is bound with its observance in a specific historical time, then the Christian religion is efficacious in "Christian times." Porphyry, or the one asking these questions through him, should simply change with the times and celebrate the Christian ceremonies now.

The more important question, Augustine asserts, is whether the Christian religion truly worships God and, hence, leads the human to God. In other words, is the Christian claim to singularity and universality, grounded in the incarnation of Christ, valid and efficacious? If so, how would it apply to those outside Israel before the coming of Christ (and, we might assume, to those to whom neither the Mosaic law nor the gospel has been taught)? Augustine's reply is fascinating:

se uiam dicit, gratiam et ueritatem in se que solo ponit animis sibi credentibus reditum, quid egerunt tot saeculorum homines ante Christum? ut dimittam, inquit, tempora ante Latium regnatum, ab ipso Latio quasi principium humani nominis sumamus. . . . non paucioribus saeculis ipsa Roma longo saeculorum tractu sine christiana lege fuit. quid, inquit, actum de tam innumeris animis, quae omnino in culpa nulla sunt, si quidem is, cui credi posset, nondum aduentum suum hominibus commodarat? orbis quoque cum ipsa Roma in ritibus templorum caluit. quare,' inquit, 'saluator qui dictus est, sese tot saeculis subduxit. . . . quid igitur actum de Romanis animis uel Latinis, quae gratia nondum aduenientis Christi uiduatae sunt usque in Caesarum tempus?'"

34. Gustavus Wolff, *Porphyrii de philosophia ex oraculis haurienda* (Hildesheim: Olms, 1962). See also Smith, *Porphyrius*.

All those from the beginning of the human race who believed in him [Christ] and understood him somehow or other and lived pious and just lives according to those commandments, whenever and wherever they lived, were undoubtedly saved through him. . . . The faith itself has not changed, nor is salvation itself different, because in accord with the different times there is now proclaimed as already having happened what was then foretold as coming. . . . Hence, one and the same true religion was signified and observed by other names and signs then [and] now, earlier in a more hidden way, while later more openly, and earlier by fewer, but afterwards by many.[35]

Here Augustine has advanced or elaborated the argument put forward in *De consensu euangelistarum*. He has not abandoned the prophetic dimension that points to Christ's universal function and sacrifice. He also does not waver in his commitment to the importance he gives to the historical development of "these Christian times." All who truly worshiped God, Augustine claims, worshiped the Son. They all, in some form, looked forward to what was effected in the incarnation. What has followed the incarnation in the worship and customs of the church and the spread of Christianity is the fullness of what had come before.

In addition to his assertion concerning Christ and the continuity of worship throughout time, Augustine also addresses God's providence. The Platonists believe in God's providence—that is, that the ages of time do not pass by in chance, but rather are ordered. Christians share a belief in this providence, which was active well before the advent of Platonism or the wisdom of Socrates and well beyond the boundaries of the Roman Empire:

From the beginning of the human race, at times in a more hidden way, at times in a more evident way, as God saw that it was appropriate to the times, he did not cease to speak in prophecies, and there were not lacking those who believed in him, both from Adam up to Moses and in the people of Israel, which was by a particular mystery a prophetic people, as well as in other peoples before Christ came in the flesh. For some are already mentioned in the holy books of

35. *Ep.* 102.12 (CCSL 31B:15; trans. Teske, WSA II/2, 26–27): "itaque ab exordio generis humani quicumque in eum crediderunt eum que utcumque intellexerunt et secundum eius praecepta pie iuste que uixerunt, quandolibet et ubilibet fuerint, per eum procul dubio salui facti sunt. . . . nec quia pro temporum uarietate nunc factum adnuntiatur, quod tunc futurum praenuntiabatur, ideo fides ipsa uariata uel salus ipsa diuersa est. . . . proinde aliis tunc nominibus et signis aliis autem nunc et prius occultius postea manifestius et prius a paucioribus post a pluribus una tamen eadem que uera religio significatur et obseruatur."

the Hebrews from the time of Abraham, people not his descendants according to the flesh, nor members of the people of Israel, nor those who joined the people of Israel from another society; they were, nonetheless, sharers in this mystery. Why, then, should we not believe that there were also others now and then at other times and in other peoples, even though we do not find them mentioned in the same authorities? In that way the salvation brought by this religion, the only true religion by which true salvation is also truly promised, was never lacking to anyone who was worthy of it, and anyone to whom it was lacking was unworthy of it.[36]

Here Augustine has deepened the claims he made in *De consensu euangelistarum*. "Sharers in the mystery" of God's action to unite humanity to Christ, both priest and king, are not limited either temporally or locally. Augustine's common example, especially in later works, is the righteous Job, who was neither Jewish nor had the Mosaic law. Hence, Augustine responds to the suggestion that there is no universal way presented in time (a point he takes up more fully in *De ciuitate dei*) with the articulation of his understanding of the extension of Christ's activity beyond the limit placed by Porphyry's objections to localization and temporal boundedness.

Augustine's reply to the third objection, concerning how Christians reject the worship and sacrifice of both the ancient Jews and pagans, restates this point. For Augustine, true sacrifice and worship are offered only to the one God. The pagan rites, and other religious ceremonies such as Job's, are not faulted because they have temples or sacrifices of animals. They are in error if they are offered to the *daimones* and not to the one God. *Latreia* (λατρεία), Augustine observes, should not be offered to anything other than the Creator.[37]

---

36. *Ep.* 102.15 (CCSL 31B:17–18; trans. Teske, WSA II/2, 28): "et tamen ab initio generis humani alias occultius alias euidentius, sicut congruere temporibus diuinitus uisum est, nec prophetari destitit nec qui in eum crederent defuerunt ab Adam usque ad Moysen et in ipso populo Israhel, quae speciali quodam mysterio gens prophetica fuit, et in aliis gentibus, antequam uenisset in carne. cum enim nonnulli commemorantur in sanctis Hebraicis libris iam ex tempore Abrahae nec de stirpe carnis eius nec ex populo Israhel nec aduenticia societate in populo Israhel, qui tamen huius sacramenti participes fuerunt, cur non credamus etiam in ceteris hac atque illac gentibus alias alios fuisse, quamuis eos commemoratos in eisdem auctoritatibus non legamus? ita salus religionis huius, per quam solam ueram salus uera ueraciter que promittitur, nulli umquam defuit qui dignus fuit, et cui defuit dignus non fuit." Concerning providence, see *ep.* 102.13 (CCSL 31B:16).

37. *Ep.* 102.18–20 (CCSL 31B:19–21). See also *ciu.* 10.1 (CCSL 47:271–74) and 10.19 (CCSL 47:293–94).

Not even the lofty noetic *daimones* of Porphyry should receive true worship and sacrifice. True worship should only be offered to God. Therefore, while the sacrifices of the Old Testament under the Mosaic law were different, just as they were different from those offered before the Mosaic law, they were both congruent with the times of God's dispensation. Now at the initiation of "Christian times," the true sacrificial victim of the one priest has been furnished by the shedding of the blood of Christ. This is not a change in God or religion; rather, Augustine gives the example of the same individual offering a sacrifice in the morning and the evening both in accord with the appropriateness of the hour.[38]

Augustine's *Epistula* 102 significantly refines and develops his articulation—if not also his understanding—of the incarnation and its effects. Porphyry's objections drive at Augustine's very points of emphasis in *De consensu euangelistarum*. In his response to these six objections, Augustine continues to develop the implications of Christ as true priest and king, both universal and yet in the fullness of time in the incarnation. He stresses the universality of the "return" to God through Christ's sacrifice. He is, however, pressed in *Epistula* 102 to consider how this extends in both directions: before Christ in the worship and sacrifice of those not of Israel, and afterward in the resurrection. Despite these advances, Augustine has still not engaged Porphyry's own philosophy as it relates to his criticisms of Christianity. It is perhaps as a consequence of *Epistula* 102 that Augustine returns to Porphyry more pointedly around 411 CE.

Sermones 240–42

In a series of homilies given during Easter week of 411 CE, Augustine discussed the Christian teaching on the resurrection. His opponents in these homilies were the philosophers, specifically Porphyry. Augustine begins the first homily, Sermon 240, by stressing the same point he had made in *De consensu euangelistarum*: the four evangelists do not contradict one another.[39] This claim as well as much of the material in these homilies functions as a summary of *De consensu euangelistarum* and *Epistula* 102. Yet in these homilies, Augustine does not simply rehearse

---

38. *Ep.* 102.21 (CCSL 31B:21–22).

39. He is very likely referring to Porphyry when in *s.* 240.1 he says, "Some people have supposed that the Gospels contradict each other" (trans. is my own). Cf. PL 38:1130: "nonnulli enim putauerunt eos inter se esse contrarios."

his earlier explanations; he also addresses Porphyry's own system, including his beliefs regarding the soul and its fate.

Augustine turns directly to the philosophers, particularly the Platonists, who argued for the immortality of the soul. From their position concerning the soul, these philosophers speculated that the soul was embodied in the "prison" (*carcer animae*) of this body because of sins that occurred in a previous life. For the Platonists, these mortal and sensuous bodies were incurred through the desire for lesser things. Hence, after this mortal life, the wicked are returned to other bodies to pay the penalty for their previous life's evils. In contrast, the good ascend from these bodies to the highest heavens and forget every evil. Yet, through their splendid forgetfulness, these souls of the just, dwelling in the highest bodiless bliss, rekindle the desire to return to bodies so that they may once again experience the passions and sufferings of the physical world. As a result, the body is understood by these philosophers only as a vehicle for the descent of the soul into suffering. The body is always situated in relation to descent, desire, and suffering. In a similar way, these philosophers conceive of the highest bliss of the immortal soul only as an interval of rest between unending descents.

Augustine finds the solution of the philosophers to be absurd. In fact, Christianity remedies the difficulties that the philosophers are either unable or unwilling to overcome. For Augustine, there is no enduring temptation to "return" to bodies because, in bliss, in the fullness of beatitude, the body is resurrected. The final state of the soul is embodied. Moreover, the endless cycle of the falls and returns proposed by the philosophers is rejected in Christianity because of the work of Christ, who, as the mediator between God and humanity, effects through his divine power a complete solution. The divine as human restores us so that humanity may be uplifted into perfect blessedness.[40]

In the next homily, Sermon 241, Augustine reiterates another point made in *Epistula* 102. God was speaking to the philosophers through the works and beauty of the world. Though they had never received the Mosaic law, they were plainly shown the truth by God. Indeed, they erred, not because they did not know God, but because they *did* know yet still failed to glorify God. Through their inquiries into the soul and the body, the philosophers raised themselves up to God, but only in order to plunge God down into their own image or, as Augustine notes, the images of beasts and other idols.[41] Much of this recalls

40. S. 240.4–5 (PL 38:1132–33).
41. S. 241.1–3 (PL 38:1133–35).

Augustine's discussion of *latreia* and true worship in *Epistula* 102. However, what follows is a development of his earlier treatment.

Augustine first cites Virgil as a witness to the inconsistency of the notion that the souls of the blessed return—indeed, they long to return—to sluggish bodies. Beatitude should be complete enjoyment of intelligible reality, where the soul is forgetful of all things in the lower realms, especially of bodies. Why would the soul, forgetful of all lesser things, return to the physical body? For the philosophers Pythagoras, Plato, and Porphyry, the soul returns to the body because of its love of bodies.[42] The body, then, is the cause for the descent from the intelligible bliss of God; it is also a punishment caused by that very descent. Love of the body and even the body itself must be rejected.

The standard bearer for the philosophical necessity to disdain the body is Porphyry, whom alone Augustine quotes as a testimony of the claim. To introduce Porphyry's quote, Augustine for the first time describes Porphyry as "the most bitter enemy of the Christian faith" (*fidei christianae acerrimus inimicus*) and a philosopher who lived during "Christian times." It is from this anti-Christian, philosophical framing that Augustine quotes Porphyry's famous dictum: *corpus est omne fugiendum* (every kind of body must be shunned).[43]

In his previous treatments of Porphyry, Augustine had not used the phrase. He had already addressed pagans such as Porphyry who rejected the Christian conception of the resurrection of the body. Augustine, however, had made neither the philosopher's positive views nor negative advice part of his response to Porphyry's objections. His increased awareness of Porphyry's thought perhaps suggested to him an important insight that he will introduce in *De ciuitate dei*: Porphyry is the closest to and yet the most direct philosophical opponent of Christianity. He is an opponent who had not only lived in "Christian times," but who had also composed philosophical critiques of Christianity in his defense of intellectual paganism.

Seeing Porphyry as a supreme representative of the philosophical pagan position concerning the body, Augustine interprets "*corpus est omne fugiendum*" in light of the position that the body is an oppressive fetter (*aerumnosum uinculum*) for the soul. He continues to quote Porphyry as saying, "You have no grounds to praise the body to me; whatever sort of body it might be, if the soul wishes

---

42. S. 241.5–6 (PL 38:1135–37). Cf. Virgil, *Aeneid* 6.719–21 (LCL 63:582): "o pater, anne aliquas ad caelum hinc ire putandum est sublimis animas iterumque ad tarda reuerti corpora? quae lucis miseris tam dira cupido?"

43. S. 241.7 (PL 38:1137–38; trans. Hill, *Sermons 230–272B*, WSA III/7, 73–74).

to be happy, every kind of body is to be shunned."[44] The fuller quotation reveals more of Porphyry's claim. The beatitude of the soul is free from every kind of body. Hence the body, both originally and ultimately, is a hindrance to the full intellectual beatitude of the soul.

Augustine's reply affirms the beauty of the body, even now in its decay and mortality.[45] If the mortal body is beautiful, the resurrected body is even more magnificent; it will be immortal and imperishable, as well as swift and free in its movements.[46] The soul is not made to "float" in intellectual nothingness but to rule the body. To stress the possibilities of a perfected body, Augustine appeals to the philosophical notion of the World-Soul against Porphyry. The World-Soul is an animating principle or soul that governs the whole universe. For Platonists, such as Porphyry, the World-Soul always clings to God and yet is always bound to the eternally existing universe. While not committed to the Platonic notion of the World-Soul, Augustine argues that if in Porphyry's system the World-Soul is to find the highest bliss, then it must destroy the universe. Augustine comments, "You tell me I must run away from and shun my flesh; let your Jupiter (the World-Soul) run away from and shun heaven and earth." Rather than give into this strange inconsistency, Augustine asserts, "What I say is that blessed souls are always going to inhabit imperishable bodies."[47] Porphyry should have been open to this realization; not only is this evidenced in the Platonic notion of the World-Soul, but it was also asserted by Plato himself. In his *Timaeus*, Plato described the highest "deities" who are granted perpetual, though bodily, bliss.[48] All bodies are not to be shunned; not even the Platonists could reasonably hold this. The Christian extends this position to the human, avoiding the endless cycle of fall from God and intelligible bliss. As Augustine has asserted repeatedly—but this time against Porphyry's strong philosophical position—human perfection is realized in the resurrected body.

The last sermon in this sequence, Sermon 242, treats the resurrection of the body directly in relation to the resurrection of Christ. Christ has demonstrated

---

44. S. 241.7 (PL 38:1137; trans. Hill, WSA III/7, 73): "sed ait Porphyrius: 'sine causa mihi laudas corpus; qualecumque sit corpus, si uult esse beata anima, corpus est omne fugiendum.'"

45. In *s. 242A.3* (= *s. Mai 87* [*MA* 1:329–30]) Augustine repeatedly asks a hypothetical objector, "Why are you so offended by the body?" ("quid tibi in corpore displicet?"). The objector's response is similar to Porphyry's as found in *ep.* 102.

46. S. 241.7 (PL 38:1137; trans. Hill, WSA III/7, 73).

47. S. 241.7 (PL 38:1137–38; trans. Hill, WSA III/7, 74): "ego dico beatas animas incorruptibilia corpora semper habituras. tu qui dicis, 'corpus est omne fugiendum, occide mundum.' tu dicis ut fugiam de carne mea: fugiat Iupiter tuus de coelo et terra."

48. Plato, *Timaeus* 41B–C (LCL 234:88); cf. *s.* 241.8 (PL 38:1138).

what is promised to the Christian. He has shown that the resurrected body is not a spirit by displaying the firmness of the resurrected body (*soliditatem corporis*). Augustine even calls "carnal" those who reject the resurrected body and assume that Christ was only a "spirit" after the resurrection. The carnal do not understand anything beyond what they see. Hence, they limit God to their own imaginative framework. They must hold that even God could not make such a body as that one revealed by Christ in his resurrection. Augustine then returns to Porphyry's objection in *Epistula* 102 and explains why Christ ate and why he had scars.[49] His answer is identical to what he wrote some ten years earlier: Porphyry has a limited understanding of God's power.

Augustine concludes the sermon by treating the general objection of how a body might exist in heaven. He notes that Christ demonstrated the kind of body that will be possessed after the resurrection. The resurrected will have a body such that "where one wishes to be, when they wish it, they are there."[50] This body will be in perfect harmony with the soul; it will not be a spirit, but a "spiritual" body in the image of Christ's after his resurrection. The very reason Christ rose from the dead was for humanity. Augustine describes Christ's resurrection as a humiliation (*humiliatio*) carried out for the sake of his body—that is, the church. He did not need to rise in his divinity; he rose solely for humanity.[51]

This sequence of homilies makes it clear that by about 411 CE Augustine was reading Porphyry as a primary opponent of Christianity. Augustine has realized the separation of Christianity from Platonism, even from one as proximate as Porphyry. The body is not the problem for Augustine. Indeed, the very attempt to remove or flee from the body as Porphyry urges is to reject what Christ specifically offered to humanity in his own resurrection. Christ's resurrection was a humiliation undertaken for the sake of humanity, through which Christ offered the perfected body. To flee or shun the body is, as Augustine makes abundantly clear, to flee from Christ. Yet this does not mean that one simply scourges this mortal body. Just as Porphyry's reduction of Christ to a mere man is not resolved by simply asserting Christ's divinity, so too his call to shun every kind of body is not fully answered by the assertion of the perfection of the resurrected body. The effects of the incarnation of Christ as true priest and king, who offers true

---

49. S. 242.1–3 (PL 38:1139–40).

50. S. 242.5 (PL 38:1140; trans. Hill, WSA III/7, 79): "credere enim debemus talia corpora nos habituros, ut ubi uelimus, quando uoluerimus, ibi simus."

51. S. 242A.1 (= s. Mai 87 [MA 1:327]).

sacrifice in his humanity, are at the center of Augustine's response to Porphyry. This is why Augustine continues to stress the importance of these "Christian times." In a similar way, the perfection of the resurrected body points to what is offered to the human in this mortal life through Christ and his body, the church. In *De ciuitate dei* Augustine elaborates his understanding of this social vision, once again in relation to Porphyry.

DE CIUITATE DEI

More than other figures, Porphyry stands as the primary opponent and, at times, as interlocutor through large portions of *De ciuitate dei*, especially in books 9, 10, 19, and 22. In responding to Porphyry, Augustine restates many of his claims from *Epistula* 102 and *Sermones* 240–42. He also greatly advances his treatment of Porphyry with direct quotations—some of which are quite extensive—drawn from *Philosophy from Oracles*, *Letter to Anebo*, and *De regressu animae*.

Augustine's engagement with Porphyry builds through books 8 and 9 to a crescendo in book 10. In book 10 Augustine takes up and qualifies Porphyry's claim that there is no universal way for the return of the soul, a claim that is nearly identical in substance to the objection Porphyry raised in *Epistula* 102 concerning salvation before Christ. Augustine writes:

> When, near the end of the first book of *On the Return of the Soul*, Porphyry says that no view containing a universal way of the soul's liberation has as yet been received into any specific philosophical school—not from any supremely true philosophy, not from the morals and practice of the Indians, not from the initiations of the Chaldeans, nor from any other way—and that no such way has as yet come to his knowledge from his historical inquiries, he acknowledges beyond any doubt that there is such a way, but it has not yet come to his knowledge.[52]

---

52. *Ciu.* 10.32 (CCSL 47:309–10; trans. Babcock, WSA I/6, 344): "cum autem dicit Porphyrius in primo iuxta finem de regressu animae libro nondum receptum in unam quondam sectam, quod uniuersalem contineat uiam animae liberandae, uel a philosophia uerissima aliqua uel ab Indorum moribus ac disciplina, aut inductione chaldaeorum aut alia qualibet uia, nondumque in suam notitiam eandem uiam historiali cognitione perlatam: procul dubio confitetur esse aliquam, sed nondum in suam uenisse notitiam."

Augustine observes that Porphyry admitted that there is a universal way, but that he had not found it. Augustine then turns the objection from *Epistula* 102, the one concerning salvation before Christ to those outside Israel, against Porphyry. Porphyry wanted to divide humanity by nation or group. In effect, he was blinded by his desire for there not to be a universal way. Augustine challenges Porphyry by asking him what he might have discovered had he searched for a way that was "divinely imparted not as the exclusive property of any one people but as the common property of all peoples?"[53]

In his reformulation of Porphyry's claims in *De ciuitate dei*, Augustine has united his criticism of the philosopher's tepid claim about a universal way with his commitment to divine providence. Porphyry was firmly committed to the Platonic notion of providence (a detail noted by Augustine in both *ep.* 102 and *ss.* 240–42). According to Augustine, Porphyry was also the Platonic philosopher who came closest to having a notion of grace. Porphyry claimed that the intellectual end of beatitude has been "granted" by God to only a few.[54] Therefore, Porphyry must not hold that "divine providence could have left humanity without such a universal way of the soul's liberation."[55] Why then does he seem to think that God's providence did not secure such a way, and why does he think that God provided it to so few?

Augustine identifies several factors that led Porphyry to his pessimistic philosophy. The first is that Porphyry was afraid of being persecuted as Christians were. For Porphyry, persecution was a sign of failure—that is, of bad philosophy. The second is that Porphyry viewed the majority of people as unequipped or unwilling to pursue the life of the intellect. For these commoners there is local and civic piety, a low form of justice, and perhaps an ascent attained through virtue, such as Porphyry allows for Christ. For others there is the mediation offered through theurgic rites or other means of spiritual purification. However, for both of these groups— excluding those who are simply wicked—the highest end of blessedness is not attained. Thus, as Gillian Clark has observed, Porphyry's theology is bound by the limits of his philosophy. It is elitist and the highest end is rarely attained.[56]

---

53. *Ciu.* 10.32 (CCSL 47:310): "quaenam ista est uniuersalis uia, nisi quae non suae cuique genti propria, sed uniuersis gentibus quae communis esset diuinitus inpertita est?"

54. *Ciu.* 10.29 (CCSL 47:304–5).

55. *Ciu.* 10.32 (CCSL 47:310; trans. Babcock, WSA I/6, 345): "prouidentiam quippe diuinam sine ista uniuersali uia liberandae animae genus humanum relinquere potuisse non credit."

56. Gillian Clark, "Augustine's Porphyry and the Universal Way of Salvation," in Karamanolis and Sheppard, *Studies on Porphyry*, 127–40, esp. 139–40; cf. Smith, *Porphyry's Place in the Neoplatonic Tradition*.

As in *Epistula* 102, Augustine's response to Porphyry centers on the universality of Christ's sacrifice, which is offered by Christ as both priest and oblation. Augustine writes that Christianity is the "universal way of the soul's liberation, that is, the way granted by divine mercy to all peoples."[57] For Augustine, God acts on behalf of the weak, the wicked, and even the intellectual philosopher. Thus, even the highest blessedness is obtained for every nation and every kind of individual through Christ.

Augustine also deepens his understanding of a second dimension of Porphyry's philosophy: his rejection of the body. Here, as in Sermon 242, Augustine quotes Porphyry's dictum "*omne corpus fugiendum est.*" Augustine restates answers he has already rehearsed concerning the incorruptible and immortal resurrected body, the virgin birth, and even the intra-Platonic point about the body of the World-Soul. More directly than he did in Sermon 242, Augustine asks, "Why do you persist in the opinion that, for us to be happy, we must flee from all bodies? Why do you persist in this opinion, trying to make it look as though you have rational grounds for fleeing from the Christian faith?"[58] The answer is simply pride (*superbia*).

While he strongly criticizes Porphyry, Augustine has also come to realize—perhaps through his preparation for composing *De ciuitate dei* book 10—that the philosopher was willing to diverge from his fellow Platonists on several positions. Porphyry possessed a strong commitment to the notion of divine mediation, though, for Porphyry, this is the activity not of the One but of the lofty *daimones*, gods, or "angels," as Augustine calls them. These lower "divine" entities aid humans in their spiritual ascent. Because of his distinct conception of the soul at three levels or modalities—the intellectual, the spiritual, and as extended into the corporeal body—Porphyry was able to place a clear limit on the mediation or aid that these lower "divine" *daimones* may effect. They may aid in the purification of the lower "spiritual" soul, which is the best possible end for most of humanity. Porphyry attributed to the One only the loftiest purification of the intellectual soul.

Perhaps even more impressive to Augustine is Porphyry's willingness to depart from Plato. Porphyry denied the reincarnation of souls into animal bodies. Hu-

---

57. *Ciu.* 10.32 (CCSL 47:311; trans. Babcock, WSA I/6, 345): "haec est igitur animae liberandae uniuersalis uia, id est uniuersis gentibus diuina miseratione concessa."

58. *Ciu.* 10.29 (CCSL 47:306; trans. Babcock, WSA I/6, 340): "quid est quod, ut beati simus, omne corpus fugiendum esse opinamini, ut fidem Christianum quasi rationabiliter fugere uideamini."

mans will return only as humans.[59] Porphyry also rejected the perpetual descent and ascent of souls, a difficulty Augustine identified in Sermon 241. However, he had not previously discussed Porphyry's distinctive position. In *De ciuitate dei* 10.30 Augustine quotes Porphyry as writing, "God put the soul into the world so that, having come to recognize the evils of matter, it might return to the Father and never again be held down in the defiling pollution of such things."[60] According to Augustine, Porphyry has thus done away with one of the principal features of Platonism—namely, "that just as the dead come from the living, so the living always come from the dead."[61] Porphyry even exposes the falsehood of Virgil, who, following Plato, asserted that the blessed become forgetful so that they may once more desire to inhabit a mortal body.[62] Alone among the philosophers, Porphyry rejects the Platonic notion that beatitude entailed a longing for renewed defilement, such that "supreme happiness will turn out to be the cause of unhappiness, and perfect wisdom the cause of foolishness, and supreme purity the cause of impurity."[63] Porphyry, Augustine avers, values truth more than the man Plato.

Augustine has also discovered Porphyry's distinction of the soul into three aspects, the intellectual, the spiritual, and as extension into the physical body. In book 10 of *De ciuitate dei*, Augustine glosses Porphyry's distinctions in light of several of the topics discussed above. For example, Augustine writes of Christ's universal and efficacious sacrifice: "This way cleanses the whole man and prepares mortal man for immortality in all his constituent parts. In fact, it was precisely so that there would be no need to seek out one purification for the part which Porphyry calls intellectual, another for the part which he calls spiritual, and yet another for the body itself."[64]

---

59. *Ciu.* 10.30 (CCSL 47:307). For a qualification, see Andrew Smith, "Did Porphyry Reject the Transmigration of Human Souls into Animals?," *Rheinisches Museum für Philologie* 127, no. 3/4 (1984): 276–84.

60. *Ciu.* 10.30 (CCSL 47:307; trans. Babcock, WSA I/6, 342): "dicit etiam ad hoc deum animam mundo dedisse, ut materiae cognoscens mala ad patrem recurreret nec aliquando iam talium polluta contagion teneretur."

61. *Ciu.* 10.30 (CCSL 47:307): "ut mortuos ex uiuis, ita uiuos ex mortuis semper fieri."

62. Virgil, *Aeneid* 6.750–51 (LCL 63:584): "scilicet immemores super aut conuexa reuisant rursus, et incipient in corpora uelle reuerti." This is drawn directly from Augustine's criticism in *s.* 241.4–5 (PL 38:1135–36).

63. *Ciu.* 10.30 (CCSL 47:308; trans. Babcock, WSA I/6, 342): "profecto erit infelicitatis causa summa felicitas et stultitiae causa perfectio sapientiae et inmunditiae causa summa mundatio."

64. *Ciu.* 10.32 (CCSL 47:312; trans. Babcock, WSA I/6, 346–47): "haec uia totum homi-

For Augustine, Christ as the universal way of return solves many of the difficulties of Porphyry's system. He is able to keep Porphyry's division of the human as explanatory without the enduring division of humanity into different statuses. The sacrifice of Christ in his very flesh purifies at each level. The whole human is restored and uplifted, not just the lofty intellectual soul. Moreover, Augustine observes that this sacrifice is offered and shared in the Eucharist, as he makes clear in book 10. Hence, it is universal, localized, and effective for the purification and uplifting of the whole human.

Built and sharpened through a range of prior works, Augustine's accomplishment in book 10 of *De ciuitate dei* is the result of his prolonged engagement with Porphyry. The Christian confession concerning Christ as truly God and truly human, high priest and king, offering the complete sacrifice of himself for humanity functions as a complex response to Porphyry. Augustine articulates how he himself conceives of religion: not as an elite, individualistic endeavor, which brackets off the highest end to just a few and merely nods at public and cultic piety. By contrast, Augustine conceives of Christianity as a binding in Christ of the whole human, indeed of the whole *ciuitas dei*, effected through God's action in time.

Thus, in book 10 Augustine has diagnosed Porphyry's broader philosophical system and its valuation of religion. He responds to the tendency to exalt the individual—particularly the intellectual soul—while relegating both the physical body and society to a remedial level of meaning. It is this social dimension that drives Augustine to return to Porphyry in book 19 of *De ciuitate dei*.

In book 19 Augustine's analysis comes full circle to *De consensu euangelistarum*. Augustine addresses at length Porphyry's interpretation of several oracles about Christ. At first glance, it is not apparent how Porphyry's treatment of Christ relates to Augustine's emphasis on a true *societas* joined by true justice or a common understanding of right (*ius*).[65] Yet, in the context of book 19, it appears that Augustine has become convinced that Porphyry's process of commentary on oracles concerning Christ is linked to the philosopher's broader social thinking. Through his use of oracles, Porphyry is not simply mocking or relegating Christ to a lower *daimon*. He is rejecting the implications of the incarnation, par-

---

nem mundat et inmortalitati mortalem ex omnibus quibus constat partibus praeparat. ut enim non alia purgatio ei parti quaereretur, quam uocat intellectualem Porphyrius, alia ei, quam uocat spiritalem, aliaque ipsi corpori." I have omitted the important reference to the three types of vision in book 12 of *Gen. litt.* (CSEL 28/1:379–435), composed ca. 414 CE—after Augustine seems to have encountered Porphyry's distinctions.

65. *Ciu.* 19.21 (CCSL 48:688).

ticularly the society unified around the true worship of one sacrifice. Augustine perceives Porphyry's rejection of Christ's divinity, the church, and Christianity as a proposal for a different social order. This proposal, he argues, possesses no true "society" and has no common *res* uniting humanity; hence, it is one that is constituted not of a populace but of individuals.[66]

By the time that he composes book 19, Augustine has clearly expanded and deepened his reading of Porphyry. In *De consensu euangelistarum* he had used Porphyry as a check against repudiations of Christ. In book 19 he has collected several of Porphyry's discussions of Christ from his *Philosophy from Oracles*. He now asserts that Porphyry's use of oracles in order to "snatch" Christ from the Christians is not simply an attempt to relegate Christ to a human who ascended to a lower divine being. Rather, it is a complex rejection of the importance of the body, the *societas* of humanity bound by God in worship of God, and the belief that God, the high God, acts in time to effect such an end.

Porphyry's argument is a defense of the status quo of the Roman Empire and of Roman religion. Cultic piety should be maintained in its variances. The One needs no worship, no sacrifice, but only a good life lived in virtue. A Roman justice, which could be as easily translated to an imperial justice of Greece or Assyria, determines what justice unites society. Porphyry's philosophical justice hovers above this justice, above the material world in the ether of intellectual ascent. Instead of sacrifice to the one God, a sacrifice that the Christian holds is offered in Christ and, hence, forms the church in this sacrifice, Porphyry permits—even argues for—obedience and sacrifice to Rome, to the lower and higher *daimones*, but not to the high God. Porphyry's higher end of religion has been individualized and reified. Religion as social and localized is an important concern, though it is utterly separated from the highest aims of the intellectual soul. It is Christianity that risks wedding the lofty One with the physical world. It is unsurprising that Augustine has judged Porphyry to be not merely a strong critic of Christianity but also a true servant of Rome.

Conclusion

By the end of his career, Augustine developed such respect for Porphyry as a philosopher that he doubted that the questions to which he responded in *Epistula*

---

66. *Ciu.* 19.23 (CCSL 48:694–95).

102 could have actually been Porphyry's.[67] Augustine's suspicion is rather dubious. When he quotes from *Epistula* 102 in *De praedestinatione sanctorum* (*praed. sanct.*), shortly after completing his *Retractationes,* Augustine simply refers to these objections as from Porphyry. Nevertheless, both references indicate the significance of Porphyry. As the *Retractationes* suggests, Augustine continued to hold Porphyry in high regard, even if as a bitter opponent. His citation of *Epistula* 102 in *De praedestinatione sanctorum* reveals why Porphyry possessed such enduring importance for Augustine.

In a letter that prompted him to write *De praedestinatione sanctorum,* Augustine was asked to explain his statement from *Epistula* 102 that "Christ willed to appear to human beings and willed that his teaching be preached when he knew and where he knew that there would be people who would believe in him."[68] Augustine defends how his comment from *Epistula* 102 does not disagree with his articulation of the grace of perseverance by quoting the letter at length.[69] Yet in Augustine's explanation we perceive the development in his own understanding of grace.[70] We also observe the importance of Augustine's engagement with Porphyry.

Augustine views Porphyry as a most important philosopher because he possesses so many affinities to Christianity. This is not to claim that Plato, Plotinus, or other philosophers are unimportant. However, Porphyry's philosophy treats mediation, prophecy, religion, public piety, and the salvation of the soul in a manner that engages Christianity. Pierre Courcelle seems on firm ground when he claims that *De ciuitate dei* is *in toto* a response and plea to Porphyrians.[71] Certainly, Porphyry is incredibly important in Augustine's work between 404 and 424 CE. Porphyry's thought and writings work their way into every genre of Au-

---

67. *Retr.* 2.31 (CCSL 57:115–16). Most modern scholars disagree with Augustine's assessment. See, e.g., Isabelle Bochet, "The Role of Scripture in Augustine's Controversy with Porphyry," *AugStud* 41, no. 1 (2010): 7–52, esp. 11–16.

68. *Letter of Hilary* 3 (CSEL 57:471; trans. Teske, *Answer to the Pelagians IV,* WSA I/26, lxix): "quod dixit sanctitas tua in quaestione contra Porphyrium de tempore Christianae religionis: 'tunc uoluisse hominibus apparere Christum et apud eos praedicari doctrinam suam, quando sciebat et ubi sciebat esse, qui in eum fuerant credituri.'"

69. *Praed. sanct.* 9.17–10.19 (BA 24:515–25).

70. See J. Patout Burns, *The Development of Augustine's Doctrine of Operative Grace* (Paris: Études Augustiniennes, 1980), 162–81.

71. Pierre Courcelle, *Late Latin Writers and their Greek Sources,* trans. Harry Wedeck (Cambridge, MA: Harvard University Press, 1969), 181.

gustine's writings, even his homilies. Moreover, Augustine returns several times to reread and even draw from new writings of Porphyry. He clearly understood the philosopher to be more than an opponent, as he incorporated even more of Porphyry's thought than this chapter has been able to show. Augustine returns to Porphyry (and at times Porphyry is brought to him for reply); as a result we see how his own thought develops. We clearly see this in the culmination of *De ciuitate dei* as Augustine diagnoses Porphyry's system for both its individual and its social implications. While there is certainly more to Porphyry's thought than Augustine knew, and more to Augustine's theology than his responses to Porphyry reveal, Augustine's engagement with Porphyry and the intellectual paganism he represents is of crucial importance for understanding Augustine.

Chapter 8

Augustine and the End of Classical Ethics

James R. Wetzel

Prelude

Consider two very different memorials to a grief. One comes from Cicero, the other from Augustine.

First Cicero. The year 45 BCE is a wounding time for Cicero, the eloquent but ultimately ineffectual defender of the Roman Senate and Republican values. He has already arrived at the beginning of his political end when he backs Pompey against Caesar in the Roman civil war and Caesar roundly defeats Pompey at the Battle of Pharsalus in August of 48 BCE. Cicero finds himself, in the delicate years to follow, a Republican without a Republic. In mid-February of 45 BCE, his political destitution gets reframed by personal loss: his beloved daughter Tullia dies in childbirth at the family estate at Tusculum; her newborn son is soon to follow. Cicero withdraws brokenhearted into mournful seclusion and remains out of politics long enough to begin to alarm his good friend and frequent correspondent Atticus, who worries about the rumor mill in and around Rome, the times being what they are—precarious. (And Cicero will indeed suffer a very violent end.)

Cicero reassures his friend that he has not simply been languishing. He has taken up philosophy, the contemplative alternative to politics, and the result has been a devoted, if also distracting, outpouring of philosophical writings. This includes what he describes to Atticus as a literary effort at self-consolation: "My grief defeats all consolation, but still," he tells Atticus, "I have done what surely no one has before: I have consoled myself through writing [*per litteras*]."[1] The idea of a book of consolation that takes the form of self-consolation, where one is for a time both within one's grief and on the outside looking in, fits well the conception of philosophy that Cicero articulates near the beginning of book 3 of the *Tusculan Disputations* (*Tusc.*), written a scant six months after Tullia's death. There, Cicero tries to think of grief (*aegritudo*) strictly as a malady of mind (*animus*) and of philosophy as mind-cure. Even more strikingly, he tries to think of the diseased mind as a self-healer, able from the murky depths of mental distress to remember and become one with its own inalienable sanity.[2]

From the evidence of the letters, the physician, in Cicero's case, fails to heal himself. While Cicero does manage to find distraction in literary pursuits and writerly self-portraiture, none of this brings him lasting peace of mind. In the *Consolatio*, the specific work of self-consolation that is now largely lost to us, Cicero moves from massaging his grief to subliming his loss: he entertains the idea of divinizing his deceased daughter.[3] He intends this to be more than a mind game. In a letter to Atticus, dated March 11 of 45 BCE, Cicero asks his friend, somewhat circumspectly (he knows the request is unusual, even suspect), for help with finding a suitable location for a shrine to Tullia, whose immortal virtue, evident in life and consecrated in death, he imagines will earn her cult. A father's love gone on holiday? Let us add to the picture these words from *Tusc.*, drawn from book 3, the book of grief, the part where Cicero ponders, briefly, the proportions of loving those we hold dear:

---

1. *Att.* 251, 12.14.3 (LCL 97:280–83): "sed omnem consolationem uincit dolor. quin etiam feci, quod profecto ante me nemo, ut ipse me per litteras consolarer."

2. *Tusc.* 3.3.5–6 (LCL 141:228–31). For a complete and much more recent translation of books 3 and 4 as well as a commentary, see Margaret Graver, *Cicero on the Emotions: Tusculan Disputations 3 and 4* (Chicago: University of Chicago Press, 2002). The translations of the Latin in this chapter—both Cicero's and Augustine's—are my own, but I have consulted Graver for Cicero as well as both *Confessions*, trans. Sarah Ruden (New York: Modern Library, 2017), and *Confessions*, trans. Henry Chadwick (Oxford: Oxford University Press, 1991), for Augustine.

3. The divinization passage shows up in Lactantius. For both the reference and a fuller account, see the introduction to Spencer Cole, *Cicero and the Rise of Deification at Rome* (Cambridge: Cambridge University Press, 2013). Cole makes the case for the part Cicero's text played in "a distinctly Roman contribution to divinization."

It is a lustrous thing and, if you look into it, a thing also right and true that we should love as much as we love ourselves those who claim our affections most. More than that is not doable. In friendship it is not even desirable that my friend love me more than himself or I him more than me. If such were the case, it would be the disordering of life and all of its proper offices.[4]

The sentiment here reads less like an inducement to selfishness than a sober caution against subliming a beloved and confusing love with craving and self-abasement. Have we left, then, the orbit of Tullia's deification? Cicero writes this to Atticus, out of another kind of caution, on May 5 of the same year: "You urge me not to sink into sorrow; you will do much to lift me up if you furnish me with a site for the shrine. Many things occur to me about what makes for divinity, but my crying need is for a site."[5]

Now Augustine. When Augustine is still a young and willing student of desire, in love with love and fully loosed upon the city of Carthage, his self-described "skillet" (*sartago*) of sexual indiscretions, he comes across the work, as he puts it, "of a certain Cicero" (*cuiusdam Ciceronis*).[6] Of course, as an aspiring speechmaker, eager for the recognition that buys him out of hometown life and transports him to mythical places, like Carthage and Rome, Augustine is already well familiar with Cicero; in fact, the work to which Augustine alludes—Cicero's *Hortensius*—has become, centuries after Cicero's death, a traditional part of a late Roman rhetor's curriculum. It is hardly a surprise that Augustine would have come across it. Still, there is a sense in which this particular Cicero, the Cicero of the *Hortensius,* can be fairly thought of as new and unfamiliar to the young Augustine, then in his nineteenth year. The *Hortensius,* a work of exhortation, draws deep from the well of Cicero's grief over Tullia; it is his spirited defense, set against the cynicism of Roman realpolitik, of philosophy's essential place in the architecture of human happiness. Augustine will have encountered in the *Hortensius* a Cicero who seems disillusioned with the very goods—worldly and

4. *Tusc.* 3.29.73 (LCL 141:310–11): "praeclarum illud est et, si quaeris, rectum quoque et uerum, ut eos, qui nobis carissimi esse debeant, aeque ac nosmet ipsos amemus; ut uero plus, fieri nullo pacto potest. ne optandum quidem est in amicitia, ut me ille plus quam se, ego illum plus quam me; perturbatio uitae, si ita sit, atque officiorum omnium consequatur."

5. *Att.* 277, 12.37a (LCL 97:336–37): "quod me a maestitia <a>uocas, multum leuaris si locum fano dederis. multa mihi εἰς ἀποθέωσιν in mentem ueniunt, sed loco ualde opus est."

6. *Conf.* 3.4.7. My source for the Latin of *conf.* is James J. O'Donnell, *Augustine: Confessions,* vol. 1, *Introduction and Text* (Oxford: Clarendon, 1992). For 3.4.7, see 25.

divisive—that Augustine has, up to this point in his desire-rich adolescence, been looking to Cicero to help fund.

Augustine describes his encounter with "a certain Cicero" as having changed his "affect" (*affectum*). There are other ways to translate *affectus* in this context. Henry Chadwick, a well-tried translator of the *Confessiones* (*conf.*), goes for feeling, and more than one: "The book changed my feelings."[7] Sarah Ruden, newer to Augustine but a gifted translator of Latin literature, prefers dispositional language: "That work did renovate my attitude."[8] The problem with both of these translations is that they suggest more of a transformation in Augustine (in Ruden's version, a full-on conversion) than Augustine himself is prepared to remember. Cicero certainly seems to have evoked in him new desire, sublime and obscure, for the love of wisdom, and, as a result, his heart catches fire.[9] But he is already used to the heartburn of desiring desire and to noticing only the acrid aftereffects of a beloved's inevitable eclipse. Why would a desire for a sublimer desire, for the sublimest desire of all, be any different? If I give myself over to a desire for *the desire* of wisdom, the way that Augustine, the lover of being in love, professes to, I will be more apt to disavow wisdom than to claim it. That sounds good; it even sounds like humility, unless of course I am not giving myself even the chance to be satisfied. Then my desire is not humble at all; it is armor.

If we translate Augustine as having had his affect changed—not so much his range of feelings or his disposition toward what he takes it to be good to want—we risk picking up affect's connotation of artifice or inauthenticity. If I am affected or indulging in affectation, I am being false. I veil my true self from others, for better or for worse, but in either case for the love of dramatic effect. Along these lines, it is just too easy to envision the eighteen-year-old footloose in Carthage, giving himself over to a great orator's gallows nobility, but detaching it from raw fear of death and shame of survival and entering imaginatively into the romance of a world-despising quest. All of this would be happening to Augustine as he continues to pay good money for the development of his oratorical skills and leans on his mother for help with his tuition. His father, who in life relished the thought of his son's worldly advancement through the persuasive arts, will have already been dead for several years, but not before being able to foresee that his eldest son and heir, having arrived at the precipice

---

7. *Confessions*, trans. Chadwick, 39.
8. *Confessions*, trans. Ruden, 57.
9. *Conf.* 3.4.8 (O'Donnell, 1:25–26).

of a burgeoning sexual desire, would soon father a child of his own.[10] Augustine and his lover—the great unnamed presence in *Confessiones*—conceive together what will turn out to be their son, Adeodatus ("God's Gift"), right around the time Augustine is acclimating to Carthage and discovering his inner philosopher among his other adolescent enthusiasms. It is hard not to conclude, and I do not resist this conclusion, that there is an element of affectation or pretense in Augustine's philosophical persona. But I do not take him to be faking philosophy. That would presume that there is something closer to the bone and thus more authentic that he could be doing.

Augustine does not tell us much about the circumstances of his son's death. Adeodatus dies within about a year of their return from the family's Italian sojourn, a period of years that has stripped Augustine both of his partner in the flesh (she returns, without him, to Africa) and his mother, the self-appointed guardian of his prodigal spirit (she was buried in Ostia). Adeodatus, at the time of his death, is around Augustine's age when Augustine became a father. But Augustine takes himself to be memorializing a son who is markedly different from his paternal alter ego, different, that is, from the seventeen-year-old who enters into a pact of (he hopes) conception-free sex with a woman who, though not his lawful spouse, will end up being his one and only intimate for some thirteen years—until he sends her away.[11] "Born of me, carnally, from my sin": this is how Augustine in retrospect pairs the son and the paternal alter ego.[12] What unsettles here is the proximity of sin to procreation. Apart from sexual transgression (*praeter delictum*), Augustine claims to have had no part in the boy. "You were the one who had made him good," he tells God. And so, what does that leave for transgression? If God is fathering the goodness of the boy, all of it, Augustine is relieved of his paternity and, in a really dispiriting way, no longer has a son to mourn.

But this cannot be right. When Augustine insists on dissociating his son from his father's sin, from a legacy of solipsistic sexual desire, he is not disavowing Adeodatus and stigmatizing himself; he is gratefully accepting forgiveness. It is precisely because he is still so deeply connected to the boy that the maker of all of us, "able to shape what is misshapen in us" (*potens formare nostra deformia*),

10. *Conf.* 2.3.6 (O'Donnell, 1:17–18).
11. *Conf.* 4.2.2 (O'Donnell, 1:33); cf. *conf.* 6.15.25 (O'Donnell, 1:71).
12. *Conf.* 9.6.14 (O'Donnell, 1:108): "ex me natum carnaliter de peccato meo."

can, through the love of a beloved son, remake Augustine.[13] The passage in *Confessiones* that Augustine uses to memorialize Adeodatus—*Confessiones* 9.6.14—is strikingly short and remarkably free of the self-mortification that tends to infiltrate his longer descriptions of a grieving process. It suffices for Augustine to recall about the dialogue *De magistro* (*mag.*)—a dialogue had with Adeodatus shortly before his death—that he did not invent his son's voice. A dialogue dedicated to words and how properly to learn from them might have given Augustine, the master rhetor, scope for just such a preemption. But love does not invent its beloved. There is always something unbidden, something undeniable, in the love that runs contrary to plan. Even the seventeen-year-old had a sense of this truth, *in nuce*, while still in the fog of a new sexual adventure. Here is Augustine hinting at an unbidden, but undeniable, gift of sex: "Along with her, I learned directly from experience what the difference is between a wedding bond, sealed for the sake of bringing new life into being, and a pact of licentious love, steeled against progeny—although once born, the child compels love."[14]

The baby boy whose new flesh interrupts sexual desire and evokes parental love grows up to become flesh that talks, and his father wants us to remember the distancing things about his son: that he is not the product of his father's desire, that he is not the echo of his father's voice. The boy is not his father, never was, and therein lies the father's consolation, in that fecund abyss.

A TRIPTYCH OF LOSS

There are two sublimings of a beloved here, and they speak to two different experiences of loss.

Cicero wants the stellar version of his daughter. Tullia is to be posthumously situated in the empyrean as the paragon of virtue, sublime and impregnably self-contained, as virtue itself essentially is. Consider a few choice words of Cicero's on the nature of virtue. In this part of *Tusculan Disputations*, he imagines himself advancing the Stoic view of virtue against Epicurus, the venerable but (to

13. *Conf.* 9.6.14 (O'Donnell, 1:108).

14. *Conf.* 4.2.2 (O'Donnell, 1:33): "in qua sane experirer exemplo meo quid distaret inter coniugalis placiti modum, quod foederatum esset generandi gratia, et pactum libidinosi amoris, ubi proles etiam contra uotum nascitur, quamuis iam nata cogat se diligi."

Cicero's mind) un-Roman sage who looks to nature for pleasure, not constancy. The Stoic view of virtue is Cicero's ideal, if not quite his conviction:

> What will you say to wisdom [*prudentiae*] when she teaches you that virtue is itself the content of the life well lived and so lived happily? If virtue were tied and bound to external things and did not emerge from itself, return to itself, and seek to embrace nothing but itself, I fail to understand why it would seem so worthy of extravagant praise or worth the arduous work of pursuing.[15]

It is unlikely that Cicero ever finds his desired site for enshrining Tullia's virtues. There is the obstacle of his enemies, the agents of Mark Antony who are out to get him, as they eventually do, for his defamation of their commander in the *Philippics* and his incautious praise of Caesar's assassins. There is also the obstacle that is closer to home. If virtue speaks to the self-sufficient self, the self that is contaminated by the mere externality of sources of value, then a shrine to virtue would be at best a memorial to what virtue excludes: a concern for fame and a life larger than life.

Cicero insists near the end of his book on grief that the pain of grief (*aegritudo*) is fueled by false belief, the belief, in this case, that the loss of a beloved has to be self-rending; for this is what love, when construed as an intimate form of attachment, seems to demand. Correct the belief, cut off the fuel, and the pain ends—for the most part. There remains, Cicero concedes, an involuntary bite (*morsus*) of grief, one that compels the mind to recoil from pain and shrink into itself.[16] While he is adamant about not calling this kind of self-shrinkage

---

15. *Tusc.* 3.17.37 (LCL 141:270–71): "prudentiae uero quid respondebis docenti uirtutem sese esse contentam quo modo ad bene uiuendum, sic etiam ad beate? quae si extrinsecus religata pendeat et non et oriatur a se et rursus ad se reuertatur et omnia sua complexa nihil quaerat aliunde, non intelligo cur aut uerbis tam uehementer ornanda aut re tanto opere expetenda uideatur." I follow Graver in taking *uirtus* and not *prudentia* to be the subject of the conditional sentence.

16. Here Cicero is invoking the Stoic doctrine of the pre-passions (*propatheiai*), or less than fully fledged emotions that disrupt but do not corrupt a sage's essentially passion-free disposition. I have written elsewhere about this doctrine and Augustine's reception of it. See esp. "Augustine: Prodigal Heart," in *The Oxford Handbook of Religion and Emotion*, ed. John Corrigan (Oxford: Oxford University Press, 2008), 349–63. Cf. Richard Sorabji, *Emotion and Peace of Mind: From Stoic Agitation to Christian Temptation* (Oxford: Oxford University Press, 2000), 373–417, and Sarah Byers, "Augustine and the Cognitive Cause of the Stoic Preliminary Passions," *Journal of the History of Philosophy* 41, no. 4 (2003): 433–48.

grief—"a name for what cannot co-exist and, so to speak, share a home with wisdom"[17]—he has no way to distinguish virtuous self-sufficiency from involuntary self-shrinkage without passing through a memory of real, self-rending sorrow. And properly to pass through that memory is, for Cicero, to evacuate sorrow of content and render the remaining husk of feeling an empty signifier, devoid of significance: "All grief is far removed from the wise person, being that it is empty, that it is a pointless experience, that it has its source not in nature but in judgment, in opinion, in a certain call to grief that comes whenever we resolve that grieving is called for."[18] Cicero resolves not to know what he feels. His bite of grief, like his shrine to Tullia, is always going to be impossible for him to locate. For when he arrives there, where love and loss meet and meet without evasion, he is determined not be the person who can recognize the place.

When Augustine brackets his own paternity and leaves the fathering of Adeodatus largely to God, I do not read him to be rendering his dead son into a paragon of virtue. The implication of his pious self-deprecation is not that Adeodatus, unlike all other sons but one, manages to slip out from under original sin and enter into this laborious life of ours unburdened by a father's shortcomings; it is that Adeodatus lives and dies as God's beloved. The boy, his mortal father assures us, is safe: "You have plucked his life from the earth early, and I am all the more untroubled in my memory of him, fearing nothing from his boyhood or teenage years, or from anything having to do with his person [*nec omnino homini illi*]."[19]

If we care to wonder about what makes Augustine so sure of his son's sanctity, the answer is probably somewhere in the neighborhood of this: that he cannot imagine God's love of the boy being *less* than his own. Adeodatus seems to have gotten the point. At the end of a long and meandering dialogue, mostly on the theme of the limitation of words for conveying shared understanding, he draws an unexpected, but not undiscerning, moral: while words are always imperfectly revelatory, even of a speaker's thoughts, they prompt us to turn to the divine teacher within, who alone renders human interiority into a learning space (*eum*

---

17. *Tusc.* 3.34.83 (LCL 141:324–25): "quod cum sapientia esse atque, ut ita dicam, habitare nullo modo possit."

18. *Tusc.* 3.34.82 (LCL 141:322–23): "aegritudinem omnem procul abesse a sapiente, quod inanis sit, quod frustra suscipiatur, quod non natura exoriatur, sed iudicio, sed opinione, sed quadam inuitatione ad dolendum, cum id decreuerimus ita fieri oportere."

19. *Conf.* 9.6.14 (O'Donnell, 1:109): "cito de terra abstulisti uitam eius, et securior eum recordor non timens quicquam pueritiae nec adulescentiae nec omnino homini illi."

docere solum, qui se intus habitare) and who evokes there the love that nudges us, without violence, back into a world that is always wider than words.[20] The boy, for all his father's rhetorical excesses and libidinal distractions, clearly feels loved. The love courses through his being, reconciling his life's interiority with its extroversion, or perhaps relieving him of the very need for that distinction.

Two losses, two sublimings. How do we take the measure of the difference?

Imagine an ideal of subjectivity—the sort that makes for a sage or a saint—cast in the language of form and matter. Let the material part, as uninformed, represent the chaotic reserve of selfhood, or, more precisely, the liability of a well-formed self, a virtuous self, either to lose its form to adventitious forces, like the onset of a mental disease, or, more mysteriously, to give into a power of self-undoing—as when a virtuous self intentionally picks vice over virtue and occludes its own self-knowledge. Let the formal part, as dematerialized, define the content of ideal selfhood, or the constancy to which a material self, normally subject to natural and moral corruption, ideally conforms. Formalization here has essentially to do with perfection, and perfection within the paradigm I am asking you to imagine admits of two different conceptions.

In one, the ethical subject, a mix of form and matter, self-perfects by holding the fort, once and for all, against matter. Virgil illustrates this kind of perfectionism in book 1 of the *Aeneid* (*Aen.*), the part where we find Jupiter reassuring Venus, mother of Aeneas, that her semidivine son, however hopeless his current travails may seem, is the founding figure of an eternal empire. His heirs will have perfected their forefather's travails when they are able to bolt shut Rome's Gates of War and keep forever confined inside, behind unyielding bars, "impious Fury" (*Furor impius*),[21] or the sum total of the material resistance, today or any day, to an imposed *pax Romana*. In perfectionism of this sort, matter retains its native potential to frustrate or corrupt form, but form has found the muscle to keep such potency forever unrealized.

In the other kind of perfectionism, matter has no such potential, and there is no true mixing in the ethical subject of form and matter. Form just is perfection, and perfection, like virtue, remains self-originating and self-sustained. Here you cannot arrive at perfection from a place where perfection is lacking. Perfection is simply *not* perfectible. So, if imperfect is what you are now, then your best fate as an embodied being is to be confined with the Fury (really your fury) behind

20. *Mag.* 14.46 (CCSL 29:203).
21. *Aen.* 1.294 (LCL 63:282–83).

bars; otherwise join Tullia in her true element. When Cicero advances his case for his daughter's posthumous deification, he may well be suggesting that she has earned by dying the perfection she never managed to perfect in life (perfectionism type one); it is at least as likely, however, that he is framing her complete disentanglement from material existence as a revelation of what she has always been (perfectionism type two).

For my purposes, the difference between the two perfectionisms is less important than their common exultation of form; materiality, by contrast, is made out to be either a veil or a corrosive. Let us call this disposition to exalt form *classicism*. (It is not such a novel use of the term.) The self that seeks perfection, above all self-perfection, in a formalization of some kind would correspondingly be pursuing a form of classical ethics. I evoke the notion of classicism as a modest gesture toward a grand scholarly preoccupation: that of properly identifying the shift in *mentalité* between the classicism of Greco-Roman antiquity and the ambivalently historicist world of late antique Roman Christians. I think here of Henri-Irénée Marrou's *Saint Augustine et la fin de la culture antique* and his subsequent *Retractatio*; Peter Brown's chapter "The Lost Future" in *Augustine of Hippo* and Martha Nussbaum's corrective; Mark Vessey's wry and brilliant take on "The Demise of the Christian Writer"; John Cooper's exasperated rationalism in *Pursuits of Wisdom*; and John Peter Kenney's irenic attempt to unearth in Augustine a "Classical Christianity," friendly to both philosophy and scripture.[22] But I think especially of that grandest of grand narratives about a fateful revision in the spiritual genealogy of Western culture, Charles Norris Cochrane's massive argument in *Christianity and Classical Culture* for Augustine's displacement of a classical focus on form and matter with the personalism of Trinitarian economy, where relations—being neither one nor other—remain irreducible.[23]

22. Henri-Irénée Marrou, *Saint Augustin et la fin de la culture antique* (Paris: de Boccard, 1938), reissued with a *Retractatio* in 1949; Peter Brown, *Augustine of Hippo: A Biography*, new ed. (Berkeley: University of California Press, 2000); Martha Nussbaum, *Upheavals of Thought: The Intelligence of Emotions* (Cambridge: Cambridge University Press, 2001); Mark Vessey, "The Demise of the Christian Writer and the Remaking of 'Late Antiquity': From H.-I. Marrou's *Saint Augustin* (1938) to Peter Brown's *Holy Man* (1983)," *JECS* 6 (1998): 377–411; John M. Cooper, *Pursuits of Wisdom: Six Ways of Life in Ancient Philosophy from Socrates to Plotinus* (Princeton: Princeton University Press, 2012); and John Peter Kenney, *Contemplation and Classical Christianity: A Study in Augustine* (Oxford: Oxford University Press, 2013).

23. Charles Norris Cochrane, *Christianity and Classical Culture: A Study of Thought and Action from Augustus to Augustine* (New York: Oxford University Press, 1940). This book was a favorite of W. H. Auden's.

While I feel the pull of the great question of the transition, the one that delegates Cicero and Augustine to different worlds, I am not so ambitious. Let us leave to classicism its dauntingly complex historical resonances—the aforementioned gesture to bigger stakes—and narrow the scope of the question. Does Augustine tend to think of goodness, while grieving its loss, ideally as a form of security, a state of perfection that outlasts sin and death, if not love? Does he, in other words, remain a classical ethicist?

The most ready-to-hand evidence that he does not, that he has become something else, proves to be an ambiguous offering. In book 19 of *De ciuitate dei* (*ciu.*), where we will encounter his famous critique of pagan virtue, Augustine begins by methodically setting out the parameters of classical ethics. Let us start with his presumption that the philosophical life aims at attaining the highest good (*summum bonum*) and avoiding the greatest evil (*summum malum*). Formally speaking, the highest good is the good for the sake of which I pursue any and all other goods; meanwhile, the greatest evil is whatever it is that prevents me, in my pursuit of goods, from having access to or awareness of the highest good. Augustine continues along this analytic vein but soon shifts his focus from form to content. There are basically four ingredients to the life that is blessed with highest or supreme goodness: pleasure, repose, basic resources (*primigenia*), and virtue.[24] Pleasure and repose can be considered states of body, soul, or some combination of the two; the term *primigenia* refers to the social and material conditions that allow for greater access to pleasure and repose—for example, health, money, and citizenship. The key ingredient in the mix is virtue, which turns out to be less an additional ingredient than the means by which I make my happiness (*beatitudo*) genuinely my own. Suppose I experience pleasure as an object that lies outside my self-determination; to get my fill of this object—say it is a person whose sensual beauty excites me—I use my alienated virtue to make this object mine. More bluntly, I bend another person to my will. Augustine thinks of this as an ugly way to live, and he would get no argument from a classical ethicist (not even from an Epicurean). The classical ideal would have

---

24. *Ciu.* 19.2 (CCSL 48:660–61). I am departing from a strict adherence to the details of Augustine's exposition (which follows Varro's in *De philosophia*) but staying within its unfolding logic. Augustine lists as a separate ingredient of the happy or blessed life a combination of pleasure and repose and leaves virtue off the list. I think it makes more sense for him to allow the listing of peace and repose as separate ingredients, to imply the desirability of their sometime combination, and to treat virtue as a peculiarly important part of happiness—and so as on the list, but with explanation.

me take pleasure *only* from virtue and in that way experience the exercise of noncoercive self-governance (perfect self-acceptance) as the first and final form of happiness. Recall the terms of Cicero's praise of virtue: virtue is a wondrous thing, worthy of reverential praise, just because it depends on nothing outside itself for its goodness.

If I find my pleasure and repose wholly within virtue, then I am never tempted to violate the self-determination of another soul in a bid to serve my own (corrupted) sense of well-being. If I find my basic resources for living, the *primigenia*, wholly within virtue, then I can be happy in any set of circumstances: war or peace, fire or flood. I live at home in the citadel of virtue and know no want. Among the classical virtue theorists, it is the Stoics who insist most on the absolute sufficiency of virtue for the *beata uita*, the estimable life.[25] The Peripatetics centralize virtue but make room in the marginalia of ethics for external goods (*bona externa*)—goods that are good independently of the exercise of anyone's virtue. You may be quite disinclined, being a person of virtue, to trade in a virtuous life for a disease-free but virtueless one, but you ought to be able to value, from within virtue, health over sickness. When Augustine sets his sights on the intramural debate within classical ethics over the propriety of admitting external goods into the kingdom of virtue, he concurs with Cicero's view of the matter in *De finibus bonorum et malorum* (*Fin.*), yet another of Cicero's post-Tullia literary productions. Peripatetics concede a place within virtue to external goods, and Stoics do likewise, provided those goods are deemed "conveniences" (*commoda*) rather than "goods" (*bona*). Here, Cicero argues, we have a distinction without a difference.[26] Both sides agree that virtue's formalizing function renders the sheer

---

25. I follow a line of thought in Nicholas Wolterstorff about *eudaimonia* when I render the *beata* in *beata uita* as "estimable." The point of that rendition is to pull together happiness and goodness and prevent them from ever going their separate ways (admittedly a concern more of ancient than of modern ethics). Wolterstorff has recently advanced the provocative argument, still very much a minority view, that Augustine breaks with classical ethics because he breaks with eudaimonism. I have felt the pull of his argument—which I think is deeply insightful—but it does not centrally inform what I am doing here. For more on Wolterstorff and the question of Augustinian eudaimonism, see his essay "Augustine's Rejection of Eudaimonism," in *Augustine's "City of God": A Critical Guide*, ed. James Wetzel (Cambridge: Cambridge University Press, 2012), and chaps. 8 and 9 of his magnum opus, *Justice: Rights and Wrongs* (Princeton: Princeton University Press, 2008). For counterpoint, see Jennifer Herdt, *Putting on Virtue: The Legacy of the Splendid Vices* (Chicago: Chicago University Press, 2008).

26. *Ciu.* 9.4 (CCSL 47:251–53); cf. *Fin.* 5.29.89 (LCL 40:492–93).

materiality of value—the stuff that, pre-virtue, is nakedly desirable—"meager and unimportant" (*parua et exigua*). So not much good there, call it what you will.

When Augustine is not working with Cicero to tidy up classicism's house, he appears to be laying waste to its foundations. In the crucial fourth chapter of *De ciuitate dei* 19, we find him taking aim at virtue itself, the good that supervenes upon and supplies good things with (nearly) all of their goodness. Virtue, to his way of thinking, is a house irreparably divided against itself. Where classicism identifies external goods or conveniences as virtue's inside other, or what sets a limit, however modest, to any quest for moral perfection, Augustine references vice. Take the case of temperance. To a classical ethicist, temperance is the virtue of having virtuous or purified desire. I do not resist having the illicit love affair; I just have no desire for it. Indeed, I have no desire for anything that is illicit. The well-tempered life is supposed to transcend temptation and leave a person feeling blessedly unconflicted. But not for Augustine. He *defines* temperance (Greek σωφροσύνη; Latin *temperantia*) as the temporary triumph of virtuous resolve in the face of spirit's perpetual struggle with flesh.[27] Yes, I resist having the illicit love affair, and perhaps do so without fail, but not because I have no desire for it. Not only do I have the desire for fleshly transgression; I have the desire, here taking the form of a partial will, to be desirous.

Augustine translates Paul's eschatological interests in the opposition between spirit and flesh into the psychology of a divided will. I have a partial will to spirit, a partial will to flesh, and these partialities line up along a fault line without ever conjoining. Temptation is now no mere dross of desire; it is a deep and painful severance. Having a *will* to incorporate spirit into flesh means that I experience such alchemy, somewhere deep within my soul, to be good. If matters were otherwise, my contrary will to liberate spirit from flesh would be no more morally fraught than my will to reduce my cholesterol intake or to get more sleep. When I will single-mindedly, I face opposition but not division; the thing that I will—for example, running a marathon—may be hard for me to do. When my will is divided, I lack the internal articulation that would, like a pregnancy, be generative. So, what does the offspring of a reconciled will, where spirit and flesh

---

27. Augustine bases his conception of inner conflict—spirit versus flesh—on what he imagines Paul to be describing in, e.g., Gal. 5:16–22 and Rom. 7:14–25. It isn't obvious that Augustine gets Paul right. But in this case, his mistake is too interesting, too fertile to be a simple mistake. See Krister Stendahl, "The Apostle Paul and the Introspective Conscience of the West," *HTR* 56 (1963): 199–215.

intimately conjoin, look like? I honestly do not know, but I assume that the child would compel love—just like Adeodatus did.

The logic of a divided will is, in any case, devastatingly clear. If the whole of my will has fragmented into incongruent parts, then I am in no position to step outside myself and will the wholeness back. I will need another will, greater than my own but still somehow not alien to me, either to restore me to myself or to facilitate my self-transcendence. This will—let's call it the will of God—is a will over which I have no control, however intimate I may find my relationship to it (and the relationship is certainly that, even on my worst day). In book 8 of *Confessiones*, where Augustine recalls his struggle to square his aspiration for celibacy with his habit of sexual craving, he gives us his best description of a divided will and the peculiar angst it generates: "I willed in favor; I willed against. That was me, not wholly willing, not wholly unwilling. In this way I was stretching myself against me and becoming scattered; the scattering itself was happening to me against my will."[28]

Late in *De ciuitate dei*, Augustine invokes the hierarchy that restrains, but likely fails to heal, self-scattering (*dissipatio*). Let the body and its chaotic propensities be ruled by soul (rule by virtue); let the soul and its bend toward chaos be ruled by God (rule by grace). Classicism goes wrong, Augustine suggests, when it affects to know no higher principle of ordering than virtue and then relegates an unfathomable well of grace to the status of a lucky break—to a problematic good, best not relied on, and so best minimized. The aspiration to perfect a self-imposed self-containment, where ideally I meet myself coming and going, serves in Augustine's mind only to deepen the internal division that makes a mockery of virtue's rule: "Some permit themselves the thought," he writes, "that the virtues are admirable and true when they are self-referential and sought for the sake of nothing else; in truth, such virtues are inflated and vain and for that reason must be accounted vices."[29] Gracelessly virtuous people take pride in lording over their troublesome desires and then refuse to notice how dissociated they have become from themselves; in that regard, their temptations prove to be more honest than their vir-

28. *Conf.* 8.10.22 (O'Donnell, 1:98): "ego eram qui uolebam, ego qui nolebam: ego eram. nec plene uolebam nec plene nolebam. ideo mecum contendebam et dissipabar a me ipso, et ipsa dissipatio me inuito quidem fiebat"; cf. 8.8.20 and 8.9.21 (O'Donnell, 1:97 and 97–98), which are also rich descriptions of the phenomenon of a divided will.

29. *Ciu.* 19.25 (CCSL 48:696): "nam licet a quibusdam tunc uerae atque honestae putentur esse uirtutes, cum referuntur ad se ipsas nec propter aliud expetuntur: etiam tunc inflatae ac superbae sunt, ideo non uirtutes, sed uitia iudicanda sunt."

tues. Augustine is happy to expose the conceit, but it is fair to wonder whether his alternative to classical ethics amounts to more than a wounded idealism.

Consider the last few chapters of *Confessiones* 8, the part that is most likely to make us think that Augustine has resolved or at least restrained the divisiveness of his will. There he reports having received the sudden ability to take to heart this Pauline verse: "No more wild parties and drunken fits, bedroom antics and indecencies, rivalries and wrangling; just put on Jesus Christ, your master, and don't look to lusts to care for your flesh."[30] So imagine: his flesh wants sex; his spirit wants purity; his God wants him to have what his spirit wants. To end his conflict of spirit with flesh, Augustine need only take up God's generous offer to him of spirit-nurtured flesh, or flesh as it exists ideally—sin-free, secured in Christ, luminous: "As soon as I finished reading the verse, it was as if a securing light poured into my heart and scattered the shadows of my hesitation."[31] Augustine will soon tell his mother not to expect another Adeodatus; her son's child-conceiving days are definitively over. But do we have the right framing yet of his "hesitation" (*dubitatio*), the framing that leaves room for a father, whether inwardly resolved or still scattered, to grieve the loss of a son?

The question takes us to the crossroads of Augustinian piety. Along one direction we will meet up with the residually classical Augustine, a reverential student of postmortem perfection, but a cynic when it comes to the prospects for perfection in this life, where materiality weighs down the soul. This Augustine will not be confessing to a conversion that is other than a heavy lift. He will continue to struggle with temptation, and temptation, post conversion, is retrograde motion; the soul descends into obscurity, defies its own moral calculus, and seems to confuse goodness with its lack. And yet it is also this Augustine who trusts himself to be able to take in his son's beauty and goodness without illusion. He finds that he can grieve for the boy *without fear*, and this ease of grief, unlike Cicero's busy sorrow over Tullia, does not demand a deification.

Along the other way, the residually classical Augustine relinquishes his residuals and ceases to cast the materiality of a beloved as a gesture toward (or away from) final form. For this postclassical Augustine, the disposition to subordinate materiality to form speaks to the painful eclipse of the mother, whose intimacy

30. *Conf.* 8.12.29 (O'Donnell, 1:101): "non in comessationibus et ebrietatibus, non in cubilibus et impudicitiis, non in contentione et aemulatione, sed induite dominum Iesum Christum et carnis prouidentiam ne feceritis in concupiscentiis"; cf. Rom. 13:13-14.

31. *Conf.* 8.12.29 (O'Donnell, 1:101): "statim quippe cum fine huiusce sententiae quasi luce securitatis infusa cordi meo omnes dubitationis tenebrae diffugerunt."

with the divine recalls the Spirit that broods over dark and unformed waters and sheds love into fearful hearts.[32] The ecstasy of her return will be hued in the language of grief. For there needs to be some acknowledgment of loss, again without fear, before the doors of a tomb can fly open and portend a resurrection. In *Confessiones*, grieving the mother is indeed sacred business.

DESCENDING, DISTENDING: TWO TAKES

Ascent is a common metaphor for union with higher being. I begin at the base-camp of my unruly mob of desires, and as I step over the noisiest portion—my narcissistic desires for power, prestige, and pleasure—I gain clarity of purpose and ultimately, after further steps over smaller, more cunning narcissisms, a singular aim. I come to desire the one thing and only the one thing that narcissism cannot translate, the God who is forever other to me, albeit far from alien. In the thin air of desire's summit, I cling to God for support, and God, I pray, clings back. Assuming that I have had my mobbish desires truly superseded by the highest high, securing me from above, what need have I to fear the bloodless shades that clamor for reconstitution and my descent back into laborious flesh?

In *Confessiones* Augustine reports having two distinctive experiences of ascent, where he will come to participate in, or feel a deep kinship with, the source of being itself. It matters to him that his readers, especially his brothers and sisters in Christ, understand that his communion has been with something lacking in a body and that he, while taken up into the experience, also lacks a body or at least the burden of one. Personally, I find it very hard, if not impossible, to envision any kind of relationship, let alone a deeply intimate one, between two immaterial things (one stumbles over the notion of a thing). But I have a vivid sense of what Augustine seems to be ruling out. The relationship between God and soul, devoid of even a hint of incarnation, is not sexual and has no possibility of being such. To speak metaphorically, perfect asexuality, here a feat of ecstasy without entanglement, completes ascent.

We might be tempted to say that ascent is, come to think of it, just like sex, only without body parts and the bother of mortality thrown in. But in the ecstasy at Milan, sex enters into the picture as a problem and not a simile. Augustine describes losing his ethereal standing the very instant he finishes his disincarnating

---

32. *Conf.* 13.7.8 (O'Donnell, 1:186); cf. Gen. 1:2 and Rom. 5:5.

climb. There he is, soul-liberated, loving God, and descending wildly into a world with bodily meetings and partings. He seems disappointed:

> It astonished me that I already loved you, not some figment in your place, and I was not standing firm in my enjoyment of my God; I was snatched away to you by your beauty and just as quickly snatched back by my weight. I crashed with a groan into all-too-familiar things; that weight was sexual habit.[33]

The Latin for "sexual habit" is *consuetudo carnalis*. A blander translation of the phrase would be "carnal or bodily habit" (whatever that is), but *consuetudo* readily carries the connotation of sexual intercourse, especially when illicit,[34] and Augustine is not unknown to complain about the tyranny of his sex drive (*conf.* 8 is something of a rant). If he is saying something like "I really love God, but not, apparently, more than I love sex," then it doesn't make much sense to render his summit experience as sexual, and this for the simple reason that sublime sex beats stupid sex. But why in any case would Augustine feel a tug of flesh while still in the teeth of a transcendent ecstasy? Habit? That just restates the puzzle.

Matters are not much clearer with the other ascent experience that he describes—the ecstasy at Ostia—although that ascent seems, on the surface, to have been less mortgaged to the entanglements of sexual desire. Augustine and his mother, Monica, lean out of a window overlooking a garden at their temporary residence in Ostia and together ponder the quality of the saintly life in eternity. Their conversation intensifies and, at some point, if the description is to be believed, transcends language, or, more precisely, transcends language insofar as language requires articulation—a continual renegotiation of partial intelligibility. Mother and son suddenly find themselves, inarticulate but fully and mutually aware, in the *caelum caeli*, the heaven of heaven, where wisdom has no past or future but only being. Within the space of a heartbeat (*toto ictu cordis*), they touch on what is. Then departure:

---

33. *Conf.* 7.17.23 (O'Donnell, 1:84): "Et mirabar quod iam te amabam, non pro te phantasma, et non stabam frui deo meo, sed rapiebar ad te decore tuo moxque diripiebar abs te pondere meo, et ruebam in ista cum gemitu; et pondus hoc consuetudo carnalis."

34. Charlton T. Lewis and Charles Short, *A Latin Dictionary* (Oxford: Clarendon, 1879), s.v. "consuetudo," IIB: "intercourse in love, in an honorable, and more freq. in a dishonorable sense, a love affair, an amour, love intrigue, illicit intercourse." Attested in Terence, Livy, Suetonius, Sallust, and Quintillian. For Augustine's use of the term in this way, see Peter King, "Augustine's Anti-Platonist Ascents," in *Augustine's "Confessions": Philosophy in Autobiography*, ed. William E. Mann (Oxford: Oxford University Press, 2014), 10–12.

With a sigh we left captive there the firstfruits of the spirit [*primitias spiritus*] and made our way back to a noisy mouth, where a word that begins also ends. How is that word like your word, the word that masters us, that abides in you without aging, that makes all things new?[35]

This exit or perhaps fall from a place of sublime retreat comes across as less forced than the Milan denouement and its invocation of an anxious and un-kempt sexuality, still clamoring to be reckoned with. Here Augustine is almost matter-of-fact about his return with his mother to the earthiness of love and language and the tides of absence that roll out from death, a source of unmas-terable difference. Post ecstasy, Monica is ready to disappear into that source. She feels too fulfilled to stay in a world of irredeemably partial pleasures, even if Augustine should be one of them: "My son, as for me, I no longer delight in this life." "What I am doing here?"[36] The final gift she bequeaths to him is the space of her absence; this will become the site in his heart reserved for inarticulacy. If Augustine ever had the words to convince his mother not to want to go, he lacks them now: "I do not well recall what I said to her in response."[37]

Whatever the differences are between the two ecstasies thus described—and the differences are profound—both Milan and Ostia appear to give the lie to ascent. Let Augustine undertake the arduous climb to love's purification; let him take his mother along (that should help him sideline his sex drive); let him be furnished with an abundant share of grace (that will illuminate the way). When he gets to the top of the mountain, he invariably discovers that he is not all there. The missing part calls to him from below, and down he tumbles, back into his labored life, like some Christian Sisyphus.

There is a classically informed way to read this failure to ascend fully, and that reading will leave Augustine with what John Peter Kenney has aptly named "a Classical Christianity."[38] The classical part concerns contemplation. Augustine,

35. *Conf.* 9.10.24 (O'Donnell, 1:113): "et suspirauimus et reliquimus ibi religatas primitias spiritus et remeauimus ad strepitum oris nostri, ubi uerbum et incipitur et finitur. et quid simile uerbo tuo, domino nostro, in se permanenti sine uetustate atque innouanti omnia?"

36. *Conf.* 9.10.26 (O'Donnell, 1:114): "fili, quantum ad me attinet, nulla re iam delector in hac uita. quid hic faciam adhuc et cur hic sim, nescio."

37. *Conf.* 9.11.27 (O'Donnell, 1:114): "ad haec ei quid responderim non satis recolo."

38. Kenney, *Contemplation and Classical Christianity.* I am greatly indebted, not only to Kenney's brilliant study of Augustine's place in a contemplative tradition of philosophy, but also to his previous study of Augustine's mystic ecstasies: *The Mysticism of Saint Augustine: Rereading the "Confessions"* (New York: Routledge, 2005).

from a high point of desire, comes to know God as transcendent being, beauty, and goodness; he also apprehends, as part of the same knowing, his distance from this God on high. The Christian part concerns conversion. The distance between God and the knowing mind or soul is not simply a function of finitude. God, being limitless, is still knowable to a mind that knows what a limit is and how to look beyond it. A sin-infected mind, unlike a merely finite one, affects to have direct knowledge of the limitless and so imposes a limit, that of its own way of seeing (or not), on God. I am the Adam who knows the good that is God's; I reject that good and hold out for the good that is not God's, the good that is mine alone. So thinks sin. Here the thinking is not simply limited; it is perverted. As finite but God-oriented, I seek a good that is less limited than I am; as sinful, finite, and God-oriented, I reject or illicitly limit goodness that would come to me in that "form." No wonder ascents are ambivalent things. "The fallen soul," writes Kenney (alluding to T. S. Eliot), "cannot bear very much reality."[39] God will have to do for the soul what the soul cannot do for itself: secure wholeness.

There is much to be said for this reading, and Kenney has already said it. I am not going to pursue further a classical reading of Augustine's failed ascents. I am not even going to assume that his ascents are failures. I have in fact an alternative way of looking at them. But first let me concede the appeal of the classical reading and its subliming of form. By way of the metaphor of ascent, Augustine expresses his desire for a final form of desire. He will have "arrived" at that form when he is able to desire the good and only the good in a perfectly secure manner. Security, being itself a good, enters into the content of what desire wants; at the same time, security refers to what contains or secures that content. Security, relative to the good, shows up inside and out. The problematic of classicism is precisely the (interminable) negotiation of the difference. Placed outside the good, as its exterior boundary, security is not, strictly speaking, part of goodness. Placed within, by virtue of being a good, security emerges out of containment as an indeterminate limit, or something that defines without fixation. As a disposition to idealize form, classicism tends to favor a fixed exterior (e.g., a wall) over something as murky as an indeterminate limit (e.g., skin).[40] That is bad news for materiality, the "stuff" of indeterminacy.

---

39. Kenney, *Contemplation and Classical Christianity*, 157.

40. Just to be clear about the examples: I am, relative to a wall, unambiguously on one side or the other. My skin both connects me to my world (a oneness) and differentiates me from it (an otherness). Think especially of skin-on-skin contact and the intimacy and alienation of

But Augustine turns out not to be that kind of classicist—and perhaps not any kind of classicist at all.

Return to Milan and Augustine's Milanese ecstasy. The setup is important. Before he recalls his recent reading in Platonist literature and heeds the directive he finds there to dive deep into his true self (*redire ad memet ipsum*)[41]—a descent—Augustine undertakes a leisurely lament over the wasteland of his desire and the problem of evil that he has become. At the end of *Confessiones* 6, we find him nearly endorsing the view that pleasurable physical stimulation without end is the best vision any of us can have of the good life. Just before this part of the narrative, he describes having sent his lover, the mother of Adeodatus, back to Africa to live apart from him, presumably for good. Augustine implies that his long relationship with her has been one of undeniable lust (*libidinis seruus eram*), but for a lust relationship its end has been peculiarly heartbreaking for both sides.[42] At the beginning of *Confessiones* 7, he tells us that his adolescence is dead and that he is growing old; he is hardly sanguine, however, about the quality of his maturation. Sexual desire, though no longer a conflagration, persists in him as an arid, desiccated plain. He feels barren inside and sealed off from his life's source; he simply cannot imagine how he could exist like this and still be a child of God. It is all the more significant, then, that when he does enter into his underworld (*in intima mea*) by way of introspection but with God as his Virgil, his tour guide (*duce te*), he feels fundamentally loved there. The love establishes the necessary context for the revelation—and the ecstasy.

Here is Augustine to God:

> When I first recognized you, you lifted me up so that I could tell that there was something for me to see, but also that I was not yet the person to see it. You forcibly beat back the infirmity of my point of view, with violent illumination, and I shook with loving awe but also fearsome dread. And I was finding myself far away from you, in a place of unlikeness [*regio dissimilitudinis*].[43]

---

sex. Inside and out slip into each other and exchange places without entirely losing definition. Can skin be a wall? Yes, but then it is no longer living.

41. *Conf.* 7.10.16 (O'Donnell, 1:81–82).

42. *Conf.* 6.15.25 (O'Donnell, 1:71).

43. *Conf.* 7.10.16 (O'Donnell, 1:82): "et cum te primum cognoui, tu adsumpsisti me ut uiderem esse quod uiderem, et nondum me esse qui uiderem. et reuerberasti infirmitatem aspectus mei, radians in me uehementer, et contremui amore et horrore. et inueni longe me esse a te in regione dissimilitudinis."

This is not an ascent that is bringing any kind of obvious wholeness to Augustine and his desire for God. Notice that God is still very far off; notice too that it is Augustine and not God who lingers in the unfamiliar place, the place that is constitutionally unlike all other places. The only familiar place that is flagged in Augustine's ascent is the created order itself, and its reality is what Augustine, before his time, is given to see. He sees an order of impeccable beauty: it is harmonious, perfectly integrated, impervious to assault; it is a classicist's paradise. But in order to take in this revelation—the consummate beauty of vulnerable things—he will need to put it together with the less spectacular but no less crucial offering: that of seeing himself as not yet the person who sees (*nondum me esse qui uiderem*). The preternatural light of a sudden and even violent illumination can be a flashpoint of insight, but it is not what makes for true seeing. In a flashpoint of insight, Augustine sees himself as already a lover of God, but he is also, at that very moment, forcibly exited from his place of unlikeness. This is not, I think, because his sin is so weighty or his sex drive so intrusive; it is because no true lover of God can afford to have such contempt for familiar things. Higher love requires an education in familiarity. The ecstasy at Milan lies in the descent.

Return now to Ostia. Augustine and Monica have finished entering into their own minds (*in mentes nostras*) and enjoying a heartbeat's worth of undistended time in the *caelum caeli*, the sanctuary where there is no birth, no aging, no death, and nothing, so to speak, that "matters" (no evidence, that is, of materiality). Now they are back to their senses, back to the contained but vulnerable beauty of a garden retreat on the Tiber, where they await word of available passage home. (The times, as ever, are precarious; the fleet of Maximus the usurper has been blockading the harbors of Rome.) Monica is dying; Augustine is preparing to grieve her. It seems to me that the writer of *Confessiones* has been framing the ecstasy at Ostia as part of a natural process of grieving and not as a curious otherworldly intrusion into the confessional narrative. But much turns on what we think Augustine really means by "first fruits of the spirit" (*primitias spiritus*), the fruits that he and his mother have bound up (*religatas*) and left behind (*reliquimus*) in heaven's heaven, like a sacrificial offering.[44]

Presumably the scriptural allusion is to Rom. 8:23. There, Paul speaks of the labor pains of all of creation but especially of human beings, as we groan to give birth to resurrected versions of ourselves, to bodies that are forever im-

---

44. *Conf.* 9.10.24 (O'Donnell, 1:113).

mune to the acids of time. Paul reminds us that we already have the first offering (ἀπαρχὴν) of this momentous, culmination-of-the-ages transfiguration—or we would not be having labor pains—but also that we still live in longing for the resurrection to come. If we just transport Paul's imaginary to the ecstasy at Ostia, then Augustine and Monica will be seen to have checked their resurrected bodies at the exit door of paradise, thereby relegating their earthly bodies to the status of transworldly coat checks, to be redeemed after the earthly show is over (a tragedy). There are a number of problems with this transposition. It suggests that it is possible to have a resurrected body without having to die first, it sets up the *caelum caeli* as the alternative to creation, and it underplays the sacrificial element in Augustine's description of leave-taking. But what if the material order of creation *just were* the materiality of the *caelum caeli*? What if he and Monica were relinquishing, not their berth in heaven, but, more radically, their claim on perfectible lives?

At one point in his grieving, Augustine stops to ask God to make the pain go away and straightaway heal his wound of loss. God would not. Augustine thinks he knows why and lets God in on the secret. He writes, "You were committing to my memory, by way of this one lesson, the bond [*uinculum*] that every relationship is, even for a mind that is no longer feeding on deceit."[45] We do not ascend out of relationships; we fall into them, and they remake us without end.

CONCLUSION: THE BOY AND HIS MOTHER

There is an extraordinary moment in *Confessiones* 12 where Augustine is broadly concerned with how creation begins and, more specifically, with the emergence of the *caelum caeli*, the heaven that is not noticeably earthy, if earthy at all. The *caelum caeli* is all about the perfection of form, or, more precisely, it is about the having been formed (present, perfect, passive) of something that always appears perfectly beautiful, even in limitless retrospect. Still, the heaven of heaven is

---

45. *Conf.* 9.12.32 (O'Donnell, 1:116): "nec faciebas, credo commendans memoriae meae uel hoc uno documento omnis consuetudinis uinculum etiam aduersus mentem, quae iam non fallaci uerbo pascitur." I follow Sarah Ruden in translating the *consuetudo* in "omnis consuetudinis uinculum" as "relationship" (*Confessions*, trans. Ruden, 271). It is a brilliant translation, one that suggests a reversal of *consuetudo*'s dark connotation of illicit sex. See n. 34 *supra* and *conf.* 7.17.23.

not without its share of materiality—where there is form, there is matter—and Augustine wonders what it would mean for matter itself to be unchanging. He admits to a bad habit of thinking here; he has become used to imagining formless matter either as deformation or the jumbling of form and therefore as ugliness incarnate. His moment of illumination comes when he gives up trying to imagine something and allows himself the thought that changeability itself (*mutabilitas*) is what matter abidingly is. He then shifts his focus from the ephemera of form to bodies themselves (*in ipsa corpora*) and their abiding capacity for change. His big insight: "The changeability of changeable things is itself capable [*capax*] of all the forms that changeable things change into."[46]

Augustine is well aware of the paradoxical air that surrounds his attempt to render changeability the subject, and therefore the constant, of change. What kind of thing, after all, is changeability? Dig deep into what it is, and you will come up with what it is not. The capacity always to be otherwise seems, as a thing, to be a "nil-thing" or a "not-being." "I would call it either," Augustine says.[47] There is not much in the way of theoretical neatness here, but perhaps that is a part of the offering. Augustine gets loosed from having to think of formation as the enemy of change. The *caelum caeli* ceases to be an exclusive or violent perfection, however hard it may be to imagine the alternative. Monica, the imperfect mother (of us all), lives out the substance of her life on earth (her *mutabilitas*) and perdures, without distention, as one of the first fruits of heaven. The point is not to claim her there but to remember her here.

It is the boy who opens up grief for the mother. The adults try to keep it together at her funeral. Adeodatus cries out in sorrow and is quickly nudged into a quiet grieving. Augustine recalls the effect on himself: "In this way too something of the child in me, which had slipped toward weeping, was checked and silenced by the youthful voice, the voice of my heart."[48] Sometimes the father remembers the boy in himself and begins to hear a long forgotten voice. He checks his sorrow but does not deny it.

46. *Conf.* 12.6.6 (O'Donnell, 1:166): "mutabilitas enim rerum mutabilium ipsa capax est formarum omnium in quas mutantur res mutabiles."

47. The coinages are Augustine's; cf. *conf.* 12.6.6 (O'Donnell, 1:166): "si dici posset 'nihil aliquid' et 'est not est,' hoc eam dicerem."

48. *Conf.* 9.12.29 (O'Donnell, 1:115): "hoc modo etiam meum quiddam puerile, quod labebatur in fletus, iuuenali uoce cordis cohercebatur et tacebat." The enviable translation is by Henry Chadwick, who renders the ambiguous phrase "iuuenali uoce cordis" as "the youthful voice, the voice of my heart" (*Confessions*, trans. Chadwick, 174).

Cicero mourns a daughter by trying to remember her perfection. When he finds what he is looking for, he will lack a way to represent it. (No shrine will do.) Augustine mourns a son by recalling the youthful voice of the heart (*iuuenali uoce cordis*). It is his own voice; it is the voice of his son. That voice is unrepresentable too, but only because the ambiguity is generous.

Chapter 9

Augustine and the Classical Latin Literary Tradition

Dennis Trout

Introduction

Occasionally a poet seems to possess such a clear-eyed vision of the "infinite sweep of humanity" that his works rise "beyond category." Augustine, well into his literary career and staging a display of public self-analysis not unlike that of the 2016 Nobel Laureate whose observation has just been quoted, openly admitted that such enchantments were not easily dispelled by time.[1] Indeed, they might never fully recede. In a passage of the *City of God* written many years after the *Confessions* had laid bare his attachment to the epic whose "infinite sweep" had captivated him as a schoolboy, he quoted a line of that lengthy poem. It offered authoritative evidence that imperturbability was, indeed, a hallmark of the wise man: "Vergil even describes Aeneas as such a person," he noted, "when he

---

1. For the observation see Bob Dylan, *Chronicles: Volume One* (New York: Simon & Schuster, 2004), 244, on his college-age discovery of the music of Woody Guthrie: "The songs themselves, his repertoire, were really beyond category. They had the infinite sweep of humanity in them." Dylan's 2004 assessment can be framed with 1962's "Song to Woody," 1963's "Last Thoughts on Woody Guthrie," and, e.g., his analysis of Guthrie's influence offered to the *Los Angeles Times*'s Robert Hilburn in an interview of April 4, 2004, an interview wherein Guthrie is idealized as a "true" artist whose "songs were about everything at the same time." See *Bob Dylan* (Columbia Records, 1962); *The Bootleg Series, Volumes 1–3: Rare and Unreleased 1961–1991* (Columbia Records, 1991); Jonathan Cott, ed., *Bob Dylan: The Essential Interviews* (New York: Wenner Books, 2006), 430–31. For Augustine see, e.g., *conf.* 1.13.20 (CSEL 33:18) and below.

says, 'His mind remains unmoved, tears roll down in vain.'"[2] Inevitably, then, our understanding of Augustine's thought and of his thinking about himself is insep-arable from our appreciation of him as a scrupulous reader.[3] Books and writers clearly are as essential to Augustine's self-representation as they are fundamental to his formulation and expression of ideas.[4] Throughout his life, as he revealed himself in his own writing, Augustine's ever-present companions, together with the books of his Bible, were the authors of the Latin school curriculum, Cicero, Sallust, Terrence, and, of course, Vergil.[5] Yet Augustine's relationship to the clas-sical Latin tradition never presents itself as simple or naive. Nor is it stable. Time and circumstance have their way to such an extent that Augustine's varying at-titudes to the authors he first met as a student at Madauros and Carthage and those he gradually added to his bookshelf as a young teacher have often seemed amenable to a scheme of periodization that proceeds from enthusiasm to dis-trust. Moreover, such a trajectory becomes even more appealing when viewed as symptomatic of an age in which some exegetical strategies worked to recuperate classical texts for Christianity—epitomized by those aimed at establishing the

2. See *civ.* 9.4 (CCSL 47:253), which quotes *Aen.* 4.449, Aeneas's clearheaded reaction to Anna's emotional plea (on Dido's behalf) that he remain in Carthage and not continue on to Italy.

3. "Reading" is employed broadly here to describe approaching and interpreting texts. Augustine and his contemporaries often accessed "texts" aurally, and sound was a crucial component of Augustine's response to them, especially to classical poetry, in which metrical rhythms and sonic figures were fundamental to pleasure and meaning. On antiquity's "audi-tory culture," see Carol Harrison's exhaustive *The Art of Listening in the Early Church* (Oxford: Oxford University Press, 2013), immediately noting that "reading effectively became a way of speaking the text" (5).

4. Foundational is Brian Stock, *Augustine the Reader: Meditation, Self-Knowledge, and the Ethics of Interpretation* (Cambridge, MA: Belknap, 1996), with the insights of Mark Vessey at *Bryn Mawr Classical Review* 1996.9.1. The same, of course, can empathically be said of Dylan.

5. These four authors supply the overwhelming majority of the classical *testimonia* em-bedded in Augustine's works; Vergil is, after Cicero, the author most often quoted or alluded to by Augustine. Harald Hagendahl, *Augustine and the Latin Classics* (Stockholm: Almqvist & Wiksell, 1967), offers 156 Vergilian *testimonia* quoted or alluded to 251 times (321–75) and 289 Ciceronian *testimonia* (42–169). Gerhard Anselm Müller's thorough *Formen und Funktionen der Vergilzitate bei Augustin von Hippo* (Paderborn: Ferdinand Schöningh, 2003) generally supports Hagendahl's numbers (see the Vergil index at 503–7), as does James J. O'Donnell, "Augustine's Classical Reading," *RechAug* 15 (1980): 147–48. On the predominance of the four school authors in Augustine's citations, see O'Donnell's tabulation at "Augustine's Classical Reading," 166.

prophetic authority of Vergil's "messianic" Fourth Eclogue—while others overtly (if sometimes disingenuously) rejected the truth claims of any literature inspired by the pagan Muses.[6]

At the same time, however, Augustine's more sensitive modern readers have recognized that the old books never really failed to reach Augustine. Late in his days, for example, when Augustine staged his rebuttal of Christianity's opponents in *De ciuitate dei* (*ciu.*) or addressed Julian of Eclanum in a series of biting essays, Cicero and Vergil still spoke insistently to him, differently perhaps but not necessarily untruthfully.[7] As challenging now to reduce to its primary elements as it once was integral to his understanding of himself and his world, a potent blend of aesthetic pleasure and intellectual stimulation, Augustine's sympathy for those authors who represented, for so many in his age, all that was good in the Latin literary tradition conditioned his thought in ways never fully overrode by time and events.

The Songs of Vergil

There is, perhaps, no better illustration of the resiliency and complexity of Augustine's relations with the authors of his schoolroom than his persistent re-

6. On Christian exegesis of Vergil's Fourth Eclogue, see Pierre Courcelle, "Les exégèses chrétiennes de la quatrième églogue," *Revue des études anciennes* 59 (1957): 249–319, and Sabine MacCormack, *The Shadows of Poetry: Vergil in the Mind of Augustine* (Berkeley: University of California Press, 1998), 21–31. For Augustine's own understanding of the eclogue, which granted Vergil semi-prophetic authority, see *ep.* 104.3 (CSEL 34/2:590) to Nectarius and *ep.* 137.12 (CSEL 44:114) to Volusianus, with MacCormack, *Shadows of Poetry*, 29–31, and Müller, *Formen und Funktionen der Vergilzitate*, 445. On Jerome's resistance to such concessions, see Jerome, *Ep.* 53.7 (CSEL 54:454) to Paulinus, with Harald Hagendahl, *Latin Fathers and the Classics* (Göteborg: Almqvist & Wiksell, 1958), 188–89. See further below. What *Aen.* "means" is, of course, a primary theme of the first five books of *ciu.*, just as the same question about Vergil's poetry animates Prudentius. On the latter, see, e.g., Marc Mastrangelo, *The Roman Self in Late Antiquity: Prudentius and the Poetics of the Soul* (Baltimore: Johns Hopkins University Press, 2008).

7. O'Donnell, "Augustine's Classical Reading," 151–57, cataloging Augustine's reading (or rereading) of Cicero as he composed *ciu.*, and 166, noting that nearly half (115 out of 251) of Augustine's citations of Vergil appear in *ciu.* The latter is affirmed by Müller, *Formen und Funktionen der Vergilzitate*, 503–4. Cf. *infra*.

course to Vergil.[8] Vergil's allure, of course, was nearly universal. Some four centuries after the *Aeneid* (*Aen.*) had been painstakingly composed, Vergil's epic of war and wandering still stood as the premier touchstone of Latin poetics and Roman identity.[9] The Augustan poet's significance for Augustine's public image as well as his thought is evident in his earliest extant works. When in late 386 or early 387 CE—on fall break from his teaching responsibilities and pondering baptism—Augustine sent his newly penned *De ordine* (*ord.*) to his friend and confidant Zenobius,[10] he portrayed himself comfortably settled into a villa north of Milan, spending the waning autumn days coaching a group of bright young men and family members in poetry and philosophy.[11] Most afternoons,

8. On Vergil and Augustine, see now, e.g., MacCormack, *Shadows of Poetry*; Müller, *Formen und Funktionen der Vergilzitate*; Garry Wills, "Vergil and St. Augustine," in *A Companion to Vergil's Aeneid and Its Tradition*, ed. Joseph Farrell and Michael C. J. Putnam (Malden, MA: Wiley-Blackwell, 2010), 123–32; and Robin Lane Fox, *Augustine: Conversions to Confessions* (New York: Basic Books, 2015), 53–55. On the role of grammarians (such as Augustine) in establishing and maintaining Vergil's cultural authority, see Richard Lim, "Augustine, the Grammarians, and the Cultural Authority of Vergil," in *Romane Memento: Vergil in the Fourth Century*, ed. Roger Rees (London: Duckworth, 2004), 112–27.

9. For examples and variety, see the essays in Rees, *Romane Memento*; Scott McGill, *Virgil Recomposed: The Mythological and Secular Centos in Antiquity* (Oxford: Oxford University Press, 2005); and many of the illustrations in Helen Kaufmann, "Intertextuality in Late Latin Poetry," in *The Poetics of Late Latin Literature*, ed. Jaś Elsner and Jesús Hernández Lobato, Oxford Studies in Late Antiquity (New York: Oxford University Press, 2017), 149–75. Vergil, as Augustine knew, reached a far wider audience through the popular media of mime and pantomime; see, e.g., Suet. *Nero* 54 (*C. Suetoni Tranquilli Opera*, ed. M. Ihm [Leipzig: Teubner, 1908], 259), on Nero's intention to dance the role of "Vergil's Turnus," with the further sources collected at "Virgil as Performed or Declaimed" in Jan M. Ziolkowski and Michael C. J. Putnam, eds., *The Virgilian Tradition: The First Fifteen Hundred Years* (New Haven: Yale University Press, 2008), 162–78. Note also Regina Höschele, "From Ecloga the Mime to Vergil's *Eclogues* as Mimes: *Ein Gedankenspiel*," *Vergilius* 59 (2013): 37–60; Lane Fox, *Augustine*, 72; and Marjorie Curry Woods, *Weeping for Dido: The Classics in the Medieval Classroom* (Princeton: Princeton University Press, 2019). Vergil is cited throughout this essay from the edition of R. A. B. Mynors, *P. Vergili Maronis Opera* (Oxford: Clarendon, 1969).

10. On Zenobius, see Charles Pietri and Luce Pietri, *Prosopographie chrétienne du Bas-Empire: 2, Prosopographie de l'Italie chrétienne (313–604)* (Rome: École française de Rome, 2000), 2:2378 (Zenobius 1); with Catherine Conybeare, *The Irrational Augustine* (Oxford: Oxford University Press, 2006), 22–23.

11. For context here (and throughout this essay) I rely especially on Peter Brown, *Augustine of Hippo: A Biography*, new ed. (Berkeley: University of California Press, 2000), 108–20; Serge

he informed Zenobius (and the cognoscenti among his Milanese audience), included the reading and discussion of Vergil's poetry, typically as a prelude to the evening meal.[12]

Yet, as the dialogue also made clear, Vergil's words rolled no less easily off the tongue in the midst of philosophical colloquy.[13] Even the dialogue's closing image was founded on a Vergilian simile, presenting the philosophical *sapiens* as the *Aeneid*'s embattled King Latinus, standing rock-firm against the tempest's buffeting surge.[14] The same dramatization of life at Cassiciacum colors the contemporary *De beata uita* (*beata u.*) and *De Academicis* (*Acad.*). The preface to the former, dedicated to the Milanese aristocrat Manlius Theodorus, promptly let slip Augustine's own Vergilian fluency with a subtle intertextual allusion.[15] One of the latter's key interlocutors, the young Licentius, is the embodiment of poetry's allure and the seductions of verse composition.[16] Vergilian lines and expressions echo so loudly through these works that, as we will see, more than one modern scholar has read them as Augustine's attempt to secure a place for Vergil's poetry as he set about reconceptualizing Christian paideia in anticipation of his resignation from his Milanese teaching post.

Lancel, *St. Augustine*, trans. Antonia Neville (London: SCM, 2002), 99–111; and Lane Fox, *Augustine*, 297–323. For a recent review of scholarship on Augustine's early dialogues, see Eric Kenyon, *Augustine and the Dialogue* (Cambridge: Cambridge University Press, 2018), 1–13. For temporal distribution of Augustine's Vergilian citations, see O'Donnell, "Augustine's Classical Reading," 166. The family group included Monica: see Conybeare, *Irrational Augustine*, 63–138, and Gillian Clark, *Monica: An Ordinary Saint* (Oxford: Oxford University Press, 2015), 80–115.

12. *Ord.* 1.8.26 (CSEL 63:138).

13. E.g., *Ord.* 1.4.10, 2.11.34, 2.20.54 (CSEL 63:128, 172, 185).

14. *Ord.* 2.20.54 (CSEL 63:185), which quotes *Aen.* 7.586. Vergil's simile is applied to the wisdom of Pythagoras, an association Augustine later regretted; see *retr.* 1.3 (CSEL 36:21–22).

15. *Beata u.* 1.4 (CSEL 63:91): "labentia in Oceanum astra," with allusion (appropriately not quotation considering the dedicatee's own erudition) to *Aen.* 3.515, "sidera . . . tacito labentia caelo." In *Aen.* those stars guide Aeneas to his new *patria*, but in the *beata u.* they symbolize the glittering objects that have distracted Augustine from his search for truth (astrology, perhaps, and Manichaeanism).

16. *Acad.* 1.5.15 (CSEL 63:15): a day spent "in recensione primi libri Vergilii"; 2.4.10 (CSEL 63:30): reviewing Vergil and Licentius's passion for the poet; 3.1.1 (CSEL 63:46): "et Licentius fingendis uersibus uacauit, quorum amore ita perculsa est." See also *ord.* 1.2.5, "poeticae deditus," and 1.7.20, "poeticae studiosum" (CSEL 63:124 and 135). On the one extant example of Augustine's hexameters, see Gillian Clark, "In Praise of the Wax Candle: Augustine the Poet and Late Latin Literature," in Elsner and Hernández Lobato, *Poetics of Late Latin Literature*, 424–46.

In time such exuberance would, at least on the surface of things, be damped down. Little more than a decade after his Cassiciacum retreat, Augustine took pains to recall at length how he himself had once been a bright student led astray by the wanderings (*errores*) of "some fellow called Aeneas."[17] His no less imprudent teachers lavished him with praise.[18] Command of Vergil, everyone understood, was requisite for social advancement and political preferment, for Vergil's poetry provided the privileged and the aspiring with a lingua franca of exclusive ideas and expressions. The *Confessiones* (*conf.*), of course, belittled such ambitions while apologizing directly and indirectly for the indulgences of Cassiciacum (though simultaneously reassuring readers of Augustine's pedigree by flaunting Vergilian allusions).[19] Perhaps inevitably, then, the opening books of *De ciuitate dei*, addressing learned contemporaries on matters of empire and identity in the wake of Alaric's sack of Rome, are often legible as commentary on the *Aeneid*, whose historical framework (if not all its values) Augustine endorsed even then.[20] Augustine's first Virgilian quotation in *De ciuitate dei* appears in the preface to that work's first book. The line was the artfully crafted hexameter into which Vergil had condensed Roman exceptionality: Your calling, Roman, Anchises informed Aeneas, is to rule the world, to impose law upon peace, "to spare the vanquished and beat down the proud" (*parcere subiectis et debellare superbos*).[21] Now, however, as Augustine set out to reassess Roman grandeur, Anchises's mandate presented itself as an unvarnished (if presciently accurate) illustration of the earthly city's enslavement to both arrogance (*fastus*) and the lust for dominion (*dominandi libido*).[22] Nothing, not even Vergil's vision of humanity's vast sweep, was quite as it seemed. Augustine had made the same point

---

17. *Conf.* 1.13.20 (CSEL 33:18): "Aeneae nescio cuius errores," with the translation of Maria Boulding in Augustine, *The Confessions*, ed. David Vincent Meconi, Ignatius Critical Editions (San Francisco: Ignatius, 2012), 22. On the "air of mild disdain" implied by Augustine's words, see James J. O'Donnell, *Augustine: Confessions*, vol. 2, *Commentary, Books 1–7* (Oxford: Clarendon, 1992), 77.

18. *Conf.* 1.13.20–21 (CSEL 33:18–19).

19. For oblique apology, see *conf.* 1.16.26–1.18.29 (CSEL 33:23–27); directly at *conf.* 9.4.7 (CSEL 33:201). For the citations and allusions, see the index at James J. O'Donnell, *Augustine: Confessions*, vol. 3, *Commentary, Books 8–13* (Oxford: Clarendon, 1992), 460–61, with Müller, *Formen und Funktionen der Vergilzitate*, 504.

20. MacCormack, *Shadows of Poetry*, 190–204.

21. *Aen.* 6.851–53 and *ciu.* 1 *praef.* (CCSL 47:1). Augustine quotes only 6.853.

22. *Ciu.* 1. *praef.* (CCSL 47:1). The passage (*Aen.* 6.847–53) reappears in similar terms at *ciu.* 5.12 (CCSL 47:144).

in a recent sermon: Vergil knew when he flattered his Augustan audience with Jupiter's grant to Rome of "empire without end" that the prophecy was a sham. That was why, Augustine pointed out, Vergil spoke not in his own *persona* but in that of Jupiter. Even so, if the god was false, the poet was a liar (*mendax*).[23]

In short, while Vergil's spirit pervades Augustine's corpus—rising and subsiding, to be sure, but seldom far below the surface—the relationship is rarely straightforward. Augustine would, on the one hand, acknowledge and praise the majesty of Vergil's "meaning" (*sententia*) as well as his "verse" (*metra*).[24] He would readily quote a well-known hexameter of the *Georgics*—*felix qui potuit rerum cognoscere causas* (fortunate is he who was able to understand the workings of the universe)—and generously dub it a *nobilissimus uersus*, acknowledging the line's poetic repute.[25] And he knew that most of his peers, raised (as he remarked) on Vergil and able to recall the poet's lines at the drop of a hat, considered him "a great poet, the best and most renowned of all," an assessment that he chose not to refute.[26] Yet even in the discussions at Cassiciacum caution is evident. Augustine (the character) would summon Vergil's oracular Apollo by excitedly quoting a line of the *Aeneid*—"so let the father of the gods grant, so lofty Apollo"—only to catch himself. It was "another" (*alius ille*), Augustine demurred, who not only was "truth-telling" (*ueridicus*) but truth (*ueritas*) itself.[27] Moreover, Licentius's Vergilian passion was at once admirable and excessive, an attachment, it was duly noted, to be tamed and rechanneled.[28] This, of course, was the opinion of a bishop who would soon lament his own youthful devotion to the *Aeneid* and publicly castigate the boyhood tears he had wept for Dido.[29] In time, after the shocking events of August 410 CE, Vergilian poetry may have remained common ground, but it just as readily offered Augustine and his pagan interlocutors a space for confrontation as for conciliation and compromise. In these latter times, the songs of the poets (*poetarum carmina*) might still ring true, but now

23. *S.* 105.7 (PL 38:622); cf. MacCormack, *Shadows of Poetry*, 188–90.
24. *Ord.* 2.11.34 (CSEL 63:172) on *Geo.* 2.481–82.
25. *Ciu.* 7.9 (CCSL 47:193). The line quickly attracted attention, being echoed by Propertius (1.12.16) and Lucan (4.393–94).
26. *Ciu.* 1.3 (CCSL 47:3): "poeta magnus omniumque praeclarissimus atque optimus."
27. *Ord.* 1.4.10 (CSEL 63:128), following the reading of mss A and T, which give the full line of *Aen.* 10.875.
28. *Acad.* 2.4.10 (CSEL 63:30): "in poeticae studium sic inflammatus est, ut aliquantum mihi etiam reprimendus uideretur." Cf. *Acad.* 3.1.1 (CSEL 63:46).
29. *Conf.* 1.13.20 (CSEL 33:18).

what they often said to Augustine would have surprised Vergil and those who followed him.[30] The same might be said of any number of writers whose books had ended up on Augustine's library shelves in earlier days.

Bookshelves

Do such moments of engagement with Vergil constitute evidence that can truly help us understand Augustine's relationship with the classical Latin literary tradition? Indeed, just what do we mean by the latter concept? On the one hand, the Latin literary tradition, as it came to be formulated by the late fourth century, can be narrowly viewed as a library shelf stocked with very select works, especially those whose authors formed the core of the late ancient school curriculum (Terence, Cicero, Sallust, and Vergil), augmented by the "further reading lists" assembled by contemporary representatives of high culture and good taste, the kind of men who, like the young Augustine, might aspire to a career as an advocate, a court official, or a provincial governor. That literary tradition, of course, which could embrace the poet Lucan as well as the historian Livy, deeply influenced elite ways of speaking and writing because it provided not only themes for declamations (such as the schoolboy Augustine's voicing of Juno's anger over the inevitability of Aeneas's arrival in Italy—a rhetorical *ethopoeia*)[31] but also set high standards of grammar, diction, and pronunciation. Such guidelines were necessary because the literary and professional registers had already drifted away from the colloquial by Augustine's day.[32] In other words, not only what one said or wrote but also how one said and wrote it announced social class, station, and ambition. This Augustine knew well, for he had himself been a seller of words and their winning ways to social and political climbers hovering around the centers of power at Carthage, Rome, and Milan.[33] From this perspective, to establish

30. *Carmen, -is* appears an unmatched twenty-seven times in *ciu.*, often in the combination *carmina poetarum*. Second place goes to *conf.* and the letters, with nine each. Statistics from Brepols's Library of Latin Texts Online. For the interpretative moves that allowed the grammarian to find truth in a text that the text's author did not recognize, see Lim, "Augustine," 119–20.

31. *Conf.* 1.17.27 (CSEL 33:24–25). It was a prose paraphrase of *Aen.* 1.38; Hagendahl, *Augustine and the Latin Classics*, 320, 392.

32. Succinctly at Clark, "In Praise of the Wax Candle," 435–38.

33. *Conf.* 4.2.2 (CSEL 33:64): "uictoriosam loquacitatem uictus cupiditate uendebam"; cf. *conf.* 1.13.22 (CSEL 33:19–20): "uenditores grammaticae uel emptores."

Augustine's particular relationship with the Latin literary tradition begins with cataloging his personal library and tracing the presence of those works in his own thought and writing. The foundation for such an enterprise was solidly established a half century ago by Harald Hagendahl in a study that he categorized as "a work of philological research on Augustine's knowledge and use of profane Latin literature." Hagendahl's two-volume study required 769 pages, even though he tried to steer clear of the "theological and philosophical questions" related to Augustine's influences and appropriations.[34]

Yet Hagendahl could hardly be content merely to inventory. He understood that cataloging Augustine's bookshelves, or accessing his memory bank, was only a first—albeit crucial—step toward assessing Augustine's relationship with the Latin literary tradition.[35] His second volume, therefore, following a first devoted to assembling the *testimonia*, confronted "Augustine's attitude"—that is, the many ways in which Augustine the Christian writer responded to the "old literary tradition."[36] His final assessment of Augustine's "appreciation" of Vergil, which "rises and falls like a wave" and vacillates "between admiration and dislike," summarizes well his overall view of Augustine and the classics, just as it anticipates the conclusions of so many who have followed his lead.[37] As one of Augustine's more sensitive readers observed, no single answer can ever express what "Vergil meant for Augustine."[38]

Nevertheless, a certain amount of waffling and ambivalence on Augustine's part is to be expected. By the late fourth century, "attitudes" to the "old literary tradition" were both dividing and divisive, mired in the kind of identity politics that informed the debate about Vergil's Fourth Eclogue. Late ancient men and women, that is, could be characterized by what they read—or at least how they read what they read. The disgruntled historian Ammianus Marcellinus, Augustine's contemporary, belittled Rome's selfish and frivolous (in his view) aristocrats by accusing them of locking up their libraries like tombs while reading only

34. Hagendahl, *Augustine and the Latin Classics*, 9 (both quotations).

35. On Augustine's "modes of citation" of classical texts and the debate over his reliance on citation from memory, see, e.g., Hagendahl, *Augustine and the Latin Classics*, 459–62; O'Donnell, "Augustine's Classical Reading," 166–71; Danuta Shanzer, "Augustine and the Latin Classics," in *A Companion to Augustine*, ed. Mark Vessey (Malden, MA: Wiley-Blackwell, 2012), 168–71; and Lane Fox, *Augustine*, 66.

36. Hagendahl, *Augustine and the Latin Classics*, 14–15.

37. Hagendahl, *Augustine and the Latin Classics*, 445 and 458, with, e.g., Lim, "Augustine," 112.

38. MacCormack, *Shadows of Poetry*, 226.

the racy satires of Juvenal and the salacious biographies of Marius Maximus.[39] Jerome, another contemporary, would express his own anxieties by recounting how in a feverish dream he was hauled before the heavenly judge, who targeted Jerome's transgressions with a concise wordplay worthy of the exemplar of classical prose style that it denigrated: "*Ciceronianus es, non Christianus*; where your treasury is, there, too, is your heart."[40] The harrowing vision, Jerome later informed his addressee Eustochium, came upon him when he was living in a desert retreat surrounded by his cherished library of "worldly books" (*codices saeculares*), his Plautus and his Cicero. Beaten but given a second chance, as he told Eustochium, he vowed never to read such works again (though expunging memory was another matter). Finally, in the same years that Augustine was adjusting to his new life as a priest at Hippo, Paulinus of Bordeaux (then in Spain but soon to be at Campanian Nola) and his former teacher, the poet and man of court Ausonius, were trying to make sense of Paulinus's ascetic withdrawal by zeroing in on his newfound relationship to the Latin Muses. Songs (*carmina*) were the heart of the matter. In response to Ausonius's plea for his return to his former (and sensible) ways, Paulinus issued an ultimatum coded in literary terms:

> Why, father, do you bid the Muses [*Musae*] I have disowned
>> to return to my keeping?
> Hearts devoted to Christ deny the Camenae
>> and are closed to Apollo.
> There was a time when you and I made common cause,
>> equal in zeal if not ability,
> in summoning deaf Apollo from the Delphic cave,
>> in calling upon the Muses as deities [*numina*],
> in seeking out in groves and mountain ridges
>> the gift of poetic utterance bestowed by the gift of a god [*deus*].
> Now another force stirs my mind, a greater God [*maior deus*],
>> and demands other ways [*mores*].[41]

39. *Amm. Marc.* 14.6.18 and 28.4.14; C. U. Clark, *Ammiani Marcellini rerum gestarum libri qui supersunt* (Berlin: Weidmann, 1910), 16 and 469. See also John Matthews, *The Roman Empire of Ammianus* (Baltimore: Johns Hopkins University Press, 1989), 414–16.

40. Jerome, *Ep.* 22.30 (CSEL 54:190). Cf. Matt. 6:20–21.

41. Paulinus of Nola, *Carm.* 10.19–30 (CSEL 30:25 = CCSL 21:530; ET *The Poems of Paulinus of Nola*, trans. P. G. Walsh, ACW 40 [New York: Newman, 1975], 58–59): "quid abdicatas in meam curam, pater, / redire Musas praecipis? / negant Camenis nec patent Apollini /

In short, claims about books and the value assigned them did not simply announce literary tastes but also signaled allegiances within a range of weighty issues then encroaching on the terrain of history, religion, and Roman mores.

It was natural, therefore, that when Augustine responded to the recriminations let loose by Alaric's sack of Rome with the first books of *De ciuitate dei,* he spent so much energy recalibrating Vergil's *Aeneid,* Livy's *Ab urbe condita,* Sallust's historical monographs, and the venerable *Antiquities* of Marcus Terentius Varro.[42] Furthermore, it is for the same reason that disentangling the threads of Augustine's attitude to the Latin literary tradition is such a formidable task, one not made simpler by the apparent depth and perspicacity of many of the very texts with which Augustine engaged. He was neither the first nor the last to be enthralled or troubled by Cicero's *De re publica* (*Rep.*) or to be beguiled by Vergil's *carmen* of statecraft, willpower, and destiny. Moreover, such dilemmas could hardly be divorced from reexamination of the foundational disciplines that made it possible in the first place to appreciate the aesthetic delights and philosophical insights of such venerable works—or to begin to find the same qualities in the books of Christian scripture.

LIBERAL ARTS

Sabine MacCormack observed that Augustine's relationship to the classical literary and intellectual legacy evolved through three broad stages: a period of dedication to the study of the classical authors (especially Vergil) and classical philosophy (especially Platonism at the time of his conversion and baptism in Italy); a stage of more "selective scrutiny" of classical texts and their content following his return to North Africa; and a renewed engagement, though now intensely apologetic and polemical, in the pages of *De ciuitate dei* and throughout the strident debate with Julian of Eclanum.[43] In part this scheme resonates

---

dicata Christo pectora! / fuit ista quondam, non ope sed studio pari, / te cum mihi concordia / ciere surdum Delphica Phoebum specu, / uocare Musas numina / fandique munus munere indultum dei / petere e nemoribus aut iugis; / nunc alia mentem uis agit, maior deus, / alios que mores postulat."

42. On Augustine's former esteem for Varro, note *ord.* 2.20.54 (CSEL 63:185): "quamuis Varroni quis non credat?" See also Fabio Gasti, *La letteratura tardolatina: Un profilo storico (secoli III–VII d.C.)* (Rome: Carocci, 2020), 152–55.

43. MacCormack, *Shadows of Poetry,* 225–31; more succinctly at Sabine MacCormack,

because Augustine's attitudes to classical literature and classical thought were bound up with other variables in a life that was long and full of discussion and controversy. Almost inevitably, therefore, Augustine's thoughts about classical Latin literature's truthfulness evolved in tandem with his ideas about the value of a "liberal arts education" for the elites of a Christianizing world. In this respect, too, a period of disenchantment followed upon a period of optimism. In works of the mid 380s Augustine expressed confidence that the liberal arts (*artes* or *disciplinae*) could serve as basic training in a system of truly Christian education.[44]

While still at Milan in 387 CE, whether relying on plans of his own design or drawing on Varro's (lost) *disciplinae libri*,[45] Augustine publicly committed himself to composing his own disciplinary primers, a project set in motion with a volume on grammar.[46] Though the plan would not be carried through—indeed would be abandoned before truly getting underway—the setting of its formulation is not coincidental. The prospectus must have been intended to catch the eye of the closely knit cognoscenti of a city in which the aristocratic bishop's sermons paraded his philosophical learning and the eminent Christian Platonist—and once and future Praetorian prefect—Manlius Theodorus held sway.[47] Indeed,

---

"Classical Influences on Augustine," *AttA*, 206–13, from which I quote (206). For consensus see, e.g., Müller, *Formen und Funktionen der Vergilzitate*, 445–47, and Lim, "Augustine," 112–13.

44. Mark Vessey, "Introduction," in *Augustine and the Disciplines: From Cassiciacum to "Confessions*," ed. Karla Pollmann and Mark Vessey (Oxford: Oxford University Press, 2005), 1–21.

45. Danuta Shanzer, "Augustine's Disciplines: *Silent diutius Musae Varronis*?," in Pollmann and Vessey, *Augustine and the Disciplines*, 69–112. See also Virgilio Pacioni, "Liberal Arts," *AttA*, 492–94.

46. *Retr.* 1.6 (CSEL 36:27). On the question of identifying Augustine's treatise with one of two works transmitted under his name, see Vivien Law, "St. Augustine's *De grammatica*: Lost or Found?," *RechAug* 19 (1984): 155–83; Robert Kaster, *Guardians of Language: The Grammarian and Society in Late Antiquity* (Berkeley: University of California Press, 1988), 246–47; CPL 1557–58. On Augustine's previous passion for devouring books on the liberal arts, see *conf.* 4.16.30 (CSEL 33:87–88).

47. Neil B. McLynn, *Ambrose of Milan: Church and Court in a Christian Capital* (Berkeley: University of California Press, 1994), 237–43, esp. 239 on the "learning he paraded in his sermons." For Theodorus's career and influence, see A. H. M. Jones, J. R. Martindale, and J. Morris, eds., *The Prosopography of the Later Roman Empire*, vol. 1, *A.D. 260–395* (Cambridge: Cambridge University Press, 1971), 900–902 (Flavius Mallius Theodorus 27); and Pietri and Pietri, *Prosopographie chrétiennes du Bas-Empire*, 2:2167–68 (Theodorus 2). Theodorus is likely to be the figure behind the "man swollen with immense pride" who at Milan provided Augustine with the *libri Platonicorum*; see *conf.* 7.9.13 (CSEL 33:154) with O'Donnell, *Confessions*, 2:418–20. For a recent view of the *status quaestionis* of Neoplatonism's prominence at Milan in

Theodorus's sister (or daughter), Manlia Daedalia, would be buried either in the Basilica Ambrosiana (S. Ambrogio), where in 397 the body of that bishop, Ambrose, joined both his brother's remains and the storied relics of Gervasius and Protasius, or in Ambrose's Basilica Apostolorum (S. Nazaro) on the other side of town.[48] In either case, Daedalia's verse epitaph, five elegiac couplets that echo Ovid as well as Damasus, announced—in bold Neoplatonic metaphor—her return to Christ "through the stars on high."[49] Notably, Augustine wore his own (Christian) Platonism lightly in the dialogue *De beata uita* that he had recently dedicated to Theodorus.[50]

Men and women such as Theodorus and Daedalia, erudite, philosophically inclined, and politically adept, could be counted on to appreciate the literary and intellectual currents that charged the dialogues of Cassiciacum. Moreover, the ideals of *otium liberale* that saturated these works, though codified centuries earlier in such Ciceronian philosophical dialogues as the *Tusculan Disputations* (*Tusc.*), still carried weight among the Roman elite.[51] Against this background, then, Vergilian quotations and Ciceronian conceits were never simply window dressing. Such ploys were integral to the ways and means by which the dialogues composed at Verecundus's alpine chalet presented Augustine in ways that justi-

---

the 380s and of Augustine's "primary philosophical debt" to it as expressed in the Cassiciacum dialogues, see Daniel Austin Napier, *En Route to the Confessions: The Roots and Development of Augustine's Philosophical Anthropology*, LAHR 6 (Leuven: Peeters, 2013), 3–33, quotation from 5; at 4n2 he notes that the Milanese church might well be considered "the institutional home" of Christian Neoplatonism.

48. Daedalia: Pietri and Pietri, *Prosopographie chrétiennes du Bas-Empire*, 1:528 (Manlia Daedalia). On the location of the burial and the epitaph, see Giuseppe Cuscito, *Inscriptiones Christianae Italiae XVI: Mediolanum III* (Bari: Edipuglia, 2016), no. 159, at 140–42.

49. Cuscito, *Inscriptiones Christianae Italiae*, 159.8: "rettulit ad Christum celsa per astra gradum."

50. E.g., *beata u.* 1.4 (CSEL 63:92). Cf. the background offered by Rein Ferwerda, "Plotinus' Presence in Augustine," in *Augustiniana Traiectina: Communications présentées au Colloque International d'Utrecht 13–14 novembre 1986*, ed. J. den Boeft and J. van Oort (Paris: Études Augustiniennes, 1987), 107–18. Cf. Lane Fox, *Augustine*, 316–21.

51. John Matthews, *Western Aristocracies and Imperial Court: AD 364–425* (Oxford: Clarendon, 1975), 1–12; Dennis Trout, "Augustine at Cassiciacum: Otium honestum and the Social Dimensions of Conversion," VC 42 (1988): 132–46; Alan Cameron, *The Last Pagans of Rome* (Oxford: Oxford University Press, 2011), 396–98; Michele Renee Salzman, ed., *The Letters of Symmachus: Book 1*, trans. Michele Renee Salzman and Michael Roberts (Atlanta: Society of Biblical Literature, 2011), xliv–xlvi, observations that can in many cases be transferred from Symmachus's letters to Augustine's dialogues.

fied his professional choices (especially his imminent retirement) and revealed him smartly "favouring flexibility" and *au courant* intellectual indeterminacy over the kind of "dogmatic fixity" that would have pegged him as boorish.[52]

However, Augustine's manifold allusions in the dialogues to those classical writers whose personae were inseparable from elite identity were also surely intended to signal his interest in some kind of program of literary salvage work. It has recently been argued, with some force, that the dialogues of Cassiciacum were especially fitted out to "recuperate" the classical *auctores* and give them a key role "in the articulation of Christian meaning." So might the classics, above all Vergil, "be made safe" for Christian readers.[53] To this end, Joseph Pucci maintains, the dialogues modeled a three-prong pedagogy that proceeded, schoolroom fashion, from the close review (*recensere*) of poetry, to the discussion of select passages in detail (*tractare*), to the application, or "turning" (*congruere*), of those passages to relevant issues of philosophical debate.[54] Seen from this perspective, Augustine's dismissal of the "lofty Apollo" in the passage of *De ordine* noted above, evoked by a quotation of *Aeneid* 10.875, becomes not a case of enthusiasm reined in by second thoughts but a display, as it unfolds in the ensuing conversation, of the sophisticated recuperation of a Vergilian hexameter to new ends. A complex of intertextual allusions, Pucci argues, draws Aeneas's (and Augustine's) Virgilian utterance into harmony with the growing exegetical skills (or recuperative powers) of Augustine's interlocutor, Licentius, preserving Vergil's general utility for readers in the new Christian age.[55] The argument is intricate, and the proof perhaps tenuous, but the problem the dialogues present is real. Others have also believed that one of Augustine's aims in these works was to "re-educate his readers" by modeling a "safe way" to read Vergil and other classical poets.[56] Certainly, a centuries-old literary tradition and the pedagogical system that underwrote it could not be precipitously tossed aside, as Jerome once

52. Conybeare, *Irrational Augustine*, 5 and 191.

53. Joseph Pucci, *Augustine's Virgilian Retreat: Reading the* Auctores *at Cassiciacum* (Toronto: Pontifical Institute of Mediaeval Studies, 2014), xv.

54. Pucci, *Augustine's Virgilian Retreat*, 20–26.

55. Pucci, *Augustine's Virgilian Retreat*, 107–10.

56. Camille Bennett, "The Conversion of Vergil: The *Aeneid* in Augustine's *Confessions*," *REAug* 34 (1988): 48; Clark, "In Praise of the Wax Candle," 438–45, demonstrates how the image of Licentius in the Cassiciacum dialogues was part of a maneuver by Augustine to offer sonorous classicizing verse with Christian content and accessible language a role in inspiring

impractically suggested one might offload wealth's debilitating weight.[57] Perhaps they could, however, like deleterious riches be redistributed and repurposed.

It is not, of course, just the complexity of Augustine's regard of Vergil in the Cassiciacum dialogues that suggests the ambivalence informing his approach to the liberal arts curriculum and its texts in those early days. There is also the towering figure that Augustine would then identify as "our Cicero."[58] No presence looms larger (naturally enough) in Augustine's *De beata uita* and *De Academicis* than the late-Republican author of the protreptic *Hortensius* (*Hort.*), *Tusculan Disputations*, and various works (including an *Academica*) devoted to the philosophy of the New Academy. In his own *De Academicis*, therefore, Augustine put on display some of the learning and insight that have earned him modern honors as Cicero's "most imaginative disciple."[59] Indeed, it is not only *Confessiones* that attests to the profound influence exercised by *Hortensius* upon the nineteen-year-old Augustine; that point had already made point in *De beata uita* and *De Academicis*.[60] *De Academicis* is itself, of course, an extended rumination on Academic epistemological skepticism as appropriated by Augustine via Cicero.[61]

But, as Maurice Testard noted (and others have pointed out in detail), Augustine, despite being ever seduced by Cicero, was never fully satisfied by him.[62] In *De Academicis* Augustine expressed that ambivalence by undermining Cicero's arguments against the certainty of knowledge. At the same time, however, he suggested that Cicero and such alleged New Academy skeptics as Carneades never actually held the (absurd) doctrines they publicly professed. Rather, they had sequestered their true (Platonic) beliefs, reserving them solely for the initiated

---

its audience to the praise of God. For more on the tutorial modeling of the dialogues, see Lane Fox, *Augustine*, 316–17.

57. Jerome, *Ep.* 53.11 to Paulinus (CSEL 54:465).

58. *Acad.* 1.3.7 (CSEL 63:8).

59. O'Donnell, *Confessions*, 2:162.

60. *Conf.* 3.4.7 (CSEL 33:48); *Acad.* 1.1.4 (CSEL 63:6); cf. Lane Fox, *Augustine*, 316: "*On the Happy Life* makes repeated use of phrases, arguments and imagery from Cicero's *Hortensius*, the young participants' lesson book."

61. "Citations" are assembled at Maurice Testard, *Saint Augustin et Cicéron. II: Répertoire des Textes* (Paris: Études Augustiniennes, 1958), 1–7. Depth of influence is considered at Testard, *Saint Augustin et Cicéron. I: Cicéron dans la formation et dans l'oeuvre de Saint Augustin* (Paris: Études Augustiniennes, 1958), 79–97 and 209–10, and at John M. Rist, *Augustine: Ancient Thought Baptized* (Cambridge: Cambridge University Press, 1994), 41–91.

62. Testard, *Saint Augustin et Cicéron. I*, 95: "Augustin se retrouvait au même point, toujours séduit par Cicéron en même temps qu'insatisfait."

and posterity.[63] Thus Augustine's Cicero could reasonably seem to be saved from himself and provide a trustworthy pathway to those regions of "truth" that would ultimately be ungated by Christian faith.[64] Or not—for Augustine's exculpatory move comes quite late in *De Academicis* and is preceded by a sharp-tongued Ciceronian parody that damned the epistemology of Cicero's *Academica* on multiple charges of immorality.[65] Even to some original readers of the Cassiciacum dialogues, then, unaware of what would follow, the Christian future of both Vergil and Cicero, twin pillars of the *artes liberales* and of the late antique schoolroom, must have seemed uncertain. Recuperation and dismissal vied for primacy. The next steps, advancing from such shaky ground, would only be more halting.

In the Service of Truth

By the mid 390s some of the tensions evident in Augustine's immediately "post-conversion" works were apparently resolved. In those years, it has been observed, Augustine appears increasingly pessimistic "about the possibility, or desirability, of a Christianization of the traditional curriculum."[66] Accordingly, the value of *grammatica*—that is, literary studies—so it goes, begins its steady decline. The more explicit scenes from the *Confessiones* are well enough known, and one—Augustine's denunciation of his schoolboy infatuation with the wanderings of that "fellow Aeneas"—has already been mentioned. It is, however, especially the *De doctrina christiana* (*doctr. chr.*), begun in the mid 390s, prior to *Confessiones,* that stages Augustine's disillusionment and whose agenda sheds fresh light on his relationship with the formative texts of his past.

To some extent Augustine's *De doctrina christiana* retains the mysteries long associated with its two-stage composition. Augustine began the work in the immediate wake of his episcopal ordination but abandoned it somewhat more than midway through its third book (after 3.25.35), only to take it up again in the late 420s and add a fourth book.[67] One stumbling block that led to the decades-long

---

63. *Acad.* 3.18.40–3.20.43 (CSEL 63:77–80).

64. Carol Harrison, *Rethinking Augustine's Early Theology: An Argument for Continuity* (Oxford: Oxford University Press, 2006), 35–36 and 68–69.

65. Conybeare, *Irrational Augustine,* 55–57.

66. Philip Burton, "The Vocabulary of the Liberal Arts in Augustine's *Confessions,*" in Pollmann and Vessey, *Augustine and the Disciplines,* 142.

67. For context, see Charles Kannengiesser and Pamela Bright, *A Conflict of Christian*

hiatus is sometimes held to be Augustine's (mis)apprehension of the *Book of Rules*, a treatise on biblical interpretation written by the Donatist theologian Tyconius.[68] In any case, for as much positive energy as the first instantiation of *De doctrina christiana* concedes to basic literacy's fundamental role in Christian education,[69] it grants just as little worth to the particular literary superstructure that antiquity had erected upon those foundations. The originating myth of pagan literature, embodied here by representing the nine Muses as the daughters of Jupiter and Memory, is dismissed as no more than a convenient fiction, and the poets and writers of the classical tradition are, for the most part, construed as abettors of falsehoods and purveyors of lethal superstition.[70] To be sure, Augustine admitted, pagan thought and literature should be stripped of any precious goods (even certain ethical principles) that could be reemployed in the "service of truth" (*usus ueritatis*)—just as the Israelites had once plundered the gold and silver vessels of the Egyptians—but that cache should never be carted off whole.[71] Perhaps nothing is more telling of the stance Augustine meant to project in *De doctrina christiana* than the near absence of allusions to or quotations of those classical writers who are so ever-present in the Cassiciacum dialogues. Vergil is once mentioned by name, but only in order to illustrate the utter conventionality (and, therefore, insidious potential) of Latin poetry, wherein the length of a syllable could cavalierly be shifted from short to long simply because it suited the needs of the moment.[72] Terence, another school author, provides a maxim, though anonymously.[73] Cicero is invoked through a weighty allusion at the outset,[74] but thereafter is avoided until Augustine returned

Hermeneutics in Roman Africa: Tyconius and Augustine (Berkeley: Center for Hermeneutical Studies, 1989), and Charles Kannengiesser, "The Interrupted *De doctrina christiana*," in *De doctrina christiana: A Classic of Western Culture*, ed. Duane W. H. Arnold and Pamela Bright (Notre Dame, IN: University of Notre Dame Press, 1995), 3–13.

68. Kannengiesser, "Interrupted *De doctrina christiana*," 7–9.

69. On reading skills and the interpretation of scripture, see *doctr. chr.* 2.9.14–2.16.26 (CSEL 80:41–53).

70. On the Muses, see *doctr. chr.* 2.17.27 (CSEL 80:53–54); on the dangers of reading too widely, see, e.g., *doctr. chr.* 2.39.58 (CSEL 80:73–74).

71. *Doctr. chr.* 2.40.60 (CSEL 80:75–76).

72. *Doctr. chr.* 2.38.56 (CSEL 80:72–73). A quotation of *Aen.* 7.508 appears much later at 4.20.42 (CSEL 80:151).

73. *Doctr. chr.* 2.39.58 (CSEL 80:74).

74. *Doctr. chr.* 1.1.1 (CSEL 80:8): "magnum opus et arduum," with Cicero, *Orat.* 33: "magnum opus omnino et arduum, Brute, conamur." See Hagendahl, *Augustine and the Latin Classics*, 162–63, and O'Donnell, "Augustine's Classical Reading," 156–57. Ciceronian allusions

to the work decades later, at a time when, for reasons connected to his composition of *De ciuitate dei*, Cicero was otherwise very much on his mind and *De doctrina christiana*'s turn to the art of oratory made Cicero indispensable. Yet even then he appears obliquely as the "founder of Roman eloquence" (*Romani auctor eloquii*).[75] In short, the *De doctrina christiana* of the mid 390s distances itself from the classical literary tradition (though not from the analytical skill sets that secular education might impart) largely by eschewing direct mention of its leading representatives.

It is left to *Confessiones* to present a more granular view of Augustine's dilemma in the years after his episcopal ordination. In this work, which so exuberantly names names, Augustine demonstrates what it might actually mean to redirect classical texts and classical exempla to the service of truth. *Confessiones* does not easily bear reduction, but it is worth noting how situational is Augustine's recourse to the literary past therein. Certainly, the dangers of absorption in the fictitious worlds of Latin poetry are made explicit. Again, this cautionary tale is most evident in the self-castigation that attends his youthful fascination with the wanderings of Aeneas and the tragedy of Dido. Yet Rome's ancient history and Latin literature's lauded texts and authors, even Augustine's retrospective on his once "passionate identification with Dido," can serve a range of ends, not all of which were injurious.[76] Elsewhere, for example, Augustine will enlist Sallust's grim view of the late Roman Republic to subvert overly simplistic readings of the trajectory of Roman triumphalism. In *Confessiones*, however, as Augustine analyzed the psychological malaise underlying his boyhood theft of pears, the tortured figure of Catiline proved useful. Artfully evoked by quotation of Sallust's monograph (another school text) before being explicitly named, Catiline and his desperate grab for control of the city typified the desire for advantage that ever motivates even the most reprehensible actions, the very desire that Augustine now found inexplicably lacking in his own wanton act.[77] Two books later, revisiting the emotional turbulence stirred up by a young friend's death and querying the nature of friendship, he inevitably nodded toward Cicero's *De amicitia*[78] while simultaneously adducing Horace's description of Vergil as "the half of

---

would echo throughout book 4; see the index at CSEL 80:174; Testard, *Saint Augustin et Cicéron*, 2:27–29; and Hagendahl, *Augustine and the Latin Classics*, 558–68.

75. *Doctr. chr.* 4.17.34 (CSEL 80:143).

76. Bennett, "Conversion of Vergil," 55–57.

77. *Conf.* 2.5.11 (CSEL 33:37–38). Helpful discussion at O'Donnell, *Confessions*, 2:133–34.

78. *Conf.* 4.6.11 (CSEL 33:72–73). If the very word (*amicitia*) were not sufficient, the introduction of Orestes and Pylades should have been effective; see Cic. *Amic.* 7.24 (text and

his own soul" (*dimidium animae suae*), though explicitly naming neither poet.[79] Even now the literary gesture remains emotionally and intellectually satisfying. Although ultimately Augustine conceded that all such formulations fell short of the mark, for only friendships formed in union with God can well endure, he understood the communicative power of such past exempla among his peers.[80] Moreover, by quoting and alluding and approving, even hesitantly, Augustine found secure places for all these writers—Sallust, Cicero, Horace, and Vergil—in *Confessiones*'s webs of meaning.

Such endorsements, some more restrained than others, run throughout *Confessiones* and in the end swamp both the cool reserve of *De doctrina christiana* and the text's own lament over those tears shed for Dido. Cicero's *Hortensius*, for example, the book whose exhortation to philosophy changed Augustine's life as a student at Carthage and for which he seems to have long maintained a "sentimental affection," may have lacked the name of Christ, but its cautionary notes about charlatans masquerading as philosophers, Augustine later came to realize, harmonized well with advice Paul had given in Col. 2:8–9: "See that no one deceives you through philosophy and the hollow seductions of man-made traditions."[81] Even the "fable" (*fabella*) of "Medea in flight" was far less noxious than the lethal fantasies of Manichaean cosmology; the former, the stuff of the schoolroom, no one was encouraged to accept as truth (and it might even provide a prodigal son the means of making a living).[82] Moreover, in this case as in his treatment of friendship, Augustine played to contemporary literary tastes, highlighting the manifest falsehood of *Medea uolans* by alluding to Cicero's *De inuentione*, which had illustrated the nature of *fabulae* by quoting a line from the *Medus* of the dramatic poet Pacuvius (a line that Augustine himself had already quoted in his *Soliloquies* [*sol.*]).[83] Clearly, it was hard to reroute old ways of making meaning. Naturally enough, then, when Augustine envisioned his own

---

trans. Falconer, LCL 154:134–35). See further Tarsicius J. van Bavel, "The Influence of Cicero's Ideal of Friendship on Augustine," in den Boeft and van Oort, *Augustiniana Traiectina*, 59–72.

79. *Conf.* 4.6.11 (CSEL 33:72–73): "bene quidam dixit de amico suo: dimidium animae suae," with Horace, *Carm.* 1.3.8: "et serues [nauis] animae dimidium meae."

80. *Conf.* 4.9.14 (CSEL 33:75): "et uersa dulcidine in amaritudinem cor madidum."

81. *Conf.* 3.4.7–8 (CSEL 33:48–50). On Augustine's running dialogue with Cicero's philosophical treatises in this and the next books of *conf.*, see O'Donnell, *Confessions*, 2:162, and O'Donnell, "Augustine's Classical Reading," 155: "sentimental affection."

82. *Conf.* 3.6.11 (CSEL 33:52–53).

83. Hagendahl, *Augustine and the Latin Classics*, 157 and 214–15, as well as O'Donnell, *Confessions*, 2:182. Cf. *sol.* 2.15.29 (CSEL 89:85).

stealthy but divinely directed departure from both Carthage and Monica, he recalled readers to Aeneas's fate-driven desertion of Dido and escape from the enervating enticements of the same city.[84] Augustine's aim, however, was surely not to suggest a facile affinity with the heroism of Aeneas but rather to prod readers to read Vergil correctly, to discern the deeper truths in his poetry and apply those truths to their own therapeutic self-reflection.[85]

Augustine was not unique in his dilemma. Nearly all educated Latin Christians of his day had been schooled on Terence, Sallust, Cicero, and Vergil, and many were sensitive to the implications of maintaining too strong attachments to once cherished texts. By highlighting not only the dangers of misuse but also the half-truths lurking in such texts, *Confessiones* will have said many things to contemporaries about ways in which the literary past might be redeployed in the service of new ends. *Confessiones*'s readers are still energized by such tensions. Here, perhaps more so than in *De doctrina christiana*, literary texture and literary questions intersected head-on with the ethical and spiritual charges carried by late antique reading practices.

THE SURFACE OF THINGS

In the aftermath of the Visigothic sack of Rome in the late summer of 410, with a sense of urgency, Augustine undertook a crash course in Roman historiography and political science, reading closely both Cicero's *De re publica* and Livy's *Ab urbe condita*—the latter perhaps in earnest for the first time—together with the second-century epitomator Florus and the fourth-century *breuiator* Eutropius. It seems Augustine had shown little real interest in such matters before,[86] but that kind of "history" had suddenly become central to the charges and countercharges reverberating among pagans and Christians in the months and years after Alaric's troops had rampaged through Italy. In Rome, as Augustine knew, some had been spared through sanctuary at the city's churches; others had been far less fortunate, as death, rape, and pillaging fell over the city. Almost immediately, in the heated arguments of the first book of *De ciuitate dei*—before the next initiated a more systematic refutation of ingrained historical assumptions—Augustine put

---

84. *Conf.* 5.8.15 (CSEL 33:101–2).

85. Cf. Bennett, "Conversion of Vergil," 61–65.

86. O'Donnell, "Augustine's Classical Reading," 160 and 171; see also Hagendahl, *Augustine and the Latin Classics*, 631–34 (Sallust) and 542 (*Rep.*).

his research to use, offering a lucid illustration of the synergy between Augustine and the reader and Augustine the writer.[87] Sallust, long familiar to Augustine but now dusted off for review and praised for his veracity, offered the bishop an easy rebuttal of those who credited Roman decline to the success of Christianity.[88] The rot, Sallust had made clear and Augustine was pleased to recall, had set in long before, with the mid-Republican destruction of Carthage.[89] But the more emotionally charged and immediately subversive feature of Augustine's defense in this first book of what would prove in time to be a twenty-two-book enterprise, was his debunking of revered classical *exempla uirtutis*. With the stakes so public and an audience so intransigent, Augustine targeted first Lucretia, whose rape by Sextus Tarquinius and self-vindicating suicide had, it was said, precipitated the fall of the city's tyrannical monarchy. He then turned to Cato the Younger, whose self-inflicted death at Utica five centuries later, at the other end of the Republic's history, had denied Caesar the opportunity to extend his withering *clementia* to a key opponent of his emerging autocracy. Though both Lucretia and Cato had proven remarkably durable exemplars of Roman values, below "the surface of things" Augustine saw realities others had too long chosen to ignore.[90]

It was essentially Livy's Lucretia, though briefly relegated to a Vergilian underworld, whom Augustine brought to trial.[91] Livy had exploited Lucretia's story

87. Augustine's research methods and sources for particular historical episodes remain difficult to sort out, but Livy's centrality is evident, either directly or through the later summaries and epitomators; see Hagendahl, *Augustine and the Latin Classics*, 650–66. Book 1 of *ciu.* was completed by September 413 CE; some of its themes had already been broached in *exc. urb.* (CCSL 46:249–62) and, as noted earlier, esp. in *s.* 105 (PL 38:618–25).

88. *Ciu.* 1.5 (CCSL 47:5): "nobilitatae ueritatis historicus."

89. Sallust, *Bell. Cat.* 10.1 (Carthago aemula imperi Romani) is verbally echoed at *ciu.* 1.30 (CCSL 47:31); Hagendahl, *Augustine and the Latin Classics*, 233. The point, Carthage's ameliorating influence on Rome, is renewed and expanded at *ciu.* 2.18, the verbal echo repeated at *ciu.* 3.31 (CCSL 47:90), and Sallust's view of Rome's moral decline expatiated on at *ciu.* 5.12 (CCSL 47:144–45). See further MacCormack, *Shadows of Poetry*, 194–98; Anne-Marie Taisne, "Salluste chez saint Augustin (Cité de Dieu, I-V)," in *Présence de Salluste*, ed. Rémy Poignault (Tours: Centre de Recherches A. Piganiol, 1997), 119–28; and the overview at Gerard O'Daly, *Augustine's City of God: A Reader's Guide* (Oxford: Clarendon, 1999), 240–46.

90. Bob Dylan, "2016 Nobel Lecture in Literature," June 4, 2017, https://www.nobelprize .org/prizes/literature/2016/dylan/lecture/: "We see only the surface of things. We can interpret what lies below any way we see fit." For context, see Richard Thomas, *Why Bob Dylan Matters* (New York: HarperCollins, 2017), 311–19.

91. For Livy, see S. Angus, *The Sources of the First Ten Books of Augustine's "De civitate Dei"* (Princeton: Princeton Press, 1906), 28 and 77. Vergil: *ciu.* 1.19 (CCSL 47:20–21) with Ver. *Aen.*

to powerful effect in the last chapters of the first book of his monumental history *Ab urbe condita*. But in a move that still surprises, Augustine turned Lucretia's own words against her and against those who would callously use her trite *exemplum* to denigrate Christian women. "My body only has been violated; my mind is innocent," the Livian heroine had exclaimed, a conceit echoed, as Augustine recalled, by a "certain declaimer" (*quidam declamans*) who had defended Lucretia's *pudictia* by announcing that "there were two, yet only one committed adultery."[92] Given that claim, Augustine concluded, Lucretia's grandstanding suicide condemned her as a simple murderess, as perpetrator of an act of prideful self-assertion that denied her any moral authority in a Christianizing age. To save her from that charge, moreover, would have required—though here Augustine hesitated—making her own will complicit, to some degree, in the assault that had victimized her. Livy had misjudged the moral of Lucretia's tale.

For good reason, Augustine's brazen act of subversive reading has drawn significant attention in recent years.[93] Less often, perhaps because less relevant to contemporary debates over sexual violence and rape, has Augustine's Cato been spotlighted. For Augustine's immediate audience, the matter may have been otherwise. Cato's reputation as a "learned and upright man" (*uir doctus et probus*) was still intact, and his suicide, like Lucretia's, Augustine observed, was considered an authoritative endorsement of the act's nobility in certain circumstances.[94] As he had with Lucretia's story, Augustine highlighted the inconsistencies that marked Cato's actions: Why did his learned (*docti*) friends try to dissuade him, arguing that suicide was the easy way out and the sign of a weak mind? Why did he advise his own son to accept Caesar's clemency when to do so was beneath his own dignity? Nor does Augustine repeat any of the details that might, as they did, for example, in Plutarch's account of Cato's last hours, win sympathy for Cato: his dinner conversation with friends, his deathbed reading of Plato's *Phaedo*, the

6.434–439; cf. Hagendahl, *Augustine and the Latin Classics*, 342. On Augustine's understanding of the motivating power of *exempla*, note his thoughts about Marius Victorinus at *conf.* 8.4.9 (CSEL 33:176).

92. Liv. 1.58.7 (R. M. Ogilvie, *Titi Livi Ab urbe condita*, Oxford Classical Texts [Oxford: Clarendon, 1974], 73): "ceterum corpus est tantum uiolatum, animus insons"; *ciu.* 1.19 (CCSL 47:20): "duo fuerunt et adulterium unus admisit." The declaimer's identity is unknown.

93. For bibliography see, e.g., Dennis Trout, "Re-textualizing Lucretia: Cultural Subversion in the *City of God*," *JECS* 2 (1994): 53–70, and Melanie Webb, "'On Lucretia who slew herself': Rape and Consolation in Augustine's *De civitate dei*," *AugStud* 44, no. 1 (2013): 37–58.

94. *Ciu.* 1.23 (CCSL 47:24).

pleas and tears of his son, the bleakness of a first botched attempt, and the loyalty of the people of Utica, who honorably laid Cato's body to rest even as Caesar approached.[95] Such details were surely known to Augustine, if not through his literary sources, probably including Livy, then through oral tradition.[96] Utica lay on the much-traveled coastal road between Hippo and Carthage.[97] Augustine preached in the city often and in *De ciuitate dei* recorded his inspection of an enormous molar tooth (*molarem hominis dentem*) that had washed up on the shore there. In his opinion, it must once have belonged to a giant (*gigas*).[98] He does not, however, mention the statue of Cato, sword in hand, that, according to Plutarch, stood atop the former's grave near that same sea coast.[99]

Both these episodes—Augustine's cross-examination of Lucretia and his repudiation of Cato—are notable, not only for their vehemence and cynicism, but for Augustine's choice to see what he saw fit in these two encrustations of the Latin literary tradition.[100] The sack of Rome had catalyzed issues that previously had been more easily sidestepped, and identity politics had seized the foreground amid the incriminations that followed. Augustine now stepped into that territory with, it seems, impatience and frustration. In any case, resistance and ambivalence rose once more to the surface. The subsequent books of *De ciuitate dei* would engage a range of representatives of the classical tradition and the ideas their works were held to embody. The massive *Antiquities* (human and divine) of the polymath Marcus Terentius Varro, Cicero's *De re publica* and *De natura deorum*, Livy's history of early Rome, and, of course, Vergil's national epic are immediately put on the defensive. In a work intended to refute those pagans who believed that the welfare of mankind depended on worshiping many gods and to disabuse them of the notion that those same gods might provide benefits for the "life we will have after death,"[101] Augustine relied heavily on the evidence supplied by the very writers who had propped

95. Plut. *Cato Min.* 67–71 (text and trans. Perrin, LCL 100:398–407).

96. The loss of Livy's Book 114 makes reconstruction of Augustine's literary sources more difficult. Livy's importance is assumed by Angus, *Sources of the First Ten Books*, 80–81. Cicero had also written an encomium of Cato, though its survival is uncertain.

97. Othmar Perler and Jean-Louis Maier, *Les voyages de Saint Augustin*, Collection des Études Augustiniennes, Série Antiquité 36 (Paris: Études Augustiniennes, 1969), Map B.

98. On Augustine's preaching in Utica, see Perler and Maier, *Les voyages de Saint Augustin*, e.g., 50 and 274. Cf. *ciu.* 15.9 (CCSL 48:464).

99. Plut. *Cato Min.* 71 (LCL 8:406–7).

100. Cf. Dylan, "Nobel Lecture," cited in n. 90 *supra*.

101. The conspectus at Angus, *Sources of the First Ten Books*, 52–59, remains helpful. On Varro, see Hagendahl, *Augustine and the Latin Classics*, 265–316. On the twofold scheme of

up that house of cards. Yet he would read them in ways they could not have antic-ipated, seeing more fully what they could only have glimpsed. No wonder, then, that Augustine is now a primary source for reconstructing the lost works of Varro or that nearly half of Augustine's citations of Vergil occur in *De ciuitate dei*.[102]

Conclusion: Past, Present, and Future

Augustine was, like many people at other times and in other places, "forever caught up in the flow of the current moment, not just freighted with the icy inventory of the past."[103] His moment was one characterized by the significant cultural realign-ments that accompanied Christianity's recent rise to social and political promi-nence, transformations initiated decades earlier by Constantine's choices and pol-icies but accelerating rapidly during Augustine's Theodosian age. For almost all of Augustine's career-minded and ambitious Western contemporaries—regardless of their religious affiliations—the past was an imaginative realm textured above all else by the works of those canonized Latin authors who dominated the school system through a pedagogy that rewarded verbal fluency and prioritized the *enar-ratio poetarum*. Christians, like the son of Monica and Patricius, had no viable alternative. Certainly, over time and as circumstances dictated, Augustine added new texts and authors to his "classical reading," searching out other poets (Lucre-tius, Persius, Horace, and Lucan), digesting Cicero's philosophical and political dialogues, delving into the books of the Platonists (as well as the books of the Manichaeans), and reading intently Livy's history *Ab urbe condita*. And he discov-ered other pasts stored away in Christian scripture and within the pages of earlier Latin Christian writers such as Tertullian and Lactantius, men who had in like manner—though in a different age—observed the world from a cultural divide. Yet the tally of Augustine's *testimonia* stands witness to the abiding influence of his school days, as teacher as well as student. As the tides of dilemma, debate, and controversy swirled within and around him, Vergil and Cicero were seldom long absent from his thought. As he scanned the immediate and far reaches of the future, those authors continued to cast light forward.

---

the first ten books of *ciu.*, see Augustine's assessment at *retr.* 2.69 (CSEL 36:181): "propter uitam post mortem futuram."

102. O'Donnell, "Augustine's Classical Reading," 166.

103. David Treuer, *The Heartbeat of Wounded Knee: Native America from 1890 to the Present* (New York: Riverhead, 2019), 417.

Consequently, during his last years, mired in acrimonious debate over concupiscence and original sin with the glib Julian of Eclanum, for whom Paulinus of Nola had once penned a wedding poem thoroughly scrubbed of the old gods,[104] Augustine would have recourse again to the larger-than-life figures who had been his companions for so many decades. In the fourth book of the *Contra Iulianum* (*c. Iul.*), Cicero and Sallust, Terence and Vergil all reappear.[105] *Hortensius* was called into service to rebut Julian's own "crowd of philosophers."[106] Vergil was quoted to verify the difference between basic hunger (*fames*) and an extravagant love of eating (*edendi amor*).[107] Certainly, here as elsewhere scriptural citations outweigh Augustine's classical allusions and quotations, but the very presence of the latter in the *Contra Iulianum* is witness to their abiding influence on Augustine's patterns of thought. In this sense, his exchange with the Christian Julian of Eclanum overlaps his earlier debate with the cultivated pagan Nectarius of Calama, against whose claims of (misplaced) patriotism Augustine enlisted both Cicero (via *Rep.*) and that "most illustrious poet of your literature."[108] The possessive adjective (*uestrarum*) may have been intended to distance Augustine safely from Vergil, but it belies just how long and how profoundly the *Aeneid* spoke to Augustine of values and ideas whose vibrancy seems never to have dulled.

In the end, there can be no uncomplicated version of Augustine's relationship to the classical literary tradition. Nor should we expect it of those who live in a "house of words," nourishing a romance with "the world of the past."[109] The classical tradition's grip on Augustine's life and Rome's history was as inescapable

---

104. Paulinus of Nola, *Carm.* 25 (CSEL 30:235–45 = CCSL 21:652–60). The poem, fittingly enough given its learned recipient, is not bereft of Vergilian allusions; see Dennis Trout, *Paulinus of Nola: Life, Letters, and Poems* (Berkeley: University of California Press, 1999), 215–17.

105. References conveniently assembled at Teske, *Answer to the Pelagians II*, WSA I/24, 429–31. For Julian's use of Cicero and Sallust, often in terms of his own self-representation, see Josef Lössl, *Julian von Aeclanum: Studien zu seinem Leben, seinem Werk, seiner Lehre und ihre Überlieferung* (Brill: Leiden, 2001), e.g., 105–7, and Lössl, "Sallust in Julian of Aeclanum," *VC* 56 (2004): 179–202.

106. *C. Iul.* 4.15.75–78 (PL 44:477–79); see esp. 4.15.75: "turbam philosophorum." See also Hagendahl, *Augustine and the Latin Classics*, testimonia, 87–88.

107. *C. Iul.* 4.14.67 (PL 44:771) with *Aen.* 1.216 and 8.184.

108. *Ep.* 91.2–3 (CSEL 34/2:428): "poeta ille uestrarum clarissimus litterarum." For the episode, see MacCormack, *Shadows of Poetry*, 185–88. See also *ciu.* 5.12 (CCSL 47:143): "poeta insignis illorum."

109. Norman Ravvin, *A House of Words: Jewish Writing, Identity, and Memory* (Montreal: McGill-Queen's University Press, 1997), 1.

as was its influence on the very language and images with which he probed and articulated his understanding of the "infinite sweep of humanity." It is hardly surprising, then, that at Cassiciacum, as he pondered the imperturbability of the wise man, a line of the *Aeneid* leapt to mind, or that three decades later, as he was at work on *De ciuitate dei* and considering whether the soul of the *sapiens* can be disturbed by emotions (*perturbationes*), Aeneas stepped forth to epitomize the mind's "sovereign rule of virtuous excellence."[110] For Augustine, Vergil was ever *hors catégorie*.

110. *Ord.* 2.20.54 (CSEL 63:185), which quotes *Aen.* 7.586 and *ciu.* 9.4 (CCSL 47:253): "regnum virtutis," both discussed above.

PART III

·

Augustine and the Greek Patristic Tradition

Chapter 10

Augustine's Reception of Origen

Joseph W. Trigg

Athens and Jerusalem

After the New Testament, Augustine's *Confessiones* (*conf.*) is by far the most commonly read work of early Christian literature. Next might be *De ciuitate dei* (*ciu.*). Both, especially *Confessiones*, articulate a fusion of the Bible and Platonism.[1] Using the Pauline letters as a key and often employing figurative interpretation, they make the Old and New Testaments a coherent revelation of one God. The Bible's one God is, furthermore, the Platonic One, incorporeal because beyond space and time, the source and sustainer of all that comes into being. Augustine's works, spanning multiple genres, transmitted this fusion, which was foundational to Western thought for at least a thousand years.

For those who do not read beyond *Confessiones* and *De ciuitate dei*, this may appear to be Augustine's distinctive achievement. In *Confessiones* Augustine tells how he needed to learn that the Bible could be interpreted figuratively and to conceive of the God of the Bible in Platonic terms before he could commit himself as a Christian. Even though he calls what he learned the long-standing teaching of Catholic Christianity, a superficial reading of *Confessiones* could leave the impression that Augustine himself did the work of connecting Platonic metaphysics to the Christian faith. This probably led John Gray to write recently, as

---

1. Understanding "Platonism" as the philosophy exemplified by Plotinus and Porphyry. For this terminology, see Lloyd P. Gerson, *Platonism and Naturalism: The Possibility of Philosophy* (Ithaca, NY: Cornell University Press, 2020).

if it were received wisdom, that "Augustine's Christian Platonism was only the first" attempt to join Athens and Jerusalem.[2] Students of early Christianity, of course, are well aware that Philo in the first century—if not the Alexandrian Jews two centuries earlier who translated אֶהְיֶה ("I Am") in Exod. 3:14 as ὁ ὤν ("He Who Is" or "Being")—already interpreted the Hebrew Bible in Platonic terms. They also know that, building on that foundation and incorporating an understanding of the Hebrew Bible that he took from Paul, Origen had joined Athens to Jerusalem some two centuries before Augustine was born.

Considering how momentous this legacy was, surprisingly little attention has been paid to Augustine's debt to his great predecessor. With a few exceptions, those who have examined Augustine's use of and attitude to Origen have generally discussed narrow issues: what Augustine can be documented to have known about Origen by reading his works or hearing about them and what Augustine said about Origen.[3] Few works consider Origen's influence on Augustine's intellectual formation. It is true that Augustine scarcely referred to Origen at all and never in connection with his own formation, but this proves little. Harold Bloom showed in *The Anxiety of Influence* that antagonism or seeming indifference often masks the profound influence of one author on another. A compelling case has been made that Origen's work entailed the reception of Valentinus, whom he openly disdained.[4] Augustine scarcely shows up in Dante's *Comedy*, but Dante's construction of his own persona is inconceivable without the model of Augustine's *Confessiones*, and the whole poem struggles with the assessment of Rome in *De ciuitate dei*.[5]

---

2. John Gray, *Seven Types of Atheism* (New York: Farrar, Straus & Giroux, 2018), 29.

3. See Alfons Fürst, "Origenes," *AugLex* 4:380–88, for works that have addressed Augustine's indebtedness to Origen and his criticism of him. Robert J. O'Connell's works, *St. Augustine's Early Theory of Man, A.D. 386–391* (Cambridge, MA: Harvard University Press, 1968) and *The Origin of the Soul in St. Augustine's Later Works* (New York: Fordham University Press, 1987), are exceptional in dealing with Origen as a serious influence on one aspect of Augustine's thought, as is Elizabeth Clark's *The Origenist Controversy: The Cultural Construction of an Early Christian Debate* (Princeton: Princeton University Press, 1992). The other major exception is György Heidl, whose work will be discussed further below.

4. See Holger Strutwolf, *Gnosis als System: Zur Rezeption der valentinianischen Gnosis bei Origenes* (Göttingen: Vandenhoeck & Ruprecht, 1993).

5. On Dante's reception of Augustine, see Peter S. Hawkins, *Dante's Testaments: Essays in Scriptural Imagination* (Stanford, CA: Stanford University Press, 1999), esp. 197–228, and Simone Marchese, *Dante and Augustine: Linguistics, Poetics, Hermeneutics* (Toronto: University of Toronto Press, 2011).

Reading Origen at first hand, however, seems to be ruled out during Augustine's formative years because, although he could read Greek, he did not do so well enough to dispense with translations that, for the most part, only became available after 400.[6] He states in *Confessiones* that he knew Plotinus, one writer in Greek whom he does credit as an influence, through Marius Victorinus's now lost translation.[7] Thus, Frederick Van Fleteren, aware of the affinity between Origen's thought and the faith Augustine came to accept in Milan, has suggested that Origen was "in the air" there, even if, he thought, Augustine did not yet have firsthand knowledge of his work.[8] Goulven Madec imagines that when Augustine watched Ambrose read, he was absorbing a commentary of Origen that would inform his homilies.[9]

THE *LIBRI PLENI*

In 2003, however, György Heidl marshaled evidence that Augustine, in Milan, did indeed know some of Origen's works in translation and that he himself testified to their crucial role in his intellectual development.[10] Unfortunately, Heidl's work has not received the attention it deserves.[11] In making the case, Heidl starts

6. Berthold Altaner's 1939 article "Augustinus und die griechische Sprache," republished in *Kleine patristische Schriften*, ed. Günter Glockmann, TUGAL 83 (Berlin: Akademie, 1967), 129–53, established that Augustine could not read Greek well enough to dispense with translations. In 1958 H. I. Marrou, who did not cite Altaner, came to the same conclusion (*Saint Augustin et la fin de la culture antique* [republished with *Retractatio*, Paris: de Boccard, 1983], 25–46). On Augustine's Greek study, see *conf.* 1.13.20–1.14.23.

7. *Conf.* 7.9.14 and 8.2.3. Marius Victorinus also translated Aristotle's *Categories*.

8. In Frederick Van Fleteren and Joseph C. Schnaubelt, eds., *Augustine: Biblical Exegete*, ColAug 4 (New York: Lang, 2001), 4.

9. Goulven Madec, *Lectures Augustiniennes* (Paris: Études Augustiniennes, 2001), 40: "Lorsqu' Augustin nous présente Ambroise concentré, absorbé dans sa lecture silencieuse [*conf.* 5.13.13], j'imagine volontiers qu'il lisait un ouvrage d'Origène, le commentaire du Cantique des cantiques, par exemple. Il s'imprégnait de cette interprétation chrétienne pour préparer ses propres homélies. Et lorsque, la nuit venue, il s'installait à son pupitre pour écrire de sa propre main . . . les formules et les pensées du grand alexandrin lui revenait spontanément."

10. György Heidl, *Origen's Influence on the Young Augustine: A Chapter of the History of Origenism* (Piscataway, NJ: Gorgias Press, 2003).

11. For example, Carol Harrison does not refer to Heidl in *Rethinking Augustine's Early Theology: An Argument for Continuity* (Oxford: Oxford University Press, 2006). Alfons Fürst

with a vivid yet curious passage in *Contra Academicos* (*c. Acad.*), Augustine's earliest account of his spiritual formation, written in 386:

> Therefore, when you [Romanianus] left after the tinder had been kindled in us, we never stopped gawking after philosophy, and we did not think about anything else beyond that life which, among us, found favor and commended itself. And we constantly maintained our activity, to be sure, even if less keenly, though we thought we were acting keenly enough. And nonetheless that flame was not yet at hand that would completely consume us, but we reckoned that the low flame that warmed was a very big one. When, look, certain full books, as Celsinus says, at that point breathed out good Arabian things onto us, when these little flames were instilling tiny drops of most precious ointment. They incited an unbelievable conflagration, unbelievable, Romanianus, unbelievable, beyond what perhaps even you would believe from me, and—what more can I say?—beyond even what I could believe from myself. What honor, what human triumph, what desire of empty fame, in the end, what comfort or curb of this moral life moved me then? Swiftly I was returning completely right into myself. I looked back, to be sure, I confess, as from a journey, at that religious observance that was implanted in us as boys, and enmeshed in our marrow, while, unbeknownst to me, it was pulling me to itself. Consequently—stumbling, hurrying, faltering—I grabbed hold of the apostle Paul.[12]

---

dismissed Heidl in a footnote, stating incorrectly that Heidl identified the *libri pleni* with the "books of the Platonists" of *conf.* 7, which *beata u.* ascribes to Plotinus. See *Von Origenes und Hieronymus zu Augustinus: Studien zur antiken Theologiegeschichte* (Berlin: de Gruyter, 2011), 490n10.

12. *C. Acad.* 2.2.5 (CSEL 63:20–21; all translations are my own): "itaque cum admoto nobis fomite discessisses, nunquam cessauimus inhiantes in philosophiam, atque illam uitam quae inter nos placuit atque conuenit, prorsus nihil aliud cogitare: atque id constanter quidem, sed minus acriter agebamus; putabamus tamen satis nos agere. et quoniam nondum aderat ea flamma, quae summa nos arreptura erat; illamqua lenta aestuabamus, arbitrabamur uel esse maximam. cum ecce tibi libri quidam pleni, ut ait Celsinus, bonas res arabicas ubi exhalarunt in nos, ubi illi flammulae instillarunt pretiosissimi unguenti guttas paucissimas; incredibile, Romaniane, incredibile, et ultra quam de me fortasse et tu credis; quid amplius dicam? etiam mihi ipse de meipso incredibile incendium concitarunt. quis me tunc honor, quae hominum pompa, quae inanis famae cupiditas, quod denique huius mortalis uitae fomentum atque retinaculum commouebat? prorsus totus in me cursim redibam. respexi tantum, confiteor, quasi de itinere in illam religionem, quae pueris nobis insita est, et medullitus implicata:

This breathless account of *libri pleni* that set him on fire, drawing him back to the religion of his childhood, has long puzzled scholars. It has been widely assumed that the *libri pleni* are "the books of the Platonists turned from the Greek tongue into Latin" of *Confessiones* 7.9.13, specified as "books of Plotinus" in *De beata uita* (*beata u.*) 5.1.4. But if Augustine was also discussing those same books in *Contra Academicos*, it is hard to explain why the books are *pleni*, "full," or what "good Arabian things" and "tiny drops of most precious ointment" might have to do with the *Enneads*.

Heidl argues from this passage in *Contra Academicos* that Romanianus had been with Augustine reading the books by Plotinus mentioned in *De beata uita* and *Confessiones* and that the *libri pleni* were a separate set of books encountered after Romanianus returned to Africa. Heidl suggests that Simplicianus, whom Augustine consulted after reading Plotinus, did not simply counsel him as recounted in *Confessiones*, but gave him books by Origen that would make up for Plotinus's limitations.[13] These books were "full" or "complete" because they made the connection Plotinus did not make between the *nous* of Platonic philosophy and the biblical Logos incarnate in Jesus Christ.[14] One of these "full books," according to Heidl, was Jerome's translation of Origen's two *Homilies on the Song of Songs* (*Hom. Cant.*), which Jerome had prepared for Damasus during his Roman sojourn (382–384); the second homily discusses perfumes, for which Arabia was renowned, and interprets *gutta*, "drop," figuratively as the incarnate Christ.[15] A decade after writing *Contra Academicos*, raging controversy over Origen made it prudent for Augustine to omit the *libri pleni* from *Confessiones*.[16]

Heidl believes that two *epistulae* (*ep.*) in Augustine's correspondence strengthen his case, admittedly speculative, that Augustine knew Origen in translation: *Epistula* 28, well known as the opening letter of Augustine's correspondence with Jerome, and *Epistula* 27*, a letter by Jerome to Aurelius of Carthage that Johannes Divjak discovered in 1975.[17] Augustine wrote *Epistula* 28 to Jerome after being ordained as a presbyter in 391 but before becoming a bishop in 395.

uerum autem ipsa me ad se nescientem rapiebat. Itaque titubans, properans, haesitans arripio apostolum Paulum."

13. Heidl, *Origen's Influence*, 5–36. See *conf.* 8.3–5.

14. See *conf.* 8.2.3 and *ciu.* 10.29.

15. Origen, *Hom. Cant.* 2.3.

16. Heidl, *Origen's Influence*, 63–73.

17. The asterisk indicates that *ep.* 27* belongs to the additional series constituted by these twenty-nine recently discovered letters. Heidl, *Origen's Influence*, 69–73.

The reader may find nothing remarkable in Augustine's intellectual assurance and his relentless insistence on arguing for his understanding of scriptural authority. Considering when it was written, however, *Epistula* 28 appears brash and provocative. By the early 390s Jerome, in Bethlehem, was well on his way to being Jerome as we remember him, the most respected scholar in Western Christianity. Augustine, by contrast, had scarcely begun to be Augustine, the towering figure who would long dominate Western Christian thought. Furthermore, *Epistula* 28 made clear that Augustine lacked one seemingly crucial prerequisite for becoming an intellectual heavyweight: he could not read Greek well.

In *Epistula* 28 Augustine addresses Jerome as an equal, *copresbyter*. He tells Jerome that his friend and colleague, Alypius, had returned from seeing him and that "when he was there [in Bethlehem] seeing you, I was seeing you."[18] The bulk of the letter attacks Jerome's interpretation of Gal. 2:11–14: that Paul and Peter had simulated their quarrel in order to impress the Galatians. Augustine complains that ascribing deliberate deceit to Paul brought the reliability of holy scripture into doubt: "Once an inopportune lie is admitted at such an apex of authority, not a shred of those books will be left, where, because it seems to someone to be hard to practice or difficult to believe, by this most pernicious rule it may be ascribed to the deliberation and employment of a lying author."[19] Before that, Augustine took Jerome to task for questioning the authority of the church's Septuagint translation of Hebrew scripture by translating from Hebrew. Jerome was wasting his talents doing so and would make better use of them by providing additional translations of Greek commentaries, especially those of the unnamed author whom he "so gladly celebrates in his writings."[20]

Jerome would eventually receive *Epistula* 28, but not until long after he had heard that Augustine was circulating in Italy a booklet attacking him. In later correspondence with Augustine, Jerome would disingenuously suggest that *Epistula* 28 was a forgery by a heretic who had appropriated Augustine's name.[21] Questioning his judgment and suggesting that he refocus his life's work is no way

18. *Ep.* 28.1 (CSEL 34/1:104): "cum te ille ibi uidebat, ego uidebam."

19. *Ep.* 28.3 (CSEL 34/1:108): "admissio enim semel in tantum auctoritatis fastigium officioso aliquo mendacio, nulla illorum particula remanebit, quae non ut quique uidebitur uel ad mores difficilis, uel ad fidem incredibilis, eadem perniciossima regula ad mentientis auctoris concilium officiumque referatur." The issues become harder to determine the longer epistolary argument continues. See Fürst, *Von Origenes*, 275–92 and 337–58.

20. *Ep.* 28.3 (CSEL 34/1:108): "quem tu libentius in tuis litteris sonas."

21. *Ep.* 68.1 = Jerome, *Ep.* 102.1.

to introduce oneself to a scholar. Jerome reasonably assumed that an aspiring provincial presbyter was attacking him in order to make a name for himself. James O'Donnell, agreeing with Jerome, makes the telling point that in their subsequent correspondence Augustine never denied circulating *Epistula* 28 among his own network in Italy. Nonetheless, O'Donnell thinks that Augustine did intend Jerome to receive *Epistula* 28: a response would enhance his own reputation.[22] More charitably, Peter Brown, in 1967, ventured that Augustine wrote *Epistula* 28 as an effort by a "cosmopolitan *manqué*" to make up for his inability to read Greek.[23] Lacking the context subsequently provided by *Epistula* 27*, Brown dated *Epistula* 28 to 392, when Augustine, newly ordained, asked his bishop in *Epistula* 21 for time to study scripture intensively before he undertook pastoral responsibilities.[24] Though he assumed that the letter was a good-faith effort, Brown noted its brash tone: "Like many people anxious to be innocent in his own aggressive behavior, Augustine declared himself always ready to accept criticism."[25]

Epistula 27*, the one Divjak letter neither from Augustine nor addressed to him, throws new light on *Epistula* 28. It is Jerome's response to a (lost) letter from Aurelius. From it we gather that Aurelius had announced his consecration as bishop of Carthage and had asked Jerome to send him translations of Origen other than three works that Aurelius already had: Jerome's translations of Origen's *Homilies on the Song of Songs* and *Homilies on Jeremiah* (*Hom. Jer.*)[26] and a *Commentary on Matthew* (*Comm. Matt.*) that he mistakenly thought was Jerome's. In *Epistula* 27* Jerome in turn invited Aurelius to send an emissary to Bethlehem to copy works of his that he wanted. *Epistula* 27* is in line with Brown's suggestion that Augustine desired translations of Origen's work to assist him in his own study of scripture. Because of their close working relationship, Aurelius would have known that Augustine sought these. As bishop of Carthage, he could reasonably expect what a *copresbyter* could not.[27] We may thus assume

22. James J. O'Donnell, *Augustine: A New Biography* (New York: HarperCollins, 2005), 92–93.

23. See Peter Brown, *Augustine of Hippo: A Biography*, new ed. (Berkeley: University of California Press, 2000), 268.

24. *Ep.* 21.3–6.

25. Brown, *Augustine of Hippo*, 272.

26. Jerome translated fourteen of Origen's *Hom. Jer.*, doing so either when he was in Antioch in 373 or in Constantinople in 380. See Pierre Nautin, SC 232:33–58. Twelve of them are among the twenty *Hom. Jer.* that survive in Greek.

27. Heidl, *Origen's Influence*, 70.

that Augustine already had access to Jerome's translations of the works by Origen that Aurelius had mentioned: *Homilies on the Song of Songs, Homilies on Jeremiah,* and, possibly, the anonymously translated *Commentary on Matthew.*[28] Jerome had already translated both sets of homilies before Augustine left Milan; Augustine himself, had he acquired them from Simplicianus, could have brought them to Africa and shared them with Aurelius.

Alypius's visit with Jerome in Bethlehem mentioned in *Epistula* 27* indicates a later date than 392 for *Epistula* 28, since Augustine could not have written it before Alypius returned. Aurelius's original letter was written after his own consecration as bishop, probably in 391, but before Augustine became a bishop in 395. Augustine's *Epistula* 22 thanks the newly elevated Aurelius for allowing Alypius to beg off an assignment and stay in the monastic community Augustine set up in Hippo. This indicates that, initially, Alypius hesitated to undertake that errand or that Augustine did not want him to go.[29] *Epistula* 27* would have survived among Augustine's correspondence because Aurelius had forwarded it to justify Alypius's proposed mission. Allowing time for letters to make their slow way back and forth during sailing season and for Alypius's eventual journey, *Epistula* 28 must be dated to 394 or early 395.[30]

This chronology makes it likely that Alypius was in Bethlehem in 393, where he would have witnessed the start of the First Origenist Controversy. This began when Epiphanius of Salamis canvassed support for his letter denouncing Bishop John of Jerusalem for holding purportedly heretical Origenist doctrines. In 393 Epiphanius exploited a weakness that was fatal to Origen's reputation: already controversial, Origen was increasingly vulnerable in the course of the fourth century because his teaching that the Son is subordinate to the Father did not fit emerging orthodoxy after the Councils of Nicaea and Constantinople. This gravely compounded earlier objections to Origen both in the Greek-speaking East and the Latin-speaking West.[31] Discussing Ambrose's *On the Hexaemeron,*

28. Fürst agrees that *ep.* 27* indicates that Augustine had access to these works by Jerome, although he does not speculate on how Aurelius obtained them or why Aurelius would have forwarded Jerome's letter to Augustine (*Von Origenes,* 490).

29. *Ep.* 22.1.

30. Peter Brown, in the epilogue to his new edition of *Augustine of Hippo,* revises the date of *ep.* 28 to 394 without comment (449), probably on the basis of *ep.* 27*.

31. See the *dossier annexe* in Marguerite Harl, Gilles Dorival, and Alain Le Boulluec, ed. and trans., *Origène, Traité sur les principes (Peri Archôn)* (Paris: Études Augustiniennes, 1976), 253–300.

composed no later than 390, and so antedating the Origenist controversy, Jean Pépin notes that, even when they made use of Origen, Latin authors avoided citing him by name. He thinks this was because Origen was suspect as a theologian even when he enjoyed prestige as an exegete.[32] Under pressure from Epiphanius, Jerome, after promoting Origen's writings in the West, underwent an apparent change of heart and subscribed.[33] Assuming that Alypius had been in Bethlehem in 393, Augustine, in *Epistula* 28, was insinuating to Jerome that he knew all about this.

Traces of Origen in Early Exegetical Works and *Confessiones*

Heidl found another indication that Augustine had read Origen or had detailed information about his works while in Milan. In *De Genesi aduersus Manicheos* (*Gn. adu. Man.*), written by 389, Augustine follows Origen's interpretation of Gen. 1:1, which Origen interpreted as God's creation of the spiritual world, and his interpretation of the "coats of skins" (Gen. 3:21) with which God clothed Adam and Eve after the fall as human bodies. Berthold Altaner cited the lack of precedent for these interpretations in any extant Latin works, including works by Ambrose that Augustine used, as evidence that Augustine took them directly from Origen.[34] We find these interpretations in Origen's *Homilies on Genesis* (*Hom. Gen.*), but, given that Rufinus would not translate those homilies until long after Augustine wrote *De Genesi aduersus Manicheos*, Heidl thinks it likely that Augustine had access to a now-lost translation of Origen's *Commentary on Genesis* (*Comm. Gen.*).[35] That commentary and any translation of it are lost, but

32. Jean Pépin, *Théologie cosmique et théologie chrétienne* (Paris: Presses Universitaires de France, 1964), 403.

33. On Jerome's role in this controversy, see Megan Hale Williams, *The Monk and the Book: Jerome and the Making of Christian Scholarship* (Chicago: University of Chicago Press, 2006), as well as J. N. D. Kelly, *Jerome: His Life, Writings, and Controversies* (London: Duckworth, 1975). Clark's lively account in *The Origenist Controversy* reveals the role of intersecting networks of friends in the exacerbation of the controversy.

34. See Altaner, "Augustinus und Origenes," 236–38.

35. Heidl, *Origen's Influence*, 81–163. On the evidence that Augustine used Origen in the *Gn. adu. Man,* see also Altaner, "Augustinus und Origenes," 224–52, 234–38, and Madec, *Lectures Augustiniennes,* 102. Pace Fürst ("Origenes," *AugLex* 4:383–84), it is unlikely that Augustine was directly influenced by Origen's *Hom. Gen.* in this work, since they had not yet been translated.

Origen is so consistent across his entire oeuvre that interpretations of Genesis in his surviving works almost certainly reflect it. Augustine's application, cited below, of the thorns and thistles of Gen. 3:17–19 to intellectual labor could also have come from Origen's *Commentary on Genesis*; it is attested in the newly discovered *Homily 4 on Psalm 77 (Hom. Ps.)*.[36]

Heidl also argued, on the basis of the similarity between approaches to the Lord's Prayer in Augustine's *De sermone domini in monte (s. dom. m.)*, composed in 393, and Origen's *On Prayer (Or.)*, that the *Commentary on Matthew* mentioned in *Epistula 27** as a work in Aurelius's possession was indeed the Latin version of Origen's commentary on that work.[37]

No work better exemplifies Augustine's adoption of Origen's fusion of Christianity and Platonism than *Confessiones*. In his accounts of mastering Aristotle's *Categories*[38] and tutoring the Manichaean teacher Faustus,[39] he intimates that he expected to find himself the smartest person in any room. He ascribes being a bad student of Greek to lack of motivation rather than to any lack of ability.[40] Nonetheless, discussing how his thinking changed as he associated with learned Christians in Milan, Augustine contrasts the "swiftness of understanding and sharpness of discernment"[41] that ordinarily enabled him to grasp concepts more easily than others with his cluelessness about how Catholics understood God: "But what did this reveal to me, *who supposed that you, Lord God, the Truth, were a body, luminous and measureless, and I was a fragment of that body*?"[42] That cluelessness hindered his return to the childhood faith:

> For when my soul tried to go back to the Catholic faith, I was repelled, because the Catholic faith was not what I judged it to be.... Your spiritual ones would now gently and lovingly laugh at me, if they were to read these my confessions, yet I was such a person.[43]

---

36. See *conf.* 4.16.30 and Origen, *Hom. Ps. 77*, 4.7 (*Die neuen Psalmenhomilien: Eine kritische Edition des Codex Monacensis Graecus 314*, ed. Lorenzo Perrone et al. [Berlin: de Gruyter, 2015], 398–99; hereafter *Psalmenhomilien*).

37. Heidl, *Origen's Influence*, 223–35.

38. *Conf.* 4.15.28.

39. *Conf.* 5.6.11.

40. See *conf.* 1.14.27.

41. *Conf.* 4.16.30 (CSEL 33:55): "celeritas intellegendi et dispiciendi acumen."

42. *Conf.* 4.16.31 (CSEL 33:55): "et quid mihi hoc proderat, putanti quod tu, domine deus ueritas, *corpus esses lucidum et immensum et ego frustrum de illo corpore*?"

43. *Conf.* 5.10.20 (CSEL 33:68–69): "cum enim conaretur animus meus recurrere in cath-

Only as he heard Ambrose explain the Old Testament did Augustine begin to see that what that faith actually taught was intellectually respectable:

> For the first time, also, these things now began to seem defensible, and the Catholic faith, in favor of which I supposed nothing could be said when Manichees attacked it, I now considered to be maintained without shame, especially when hearing time and again one riddle and then another from the old scriptures solved, where, when I took it in according to the letter, I was killed. Accordingly, when many passages from those books were expounded spiritually, I now found fault with my despair, insofar as I had believed that the law and the prophets could not at all be sustained against those who despised and ridiculed them.[44]

Here, whether he was aware of doing so or not, Augustine echoes Origen's identification of literal interpretation as Paul's killing letter. The *Biblia Patristica* lists eighty references to 2 Cor. 3:6, consistently understood in that sense, in Origen's works.[45] Augustine's use of "riddle" (*ainigma*) likewise reflects Origen's interpretation of Paul's ἐν αἰνίγματι, "in a riddle," in 1 Cor. 13:12. Following the usage of Hellenistic grammar, in which he was trained, Origen understood "riddle" (αἴνιγμα) as a literary conundrum—namely, the "wording" (λέξις) of scripture. Such a conundrum is a "problem" (πρόβλημα) for which the interpreter presents a "solution" (λύσις).[46] It is through such means that we see God imperfectly, as in a mirror.[47] (Translating ἐν αἰνίγματι as "darkly" obscures the likelihood that Paul understood "riddle" in the same way.) The method of figurative interpretation that Origen had employed to refute Marcion and Valentinus, who separated the God of the Old Testament from the God of the New Testament, freed Augustine from Mani, who did the same.

---

olicam fidem, repercutiebar, quia *non erat catholica fides quam esse arbitrabar.* . . . nunc *spiritales tui blande et amanter ridebunt me,* si has confessiones meas legerint, sed tamen talis eram."

44. *Conf.* 5.14.24 (CSEL 33:71): "nam primo etiam ipsa defendi posse mihi iam coeperunt uideri, et fidem catholicam, pro qua nihil posse dici aduersus oppugnantes manicheos putaueram, iam non impudenter adseri existimabam, maxime audito uno atque altero saepius aenigmate soluto de scriptis ueteribus, ubi cum ad litteram acciperem, occidebar. spiritaliter itaque plerisque illorum librorum locis expositis iam reprehendebam desperationem meam, illam dumtaxat qua credideram legem et prophetas detestantibus atque irridentibus resisti omnino non posse."

45. See J. Allenbach et al., eds., *Biblia Patristica: Index des citations et allusions bibliques dans la littérature patristique*, vol. 3, *Origène* (Paris: CNRS, 1980), 409–10.

46. Origen discusses this method in *Hom. Ps.* 77, 1.6 (*Psalmenhomilien*, 362–64).

47. See, e.g., Origen, *Contra Celsum* (*Cels.*) 7.38.

Even with this newly acquired sophistication about biblical language, still Augustine could not refute the Manichees, since he did not understand the concept of spiritual substance:

> Then, in fact, I strongly bent my efforts to determine if in some manner I could convict the Manichees of falsehood by some irrefutable teaching. If I could have conceived of spiritual substance, those devices would immediately have been dissolved and expelled from my soul, but I was not able to do so.[48]

At the root of his difficulties was his inability to conceive of incorporeality, a nonspatial reality:

> As soon as I actually found out that the man made by you in your image was not understood by your spiritual sons and daughters, whom you had regenerated by grace from the Catholic mother, as if they believed and conceived of you as confined by the form of a human body (even though, as to how it consisted of a spiritual substance, I had not the slightest inkling even in a riddle), yet rejoicing I blushed to realize that I had been barking for so many years, not against the Catholic faith, but against the inventions of fleshly ways of thinking. . . . You, nonetheless, most high and most near, most hidden and most present, whose parts are not some larger and some smaller, but you are everywhere in your entirety and not in space at all, and are certainly not in this bodily form, have still made a human being in your image, and, look, he is, head to toe, located in space.[49]

---

48. *Conf.* 5.14.25 (CSEL 33:71): "tum uero fortiter intendi animum, si quo modo possem certis aliquibus documentis manicheos conuincere falsitatis. quod si possem spiritalem substantiam cogitare, statim machinamenta illa omnia soluerentur et abicerentur ex animo me: sed non poteram."

49. *Conf.* 6.3.4 (CSEL 33:117–18): "ubi uero etiam comperi ad imaginem tuam hominem a te factum ab spiritalibus filiis tuis, quos de matre catholica per gratiam regenerasti, non sic intellegi ut humani corporis forma te determinatum crediderent atque cogitarent (quamquam quomodo se haberet spiritalis substanti, ne quidem tenuiter et in aenigmate suspicabar), tamen gaudens erubui non me tot annos aduersus catholicam fidem, sed contra carnalium cogitationum figmenta latrasse. . . . tu enim, altissime et proxime, secretissime et praesentissime, cui membra non sunt alia maiora et alia minora, sed ubique totus es et nusquam locorum es, non es utique forma ista corporea, tamen fecisti hominem ad imaginem tuam, et ecce ipse a capite usque ad pedes in loco est."

Augustine thus depicts himself as slowly coming to understand what the Catholic Church had always taught about God and the image of God in humanity, even if only the church's "spiritual sons and daughters" fully understand it. He wrote that he had maintained a childish misconception because the sin of Adam diminished his intellectual perspicuity: "For you ordered, and thus it was accomplished in me, that the earth would bear thorns and thistles for me and that I would come by my bread with toil (Gen. 3:18–19)."[50]

Another explanation is at hand: Augustine did not believe in the incorporeality of God because the concept was foreign to the Christianity in which he was reared. In a long-overdue work, *Gottes Körper*, Christoph Markschies demonstrates that we find the concept of God's incorporeality neither in the Bible, nor in Greek religious practice, nor in the teaching of all the philosophical schools, nor shared by all early Christians.[51] In particular, Tertullian, the principal thinker of North African Christianity, held the Stoic philosophical understanding of God as embodying a fine, spiritual substance, the very concept that Augustine confesses to having had such difficulty surmounting.[52] Belief in divine incorporeality is, in fact, as Markschies shows, distinctively Platonic.[53] Origen, more than anyone else, propagated among Christians the concept that God is incorporeal because God is to be identified in Platonic terms with the realm of being, beyond space and time.[54] By contrast, corporeality belongs to the realm of becoming that we experience "in space" through our bodily senses.[55]

Aware that the incorporeality of God is not expounded as such in the Bible, Origen began *Peri archōn* (*De principiis* [*Princ.*]) with a defense of the application of the word ἀσώματος, "bodiless," to God.[56] Origen was not the first person to describe the God of the Bible in Platonic terms; we can find many of the same ideas, including the term ἀσώματος, in Philo,[57] whose works Ambrose used,

---

50. *Conf.* 4.16.29 (CSEL 33:55): "iusseras enim, et ita fiebat in me ut terra spinas et tribulos pareret mihi et cum labore perueniem ad panem meum."

51. Christoph Markschies, *Gottes Körper: Jüdische, christliche und pagane Gottesvorstellungen in der Antike* (Munich: Beck, 2016), 43–85, 113–44.

52. Markschies, *Gottes Körper*, 106–8.

53. Markschies, *Gottes Körper*, 135.

54. Markschies, *Gottes Körper*, 98–106.

55. Markschies, *Gottes Körper*, 60–63.

56. Origen, *Princ.* preface 8 and 1.1.

57. On Christian use of Philo, see David Runia, *Philo in Early Christian Literature: A Survey* (Assen: Van Gorcum, 1993).

JOSEPH W. TRIGG

and in Clement of Alexandria. Nonetheless, Origen made the incorporeality of
God the common property of learned Christians, those whom Origen habitually referred to as οἱ πνευματικοί, "the spiritual," as opposed to οἱ ἁπλούστεροι,
"the simpler," whose benighted concepts of God might well induce "gentle and
loving" mirth among the spiritual. Such learned, spiritual Christians known to
Augustine included not only Simplicianus, Mallius Theodorus, and Ambrose,[58]
whom Augustine associated with in Milan, but also Latin writers whom he could
read, such as Hilary of Poitiers and Jerome.[59] Thus, although Augustine depicts
his encounters in Milan as gradually enabling him to comprehend and uphold
the faith that he had imbibed as a child, we might just as easily see his intellectual development as an education in Origen's philosophical concepts, exegetical
techniques, and even characteristic attitude. This would be true even if these
concepts and techniques and that supercilious attitude came to him at second
hand. As we have seen, there is reason to think that at Milan he did read at least
some Origen in translation.

In *Confessiones* Augustine stated that he found in the books of the Platonists
the equivalent of the Logos, who, according to the opening verses of John's Gospel, was with God, the light of human beings, and born not from the flesh but
from God (John 1:1–13). Even so, he could not find that the Logos became flesh
and dwelt among us (John 1:14). He could find that the Logos was in the form of
God, but not that he emptied himself and took upon him the form of a servant
(Phil. 2:7). He did not find that he died for the ungodly (Rom. 5:6) or that he
invites all who labor and are heavily laden to come to him (Matt. 11:28).[60] Augustine could have found in the *Homilies on the Song of Songs* the identification

58. See, e.g., Pierre Hadot, "L'entretien d'Origène avec Héraclide et le commentaire de
Saint Ambroise sur l'Évangile de Saint Luc" and "Une source de l'*Apologia David* d'Ambroise:
les commentaires de Didyme de d'Origène sur le psaume 50," in *Études de patristique et d'histoire des concepts* (Paris: Les Belles Lettres, 2010), 171–98 and 199–221. Christoph Markschies
in "Ambrosius und Origenes: Bemerkungen zur exegetischen Hermeneutik zweier Kirchenväter" (in *Origenes und sein Erbe: Gesammelte Studien*, TUGAL [Berlin: de Gruyter, 2007],
195–222) shows how thoroughly Ambrose assimilated Origen's biblical hermeneutic.
59. On Hilary, see Isabella Image, *The Human Condition in Hilary of Poitiers: The Will and
Original Sin between Origen and Augustine* (Oxford: Oxford University Press, 2017). On Jerome, see Pierre Courcelle, *Late Latin Writers and Their Greek Sources*, trans. Harry E. Wedeck
(Cambridge, MA: Harvard University Press, 1969), 90–100. See also Williams, *The Monk and
the Book*, 154–60.
60. *Conf.* 7.9.13–14. See also *ciu.* 10.29.

of Christ as one who for our sake emptied himself and took upon himself the form of a servant.[61] Origen's *Homilies on Jeremiah*, mentioned in *Epistula* 27*, is another "complete book" where he could have found Phil. 2:7, identifying the divine Logos with Christ, along with Rom. 5:6 and Matt. 11:28.[62] Here Augustine could have found in the work of Origen the link between the *Enneads* and the Bible. He also could have seen that the Manichees, like Origen's adversaries, the Valentinians and Marcionites, had misused Paul's writings to discredit the Old Testament and its God. This makes those works of Origen all the better candidates for the *libri pleni* that motivated Augustine to grab for Paul. Augustine could also have learned from them his characteristically Origenian use of Pauline language to recount Ambrose's preaching and he could even have read an allusion to 1 Cor. 13:12 in Origen's *Homilies on Jeremiah*.[63] Thus the *libri pleni* could have reinforced the lessons in Origen's philosophical outlook and exegetical methods that were "in the air" among the *spirituales* in Milan.

Augustine's account of his experience at Ostia, the high point of *Confessiones*, exemplifies how, with Origen's unacknowledged help, Augustine integrated Platonism and the Bible. After describing his intellectual ascent in terms taken directly from the *Enneads*, he reaches its goal:[64]

> Raising ourselves with more ardent affection toward the selfsame, we traveled step by step through every bodily thing and heaven itself, where the sun and moon and stars shine above the earth. And we ascended so far within as to consider and discuss and admire all these things. And we came into our minds and transcended them, so that we touched a region of unfailing abundance where you pasture Israel with truth as fodder.[65]

61. Origen, *Hom. Cant.* 2.3.

62. Phil. 2:7 in Origen, *Hom. Jer.* 1.7, 8.8, 14.9; Rom. 5:6 in *Hom. Jer.* 14.11; and Matt. 11:28 in *Hom. Jer.* 17.6.

63. Origen, *Hom. Jer.* 8.7.

64. See Pierre Courcelle, *Recherches sur les Confessions de Saint Augustin* (Paris: de Boccard, 1968), 157–74 and 224–226. See also James J. O'Donnell, ed., *Augustine: Confessions* (Oxford: Clarendon, 1992), 2:434–46 and 3:122–33.

65. *Conf.* 9.10.24 (CSEL 33:147): "erigentes nos ardentiore affectu in idipsum, perambulauimus graditim cuncta corporalia et ipsum caelum, unde sol et luna et stellae lucent super terram. et adhuc ascendebamus interius cogitando et loquendo et mirando opera tua. et uenimus in mentes nostras et transcendimus eas, ut attingeremus regionem ubertatis indeficientis, ubi pascis Israhel in aeternum ueritate pabulo."

He arrived in the biblical Land of Promise, which the Platonists had shown him from afar without enabling him to reach it.[66] It is not just Origen's identification of God with Being but his spiritual geography, identifying the Holy Land as the inner "place,"[67] so to speak, where the soul encounters God, that made Plotinus profoundly compatible with the Bible. The ascent to the Holy Land and the Platonic ascent to the One are already fused in Origen. Augustine could have found that interior, spiritual geography "in the air" at Milan or in the sixth of the *Homilies on Jeremiah* mentioned in *Epistula* 27*: "For this [i.e., this sensible land where we are] is not the land that God promised, a land flowing with milk and honey (Jer. 11:5), but it is that land about which the Savior taught, saying, 'Blessed are the meek, for they shall possess the land' (Matt. 5:5)."[68]

Augustine's accounts of his intellectual development thus indicate that, well before he asked Jerome for more translations of Origen's work in *Epistula* 28, he had already assimilated aspects of Origen's thought that his own work would give a secure place in Christian theology: figurative interpretation, the incorporeality of God, and the location in biblical geography of the soul's inner access to a God identified with the Platonic One. When he wrote *Confessiones*, Augustine also knew Origen's doctrine of five spiritual senses, which he was the first Latin author to use (without attribution) in that work.[69] Nonetheless, by the time Augustine, by then a bishop, wrote *Confessiones*, the Origenist Controversy had gone through the more virulent phase prompted by the translation of Origen's great work of systematic theology, *De principiis*, by Jerome's erstwhile friend Rufinus of Aquileia. This gave him good reason not even to hint at Origen's role in his theological formation.

66. *Conf.* 7.21.27.

67. This is, of course, a "place" in a nonspatial sense. See Origen's discussion of Ps. 67:6b (LXX), "God is in his holy place," in the newly discovered *Hom. Ps. 67*, 2.8 (*Psalmenhomilien*, 222–24).

68. Origen, *Hom. Jer.* 9.3 (Homily 6 in Jerome's translation): "haec enim non est terra quam pollicitus est deus, terra fluens lac et mel: sed ista est terra de qua saluator docuit dicens: beati mites quoniam ipsi possidebunt terram." There is also a hint in Origen, *Hom. Cant.* 1.1, the list of an ascending series of songs that can be sung by one who has left Egypt.

69. *Conf.* 10.6.27. See Altaner, "Augustinus und Origenes," 242–43. The most we find is the term "senses of the soul" (*sensus animae*) in Origen, *Hom. Ezech.* 11.1, translated by Jerome most likely in 382.

TRACES OF ORIGEN IN AUGUSTINE'S LATER WORKS

Living in Jerusalem in 393, Rufinus, unlike Jerome, had not supported Epiphanius but had sought to defend Origen. This led him, in 397, to translate *De principiis*. He evidently sought to make Origen's thought, with passages offensive to Nicene/Constantinopolitan orthodoxy cleaned up, available to the Latin West. Rufinus's statement in the preface of that work that Jerome followed the same procedures in translating Origen as he himself did exacerbated the Origenist Controversy and put an end to any remaining friendship between the two scholars.[70] Because only portions of *De principiis* survive in Greek, the faithfulness of that translation to the Greek original remains controversial.[71] In the event, Jerome accused Rufinus of mistranslating Origen in order to conceal heresy. At Bethlehem around 390, before the Origenist Controversy began, Jerome had translated Origen's *Homilies on Luke* (*Hom. Luc.*). One motive for that translation was to expose Ambrose as someone who relied extensively on Origen, without attribution, in his own work.[72] After 393 Jerome made no more translations of Origen except for a few short passages of *De principiis* meant to expose Rufinus's expurgations. Rufinus would, in the first decade of the fifth century, translate 117 of Origen's homilies on the Old Testament and his commentaries on the Song of Songs and Romans.

Although he did not recognize Augustine's use of Origen's *Commentary on Romans* (*Comm. Rom.*), Altaner showed that Augustine knew and used at least some of these translations. Augustine's use of these works was sufficiently extensive that Altaner considered Origen the Greek Christian writer with whom Augustine was best acquainted.[73] Other than demonstrating a continuing interest in Origen and receptivity to his ideas, these works by Origen that Augustine read after becoming a bishop in 395 had no impact on him remotely comparable to the impact of Origen's ideas early in his life, when he had far less direct access. Altaner documented, for example, that Augustine adopted Origen's reading of

---

70. Augustine would lament this rupture. See *ep.* 73.3.6.

71. The best discussion of Rufinus's aims is Nicola Pace, *Ricerche sulla traduzione di Rufino del "De principiis" di Origene* (Florence: La Nuova Italia Editrice, 1990). On Rufinus as translator, see also Emmanuele Prinzivalli's comparison of Rufinus's translation of *Hom. Ps. 36, 1–4*, with the newly discovered Greek original in *Psalmenhomilien*, 35–58.

72. See the allusion to a crow, Ambrose, who plumes himself with feathers stolen from a peacock, Origen, in Jerome's preface to *Hom. Luc*, discussed by Henri Crouzel in SC 87:70–74.

73. Altaner, "Augustinus und Origenes," 225.

Ps. 21:7 (LXX), "I am a worm and no man," in the *Homilies on Luke*. The *sensus eligantissimus* of this verse is that it is a prophecy of the virgin birth, since worms arise, as the ancients supposed, by spontaneous generation.[74] Origen also gave Augustine a way, as he saw it, to reconcile the dimensions of Noah's ark recorded in the Bible with its required carrying capacity.[75] Far more consequentially, Altaner proposed that Origen's spiritual geography may have suggested identifying Babylon as the city of the devil that opposes the city of God.[76]

Altaner also showed that Augustine continued to respect Origen and did not necessarily agree with Jerome's negative assessments. He did classify "Origenists" as heretics and, in *De ciuitate dei*, called out Origen by name. He also refuted Origen's supposed doctrine that God imprisoned souls in bodies.[77] He did not, however, condemn Origen by name for other purportedly false doctrines that Origen taught or had been dubiously accused of teaching.[78] Altaner considered it likely that Augustine read *De principiis* either in Rufinus's translation or in a supposed translation by Jerome, as does Alfons Fürst.[79] This is doubtful, because the few references Augustine makes to *De principiis* can be explained in other ways. Altaner suggested that Augustine learned about Origen's teaching that the stars are embodied spiritual beings from reading *De principiis*, but he is more likely to have learned this from Jerome.[80] Altaner cites Origen's interpretation of the firmament dividing the waters in Gen. 1:6–7, again without mentioning its source, as evidence that he knew Rufinus's translation of Origen's *Homilies on Genesis* at first hand.[81] He could also have known it as the seventh of eight charges against Origen in Epiphanius's *Letter to John of Jerusalem*, which Jerome

---

74. Altaner, "Augustinus und Origenes," 241–42, discussing *Hom. Luc.* 14.8 and *ep.* 140.8.21.

75. Altaner, "Augustinus und Origenes," 232–34.

76. Altaner, "Augustinus und Origenes," 243–44.

77. Altaner, "Augustinus und Origenes," 225–29, discussing, inter alia, *De haeresibus* 43 on the "Origenistae" and *ciu.* 11.23.

78. An example of the former is that God's punishment is always remedial (*ciu.* 21.11). An example of the latter is that the blessed in heaven can fall again from blessedness (*ciu.* 12.10).

79. Nonetheless, *pace* Fürst ("Origenes," *AugLex* 4:383), the citation of *Princ.* in *ciu.* 11.23 does not prove that Augustine had actually read that work.

80. Altaner, "Augustinus und Origenes," 231–32. See Jerome, *Ep. 124 ad Avitum* 2, cited as testimony 47 in Harl, Dorival, and Le Boulluec, *Traité des principes*, 278. On Augustine's dependence on Jerome, see Giulia Sfameni Gasparro, "Agostino di fronte alla 'eterodossia' di Origene," in *Origene e la tradizione origeniana in Occidente: Letture storico-religiose* (Rome: Libreria Ateneo Salesiano, 1998), 123–50. This is also a point made repeatedly by O'Connell in *Origin of the Soul*.

81. *Ciu.* 11.34. Augustine also states that the firmament should be understood allegorically

translated.[82] The willingness to entertain these two positions on which Origen had been attacked, however, shows that Augustine continued to respect Origen, maintaining independent judgment in spite of the Origenist Controversy.[83] The same applies to Origen's position on the preexistence of souls, which Augustine entertained as a possibility until, late in life, he repudiated it.[84]

AUGUSTINE AND ORIGEN'S INTERPRETATION OF PAUL: TRUTH AND GRACE

Augustine's critical reception of Origen is most apparent in his appropriation of and quarrel with Origen's interpretation of the figure at the heart of the work of them both: the apostle Paul. Heidl thinks that, when he took Jerome to task on Galatians in *Epistula* 28, Augustine had already inferred what Jerome subsequently confirmed: Jerome's interpretation came from Origen.[85] Heidl noted that *Epistula* 28 emphasized Jerome's awkward position after 393 by coyly omitting to name the author whom he had "gladly celebrated."[86] Augustine could have counted on smiles among the *spiritales* in Milan at this hint that Jerome was just as guilty as Ambrose of using Origen without attribution. *Epistula* 28 thus points to one of Augustine's most fundamental objections to Origen: his tolerance of deception in the Bible. Around 395 Augustine wrote *De Mendacio* (*mend.*), in which he had pressed the same interpretation of Gal. 2, denying that two apostles would have engaged in deliberate deception.[87] In his subsequent correspondence

---

(without identifying the waters as spiritual beings) in *conf.* 13.24.37, a position he modified in *retr.* 2.6.7, perhaps because of its connection to Origen.

82. See Harl, Dorival, and Le Boulluec, *Traité des principes*, 268. The newly discovered *Hom. Ps. 76*, 3, shows that, for what it is worth, this "charge" is accurate.

83. *Ep.* 12* from Consentius testifies to Origen's bad reputation around 419 CE.

84. *Ciu.* 11.23. See O'Connell, *Origin of the Soul*.

85. Heidl, *Origen's Influence*, 71–72. He could have found a hint to that effect in *Hom. Cant.* 1.7, where Origen cites 1 Cor. 9:19–22 to show how Paul altered his conduct to meet the needs of those to whom he ministered, being made weak for the weak and a Jew for the Jews.

86. Heidl, *Origen's Influence*, 68. If Augustine already knew Jerome's translation of the *Hom. Cant.*, he would have read in Jerome's introduction, "Even though Origen outdoes everyone else in the rest of his books, on the Song of Songs he outdoes himself . . . so that it seems to me that in him are fulfilled the words: 'The king has brought me into his chamber' (Song 1:4)."

87. See esp. *mend.* 8. See also Julia Fleming, "The Helpful Lie: The Moral Reasoning of Augustine and John Cassian" (PhD diss., Catholic University of America, 1993).

with Jerome, who would realize soon enough that Augustine had to be reckoned with, Augustine would insist on thrashing the matter out. Had Jerome translated *Homilies on Jeremiah* 20, commenting on "You have deceived me, Lord, and I was deceived" (Jer. 20:7), Augustine would have been even more dismayed at the deception Origen found justifiable.[88]

Augustine's interest in obtaining translations of additional works by Origen, stated in *Epistula* 28, involves another topic involving Pauline interpretation: the origin of the soul. *De libero arbitrio* (*lib. arb.*), also written in 395, roughly the same time as *Epistula* 28, indicates that Augustine was looking for works that would shed light on this topic:

> We should not casually affirm any of these four ways of thinking about the soul: whether they come from propagation, or are newly made in each individual who is born, whether already existing in some manner they are sent or slipped of their own will into the bodies of those who are born. For this issue either has not been opened up and illuminated by Catholic discussions of the divine books on account of obscurity and intricacy or, if that has been done, no texts of this kind have yet come into our hands.[89]

Here Augustine lays out four theories about the origin of the human soul, the third or fourth of which represents Origen's position. The last phrase makes best sense if Augustine had heard that this was Origen's "way of thinking" and hoped to encounter a translated text by Origen that discussed it.

Caroline Hammond Bammel, editor of a critical edition of Rufinus's translation of the *Commentary on Romans*, argues that Augustine found this position attractive and wanted to know more about it because it provided a way to square original sin with a just God: "The fact that each individual soul has fallen before

---

88. See my article "Divine Deception and the Truthfulness of Scripture," in *Origen of Alexandria: His World and His Legacy*, ed. Charles Kannengiesser and William L. Peterson (Notre Dame, IN: University of Notre Dame Press, 1988), 147–64.

89. *Lib. arb.* 3.21.59 (CSEL 74:138): "harum autem quatuor de anima sententiarum, utrum de propagine ueniant, an in singulis quibusque nascentibus nouae fiant, uel in corpora nascentium iam alicubi existentes uel mittantur diuinitus, uel sua sponte labantur, nullam temere affirmare oportebit. aut enim nondum ista quaestio a diuinorum librorum catholicis tractatoribus pro merito obscuritatis et peplexitatis euoluta atque illustrata est; aut si iam factum est, nondum in manus nostras huiuscemodi litterae peruenerunt." See O'Connell, *St. Augustine's Early Theory of Man*, 148–52.

being assigned to life in a mortal body as a descendent of Adam means that there is no injustice involved in the soul being born in circumstances which impede the practice of virtue."[90] Such issues would preoccupy Augustine for the rest of his life. He would look for help from Origen and would find it, thanks not to Jerome but to Jerome's erstwhile friend Rufinus. Origen's *Commentary on Romans* would have become available to Augustine in 411, the year when he became engaged in controversy with Pelagius. In Origen's interpretation of Rom. 5:12, 6:6, and 8:3 he found arguments that the pollution of sin is transmitted to Adam's descendants through concupiscence.[91] He also found in Origen two key citations, Job 14:4–5 and Ps. 51:5, that indicate that children have sin from birth. In expounding Rom. 3:10 Augustine used the same verses as Origen, Ps. 143:2 and Wis. 9:15, to argue that only Christ is sinless and that we cannot be completely sinless in our earthly life.[92] Augustine, like Origen, argues that Paul speaks of perfection in two senses illustrated by Phil. 3:12–13 and 3:15.[93] In addition, he repeats Origen's argument that an infant hitting parents does not commit sin by that act itself, since the infant is not yet subject to natural law.[94]

Hammond Bammel suggests that a year later, when he wrote *De spiritu et littera* (*spir. et litt.*), aware of the link drawn by Rufinus the Syrian between Origenism and the doctrine of original sin, Augustine took care to differentiate his own advocacy of that doctrine from positions known to be held by Origen, denying his interpretation of the letter and the spirit in 2 Cor. 3:6 as the literal and figurative senses of the Jewish law and his interpretation of Rom. 2:14–15 to affirm that unbelieving gentiles are promised rewards for their good works.[95] She also points to minor issues of interpretation where Augustine's refutation

90. Caroline P. Hammond Bammel, "Augustine, Origen and the Exegesis of Saint Paul," in *Tradition and Exegesis in Early Christian Writers* (Aldershot, UK: Variorum, 1995), 350.

91. Hammond Bammel, "Exegesis of St. Paul," 359, referencing Augustine's *pecc. mer.* 1.9, 2.11, 2.15, 2.38 and Origen, *Com. Rom.* 5.12, 6.6, 8.3.

92. Hammond Bammel, "Exegesis of St. Paul," 360, referencing Augustine, *pecc. mer.* 1.34 and Origen, *Com. Rom.* 6.6.

93. Hammond Bammel, "Exegesis of St. Paul," referencing Augustine, *pecc. mer.* 2.22 and Origen, *Com. Rom.* preface.

94. Hammond Bammel, "Exegesis of St. Paul," referencing Augustine, *pecc. mer.* 1.65–66 and Origen, *Com. Rom.* 5.13.

95. Hammond Bammel, "Exegesis of St. Paul," 361–62, referencing *spir. et litt.* 44 and Origen, *Com. Rom.* 2.7–11 on Rom. 2:10. On this obscure figure and the anti-Origenist focus of his treatise *De fide*, see Gerald Bonner, "Rufinus of Syria and African Pelagianism," *AugStud* 1 (1970): 31–47, and Clark, *Origenist Controversy*, 202–7.

of Origen's position in the *Commentary on Romans* indicates his continued engagement with that work.[96]

One might have expected that in his initial confrontation with Pelagius, Augustine, with his insistence on the necessity of grace, would regard Origen, the champion of human freedom, as an antagonist. He evidently did not, looking to Origen, if not as an ally, at least as an exegetical resource.[97] This is not incongruous. If Heidl is correct, Augustine learned from Origen's *libri pleni* that God's grace, manifested in Jesus Christ, could take him to the land that the Platonists could show him only from afar. This is not to say that Origen had a "doctrine of grace."[98] Augustine bears principal responsibility for making "grace" the term used in Christian theology for discussing that divine initiative in salvation. Origen was far more likely to speak about the divine initiative, not in terms of χάρις, "grace," but of πνεῦμα, "spirit." He also used δύναμαι, "to be able," in the passive voice to indicate the necessity of God's empowerment either for knowledge or for salvation. Although less concerned to delimit its conditions, Origen was no less insistent on our need for that divine initiative.

A passage in Origen's *Contra Celsum* (*Cels.*) best illustrates this. Celsus was a second-century Platonist who wrote *True Logos* (Λόγος Ἀληθής) in order to demonstrate that the traditional Hellenic "logos" or "discourse" is superior to Christianity. There Celsus cited a celebrated passage from Plato, *Timaeus* (*Tim.*) 28c: "Therefore to find the maker and father of this all is indeed a work and impossible for the one who finds to say to all."[99] While respecting Plato, Origen responds that Christian discourse, the discourse that proclaims and is the divine Logos, differs from Plato's in at least one crucial respect—it can reach everyone:

> But see if the divine discourse does not introduce something more benevolent,
> a god discourse in the beginning with God who has become flesh, so that what,
> on Plato's account, is "impossible for the one who finds to say to all" is [by the
> god discourse] able to reach to all.[100]

96. Hammond Bammel, "Exegesis of St. Paul," 362–63.

97. In connection with the Pelagian controversy, Fürst discusses Augustine's strong objections to Origen's cosmology and eschatology, although in his view Augustine's insight into these aspects of Origen's thought was limited ("Origenes," *AugLex* 4:386).

98. See Benjamin Drewery, *Origen and the Doctrine of Grace* (London: Epworth, 1960).

99. Plato, *Tim.* 28c: "τὸν μὲν οὖν ποιητὴν καὶ πατέρα τοῦδε τοῦ παντὸς εὑρεῖν τε ἔργον καὶ εὑρόντα εἰς πάντας ἀδύνατον λέγειν."

100. Origen, *Cels.* 7.42, alluding to John 1:1 and Matt. 7:7: "Ὅρα δὲ εἰ μὴ φιλανθρωπότερον

After expressing doubt that even Plato had truly found God, since he never worshiped God exclusively, Origen says,

> But we have as our view that human nature is not sufficient on its own in any way to seek God and to find him genuinely, unless helped by the one being sought, being found by those who confess, after doing their part, that they need him.[101]

The necessity for God's empowerment, concisely expressed here, pervades Origen's work.

Contra Celsum was not accessible to Augustine in Latin, so he did not know this particular passage. He probably did know that Origen had written an extensive philosophical defense of Christian doctrine before he himself wrote *De ciuitate dei*. In that work, responding to a passage in Porphyry alluding to *Timaeus* 28c, Augustine makes much the same point about the insufficiency of Platonism that Origen makes in *Contra Celsum* and that he himself had made in *Confessiones*. There is, however, one telling difference. In *Contra Celsum* the hallmark of God's benevolent empowerment of Christian discourse is that, in contrast to Plato's discourse, the knowledge of God reaches "to all." In *De ciuitate dei* the hallmark of God's grace is that, as Plato actually testified correctly, the knowledge of God is restricted "to few": "You testify to grace nonetheless, seeing that you say that it is granted to few to reach God by virtue of intelligence."[102] Augustine and Origen agreed that fallen human nature requires the divine enablement that comes through Christ. Throughout his life Origen never changed his confidence, set forth in the treatise on freedom of the will that constitutes *De principiis* 3.1, that human freedom is compatible with grace; Augustine, of course, would eventually find such confidence untenable.

With their common understanding of a necessity for the divine initiative, Origen and Augustine share a common approach to divine providence and specifically to what Patout Burns calls "the ways and means by which God achieves his salvific purposes," or "various internal and external influences" through which

---

ὁ θεῖος λόγος εἰσάγει τὸν ἐν ἀρχῇ πρὸς τὸν θεὸν θεὸν λόγον γινόμενον σάρκα, ἵνα εἰς πάντας δυνατός ᾖ φθάνειν ὁ λόγος, ὅν καὶ τὸν εὑρόντα εἰς πάντας ἀδύνατον λέγειν φησὶν ὁ Πλάτων."

101. Origen, *Cels.* 7.42: "ἡμεῖς δὲ ἀποφαινόμεθα ὅτι οὐκ αὐτάρκης ἡ ἀνθρωπίνη φύσις ὁπωσποτανοῦν ζητῆσαι τὸν θεὸν καὶ εὑρεῖν αὐτὸν καθαρῶς, μὴ βοηθηθεῖσα ὑπὸ τοῦ ζητουμένου, εὑρισκομένου τοῖς ὁμολογοῦσι μετα τὸ παρ' αὐτοὺς ποιεῖν ὅτι δέονται αὐτοῦ."

102. *Ciu.* 10.29.1 (CSEL 40/1:304): "confiteris tamen gratiam, quandoquidem ad deum per uirtutem intelligentiae peruenire, paucis dicis esse concessum."

"God establishes the circumstances in which a person can choose and moves the person to decide and act according to his own intention."[103] Origen refers to these devices as οἰκονομία, "arrangement," "plan," or, in biblical terms, "stewardship."[104] Although, unlike Augustine, Origen left us no account of the way God arranged his own life, his understanding of God's internal and external influences is reflected in one of the few parallels to *Confessiones* in early Christian literature, the *Address to Origen* by a student of his traditionally identified as Gregory Thaumaturgus, the apostle to Pontus. Like Augustine, the author of the *Address* recounts a spiritual odyssey, one where Origen himself plays the role of Augustine's Milanese circle.

Lorenzo Perrone has shown how, when discussing prayer, Augustine and Origen share a common understanding of the role of the divine initiative. In his magisterial work on prayer in Origen, he details how Origen continually prays to God for insight into Scripture.[105] Perrone, drawing widely on Augustine's works and especially on *De sermone domini in monte* and *Epistula* 130 (to Proba), compares of Augustine with Origen.[106] Perrone does not commit himself to Heidl's thesis that Augustine had direct knowledge of Origen's interpretation of the Lord's Prayer, but he demonstrates in considerable detail the profound similarities between their interpretations. Not only do both Origen and Augustine stress the interior dynamics of prayer, both also share an awareness of the philosophical problem (*dato aporetico*) of prayer in light of an all-superintending divine providence by a God who knows all things before we ask (Matt. 6:8).[107] Thus, Perrone concludes that Augustine "makes his own, despite all the dissimilarity of his own distinctive conceptual framework, the Origenian idea of prayer as 'impossibility made possible,' vindicated all the more urgently by Augustine with the development of his doctrine of grace in response to the theses of Pelagius and his successors."[108] As an example, Perrone cites *De dono perseuerantiae*

103. J. Patout Burns, *The Development of Augustine's Doctrine of Operative Grace* (Paris: Études Augustiniennes, 1980), 7.

104. See H. S. Benjamins, *Eingeordnete Freiheit: Freiheit und Vorsehung bei Origenes* (Leiden: Brill, 1994).

105. Lorenzo Perrone, *La preghiera secondo Origene: L'impossibilità donata* (Brescia: Morcelliana, 2012), 281–428.

106. Perrone, *La preghiera*, 609–36.

107. Perrone, *La preghiera*, 615.

108. Perrone, *La preghiera*, 633: "Pur con tutta la diversità del suo distinto quadro concettuale, l'idea origeniana dell'orazione come 'impossibilità donata,' tanto più urgentemente rivendicata dall'Ipponate con lo sviluppo della dottrina sulla grazia in risposta alle tesi di

(*perseu.*): "If then there were no other documentation, this Lord's Prayer would be enough for us in the cause of grace that we are defending, because it leaves nothing in us, in which we might, as it were, glory in what is ours."[109]

Perspectives from Origen's Recently Discovered Psalms Homilies

In his comparison of Augustine and Origen on prayer, Perrone lamented the paucity of evidence on Origen's interpretation of the Psalms, "the book of prayer par excellence of the Old Testament."[110] Ironically, that statement came into print concurrently with the sensational discovery of Origen's twenty-nine *Homilies on Psalms*, which Perrone himself would soon edit.[111] These homilies do not offer new insights into Augustine's role in the reception of Origen comparable to those we gain from the Divjak letters, but they amply vindicate Perrone's intuition. As well as discussing the Psalms as prayers, the homilies attribute exegetical insights to prayer[112] and include requests for prayers for insight into problematical passages.[113] One homily demonstrates how Origen's belief that the soul preexists its embodiment is fundamental, not only to Origen's understanding of original sin, but also of the incarnation. Christ can be fully human and yet sinless because his soul did not fall away from God and so is fully human even though it lacks the inclinations to sin beneath the level of conscious awareness common to all other human beings.[114] The homilies also reveal affinities to the understanding of the church that Augustine derived largely from Cyprian and Tyconius. Like

---

Pelagio e dei suoi seguaci." "Impossibility made possible," Perrone's subtitle, comes from Origen, *Or.* 1.1.9: "δυνατὸν ἐξ ἀδυνάτου."

109. *Perseu.* 7.13 (PL 45:1001): "si ergo alia documenta non essent, haec dominica oratio nobis ad causam gratiae, quam defendimus, sola sufficeret: quia nihil nobis reliquit, in quo tamquam in nostro gloriemur."

110. Perrone, *La preghiera*, 638.

111. *Psalmenhomilien*, translated as Origen, *Homilies on the Psalms: Codex Monacensis Graecus 314*, trans. Joseph W. Trigg, FC 141 (Washington, DC: Catholic University of America Press, 2020).

112. See, e.g., *Hom. Ps.* 73, 3.1 (*Psalmenhomilien*, 328).

113. This occurs most notably in *Hom. Ps.* 67, 1.1 (*Psalmenhomilien*, 173–74), where Origen leads his congregation in praying the opening verses of Ps. 69 (LXX) for this purpose. See also *Hom. Ps.* 15, 2.7 (*Psalmenhomilien*, 104); *Hom. Ps.* 73, 2.8 (*Psalmenhomilien*, 253); and *Hom. Ps.* 77, 4.10 (*Psalmenhomilien*, 406).

114. See Origen, *Hom. Ps.* 15, 2.3.

Augustine, Origen considered it vital to maintain the unity of the church as the body of Christ while seeing it as inevitably imperfect. Where Augustine speaks of a *corpus permixtum*, Origen reads 1 Cor. 12:27 to say that the church can never be more than Christ's body "in part."[115] On the other hand, the homilies reveal affinity with Jerome on the issue that Augustine brought up in *Epistula* 28, the authority of the Septuagint translation as opposed to its Hebrew original.[116]

CONCLUSION

How we estimate Augustine's relationship to Origen depends on what questions we ask and whether we look, not just at what Augustine said about Origen, but at what he showed without saying. If we ask what he received from a firsthand reading of Origen's work, as Altaner and Fürst did, Origen's influence is not particularly impressive. If we ask how Origen shaped Augustine's thought, with or without his being aware of it, Origen's influence was arguably immense. Augustine received and passed on Origen's fusion of Christianity with Platonic philosophy and his allegorical interpretation of the Bible, even if, as we have seen, he presents these in *Confessiones* as simply the teaching of the church understood by the spiritually mature. Back-to-back articles titled "Origenismo in Occidente" in *Origene Dizionario* illustrate these approaches. Looking narrowly for what can be documented, Basil Studer's article on the fourth through the sixth centuries claims that Origen exercised a real, if limited, influence. Looking for the afterlife of Origen's ideas, Gaetano Lettieri's article covering the seventh through the eighteenth centuries claims that Western theology "absorbed Origen's influence precociously" through the same figures, including Augustine, that were discussed by Studer.[117]

115. Interpreting ἐκ μέρους to mean the same thing it means thirteen verses later in 1 Cor. 13:9. On the church being the body of Christ "in part," see Origen, *Hom. Ps. 15*, 1.3 (*Psalmenhomilien*, 77–78). On the value of unity, see Origen, *Hom. Ps. 67*, 1.4 (*Psalmenhomilien*, 184–85); *Hom. Ps. 81*, 1 (*Psalmenhomilien*, 510–11); and *Hom. Ps. 77*, 8.2–4 (*Psalmenhomilien*, 451–56).

116. See, e.g., Origen, *Hom. Ps. 36*, 1.1 (*Psalmenhomilien* 113–117); *Hom. Ps. 77*, 8.9 (*Psalmenhomilien*, 462–63); and *Hom. Ps. 80*, 1.7 (*Psalmenhomilien*, 491–92). On Jerome's position see Fürst, *Von Origenes*, 359–83.

117. Adele Monaci Castagno, ed., *Origene dizionario: La cultura, il pensiero, le opere* (Rome: Città Nuova, 2000), 302–22, citation from Lettieri, 307.

A full assessment of Augustine's reception of Origen would entail evaluating what Augustine knew of Origen's work, either through translations or through informants, and tracing how he adopted or rejected what he learned. It would also entail tracing how Origen's ideas were mediated to him through Latin authors, such as Hilary of Poitiers and Ambrose. To accomplish this task adequately would require, at minimum, a thorough acquaintance with the Latin traditions on which Augustine drew as well as with his work and the surviving works of Origen. It would also require facing difficult methodological issues. Robert O'Connell's illuminating, if controversial, work on one vital aspect of Origen's legacy, Augustine's understanding of the origin of the soul, illustrates one of these issues: how to evaluate the impact of Origen's thought when it remains an open question just what Origen taught. Augustine seems to have believed that Origen left open the possibility of a fall from blessedness, when he likely believed no such thing.[118] O'Connell himself seems to think that Plotinus had a higher assessment of the cosmos than Origen, which is even more doubtful.[119]

Though daunting, such an enterprise would be rewarding. Sabine MacCormack has shown, tracing Augustine's use of Vergil, the rewards of watching Augustine wrestle throughout his life with an influential figure.[120] Augustine critically appropriated Origen without having his assessments dictated by others, but Origen's increasingly questionable reputation in the larger Christian world influenced how he discussed, or failed to discuss, that appropriation. Rowan Williams suggests that Origen's reputation had become so problematic by Augustine's time because "'orthodoxy' . . . is always under construction. . . . Neither canon nor hierarchy in the abstract guarantees a secure and rational world for the believer to inhabit."[121] One might say that Origen had too much ability to remain open and uncertain, what John Keats called "negative capacity," to remain acceptable once Catholic Christianity, having become a state religion in the course of the fourth century, would no longer put up "with the idea of a community at whose center lies the continuing process of a search for unifying meanings of scripture and

118. O'Connell, *Origin of the Soul*, 74–76, 292–93.

119. O'Connell, *Origin of the Soul*, 140–44.

120. Sabine MacCormack, *The Shadows of Poetry: Vergil in the Mind of Augustine* (Berkeley: University of California Press, 1998).

121. In R. D. Williams, "Origen: Between Orthodoxy and Heresy," in *Origeniana Septima: Origenes in den Auseindersetsetzungen des 4. Jahrhunderds*, ed. W. A. Bienert and U. Kühneweg (Leuven: Leuven University Press, 1999), 9.

cosmos."[122] As a result, he fell victim to what Diarmaid MacCulloch has termed "purposeful forgetfulness."[123] Origen became the most influential thinker in the history of Western thought that otherwise well-educated persons still feel safe in ignoring. It is time for that to change. Augustine took much from Origen, but often those elements that he did not take are ones we can use now.

122. Williams, "Origen," 10.

123. For the term, see Diarmaid MacCulloch, *Silence: A Christian History* (New York: Penguin, 2013), 194.

Chapter 11

AUGUSTINE'S ANTI-PELAGIAN RECEPTION OF
BASIL OF CAESAREA AND GREGORY OF NAZIANZUS

Mark DelCogliano

INTRODUCTION

In both patristic scholarship and modern theological writing there is a long tradition of opposing Augustine and the Cappadocian Fathers on the grounds of
their supposedly divergent approaches to such issues as Trinitarian theology and
grace and free will. A massive amount of scholarship has been produced since (at
least) the late nineteenth century on the vexed issue of the Cappadocian Fathers'
influence on Augustine. Some have attempted to delineate the precise ways in
which Augustine was influenced by and used the Cappadocian Fathers. In this
regard the pioneering studies by Berthold Altaner in the 1940s and 1950s remain
foundational.[1] In a 2008 essay that constitutes a kind of *status quaestionis* on this
issue, Joseph Lienhard enumerates three approaches to the topic of Augustine
and the Cappadocians that scholars have taken.[2] The first is the "impressionistic"
approach, in which Augustine's use of the Cappadocians is posited on the basis
of similar ideas without much or any textual evidence. This approach, comments

---

My first academic study of Augustine and the Cappadocian Fathers came in the four graduate
seminars I took with J. Patout Burns in 2002–2004. Not only were these classes deeply formative for me as a developing scholar, but the bonds formed during those years, his friendship,
and his support since then have also been of inestimable value to me. I am thrilled to take up
the subject of Augustine and Cappadocians in honor of Patout.

    1. Altaner's essays are collected in Günter Glockmann, ed., *Kleine patristische Schriften*,
TUGAL 83 (Berlin: Akademie, 1967). As the notes below attest, I have benefited from several
of his studies.

    2. Joseph T. Lienhard, "Augustine of Hippo, Basil of Caesarea, and Gregory Nazianzen,"

Lienhard, is "the most intriguing, perhaps, but also the least trustworthy" and "cannot offer clear historical certitude."[3] The second is the "census" approach, which determines how often Augustine mentions a Cappadocian Father by name, but Lienhard notes that this approach does not tell us much more than that Augustine esteemed the Cappadocian Fathers and considered them among the Greek and Latin patristic authorities. The third is the "textual" approach, in which Augustine's use of the Cappadocian Fathers is demonstrated on the basis of the identifiable quotations from them, often with explicit mention of the author of the excerpt. This third approach is, according to Lienhard, "the surest—if not the most fruitful," but ultimately it is also "disappointing" because of the meager results.[4] Taking the textual approach, Lienhard catalogs and quotes the nine Cappadocian testimonies used by Augustine in his corpus.[5]

Building on the work of Lienhard, my goal here is to set Augustine's engagement with the Cappadocians in its literary context. In other words, building on the summative or global view of Augustine's use of the Cappadocians that emerges from the textual approach, I take a diachronic literary approach that explores not only what passages of the Cappadocians Augustine used but also how, why, and when he deployed those passages in his writings. I also investigate what "literary" challenges Augustine faced when using excerpts from the Cappadocians. This approach enables us to draw more refined conclusions about Augustine's use of the Cappadocian Fathers.[6]

---

in *Orthodox Readings of Augustine*, ed. George E. Demacopoulos and Aristotle Papanikolaou (Crestwood, NY: St. Vladimir's Seminary Press, 2008), 81–99.

3. Lienhard, "Augustine of Hippo," 85, 98.

4. Lienhard, "Augustine of Hippo," 87, 98.

5. Lienhard, "Augustine of Hippo," 88–98. Augustine quotes seven unique passages of Gregory from five orations; five of these passages he quotes or paraphrases more than once, though the extent of the quotation varies: *Oration (Or.)* 2.91 (PG 35:493) (*c. Iul.* 2.3.7; *c. Iul. imp.* 1.67, 1.69, 6.14); *Or.* 16.15 (PG 35:953–56) (*c. Iul.* 1.5.15, 1.7.32); *Or.* 17.5 (PG 35:971–72) (*c. Iul.* 2.3.7); *Or.* 38.4 (PG 36:315) (*c. Iul.* 1.5.15, 1.7.32); *Or.* 38.17 (PG 36:330–31) (*c. Iul.* 1.5.15, 1.7.32; *c. Iul. imp.* 1.52, 1.53, 1.70); *Or.* 41.8 (PG 36:440b) (*perseu.* 19.49); and *Or.* 41.14 (PG 36:448) (*c. Iul.* 1.5.15, 1.7.32; *c. Iul. imp.* 1.70). Augustine quotes two unique passages of Basil from two homilies; only one of these is quoted or paraphrased more than once: *De ieiunio I* 3–4 (PL 44:652) (*c. Iul.* 1.5.18, 1.7.32; *c. Iul. imp.* 1.52) and *Homilia exhortatoria ad sanctum baptisma* 2 (PG 31:428) (*c. Iul.* 2.6.18). For the Latin text of Augustine's *c. Iul.* and *c. Iul. imp.*, see PL 44:641–874 and PL 45:1049–1608, respectively.

6. Another approach would be to study how Augustine was influenced by the Cappadocians *indirectly* through the work of Latin authors such as Ambrose. Still another would be

In his classic study *Late Latin Writers and Their Greek Sources*, Pierre Courcelle has this to say about Augustine:

> Augustine is convinced of the fundamental unity of the Church. He believes that the faith is precisely the same among the Greeks and the Latins. Thus he does not feel the need, as a general rule, to appeal to Greek authorities for his Latin readers. He does not depart from this method except on two occasions that are quite exceptional. The first time, to bring back to the Catholic faith some obscure bishops, he draws his argument from the authority of the Greek and Roman Fathers where these agree. On another occasion, it is because the Pelagians support their heretical theories with several Greek texts that Augustine follows them on this ground and considers it his duty to quote the principal Greek writers who have treated the question.[7]

Courcelle is certainly correct that Augustine's debate with the Pelagians—or, to be more precise, Julian of Eclanum—marked a new stage in his reading of Greek patristic literature in general and the Cappadocian Fathers in particular. Augustine's debate with Julian occupied the last twelve years of his life. It began in the summer of 418 CE when Julian, in a letter to Count Valerius, accused Augustine of condemning marriage on account of his doctrine of original sin.[8] The accusation soon made its way to Augustine, who responded to it in the winter of 418–419 with the first book of *De nuptiis et concupiscentia* (*nupt. et conc.*), to which in turn Julian responded with the four books of *Ad Turbantium* (*Turb.*) in the summer of 419. A collection of excerpts from *Ad Turbantium* was compiled by some unknown person who occasionally altered Julian's words. Valerius forwarded these excerpts to Augustine, who responded to them in 420 or 421 with the second book of *De nuptiis et concupiscentia*. Soon, however, Augustine received the complete text of

---

to determine whether there are any clear indications beyond a similarity of ideas (such as similar argumentative logic, similar interpretations of clusters of scriptural verses, or similar terminology) that Augustine borrowed from the Cappadocians without verbatim citations or explicit acknowledgment. But these are beyond the scope of this essay.

7. Pierre Courcelle, *Late Latin Writers and Their Greek Sources*, trans. Harry E. Wedeck (Cambridge, MA: Harvard University Press, 1969), 196–97. The quotation continues: "It is therefore not necessary to think that Augustine is unacquainted with, or systematically disregards, Greek ecclesiastical literature. What strikes me, on the contrary, is the effort he makes to get to know it, either through translations or even from the original texts."

8. *Nupt. et conc.* 1.1.1 (PL 44:413).

the four books of *Ad Turbantium* and responded to them in 421 or 422 with the six books of *Contra Iulianum* (*c. Iul.*). Apparently these six books never reached Julian. Between 423 and 426 Julian responded to the second book of *De nuptiis et concupiscentia* with the eight books of *Ad Florum* (*Flor.*). Augustine began a response to these books in 427 or 428. Having reached six books, it remained unfinished at his death in 430 and thus is called *Contra Iulianum opus imperfectum* (*c. Iul. imp.*). Julian had appealed to Greek fathers such as John Chrysostom in support of his Pelagian viewpoint. Augustine realized that he needed to reclaim the Greek fathers for the Catholic position in order to refute Julian as effectively as possible. This required him not only to give alternative interpretations to the patristic passages cited by Julian but also to adduce other passages from the same Eastern patristic writers that, in his opinion, confirmed the Catholic position.[9] It is in his writings against Julian that we find all but one of his explicit references to and uses of the Cappadocian Fathers—or, more precisely, Basil of Caesarea and Gregory of Nazianzus. In every case Augustine has cited testimonies of Basil or Gregory as corroborating evidence from Eastern bishops for his doctrine of original sin, which Augustine takes to be Catholic teaching.

CHALLENGES

Augustine faced at least three "literary" challenges in using the Cappadocian Fathers when refuting Julian. First, in his corpus Augustine evinces almost no biographical knowledge of Basil and Gregory of Nazianzus and no knowledge at all of Gregory of Nyssa, making neither (clear) reference to nor use of him.[10] I write "clear" because there is actually a garbled reference. Once when lauding Basil and Gregory of Nazianzus, Augustine writes, "They are outstanding men endowed with obvious holiness and, it is said, brothers in the flesh" (*et, sicut fer-*

---

9. On Augustine's foray into argument from patristic citations in the Pelagian controversy, see Éric Rebillard, "A New Style of Argument in Christian Polemic: Augustine and the Use of Patristic Citations," *JECS* 8 (2000): 559–78.

10. See Karl Adam, *Die Eucharistielehre des hl. Augustin* (Paderborn: Ferdinand Schöningh, 1908), 43; Berthold Altaner, "Augustinus und Gregor von Nazianz, Gregor von Nyssa," in Glockmann, *Kleine patristische Schriften*, 285; and Lienhard, "Augustine of Hippo," 81. Altaner attributes Augustine's unfamiliarity with Gregory of Nyssa to the fact that nothing of his corpus had been translated into Latin in Augustine's time.

tur, etiam carne germani).[11] Augustine, it seems, had heard or read some report (as the *sicut fertur* indicates) that Basil had a brother named Gregory and mistakes this *carne germanus* to be the Nazianzen instead of the Nyssen.[12] If Augustine knew any other biographical details about Basil or Gregory, either from Rufinus's continuation of the *Historia ecclesiastica* (*Hist. eccl.*) of Eusebius, or from the details about each recounted by Rufinus in his prefaces to his translations of their works, or from the notices on the pair in Jerome's *De uiris illustribus* (*Vir. ill.*), or from some other source, he gave no evidence of it in his writings.[13] Apart from knowing that they were bishops and correctly identifying where they were from,[14] he thought he knew an additional biographical datum about them, but he got this wrong too.[15] In spite of this meager knowledge of them, Basil and Gregory—whom Augustine routinely labels *sanctus* or *beatus*[16]—feature prominently

11. *C. Iul.* 1.5.19 (PL 44:652; trans. Teske, *Answer to the Pelagians II*, WSA I/24, 280).

12. One possible source of this information is Rufinus's continuation of Eusebius's *Hist. eccl.* See Altaner, "Augustinus und Gregor von Nazianz," 277, and Altaner, "Augustinus und Basilius der Große," in Glockmann, *Kleine patristische Schriften*, 267. Rufinus concluded his chapter on Basil and Gregory of Nazianzus with a brief mention of Gregory of Nyssa (*Hist. eccl.* 11.9). Augustine may have either misread or misremembered this chapter. Altaner assumed that Augustine had read both this work of Rufinus and the entries on Basil and Gregory of Nazianzus in Jerome's *Vir. ill.* 116–17. Gregory of Nyssa is mentioned only in the former, and Altaner speculated that because Augustine had read Rufinus "ungenau," he mixed up the Gregorys.

13. Henceforward all references to "Gregory" without further qualification are to the Nazianzen.

14. References to their episcopal status are numerous. The following are the references to their location: "Cappadoci Basilio" (*c. Iul.* 1.6.22 [PL 44:655]); "Basilii Caesareensis" (*c. Iul.* 6.22.69 [PL 44:865]); "Nazianzeno Gregorio" (*c. Iul.* 1.6.22 [PL 44:655]); "Graecus Gregorius" (*c. Iul. imp.* 2.33 [PL 45:1155]).

15. Augustine's chance of knowing any correct biographical details about Basil and Gregory of Nazianzus was hampered by Rufinus's inaccurate account of them. "The errors in Rufinus's biographical sketch of Basil and Gregory are so egregious as to seem almost deliberate," writes Philip R. Amidon, *The Church History of Rufinus of Aquileia: Books 10 and 11* (Oxford: Oxford University Press, 1997), 93. Cf. Rufinus of Aquileia, *History of the Church*, trans. Philip R. Amidon, FC 133 (Washington, DC: Catholic University of America Press, 2016), 445n16, where this sentence is repeated verbatim.

16. "Sanctus Basilius" (*c. Iul.* 1.5.16 *bis* [PL 44:650], 1.5.18 [PL 44:652], 1.7.32 [PL 44:663], 6.22.69 [PL 44:865]); "Beatus Gregorius (*c. Iul.* 2.3.7 [PL 44:678]; *c. Iul. imp.* 6.14 [PL 45:1528]); "Sanctus Gregorius" (*c. Iul.* 1.5.15 [PL 44:649], 1.7.32 [PL 44:663], 2.3.7 [PL 44:677]; *perseu.* 19.49 [PL 45:1024]).

in the lists of Latin and Greek church fathers that Augustine often provides in his works against Julian to indicate which Catholic authorities support his position rather than his opponent's: Cyprian of Carthage, Ambrose of Milan, Hilary of Poitiers, and John Chrysostom are the others.[17] Augustine leaves no doubt that he held Basil and Gregory in the highest esteem, even if he knew almost nothing about them.

His ability to use the Cappadocians was hampered in a second way, for he took texts not by one of them to be by one of them, and texts by one of them to be by someone else. There are three instances of this in his corpus. First, in a letter to Fortunatian of Sicca from 413 or 414, Augustine cites, inter alia, "Saint Gregory, an Eastern bishop" on the topic of the essential invisibility of the Father, Son, and Holy Spirit.[18] But it is not Gregory of Nazianzus that he cites, but the Latin-speaking Western bishop Gregory of Elvira. The text from which Augustine quoted is the *Tractatus de fide*, an anti-Arian tract first issued by Gregory of Elvira anonymously around 360 and then revised for a second edition a few years later in response to criticisms. The first edition came to be preserved among the works of Ambrose of Milan, while the second edition came to be bundled in manuscripts with Rufinus's Latin translation of nine orations of Gregory of Nazianzus.[19] Given that Augustine had access to Rufinus's translation of Gregory,

---

17. See *c. Iul.* 1.6.22, 1.7.35, 2.4.8, 2.4.9, 2.8.30, 2.10.33, 2.10.35, 2.10.37, 3.17.32, 6.23.70; *c. Iul. imp.* 1.6, 1.9, 1.59, 1.117, 2.33, 2.37, 4.72, 4.73. Lienhard, "Augustine of Hippo," 85–86, provides statistics: Basil (mentioned in 11 lists), Gregory of Nazianzus (13), Cyprian (13), Ambrose (12), Hilary (12), John Chrysostom (11); the others appearing in such lists are Irenaeus of Lyon (6), Innocent of Rome (4), Jerome (4), Olympius of Spain (4), Reticus of Autun (4), and Theodore (1).

18. *Ep.* 148.10 (PL 33:626; trans. Teske, *Letters 100–155*, WSA II/2, 355). The same "Gregory" is mentioned again at *ep.* 148.15 in a reference to the earlier passage.

19. As far back as the seventeenth century, scholars realized that the attribution to both Ambrose and Gregory was mistaken. Vigilius of Thapsus, Phoebadius of Agen, and Gregory of Elvira were proposed as the correct author, with consensus eventually emerging around the third. For a summary of the debates over the authorship of *De fide*, see Manlio Simonetti, *Gregorio di Elvira: La fede* (Turin: Società Editrice Internazionale, 1975), 26–28; Joaquín Pascual Torró, *Gregorio de Elvira: La fede*, Fuentes Patrísticas 11 (Madrid: Ciudad Nueva, 1998), 17–22. The work is printed three times in Migne: PL 17:579–98 (Ambrose), PL 20:31–50 (Phoebadius), and PL 62:465–72 (Vigilius). In *Ep.* 148.10 (PL 33:626) Augustine quotes from *De fide* 8 (Simonetti, *Gregorio di Elvira*, 114). For the manuscripts that bundle the *Tractatus de fide* with Rufinus's Latin translation of Gregory of Nazianzus, see Simonetti, *Gregorio di Elvira*, 29–35. Teske, WSA II/2, 355n13, mistakenly identifies Phoebadius as Augustine's source.

it seems quite likely that the manuscript he used had already misattributed the *Tractatus de fide* to Gregory of Nazianzus.[20]

Second, when writing against Julian, Augustine misattributed a passage from Basil's *Homilia exhortatoria ad sanctum baptisma* (*Bapt.*) to John Chrysostom.[21] In this homily, preached on Epiphany at some point during his episcopate, Basil urges catechumens to be baptized without any further procrastination.[22] No ancient Latin translations of this homily are known to have been made or are extant.[23] Some have speculated that Augustine came across a translation of this homily in a Latin collection of John Chrysostom's preaching.[24] At any rate, even if in this case Augustine was unaware that he was quoting Basil, we should count it as a use of Basil.[25]

20. André Wilmart, "Les tractatus sur le cantique attribués à Grégoire d'Elvire," *Bulletin de littérature ecclésiastique* 8 (1906): 233–99; Augustus Engelbrecht, CSEL 46:ix–xvi; Altaner, "Augustinus und Gregor von Nazianz," 277; and Courcelle, *Late Latin Writers*, 203n36. There is some question about whether it was Rufinus himself who attached the *Tractatus de fide* to his translation of Gregory (as Wilmart suggested), or whether it was a misattribution that arose because of the identical names. Adjudicating this debate is beyond the scope of this essay.

21. *C. Iul.* 2.6.18. Altaner, "Augustinus und Basilius der Große," 274; Courcelle, *Late Latin Writers*, 203–4; Lienhard, "Augustine of Hippo," 89–90. The homily of Basil is CPG 2857 (PG 31:423–43); it is traditionally numbered as his thirteenth. The most recent translation is by Susan R. Holman, for which see St. Basil the Great, *On Fasting and Feasts*, trans. Susan R. Holman and Mark DelCogliano, Popular Patristics Series 50 (Yonkers, NY: St Vladimir's Seminary Press, 2013), 41–54. Augustine quotes from *Bapt.* 2 (PG 31:428a; trans. Holman in *On Fasting and Feasts*, 43).

22. See Jean Bernardi, *La prédication des pères cappadociens* (Paris: Presses universitaires de France, 1968), 68.

23. See Paul Jonathan Fedwick, *Bibliotheca Basiliana Vniversalis* II/2 (Turnhout: Brepols, 1996), 1047–51.

24. Courcelle, *Late Latin Writers*, 204 as well as 205n47; Altaner, "Augustinus und Basilius der Große," 275. Courcelle conjectures that Augustine used a Latin translation, produced by Pelagians, of selected homilies of Basil and Chrysostom and misidentified the homily's true author because of missing *incipit*, whereas Altaner, rejecting Courcelle's theory, suggests that the homily was attributed to Chrysostom in the manuscript Augustine used. See also the judicious remarks of Paul Jonathan Fedwick, "The Translations of the Works of Basil before 1400," in *Basil of Caesarea: Christian, Humanist, Ascetic; A Sixteen-Hundredth Anniversary Symposium*, ed. Paul Jonathan Fedwick (Toronto: Pontifical Institute of Mediaeval Studies, 1981), 456n89.

25. Ambrose, *De Helia et ieiunio* 79, 83, 84 (CSEL 32:460, 463), quoted different passages from the same baptism homily of Basil, but Altaner, "Augustinus und Basilius der Große," 275, denied that this accounted for Augustine's use in any way since Ambrose could read Greek.

Third, also when writing against Julian, Augustine quoted as Basil's some passages from a treatise *Adversus Manichaeos*.[26] But Basil is not known to have written such a treatise, and the source of the quotations has been identified as the anti-Manichaean treatise of Serapion of Thmuis.[27] Julian of Eclanum had cited these passages in his *Ad Turbantium*, without dissembling we must assume, as Eastern patristic testimony for his position. Accordingly, the only reason that Augustine cited them in *Contra Iulianum* was to refute Julian's interpretation of the passages and to undermine his opponent's appeal to Basil. He argued that the passages did not contradict the doctrine of original sin; instead, they emphasized the freedom of the human will and denied the substantial existence of evil. It appears that Augustine only knew of this treatise through Julian, quoted only the Latin citations provided by Julian, and accepted its authenticity on the authority of Julian.[28]

We now see some of the challenges Augustine faced: he knew next to nothing about the biographical details of Basil and Gregory, and he was mistaken in some cases about which works of theirs were authentic. He faced a third challenge: the language barrier. Augustine's knowledge of Greek has been a perennial issue in scholarship, and opinions vary widely on his facility with the language. It may not have been as poor as it has sometimes been made out to be, though it is hard to say with certitude. In any event, it seems that Augustine relied exclusively on Rufinus's Latin translation of nine orations of Gregory for his access to the Nazianzen's writings. Indeed, Augustine admitted as much before he quoted Gregory for the first time when he wrote, "Because of their deservedly great popularity, [Saint Gregory's] sermons have even been translated into Latin and become known far

26. *C. Iul.* 1.5.16–17 (PL 44:650–52). For discussion, see Altaner, "Augustinus und Basilius der Große," 273; Fedwick, "Translations," 462; and Lienhard, "Augustine of Hippo," 90.

27. Nello Cipriani, "L'autore dei testi pseudobasiliani riportati nel *c. Iul.* (1.16–17) e la polemica agostiniana de Giuliano d'Eclano," in *Congresso internazionale su s. Agostino nel XVI centenario della conversione: Atti* (Rome: Institutum Patristicum Augustianum, 1987), 1:439–49. Fedwick, *Bibliotheca Basiliana Vniversalis* II/2, 1247, lists this treatise among the Latin *spuria* of Basil.

28. Altaner, "Augustinus und Basilius der Große," 273, and Lienhard, "Augustine of Hippo," 90. Cf. Augustine's comment in *cat. rud.* 8.12.4 (PL 40:318–19) that the books that prompted a person to join the church should be approved if personally known or accepted by ecclesiastical tradition as Catholic. As Augustine couldn't have personally known an *Adversus Manichaeos* of Basil, he seems to have trusted Julian's familiarity with the ecclesiastical tradition. It is worth noting that Augustine and Julian did not disagree on which Latin and Greek church fathers were authorities.

and wide."[29] All of his quotations from Gregory are taken more or less verbatim from Rufinus.[30] Augustine's dependence on the translation of Rufinus is also supported by the fact that he did not use other passages of the Nazianzen that would have suited his purposes quite well.[31] There are no other certain citations or uses of Gregory in Augustine's corpus, either explicit or unattributed.[32]

The case is somewhat different with Basil. Augustine quoted from only one homily of Basil besides the above-mentioned—but wrongly attributed—*Homilia exhortatoria ad sanctum baptisma*: the first *Homilia de ieiunio* (*Iei1*). Like *Homilia exhortatoria ad sanctum baptisma*, this homily is not one of the eight sermons translated into Latin by Rufinus.[33] Before quoting this homily for the first time, Augustine wrote, "Although I found it already translated, I preferred, nonetheless, to translate it word by word from the Greek to obtain a more exact fidelity to the original."[34] An ancient Latin translation of Basil's two homilies on fasting is extant. Some scholars have suggested that Rufinus is also the translator of these homilies; however, even if

29. *C. Iul.* 1.5.15 (PL 44:649; Teske, WSA I/24, 276): "cuius eloquia ingentis merito gratiae, etiam in linguam latinam translata usquequaque claruerunt."

30. Rufinus translated nine orations of Gregory: *Or.* 2 (*Apologeticus*), *Or.* 38 (*De epiphaniis*), *Or.* 39 (*De luminibus*), *Or.* 41 (*De pentecoste*), *Or.* 26 (*In semetipsum de agro regressus*), *Or.* 17 (*Ad cives Nazianzenos*), *Or.* 6 (*De reconciliatione et unitate monachorum*), *Or.* 16 (*De grandis uastatione*), and *Or.* 27 (*De Arrianis*). For critical editions, see CSEL 46.

31. Altaner, "Augustinus und Gregor von Nazianz," 279; Lienhard, "Augustine of Hippo," 91.

32. Some scholars have claimed that Augustine used Gregory without acknowledgment on the basis of a similarity of ideas or arguments (examples of Lienhard's "impressionistic" approach mentioned above). E.g., Altaner, "Augustinus und Gregor von Nazianz," 281–84, claims that in *trin.* 15.20.38 (as well as *c. s. Arrian.* 1.2) Augustine borrowed from Gregory's argument from *Or.* 29.6. Altaner goes on to posit the existence of a Latin translation of *Or.* 29 not by Rufinus but also no longer extant. But the argument adduced by Gregory and Augustine was common in pro-Nicene literature, and a claim of a direct literary relationship between the two need not be made to explain its presence. Some scholars have even made claims for influence based on general similarities without citing specific passages: see, e.g., Adam, *Die Eucharistielehre*, 41, which discusses eucharistic doctrine.

33. Rufinus translated the following sermons: (1) *In Psalmum* i; (2) *In illud, Attende tibi ipsi*; (3) *In illud, Destruam horrea mea*; (4) *De invidia*; (5) *In principium Proverbiorum*; (6) *De fide*; (7) *Ad virginem lapsum* [= Ep. 46]; and (8) *In Psalmum lix*. For critical editions, see CSEL 20.

34. *C. Iul.* 1.5.18 (PL 44.652; Teske, WSA I/24, 279): "quod etsi reperi interpretatum, tamen propter diligentiorem ueri fidem uerbum e uerbo malui transferre de graeco." Note that Augustine translated only an excerpt, not the whole homily.

this attribution is incorrect, the fact remains that these two Latin homilies on fasting are more adaptations of Basil than they are strict translations.[35] A comparison of the original Greek of the excerpt cited by Augustine with the Latin translations of Augustine and Rufinus (if the latter attribution is correct) corroborates Augustine's statement that he sought to produce a literal translation more faithful than the existing Latin translation. Augustine's translation of the brief excerpt is word for word, usually following the same word order as the Greek, with one or two slight differences. This is perhaps due to Augustine having a corrupt text before him or simply being more idiomatic than literal; in any case, the meaning is essentially the same.[36] By contrast, the translation of Rufinus follows Basil in substance but has a habit of expanding on the original. Thus, if this was the translation of the first homily that Augustine had access to, it would explain his decision to produce a literal translation of his own from the Greek.[37] One wonders what it was about the Latin translation he had that prompted him to check it against the Greek. In other words, he could have judged the translation too free only after comparing it with the Greek. Augustine must have had easy access to the Greek version of this homily, enabling him both to check the existing Latin translation against it and then to produce his own translation "to obtain a more exact fidelity to the original." At any rate, this brief excerpt from the first *Homilia de ieiunio* appears to be the only instance in which Augustine read Basil or Gregory in the original Greek. There are no other certain citations or uses of Basil in Augustine's corpus, either explicit or unattributed.[38]

35. Heinrich Marti, "Rufinus' Translation of St. Basil's Sermon on Fasting," *StPatr* 16, no. 2 (1985): 418–22. Heinrich Marti, *Rufin von Aquileia De ieiunio I, II: Zwei Predigten uber das Fasten nach Basileios von Kaisareia; Ausgabe mit Einleitung, Übersetzung und Anmerkungen*, VCSup 6 (Leiden: Brill, 1989). See also Berthold Altaner, "Altlateinische Übersetzungen von Basiliusschriften," in Glockmann, *Kleine patristische Schriften*, 409–15, esp. 409–13; Fedwick, "Translations," 466–68. Fedwick, *Bibliotheca Basiliana Vniversalis* II/2, 1242–43, lists these Latin homilies on fasting among Basil's Latin *spuria*.

36. Lienhard, "Augustine of Hippo," 89, observes, "Augustine's literal interpretation of Basil's Greek is quite accurate, with perhaps some slight adaptation to Latin style."

37. On Augustine's ability during his debate with Julian to produce literal translations from Greek, see Mathijs Lamberigts, "Augustine as Translator of Greek Texts: An Example," in *Philohistôr: Miscellanea in honorem Caroli Laga septuagenarii*, ed. A. Schoors and P. Van Deun (Leuven: Peeters, 1994), 151–61.

38. As with Gregory (cf. n. 32 *supra*), some scholars have claimed that Augustine used Basil without acknowledgment on the basis of a similarity of ideas or arguments (examples of Lienhard's "impressionistic" approach mentioned above). For example, Berthold Altaner, "Eustathius, der lateinische Übersetzer der Hexaemeron-Homilien Basilius des Großen," in

A LITERARY APPROACH

The challenges that Augustine faced when it came to Basil and Gregory, however, did not prevent him from using their writings polemically in his debate with Julian. According to *Retractationes* (*retr.*), the first two books of the *Contra Iulianum* "refuted the impudence of Julian by the testimonies of the saints who defended the Catholic faith after the apostles."[39] Written between 421 and 422 CE, the first two books of the *Contra Iulianum* are the first steps and, as we shall see, the foundation of Augustine's anti-Pelagian reception of Basil and Gregory. The bulk of Augustine's testimonies from Gregory and Basil are found in these two books. Writing in response to the four books of Julian's *Ad Turbantium*, Augustine was now aware to what extent Julian appealed to the Eastern fathers in support of his views and needed to reclaim them for his side. This was the first order of business in *Contra Iulianum*.

In his preliminary remarks in book 1, Augustine, inter alia, spells out the key disagreement between him and Julian.[40] Augustine teaches that infants are born having contracted the infection of original sin and thus stand in need of baptism, but Julian sees this as indicting marriage as blameworthy since what is born of it is not free of the debt of original sin. Thus, he interprets Augustine's teaching as tantamount to the Manichaean understanding of natural evil. In response to this charge, Augustine's tactic is to present testimonies of Catholic authorities—au-

---

Glockmann, *Kleine patristische Schriften*, 437–47, suggested that Augustine's reference to a Syrian exegete (probably Ephrem) in *Gen. litt.* 1.18.36 (PL 34:260) was borrowed from Basil's *Hexaemeron* 2.6 (PG 29:44a) through the intermediary of the Latin translation of this work by Eustathius (PL 30:888c). Similarly, John F. Callahan, "Basil of Caesarea: A New Source for St. Augustine's Theory of Time," *Harvard Studies in Classical Philology* 63 (1958): 437–54, argued that Augustine borrowed from Basil's *Contra Eunomium* 1.21 for his own account of time in *conf.* 11.23.30–11.31.41. Infamously, Jean Chevalier, *Saint Augustin et la pensée grecque: Les relations trinitaires*, Collectanea Friburgensia 33 (Fribourg: Librairie de l'Universite, 1940), 127–52, asserted that Augustine knew and read the dogmatic writings of both Basil and Gregory, even if it was difficult to pinpoint the precise sources used by Augustine. This claim was posited on the demonstration of similar ideas: "Il importe de souligner en terminant d'autres affinités doctrinales entre les deux évêques de Césarée et d'Hippone. Elles confirmeront cette opinion que Basile a exercé une influence réelle sue la doctrine trinitaire d'Augustin" (138), and, speaking of Gregory, "Ces affinités, dont on n'a donné qu'une esquisse, suffisent-elles à déceler une dépendance? Prises dans l'ensemble, elles paraissent bien confirmer la conclusion" (140).

39. *Retr.* 2.88(62) (PL 32:655; trans. Teske, WSA I/24, 222): "sed meorum duo primi testimoniis sanctorum, qui fidem catholicam post Apostolos defenderunt, Iuliani impudentiam redarguunt."

40. *C. Iul.* 1.1.1–1.2.4 (PL 44:614–43).

thorities recognized by both Augustine and Julian—whom Julian will also have to accuse of Manichaeanism if the Pelagians insist that Augustine's teaching on original sin is essentially Manichaean.[41] Augustine begins by citing Western fathers: Irenaeus, Cyprian, Reticus, Olympius, Hilary, Ambrose, and Innocent.[42] Although some are clearer and more direct than others, the consensus of all these testimonies attests that "newborn infants contract original sin from Adam" is a teaching found in the staunchest Catholic thinkers.[43] In other words, then, in *Contra Iulianum*, book 1, Augustine aims to demonstrate that his teaching on the subject of original sin agrees with the consensus doctrine of authoritative Western Catholic thinkers.

But, having read *Ad Turbantium*, Augustine also knew that Julian considered original sin a peculiarly Western idea and, for polemical reasons, had appealed to Eastern church fathers—specifically John Chrysostom and Basil—to show the division between East and West on this matter and, by doing so, to refute Augustine in the bargain.[44] Augustine chides Julian for his appeal to Eastern bishops, since "they too are Christians and this faith is one in both parts of the world, because this faith is the Christian faith."[45] Given the need to adduce both Greek and Latin fathers against Julian to demonstrate the Catholic consensus, Augustine begins his compilation of testimonies from Eastern church fathers with Gregory, "a man with a great name and glorious reputation, from the East as well."[46] Augustine further validates the authority of Gregory by adding that his deservedly popular sermons have even been translated into Latin and become widely disseminated in the West.[47] He then quotes four passages of Gregory in quick succession without any intervening commentary in order to rebut Julian's accusations that (a) Eastern bishops denied that newborn infants contracted

---

41. Rebillard, "New Style," 575–76.

42. *C. Iul.* 1.3.5–1.4.13 (PL 44:643–48).

43. *C. Iul.* 1.4.12 (PL 44:6488; trans. Teske, WSA I/24, 274).

44. Apparently, Julian never dropped the claim that Eastern bishops agreed with him. E.g., in his *Flor.* (cf. *c. Iul. imp.* 3.111), written between 423 and 426 CE, Julian lists John Chrysostom, Basil, and Theodore of Mopsuestia as authorities who support his opinions.

45. *C. Iul.* 1.4.14 (PL 44:649; trans. Teske, WSA I/24, 275): "quia et ipsi utique christiani sunt, et utriusque partis terrarum fides ista una est; quia et fides ista christiana est."

46. *C. Iul.* 1.5.15 (PL 44:649; trans. Teske, WSA I/24, 276): "magni nominis et fama celeberrima illustris episcopus etiam de partibus Orientis."

47. *C. Iul.* 1.4.15 (PL 44:649). The passage is cited above, pp. 268–69.

original sin from Adam and needed baptism for its removal and (b) those who subscribed to such ideas were nothing more than Manichaeans. The first excerpt is from Oration 16, *De grandis uastatione* (*On the Devastation from Hail*); the second and third are from Oration 38, *De epiphaniis* (*On the Theophanies*); and the fourth is from Oration 41, *De pentecoste* (*On Pentecost*).[48]

> **G1** Let the image of God wash away the stain of immersion in the body, and let it raise up by the wings of the word of God the flesh joined to it. It would have been better for it not to need any such cleansing and to have remained in its original dignity, to which we hastily return after our present conversion, and it would have been better not to fall from the tree of life by the most bitter taste of sin. It is, nonetheless, better in the present condition to mend one's ways and to be converted after the fall rather than to remain in sinfulness.[49]

> **G2** Just as we all died in Adam, so let us come to life in Christ. Let us, then, be born with Christ, and let us be crucified with Christ and buried with him into death so that we may also rise with him for life. It is necessary, after all, that we suffer this change which is both beneficial and necessary so that, as we have changed from a good to a sad state, we might also be restored from our sad state to a good one. For, where sin abounded, there grace was even more abundant; by a greater grace the cross of Christ made righteous those whom the taste of the forbidden tree condemned.[50]

48. Sigla have been given to the quotations for easy reference.

49. *C. Iul.* 1.5.15 (PL 44:649; trans. Teske, WSA I/24, 276) = Gregory, *De grandinis uastatione*, oration 16.15 (PG 35:953–56) = Rufinus, *De grandinis uastatione*, oration 8.15 (CSEL 46:253–54): "imago inquit dei labem corporeae inundationis expurget, et coniunctam sibi carnem uerbi dei subleuet pennis. et quamuis melius fuisset, ne egere quidem huiuscemodi expurgatione, sed in illa prima dignitate permansisse, ad quam et refestinamus, post praesentem emendationem, et melius fuisset non excidere a ligno uitae gustu amarissimo peccati; tamen in secundo loco expedit emendari et corrigi post lapsum, quam in nequitiis permanere."

50. *C. Iul.* 1.5.15 (PL 44:649–50; trans. Teske, WSA I/24, 276–77) = Gregory, *In Theophaneia, sive natalitia Salvatoris*, oration 38.4 (PG 36:315) = Rufinus, *De epiphaniis*, oration 2.4 (CSEL 46:89–90): "sicut in Adam omnes inquit mortui sumus, ita et in Christo omnes uiuificemur. cum Christo ergo nascamur, et cum Christo crucifigamur, et consepeliamur ei in mortem, ut cum ipso etiam resurgamus ad uitam. necesse est enim nos perpeti utilem hanc et necessariam uicissitudinem: ut sicut ex bonis ad tristia deuoluti sumus, ita ex tristibus ad

G3 (a) Show reverence for the birth through which you were set free from the chains of earthly birth. (b) Honor small and tiny Bethlehem through which the return to paradise has been opened for you.[51]

G4 (a) On this point let Christ's words persuade you, when he says that no one can enter the kingdom of heaven, unless he has been reborn of water and the Spirit. (b) This baptism washes away the stains of the first birth because of which we are conceived in iniquities and our mothers bore us in sins.[52]

Augustine concludes these four citations with a rhetorical question, "Are you going to say that this man too thinks and spreads poison like a Manichee?"[53] On the contrary, retorts Augustine, Gregory echoes the one Catholic faith found in Western and Eastern fathers alike.[54] Though Augustine does not explicitly indicate why he chose these excerpts, we can surmise that he did so because all four mention a fallen condition precipitated by the first sin of eating from the forbidden tree, a condition marked by stain, sinfulness, iniquity, chains, death, and the like. Furthermore, all four speak of the dissipation of this fallen condition, conceived of as a restoration to the prelapsarian state. Only the fourth quotation, however, mentions baptism as the means through which the original condition is regained, the others speaking of other means such as grace, cleansing, conversion, and so forth, all of which, of course, presume or at least do not preclude baptism.

Augustine next turns to Basil, not only as another example of an Eastern bishop who supports the doctrine of original sin, but also because Julian had cited

---

meliora reparemur. ubi enim abundauit peccatum, superabundauit gratia: ut quos gustus ligni uetiti condamnauit, Christi crux gratia largiore iustificet."

51. *C. Iul.* 1.5.15 (PL 44:650; trans. Teske, WSA I/24, 277) = Gregory, *In Theophaneia, sive natalitia Salvatoris*, oration 38.17 (PG 36:330–31) = Rufinus, *De epiphaniis*, oration 2.17 (CSEL 46:105): "uenerare inquit natiuitatem, per quam terrenae natiuitatis uinculis liberatus es. honora Bethlehem pusillam et minimam, per quam tibi regressus ad paradisum patefactus est."

52. *C. Iul.* 1.5.15 (PL 44:650; trans. Teske, WSA I/24, 277) = Gregory, *In Pentecosten*, oration 41.14 (PG 36:448) = Rufinus, *De Pentecoste et de Spiritu Sancto*, oration 4.14 (CSEL 46:158): "persuadeat inquit tibi de hoc quoque sermo Christi dicentis, neminem posse introire in regnum caelorum, nisi renatus fuerit ex aqua et spiritu. per hunc primae natiuitatis maculae purgantur, per quas in iniquitatibus concipimur, et in delictis genuerunt nos matres nostrae."

53. *C. Iul.* 1.5.15 (PL 44:650; trans. Teske, WSA I/24, 277): "numquid et istum manichaei sapere uel iacere uenena dicturus es?"

54. *C. Iul.* 1.5.15 (PL 44:650).

an anti-Manichaean work attributed to Basil in support of his own position.[55] Unaware that the anti-Manichaean work is not Basil's,[56] Augustine dismantles Julian's use of the anti-Manichaean work by showing that the passages adduced by Julian are irrelevant to the topic of original sin and in fact contain nothing but the true Catholic faith.[57] But Augustine is not yet done with demolishing Julian's appeal to Basil. He quotes a passage from Basil's first *Homilia de ieiunio* in the Latin translation he himself produced from the original Greek (cf. *supra*):

> **B1 (a)** Fasting was established by law in paradise. For it was the first command that Adam received: "You shall not eat from the tree of the knowledge of good and evil" (Gen 2:17). "You shall not eat" legislates fasting and it is the beginning of the establishment of law. If Eve had fasted from the tree, we would not need this [present] fasting. "For those who are well have no need of a physician, but those who are sick" (Matt. 9:12). We have been injured by sin; let us be healed by repentance. But repentance without fasting is futile. "Cursed is the ground; thorns and thistles it shall bring forth" (Gen 3:17–18). You have been ordered to be sorrowful, why do you indulge yourself? . . . **(b)** It is because we did not fast that we fell from paradise. So let us fast that we may return to it.[58]

According to Augustine's interpretation of Basil, fasting would not be needed now unless the first human beings broke the law of fasting in paradise, and thus "the rest of us are born subject to the sin of those human beings," and "by the sin

---

55. *C. Iul.* 1.5.16–17 (PL 44:650–52). See also *c. Iul.* 6.22.69 (PL 44:865), where Augustine mentions that Julian tried to claim that both Basil and Chrysostom agreed with his views.

56. Cf. *supra*.

57. See also *c. Iul.* 1.7.30 (PL 44:661), where Augustine is summarizing how the various testimonies he had cited refute Julian. In reference to Basil he writes, "Here is also Basil by whose words you thought you were somehow helped, though they had nothing to do with the topic now being discussed" ("hic est Basilius, cuius te uerbis ad id quod nunc agitur non pertinentibus, putasti aliquid adiuuari") (trans. Teske, WSA I/24, 289).

58. *C. Iul.* 1.5.18 (PL 44:652; trans. is my own): "ieiunium inquit in paradiso lege constitutum est. primum enim mandatum accepit Adam: a ligno sciendi bonum et malum non manducabitis. non manducabitis autem, ieiunium est, et legis constitutionis initium. si ieiunasset a ligno Eua, non isto indigeremus ieiunio. non enim opus habent ualentes medico, sed male habentes. aegrotauimus per peccatum, sanemur per paenitentiam. paenitentia uero sine ieiunio uacua est. maledicta terra spinas et tribulos pariet. constristari ordinatus es, numquid deliciari? et paulo post in eodem sermone, idem ipse: quia non ieiunauimus inquit decidimus de paradiso. ieiunemus ergo, ut ad eum redeamus."

of those human beings we have lost the good health in which we were created,"
and "there belongs to us the sin of those human beings, the only ones who were
then in paradise and in whom we also existed."[59] For Augustine, then, Basil's
remarks demonstrate the Catholic teaching that the original sin of the first human beings continues to harm their descendants. There can be little doubt that
Augustine provides an explicitly anti-Pelagian interpretation of Basil, in contrast
to letting the excerpts from Gregory speak for themselves, because Julian had
tried to corral Basil for his side in the debate.

After citing testimonies from Gregory and Basil in the first book of *Contra
Iulianum*, Augustine claims the fourteen Eastern bishops at the Council of Dio-
spolis held in December of 415 for his side[60] and then turns to John Chrysostom,
the other Eastern bishop whom Julian had claimed denied original sin. Augustine
disputes Julian's interpretation of the passage of John Chrysostom that he had
adduced in support of his position, arguing that John meant that infants have no
personal sin, even citing the original Greek to prove his point.[61] Augustine then
cites other testimonies of John to demonstrate that he did in fact hold to the
doctrine of original sin.[62] In the remainder of the first book, Augustine challenges
Julian to reconsider his views in the light of all the evidence he has presented
against him and ends by showing how it is Julian's views that are really tantamount to Manichaeanism.[63] While they are not his only sources, Gregory and
Basil are at the forefront in the arsenal of Eastern patristic texts that Augustine
assembles in response to Julian.

In the second book of *Contra Iulianum*, Augustine again refutes Julian by
means of appeal to ecclesiastical authorities. But his purpose has shifted slightly
from the first book: it is not to show that Augustine's views on original sin agree
with the consensus of authoritative Western and Eastern church fathers and,

59. *C. Iul.* 1.5.18 (PL 44:652; trans. Teske, WSA I/24, 279): "audis quod isto non indigeremus ieiunio, si homo ieiunii legem non fuisset in paradisi felicitate transgressus; et negas peccato illorum hominum obnoxios ceteros nasci. audis adiunctum: non enim sani indigent medico; et negas nos sanitatem, in qua creati sumus, peccato illorum hominum perdidisse? audis
sententiam, quae prolata est in primum hominem peccatorem: spinas et tribulos terra pariet
tibi, ad nos etiam pertinere; et negas obnoxios esse peccato, quos eidem cernis obnoxios esse
sententiae? audis ad paradisum nos, unde decidimus, redire debere; et negas ad nos eorum
peccatum, qui soli tunc homines in paradiso fuerant, in quibus et nos fuimus, pertinere?"
60. *C. Iul.* 1.5.19–20 (PL 44:652–54).
61. *C. Iul.* 1.6.21–22 (PL 44:654–56).
62. *C. Iul.* 1.6.23–28 (PL 44:656–60).
63. *C. Iul.* 1.7.29–33 (PL 44:660–65) and 1.8.36–1.9.46 (PL 44:666–72).

thus, represent nothing but the true Catholic faith. Rather, here it is to refute Julian's denial of original sin by again appealing to both Western and Eastern patristic authorities.[64] Augustine articulates five erroneous conclusions drawn by Pelagians from the Catholic defense of original sin. The Pelagians think that the Catholics (1) teach that "the devil is the author of newborn human beings," (2) "condemn marriage," (3) deny that all sins are forgiven in baptism, (4) accuse God of the crime of injustice, and (5) inculcate a despair of attaining perfection.[65] Augustine's procedure in book 2 is not to take up each of these five arguments individually and to refute each by appeal to some testimony of a certain church father; rather, he proceeds through the testimonies he has at his disposal, using each testimony to refute the various individual arguments. In other words, Augustine makes a cumulative case. The testimonies he cites are drawn mostly from Ambrose, but there are also excerpts from Cyprian, Gregory, Basil, Chrysostom, and Hilary.[66]

Augustine provides two testimonies from Gregory in the second book of *Contra Iulianum* to demonstrate that the effects of original sin (i.e., concupiscence) remain even after original sin is forgiven through baptism. In contrast to how he handled the Gregorian excerpts cited in book 1, here Augustine supplies an interpretation of each passage. The first testimony is taken from Oration 17, *Ad ciues Nazianzenos graui timore perculsos* (*To the Citizens of Nazianzus Stricken with Grave Fear*):

64. *C. Iul.* 2.1.1 (PL 44:671–72).

65. *C. Iul.* 2.1.2 (PL 44:672–73): "haec sunt certe uelut capita argumentorum quasi formidanda uestrorum, quibus terretis infirmos, et minus quam contra uos expedit, sacris litteris eruditos. dicitis enim: nos asserendo originale peccatum, diabolum dicere hominum nascentium conditorem, damnare nuptias, negare in baptismo dimitti uniuersa peccata, deum crimine iniquitatis arguere, desperationem perfectionis ingerere. haec quippe omnia consequentia esse contenditis, si credamus nasci paruulos peccato primi hominis obligatos, et ob hoc esse sub diabolo, nisi renascantur in Christo. diabolus enim creat dicis si ex hoc uulnere creantur, quod diabolus naturae, quae primum condita est, inflixit humanae: et damnantur nuptiae, si aliquid unde damnabiles generantur, habere creduntur: nec omnia peccata dimittuntur in baptismo, si aliquod in baptizatis coniugibus remanet malum, ex quo generentur mali. quemadmodum autem non est iniquus deus, qui cum baptizatis remittat peccata propria, paruulum damnat, quia cum ab illo crearetur, nesciens nec uolens etiam ex illis parentibus, quibus remissa fuerant, traxit aliena? nec uirtus, cui uitiositas intelligitur esse contraria, posse creditur perfici; quia ingenerata uitia incredibile est posse consumi: quae iam nec uitia deputanda sunt. non enim peccat, qui non potest aliud esse quam creatus est."

66. *C. Iul.* 2.2.4–2.3.5 (Ambrose), 2.4.6 (Cyprian), 2.4.7 (Gregory), 2.4.8–2.6.16 (Ambrose), 2.7.17 (Chrysostom), 2.7.18 (Basil), 2.7.19–2.8.24 (Ambrose), 2.8.25 (Cyprian), and 2.8.26–30 (Hilary). For the Latin text of Augustine's *c. Iul.*, see PL 44:641–874.

G5 When the soul is in labors and trials, when it is hostilely attacked by the flesh, it has recourse to God and knows from whom it ought to demand help.[67]

Rather than understanding this in a Manichaean way, such that the attacks on the flesh come from an opposing evil nature, Augustine says that Gregory teaches that flesh and spirit are opposed "for no other reason than that both might be called back to their author after their fierce combat in this life, for in that combat the life of all the saints must struggle."[68] While not the clearest proof, Augustine sees its point as this: that even after baptism and the forgiveness of original sin, the struggle of concupiscence, which is the legacy of original sin, continues and indeed is constitutive of the Christian life.

Augustine regards the second Gregorian testimony he cites in book 2 as making the same point as the previous testimony did. It comes from Gregory's Oration 2, *Apologeticus* (*Apology*), the self-defense for his flight to Pontus:

G6 I do not as yet make mention of those blows by which we are attacked within ourselves by our own vices and passions and are day and night oppressed by the burning temptations of the body of this lowly state and of the body of death. In it the snares of visible things entice and arouse us at times in a hidden way and at other times quite openly, and the clay of these dregs to which we cling breathes forth the foul odor of its filth through its larger passages. The law of sin which is in our members resists the law of the spirit, as it strives to take captive the royal image which is within us so that all that has been poured into us by the gift of our original and divine creation becomes his booty. From there, though they govern themselves with a long and uncompromising pursuit

67. *C. Iul.* 2.3.7 (PL 44:677; trans. Teske, WSA I/24, 309) = Gregory, *Ad ciues Nazianzenos graui timore perculsos et praefectum irascentem*, oration 17.5 (PG 35:971–72) = Rufinus, *Ad ciues Nazianzenos graui timore perculsos et praefectum irascentem*, oration 6.5.1 (CSEL 46:199): "anima namque cum in laboribus fuerit et in angustiis cum hostiliter urgetur a carne tunc ad deum refugit et cognoscit unde debeat auxilium poscere." Teske, WSA I/24, 335n11, indicates that Rufinus's Latin rather freely translates Gregory's Greek, a comment that renders the original Greek excerpt less pertinent than Augustine took it to be.

68. *C. Iul.* 2.3.7 (PL 44:677; trans. Teske, WSA I/24, 309): "ac ne quisquam in his uerbis episcopi Gregorii hostiliter urgentem carnem tamquam ex contraria natura mali secundum Manichaeorum insaniam suspicetur; etiam ipse uide quemadmodum suis fratribus et condoctoribus concinat docens non ob aliud aduersus carnem spiritum concupiscere nisi ut suo utrumque reuocetur auctori post grauissimum in hac uita rei utriusque conflictum in quo laborat omnium uita sanctorum."

of wisdom and gradually recover the nobility of their soul, hardly any summon back and turn back to God the nature of the light which is joined in them to this humble and dark clay. Or if they do this with God's help, they will call both of them back equally, if by long and constant meditation they become used to always looking upward and to pulling up by tighter reins the matter bound to them that always wrongly drags them downward and weighs them down.[69]

Once again, Augustine stresses that Gregory is describing baptized Christians and the continued struggle with concupiscence that baptized Christians experience. "In baptism," writes Augustine, "all sins are forgiven," but "there remains for the baptized a civil war, as it were, with their inner faults."[70] He goes on to describe these faults, which are not sins per se, but interior passions and vices that trouble the Christian and must be healed for Christian progress to occur. Accordingly, this excerpt supplies Augustine with solid proof from the teaching of an Eastern father that the effects of original sin linger after baptism.

Augustine also cites a testimony from Basil in *Contra Iulianum*, book 2, though he mistakenly attributes it to John Chrysostom (cf. *supra*). This excerpt comes from Basil's *Homilia exhortatoria ad sanctum baptisma*:

69. *C. Iul.* 2.3.7 (PL 44:677; trans. Teske, WSA I/24, 309–10) = Gregory, *Apologetica*, oration 2.91 (PG 35:493) = Rufinus, *Apologeticus*, oration 1.91 (CSEL 46:67.20–68.17): "illorum uero inquit uerborum nondum facio mentionem quibus intra nosmetipsos propriis uitiis ac passionibus impugnamur et die noctuque ignitis stimulis corporis humilitatis huius et corporis mortis urgemur nunc latenter nunc etiam palam prouocantibus ubique et irritantibus rerum uisibilium illecebris luto hoc faecis cui inhaesimus caeni sui fetorem uenis capacioribus exhalante; sed et lege peccati quae est in membris nostris legi spiritus repugnante; dum imaginem regiam quae intra nos est captiuam ducere studet: ut spoliis eius cedat, quidquid illud est quod in nos beneficio diuinae ac primae illius condicionis influxit: unde uix aliquis fortasse longa se et districta regens philosophia et paulatim nobilitatem animale suae recolens naturam lucis quae in se est humili huic et tenebroso luto coniuncta reuocet ac reflectat ad deum: uel si certe propitio deo agat utrumque pariter reuocabit; si tamen longa et assidua meditatione insuescat sursum semper aspicere et deorsum male trahentem ac degrauantem materiam sibimet astrictam frenis arctioribus subleuare." In *c. Iul. imp.* 1.67, 1.69, and 6.14 Augustine cites **G6** three times to varying, overlapping extents. For ease of reference, the following abbreviations are used for these quotations. **G6a** = "We are attacked within ourselves . . . resists the law of the spirit." **G6b** = "The law of sin which is in our members . . . drags them downward and weighs them down." **G6c** = "We are attacked within ourselves . . . becomes his booty."

70. *C. Iul.* 2.3.7 (PL 44:678; trans. Teske, WSA I/24, 310): "et in baptismate fieri omnium remissionem peccatorum et cum baptizatis quasi ciuile bellum interiorum remanere uitiorum."

B2 See how the Jews do not postpone circumcision on account of the threat that every soul who has not been circumcised on the eighth day will be cut off from its people. But what you postpone is not a circumcision made by the hand which is accomplished by the removal of flesh from the body, for you hear the Lord saying: "Truly, truly, I say to you, no one has not been reborn of water and the Spirit will enter into the kingdom of heaven" (John 3:5).[71]

Following Basil's lead, Augustine interprets the circumcision of the flesh figuratively as a sign of baptism (a circumcision not made by the hand) and the foreskin removed in the circumcision as a sign of sin, "especially of the sin which is contracted in our origin."[72] According to Augustine, the symbolism here shows that, just as the circumcision of infants removes the foreskin, so too the baptism of infants removes a sin, particularly original sin.

Elsewhere in the first two books of *Contra Iulianum* and indeed throughout his works against Julian—that is, in the last four books of *Contra Iulianum* and the six books of *Contra Iulianum opus imperfectum*—Augustine cites no new testimonies of either Gregory or Basil. But on thirteen occasions—Basil twice and Gregory eleven times—he quotes snippets of the excerpts already cited in the first and second books of *Contra Iulianum*, a feature that makes books 1 and 2 foundational for Augustine's anti-Pelagian reception of Basil and Gregory. Nine of these brief quotations appear in three distinct sections where Augustine rapidly summarizes the views of several church fathers he has previously cited, usually quoting a sentence or two of each to demonstrate their endorsement of the doctrine of original sin or some related teaching.[73] In these cases Augustine provides no new commentary on the testimonies, presumably because his readers would remember his discussion from when the passages were originally cited. In each of these

---

71. *C. Iul.* 2.6.18 (PL 44:685–86; trans. Teske, WSA I/24, 319) = Basil, *Bapt.* 2 (PG 31:428): "et uide quomodo Iudaeus inquit circumcisionem non differt propter comminationem quia omnis anima quaecumque non fuerit circumcisa die octauo exterminabitur de populo suo. tu autem inquit non manufactam circumcisionem differs quae in exspoliatione carnis in corpore perficitur ipsum dominum audiens dicentem: amen, amen dico uobis nisi quis renatus fuerit ex aqua et spiritu, non introibit in regnum caelorum."

72. *C. Iul.* 2.6.18 (PL 44:686; trans. Teske, WSA I/24, 319): "non enim eos fatemini mortuos in praeputio carnis suae quo peccatum significatur maxime quod originaliter trahitur."

73. In *C. Iul.* 1.7.32 (PL 44:663) G1, G2, G3, G4, and B1 are paraphrased; in *c. Iul. imp.* 1.52 (PL 45:1075) B1b and G3a are paraphrased; in *c. Iul. imp.* 1.70 (PL 45:1093) G3a and G4b are paraphrased.

three instances, however, Augustine included G3a, making it a kind of favorite of his to employ against Julian. Augustine quotes the same excerpt a fourth time in a different context, where he affirms that baptism sets free from original sin and insinuates that Julian denies what Gregory teaches: "You, therefore, in no way acknowledge that little ones have any share in this grace [of baptism] as long as you deny that by their heavenly birth they are set free from the bonds of their earthly birth."[74] Augustine also cites G6 three times, to varying extents. Because G6 uses the Pauline expression "body of death" from Rom. 7:24, Augustine appeals to this testimony of Gregory in his debate with Julian over the correct interpretation of that biblical verse. Along with a passage from Ambrose, Augustine adduces G6a as an example of a Catholic father who understood the "body of death" as a reference to the mortality that is a consequence of original sin.[75] Augustine asserts that Gregory attributed "the law of sin which is in our members and resists the law of the spirit" (G6b) to the mortal and earthly body. Augustine goes on to say that the interior struggle that all—including the saints—experience is due to the body that weighs down the soul. The human condition, in which there is struggle because of the mortal and corruptible body, is the result of original sin. In paradise, however, body and soul were in perfect harmony.[76] Augustine cites G6c as part of his demonstration that, because of the effects of original sin, even the saints experience interior struggle.[77] Finally, as in the first two books of *Contra Iulianum*, Augustine naturally includes the two Cappadocians in lists of Latin and Greek authorities who support his position rather than Julian's.[78] In sum, then, after the second book of *Contra Iulianum*, Augustine continues to exploit, but does not expand, the testimonies of Gregory and Basil in his campaign against Julian.

There is one more testimony of Gregory used by Augustine in his corpus—namely, in *De dono perseuerantiae* (*perseu.*). This work is not against Julian, nor

74. *C. Iul. imp.* 1.53 (PL 45:1077; trans. Teske, *Answer to the Pelagians III*, WSA I/25, 82): "nullo itaque modo ad istam gratiam pertinere paruulos confitemini quamdiu negatis eos natiuitate caelesti a terrenae natiuitatis uinculis liberari." G3a is thus cited no less than five times by Augustine.

75. *C. Iul. imp.* 1.67 (PL 45:1089).

76. *C. Iul. imp.* 1.69 (PL 45:1092).

77. *C. Iul. imp.* 6.14 (PL 45:1528).

78. *C. Iul.* 1.6.22, 2.10.33, 2.10.37 bis, 3.7.32; *c. Iul. imp.* 1.59, 2.37, 4.72, 4.73 (both Gregory and Basil); *c. Iul.* 1.7.35 (Basil); *c. Iul.* 2.4.8. 2.4.9, 2.8.30, 2.10.33, 2.10.35, 6.23.70; *c. Iul. imp.* 1.6, 1.9, 1.117, 2.33 (Gregory). For the Latin text of Augustine's *c. Iul.* and *c. Iul. imp.*, see PL 44:641–874 and PL 45:1049–1608, respectively.

is it even, strictly speaking, anti-Pelagian. It does, however, deal with issues that arose among certain monks of Provence in southern Gaul because of the doctrines of grace and predestination that Augustine articulated in the Pelagian controversy. In fact, it was written at the same time as Augustine was working on *Contra Iulianum opus imperfectum.* Toward the end of *De dono perseuerantiae,* Augustine argues that his doctrine that divine predestination, the beginning of faith, and final perseverance are all unmerited gifts of God is found in both scripture and the Catholic fathers, citing testimonies of Cyprian and Ambrose by way of support.[79] He then provides the testimony of Gregory, from Oration 41, *De pentecoste*:

> **G7** Confess, I beg you, the Trinity of one deity or, if you want to put it otherwise, say, "of one nature," and God will be entreated to give you a voice by the Holy Spirit. For he will give it, I am certain: he who has given what is first will also give what is second; he who has given our belief will also give our confession of it.[80]

79. *Perseu.* 19.48–49 (PL 45:1023–1025).

80. *Perseu.* 19.49 (PL 45:1025; trans. Teske, *Answer to the Pelagians IV*, WSA I/26, 226, modified) = Gregory, *In Pentecosten*, oration 41.8 (PG 36:440b) = Rufinus, *De Pentecoste et de Spiritu Sancto*, oration 4.8 (CSEL 46:150.15–19): "unius deitatis, quaeso uos, confitemini trinitatem: si uero aliter uultis dicite unius esse naturae; et deus uocem dari uobis a sancto spiritu deprecabitur: id est, rogabitur deus. dabit enim, certus sum; qui dedit quod primum est, dabit et quod secundum est; qui dedit credere, dabit et confiteri." In the first sentence Rufinus has "dei" for "deus" and "deprecabimur" for "deprecabitur," which better reflects Gregory's original Greek of the last bit: καὶ τὴν θεὸς φωνὴν παρὰ τοῦ πνεύματος ὑμῖν αἰτήσομεν, "and we will pray that the term 'God' be given to you by the Spirit." As Teske, WSA I/26, 239n83, comments, "In both Gregory's words and Rufinus' translation the homilist prays that those who do not believe in the divinity of the Holy Spirit may be given the word, 'God,' to speak of him." Teske adds that Augustine's changes are "difficult to explain." After the first sentence of the testimony, Augustine interrupts his quotation and offers an interpretative paraphrase of what he has just quoted: "that is, we will ask God that he permit that you be given a voice by which you may be able to confess what you believe" (ut permittat uobis dari uocem qua quod creditis confiteri possitis) (PL 45:1024). This interjection perhaps indicates that Augustine found Rufinus's Latin hard to parse, a fact that might explain both his adjustments to Rufinus's Latin and why he felt the need to provide an interpretive paraphrase. In the second sentence of the testimony, Augustine follows the Latin translation of Rufinus verbatim. Note, however, that "qui dedit credere, dabit et confiteri" does not correspond to anything in Gregory's original Greek and seems to be a kind of explanatory gloss of Rufinus—one that also served Augustine's purposes well. In his English translation Teske mistakenly does not include "he

Augustine had introduced this testimony by saying, "But to these men who ought to have been enough, we also add Saint Gregory as a third who testifies that both our believing in God and our confessing what we believe are gifts of God."[81] Note how Augustine's statement of what this excerpt "testifies" to borrows from the language of Gregory himself in the last part of the testimony. In this remark, however, Augustine also admits that the testimony of Gregory is essentially superfluous, adding nothing to what Cyprian and Ambrose had said—namely, that initial belief, conversion, confession, final perseverance, and so on are all unmerited gifts of God. So why did Augustine cite Gregory here? It was not because the monks of Provence, like Julian, had appealed to authoritative Eastern fathers to support their position, sparking Augustine to reclaim them for his side. And it seems unlikely that Augustine trolled again through Rufinus's translation of Gregory in search of helpful excerpts as he had in his anti-Julian works. I suspect, rather, that Augustine had come across this passage from Gregory's oration *On Pentecost* earlier, perhaps even during the writing of *Contra Iulianum* (cf. *supra*), and saved it for future use.

Conclusion

We know far more about the Cappadocian Fathers than Augustine ever did. There is enough surviving evidence that we can become acquainted with them not only as historical figures but also as all-too-human persons with strengths and weaknesses who experienced successes and failures. Their authentic writings have been identified, edited, and translated into modern languages, even if a few questions and gaps remain. None of this was possible in Augustine's day. While it is safe to say that Augustine esteemed Gregory and Basil as preeminent among Eastern patristic authorities, he gives no evidence of knowing much about them and faced several challenges accessing their writings. Misattributed texts were a problem for Augustine as much as they were for his contemporaries. Augustine's reading of Gregory was made easier by Rufinus's Latin translations of Gregory's

---

who has given our belief will also give our confession of it" as part of the Gregorian testimony that Augustine quoted from the translation of Rufinus.

81. *Perseu.* 19.49 (PL 45:1024; trans. Teske, WSA I/26, 226): "sed his duobus, qui sufficere debuerunt, sanctum Gregorium addamus et tertium, qui et credere in deum et quod credimus confiteri, dei donum esse testatur." In fact, Augustine cited another passage from this same oration in book 1 of this treatise.

orations, but he provides no evidence of having benefited from Rufinus's trans-lations of Basil. Perhaps this explains why Augustine cites only two homilies of Basil (albeit one under someone else's name). The fact is that Augustine did not have access to Gregory's and Basil's complete corpora as we do today, and this greatly limited the extent to which he could engage their thought. It seems that he simply made use of whatever subset of their corpora was available to him.

Augustine did not study the Cappadocian Fathers to educate himself or to deepen his theological understanding. Rather, his engagement with the Cappa-docians was strictly polemical and necessitated by Julian's attempt to bolster his positions by appeal to Eastern patristic authorities, particularly Basil and John Chrysostom. Augustine had to reclaim these authorities for the Catholic side, and his method was to overwhelm Julian with excerpts of theirs that Augustine thought corroborated his doctrine of original sin. Julian had not cited Gregory, but Gregory was the chief Eastern father that Augustine deployed against him. This is probably because—apart from Gregory's stellar reputation in the West—Augustine found the majority of the excerpts that were useful for refuting Julian in Rufinus's recent Latin translation of Gregory's orations.

The ideas found in the testimonies of Gregory and Basil that Augustine cites can be put into four broad categories: (1) there is a multifaceted fallen condition that is a consequence of original sin; (2) baptism is necessary for undoing this sin; (3) even after baptism the Christian continues to struggle with the effects of original sin—particularly in the conflict between body and soul—and this struggle is constitutive of the Christian life; and (4) the eventual overcoming of these effects, which is conceived as a return to paradise, is made possible by the grace of God. None of these topics were central in any of the writings of Gregory or Basil that Augustine cited; rather, both made the comments cited by Augustine in the service of other themes and concerns. Nonetheless, Augustine saw in their remarks teachings on sin and grace that were the common heritage of the Catholic church, both East and West. Of course, none of these ideas was new to Augustine, but the excerpts conveniently reinforced his own thinking and, therefore, he put them to good polemical use.

It almost goes without saying that Augustine was not influenced by the Cappadocian Fathers in any formative or even significant way. Coming to them during the writing of *Contra Iulianum* in 421 or 422 CE, Augustine was already theologically mature. Even if his thought continued to evolve, it was not because of his reading of Gregory and Basil. Indeed, after 421–422 there is no evidence that Augustine continued to read either of them. In the *Contra Iulianum opus imperfectum*, with which he was occupied from 427 or 428 until his death in 430, Augustine merely recycles the testimonies he cited years earlier in the first two books of *Contra Iulianum*. The lone exception is the new testimony of Gregory in *De dono perseuerantiae*, though, as suggested above, this text is probably a leftover from his earlier study of Gregory. Thus, except for that small window of time in 421–422, it seems that Augustine did not read the writings of Basil and Gregory in any meaningful or, at least, detectable way.

Perhaps Courcelle was right to say that it was because of Augustine's belief in the sameness and unity of the Catholic faith in East and West that he did not feel the need to engage the Eastern fathers. Given our detailed knowledge of Basil, Gregory, and Augustine—those titans of the late fourth and early fifth centuries whose magnificent works changed the course of Christian theology and spirituality, those luminaries rightly recognized as Doctors of the Church whose *eminens doctrina* and *insignis uitae sanctitas* have exercised enormous influence through the centuries—it is difficult to imagine that the two great Cappadocian Fathers did not have much of an impact on Augustine. But wishing that they did cannot make it so.

·

PART IV

Augustine and His Latin Contemporaries/Successors

Chapter 12

AUGUSTINE AND MARIUS VICTORINUS

Stephen A. Cooper

INTRODUCTION

No reader of *Confessiones* (*conf.*) can escape the impression that Marius Victorinus was a figure of special significance for Augustine, and not only in one respect. Everything we know of Victorinus's conversion we owe to Augustine's marvelous vignette in *Confessiones* 8.2.3–5, in which he tells how the old professor of rhetoric through his friendship with Simplicianus at Rome eventually came to seek baptism in the church whose doctrine he avowed to have already accepted.[1] This is not the only feature of Victorinus's *uita et opera* for which Augustine is our sole source. The *libri Platonicorum*, the "books of the Platonists" that Victorinus translated (*conf.* 7.9.13), made a tremendous impact on Augustine, leading to his intellectual—or supra-intellectual—vision of God that alleviated a major obstacle to his conversion.[2] By these books, says Augustine, "I was admonished

---

1. Jerome also relates the fact of his conversion in *uir. ill.* 101 (Carl A. Bernoulli, ed., *Hieronymus und Gennadius: De viris illustribus*, SAQ 11 [Leipzig: Mohr, 1895], 49). The ancient testimonia to Victorinus have been collected and discussed by Pierre Hadot in his unsurpassed monograph *Marius Victorinus: Recherches sur sa vie et ses œuvres* (Paris: Études Augustiniennes, 1971), 13–34, and Italo Mariotti, *Marii Victorinii Ars grammatica, introduzione, testo critico e commento* (Florence: Felice Le Monnier, 1976), 13–18. For a general presentation, see Michael von Albrecht, *A History of Roman Literature from Livius Andronicus to Boethius*, rev. ed., trans. Frances and Kevin Newman (Leiden: Brill, 1997), 1616–27.

2. See the seminal discussion of Paul Henry, "Augustine and Plotinus," *JTS* 38 (1937): 1–23, and the monograph of Brian Dobell, *Augustine's Intellectual Conversion: The Journey from Platonism to Christianity* (Cambridge: Cambridge University Press, 2009).

to return into myself" and "saw above that same eye of my soul the immutable light higher than my mind."[3] Those works of Plotinus and Porphyry had reached his hands through the agency of "a man puffed up with monstrous pride"—a providential provision, Augustine avers, to reveal by contrast "the way of humility" (*uia humilitatis*) provided by divine mercy.[4] But the emphatic element in Augustine's account of Victorinus's conversion, as Patout Burns has noted, is his submssion "to the teaching authority and the rituals of the church as an act of humility, in reverence for the incarnation of the divine Word."[5] This was the man whose example Augustine "was ardent to follow."[6] But was Victorinus's example in baptism, with its implicit acknowledgment of Cyprian's axiom "salus extra ecclesiam non est,"[7] the only aspect of the converted rhetor's Christianity that influenced Augustine?

Despite the evident admiration Augustine had for his fellow Roman African professor of rhetoric,[8] whose commentary on Cicero's *De inuentione* he likely knew and whose learning in philosophy he could not with his inadequate Greek hope to match,[9] scholars have been puzzling for well over a century as to whether he had read Victorinus's Christian works. Newly converted to Christianity, Victorinus composed treatises and hymns around 357–363 CE in defense of the Nicene Creed,[10] and he subsequently produced an incomplete series of com-

---

3. *Conf.* 7.10.16 (CCSL 81:103): "et inde admonitus redire ad memet ipsum, intraui in intima mea duce te, et potui, quoniam factus es adiutor meus. intraui et uidi qualicumque oculo animae meae supra eundem oculum animae meae, supra mentem meam, lucem incommutabilem." Unless otherwise noted, translations of *Confessiones* in this chapter are those of Henry Chadwick; see Augustine, *Confessions*, trans. Henry Chadwick (Oxford: Oxford University Press, 1991); for 7.10.16, see 123.

4. *Conf.* 7.9.13 (CCSL 81:101).

5. Patout Burns, "Christ and the Holy Spirit in Augustine's Theology of Baptism," in *Augustine: From Rhetor to Theologian*, ed. Joanne McWilliam (Waterloo, ON: Wilfrid Laurier University Press, 1992), 161n1.

6. *Conf.* 8.5.10 (CCSL 81:119): "exarsit ad imitandum."

7. *Ep.* 73.21.2 (CSEL 3/2:795).

8. For discussion of his *uita*, see Stephen Andrew Cooper, *Marius Victorinus' Commentary on Galatians: Introduction, Translation, and Notes*, OECS (Oxford: Oxford University Press, 2005).

9. The most recent critical edition is Thomas Riesenweber, ed., *C. Marius Victorinus, Commenta in Ciceronis Rhetorica*, BSGRT (Berlin: de Gruyter, 2013).

10. The critical edition is CSEL 83/1; for an English translation, see Marius Victorinus, *Theological Treatises on the Trinity*, trans. Mary T. Clark, FC 69 (Washington, DC: Catholic University of America, 1981). For the most up-to-date translation (into Italian, with facing Latin and superb introduction and notes), see Claudio Moreschini and Chiara O. Tom-

mentaries on the Pauline Epistles, the first in Latin.[11] Surely Augustine would
have been eager to read the works of the one to whom he gave such a striking
cameo appearance in *Confessiones*. Yet, as the author of the first monograph on
Victorinus, Gustav Koffmane, noted in his 1880 dissertation, "Augustine, who is
so copious in narrating the conversion of Victorinus, does not mention his Christian works."[12] And in a contemporaneous entry for the *Dictionary of Christian
Biography*, Charles Gore concluded,

> It is worth while calling attention to the evidence, suggested by a good deal of
> Victorinus's theology, of a closer connexion than has been yet noticed between
> him and St. Augustine. His strong insistence in his Trinitarian theology on the
> double Procession of the Holy Spirit—his conception of the Holy Spirit as the
> "Bond" of the Blessed Trinity—his emphasis on the unity of Christ and His
> church—his strong predestinarianism—his vehement assertion of the doc-
> trines of grace—his assertion of the priority of faith to intelligence—all reap-
> pear in St. Augustine, and it may be that the (hitherto unsuspected) influence
> of the writings of the old philosopher whose conversion stirred him so deeply
> was a determining force upon the theology of St. Augustine.[13]

Harnack agreed: Victorinus with his blend of Paulinism and Platonism was "Augustine before Augustine."[14]

---

masi, ed. and trans., *Opere teologiche di Mario Vittorino* (Turin: Unione Tipografica-Editrice
Torinese, 2007).

11. The critical edition is CSEL 83/2. For an earlier version by the same editor (with facing Italian translation), see Marius Victorinus, *Commentari alle Epistole di Paolo agli Efesini,
ai Galati, ai Filippesi*, ed. and trans. Franco Gori, Corona Patrum 8 (Turin: Società Editrice
Internazionale, 1981).

12. Gustavus Koffmane, *De Mario Victorino philosopho christiano* (Breslau: Lindner, 1880),
34: "Augustinus qui tam uber est in narranda conuersione Victorini libros Christianos non
recenset. quamuis alia notio sit Victoriniani illius 'sola fide' alia Augustini, tamen si nouisset
inter testes antiquiores Afrum enumerauisset." Victorinus, moreover, "did not distinguish
between the natural will and the will as recreated by divine power" and thus fell short of
Augustine's mature theology (22–23).

13. Charles Gore, "Victorinus Afer," in *A Dictionary of Christian Biography, Literature, Sects
and Doctrines*, ed. Henry Wace and William Smith (London: Murray, 1877–1887), 4:1138.

14. Adolf Harnack, *History of Dogma*, trans. Neil Buchanan (Boston: Little, Brown, 1988),
5:35 (trans. of *Dogmengeschichte* [Freiburg i. B: Mohr, 1897], 3:32). On the relation of Neoplatonism to the developing interest in Paul in the Latin church, see the comments of Almut
Mutzenbecher in CCSL 44:xvi–xxiv.

This enthusiasm was soon quashed by the dissertations of Godhard Geiger and Reinhold Schmid, who pointed out significant differences in both Paulinism and Trinitarian thought, as well as a manifest lack of literary parallels.[15] Yet the question of Victorinus's influence on Augustine continued to haunt scholarship. In 1924 the dissertation of Werner Karig could venture not much more on the subject than that Victorinus had an affinity for Pauline piety.[16] Alberto Pincherle in 1947 notably argued for a claim of influence in the exegesis of Paul, identifying as evidence some general exegetical parallels between Victorinus and Augustine on Galatians.[17] Paolo Frassinetti found in Victorinus's hymns a foreshadowing of the Pauline inflections of Augustine in *Confessiones*.[18] The 1950 article of L. J. van der Lof concluded that "direct influence" of Victorinus on Augustine is at most possible and that Harnack's notion of him as *Augustinus ante Augustinum* should be modified to indicate that Victorinus was simply "a man like Augustine," one whose way into orthodox Christianity came through combining it with Neoplatonism.[19] The late Pierre Hadot, who has done more than any other scholar to introduce Marius Victorinus as an exemplary figure of fourth-century Latin intellectual life, found the evidence lacking and suggested that any influence was more likely to be through the commentaries on Paul than the Trinitarian treatises,[20] as convincing literary parallels were absent in the latter.[21]

15. See P. Godhard Geiger, *C. Marius Victorinus Afer, ein neuplatonischer Philosoph*, Beilage zum Jahres-Berichte der Studien-Anstalt Metten (Landshut: Thomann, 1888), 116–17, and Reinhold Schmid, *Marius Victorinus Rhetor und seine Beziehungen zu Augustin* (Kiel: Uebermuth, 1895), 79–80. The skeptical view was opposed by Alberto Pincherle, who pointed to the evidence of general exegetical parallels between Victorinus and Augustine on Galatians, in his *La formazione teologica di Sant'Agostino* (Rome: Edizioni Italiane, 1947), 118.

16. Werner Karig, "Des C. Marius Victorinus Kommentare zu den paulinischen Briefen" (Inaugural diss., University of Marburg, 1924), 95.

17. Pincherle, *La formazione teologica*, 118.

18. Paolo Frassinetti, "Le Confessioni agostiniane e un inno di Mario Vittorino," *Giornale italiano di filologia* 2 (1949): 50–59. Paul Monceaux had previously recognized that these hymns "mystique et métaphysiques" were patterned after the Psalms and were groundbreaking in their form and content (*Histoire littéraire de l'Afrique chrétienne depuis les origines jusqu'à l'invasion arabe*, vol. 3, *Le IVᵉ siècle, d'Arnobe à Victorin* (Paris: Leroux, 1905; repr., Brussels: Culture et Civilisation, 1963), 409–10.

19. L. J. van der Lof, "De Invloed van Marius Victorinus Rhetor op Augustinus," *Nederlands Theologisch Tijdschrift* 5 (1950–1951): 307.

20. Pierre Hadot, "L'image de la Trinité dans l'âme chez Victorinus et chez saint Augustin," *StPatr* 6 (1962): 433.

21. Pierre Hadot, *Porphyre et Victorinus* (Paris: Études Augustiniennes, 1968), 1:15.

Only in the final decade of the last century did scholars again venture to press the case. Nello Cipriani[22] and Eric Plumer,[23] working independently of each other in the first round of their investigations, have presented evidence they maintain can overcome the skeptical consensus. Cipriani argues that Victorinus's language and ideas from his Trinitarian treatises and hymns appear in a range of Augustine's works, from his early dialogues to *De Trinitate* (*Trin.*), and that traces of his commentaries on Paul are discernable in Augustine's treatment of Galatians. Plumer's claims are restricted to the question of influence in the exegesis of Galatians, where he makes the original observation that Augustine's frequent repetition of the Pauline phrase *spes salutis*, "hope of salvation" (from 1 Thess. 5:8), features prominently in Victorinus's commentary on Galatians.[24] Around the same time, other scholars of Latin exegesis came to different conclusions. Antoon Bastiaensen, studying Augustine's commentaries on Romans and Galatians in light of his Latin predecessors, has found that Augustine's commentary on Galatians shows the influence of Ambrosiaster and Jerome but not Victorinus.[25] Bastiaensen's conclusions have in part been supported by Martine Dulaey in a series of articles on Augustine's "apprenticeship in biblical exegesis."[26]

22. Nello Cipriani, "Le fonti cristiane della dottrina trinitaria nel primi dialoghi di S. Agostino," *Augustinianum* 34 (1994): 253–312; Cipriani, "La retractatio Agostiniana sulla processione-generazione dello Spirito Santo (*Trin.* V.12.13)," *Augustinianum* 37 (1997): 431–39); Cipriani, "Agostino lettore dei commentari paolini di Mario Vittorino," *Augustinianum* 38 (1998): 413–28; Cipriani, "La presenza di Mario Vittorino nella riflessione trinitaria di Agostino," *Augustinianum* 42 (2002): 261–313; Cipriani, "Le fonti patristiche e filosofiche del De Trinitate di S. Agostino," *Augustinianum* 55 (2015): 427–60. For his work, see Cipriani, "Augustine and the Writings of Marius Victorinus," in *Marius Victorinus: Pagan Rhetor, Platonist Philosopher, and Christian Theologian,* ed. Stephen Cooper and Václav Němec, Writings from the Greco-Roman World, Supplement (to be published by SBL Press).

23. Eric Plumer, "The Influence of Marius Victorinus on Augustine's Commentary on Galatians," *StPatr* 33 (1997): 221–28; Plumer, *Augustine's Commentary on Galatians: Introduction, Text, Translation, and Notes,* OECS (Oxford: Oxford University Press, 2003).

24. Plumer, *Augustine's Commentary on Galatians,* 28–29.

25. Antoon A. R. Bastiaensen, "Augustin commentateur de saint Paul et l'Ambrosiaster," *Sacris Erudiri* 36 (1996): 37–65. See also Bastiaensen's earlier article "Augustin et les prédécesseurs latins chrétiens," in *Augustiniana Traiectina: Communications présentées au colloque international d'Utrecht, 13–14 novembre 1986,* ed. J. den Boeft and J. van Oort (Paris: Études Augustiniennes, 1987), 25–57.

26. Martine Dulaey, "L'apprentissage de l'exégèse biblique par Augustin, Première partie: Dans les années 386–389," *REAug* 48 (2002): 268; Dulaey, "L'apprentissage de l'exégèse biblique par Augustin (2): Années 390–392," *REAug* 49 (2003): 43–84; Dulaey, "L'apprentissage

STEPHEN A. COOPER

Focusing on his theological works composed before 395 and his commentaries on Romans and Galatians, Dulaey reports evidence of Augustine reading numerous Christian authors, including Ambrose, Tertullian, Cyprian, Origen in translation, Victorinus of Petau, Lactantius, Fortunatian of Aquila, and Ambrosiaster,[27] but not Marius Victorinus.

In discussing methodological issues, Dulaey sets out stringent criteria to determine whether the interpretation of a given biblical passage by Augustine was (a) attributable to his reading of another Christian author, (b) a commonplace, or (c) a conclusion he could have independently reached.[28] Cipriani also has explicitly addressed the methodological issue of establishing literary dependence on the basis of anything short of literary citation.[29] But because the passages on which the strongest part of his case rests consist of non-exegetical material, the precise criteria of Dulaey do not apply, and these criteria are more potent in casting doubt on claims based on exegetical parallels, both those of Plumer and the additional exegetical parallels I have adduced in my own work on Victorinus's commentary on Galatians.[30]

Clearly the matter is not so obvious as to command easy consensus. Cipriani and Plumer have convinced some scholars, but not all agree.[31] There is little else to

---

de l'exégèse biblique par Augustin (3): Années 393–394," *REAug* 51 (2005): 21–65. This last article covers Augustine's work up to 394, just before he wrote his commentary on Galatians.

27. Dulaey, "L'apprentissage de l'exégèse biblique" (2002), 294, reports that the traces of Ambrosiaster she found in Augustine are from his *Questions on the Old and New Testaments*, not his commentaries on Paul.

28. Dulaey, "L'apprentissage de l'exégèse biblique" (2002), 268.

29. Cipriani, "Le fonti cristiane," 261–62.

30. See chap. 6 in Cooper, *Marius Victorinus' Commentary on Galatians*.

31. E.g., the influence of Victorinus on the early Augustine has been accepted by Carol Harrison, *Rethinking Augustine's Early Theology: An Argument for Continuity* (Oxford: Oxford University Press, 2006); Francesco Cocchini, *Agostino, Commento alla Lettera ai Galati* (Bologna: Dehoniane, 2012), 10–11; and Gerald P. Boersma, *Augustine's Early Theology of Image: A Study in the Development of Pro-Nicene Theology* (Oxford: Oxford University Press, 2016). More skeptical is Thomas G. Ring, *Aurelius Augustinus, Schriften gegen die Pelagianer, Prologomena*, Band 2, *Die Auslegung des Briefes an die Galater, Die angefangene Auslegung des Briefe an die Römer, Über dreiundachtsig verschiedene Fragen* (Würzburg: Augustinus-Verlag, 1997), 41–43, who accounts for the parallels mostly by a common exegetical method as well as shared catechetical and exegetical traditions. Some scholars consider the case so closed that there is no need to revisit the question—e.g., Dobell, *Augustine's Intellectual Conversion*, who refers to Victorinus's conversion as influential on Augustine through Simplician's re-

do than consider the proposed textual parallels as a whole, but on a case-by-case basis in light of criteria that screen out mere coincidence of ideas and exegeses. First we examine the passages alleged by Cipriani for Augustine's reading of Victorinus's Trinitarian treatises and hymns, then we turn to the arguably more tricky demonstrations concerning the material from their commentaries on Paul, and finally we turn to *De Trinitate*, where one finds Augustine distancing himself from a number of Victorinus's notions but sharing aspects of his understanding of the Holy Spirit.

NEW CHALLENGES TO THE CONSENSUS

Eric Plumer renewed the observation of Alexander Souter that "nothing is more antecedently probable than that Augustine, who knew and esteemed the works of his fellow-countryman, consulted his commentaries on the Pauline Epistles in the course of his own work."[32] Such "antecedent probability" means that any exegetical parallels in their commentaries on Galatians indicate "not that Augustine's dependence on Victorinus has been demonstrated beyond all doubt, but rather that such dependence is in the highest degree probable."[33] A great part of that probability, Plumer maintains,[34] rests on the only other place in his works besides *Confessiones* where Augustine mentions Victorinus: *De doctrina christiana* (*doctr. chr.*) 2.40.61, which lists him among other orthodox authorities who made good Christian use of the spoils of Egypt (Exod. 11:2)—namely, philosophy and liberal arts:

> These treasures which were used wickedly and harmfully in the service of de-
> mons must be removed by Christians, as they separate themselves in spirit
> from the wretched company of pagans, and applied to their true function, that
> of preaching the gospel. As for their clothing . . . this may be accepted and kept
> for conversion to Christian purposes [*in usum conuertenda christianum*]. This
> is exactly what many good and faithful Christians have done. We can see, can

counting of it but does not even mention Victorinus's Christian writings as a possible source for Augustine's theology.

32. Alexander Souter, *The Earliest Latin Commentaries on the Epistles of St. Paul* (Oxford: Clarendon, 1927), 199 (cited in Plumer, "Influence of Marius Victorinus," 221 and 227n45).

33. Plumer, *Augustine's Commentary on Galatians*, 31.

34. Plumer, "Influence of Marius Victorinus," 223.

we not, the amount of gold, silver, and clothing with which Cyprian, that most attractive writer and most blessed martyr, was laden when he left Egypt; is not the same true of Lactantius, and Victorinus, of Optatus, and Hilary, to say nothing of people still alive, and countless Greek scholars.[35]

Clearly Augustine credits Victorinus with having made a substantial contribution to the life of the church, but does this mean he read his works?[36]

Cipriani also prefaces his claims for probative parallels by a similar argument: it is "more than probable that from the beginning of his conversion Augustine, in order to deepen his understanding of the Christian faith, was not content to hear about it from authoritative figures but had recourse beyond the books of the Holy Scriptures to some works of patristic literature."[37] In support of this perspective, Cipriani adduces Augustine's own words in *Soliloquies* (*sol.*): "In order that we may not express opinions of that concerning which we are ignorant, we have within reach writings concerning this subject [i.e., the immortality of the soul], both in prose and in verse, by men whose works are not unknown to us, and whose talents we know well."[38] Whose works could these be? Ambrose certainly; and Cipriani maintains that Marius Victorinus is also likely.[39] Plumer also observes that Augustine knew of the existence of Victorinus's treatment of

35. Augustine, *De Doctrina Christiana*, ed. and trans. R. P. H. Green, OECT (Oxford: Clarendon, 2004), 124–27: "quod eorum tamquam aurum et argentum, quod non ipsi instituerunt sed de quibusdam quasi metallis diuinae prouidentiae, quae ubique infusa est, eruerunt, et quo peruerse atque iniuriose ad obsequia daemonum abutuntur, cum ab eorum misera societate sese animo separat debet ab eis auferre Christianus ad usum iustum praedicandi euangelii. uestem quoque illorum, id est hominum quidem instituta, sed tamen accommodata humanae societati qua in hac uita carere non possumus, accipere atque habere licuerit in usum conuertenda christianum. nam quid aliud fecerunt multi boni fideles nostri? nonne aspicimus quanto auro et argento et ueste suffarcinatus exierit de Aegypto Cyprianus et doctor suauissimus et martyr beatissimus? quanto Lactantius? quanto Victorinus, Optatus, Hilarius, ut de uiuis taceam? quanto innumerabiles Graeci?"

36. The salience of the passage was first noted by Schmid, *Marius Victorinus Rhetor*, 70.

37. Cipriani, "Le fonti cristiane," 255. Cf. 259, where he amplifies this argument.

38. Cf. Cipriani, "Le fonti cristiane," 255n10. For the quotation (*The Soliloquies of St. Augustine*, trans. Rose E. Cleveland [Boston: Little, Brown, 1910], 92), see *Sol.* 2.14.26 (CSEL 89:80): "nam et multos ante nostram aetatem scriptos esse arbitror, quos non legimus, et nunc, ut nihil, quod nescimus, opinemur, manifestum habemus et carmine de hac re scribi et soluta oratione et ab iis uiris, quorum nec scripta latere nos possunt, et eorum ingenia talia nouimus, ut nos in eorum litteris, quod uolumus, inuenturos desperare non possimus."

39. Cipriani, "Le fonti cristiane," 259–60.

Paul, because, by the time he wrote his own commentary on Galatians around 395 CE, he had read Jerome's,[40] which in its prologue slightingly mentions Victorinus's work on the Pauline letters.[41]

VICTORINUS AND AUGUSTINE'S CASSICIACUM DIALOGUES

Among these early works of Augustine, *De ordine* (*ord.*) 2.5.16 is "certainly the most significant" for the question, since it contains unusual lexical parallels.[42] The first is *principium sine principio*, "a beginningless beginning," a descriptor for God taken up by Victorinus from his fictive Arian interlocutor, Candidus,[43] in light of John 1:1 (the Vetus Latina [VL] rendered the opening ἐν ἀρχῇ as *in principio*). The terms come up in *De ordine* 2.5 amidst Augustine's elucidation of the *duplex uia* (twofold path) of reason and authority, noting how *ratio* as philosophy succeeds in freeing only a tiny minority of people (*paucissimos liberat*), whereas the *auctoritas* of "the venerable mysteries" gives instruction on the nature of God to all comers. Can these paths be reconciled?

Augustine: "That true philosophy—the genuine philosophy, I would say—has no other concern than to teach what is the beginningless beginning of all things [*omnium rerum principium sine principio*], and what magnitude of mind dwells in it [*quantusque intellectus*], and what without any degeneration has flowed

40. Plumer, *Augustine's Commentary on Galatians*, 20.

41. Jerome, *Commentarii in epistulam Pauli ad Galatas, praef.* (CCSL 77A:6; ET *Commentary on Galatians*, trans. Andrew Cain, FC 121 [Washington, DC: Catholic University of America Press, 2010], 56–57): "I am not unaware that Gaius Marius Victorinus, who taught rhetoric at Rome when I was a boy, produced commentaries on the Apostle. Engrossed in secular learning as he was, however, he was completely ignorant of Scripture, and nobody—no matter how eloquent he may be—is able to discuss competently what he does not know." ("non quod ignorem Gaium Marium Victorinum, qui Romae me puero rhetoricam docuit, edidisse commentarios in apostolum, sed quod occupatus ille eruditione saecularium litterarum scripturas omnino ignorauerit et nemo possit, quamuis eloquens, de eo bene disputare quod nesciat.") On Jerome's hostility to Victorinus's exegetical work, see Cooper, *Marius Victorinus' Commentary on Galatians*, 107–10.

42. Cipriani, "Le fonti christiane," 263. Cipriani discusses many more passages of *ord.*, *beata u., Sol.*, etc. than can be fully treated here. See his articles in Italian (cited at n. 22 *supra*) for the relevant evidence in its entirety.

43. *Cand. 1,* 3 (CSEL 83/1:4; trans. is my own): "principium autem sine principio."

from there [*sine ulla degeneratione manauerit*] for our salvation. This one omnipotent God, the venerable mysteries teach, is tripotent [*tripotentem*]: Father, Son, and Holy Spirit."[44]

Victorinus: "It has been said that *in the beginning was the* λόγος. And, as you say, that is not a beginning if another beginning precedes it. For God[45] is a beginningless beginning [*sine principio enim principium*], since indeed God both is and is called a beginning.[46] This is God, this the Father . . . spirit tripotent [*tripotens*] in its oneness, perfect and above spirit."[47]

The words *tripotens*[48] and *principium sine principio* are rare, used prior to Augustine only by Victorinus (and *tripotens* is a *hapax* in Augustine).[49] Not just the rare terms but the conceptual context, Cipriani maintains, is important for the case.[50] Augustine is intent on distinguishing a second principle that remains in the first principle—the *principium sine principio*—but also has a dynamic aspect in that it flows forth "for our salvation" (perhaps an echo of the Nicene Creed). The Trinitarian thought here, Cipriani argues, is closely patterned after Victorinus's conception of the Trinity, where the divine begetting involves the emergence of a double dyad—Father–Intellect/Son and Son–Christ/Spirit—where

44. *Ord.* 2.5.16 (CCSL 29:116; trans. is my own): "nullumque aliud habet negotium, quae uera, et, ut ita dicam, germana philosophia est, quam ut doceat, quod sit omnium rerum principium sine principio quantusque in eo maneat intellectus quidne inde in nostram salutem sine ullla degeneratione manauerit, quem unum deum omnipotentem cum quo tripotentem, patrem et filium et sanctum spiritum, docent ueneranda mysteria."

45. I have supplied "God" as the subject, as this seems to be indicated from Candidus's discussion in *Cand. 1, 3,* and Victorinus's elucidation of John 1:1 here.

46. *Ad Cand.* 16 (CSEL 83/1:33–34; trans. is my own): "dictum est autem quoniam *in principio fuit* λόγος. et, ut tu dicis, non est principium quod praecedit aliud principium."

47. *Ar. 1B,* 50 (CSEL 83/1:144–45; trans. is my own): "hic est deus, hic pater . . . tripotens in unalitate spiritus, perfectus et supra spiritum." Cf. the parallel expression in *Ar. 4,* 21 (CSEL 83.1:144–45; trans. is my own): "τριδύναμος . . . id est tres potentias habens" ("triple powered . . . i.e., having three powers").

48. On the term *tripotens* (= τριδύναμος) and the possibility that Victorinus derived it from its use in the Nag Hammadi tractates *Zostrianus* (VIII 1.24.12) and *Allogenes* (XI 3.51.7), see Chiara O. Tommasi, "Tripotens in unalitate spiritus: Mario Vittorino e la gnosi," *KOINΩNIA* 20 (1996): 52–75.

49. Cipriani, "Fonti christiane," 264.

50. Cipriani, "Le fonti patristiche e filosofiche," 430.

the Son stays in God and also proceeds into the world in the incarnate Christ, remaining there as the Holy Spirit after the ascension.[51] Thus in *De ordine* 2.5 Augustine differentiates a double dyad in this passage by coupling the Father and the Son with the verbs *maneo* (to remain) and *mano* (to flow, proceed, emanate). The Son, whom he calls *intellectus* remains (*maneat intellectus*) within the principle (= the Father), but from there (*quidne inde*) something else (= the Holy Spirit) "flowed forth [*manauerit*] without any degeneration for our salvation." Augustine's stipulation that the procession of the latter occurs *sine ulla degeneratione* follows Victorinus, who states in one of his Trinitarian treatises that both Son and Holy Spirit are begotten without any change (*nulla sui per motum mutatione generarunt*).[52] Ambrose in *De fide* 1.6.43,[53] Cipriani points out, explicitly excluded such language (*degenerasse*) pertaining to Christ without mentioning the same in regard to the Spirit.[54]

The same section of *De ordine* also contains two brief passages likewise combining Trinitarian and soteriological reflections. Here Cipriani points to Victorinus's commentary on Ephesians with similar terminology:[55] *liberare* to express the salvific work of Christ in terms of its effects on those to be saved; and *mysteria* or *mysterium* as a term for the saving remedy.

> Augustine: "But if they be sluggish, preoccupied with other business, or already hardened against instruction, let them obtain the resources of faith for themselves by that bond through which the one who allows no one believing well in him through the mysteries [*mysteria*] to perish draws them to himself and frees them [*liberet*] from those awful entwining evils."[56]

51. For his account of Victorinus's theology, Cipriani ("Augustine and the Writings of Marius Victorinus") cites Manlio Simonetti, "Mario Vittorino," in *Patrologia*, ed. Angelo Di Berardino (Casale Monferrato: Marietti, 1978), 3:73; ET by Placido Solari in Quasten, *Patrology*, 4:78–79.

52. *Ar. 4*, 21 (CSEL 83/1:257).

53. PL 16:537–38: "non potest bono patri placere, si filius degenerasse potius a patre, quam patrem aequasse credatur."

54. Cipriani, "Le fonti christiane," 267.

55. Cipriani, "Agostino lettore," 419–21.

56. *Ord.* 2.5.15 (CSEL 29:115; trans. is my own): "si autem aut pigriores sunt aut aliis negotiis praeoccupati aut iam duri ad discendum, fidei sibi praesidia parent, quo illos uinculo ad sese trahat atque ab his horrendis et inuolutissimis malis liberet ille, qui neminem sibi per mysteria bene credentem perire permittit."

Victorinus: "By means therefore of the Mystery [*mysterium*], which Christ fulfilled here by his flesh, cross, death, and resurrection, help is come unto souls.
And if faith in Christ is taken up, Christ takes in souls of this sort, comes to
their aid and frees [*liberat*] them."[57]

More such overlap with Victorinus's characteristic vocabulary for salvation
occurs in the following section of *De ordine*:

Augustine: "The mysteries that free [*liberant*] people because of their sincere
and unshaken faith are to be venerated."[58]

Victorinus: "I have pointed out frequently that this is the door of our liberation:
if we just believe in Christ. For his Mystery has freed [*liberauit*] us, if we just
follow him . . . if we have faith in him."[59]

Likewise, in *De beata uita* (*beata u.*) Cipriani finds aspects of Victorinus's
Trinitarian theology, especially the Son and Spirit as a double dyad.[60] He refers
to *De beata uita* 4.34–35, which features Neoplatonist ideas of the procession and
reversion of the divine *nous* and the divine outreach to souls. Augustine would
have encountered such ideas in the *libri Platonicorum* but was also influenced by
how they were already filtered through Christian sources—namely, Ambrose
and, *ex hypothesi*, Victorinus.[61]

The opening phrase of *De beata uita* 4.34, as well as the parallel Cipriani adduces from *Adversus Arium* (*Ar.*) 1A, 13, are both peculiar in seeming to suggest
a coming-into-being of the Son. Victorinus did not intend to violate the dictum
that enraged Arius as he listened to Bishop Alexander: "always Father, always

---

57. *Ephes.* 1:4 (CSEL 83/2:9; trans. is my own): "ergo mysterio, quod hic inpleuit et carne
et cruce et morte et resurrectione, subuentum est animis, et, si in Christum fides sumatur,
ille suscipit huiusmodi animas et adiuuat et liberat."

58. *Ord.* 2.5.16 (CSEL 29:115; trans. is my own): "ueneranda mysteria, quae fide sincera et
inconcussa populos liberant."

59. *Ephes.* 3:12 (CSEL 83/2:50; trans. is my own): "monui et saepe monui eam esse ianuam
liberationis nostrae, si in Christum credamus; mysterium enim eius liberauit nos, si eum
sequamur. . . . si fidem in eum habeamus."

60. Cipriani, "Le fonti christiane," 268–71.

61. Cipriani, "Le fonti christiane," 270.

Son."[62] Rather, Victorinus is discussing two statements in the Fourth Gospel crucial to the Trinitarian controversy—"I and the Father are one" (10:30) and "the Father is greater than I" (14:28)—to argue "that the Logos, meaning Jesus or Christ, is both equal to and inferior to the Father" (*Ar. 1A*, 13). The "inferior" aspect comes from the Son receiving all from the Father (a motif in his discussion of Christ and the Spirit treated *infra* in relation to Augustine's *trin.*).

We consider the Latin first, the better to observe the resemblance in the syntax and sense of the opening phrase. Augustine opens the passage by citing John 14:18—*ego sum ueritas*—and I have translated what follows accordingly:

Augustine: "Veritas autem ut sit, fit per aliquem summum modum, a quo procedit et in quem se perfecta conuertit." ("But in order that he may be the Truth, he comes to be through a certain supreme Measure, from which the Truth proceeds and to which the Truth returns when perfected.")[63]

Victorinus: "Filius autem, ut esset, accepit et in id quod est agere ab actione procedens in perfectionem ueniens, motu efficitur plenitudo." ("But the Son has received his being also in respect of that which is 'to act': proceeding from action and coming to perfection, his fullness is completed by movement.")[64]

Some of the phraseology of *De beata uita* 4.34 not found in *Adversus Arium 1A*, 13—*se perfecta conuertit*—appears in a passage from another of Victorinus's Trinitarian treatises: *Adversus Arium 1B*, 51: "Rursus in semet ipsam conuersa, uenit in patricam exsistentiam . . . et perfecta in omnipotentem uirtutem."[65] Cipriani argues that "all the doctrinal elements contained in this text [of Augustine] are found on a page of the first anti-Arian treatise, with exception of the notion of

---

62. Victorinus quotes the sayings of Alexander from Arius's letter (preserved in Epiphanius, *Haer.* 69.7) to Eusebius of Nicomedia in *Ar. 1*, 34, to signal that the begetting of the Son is "by a begetting always begetting" (CSEL 83/1:116; trans. Clark, 145): "semper generante generatione."

63. *Beata u.* 4.34 (CCSL 29:84; trans. is my own).

64. *Ar. 1A*, 13 (CSEL 83.1:72; trans. is my own).

65. *Ar. 1B*, 51 (CSEL 83/1:147). Here Victorinus is discussing how "life" enters into "the virginal power" and is thus born a human Son of God (trans. Clark, 175): "When it once again turned towards itself, it returned toward the existence that it has in the Father. . . . And having come to the full completion of its all-powerful vigor, life became perfect Spirit."

the *summus modus*."[66] These doctrinal agreements include the identification of Christ with truth and the claim that Father is the cause of the Son,[67] along with the idea that the Christ proceeds from the Father.[68] The term *procedere* occurs in both texts to describe the movement of the Son from the Father. Augustine's term for the Father, "supreme Measure" (*summus modus*), does not recur as such in Victorinus, but Cipriani maintains its meaning is the same as the language for the Father employed by Victorinus in his hymns, where he calls the Father *inmensus*, "the Unmeasured," and the Son as *mensus atque inmensus*, "measured and unmeasured" (*Hymn.* 1.11; cf. *Hymn.* 3.172).[69] In any case, the match in *De beata uita* 4.34 of vocabulary (*procedere, perficere, conuertere*) and subject matter with *Adversus Arium 1A* 13 and *Adversus Arium 1B* 51 proves Cipriani's point (against Hadot) that the early Augustine, like Victorinus, conceived the Trinity as a movement of procession and retrogression.[70]

De beata uita 4.35 contains more of Augustine's Trinitarian ideas, including the mention of an *admonitio* that Cipriani relates to the Spirit,[71] identified here as the means by which people are connected to God:

> A certain admonition, flowing to us from the very fountain of truth [*de ipso ad nos fonte ueritatis emanat*], urges us to remember [*recordemur*] God, to seek Him, and thirst after Him tirelessly. This hidden sun pours into our innermost

66. Cipriani, "Le fonti christiane," 270.

67. *Ar. 1*, 13 (CSEL 83/1:73 and 72): "causa est ipsi filio, ut sit et isto modo sit. . . . Christus enim ueritas."

68. *Ar. 1*, 14 (CSEL 83/1:73): "Christus et a patre processit" (cf. John 16:27–28).

69. Cipriani, "Le fonti christiane," 271. Plotinus uses similar expressions of the Good (cf., e.g., I 8.2: μέτρον πάντων καὶ πέρας) and the One (V 5.4: μέτρον . . . οὐ μετρούμενον), but Cipriani maintains that the other traces of Victorinus's language suggest his Christian works were a mediating filter through which Augustine found Neoplatonist ideas already adapted to a pro-Nicene Trinitarian theology. For *summus modus*, see Luigi F. Pizzolato, "Il modus nel primo Agostino," in *La langue latine, langue de la philosophie: Actes du colloque de Rome (17–19 mai 1990)*, Publications de l'École française de Rome 161 (Rome: École française de Rome, 1992), 245–61.

70. Cipriani, "Le fonti christiane," 270, citing (in n. 73) Hadot, *Porphyre et Victorinus*, 1:477: "nulle trace chez Augustin d'un déploiement de la monade en triade, d'un mouvement de procession et de conversion." (Cipriani admits Hadot was likely generalizing about *De Trinitate*, not the early dialogues.)

71. Cipriani, "Le fonti christiane," 272, arguing against scholars who have denied that this *admonitio* refers to the Holy Spirit—namely, Jean Doignon, "La 'praxis' de l'admonitio dans les dialogues de Cassiciacum de St. Augustin," *Vetera Christianorum* 23 (1986): 21–37, and Otto du Roy, *L'intelligence de la foi en la Trinité selon saint Augustin: Génèse de sa théologie trinitaire jusqu'en 391* (Paris: Études Augustiniennes, 1966), 163.

eyes that beaming light. His is all the truth that we speak.... This light appears to be nothing other than God, perfect without any degeneration [*nulla degeneratione inpediente*].... But, as long as we are still seeking, and not yet satiated by the fountain itself and—to use that word—by fullness [*plenitudine*], we must confess that we have not yet reached our measure [*modum*]; therefore, notwithstanding the help of God now, we are not yet wise and happy. This, then, is the full satisfaction of souls, that is, the happy life: to recognize piously and completely the One through whom [*a quo*] you are led into the truth, the nature of the truth [*qua ueritate*] you enjoy, and that through which you are connected [*per quid conectaris*] with the supreme measure.[72]

Cipriani cites for comparison a passage in Victorinus (*Ar. 4, 17*) that depicts the Holy Spirit as the divine stimulator of faith:

But because the memory [*memoriam*] of Christ and of God is obscured in human souls, there is need of the Holy Spirit. If knowledge and understanding "what is the breadth, and length and height and depth" (Eph. 3:15–16) is added to love and faith in Christ, through the Holy Spirit who is knowledge, people "will be saved" (cf. Matt. 16:16). For the Holy Spirit fully gives "testimony" of Christ and "teaches" (cf. John 14:24 and 15:26) all things and is the interior force of Christ, giving knowledge and advancing us to salvation; whence, he is "another Paraclete" (John 14:15). Indeed, to people dead through sin, life first had to be given so they might be raised up [*erigerentur*] to God through faith.... That is why, to those strengthened through faith, through Christ the

---

72. *Beata u.* 4.35 (CSEL 63:115; ET Augustine, *The Happy Life; Answer to Skeptics; Divine Providence and the Problem of Evil; Soliloquies*, trans. Ludwig Schopp, Denis J. Kavanagh, Robert P. Russell, and Thomas F. Gilligan, FC 5 [Washington, DC: Catholic University of America Press, 1948], 83, modified): "admonitio autem quaedam, quae nobiscum agit, ut deum recordemur, ut eum quaeramus, ut eum pulso omni fastidio sitiamus, de ipso ad nos fonte ueritatis emanat. hoc interioribus luminibus nostris iubar sol ille secretus infundit. huius est uerum omne, quod loquimur, etiam quando adhuc uel minus sanis uel repente apertis oculis audacter conuerti et totum intueri trepidamus, nihilque aliud etiam hoc apparet esse quam deum nulla degeneratione inpediente perfectum. nam ibi totum atque omne perfectum est simulque est omnipotentissimus deus. sed tamen quamdiu quaerimus, nondum ipso fonte atque, ut illo uerbo utar, plenitudine saturati nondum ad nostrum modum nos peruenisse fateamur et ideo quamuis iam deo adiuuante nondum tamen sapientes ac beati sumus. illa est igitur plena satietas animorum, hoc est beata uita, pie perfecteque cognoscere, a quo inducaris in ueritatem, qua ueritate perfruaris, per quid conectaris summo modo. quae tria unum deum intellegentibus unamque substantiam exclusis uanitatibus uariae superstitionis ostendunt."

Son of God, it was necessary, it seemed, to give also the knowledge of Christ and in like manner of God, and also of the world, "to judge it" (John 16:8). When they will have understood these things, people would be more easily freed [*liberarentur*] by their knowledge of themselves and of divine things to attain the light of God because of their contempt for worldly and earthly things and by the desire which knowledge of divine things stirs up [*excitat*].[73]

This passage, Cipriani claims, inspired Augustine's formulations in *De beata uita* 4.35 as well as part of the opening prayer in *Soliloquies* (note the two verbs found in the above-quoted passage):[74] "God, to whom faith stirs us up [*excitat*], to whom hope raises us up [*erigat*], and to whom love joins [*iungit*] us."[75]

In sum, beyond the elements of vocabulary common with Victorinus, Augustine's Cassiciacum dialogues share a coordination of Trinitarian discussion with soteriological concerns in which the action of the Holy Spirit liberates souls through faith and knowledge.

The Case for Influence in the Exegesis of Galatians

The question of the influence of Victorinus on Augustine in the matter of Pauline exegesis is complicated by a number of factors. On the one hand, the basis for comparison is practically limited to their commentaries on Galatians, since Victorinus's Romans commentary, the existence of which is established by internal

73. *Ar.* 4, 17 (CSEL 83/1:250; trans. Clark, 276–77, modified): "propter uero hominum obrutam sui et dei memoriam opus est spiritus sanctus. si accesserit scientia et intellegere quae sit latitudo dei, quae longitudo, quae profunditas et altitudo, et comfirmata fuerit caritas et fides in Christum per spiritum sanctum, qui scientia est, fiet saluus. plene namque ipse dicit testimonium de Christo et docet omnia et est interior Christi uirtus, scientiam tribuens et ad saluationem proficiens, unde alter paraclitus. etenim mortuis per peccata hominibus uita prius danda fuerat, ut erigerentur in deum per fidem. . . . quare, confirmatis hominibus per fidem, per Christum filium dei, etiam scientia danda uidebatur et de Christo et perinde de deo, item de mundo, ut eum argueret. quae cum intellexissent, facilius ad dei lucem homines sui diuinorumque intellegentia liberarentur terrenorum mundanorumque contemptu et desiderio quod excitat scientia diuinorum." Cipriani presents this passage in a more abbreviated form.

74. Cipriani, "Le fonti christiane," 277–79.

75. *Sol.* 1.3 (CSEL 89:6). It is noteworthy that *beata u.* 4.35 concludes with a similar allusion to the Pauline triad of faith, hope, and love from the mouth of Monica.

references, has not survived.[76] On the other hand, we know that Augustine read Jerome on Galatians and, by the time of his anti-Pelagian works, if not earlier, had also read Ambrosiaster's commentaries on Paul.[77] As previously noted, Bastiaensen maintains that Augustine had read Ambrosiaster by the time he wrote his early exegetical works on Paul and that it was Ambrosiaster—not Jerome or Victorinus—whose influence on Augustine is most evident.[78]

I have treated the exegetical parallels on Galatians proposed by Cipriani, Plumer, and myself elsewhere, concluding that eleven show elements of Victorinus in Augustine.[79] These results, however, do not in all cases meet the stricter criteria of Dulaey.[80] She is correct that one cannot eliminate the possibility that the two rhetorically trained readers of texts could have noticed the same features and problems of a Pauline passage and reached a similar interpretation. This consideration weakens the case, for example, that I made about their exegesis of the *infirma et egena elementa* in Gal. 4:9–10, where "they share a specific literary-critical perspective on the passage."[81] In what follows I will present a smaller sample of material, instances of parallel exegeses where the case for literary borrowing is strongest.

The Hope of Salvation

The place of "hope" in any Christian theology is guaranteed by the centrality of eschatology to the faith and, more particularly, by its prominent place in the Pauline letters, not least in the triad "hope, faith, and love" (1 Cor. 13:13; cf. 1 Thess. 1:3). Basil Studer has even proposed that "it is precisely by means of the

76. Cf. his comments on Gal. 4:7 and 5:8 (CSEL 83.2:144 and 161, respectively).

77. Thus James Houston Baxter, "Ambrosiaster cited as 'Ambrose' in 405," *JTS* 24 (1922–1923): 187. Opposed to the claim that Augustine knew Ambrosiaster's commentaries is Bernard Leeming, "Augustine, Ambrosiaster and the *massa perditionis*," *Gregorianum* 11 (1930): 58–91. See also A. C. de Veer, "Saint Augustin et l'Ambrosiaster," BA 23:817–24, and Nello Cipriani, "Un'altra traccia dell'Ambrosiaster in Agostino (*De pecc. mer. remiss.* II, 36, 58–59)," *Augustinianum* 24 (1984): 515–25.

78. Bastiaensen, "Augustin commentateur de saint Paul," 57. Plumer (*Augustine's Commentary on Galatians*, 54–55) is skeptical that Augustine had read Ambrosiaster on Paul prior to 405 CE.

79. Cooper, *Marius Victorinus' Commentary on Galatians*, 241. Chap. 6 of this work examines all the possible parallels *in extenso*.

80. Cf. n. 28 *supra*.

81. Cooper, *Marius Victorinus' Commentary on Galatians*, 219.

Augustinian theology of hope that one can best measure the extent to which Augustine followed the apostle."[82] Plumer's observation that both Victorinus and Augustine frequently invoke the phrase *spes salutis* ("the hope of salvation") from 1 Thess. 5:8 is his key contribution to the claim that the latter was familiar with Victorinus's commentaries on Paul.[83] Yet Victorinus and Augustine do not use *spes salutis* to exposit the identical verses of Galatians, although the matter is not so clear, given that their two works are formally different. While Victorinus's work quotes the entire lemmatized text of the commentaries, Augustine does not follow this method but still considered his work on Galatians a full commentary on the letter.[84] Nonetheless, there are two passages in their commentaries in which their uses of *spes salutis* fall in proximate verses.

There are objections to Plumer's position.[85] First, Augustine could have absorbed the phrase from his reading of 1 Thessalonians and used it on his own, both in his commentary on Galatians and in two earlier anti-Manichaean works.[86] Second, Augustine could have encountered this phrase, along with a pronounced theology of hope, in Ambrosiaster's commentaries on Paul. But *spes salutis* occurs only once in these works, at Rom. 1:7.[87] Ambrosiaster has left ample traces of having read Victorinus, which include the incorporation of the latter's theology of hope as a central expression of soteriology and apologetics

---

82. Basil Studer, "Augustine and the Pauline Theology of Hope," in *Paul and the Legacies of Paul*, ed. William S. Babcock (Dallas: Southern Methodist University Press, 1990), 220.

83. Plumer, *Augustine's Commentary on Galatians*, 28–29.

84. *Retr.* 1.23.1 (CSEL 536:111): "eiusdem apostoli epistulam ad Galatas non carptim, id est aliqua praetermittens, sed continuanter et totam." See Ludwig Fladerer, *Augustinus als Exeget: Zu seinen Kommentaren des Galaterbriefes und der Genesis* (Vienna: Österreichische Akademie der Wissenschaften, 2010), 44–53, who concludes that Augustine considered his work on Galatians a complete commentary on the grounds that it covers the progression of the thought (*Gedankengang*), even without a full citation and discussion of the words of the text.

85. Plumer, *Augustine's Commentary on Galatians*, 21–22.

86. Plumer (*Augustine's Commentary on Galatians*, 29nn144–45) notes its occurrence in Augustine's remarks on Gal. 2:3, 2:11–14; 5:2, 5:25, 6:15 (in *exp. Gal.* 11.2, 15.2, 41.5, 54.5, 63.2; CSEL 84:65, 69, 112, 139) and also in two earlier works, *c. Adim.* 11 (CSEL 25:136) and *mor.* 1.28.55 (CSEL 90:58).

87. CSEL 81/1:18; ET *Ambrosiaster's Commentary on the Pauline Epistles: Romans*, trans. Theodore S. de Bruyn, ed. Andrew Cain, WGRW 41 (Atlanta: SBL Press, 2017), 13–15n41: "For those who operate under the law understand Christ in the wrong way and do God the Father an injustice when they doubt whether there is complete hope of salvation in Christ." Ambrosiaster's comment here appears only in his first two recensions of his commentary on Romans, but, as de Bruyn has noted (97n51 on Rom. 5:14), Augustine read the second recension (*recensio* ß).

in the face of rival religious hopes.[88] *Prima facie*, however, the case for Augustine having been influenced in his use of *spes salutis* by Ambrosiaster is rather weak given its infrequency in his commentaries.

By contrast, Victorinus repeats this motif and the phrase *spes salutis* many times in his commentary on Galatians.[89] In his preface to that work he states, "Paul writes the letter wanting to correct them and to summon them back from Judaism, so they would keep faith in Christ alone and have the hope of salvation from Christ, the hope of his promises, as clearly no one is saved based on the works of the law."[90] His remarks on Paul's thanksgiving prayer in Gal. 1:3–5 likewise emphasize the place of hope in Christian faith as he sketches the apostle's goal in this letter:

> Let us recall what the apostle is doing in this letter. He is reprimanding the Galatians and trying to correct them, in order that they might have faith in Christ and look for the hope of salvation [*spem salutis*], for the hope of eternity, for the remission of sins, and for all things, from him alone [*ab ipso solo*]. He does this to prevent them from believing that the works of the Law, sabbath, or circumcision are advantageous for them.[91]

A similar summary occurs on the next lemma, where, while treating Gal. 1:6, Victorinus asserts that "all hope for salvation [*spem salutis*] and for the grace of God pertaining to us lies in faith pertaining to Christ."[92] He also applies this idea

---

88. Cooper, *Marius Victorinus' Commentary on Galatians*, 190–92, 201–2. Ambrosiaster's preface on Galatians presents the situation of the letter as one in which false hopes for salvation from the law are correlated with a failure to understand Christ as God (CSEL 81/3:95). Further remarks on hope occur in his commentary on Gal. 1:6 (CSEL 81/3:9); 3:16 (36); 4:3 (43); 6:14 (67); see also on Eph. 3:9 (89).

89. *Spes salutis* appears in Victorinus's preface to his commentary on Galatians (CSEL 83/2:95) and also in his comments on 1:3–5 (99); 1:6 (99); 2:10 (117); 3:24 (135); 4:17 (150); and 6:16 (172).

90. *Gal.* (CSEL 83/2:95): "Paulus scribit hanc epistolam eos uolens corrigere et a Iudaismo reuocare, ut fidem tantum in Christum seruent et a Christo spem habeant salutis et promissionem eius, scilicet quod ex operibus legis nemo saluetur."

91. *Gal.* (CSEL 83/2:98–99): "memores simus quid in hac epistola agat apostolus: quod Galatas reprehendit et corrigere cupit, ut in Christum fidem habeant, ab ipso solo spem salutis, spem aeternitatis exspectent, remissionem peccatorum et omnia, ne sibi credant prodesse uel opera legis uel sabbata uel circumcisionem."

92. *Gal.* (CSEL 83/2:99): "sed omnem spem salutis et gratiae dei circa nos in fide esse circa Christum."

programmatically to the exposition of Paul's soteriology found in his commentary on Ephesians.[93]

Victorinus returns to the same phrase in treating Gal. 2:10, where he notes that John, Peter, and James confirmed Paul's preaching of the gospel but requested, in Paul's word, that "we remember the poor." Victorinus maintains this betokened no departure in their agreement as regards soteriology: "Thus they came to agree even on this matter: that if we perform works for the poor, the hope of salvation is not to be found there [*non ibi esse spem salutis*]."[94] Augustine does not use *spes salutis* in his discussion of this verse, but it does occur in his remarks on Gal. 2:3–5 (*exp. Gal.* 11) and directly after he treats Gal. 2:10, in the excursus (*exp. Gal.* 15.1–5) prefacing his discussion of Gal. 2:11–21 (*exp. Gal.* 15.6–17.14). Indeed, on this basis Ralph Hennings, in his study of the epistolary dispute between Augustine and Jerome about this passage,[95] concludes that Augustine "follows Cyprian, Marius Victorinus, and Ambrosiaster in his interpretation."[96] Operating with the strictest criteria, however, elements common to Victorinus, Ambrosiaster, and Augustine—as one finds in some aspects of their interpretations of this and other passages (e.g., on Gal. 1:17, 1:20, and 4:12)—are not probative. In fact, the remarks of these three on Gal. 2:11–14 resemble each other precisely in their insistence on the genuineness of Paul's rebuke of Peter and on the reality of the latter's error.

To track Augustine's employment of *spes salutis*, we begin with his exegetical remarks about Titus:

"But not even my companion Titus, although he was a Greek, was compelled to be circumcised" (Gal. 2:3). Though Titus was Greek and not obliged by any custom or parental relationship to be circumcised (as was the case with Timothy), yet the apostle might easily have allowed even him to be circumcised. For he was not trying to teach that salvation is taken away by such circumcision but rather to show that it is contrary to salvation to place one's hope for

93. See, e.g., his use of *spes salutis* and similar phrases in his commentary on Ephesians: *Ephes.* 1:4 (CSEL 83/2:9); 3:1–2 (42: "spes omnis in Christo"); and 3:13 (51: "solam spem de Christo habeatis").

94. *Gal.* (CSEL 83/2:117; trans. is my own): "ita et ipsum consentiunt non ibi esse spem salutis, si in pauperes operas efficiamus."

95. Cf. *epp.* 28, 40, 75, and 81; trans. Teske, *Letters 1–99*, WSA II/1, 90–94, 148–52, 280–96, 313–34.

96. Ralph Hennings, *Der Briefwechsel zwischen Augustinus und Hieronymus* (Leiden: Brill, 1994), 257.

it [*constitueretur spes salutis*] in circumcision. Thus, he could calmly tolerate it as something superfluous, as when he says elsewhere [he cites 1 Cor. 7:19].[97]

A number of points are common to Augustine and Victorinus here. They both emphasize not putting any hope for salvation in Jewish practices, and they also agree that the apostle could have circumcised Titus just as he did Timothy. Thus Victorinus on Gal. 2:4–5, defending the positive reading of Gal. 2:5—"for an hour we submitted in subjection"—that he (along with Ambrosiaster) found in the VL, says quite frankly, "Paul really did submit, for in fact he also circumcised Timothy on account of the Jews, as it says in the Acts of the Apostles. So the apostle was under no pressure to lie [*mentiri non debuit*]."[98] He then explains that Paul's policy of submitting in unessential matters was a regular part of his mission strategy, something "we have shown was approved and done by Paul in many places." Like Augustine, Victorinus goes on to allude to Paul's discussion in 1 Cor. 7, citing in particular the concessions (1 Cor. 7:18–8:13) Paul allowed in the matter of second marriages, marriage itself, and "all foods, even meats from idol-sacrifices."[99]

Augustine's remarks prefacing his discussion of the conflict between Peter and Paul at Antioch are much to the same point, although more directly aimed to combat Jerome's claims in his commentary, which Ludwig Fladerer has argued were directed primarily against Victorinus's exegesis.[100] Jerome, following Origen and other Greek commentators, maintained that various biblical figures resorted "to temporary dissimulation for the sake of their own or others' salvation,"[101] and that "Paul likewise employed the same pretense as Peter and confronted him and spoke in front of everyone, not so much to rebuke Peter as to correct those for

97. *Ex. Gal.* 11.2 (CSEL 84:65; trans. Plumer, *Augustine's Commentary on Galatians*, 139): "sed neque Titus, qui mecum erat, inquit, cum esset graecus, compulsus est circumcidi. quamuis Titus Graecus esset et nulla eum consuetudo aut cognatio parentum cogeret, sicut Timotheum, facile tamen etiam istum circumcidi permisisset apostolus. non enim tali circumcisione salutem docebat auferri, sed si in ea constitueretur spes salutis, hoc esse contra salutem ostendebat. poterat ergo ut superfluam aequo animo tolerare secundum sententiam, quam alibi dixit."

98. *Gal.* (CSEL 83/2:114): "quia uere cessit: nam et Timotheum circumcidit *propter Iudaeos*, ut ait in Actibus Apostolorum. ergo mentiri non debuit apostolus."

99. *Gal.* (CSEL 83/2:115).

100. Fladerer, *Augustinus als Exeget*, 22.

101. *In Gal.* 2:11–13 (CCSL 77A:54; trans. Cain, 107): "utilem uero simulationem et adsumendam in tempore et Hieu regis Israel nos doceat exemplum."

whose sake Peter had engaged in simulation."[102] Without mentioning Jerome's views in his commentary, Augustine argues against any such harmonization. We see this in his opening remarks that form the transition from his discussion of Gal. 2:10 to the controverted issue, first mentioned in his preface, of Paul's rebuke of Peter at Antioch (Gal. 2:11–14):[103]

> The fact that Paul observed what were regarded as the accepted practices in all circumstances—whether dealing with Gentile or Jewish churches—does not mean that he had fallen into hypocrisy [*simulatione*]. Rather, his aim was to avoid detracting from any local custom [*consuetudinem*] whose observance did not hinder the kingdom of God. He merely warned against placing one's hope for salvation [*spem salutis*] in unessential things, even though he himself might honour a custom among them so as not to offend the weak. As he says to the Corinthians [he quotes 1 Cor. 7:18–20].[104]

Given that any interpreter who had thoroughly read the Pauline corpus could cite that discussion apropos of the problems of the conduct of Peter and Paul in Antioch, the common reference of Victorinus and Augustine to 1 Cor. 7 cannot be made the basis of a claim for literary influence. Apart from the use of *spes salutis*, then, the common elements of their interpretation of this passage, noted in greater detail by both Plumer and myself, fall short of a truly compelling case.

Galatians 2:19–21

Cipriani finds this passage highly significant in that both Victorinus and Augustine offer two possible interpretations, both of which are different from those of either

---

102. *In Gal.* 2:14a (CCSL 77A:57; trans. Cain, 110): "unde et Paulus eadem arte qua ille simulabat ei restitit in faciem et loquitur coram omnibus non tam ut Petrum arguat quam ut hi quorum causa Petrus simulauerat corrigantur."

103. See Cooper, *Marius Victorinus' Commentary on Galatians*, 203–11, for discussion of the history of Latin patristic exegesis on these verses and for references to the scholarly literature.

104. *Exp. Gal.* 15.1–3 (CSEL 84: 69; trans. Plumer, *Augustine's Commentary on Galatians*, 143): "in nulla simulatione Paulus lapsus erat, quia seruabat ubique, quod congruere uidebat, siue ecclesiis gentium siue Iudaeorum, ut nusquam auferret consuetudinem, quae seruata non impediebat ad obtinendum regnum dei, tantum admonens, ne quis in superfluis poneret spem salutis, etiam si consuetudinem in eis propter offensionem infirmorum custodire uellet. sicut ad Corinthios dicit. . . ."

Ambrosiaster or Jerome.[105] I have argued elsewhere that Ambrosiaster actually reproduces one of Victorinus's explanations—his first interpretive option—while Augustine reiterates the second.[106] For simplicity, we will first examine what Victorinus and Augustine said about these verses before considering whether the latter might have obtained his interpretation through Ambrosiaster.

> Victorinus: "Paul could seem to have spoken of two laws, one of Christ and another of Moses, so as to say that 'through the law' which was given by Christ, he died *to the very law that was given to the Jews*. This would then be the meaning of *through the law I died to the law*—that is, through the law of Christ I died to the law of the Jews that was given previously. But it could seem that he has here mentioned two laws . . . for the reason that *this same law* [*eadem ipsa*] is twofold, so to speak: one when it is *understood carnally* [*una cum carnaliter*] and another law when it is *understood spiritually* [*altera cum spiritaliter intellegitur*]. Previously it was understood carnally, and one kept the law based on its works, on circumcision, and with its other observances understood carnally [*obseruationibus carnaliter intellectis*]."[107]

> Ambrosiaster: "'For I through the law died to the law that I might live to God.' He is saying this since 'through the law' of faith, he has 'died to the law' of Moses. One who is freed from that law dies, and he lives *to God*, whose slave he becomes, having been bought by Christ."[108]

> Augustine: "Now he says he 'died to the law' and so is no longer under the law, but nevertheless he did this 'through the law.' Why does he say this? One ex-

---

105. Cipriani, "Agostino lettore," 414–15. Plumer (*Augustine's Commentary on Galatians*, 29–30) accepts Cipriani's arguments on this point.

106. Cooper, *Marius Victorinus' Commentary on Galatians*, 212–14.

107. *Gal.* 2:19 (CSEL 83/2:123; trans. is my own): "potest uideri duas leges dixisse Paulus, unam Christi, alteram Moysi, ut ipsi legi mortuum se dicat quae fuit Iudaeis data, per legem quae a Christo data sit, ut hoc sit: per legem legi mortuus sum, id est per legem Christi mortuus sum legi Iudaeorum ante datae. potest autem uideri, quod frequenter ait Paulus, sed et ipse saluator, ut idcirco duas leges hic nominauerit, quoniam eadem ipsa uelut duplex est: una cum carnaliter, altera cum spiritaliter intellegitur. ante cum carnaliter intellegebatur, et ex operibus et ex circumcisione et ceteris obseruationibus carnaliter intellectis legi seruiebatur."

108. CSEL 81/3:28; trans. is my own: "ego enim per legem legi mortuus sum, ut deo uiuam. hoc dicit quia per legem fidei mortuus est legi Moysi. moritur enim qui liberatur ab ea, et uiuit deo, cuius fit seruus emptus a Christo."

planation is that he said it *because he was a Jew and had received the law* as a kind of 'disciplinarian,' as he shows later. . . . Another explanation is that 'through the law' *understood spiritually [spiritualiter intellectam]* he 'died to the law,' in order that he might not live under it carnally [*carnaliter*] . . . so that through *the same law [eandem legem], understood spiritually [spiritualiter intellectam]*, they might die to carnal observances of the law [*carnalibus obseruationibus legis*]."[109]

Ambrosiaster's typically concise remarks match the first part of what Victorinus and Augustine have to say about the verse. Beyond that point, however, we note the common vocabulary of the latter two, part of which is Pauline (both VL and the Vulgate rendered πνευματικῶς from 1 Cor 2:14 as *spiritaliter*, a term used in an exegetical sense as early as Tertullian[110]). The chief argument here, as Cipriani maintains, is that both exegetes offer two explanations: one in which "law" has the Jewish meaning (= Torah), and another in which Paul could have intended a dual sense as Christians might well apprehend it (i.e., the Old Testament law understood either "spiritually" or "carnally"). Jerome supports the second interpretative option, but he does not employ the same adverbial language.[111] This offers fairly strong evidence for thinking that Augustine has taken over Victorinus's exegesis, including some of his exact language.

Proscription of Jesus Christ (Gal. 3:1)

Among his proofs of influence, Plumer has taken up the suggestion of Alexander Souter that Augustine's exegesis of Gal. 3:1 resembles that of Victorinus.[112] The VL versions found in their commentaries both rendered προεγράφη (RSV, "publicly portrayed") as *proscriptus*; and Souter noticed that Victorinus's "curious view" of the meaning of this term also occurs in Augustine.[113] The verb *proscrib-*

---

109. *Exp. Gal.* 17.1–3 (CSEL 84:73; trans. Plumer, *Augustine's Commentary on Galatians*, 149): "mortuum autem se legi dicit, ut iam sub lege non esset, sed tamen per legem, siue quia iudaeus erat et tamquam paedagogum legem acceperat, sicut postea manifestat . . . siue per legem spirtualiter intellectam legi mortuus est, ne sub ea carnaliter uiueret. . . . ut per eandem legem spiritualiter intellectam morerentur carnalibus obseruationibus legis."

110. E.g., Tertullian, *De oratione* 6.2 (CCSL 1:261).

111. *In Gal.* 2:19a (CCSL 77A:62; trans. Cain, 114): "Therefore, he lives for God who through the spiritual Law dies to the literal Law" ("qui per legem igitur spiritalem legi litterae moritur deo uiuit").

112. Plumer, *Augustine's Commentary on Galatians*, 28.

113. Souter, *Earliest Latin Commentaries*, 24 and 193.

ere originally signified the public notice or exhibition of an item for sale (e.g., at an auction), but this original sense was altered by the provision of Sulla to refer to the sale of the goods of those he had executed; these unfortunate persons were known as *proscripti*.[114] Both Victorinus and Augustine interpret the word in light of this latter use. The close coincidence of their exegesis of *proscriptus* is apparent, but their opening discussions of the verse also have similarities.[115]

Victorinus: "People do not suffer from a spell unless they are *going strong in something good* [*in bono aliquo pollent*], and then come under affliction by the doings of spiteful and jealous people. Because the Galatians really had received something good from the gospel (they believed in Christ and put hope in his promises), now, since they have begun to add on Judaism's teaching, he says, 'Who put a spell on you' to make you *back away from your own good* [*a bono uestro recederetis*]? Therefore, you are 'foolish': you fail to understand the wrong you are doing. But what did *they allow* [*admiserunt*], what are they foolish about? That they were persuaded to observe Judaism. So Christ has been 'proscribed,' meaning his goods have been divided up and sold. These goods, which certainly were *amidst us* [*in nobis*], have been 'proscribed,' sold, and lost by the persuasion of Judaism. So you are foolish, you before whose eyes Jesus Christ was 'proscribed.' The result is that the goods *amidst you* [*in uobis*] disappeared, though you were present all the while. Inasmuch as the things proscribed disappeared because you did not resist, because you did not fight back, you are on that account foolish. Finally, in this line of thought as well is also the fact that Christ was crucified *'even amidst you'* [*et in uobis*]. The Jews who were persuading you to pursue Judaism did to you too what they did to Christ when they put him on the cross. Thus, by persuading you to accept Judaism's teaching, they crucified Christ even among you [*et in uobis*]. So you Galatians are foolish: you have lost [*perdistis*] Christ and his goods from your souls."[116]

114. See William Smith, ed., *A Dictionary of Greek and Roman Antiquities* (London: Murray, 1875), 963–64, s.v. *"Proscriptio."* For a full discussion, see François Hinard, *Les Proscriptions de la Rome republicaine*, Collection de l'École française de Rome 83 (Rome: École française de Rome, 1985).

115. Plumer, *Augustine's Commentary on Galatians*, 28.

116. *Gal.* 3:1 (CSEL 83/2:125–26; trans. is my own): "non patiuntur fascinum nisi quo in bono aliquo pollent, et patiuntur a malignis et inuidis, et cum bonum ex euangelio uero accepissent ut in Christo crederent et eius promissia sperarent, nunc cum adiungere coeperint etiam iudaismi disciplinam, quis, inquit, uos fascinauit ut a bono uestro recederetis? estis igitur stulti, id est non intellegentes quid mali feceritis. quid autem admiserunt, unde stulti

Augustine: "He rightly says to these people: 'You foolish Galatians, who put a spell on you?' It would not be right to say this of people who had never made progress [*profecissent*], but it is right to say it of people who had turned away from the progress they had made [*ex profectu defecissent*]. 'Before whose eyes Jesus Christ was proscribed—after being crucified!' In other words, they saw Jesus Christ lose [*amisit*] his inheritance and his possession, specifically to those who were taking it away and banishing the Lord. They, in order to take away Christ's possession (meaning the people in whom he dwelt by right of grace and faith), were calling those who had believed Christ back—back from the grace of faith whereby Christ has possession of the Gentiles to works of the law. The Apostle wants the Galatians to realize that this has happened in their very midst [*in ipsis*], which is why he says: 'before whose eyes.' What has happened before their eyes so much as what has happened in their very midst [*in ipsis*]? Moreover, when he said, 'Jesus Christ was proscribed,' he added, 'after being crucified!,' so as to move them very deeply when they considered the price Christ paid for the possession he was losing [*amittebat*] in them."[117]

Despite the notable differences in their treatments of the verse—Victorinus's second-person recreation of Paul's hortatory style, his explicitly anti-Jewish rep-

---

sunt? quod illis persuasum est colere iudaismum. ergo proscriptus Christus est, id est bona eius distracta et uendita sunt, quae utique in nobis erant, iudaismi persuasione proscripta sunt, uendita et perdita. ergo stulti, quorum ante oculos Iesus Christus proscriptus est, ut ea bona in uobis uobis praesentibus perirent, ut pereunt illa quae proscribuntur, quod non restitistis, non repugnastis, et idcirco stulti. denique et in hac sententia etiam illud est quod in uobis crucifixus est Christus. hoc enim fecerunt et in uobis illi Iudaei qui uobis persuaserunt ut Iudaismum sequeremini, quod fecerunt Christo ut in crucem tollerent. sic et persuadendo uobis Iudaismi disciplinam et in uobis Christum crucifixerunt. stulti ergo uos, Galatae: perdistis ex uestris animis Christum et eius bona."

117. *Exp. Gal.* 18:1–4 (CSEL 84:75–76; trans. Plumer, *Augustine's Commentary on Galatians*, 151–53, slightly modified): "quibus recte dicit: o stulti galatae, quis uos fascinauit? quod non recte diceretur de his, qui numquam profecissent, sed de his, qui ex profectu defecissent. ante quorum oculos Christus Iesus proscriptus est, crucifixus, hoc est, quibus uidentibus Christus Iesus hereditatem suam possessionemque suam amittebat, his utique auferentibus eam dominumque inde expellentibus, qui ex gratia fidei, per quam Christus possidet gentes, ad legis opera eos, qui crediderant Christum, reuocabant auferendo illi possessionem suam, id est, eos in quibus iure gratiae fideique inhabitabat. quod in ipsis Galatis accidisse uult uideri apostolus, nam ad hoc pertinent, quid ait: ante quorum oculos. quid enim tam ante oculos eorum contigit, quam quod in ipsis contigit. cum autem dixisset: Iesus Christus proscriptus est, addidit, crucifixus, ut hinc eos maxime moueret, cum considerarent, quo pretio emerit possessionem, quam in eis amittebat, ut parum esset gratis eum mortuum, quam superius dixerat."

resentation of the apostle's arguments, and his closeness to the legal terminology of the *proscriptio bonorum*—we observe a number of similarities even beyond the interpretation of *proscriptus* in light of Roman law.[118] They both begin on the note that Paul's question to the Galatians implies they had been making progress and then lost something on account of their deviation from Paul's gospel. Here is where, *ex hypothesi*, Augustine offers a correction to Victorinus, who had pointed to the loss of goods that occurs in a *proscriptio* but pointed to the Galatians' loss rather than that of Christ. Augustine, focusing on Christ's loss of the Galatians, is actually interpreting the passage more consistently in terms of the law of proscription, where it is those condemned who lose their goods. This shift in focus from the Galatians' loss of Christ to Christ's loss of them is notable in the vocabulary shift from Victorinus's verb *admitto* (to allow, admit, grant access to) to Augustine's *amitto* (to dismiss, let go, lose); it is also significant that they conclude the passages cited above with the synonyms *perdo* (Victorinus) and *amitto* (Augustine).

The Case for Influence in *De Trinitate*

Cipriani has argued that *De Trinitate* contains numerous traces of Victorinus's theology, most of which are presented by Augustine as erroneous positions, the author(s) of which he declines to name or to denounce anonymously as heretical. The first of these occurs early in book 1, where Augustine specifically rejects any notion that God is self-begetting: "Those who maintain that it is in the power of God that he would beget himself [*ut seipsum ipse genuerit*] are ... so much more mistaken."[119] As Cipriani points out, this is a doctrine that Victorinus exposited in *Adversus Arium 1*—namely, that God the Father is "the begetter of his own substance [*suae ipsius substantiae generator*]."[120] Cipriani admits that we cannot really be certain Augustine had Victorinus in mind, since Plotinus himself had discussed the auto-creation of the One.[121]

---

118. On the "proscriptio bonorum," see Hinard, *Proscriptions de la Rome republicaine*, 21–22.

119. *Trin.* 1.1.1 (CCSL 50:28; trans. is my own): "qui autem putant eius esse potentiae deum ut seipsum ipse genuerit, eo plus errant quod non solum deus ita non est sed nec spiritalis nec corporalis creatura. nulla enim omnino res est quae se ipsam gignat ut sit."

120. *Ar.* 1, 55 (CSEL 83/1:152–53): "neque igitur praeextitit exsistentia—pater enim suae ipsius substantiae generator et aliorum secundum uerticem fontana est exsistentia." Likewise, in *Ar.* 1, 40, he claimed that the Father "is the begetter of his own existence" (CSEL 83.1:127; trans. Clark, 155): "sui generator est exsistentis."

121. Cf. Plotinus, *Enn.* VI 8.20 (LCL 468:290–94) and V 3.17 (LCL 444:130–32).

He makes a stronger case in regard to Augustine's interpretation of John 16:13–15 in *De Trinitate* 2.3.5 when compared with Victorinus's treatment of this passage in *Adversus Arium 1*, 13.[122] The parallels are provided below, beginning with the text of Victorinus that, *ex hypothesi*, elicited Augustine's correction:

Victorinus: "That there is a twofold power of the Logos with God, one visible, Christ in the flesh, the other in hiding, the Holy Spirit—therefore while the Logos was in presence, that is, Christ, the Logos in hiding, that is, the Holy Spirit, could not come: 'Indeed, if I do not go, the Paraclete will not come to you' (John 16:7). Therefore, these are also two, one coming from the other, the Holy Spirit from the Son just as the Son comes from God [*ex filio spiritus sanctus, sicuti ex deo filius*] and, as a logical consequence, the Holy Spirit also comes from God. That all three are one. . . . Then he adds: 'All things that the Father has are mine' (John 15:16). Therefore he says: 'he receives from me' (John 16:14), because Christ and the Holy Spirit are one sole movement."[123]

Augustine, quoting John 16:13–14 and then discussing it: "If he had not immediately gone on to state, 'All that the Father has is mine; that is why I said, he will receive of mine and will tell it to you' (John 16:14), one could believe that the Holy Spirit was begotten of Christ, as he himself is begotten of the Father [*ita natus de Christo spiritus sanctus quemadmodum ille de patre*]."[124]

Victorinus's text does not contain Augustine's more specific language—*natus de Christo/patre*—but Cipriani is surely correct to claim that Augustine is reject-

---

122. Cipriani, "Le fonti patristiche e filosofiche," 435.

123. *Ar. 1A*, 13 (CSEL 83/1:72; trans. Clark, 106): "quod duplex potentia τοῦ λόγου *ad deum*, una in manifesto, Christus in carne, alia in occulto, spiritus sanctus—in praesentia ergo cum erat λόγος, hoc est Christus, non poterat uenire λόγος in occulto, hoc est spiritus sanctus—: etenim si non discedo, paraclitus non ueniet ad uos. duo ergo et isti, ex alio alius, ex filio spiritus sanctus, sicuti ex deo filius, et conrationaliter et spiritus sanctus ex patre. quod omnia tria unum. . . . deinde adiungit: omnia, quae habet pater, mea sunt. dicit ergo: ex meo accipiet, quod una motio, hoc est actio agens, Christus est et spiritus sanctus."

124. *Trin.* 2.3.5 (CCSL 50:85; trans. is my own): "post haec uerba nisi continuo secutus dixisset: omnia quaecumque habet pater mea sunt; propterea dixi quia de meo accipiet et annuntiabit uobis, crederetur fortasse ita natus de Christo spiritus sanctus quemadmodum ille de patre."

ing the key idea of Victorinus's proposal to treat the begetting of the Son and the procession of the Spirit as parallel processes.

Augustine also discusses a similar misunderstanding in *De Trinitate* 5.12.13. Here the issue is the use of relative terms in Trinitarian discourse, particularly with reference to the Holy Spirit. Cipriani noted a couple of passages where Augustine might have found this sort of confusion in Victorinus:[125]

> Victorinus: "As for the Holy Spirit, we have already set forth in many books that he is Jesus Christ himself but in another mode, Jesus Christ hidden, interior, dialoguing with soul, teaching these things and giving these insights; he has been begotten by the Father through the mediation of Christ and in Christ since Christ is the only-begotten Son."[126]

> Augustine: "For we speak of the Holy Spirit of the Father; but, on the other hand, we do not speak of the Father of the Holy Spirit, lest the Holy Spirit should be understood to be His Son. So also we speak of the Holy Spirit of the Son; but we do not speak of the Son of the Holy Spirit, lest the Holy Spirit be understood to be His Father."[127]

Besides the problem of taking the Holy Spirit as the Son of the Father, which Victorinus seems to have done by claiming the Spirit is "*a patre . . . genitus*," an expression in one of his hymns also appears to have been problematic for Augustine—namely, when Victorinus speaks of the Holy Spirit as "begotten from the Begotten" (*genito genitus*).[128]

Augustine mentions more such misunderstandings about the attribution of names and terms for the Holy Spirit (or his procession) a little later. Augustine's

---

125. Cipriani, "Le fonti patristiche e filosofiche," 437–38.

126. *Ar.* 4, 33 (CSEL 83/1:276; trans. Clark, 302): "iam uero spiritum sanctum alio quodam modo ipsum esse Iesum Christum, occultum, interiorem, cum animis fabulantem, docentem ista intellegentiasque tribuentem, et a patre per Christum genitum et in Christo, quippe cum unigenitus filius Christus sit, multis nos libris exposuimus."

127. *Trin.* 5.12.13 (CCSL 50:220; trans. *NPNF¹* 3:93–94): "dicimus enim spiritum sanctum patris, sed non uicissim dicimus patrem spiritus sancti ne filius eius intellegatur spiritus sanctus. item dicimus spiritum sanctum filii, sed non dicimus filium spiritus sancti ne pater eius intellegatur spiritus sanctus."

128. *Hymn.* 3.81 (CSEL 83/1:290; trans. Clark, 326).

summary is offered first, since the corresponding ideas in Victorinus are drawn from several of his treatises:

> The Father is called so, therefore, relatively, and He is also relatively said to be the Beginning, and whatever else there may be of the kind; but He is called the Father in relation to the Son, the Beginning in relation to all things, which are from Him. So the Son is relatively so called; He is called also relatively the Word and the Image. And in all these appellations He is referred to the Father, but the Father is called by none of them.[129]

Victorinus seems to have fallen into this error of giving Father and Son the same appellations on account of his desire to establish that they are one substance. This is evident in *Adversus Arium* 3, 8, the first passage Cipriani cites in this regard: "The Father also is word—although he is a silent word, he nevertheless is word—and the Son is word; and this also is *ousia* (substance)."[130] Similarly, with regard to the word "image," Victorinus made the mistake of giving the Father this appellation, as we see in *Adversus Arium 1A*, 20: "Therefore both Father and Son are one image. If the image of the Father is the Son and if the image itself is the Father (*et ipsa imago pater*), they are therefore *homoousioi* (consubstantial) in respect to image."[131] Augustine explicitly opposed this position in *De Trinitate* 6.2.3, where he states that "the Father and Son are not both together the Image, but the Son alone is the Image of the Father."[132]

Cipriani also cites other passages from *De Trinitate*, book 6, in which Augustine criticizes an aspect of Victorinus's Trinitarian thought using Victorinus's own terminology. He makes the point twice: "Neither, since He is a Trinity, is He therefore to be thought triple (*triplex*) otherwise the Father alone, or the

---

129. *Trin.* 5.13.14 (CCSL 50:220–221; trans. *NPNF¹* 3:94): "dicitur ergo relatiue pater idemque relatiue dicitur principium et si quid forte aliud; sed pater ad filium dicitur, principium uero ad omnia quae ab ipso sunt. item dicitur relatiue filius; relatiue dicitur et uerbum et imago, et in omnibus his uocabulis ad patrem refertur; nihil autem horum pater dicitur."

130. *Ar.* 3, 8 (CSEL 83/1:204; trans. Clark, 233): "ergo et uerbum pater—licet tacens uerbum, uerbum tamen—et uerbum filius et hoc οὐσία."

131. *Ar.* 1A, 20 (CSEL 83/1:86; trans. Clark, 117–18): "ergo et pater et filius imago una. si imago patris filius est et ipsa imago pater, imagine ergo ὁμοούσιοι."

132. *Trin.* 6.2.3 (CCSL 50:230; trans. *NPNF¹* 3:98): "sic enim uerbum quomodo imago; non autem pater et filius simul ambo imago, sed filius solus imago patris quemadmodum et filius; non enim ambo simul filius."

Son alone, will be less than the Father and Son together";[133] "whether it be the Father, or the Son, or the Holy Spirit, He is perfect, and God the Father the Son and the Holy Spirit is perfect; and therefore He is a Trinity rather than triple (*triplex*)."[134] This terminology is found in Victorinus, in both *Adversus Arium 4*, 21 (*triplex igitur in singulis singularitas et unalitas in trinitate*),[135] and *Hymni* 1 (*sed quo, progressu actuum, sit ter triplex alterum*).[136]

Book 9 of *De Trinitate* also contains a notable correction of Victorinus on the question of what kind of mental "birth" (*partus*) might be a suitable analogy for grasping the Trinity. Cipriani maintains that Augustine had in view a passage from Victorinus's commentary on Eph. 1:1 quoted just below.[137] This passage is one Hadot treats as among the few texts from his exegetical work with an "allure préaugustinienne,"[138] and Henry notes it as displaying the third of the four ways in which Victorinus had anticipated Augustine's *De Trinitate*, "the psychological doctrine of the Divine Processions according to thought and will."[139]

Victorinus: "At the same time, it must be noted rather carefully how the Son exists and how the Father exists. For although the begetting is not known, the analogy must nonetheless be grasped: by some birth in the mind [*quodam partu mentis*], as it were, by a thought, the will that has been conceived [*uelle conceptum*] breaks forth and is poured out. The thoughts of the soul, surely, are in a manner of speaking its children [*quasi filii*]."[140]

---

133. *Trin.* 6.7.9 (CCSL 50:237; trans. *NPNF¹* 3:101): "nec quoniam trinitas est ideo triplex putandus est; alioquin minor erit pater solus aut filius solus quam simul pater et filius."

134. *Trin.* 6.8.9 (CCSL 50:238; trans. *NPNF¹* 3:102): "perfectus autem siue pater siue filius siue spiritus sanctus, et perfectus deus pater et filius et spiritus sanctus, et ideo trinitas potius quam triplex." Cipriani ("Le fonti patristiche et filosofiche," 442) also mentions a similar passage in *trin.* 15.3.5 (CCSL 50A:464; trans. is my own): "et non deus triplex sed trinitas" ("God is not triple but a trinity").

135. *Ar.* 4, 21 (CSEL 83/1:258; trans. is my own): "For that reason there is a triple individuality in each individual, and a triple unity in the trinity."

136. *Hymn.* 1 (CSEL 83/1:287; trans. Clark, 318): "So that by the progression of acts there are thrice a triple singularity."

137. Cipriani, "Le fonti patristiche et filosofiche," 456.

138. Hadot, "L'image de la Trinité," 432. Hadot also reckons among these passages Victorinus's comments on Gal. 4:6 (CSEL 83/2:142–43).

139. Paul Henry, "The *Adversus Arium* of Marius Victorinus, the First Systematic Exposition of the Doctrine of the Trinity," *JTS* 1 (1950): 53–54.

140. *Ephes.* 1:1 (CSEL 83/2:3; trans. is my own): "simul et hoc adtentius uidendum, quo-

Augustine: "A birth in the mind [*partum ergo mentis*] is therefore preceded by some desire, by which, through seeking and finding what we wish to know, the offspring—the knowledge itself—is born. And for this reason, that desire by which knowledge is conceived [*concipitur*] and brought forth, cannot rightly be called a birth and an offspring [*partus et proles*]."[141]

While Hadot rules out this passage as betraying the influence of Victorinus on Augustine because of the dissimilarities—"Augustine would never have admitted the will was engendered by a thought"[142]—Cipriani argues on the basis of *De Trinitate* 11.5.9 and 15.20.38 that Augustine, who associates *uoluntas* (and *caritas*) with the Holy Spirit rather than the Son,[143] is correcting Victorinus's conception of the Son as will, which he enunciated just prior to the passage quoted above.[144]

The Holy Spirit as Bond of the Trinity

Charles Gore's claim that Victorinus influenced Augustine in conceiving of the Holy Spirit as the "bond" of the Trinity was reprised by Bertrand de Margerie and taken up by Cipriani.[145] De Margerie concludes that "the Augustinian pneumatology of *communio* is doubtless ... the most original contribution of the great African *doctor* to trinitarian theology."[146] De Margerie opens with a passage from Augustine's sermon *De fide et symbolo* (*f. et symb.*):

---

modo filius sit et quomodo pater. non enim generatione nota, sed similitudo capienda est, quasi quodam partu mentis cogitatione prorumpit uelle conceptum et effunditur. etenim cogitationes animae quasi filii sunt animae. porro cum deus uniuersali cogitatione unam uoluntatem habeat, unus et filius et unicus."

141. *Trin.* 9.12.18 (CCSL 50:310; trans. *NPNF¹* 3:133, modified): "partum ergo mentis antecedit appetitus quidam quo id quod nosse uolumus quaerendo et inueniendo nascitur proles ipsa notitia, ac per hoc appetitus ille quo concipitur pariturque notitia partus et proles recte dici non potest."

142. Hadot, "L'image de la Trinité," 432.

143. Cipriani, "Le fonti patristiche et filosofiche," 456–57.

144. *Ephes.* 1:1 (CSEL 83/2:3): "Christum uero, id est, λόγον eum qui in Christo fuit, dei uoluntatem."

145. Cf. n. 13 *supra*; see also Bertrand de Margerie, "La doctrine de Saint Augustin sur l'Esprit-Saint comme communion et source de communion," *Augustinianum* 12 (1972): 107–19, and Cipriani, "Le fonti patristiche et filosofiche," 443.

146. De Margerie, "La doctrine," 117. If correct, this makes it clear that the case for the

Some have even dared to believe that the Holy Spirit is the communion [*ipsam communionem patris et filii*] or deity, so to speak, of the Father and the Son, their θεότης as the Greeks call it. So, as the Father is God and the Son is God, the very deity which embraces [*qua sibi copulantur*] both—the Father who begets the Son and the Son who cleaves to the Father—is equated with God by whom the Son is begotten. This "deity" by which they would have understood the mutual love and charity of both Father and Son, they say is called the Holy Spirit, and they adduce many proofs from Scripture for their opinion.[147]

De Margerie cites five passages from Victorinus's first and third hymns that "present the Spirit as the bond [*lien*] between the Father and the Son."[148]

> Holy Spirit, assist us, the bond [*copula*] of Father and Son! . . .
> And binding [*nectis*] all in one, you are the Holy Spirit.[149]

> All therefore are one in the Spirit . . .
> Hence for each the substance is real, hence for the Three it is one,
> A substance gone forth from the Father to the Son and returned by
>   the Spirit.[150]

---

influence of Victorinus on this particular point is via the stimulus he provided Augustine toward creative reflection and further development.

147. *F. et symb.* 9.19 (CSEL 41:23; ET Augustine, *Earlier Writings*, trans. J. H. S. Burleigh, Library of Christian Classics [London: SCM; Philadelphia: Westminster, 1953], 364): "ausi sunt tamem quidam ipsam communionem patris et filii atque, ut ita dicam, deitatem, quam graeci θεότητα appellant, spiritum sanctum credere: ut, quoniam pater deus et filius deus, ipsa deitas, qua sibi copulantur et ille gignendo filium et ille patri cohaerendo, ei a quo est genitus aequetur. hanc ergo deitatem, quam etiam dilectionem in se invicem amborum caritatemque uolunt intellegi, spiritum sanctum appellatum dicunt multisque scripturarum documentis adsunt huic opinioni suae."

148. De Margerie, "La doctrine," 109–10.

149. *Hymn.* 1.4–6 (CSEL 83/1:285; trans. Clark, 315, modified): "adesto, sancte spiritus patris et filii copula. . . . in unum qui cuncta nectis, tu es sanctus spiritus."

150. *Hymn.* 1.74–76 (CSEL 83/1:289; trans. Clark, 319, modified): "omnes ergo unum spiritu . . . hinc singulis uera, hinc tribus una substantia est. progressa a patre filio et regressa spiritu."

> One, uniting all [*unitor omnium*], the working power of one,
> So that all may become one.[151]

> These two you joined [*iunxisti*] as one by the Holy Spirit.[152]

> You, Holy Spirit are a bond [*conexio*]; but a bond is whatever unites
>   two;
> In order to unite [*conectas*] all, you first unite the two;
> You, the third, are the embrace [*conplexio*] of the two, an embrace dif-
>   fering in nothing from the one, since you make the two one.[153]

As proof for the claim that Augustine has borrowed this motif from Victorinus, de Margerie cites three passages from *De Trinitate*. At 6.5.7 Augustine writes, "Therefore the Holy Spirit, whatever it is, is something common both to the Father and Son [*commune aliquid est patris et filii*]. But that communion [*communio*] itself is consubstantial and co-eternal; and if it may fitly be called friendship, let it be so called; but it is more aptly called love."[154] In book 15, however, he takes care to point out the scriptural grounds for this understanding of the Spirit as love (i.e., *dilectio* and *caritas*). And a bit later in the same book, he returns to the term *communio* for the Spirit,[155] which he seems to have preferred to the expression he used in 6.10.11—namely, "unspeakable conjunction of the Father and the Image."[156]

---

151. *Hymn.* 3.98–99 (CSEL 83/1:298; trans. Clark, 327): "unus, unitor omnium, uirtus unius operans, unum ut fiant omnia."

152. *Hymn.* 3.138 (CSEL 83/1:299; trans. Clark, 329): "haec duo unum sancto <i>unxisti spiritu."

153. *Hymn.* 3.242–246 (CSEL 83/1:303; trans. Clark, 333, modified): "tu, spiritus sancte, conexio es; conexio autem est quicquid conectit duo; ita ut conectas omnia, primo conectis duo; esque ipsa tertia conplexio duorum atque ipsa conplexio nihil distans uno, unum cum facis duo."

154. *Trin.* 6.5.7 (CCSL 50:235; trans. *NPNF¹* 3:100): "spiritus ergo sanctus commune aliquid est patris et filii, quidquid illud est, aut ipsa communio consubstantialis et coaeterna; quae si amicitia conuenienter dici potest, dicatur, sed aptius dicitur caritas."

155. Cf. *trin.* 15.17.31, 15.18.32, and 15.19.37. For the original of the latter, see CCSL 50A:513: "et si caritas qua pater diligit filium et patrem diligit filius ineffabiliter communionem demonstrat amborum, quid conuenientius quam ut ille proprie dicatur caritas qui spiritus est communis ambobus?"

156. *Trin.* 6.10.11 (CCSL 50:242; trans. *NPNF¹* 3:103): "ineffabilis quidam complexus patris et imaginis."

If this formulation were not enough to convince skeptics that Victorinus's language and understanding of the Holy Spirit in his hymns as *patris et filii copula, conexio, conplexio duorum* impacted Augustine, Cipriani points out that just before Augustine calls the Spirit *complexus patris et imaginis*, there occurs a passage in which Augustine both takes issue with a point of Victorinus's Trinitarian thought—the notion of the Son as both equal and unequal, discussed above in regard to *De beata uita* 4.34—and then incorporates some of his main terminology into a positive formulation. The passage opens with a (loose) quotation from Hilary's *De Trinitate* 2.1,[157] where his use of the term "image" allows Augustine to offer the needed correction:

> And in respect to this image he [Hilary] has named form, I believe in account of the quality of beauty, where there is at once such great fitness, and prime equality, and prime likeness, differing in nothing, and unequal in no respect, and in no part unlike, but answering exactly to Him whose image it is: where there is prime and absolute life, to whom it is not one thing to live [*uiuere*], and another to be [*esse*], but the same thing to be and to live; and prime and absolute intellect [*summus intellectus*], to whom it is not one thing to live, another to understand [*intellegere*], but to understand is to live, and is to be. [158]

Thus, Augustine propounds the mutual implication and consubstantiality of the members of the Trinity[159] that occurs in Victorinus's original employment of the infinitives *esse*, *uiuere*, and *intellegere*,[160] which he intended as pro-Nicene but

---

157. CCSL 62:38: "nec deesse quidquam consummationi tantae reperietur, intra quam sit, in patre et filio et spiritu sancto, infinitas in aeterno, species in imagine, usus in munere" (trans. *NPNF²* 9:52: "Nothing can be found lacking in that supreme Union, which embraces, in Father, Son and Holy Spirit, infinity in the Eternal, His Likeness in His express Image, our enjoyment of Him in the Gift").

158. *Trin.* 6.10.11 (CCSL 50:241; trans. *NPNF¹* 3:103).

159. *Trin.* 6.10.11 (CCSL 50:241): "ubi est prima et summa uita cui non est aliud uiuere et aliud esse, sed idem et esse et uiuere, et primus ac summus intellectus cui non est aliud uiuere et aliud intellegere, sed id quod est intellegere, hoc uiuere, hoc esse est unum omnia tamquam uerbum perfectum cui non desit aliquid et ars quaedam omnipotentis atque sapientis dei plena omnium rationum uiuentium incommutabilium, et omnes unum in ea sicut ipsa unum de uno cum quo unum."

160. See Michael D. Metzger, "Marius Victorinus and the Substantive Infinitive," *Eranos* 72 (1974): 65–70.

which, unfortunately, assigned each of the persons a predominance of just one of the infinitival divine descriptors.[161]

Acknowledging that Victorinus's formulation about the Holy Spirit as the bond uniting Father and Son spurred Augustine toward his mature formulations of Trinitarian doctrine (as found in *trin.*) does not diminish the originality of the bishop of Hippo; rather, it extends our understanding of how he creatively drew on earlier Christian thinkers who applied themselves to the mysteries that he also sought to understand.

Conclusion

Given the difficulty of making claims for literary dependence on the basis of similar exegeses using only a handful of common phrases, it seems fair to conclude that the strongest evidence in favor of Augustine's knowledge of Victorinus comes via the traces of his Trinitarian treatises and hymns that Cipriani has found in Augustine's Cassiciacum dialogues and in *De Trinitate*. Several elements of Victorinus's vocabulary and Trinitarian thought appear in a raw form in *De ordine* and *De beata uita*, while *De Trinitate* displays a more considered approach in which Augustine clearly distinguished between aspects of Victorinus's theology that were acceptable and aspects that had to be discarded. On the question of Pauline exegesis, although the picture is less clear given the fewer lexical traces of Victorinus's language, the presence of *spes salutis* would appear to tip the scale in the direction of an influence of Victorinus on Augustine here as well. While it is not impossible that the frequent repetition of this phrase and motif in both of their commentaries on Galatians is pure coincidence, it is a very striking parallel. Given the case alleged by Plumer for antecedent probability and the echoes of Victorinus's language and doctrine in both Augustine's early and his later works, one must ask whether coincidence is the most likely explanation. There is a fairly strong cumulative case for Augustine's reading of Victorinus's Christian works and an ongoing reflection on what elements in them were worthy of preservation, refinement, or rejection. Augustine's mention of Victorinus in *De doctrina chris-*

161. Cipriani ("Le fonti patristiche et filosofiche," 443) cites Victorinus, *Ar.* 4, 16 and 21–22. The briefest passage (*Ar.* 4, 21 [CSEL 83/1:257–58; trans. Clark, 284]) reads, "God is *tri-dunamos* (tri-powered), that is, one having three powers, 'to be,' 'to live,' 'to understand,' so that in each one power there are three powers, and anyone of the three is three powers, receiving its name by the power wherein it predominates, as I have taught above and in many places."

tiana cannot be overlooked as a piece of clear evidence amidst the admittedly sparse number of literary parallels.

Perhaps the most important question is: What difference does the case for influence make for our understanding of Augustine? Cipriani is helpful when he asks: Are we to understand that Augustine produced his first Christian works guided only by some acquaintance with sermons and writings of Ambrose and conversation with Catholic thinkers like Simplician? Are we to imagine that the synthesis of Neoplatonism and Christianity found in the Cassiciacum dialogues can be accounted for by Augustine's reading of the *libri Platonicorum*, with some help from Ambrose's incorporation of Plotinus's psychagogy in his sermons? Or did Augustine have the benefit of Victorinus's own creative synthesis that strove to be an orthodox expression of Christian truth? Given that the evidence is to some degree ambiguous and that Augustine chose not to mention Victorinus's works, these questions are still answered very differently by competent scholars.

Marius Victorinus may not have been an *Augustinus ante Augustinum* exactly as Harnack imagined, but there seems to be enough evidence to suggest that Victorinus's Christian works were an important stimulus to Augustine's continual theological reflections and that Augustine considered him a predecessor in his appropriation of the "spoils of Egypt" for the needs of the church.

Chapter 13

Augustine and Ambrose

John C. Cavadini

Introduction

"*Deus Creator Omnium.*" Of the four Ambrosian hymns that Augustine cites, this is the one "most often quoted or referred to by St. Augustine."[1] He refers to it eight times in all, four times in *Confessiones* (*conf.*), once in *De beata uita* (*beata u.*), and three times in *De musica* (*mus.*). What ought we to make of that? In the literature attempting to gage the influence of Ambrose on Augustine,[2] very little is made of

I dedicate this essay not only to Patout Burns but also to Jaroslav Pelikan, our common teacher, who always encouraged his students to ponder the meaning of the development of Christian doctrine.

1. Barbara Beyenka, "St. Augustine and the Hymns of St. Ambrose," *American Benedictine Review* 8 (1957): 128; see also her "The Names of St. Ambrose in the Works of St. Augustine," *AugStud* 5 (1974): 19–28. Brian Dunkle, SJ, "'Made Worthy of the Holy Spirit': A Hymn of Ambrose in Augustine's *Nature and Grace*," *AugStud* 50, no. 1 (2019): 1–12, provides an analysis of a use of an Ambrosian hymn in Augustine's theology. J. Warren Smith, "Justification and Merit Before the Pelagian Controversy," *Pro Ecclesia* 16 (2007): 195–217, shows how Ambrose (like Origen) can use language which implies that "grace is somehow contingent on human merit," but actually "in no sense is arguing that God's saving mercy is merited by human initiative or effort" (216), which shows that Augustine's use of this hymn is not a reinterpretation against the grain of Ambrose but a development of his intent. This is relevant also to Han-luen Kantzer Komline, "From Building Blocks to Blueprints: Augustine's Reception of Ambrose's *Commentary on Luke*," *StPatr* 84 (2017): 153–66, who worries about Augustine's apparent use of Ambrose contrary to the latter's intentions.

2. Vittorino Grossi, "Sant' Ambrogio e sant' Agostino: Per una rilettura dei loro rapporti," in *Nec timeo mori: Atti del congresso internazionale di studi ambrosiani nel XVI centenario della*

it, despite the fact that it has left an indelible mark on Augustine's earlier works. Citation of this hymn connects Augustine and Monica in both of their literary appearances in Augustine's oeuvre, since it is Monica who sings part of the hymn at the close of *De beata uita*, while in *Confessiones* it is Augustine's silent intoning of this hymn in the peace of the evening that allows him finally to vent his grief after his mother's death and burial. Perhaps its evocation of night as a time provided by the Creator to salve the anxieties and griefs of the day allowed Augustine the space to grieve despite his worries that, in doing so, he was indulging his passions instead of controlling them. According to Ambrose, whom Augustine names as the author of the verses (*conf.* 9.12.32), the Creator's providence extended even to our grief. Permission to grieve seemed granted both by God and by Ambrose.

DEUS CREATOR OMNIUM

The first use of the line *Deus Creator Omnium* in *Confessiones* is also associated with death, as Augustine reflects in book 4, after the death of his unnamed friend, on the transient nature of creatures, comparing them to the transient character of a vocal utterance, and prays that he would be able to use the things of creation to praise their Creator rather than cling to them as though they were unchanging, as only God can be (4.10.15). Like a hymn, creation is beautiful because of the way the parts, transient in themselves, fit together in the Creator's plan. In book 10, speaking of the temptations afforded by the sense of sight, and prompted by the Ambrosian hymn's praise of the Creator for "clothing the day in the beauty of light," Augustine uplifts the beauty of physical light yet warns against the Manichaean error of divinizing the light rather than learning to praise God "for light as well as for your other gifts, *Deus Creator Omnium*."[3]

In book 11, as Augustine begins his extended exegesis of the Hexameron, the first line of the hymn is intoned for the reader as an illustration of the conceptual

---

more di sant' Ambrogio: Milano, 4–11 Aprile 1997, ed. Luigi Pizzolato and Marco Rizzi (Milan: Vita e Penserio, 1998), 405–62, gives an overview of previous literature, helpfully dividing the waves of Ambrosian influence on Augustine into three periods and summarizing the convergences and divergences as he sees them. Included among convergences are "exegetical method" and "il peccato originale." See 453 and 455.

3. *Conf.* 10.34.52 (James J. O'Donnell, *Augustine: Confessions*, vol. 1, *Introduction and Text* [Oxford: Clarendon, 1992], 39; trans. Boulding, *Confessions*, WSA I/1, 271): "cum autem et de ipsa laudare te norunt, deus creator omnium."

puzzle posed by the attempt to measure time, since, even as the verse is spoken, its short and long syllables cannot be recognized as such until the speaking of it has passed into memory and it is no longer present but past (11.27.35). At the same time, the verse reminds the reader of the enduring sovereignty of the Creator, who is outside time and whom our speech vainly attempts to contain. To illustrate the passage of a metered verse through the present into the past, Augustine could have chosen any verse of any lyric, Christian or not. Yet this hymn continues to mark and to uplift a theme, perhaps the most prominent theme in *Confessiones*, that of God as Creator and the goodness of creation, against the Manichaeans. It serves to associate this theme with Ambrose and to identify *Confessiones* as in some way Ambrosian. In fact, this is the only direct quotation of anything Ambrose said or wrote that is identified as such in *Confessiones*.

Further, the use of a hymn text, especially of this specific hymn text, serves to integrate this major theme of God as Creator with another anti-Manichaean theme, that of the church as a communion of people of diverse backgrounds fundamentally united by baptism and open to all regardless of education or social status. Just before recounting the conversion of Victorinus, Augustine notes that he had gotten used to seeing the church assembled as "full," because it contained people, "some of whom chose one path, some, another."[4] Later he emphasizes that Victorinus refused to receive baptism privately (presumably with a small elite present) but wanted to make his profession in front of the "holy multitude," of the "faithful people of Rome."[5] In *Confessiones* this assembly is prominently associated with singing. About the only thing we encounter with regard to Augustine's mentioning of his baptism is his memory, "in those days" (i.e., of baptism and mystagogy afterward), of the assembly of the church, singing: "In those days . . . how copiously I wept at your hymns and canticles, how intensely was I moved by the voices of your sweetly singing church."[6] In 9.7.15, immediately after this brief account of his baptismal experience, he speaks of the custom of the Milanese church to sing and the fraternal unity it represented and mentions the Ambrosian origin of the practice in the vigil kept during the standoff with

4. *Conf.* 8.1.2 (O'Donnell, 88; trans. is my own): "uidebam enim plenam ecclesiam, et alius sic ibat, alius autem sic."

5. *Conf.* 8.2.5 (O'Donnell, 90; trans. is my own): "in conspectu populi fidelis Romae, . . . in conspectu sanctae multitudinis."

6. *Conf.* 9.6.14. (O'Donnell, 109; trans. Boulding, 199–200, slightly modified): "illis diebus . . . quantum fleui in hymnis et canticis tuis, suaue sonantis ecclesiae tuae uocibus commotus acriter!"

Valentinian and Justina. Augustine notes that, although his mother was present then, he was not. This fact emphasizes how his presence at the singing later on is a presence with her and with others like her. There is even a sense, then, in which this hymn also positions the reader as a participant in the ecclesial assembly—even if only virtually. After all, Augustine ends book 9 by inviting the reader to remember his mother and father at Mass.[7] Thus, Augustine associates Ambrose with a vision of the church that is united in worship across differences in education and class, praising the "God" who is "Creator of all things," and he invites the reader to make the same association.

Augustine's use of this hymn text, though strikingly prominent, is not usually adduced as an index of how much or how little Ambrose influenced Augustine. This chapter's argument is that Augustine's use of the hymn denominates as Ambrosian the major theme of the *Confessiones*—namely, the praise of the Creator and the acknowledgment of the goodness of creation as ecclesial acts performed by all who are bound together by baptism. In a sense, Augustine is identifying and featuring a central element in Ambrose's thought, acknowledging a debt and claiming continuity precisely by using and developing what he was given. But is this objectively Ambrosian? An answer we could easily hear in return is that the essence of someone's thought can be hard to recognize until it is masterfully taken up by a later author of great brilliance who shows you what is distinctive precisely by developing it. But let us investigate this.

In a justly influential article from 1990, Patout Burns sets out to "specify the role of Ambrose in the process of conversion and the ways in which he might have shaped Augustine's understanding of the Catholic Christianity which he embraced."[8] Burns observes that "we may recognize Ambrose's preaching as [a] major influence . . . on Augustine" (378), even if it was "not decisive" (373) for his conversion. But Burns does firmly establish some specifics, even as he rejects

---

7. *Conf.* 9.13.37 (O'Donnell, 118; trans. Boulding, 236): "at your altar" ("ad altare tuum"). Cf. 10.4.6 where the same audience is, as it were, assembled by being invoked. See my "Eucharistic Exegesis in Augustine's *Confessions*," in *Visioning Augustine* (Oxford: Wiley-Blackwell, 2019), 187. Cf. O'Donnell, *Augustine: Confessions*, 1:xxxvii n. 3, who sees a similar dynamic "at the end of Book 10, where Augustine closes the central book of the work with a passage of such dense Eucharistic imagery that it may best be thought of as perhaps the only place in our literature where a Christian receives the Eucharist in the literary text itself."

8. J. Patout Burns, "Ambrose Preaching to Augustine: The Shaping of Faith," in *Augustine: Second Founder of the Faith*, ed. by Joseph C. Schnaubelt and Frederick van Fleteren (New York: Lang, 1990): 373. Subsequent page references appear in the text.

some elements of Ambrose's supposed influence that he believes rest on hagiographical exaggeration.[9] Among the careful distinctions Burns makes, drawing mainly from evidence in *Confessiones*, is the fact that

> Ambrose convinced Augustine that the scriptures could be read in a manner which would undercut the Manichean objections to the presentation of God and of divine actions in the Hebrew scriptures. He did not, however, engender the conviction that this allegorical interpretation yielded a true understanding of the divine. Although Ambrose showed that the Catholic church did not believe that God was bodily or occupied space, he failed to provide Augustine with a way of actually understanding the nature of spiritual reality. (374)

Some further specifics: Ambrose's preaching convinced Augustine that the scriptures were "a tool used by God to guide both the educated and the ignorant" and, in turn, that "recognition of the divine authority of scripture led him to accept its account of the humanity of Christ and thus to reject Manichean Docetism." Also, partly because Ambrose "convinced Augustine" of the value of scripture for both the educated and the uneducated, since "unlike the pagan mythology, the literal reading . . . promoted a salutary way of life among the unlearned and its allegorical interpretation led the more adept deeper into Truth" (375), and partly because Ambrose was successful in answering Monica's questions about customs associated with the martyrs' shrines, "Ambrose seemed to hold open the possibility of a Christian practice in which mother and son, diverse as their religious sensibilities might be, could be equally at home" (376). This certainly tallies with what we have seen in *Confessiones* thus far.

At the same time, though Ambrose "may have informed Augustine of the actual teaching of the Catholic church on scripture, immaterial reality, evil and the humanity of Christ," he "failed . . . to provide the means for Augustine to understand these doctrines and thus did not persuade him of their truth" (375). He perhaps even posed an "unwitting obstacle" insofar as Augustine "seems to have perceived Ambrose as a model of understanding *rather than* of belief" (376; emphasis added). Having been given a hint in this direction from Ambrose, it was

---

9. Although his article is not mentioned, he is followed in this by Garry Wills, *Font of Life: Ambrose, Augustine and the Mystery of Baptism* (Oxford: Oxford University Press, 2012), with regard specifically to influences on Augustine's conversion.

left to others, most notably Simplicianus and the circle of Christian Platonists who led him to the Platonic books, to provide the "intellectual advances," confirmed in the Cassiciacum dialogues, that convinced and thus converted Augustine, at least intellectually, to the Catholic position, especially insofar as he was now able to imagine noncorporeal being and evil as a corruption of the good. With regard to God, this meant that "as Truth, God could contain and control the world without being spatially extended through it or affected by corruption within it" as the Manichaeans thought (377).

ORIGIN OF EVIL

Augustine, however, soon (i.e., by the time he completed *De Genesi aduersus Manicheos* around 390 CE) parted ways with Ambrose on the question of the origin of evil. Ambrose, whose views Augustine could have learned by reading *De Paradiso* (*Par.*) or other sources, found the origin of evil in the opposition between fleshly passions (natural to human nature) and reason (equally natural) and thought that the transmission of evil to all Adam's offspring resulted from Adam allowing the passion for bodily pleasure to dominate his soul. Augustine, probably because of his experience with Manichaeism, "had to push beyond Ambrose's dualism of eternal and temporal, mind and passion, to a more radical understanding of the origin of evil and the incarnation of the Word of God through which it is reversed."[10] Augustine, who discussed the fall of the (nonfleshly) devil as well as of humans, "consistently avoided any reference to desires of the flesh as an occasion or even condition for the temptation and fall of humanity"; rather, these very desires are derivative from "a sin committed earlier in the spirit."[11] The difference in the doctrine of the incarnation is not further specified; nevertheless, Burns concludes,

> Through his preaching and the example of his own Christian practice, Ambrose may have directed Augustine to new resources and removed some obstacles by convincing him of the intelligibility of Catholic Christianity, the value of Platonic philosophy, and particularly the significance of scripture. To attain the point of commitment described in the *conf.* and exemplified in his earliest writ-

10. Burns, "Ambrose Preaching to Augustine," 381.
11. Burns, "Ambrose Preaching to Augustine," 381.

ings, however, Augustine had to pass well beyond the Christian understanding and practice of Ambrose.[12]

I take Burns's point, yet I wonder if this fully describes Augustine's understanding of the matter, at least insofar as the evidence from *Confessiones* allows us to access it. Though understood differently, Ambrose clearly taught a version of inherited sin, and it is always hard to specify which is more fundamental, the agreement or the variations on that which is agreed, since the weighting of such differences is partly in the mind of the observer.[13] Building on scholarship not available when Burns wrote, Garry Wills argues that the most decisive impact Ambrose had on Augustine came from his catechetical and mystagogical instruction.[14] Recalling the days of his initiation in *Confessiones*, Augustine comments not only on the singing of the gathered church but also on what we could call the properly liturgical mutual coinherence of ceremony and doctrine: "Those voices flooded my ears, and the truth was distilled into my heart until it overflowed in loving devotion; my tears ran down, and I was the better for them."[15]

What truth was it that was distilled into his heart? There is no reason to think Augustine has in mind only, or even principally, an interior, wordless infusion of direct insight philosophically construed. Certainly, it was (at least) the truth of the faith expressed in the Creed which Augustine reports receiving in such a

12. Burns, "Ambrose Preaching to Augustine," 381.

13. Augustine, it should be noted, is perfectly capable of disagreeing with Ambrose on a particular point in the interests of furthering a larger Ambrosian agenda. See my "Ambrose and Augustine *de bono mortis*," in *The Limits of Ancient Christianity: Essays on Late Antique Thought and Culture in Honor of R. A. Markus*, ed. William Klingshirn and Mark Vessey (Ann Arbor: University of Michigan Press, 1999), 232–49.

14. See, e.g., Wills, *Font of Life*, 82, where he says that Augustine's "six weeks of intense daily indoctrination" in Ambrose's method of scriptural exegesis "left a lasting mark on all his later readings of the Bible," although in describing that method as "Platonist allegorizing of the Jewish scriptures" I think he mischaracterizes it, especially since most if not all of the examples Wills cites from the mystagogy are typologies that draw their inspiration from the Bible itself. The philosophical substrate of the catechetical lectures was eclectic—Platonic, Aristotelian, and Stoic in turns; see Marcia L. Colish, *Ambrose's Patriarchs: Ethics for the Common Man* (Notre Dame, IN: University of Notre Dame Press, 2005), esp. chap. 3, "Human Nature in the Patriarch Treatises."

15. *Conf.* 9.6.14 (O'Donnell, 109; trans. Boulding, 220): "uoces illae influebant auribus meis, et eliquabatur ueritas in cor meum, et exaestuabat inde affectus pietatis, et currebant lacrimae, et bene mihi erat cum eis."

way that it entered his heart, meaning it moved him and he loved it. Ambrose, we can recall, did not "hand over" the Creed to the catechumens until just before the time of baptism—that is, on Palm Sunday.[16] William Harmless points to *De quantitate animae* (*an. quant.*) 34.77, a passage in which Augustine claims to be using "the very words by which these things were taught to me," as perhaps a direct quote of the preaching that is summarized in Ambrose's *Explanatio symboli*, a summary that strongly features the confession of God as Creator.[17] Ambrose emphasized the confession of the Creed, including the orthodox confession of the coequality of all three persons of the Trinity, as a communal act.[18] Pamela Jackson and Craig Satterlee have produced admirable studies of Ambrose's mystagogical preaching,[19] which is available to the reader in Ambrose's *De sacramentiis* (*Sac.*) and *De mysteriis* (*Myst.*). Following Neil McLynn, Satterlee emphasizes that the assembled church at Milan was composed of "diverse social groups," and that Ambrose "found in congregational singing the means to reach across the barriers of social class that separated his people in their everyday lives."[20]

Sacraments

Ambrose's homilies on the sacraments are highly typological. For example, Ambrose comments that the commonplace appearance of the water of baptism

16. See Craig Alan Satterlee, *Ambrose of Milan's Method of Mystagogical Preaching* (Collegeville, MN: Liturgical Press, 2002), 153.

17. "Here, Augustine seems to be citing Ambrose's instruction on the Creed (the *traditio symboli*)." William Harmless, *Augustine and the Catechumenate* (Collegeville, MN: Liturgical Press, 1995), 93; see also 106, where Ambrose's *traditio symboli* is identified with the *Explanatio symboli*. See also 94, where a reminiscence of Augustine's catechetical experience is quoted from *f. et op.* 6.9 (see CSEL 41:44–45). On the text known as Ambrose's *Explanatio symboli*, see Satterlee, *Ambrose of Milan's Method*, 153n41. For the critical edition of these texts, see *Ambroise de Milan: Des Sacraments; Des Mystères*, SC 25, ed. and trans. Dom Bernard Botte, OSB (Paris: Cerf, 1950).

18. At least that is the lesson Augustine seems to have drawn from it; cf. Harmless, *Augustine and the Catechumenate*, 97.

19. See Pamela Jackson, "Ambrose of Milan as Mystagogue," *AugStud* 20 (1989): 93–107.

20. Satterlee, *Ambrose of Milan's Method*, 118–19, drawing at least in part from Neil B. McLynn, *Ambrose of Milan: Church and Court in a Christian Capital* (Berkeley: University of California Press, 1994). Cf. *supra* where I point out how this tactic is echoed and reproduced in literary form in *Confessiones* via the use of Ambrose's hymns.

belies the unseen efficaciousness, a feature that makes it greater than any typological significance that went before, including the passage through the Red Sea, which is but a figure of this "passage from sin to life, from fault to grace, from defilement to sanctification," since "he who passes through this font does not die but rises."[21] The water of baptism is healing because, as at the baptism of Jesus, the Holy Spirit descends and consecrates the water. Christ descended into the water too, and Ambrose explains, "Why did Christ descend, except that that flesh of yours might be cleansed, the flesh which he took over from our condition? For no washing away of his sins was necessary for Christ, 'who did no sin' (1 Pet. 2:22), but it was necessary for us who remain subject to sin."[22] The whole Trinity was present at the baptism of Jesus, and the same Trinity enables this water to be efficacious.[23] The miracle of the pool of water agitated by an angel displayed the "mystery" of baptism. The angel who came to the water was a figure of Christ, whose cross and death is the source of the sacrament of baptism: "There is all the mystery, because he suffered for you. In him you are redeemed; in him you are saved." Against any form of Docetism—that is, any refusal to believe that "our Lord Jesus Christ had taken on flesh from a virgin"— Ambrose asserts that "by a man came death and by a man the resurrection" (cf. 1 Cor. 15:21). The cleansing of Naaman the Syrian prefigured both the baptism of Christ and, through that, our own baptism, while the "girl of the captives" who advised Naaman to go to Israel to be cleansed is a figure of the church while still captive to the power of the devil.[24]

The human being was created "so that, if he had not tasted sin, he would not have died the death," but because he sinned, God "made man subject to death" and the divine sentence could not be resolved by human beings on their own. At baptism, "whoever is baptized is baptized in the death of Jesus" (cf.

21. *Sac.* 1.12 (SC 25:58; ET Ambrose, *Theological and Dogmatic Works*, trans. Roy J. Deferrari, FC 44 [Washington, DC: Catholic University of America Press, 1963], 273): "transitus a peccato ad uitam, a culpa ad gratiam, ab inquinamento ad sanctificationem,—qui per hunc fontem transit, non moritur sed resurgit."

22. *Sac.* 1.16 (SC 25:59; trans. Deferrari, 274): "quare Christus descendit, nisi ut caro ista mundaretur, caro quam suscepit de nostra conditione? non enim ablutio peccatorum suorum Christo necessaria erat qui peccatum non fecit, sed nobis erat necessaria qui peccato manemus obnoxii."

23. *Sac.* 1.19 (SC 25:60); cf. 2.14 and 2.22 (SC 25:66 and 69).

24. *Sac.* 2.6–8 (SC 25:62–64; trans. Deferrari, 281–82): "ibi est omne mysterium quia pro te passus est. in ipso redimeris, in ipso saluaris"; "dominus noster Iesus carnem suscepisset ex uirgine . . . per hominem mors et per hominem resurrectio"; "puella . . . ex captiuis."

Rom. 6:10); they are made to "cling to Christ, . . . to the nails of our Lord Jesus Christ, lest the Devil be able to take you from him." Clinging to the cross, we are stuck to the death taken on "for us," and so to this taking on of death, and this is the "reformation of our nature," our "regeneration." Creation itself is a figure of this regeneration, which is therefore a kind of re-creation: "You have read about water, 'Let the waters bring forth creatures having life' (cf. Gen. 1:20–22) . . . but for you it was reserved for water to regenerate you unto grace, just as water generated other creatures unto life."[25] Ambrose tells the neophytes to "imitate the fish, which has indeed obtained less grace, yet should be an object of wonder to you," because even though it is in the sea and a storm may rage, it still swims; "so even for you this world is a sea," complete with floods and storms, but if you are as the fish, the "water of the world" will not drown you.[26] The economy of grace, of re-creation, enables one to look at the original creation from the new perspective of redemption, and its wonder is seen anew or, at least, more fully. Creation is recontextualized by the new creation in Christ, and now creation is referred to new creation almost as a figure is referred to that which it figures.

In sum, Ambrose anticipates Augustine's magnificent use of the creation story in *Confessiones*, book 13, as a type or allegory of redemption.[27] But is that not the point? Can we not say that Augustine, in not simply repeating Ambrose but attempting to capture creatively the essence of his mystagogy and thus to make it live again in literary form for his reader, has paid Ambrose the greatest possible homage? In a sense, because Augustine took it up in this way, we can see Ambrose better than we could before.

To return to *De sacramentiis*, Ambrose goes on to comment on the footwashing that followed immediately upon the baptized coming up out of the font.[28] Just as John the Baptist demurred at the prospect of baptizing Jesus, so Peter

25. *Sac.* 2.17, 2.23, 2.17, 3.1, and 3.3, respectively (SC 25:67, 69, 67, 71, 72; trans. Deferrari, 284–85, 287, 285, 289, 290): "ut, si peccatum non gustaret, morte non moreretur . . . morti hominem fecit obnoxium"; "quicunque baptizantur in morte Iesu baptizatur . . . Christo adhaeres, claui domini nostri Iesu Christi . . . ne te diabolus possit abstrahere"; "naturae . . . reformatio"; "regeneratio"; "de aquis legisti: producant aquae animantia, et nata sunt animantia . . . sed tibi reseruatum est ut aqua te regeneraret ad gratiam sicut alia generauit ad uitam."

26. *Sac.* 3.3 (SC 25:72; trans. Deferrari, 290): "imitare illum piscem qui minorem quidem adeptus est gratiam, tamen debet tibi esse miraculo. . . . ergo et tibi saeculum hoc mare est . . . saeculi . . . unda."

27. See Cavadini, "Eucharistic Exegesis," 197–98.

28. *Sac.* 3.4 (SC 25:72–73).

demurs at the prospect of Jesus washing his feet. But, in both cases, the humility of Jesus, his "righteousness" or "justice" (cf. Matt. 3:15), is what is mediated in his actions. Jesus's washing the feet of his disciples is of a piece with his going down into the Jordan in our flesh, though without sin—the final figure of his own death as descending to our dirtiness, our sinfulness—so that he can cleanse it. And, corresponding to this interrelationship among the figures, so too the rite of footwashing is not a separate sacrament (using the word somewhat anachronistically); rather, it is the completion of the cleansing action of the water of baptism, getting to the deepest level, the level of inherited sin, the level of the poison that the devil poured out onto Adam's feet. Now, the neophytes are told, like the man born blind and healed, that they can see "what you did not see before" and can "come to the altar." They have now washed in the pool of Siloam and are permitted to see the Eucharist physically, but they can now also see both Eucharist and baptism "with the eyes of the heart," having recognized "the lot of human generation"—that is, having recognized that they had "contracted sin." Taking refuge in the baptism of Christ, they can see the full extent of their humanity: each "recognizes himself as human" in his need for the cross of Christ and the font "at which Christ redeemed the errors of all."[29] In the grace of Christ, we see the full extent of our sin and, to use the language of *Confessiones*, "we can reflect on the depths from which we must cry" to God. We do this under the guidance of the mystagogical preacher, Ambrose, or, in *Confessiones*, under the guidance of the mystagogical writer who is fixing us, by rhetorical literary art, in the grace of the baptismal moment of "seeing."[30]

Commenting on the clothing with white garments, Ambrose notes that "the church, having assumed these vestments through the laver of regeneration, says in the *Song of Songs*: 'I am black but beautiful' (cf. 1:4 and 8:5)—black through the frailty of human condition, beautiful through grace; black, because I am made up of sinners, beautiful by the sacrament of faith."[31] Thus, as the bride of Christ, the church is made through the sacrament of baptism. Further, in the

29. *Sac.* 3.7; and 3.11–14, respectively (SC 25:74 and 75–77): "uidere habes quae ante non uidebas.... uenire ... ad altare"; "coris oculis ... sortem humanae generationis ... peccartum contraxi"; "agnoscit se hominem ... in quo omium Christus redemit errores."

30. *Conf.* 2.3.5 (O'Donnell, 17): "cogitemus de quam profundo clamandum sit ad te."

31. *Myst.* 7.35 (SC 25:118–19; trans. Deferrari, 17–18): "haec uestimenta habens ecclesia per lauacrum regenerationis adsumpta dicit in canticis: nigra sum et decora, filiae Hierusalem. nigra per fragilitatem conditionis humanae, decora per gratiam, nigra quia ex peccatoribus, decora fidei sacramento."

Eucharist, it is the Lord himself, "delighted with their fertility" (that of the bride and bridegroom in baptism), who says, "I have eaten my food with my honey ... drunk my drink with my milk" (cf. Song of Sol. 5:1), because in the church's sacramental eating and drinking "he himself eats and drinks in us"; therefore, in a sense, in the Eucharist we experience ourselves as so closely bound together in Christ that—as Augustine will later develop and clarify—we are not only Christians but Christ himself.[32] To the neophytes finding the types of the Eucharist, such as the manna in the desert or the multiplication of loaves and fishes in the Gospels, which they can now see as figures, Ambrose points out that the Jewish people figured the predestined people of the church and the sacraments are even more powerful than the miracles that prefigured them. "Every creature is new in Christ" in baptism, and the power that re-creates also makes the bread and wine into the body and blood of Christ, though not in appearance: "For just as you took on the likeness of death [in baptism], so, too, you drink the likeness of precious blood, that there may be no horror of blood and yet the price of redemption may be effected."[33] This is "the sacrament of that ransom price" (*cuius pretii nostri sacramentum*) to which Monica had bound her trust, the "innocent blood" (*innocentum sanguinem*), which no one could ever "reimburse" (*refundet*).[34]

To return to Augustine's characterization of his baptismal days for a moment, we can perhaps specify more fully what "truth" was distilled into Augustine's heart. Just before that passage, he exclaims, "During those days I could not get enough of the wonderful sweetness that filled me as I meditated upon your deep design [*altitudinem consilii tui*] for the salvation of the human race."[35] This "deep design" is the focus of the wonder. It is surely none other than the "deep design"

---

32. *Myst.* 9.57 (SC 25:190; trans. Deferrari, 27, slightly modified): "fertilitate earum ... delectatus ... manducaui cibum meum cum melle meo, bibi potum meum cum lacte meo ... in nobis et ipse manducat et bibit." The whole clause reads, "that in us he himself eats and drinks, just as in us you read that he says that he is in prison" ("quod in nobis et ipse manducat et bibit sicut in nobis legisti quia et in carcere esse se dicit"; cf. Matt. 25:36). Augustine used the parable of the sheep and goats to help explicate his doctrine of the *totus Christus*, which can be seen as a development of the ideas Ambrose expresses here. See, e.g., *en. Ps.* 32.2; *s.* 1.2, which incorporates Matt. 25:35, in BA 58/B:42.

33. *Sac.* 4.16, 4.20 (SC 25:83, 84; trans. Deferrari, 303, 304): "omnis ... in Christo noua creatura"; "sicut enim mortis similitudinem sumpsisti, ita etiam similitudinem pretiosi sanguinis bibis, ut nullus horror cruoris sit et pretium tamen operetur redemptionis."

34. *Conf.* 9.13.36 (O'Donnell, 118; Boulding, 235). See also "pretium meum" used eucharistically at 10.43.70 (O'Donnell, 147).

35. *Conf.* 9.6.14 (O'Donnell, 109; trans. Boulding, 219–20, slightly modified): "nec sa-

summarized in the Creed and then displayed in all its magnificence in the typologies that Ambrose used to show how God's plan for creation came to its fulfillment in Christ and in the sacraments of his new creation. Realization of this deep design of creation brought to its fulfillment in Christ is also realization of the truth of the first line of *Confessiones*: "You are Great, O Lord" (*Magnus es, domine*). Realization of this deep design is what permits an effective defense of the truth that God is *Deus Creator Omnium*, because only awareness of this deep plan obviates Manichaean objections against the Creator, as revealed in the Old Testament, even as it displays and vindicates his intentions.

More recent scholarship on Ambrose's influence contributes to the plausibility of the case I am making. Building on the work of Gerald Bruns and Robert Dodaro, Michael Cameron has specified in great detail how "Augustine's reorientation to scripture . . . was rhetorical before it was philosophical." By listening to Ambrose's preaching, Augustine came to appreciate "the Bible's strategy of accommodating truth to people at all levels of understanding"—that is, in rhetorical terminology, its *decorum* (appropriate style), which fits speech to its particular audience and is the fruit of its *dispositio* (arrangement), including the arrangement of the parts of a discourse such that its central intention or *oeconomia* can be discerned. Ambrose helped him realize that 2 Cor. 3:6, "The letter kills but the spirit gives life," cited at *Confessiones* 6.4.6 and often by Ambrose in preaching, could be theorized using these rhetorical principles and thereby matched to the further legal and rhetorical concepts of *scriptum* (letter) and *uoluntas* (intention/spirit) of the text, which, once discovered, would permit a correct application of a law in new situations.[36] If we read scripture appropriately, its spirit or overall intention will become clearer despite—and perhaps even through—apparent contradictions and difficulties. From this perspective, one can also see God's "plan of salvation," which scripture reveals, as itself a unified work of art, one that Augustine eventually likened to a "sung poem by some indescribable artist," another image reflected in his use of *Deus Creator Omnium*.[37]

---

tiabar illis diebus dulcedine mirabili considerare altitudinem consilii tui super salutem generis humani."

36. Michael Cameron, *Christ Meets Me Everywhere: Augustine's Early Figurative Exegesis*, Studies in Historical Theology (New York: Oxford University Press, 2012), 29–31.

37. Cameron, *Christ Meets Me Everywhere*, 33. Cameron also uses as an example *conf.* 11.28.38 (O'Donnell, 163), which forms part of the section introduced by book 11's analysis of *Deus Creator Omnium*. The use of the hymn here echoes its use in *conf.* 4.10.15 (O'Donnell, 39), which discusses the unity of fleeting things in the Creator's intentions.

Thus, "for Augustine rhetoric paved the way for spiritual philosophy . . . to receive the concept of immaterial reality, first from Ambrose and then from 'the books of the Platonists.'"[38] The philosophical ideas that were so crucial for Augustine's refutation of Manichaeism did not operate independently of the biblical awareness of God's plan for salvation but were instead contextualized by it.[39] We can recognize "Ambrose's rhetorical-spiritual perspective" as, in a way, forming the *Confessiones* as Augustine uses it and develops it in the service of his overarching aim for that work—namely, to praise the Creator and discredit the Manichaean claims against the goodness of the created order.[40]

PELAGIUS AND JULIAN

Augustine's references to Ambrose play an even larger role in Augustine's anti-Pelagian works and, in particular, in that controversy's last phase against Julian.[41]

38. Cameron, *Christ Meets Me Everywhere*, 41.

39. Goulven Madec, *Saint Ambroise et la Philosophie* (Paris: Études Augustiniennes, 1974), emphasizes the eclectic nature of Ambrose's use of philosophy and that, for him, the point of integration is scripture. On 344, while commenting on Ambrose's method of using philosophical sources, he writes, "Il dissocie . . . les *verba* des *res*, pour disposer librement des premiers dans son proper discours; et celui-ci, n'en doutons pas, Ambroise entend bien qu'il soit specifiquement chretien."

40. Cameron, *Christ Meets Me Everywhere*, 41–42. In an important article, Douglas Finn, "Holy Spirit and Church in the Early Augustine," *Augustiniana* 64 (2014): 153–85, builds on the work of Cameron, as well as that of David Alexander, Catherine Conybeare, and Chad Gerber, to argue further that what I would call the "Ambrosian" character of Augustine's early theology includes important reflections on the Holy Spirit. Far from being bound to a Platonist account of the three primordial hypostases, the Spirit, as revealed in scripture, actually serves to relativize the Platonist "Trinity" to a scriptural account, drawn from the "rhetorically understood, broadly incarnational trajectory" (167), which he learned from Ambrose, including what he gleaned from his *On the Holy Spirit*. Finn demonstrates a connection between Augustine's early theology of the Spirit, to whom is attributed the unity of the two testaments in a whole narrative of God's love, and his developing ecclesiology as the "locus of the Holy Spirit's work" (180).

41. Grossi, "Sant' Ambrogio," 426–28 and 434–47, provides an exhaustive list of Augustine's citations of Ambrose in the anti-Pelagian literature. M. Lamberigts, "Augustine's Use of Tradition in the Controversy with Julian of Eclanum," *Augustiniana* 60 (2010): 11–61, is a very helpful study that dedicates a section to Ambrose (29–32), the authority to whom Augustine "most often" appeals (29); there is a list of all citations in *c. Iul. imp.* at 39n149. Andrew C.

We should not be surprised to find a familiar Ambrosian presence in this new context. Ambrose taught a version of the doctrine of original sin, without that name but with many of the features that Augustine legitimately recognized as similar to his own: "As to original sin, Ambrose represents the 'humus' of the Tradition of the church and of the Augustinian doctrine."[42] In other words, Ambrose's thought was the ground from which Augustine's teaching grew. Of course, Ambrose's doctrine is not as fully developed as Augustine's, which solidified in the course of the Pelagian controversy; indeed, it differs in several significant ways. Yet the major influence of Ambrose in the polemic against Julian is only trivialized if the quest for it is limited to precisely how much of the doctrine of original sin was present in Ambrose and how much Augustine took from it, especially since judgments about how continuous or discontinuous their respective teachings were are (partly) subject to the details that an observer might choose to emphasize. Instead, Ambrose's significance is his presence in defense of the doctrine of creation against the Manichaeans. The Ambrosian Augustine, who learned from Ambrose's catechesis and mystagogy to "meditate on your [God's] deep design for the salvation of the human race" as the essential condition for effective praise of the "God" who is "Creator of all things," is present and fully operative in the *Contra Iulianum opus imperfectum* (*c. Iul. imp.*). This is ironic, of course, because Julian accused Augustine of reverting to Manichaeism in teaching original sin, thus offending against the doctrine of the goodness of both creation and Creator.

Further, for the Ambrosian Augustine, to praise God as Creator means to view creation from the perspective of the redemption planned from all eternity in Christ, enacted on the cross, and made present in the sacraments of the church. Creation thus takes its place among the true mysteries of the Christian faith as opposed to a more or less Christianized version of a philosophical doctrine available to reason without revelation. It is a moment in an economy of absolutely gratuitous gift that is above the capacity of philosophical reason to penetrate on its own; it is seen most fully from the perspective of the incarnation, passion, death, and resurrection of the Father's coequal Son. In essence it is the doctrine of creation that is contested in the controversy with Julian.[43] The Ambrosian

---

Chronister, "Doctor Traditionum: Augustine and Appeals to Tradition in the Pelagian Controversy" (PhD diss., St. Louis University, 2016), is the most thorough recent study.

42. Grossi, "Sant' Ambrogio," 455.

43. Mathijs Lamberigts, "Julian of Aeclanum: A Plea for a Good Creator," *Augustiniana* 38, no. 1/4 (1988): 5–25, makes the case that Julian's fundamental objection to Augustine's

Augustine realizes that the contestation of the doctrine of grace is only a symptom of a deeper contestation that brings us back to anti-Manichaean basics.

According to Augustine, it is actually Julian who frames the issue this way. For Julian, what most distinguishes Manichaeans from Catholics is that Catholics "ascribe every sin to an evil will, but the Manichaeans ascribe it to an evil nature."[44] Julian argues that it is not just for anyone to be condemned for a sin they did not personally will but, rather, obtained by nature: "The roles then, of creator and creature, that is of God and human beings, are under examination here." The question of the relationship between Creator and creature resolves itself into a question of justice. Julian appeals to the Stoics, who, he says, characterize justice as the greatest of the virtues, "for it carefully serves the function of restoring to each person what is due without fraud and without favor [*gratia*]."[45] If justice did not exist, Julian exclaims, "God would not exist."[46]

Augustine responds by insistently asking "what sort of justice," then, "has recompensed the little ones with a heavy yoke of such great and obvious misery?" "For," Augustine says later, "you do not, of course, find a way to show that God is just if even in the newborn he finds no sins and yet weighs them down with a corruptible body and with so many and such great troubles besides." Later still, he points out that "many of them are . . . ailing and twisted and deformed with countless defects."[47] Augustine charges that by ignoring the

---

doctrine of original sin was based on the doctrine of creation, and this would imply that the controversy was, fundamentally, about that doctrine. Lamberigts aligns himself (along with Solinac) with Julian on the issue of the transmission of original sin by concupiscence (23) but, on the other hand, realizes that Julian does not even begin to answer Augustine's deeper questions about human suffering: "How to explain intellectual, mental deficiencies within a creationist view?" (24). Thanks to Jonathan Yates for directing my attention to this article.

44. *C. Iul. imp.* 1.24 (CSEL 85.1:21; trans. Teske, *Answer to the Pelagians III*, WSA I/25, 65): "omne peccatum uoluntati malae, illi uero malae conscribunt naturae." Throughout this section, Teske's translations are occasionally adjusted. Peter Brown, *Augustine of Hippo* (Berkeley: University of California Press, 1967), 388n4, famously notes that "Julian, significantly, skirts round Augustine's citations from Ambrose: *Op. Imp.* 4.110–13."

45. *C. Iul. imp.* 1.24 (CSEL 85.1:21; trans. Teske, WSA I/25, 65).

46. *C. Iul. imp.* 1.35 and 1.38 (CSEL 85.1:25–26 and 28; trans. Teske, WSA I/25, 68 and 69): "creatoris hic igitur et creaturae ratio uertitur id est dei et hominis . . . fungens diligenter officio ad restituendum sua unicuique sine fraude sine gratia"; and "deus non esset."

47. *C. Iul. imp.* 1.35, 3.48 (cf. 4.114), and 3.95 (CSEL 85.1:85, 388, 420; trans. Teske, WSA I/25, 68, 309, 330): "qua iustitia retributum sit paruulis graue iugum tam magnae manifestaeque miseriae"; "nam prorsus, quomodo iustum ostendatis deum, non inuenitis, si et in nascentibus

miseries of infants, who are incapable of sinning by their personal will, Julian is playing into the hands of the Manichaeans, for "Mani says that bodies of flesh do not belong to the creation of the good God, but to the evil nature, and that Christ was not raised from the dead, but did not die." "Do bodies not belong to the nature of human beings?" Augustine asks. "Or, as the Manichaeans say, is the good soul held captive in the bodies of the nation of darkness? You refuse to notice and bear in mind how much help you give, though unwittingly, to their madness." He points out that the Manichaean critique of the Catholic doctrine of creation is pointedly centered on the suffering of infants: "Look, the Manichaeans say, This mortal flesh is not a part of God's creation, but a product of the nation of darkness, so that even the bodies of human beings who you say were made to the image of God are born, not only corruptible and subject to the condition of death, but also are often born defective."[48] The doctrine of original sin, by contrast, traces infant sufferings to the damage inflicted on human nature by the willing sin of our first parents. If Julian cannot admit this, Augustine insists, "the Manichaeans will force you to attribute human bodies to an evil and unjust maker."[49]

It is in this context that Ambrose comes to the rescue precisely as the defender of creation against the Manichaeans. Augustine challenges Julian: "Put the Manichaeans and Ambrose into the ring and choose which side you favor, if you want to be Catholic, in the spectacle of the fight. I think that you will judge Ambrose the victor . . . for Ambrose undoubtedly defeats both you and the Manichaeans."[50] In fact, Augustine has been putting Ambrose in the ring from

peccata nulla inuenit et eos tamen corruptibili corpore et tot tantisque insuper calamitatibus aggrauat"; and "multa in eis innumerabili uitiositate languida distorta deformia."

48. *C. Iul. imp.* 3.94, 3.95 (CSEL 85.1:419, 420; trans. Teske, WSA I/25, 329, 330): "manicheus autem dicat carnis corpora non pertinere ad boni dei creaturam, sed ad mali naturam nec Christum a mortuis suscitatum, sed non esse mortuum"; and "numquid ad hominum naturam non pertinent corpora? aut quod manichei dicunt, quorum dementiam nescientes quidem, sed, quantum adiuuetis, aduertere et cogitare non uultis, gentis tenebrarum corporibus anima bona tenetur ammixta . . . ecce manichei dicunt: usque adeo caro ista mortalis non ad opificium dei, sed ad gentis pertinet tenebrarum, ut etiam hominum corpora, quos ad imaginem dei factos esse perhibetis, non solum corruptibilia et condicioni mortis obnoxia, uerum etiam uitiosa saepe nascantur."

49. *C. Iul. imp.* 3.104 (CSEL 85.1:425; trans. Teske, WSA I/25, 333): "ne manichei uos cogant humana corpora tribuere artifici maligno et iniusto."

50. *C. Iul. imp.* 3.178 (CSEL 85.1:480; trans. Teske, WSA I/25, 368): "manicheos Ambrosiumque committite atque in spectaculo huius certaminis, si catholici estis, cui parti faueatis,

the beginning of the work. Infants, he has said, "have a body dead on account of sin," a sin that is "present in the newborn, but it begins to be seen with them as they grow up," and yet "the origin of this sin, nonetheless, comes from the will of a sinner. 'For Adam existed, and we all existed in him; Adam perished, and all perished in him.'" Calling Ambrose his *doctor meus* or "teacher," and "a man highly praised by the lips of your teacher [i.e., Pelagius]," Augustine adds words from Ambrose's *De Paradiso* 13.67 that show that Ambrose believed that Adam clothed himself with fig leaves out of shame for sin that had been committed in paradise, and these words are followed immediately by a second citation, from book 7 of *Tractates on Luke* (*in Luc.*).[51]

He follows up with yet another passage from Ambrose, this time from his *De paenitentia* (*Paen.*) 1.3.13: "We were all born under the power of sin, and our very origin lies in guilt." Referring to Julian's reliance on "justice" for judging claims about the Creator, he cites Julian's allegation that it is unjust for newborns, if they "have not been reborn . . . before attaining the choice of their own will," to be condemned "on account of the sins of others" and, worse, that the condemnation occurs "by him who 'manifests his love in us' (Rom. 5:8), who loved us and 'did not spare his own Son, but handed him over for us' (Rom. 8:32)."[52] One reply to this, Augustine says, would be Rom. 11:22—"his judgments are inscrutable"—but he knows that this would only make his critics angrier. Stick with judges that everyone acknowledges are credible, like Ambrose, Augustine advises, quoting *Tractates on Luke* 7.234 yet again: "Adam existed, and we all existed in him; Adam perished, and all perished in him." To the objection that "they ought not to have perished for the sins of others," Augustine replies, "They are the sins of others, but they are the sins of our [first] parents, and for this reason they are ours by

eligite. puto, quod a uobis uictor Ambrosius iudicatur . . . et uos enim et manicheos sine dubio uincit Ambrosius."

51. *C. Iul. imp.* 1.47–48 (CSEL 85.1:36–37; trans. Teske, WSA I/25, 74–75): "inest eis corpus mortuum propter peccatum . . . inest quidem nascentibus, sed in eis crescentibus incipit apparere . . . origo tamen etiam huius peccati descendit a uoluntate peccantis. fuit enim Adam et in illo fuimus omnes; periit Adam et in illo omnes perierunt . . . meus, tui quoque doctoris excellenter ore laudatus." For the quotation from *In Luc.* 7.234, see SC 52*bis*:96. For *Par.* 13.67, see CSEL 32.1:325.

52. *C. Iul. imp.* 1.48 (CSEL 85.1:39–40; trans. Teske, WSA I/25, 76): "omnes . . . sub peccato nascimur, quorum ipse ortus in uitio est . . . non renati . . . ante propriae uoluntatis arbitrium, propter aliena . . . peccata . . . qui commendat caritatem suam in nobis, qui dilexit nos et filio suo non pepercit, sed pro nobis illum tradidit." Cf. 1.2 (CSEL 85.1:6–7).

the law of propagation and growth. Who set us free from this state of being lost but he who 'came to seek what was lost' (Luke 19:10)?"[53]

Reflecting on this sequence of thought, it is tempting to think that a passage like Rom. 11:22 is invoked only in order to shut down the argument. But Augustine's thought points in a different direction. The idea seems to be that one has to contemplate the mystery of human nature as created from the perspective of its redemption by the one who, in a passage invoked by Julian, "did not spare his own Son," the very Son whom we know, carrying forward Ambrose's anti-Arian theology invoked in *Confessiones*, to be both human and coequal to the Father.[54] Such lavish love! Doesn't it require us to look at the "law of human propagation and growth," an element of human nature as created, through this lens? Augustine implies that Julian's problem is really with these laws, which make it so that original sin is handed down. Are these laws, which entail a kind of solidarity that is at once physical and social, really fair?[55] After all, is it "just" that human beings are procreated this way, with no choice of their own as to their father, completely vulnerable on that score? Is this kind of primal human

---

53. *C. Iul. imp.* 1.48 (CSEL 85.1:40; trans. Teske, WSA I/25, 76): "inscrutabilia sunt iudicia eius . . . fuit . . . Adam et in illo fuimus omnes; periit Adam et in illo omnes perierunt . . . peccatis . . . alienis non utique perire debuerunt . . . aliena sunt, sed paterna sunt, ac per hoc iure seminationis atque germinationis et nostra sunt. quis ab hac perditione liberat nisi qui uenit quaerere quod perierat."

54. On the influence of Ambrose on Augustine's Christology, see Brian Daley, SJ, "The Giant's Twin Substances: Ambrose and the Christology of Augustine's *Contra sermonem Arrianorum*," in *Augustine: Presbyter Factus Sum*, ed. Joseph T. Lienhard, Earl C. Muller, and Roland J. Teske (New York: Lang, 1993), 477–95. On 487, Daley argues that 419's *c. s. Ar.* is influenced by a fresh reading of Ambrose's *De incarnatione dominicae sacramento* and *De fide* I-II, which prompts Augustine to distinguish "the human experiences and human reality of Christ . . . more unambiguously, more metaphysically, from his divine nature" in order to avoid being "drawn into the Arian error of conceiving the Word as limited by his very identity with a human soul and body." Of course, the precisely correct Christology is absolutely crucial to any defense of the Creator against the Manichaeans.

55. Augustine dwells on these laws at considerable length in *c. Iul. imp.* 6.22 (CSEL 85.2:367–68). They are the "natural laws of propagation in the creatures which God willed to be born, generation after generation, according to their kind"; they are "great and impenetrable by any thought." An element of them is the desire, implanted in the human, to know whose children are your own; another is indicated by the way we can say "Israel was a slave in Egypt," even though not all Israelites ever were in Egypt individually, etc. This is due to "some sort of invisible and intangible power." Thus the "inscrutability" of God's designs go back to before (so to speak) God's election, to creation itself.

solidarity, willed by the Creator, itself just? Or are *all* "his judgments" truly "inscrutable," including the rationale for these laws? "In those, then, whom he sets free we embrace his mercy, but in those whom he does not set free we acknowledge his judgment which is indeed most hidden, but undoubtedly most just," Augustine concludes.[56] Augustine seems to be saying: "justice" has no purchase in the universe if there is no freedom, and it is God's freedom, revealed as inscrutably gratuitous love in the redemption, that underwrites all freedom and therefore all justice and therefore all creation.[57] To insist on a justice accessible to reason alone as the criterion for the goodness of the Creator is to want to set the terms not only for redemption but for creation itself. But that would be a kind of self-creation.

As it turns out, the passage cited from Ambrose's *Tractates on Luke* is not a one-off, unrepresentative reference to that text. It comes from Ambrose's treatment of the prodigal son, part of his treatment of the three-parable sequence from Luke 15 (*In Luc.* 7.207–43) that also includes the woman in search of the lost coin and the man who searches for one lost sheep—who "came to seek what was lost" (Luke 19:10). Augustine used Luke 15 just a little earlier (1.48) in association with the Ambrose passage, with Luke 19:10 added to the mix in order to bring out the christological reference in 15:3–7,[58] a link that Ambrose suggests. In 7.208–9 of *Tractates on Luke* Ambrose says the lost sheep is the human being, who perished in Adam, and the good shepherd is Christ, who carries us in/by his body, for he took upon himself our sins. The shoulders of Christ are the arms of the cross: "Just as," Ambrose quotes Paul, "all have died in Adam, so all will receive life in Christ" (1 Cor. 15:22) because all receive life in his body, the church, "since 'we all form but one body'" (1 Cor. 10:17). The death in Adam is one way of being in solidarity as humans; the life in Christ is a new way of being in solidarity as human beings, in a communion we did not give ourselves but received as "members of his members" (1 Cor. 12:27). And the mercy we receive is the mercy, Ambrose says, of the Father, administered through the Son and assisted by the church. Here, for Ambrose, the solidarity mercifully given in Christ's body, the church, provides perspective from which to contemplate, to see fully, the old solidarity in Adam (i.e., in death). Is not this the mystagogical Ambrose we

56. *C. Iul. imp.* 1.48 (CSEL 85.1:40; trans. Teske, WSA I/25, 76).

57. Thus, Augustine later rebukes Julian, "you destroy free choice by defending it" (*c. Iul. imp.* 3.103 [CSEL 85.1:424; trans. Teske, WSA I/25, 332]: "liberum arbitrium defendendo premitis") because Julian's defense, as Augustine sees it, undercuts the doctrine of creation.

58. Augustine mentions "mercy" (*misericordia*) right after he cites Luke 19:10.

have met, alive and well, carried into Augustine's text by this invocation of his tractates on Luke?[59]

It is also interesting to notice the context of the passage from *De paenitentia*, because this, too, is not just a one-off citation taken out of context by Augustine. Ambrose begins *De paenitentia* 1.3.12–14 with a reference to Rom. 8:3–4, a passage of scripture that is very important to Augustine: "For God, sending his own Son in the likeness of sinful flesh, and for sin condemned sin in the flesh, that the justice of the law might be fulfilled in us," commenting that "he does not say 'in the likeness of flesh,' for Christ took on himself the reality not the likeness of flesh; nor does he say 'in the likeness of sin,' for he did no sin, but was 'made sin' for us."[60] That he had "our flesh" truly, but not "the failings of the flesh," is because he was "not begotten, as is every human being, by intercourse between male and female, but born of the Holy Spirit and the Virgin," and therefore "he received a stainless body, which . . . no sins polluted," unlike us, "for we are all born under sin, and our very origin is in evil, as we read in the words of David." He then quotes Ps. 51:5, a verse that leads him to Rom. 7:24: "Therefore the flesh of Paul was a body of death, as he himself says, 'Who shall deliver me from the body of this death?'" In Ambrose's words, Paul answers, "But the flesh of Christ condemned sin, which he felt not at his birth, and crucified by his death, so that in our flesh there might be justification through grace, in which before there had been pollution by guilt."[61] The point is that we have, through grace, justification *in flesh*, not just in spirit, and in *our* flesh, truly shared by Christ. Even in Ambrose flesh as "ours" is not just physical but qua physical is the locus of our most intimate social solidarity with each other. This communion is the site of the work

59. Cf. n. 30 *supra*.

60. *Paen.* 1.3.12 (SC 179:62; trans. H. de Romestin, *NPNF*[2] 10:331, slightly modified; cf. *c. Iul. imp.* 4.59–60 [CSEL 85.2:66–67]): "deus filium suum mittens in similitudinem carnis peccati, et de peccato damnauit peccatum in carne, ut iustificatio legis inpleretur in nobis. non 'in similitudinem carnis' ait, quia Christus ueritatem suscepit carnis humanae, non similitudinem; neque 'in similitudinem peccati' ait, quia peccatum non fecit, sed peccatum pro nobis factus est."

61. *Paen.* 1.3.12–13 (SC 179:62–64; trans. de Romestin, *NPNF*[2] 10:331, slightly modified): "carnem . . . nostram . . . carnis huius uitia . . . sicut omnes homines ex uiri erat et feminae permixtione generatus, sed natus de spiritu sancto et virgine inmaculatum corpus susceperat, quod non solum nulla uitia maculauerant. . . . nam omnes homines sub peccato nascimur, quorum ipse ortus in uitio est, sicut habes lectum dicente Dauid. . . . ideo Pauli caro corpus mortis erat, sicut ipse air: quis me liberabit de corpore mortis huius? Christi autem caro damnauit peccatum, quod nascendo non sensit, quod moriendo crucifixit, ut in carne nostra esset iustificatio per gratiam, ubi erat ante colluuio per culpam."

of grace and is rewoven in the justice of God's sending his Son in our flesh but with his loving acceptance of it as still subject to death and thus as the likeness of sinful flesh. The flesh is real; the "likeness" is a choice of love. "'What, then, shall we say to this,' except that which the Apostle said: 'If God is for us, who is against us? He who spared not his own Son, but gave him up for us all, how has he not with him also given us all things?'"[62]

In other words, two of the three passages of Ambrose from which Augustine borrows, seem, in the early sections of *Contra Iulianum opus imperfectum*, to provide Augustine with a cluster of Ambrosian scriptural passages, which he weaves in and out of his own argument, having begun the whole sequence with an evocation of the infant's body as the "body dead on account of sin."[63] Against Julian, Augustine emphasizes and develops Ambrose's scriptural cluster to support the assertion that the "deathly" condition of human nature goes back to the will of Adam, who deformed the solidarity of human beings. Human solidarity is primordially and irreducibly enfleshed by the "laws of propagation" at once social and physical. Its social dimension is irreducibly mediated by and in the flesh, as a solidarity in Adam's will, and the same is true for Christ's choice to take on real flesh not in its unfallen form but, as Rom. 8:3 says, in the "likeness of sinful flesh."

Augustine further peppers *Contra Iulianum opus imperfectum*, book 1, with citations from *De paenitentia* 1.3.13, which are never just citations of that passage but, like a magnet, draw along with it the scriptures with which it is grouped (at least implicitly). In two of the other references to Ambrose in book 1, two scriptural passages are drawn along explicitly—namely, Ps. 51:7 and Rom. 7:24.[64] In connection with a citation of *De paenitentia* 1.3.13, Augustine reminds Julian that he, Augustine, "received the bath of rebirth from this bishop of Italy who preached and taught this faith." We noted *supra* that Augustine, in recalling his baptism, is not recalling a brief ritual moment, however efficacious, but rather a whole season of formation and ritualized instruction. He is teaching the "faith of Ambrose," passed on in that instruction, and Ambrose was someone who was

62. Cf. Rom. 8:31–32; *Paen.* 1.3.14 (SC 179:64; trans. de Romestin, NPNF² 10:331, slightly modified): "quid ergo dicemus ad haec, nisi quod dixit apostolus: si deus pro nobis, quis contra nos? qui filio proprio non pepercit, sed pro nobis omnibus tradidit eum quomodo non etiam cum illo omnia nobis donauit?"

63. Cf. Rom. 8:10. *C. Iul. imp.* 1.47 (CSEL 85.1:33–36) and repeated at 1.49 (CSEL 85.1:41–42). Rom. 8:10 functions similarly to Rom. 7:24 in the Ambrosian cluster. Cf. *c. Iul. imp.* 4.48 (CSEL 85.2:52–53), where Rom. 7:24 and 8:3 are explicitly connected.

64. *C. Iul. imp.* 1.52 and 1.59 (CSEL 85.1:45–48 and 55–57).

"very different from, very opposed to" Augustine's various Manichaean teachers. To teach the faith of Ambrose is to defend the Creator and the doctrine of creation against them. This faith of Ambrose is that infants, who, like the rest of us, are burdened with the "body of death" with its attendant miseries through no personal fault, have the same need we all have. They "need as their savior the Creator by whose work they were born. And, thus, by being reborn they are transferred from Adam to Christ."[65] The savior is the Creator in the "faith of Ambrose." We see again the primordial mystagogic dynamic of contemplating all parts of God's plan from the perspective of its fulfillment, which shows that it is in fact a plan. So we do not contemplate generation (the laws of human propagation) apart from regeneration, birth apart from rebirth, Creation apart from salvation. In fact, we see the Creator and his work in the fullest possible resolution only by contemplating his work as savior.

Still later in book 1, Augustine quotes Ambrose: "Little ones who have been baptized are restored from evil to the original state of their nature." In the immediate context of *Tractates on Luke* 1.37, Ambrose cites Elijah's splitting the waters of the Jordan (2 Kings 2:4) so that the waters flowed backward toward their source (cf. Josh. 3:16), saying that it "signifies the future mysteries of the saving bath, by which the baptized are re-formed [*reformantur*] from evil to the original state of their nature."[66] If it is true that the baptized, including little ones, are restored to the primordial state of their nature by baptism, then it is the state of the baptized that will tell us about the primordial or original state, since that state of the baptized is what is present to us now. It is sacramentally present in those who, "by being reborn . . . are transferred from Adam to Christ." "Those," he tells Julian, "who are poisoned by your arguments must be admonished to look upon Christ and to see in the righteousness [*iustitia*] of that man, the mediator, grace apart from merits," because "human beings who are reborn in Christ are made righteous by the same grace by which Christ was born a righteous man." Since "this man was never a man

---

65. *C. Iul. imp.* 1.59–60 (CSEL 85.1:57–58; trans. Teske, WSA I/25, 86–87): "ab isto episcopo Italiae hanc praedicante et docente lauacrum regenerationis accepi . . . fidem . . . Ambrosii . . . longe his dissimilis longeque contrarius . . . quo creatore nati sunt hoc indigent saluatore et ideo renascendo ex Adam transferuntur ad Christum."

66. *C. Iul. imp.* 1.123 (CSEL 85.1:137; trans. Teske, WSA I/25, 135): "in primordia naturae suae, qui baptizati fuerint paruuli, a malitia reformantur." Here Augustine is citing Ambrose *In Luc.* 1.37 (SC 45bis:65; trans. is my own; cf. *myst.* 51 [SC 25:124–25]): "significat salutaris lauacri futura mysteria, per quae in primordia naturae suae qui baptizati fuerint paruuli a militia reformantur."

in such a way that he was not the Only-begotten Son of God on account of the Only-Begotten Word," there is no way that, as man, he could have merited this: "nor did he earn his being such by the merits of his actions coming from his own will."[67] He did not even exist as man before he was conceived of the Holy Spirit— he, too, obeyed the laws of propagation. Although conceived in an extraordinary manner, he still was conceived; he still, as human, had no way of deserving that conception and no way of humanly willing that conception. But, as Ambrose spells it out, his righteousness or justice comes from that conception: "Inasmuch as he was born of the Holy Spirit, he refrained from sin." Augustine comments that "human beings who are his members are changed from evil to good by the same grace by which that man was made good from the beginning."[68]

The relative clause "who are his members" is important. They were made his members by the grace of baptism, by being "reborn," and thus they are "transferred from Adam to Christ" by being made Christ's members. They are not taken out of the fleshly solidarity that is proper to the laws of propagation; rather, the grace of the sacrament regenerates, as it were, that fleshly solidarity so that it is now renewed or reborn in the same utter gratuity and grace in which Christ was conceived. We are, as it were, incorporated into his conception. This does not mean losing the body or leaving behind being human by removing a part of ourselves as the Manichaeans believed. Rather, it means being human in and through a physical, fleshly solidarity that is a return, sacramentally, to the primordial state of solidarity as we were created. Now we have Christ's "justice," a function of pure grace, defining our new solidarity, which, though "transferred from Adam to Christ," is still a human solidarity, a solidarity in and of human nature, a solidarity in the flesh. It is now—indeed, it always was—a solidarity in a "justice" based not on merit but on God's gratuitous and loving act, on the very same grace that made Christ truly human even though united to the Word.

---

67. *C. Iul. imp.* 1.60, 1.140, and 1.138, respectively (CSEL 85.1:58, 156–57; trans. Teske, WSA I/25, 87, 147, 145): "renascendo ex Adam transferuntur ad Christum . . . sunt ammonendi, qui uestris disputationibus uenenantur, ut Christum attendant et in illius hominis mediatoris iustitia gratiam sine meritis uideant . . . homines, qui renascuntur in Christo, qua gratia iustus homo natus . . . ipse homo numquam ita fuit homo, ut non esset unigenitus dei filius, propter unigenitum uerbum. neque enim ut hoc esset, morum suorum de propria uoluntate uenientium meritis comparauit."

68. *C. Iul. imp.* 1.138 (CSEL 85.1:154; trans. Teske, WSA I/25, 145): "quasi de spiritu natus abstinuit a delicto . . . qua . . . gratia homo ille ab initio factus est bonus, eadem gratia homines, qui sunt membra eius, ex malis fiunt boni." Cf. *Ambrose, Myst.* 59 [SC 25:128]).

Conclusion

The foregoing shows us the importance of contemplating creation from the perspective of redemption. It is the only adequate vantage point for the defense of the doctrine of creation. From this perspective, we see that there is no "justice" that can give an adequate account of itself independent of the "justice" we see revealed in the savior. There is no justice anywhere apart from freedom, and if the creation we see does not arise out of God's utterly free and unbound gratuity and grace (not just any gratuity, but that by which the Son of God was conceived as a human, that revealed in the Creator's not sparing his own Son for those who deserved the opposite), then justice is only an abstract conception of the human mind in its deformed and deforming attempt to set the terms for creation and, thus, to create itself. This so-called justice is part of the effort of the fallen mind to justify the project of self-creation. One of the benefits of seeing these latest iterations of Augustine's theology of grace through an Ambrosian lens is that it helps us think a little differently about the Pelagian controversy as a controversy not simply about grace and free will but about the very meaning of the doctrine of creation itself.[69]

---

69. One late, but clearly relevant, citation of Ambrose that is rarely noted in these discussions occurs in *doctr. chr.* 4.21.46. The citation, adduced by Augustine as an example of the plain style of eloquence, is borrowed from *De spiritu sancto* 1.prologue 2–3 (CSEL 79:16). In the context of an exegesis of Judg. 6:11–21, Ambrose mentions the "flesh [of Christ] which has flooded the hearts of thirsty people with the perennial river of his blood ... [and which,] filled with the divine Spirit, would burn up all the sins of the human condition" ("carnem [i.e., Christi] quae sitientium corda populorum perenni riuo sui sanguinis inundauit, spiritu replete diuino peccata omnia humanae conditionis exureret"; *La Doctrine Chrétienne*, BA 11/2:396; trans. Hill, *Teaching Christianity*, WSA I/11, 229). Cf. *c. Iul. imp.* 5.9 (CSEL 85.2:177–78). Note that Augustine is charging that the Pelagians defeat the logic and efficacy of the church's sacraments, though it is the reverse that is commonly received wisdom—namely, that it is Augustine's doctrine of grace that undercuts the sacraments—just as it is received wisdom that Augustine undercuts the doctrine of creation, while the Pelagians are its defenders, contrary to the argument we have adopted here.

Chapter 14

AUGUSTINE AND AMBROSIASTER

Theodore de Bruyn

INTRODUCTION

It may not be surprising that a chapter on Augustine and Ambrosiaster is included in this volume, but it should be. The two writers are incommensurable on most measures: intellectual acumen, rhetorical facility, literary production, contemporary importance, and subsequent influence. I suspect that the anonymous Roman author (probably a presbyter) known to us only by the pejorative epithet "Ambrosiaster" would himself have found his association with the later African bishop to be somewhat unexpected.[1] Indeed, had Augustine in *Contra duas epistulas Pelagianorum* (*c. ep. Pel.*) not quoted an excerpt—without context—from Ambrosiaster's commentary on Romans to support his own interpretation of Rom. 5:12,[2] and had he later not adduced the same writer, whom he mistakenly identified as Hilary, bishop of Poitiers, in *Contra Iulianum opus imperfectum* (*c. Iul. imp.*),[3] it is unlikely that Ambrosiaster would have figured as largely in Augustinian scholarship as he has or that this volume would have included a chapter on him.

Yet, despite their differences in ability, position, oeuvre, and significance, the two writers are similar in other respects. Both were committed to expounding

---

1. On the name, status, and writings of Ambrosiaster, see David G. Hunter, "The Author, Date, and Provenance," in *Ambrosiaster's Commentary on the Pauline Epistles: Romans*, trans. Theodore S. de Bruyn, ed. Andrew Cain, WGRW 41 (Atlanta: SBL Press, 2017), xxiii–xxix.
2. *C. ep. Pel.* 4.4.7 (CSEL 60:528).
3. *C. Iul. imp.* 2.33, 2.164 (CSEL 85.1:186, 285).

the teaching of the church as they understood it in their time, and the opponents they confronted in doing so were often the same, including, most notably, Manichaeans and Donatists.[4] Both turned to the scriptures as the principal source of instruction for Christians, and both persisted in their efforts to arrive at a satisfactory explanation when they encountered difficult passages in those scriptures. Both wrote as much for themselves as for others, and each employed the question-and-answer format to deal with problems that arose from a passage of scripture, a point of theology, or the teaching of an opponent. Finally, both displayed a degree of originality when dealing with such problems, and both were tenacious in holding to their positions even if others disagreed or objected.

It is likely that Augustine at one time had access to both of Ambrosiaster's principal works, the *Commentarius in epistulas Paulinas* (*In Rom.*, *In 1 Cor.*, etc.) and the *Quaestiones ueteris et noui testamenti* (*Qu.*). The commentaries Augustine wrote on Romans and Galatians in 394–395 CE—that is, during the three or four years following his ordination to the priesthood in which he began a careful study of Paul's letters—occasionally echo language and ideas found in Ambrosiaster's commentaries on those letters.[5] Scholars have also found evidence of acquaintance with Ambrosiaster's *Quaestiones* in Augustine's work.[6] That Augustine did not name Ambrosiaster is not unusual; like most writers of his time, he rarely names his sources, unless he is obliged to expose them for polemical purposes. Moreover, from an early date Ambrosiaster's work circulated either anonymously or pseudonymously.[7] Since Augustine was not slavish when using the work of other writers, but rather integrated insights gathered from them into arguments

---

4. On the polemical dimensions of Ambrosiaster's writings, see Emanuele Di Santo, *L'Apologetica dell'Ambrosiaster: Cristiani, pagani e giudei nella Roma tardoantica* (Rome: Istituto Patristico Augustinianum, 2008); for a brief overview, see Theodore S. de Bruyn, Stephen A. Cooper, and David G. Hunter, "Polemical Aspects of the Commentary," in *Ambrosiaster's Commentary*, xcvii–cxiii.

5. A. A. R. Bastiaensen, "Augustine's Pauline Exegesis and Ambrosiaster," in *Augustine: Biblical Exegete*, ed. Frederick Van Fleteren and Joseph C. Schnaubelt, ColAug 4 (New York: Lang, 2001), 33–54; cf. Eric Plumer, *Augustine's Commentary on Galatians: Introduction, Text, Translation, and Notes*, OECS (Oxford: Oxford University Press, 2003), 54–55.

6. Coelestinus Martini, *Ambrosiaster: De auctore, operibus, theologia* (Rome: Athenaeum Antonianum, 1944), 45–46; Jean Doignon, "'L'esprit souffle où il veut' (*Jean* III, 8) dans la plus ancienne tradition patristique latine," *Revue des sciences philosophiques et théologiques* 62 (1978): 356–57.

7. Theodore S. de Bruyn, "The Transmission and Editions of the Commentary," in *Ambrosiaster's Commentary*, xxxi–xxxiii; Marie-Pierre Bussières, "Introduction," in SC 512:33–34.

developed on his own terms, we should not expect to find verbatim or undigested borrowings. In addition, Augustine's writings in the decade between 386 and 396 were more philosophical in style and purpose than Ambrosiaster's works. Any debt to Ambrosiaster, whose *floruit* in Rome immediately preceded Augustine's sojourns there in 383–384 and 387–388, is bound to have been refashioned.

Therefore, I do not propose to use this chapter to unravel Ambrosiaster's influence on Augustine any further. Rather, I wish to show how different the prevailing concern of each writer was when he approached Paul's Letter to the Romans. Whereas Ambrosiaster read the letter as a narrative of the history of humankind, Augustine read the letter as a narrative of the history of each human being, especially as he himself experienced that history.

AMBROSIASTER ON GOD, THE DEVIL, AND SALVATION

Underlying Ambrosiaster's interpretation of Romans is his understanding of the overarching soteriological drama unfolding in human history: the story of how God rescues humankind from its subjugation to the devil, who had gained lawful dominion over humankind by cunning and deceit. As scholars have observed, the devil—also called "Satan" and "sin"—looms large in Ambrosiaster's universe.[8] According to Ambrosiaster, the devil's apostasy was motivated by pride in his position as one of the princes in the angelic hierarchy and by a desire, characteristic of a usurper, to claim the honor and lordship of God for himself.[9] Seeing that God had created matter, from which he shaped the earth and eventually the first human being, in order to demonstrate that he alone is God,[10] the devil set about cunningly to persuade the first human being to participate in his own transgression and thus be liable to the same condemnation.[11] As a result,

---

8. Di Santo, *L'Apologetica*, 431.

9. *Qu.* 1.2 (CSEL 50:17–18). On the devil as usurper in Ambrosiaster's thought, see Sophie Lunn-Rockliffe, *Ambrosiaster's Political Theology* (Oxford: Oxford University Press, 2007), 150–52.

10. *Qu.* 1.3 (CSEL 50:18); cf. *In Rom.* 5:14.3a (CSEL 81.1:172). References to Ambrosiaster's commentaries on the Pauline letters indicate the chapter and verse or verses to which the comment applies and, if relevant, the section of the comment. For example, *In Rom.* 5:14.3a refers to section 3a of the comment on Rom. 5:14, and *In Rom.* 4:23–25.2–3 refers to sections 2 and 3 of the comment on Rom. 4:23–25.

11. *Qu.* 1.4 (CSEL 50:19).

according to the just terms by which God governs and is governed, humankind legitimately fell under the devil's dominion.[12] Consequently, while people live on earth, they are continually beset by the devil's sinful insinuations, which are conveyed by way of bodily senses. When people die, as they now do as a result of the sin of the first human beings, they are sent to the underworld, the abode of death, often personified as an agent of the devil.

Fortunately, God was unwilling to let his creation languish under the devil's tyranny. The story of salvation thus becomes an unfolding narrative of how humankind is eventually released from the devil's dominion, despite the devil's continual efforts to subvert God's interventions.[13] God did not leave humankind without guidance after the fall, since people could infer from the natural order that the Creator should be honored and that their fellow human beings should be treated as they themselves would wish to be treated. When, over time, the guidance of nature was subverted by people believing that they could sin with impunity, God revealed that he would hold people accountable for their sins and taught people what they should avoid by giving the law to Moses.[14] However, the devil subverted the beneficial effects of the Mosaic law by encouraging unlawful behavior, so that humankind once more offended God and fell into the devil's power.[15] When God subsequently sent his Son to teach people how to return to his favor by accepting forgiveness and renouncing sin, the devil, jealous of Jesus's manifest influence, sought to kill him.[16]

This proves to be the turning point in the narrative. When the devil killed Jesus, unaware that he was the incarnate Son of God, the devil forfeited his legitimate claim over humankind, which had been established in a binding decree pursuant to the sin of the first human beings (cf. Col. 2:14–15).[17] One of the consequences of Christ's triumph over the devil is that all who honored God, even if

---

12. Lunn-Rockliffe, *Ambrosiaster's Political Theology*, 155–58.

13. For a concise summary with full documentation, see Vít Hušek, "*Duplex gratia*: Ambrosiaster and the Two Aspects of His Soteriology," in *Für uns und für unser Heil: Soteriologie in Ost und West*, ed. Theresia Hainthaler et al. (Innsbruck: Tyrolia, 2014), 151–59; for a more extensive discussion, see Di Santo, *L'Apologetica*, 461–92.

14. *In Rom.* 5:13.1–4 (CSEL 81.1:166–69).

15. *In Rom.* 7:8.2 (CSEL 81.1:224–25).

16. *In 2 Cor.* 5:18–21.4–5 (CSEL 81.2:238).

17. *In Rom.* 3:4.5a rec. γ; 3:24.2; 4:23–25.2–3; 7:4.1–3; 8:3.3–4 (CSEL 81.1:99, 118–21, 148–51, 214–17, 254–57); *in Col.* 2:13–15.2–4 rec. α (CSEL 81.3:185–86).

imperfectly, prior to Christ's coming are released from the underworld; they do not suffer the "second death," eternal punishment in Gehenna, the lowest level of the underworld. As Ambrosiaster explains in a comment on Rom. 5:12:[18]

> When [Adam] transgressed, he lost the gift of God, having become unworthy to eat of the tree of life, and as a result he died. |This death is the dissolution of the body, when the soul is separated from the body. <This death is the separation of the soul from the body.>| There is another death—called the second death—in Gehenna. We do not undergo it on account of the sin of Adam, |for it is acquired by one's own sins {it is acquired by the opportunity one has for one's own sins}|. The good are spared it, insofar as they are in the underworld, but in the uppermost level as if under house arrest, because they could not ascend to the heavens. They were held by the sentence given to Adam. This written bond with its decrees, |which continued to be in effect, was cancelled by Christ {was erased by Christ's death}|. {The decreed sentence was <this:> that the body of an individual person would decay on earth, but the soul, held by the bonds of the underworld, would suffer torments.}[19]

18. Ambrosiaster's commentary on Romans is preserved in three successive versions, identified in the CSEL edition as *recensiones* α, β, and γ. Since this chapter will trace developments in Ambrosiaster's interpretation of the letter, changes introduced in the second and third versions (*recensiones* β and γ) are indicated in the English translation (unless the Latin variations do not alter the English sense) and in the Latin text as follows: changes introduced in *recensio* β are set between curly brackets { }, and changes introduced in *recensio* γ are set between angle brackets < >. When text in a later version replaces text in a prior version, both the initial and the revised text are placed between vertical lines | |. For a detailed discussion of the versions of Ambrosiaster's Pauline commentaries and their attribution to Ambrosiaster, see de Bruyn, "Transmission," xxxv–lv.

19. *In Rom.* 5:12.3–4 (CSEL 81.1:164–67; trans. de Bruyn, *Ambrosiaster's Commentary*, 97–98, with nn. 53, 55, 58, 59–60): "hic enim beneficium dei perdidit, dum praeuaricauit, indignus factus edere de arbore uitae, ut moreretur. |mors autem dissolutio corporis est, cum anima a corpore separatur. < mors autem separatio animae a corpore est.>| est et alia mors, quae secunda dicitur in gehenna, quam non peccato Adae patimur, |propriis enim peccatis adquiritur {sed eius occasione propriis peccatis adquiritur}|. a qua boni inmunes sunt, tantum quod in inferno erant, sed |superiori {superiore}| quasi in libera, quia ad caelos ascendere non poterant; sententia enim tenebantur data in Adam. quod cirografum in decretis |manentem a Christo euacuatum est {morte Christi deletum est}|. {sententia autem decreti <haec> fuit, ut unius hominis corpus solueretur super terram, anima uero uinculis inferni detenta exitia pateretur.}"

As for those who lived during or after the coming of Christ, even more is promised if they accept who he is and what he teaches.[20] Not only are they released from the power of the devil; all their prior sins are forgiven, and the Holy Spirit, bestowed in baptism, helps them to resist sinful temptations and habits and to develop qualities that will reveal them to be children of God.

Having reviewed the prevailing soteriological narrative that runs through Ambrosiaster's commentary on Romans, I wish to turn to his interpretation of specific passages to illustrate how that narrative is animated by his interaction with Paul's text and helps him to explain Paul's text. As one reads through Ambrosiaster's comments, one comes to appreciate how odd or puzzling Paul's manner of speaking was for Christians who were reading the letters perhaps for the first time. Paul uses words such as "law" or "flesh" or "spirit"—words that are central to his argument—in more than one sense. He personifies otherwise concrete or abstract terms, such as "circumcision" or "sin" or "death." He sets up figures known to him but not necessarily to someone unfamiliar with Jewish readings of Hebrew scripture as types encompassing whole groups of people: "Adam" and "Abraham" and "Israel." This way of speaking, as well as the complex rhetoric in which such language is deployed, requires explanation for someone reading the text naively or literally.[21]

Ambrosiaster reveals the principles that guide him when dealing with the problems posed by Paul's language in a remark he makes when he is obliged to defend his preference for an older Latin translation of Paul's letters over the Greek version of the text: "But I deem a matter to be true when reasoning [ratio] and history [historia] and authority [auctoritas] are upheld."[22] In other words, one's interpretation must be argued rationally; it must make sense of what has happened in the past, which for Ambrosiaster usually means events recorded in Hebrew and Christian scriptures, but also may include other historical events; and it must agree with what the church or reputable authorities have taught—in this instance, the precedent of Latin Christian writers whose text of the verse in question was the same as Ambrosiaster's.[23] It is instructive to observe how these

20. Hušek, "Duplex gratia," 155–57.

21. For a detailed overview of the rhetorical construction of the letter, see Robert Jewett with Roy D. Kotansky, Romans: A Commentary (Minneapolis: Fortress, 2007), 23–46.

22. In Rom. 5:14.5a rec. β, γ (CSEL 81.1:176–77; trans. de Bruyn, 104): "hoc autem uerum arbitror, quando et ratio et historia et auctoritas |observatur <conseruatur>|."

23. Giacomo Raspanti, "Il peccato di Adamo e la grazia di Cristo nella storia dell'umanità: Rilettura del commento di Ambrosiaster a Rom. 5, 12–21," Augustinianum 49, no. 2 (2008): 437–38.

principles come into play as Ambrosiaster explains what Paul means, especially when he changes or supplements his initial comments. I will focus on examples that relate to the overarching narrative of salvation outlined above.

ADAM AND THE POSTLAPSARIAN HUMAN CONDITION

According to Ambrosiaster's soteriological narrative, the devil gains dominion over humankind by successfully inducing the first human beings to transgress God's command, and loses that dominion by unjustly seeking to kill Jesus and hold him in the realm of the dead. Paul's comparison between Adam and Christ in Rom. 5:12–21 obviously resonates with this narrative. As Ambrosiaster says, echoing Paul's language at Rom. 5:14, "Adam is a type of the one to come, because already at that time God in a hidden way determined to rectify through the one Christ the sin that had come about through the one Adam."[24] Or, as he says when he begins to explain Rom. 5:12, "Because the one Adam sinned in everyone, so too the one Christ, the Son of God, conquered sin in everyone."[25] What this means, exactly, requires considerable discussion and teasing out.[26]

In Ambrosiaster's Latin translation of Paul's letter, the last clause of verse 12 read "in whom all sinned" (*in quo omnes peccauerunt*). Ambrosiaster understood the masculine singular relative pronoun (*quo*) to refer to Adam, as he explains when revisiting his comments: "*in whom*{—that is, in Adam—}*all sinned*."[27] But according to the biblical account of the fall (Gen. 3:1–24), which Ambrosiaster accepts as historical,[28] Eve was the first human being to transgress God's command. Paul's language, therefore, requires explanation: "Although he is speaking of the woman, he said *in whom* because he was referring to the race [*ad genus*],

24. *In Rom.* 5:14.7 (CSEL 81.1:178–79; trans. de Bruyn, 105): "|ideo que Adam {Adam autem ideo}| forma futuri est, quia iam |tunc {tum}| in mysterio decreuit deus per unum Christum emendare, quod per unum Adam peccatum erat."

25. *In Rom.* 5:12.1 *rec.* α (CSEL 81.1:162; trans. de Bruyn, 96, with n. 44): "ut quia Adam unus peccauit in omnibus, ita unus Christus filius dei peccatum uicit in omnibus."

26. For detailed expositions, see Alessandra Pollastri, *Ambrosiaster: Commento alla Lettera ai Romani; Aspetti cristologici*, Collana di testi storici 7 (L'Aquila: Japadre, 1977), 106–85; Juan B. Valero, "Pecar en Adan segun Ambrosiaster," *Estudios eclesiásticos* 65 (1990): 147–91; and Raspanti, "Il peccato di Adamo."

27. *In Rom.* 5:12.2a *rec.* β, γ (CSEL 81.1:164–65): "in quo{—id est in Adam—}omnes peccauerunt."

28. Cf. *Qu.* 31.1 (CSEL 50:58).

not to a specific manifestation [*ad speciem*]."[29] Ambrosiaster thus reconciles, somewhat awkwardly, Pauline typology with biblical history.

Ambrosiaster goes on to explain how all people sinned in Adam, something he takes to be obvious but, in fact, is not: "It is clear {, consequently,} that all sinned in Adam {as in a lump [*quasi in massa*]}. Once he was corrupted by sin, those he begat were all born under sin. All sinners, therefore, derive from him, because we are all from him."[30] For Ambrosiaster, *massa*—a term he would have encountered elsewhere in Paul's letters (Rom. 9:21; 11:16; 1 Cor. 5:6; Gal. 5:9)— refers to the corporeal matter shared by all human beings.[31] By sinning, Eve and Adam altered the condition into which all successive generations of human beings are born; the corporeal existence of all human beings is now subject to sin, which for Ambrosiaster is a personified force or power. What this means, specifically, is that their physical body is mortal—death being defined as the separation of the immortal soul from the mortal body—and is the medium through which the devil continues to tempt the soul to consent to sinful inclinations.

THE REIGN OF DEATH

Ambrosiaster, like Paul, personifies death. Death is not merely the end of human life; it is also a cosmic power. Ambrosiaster, however, has a specific notion of the limits of death's dominion, based in part on his Latin translation of Rom. 5:14. Whereas in the majority of Greek witnesses the verse reads "death reigned from Adam to Moses even over those who did not sin after the manner of Adam's transgression," in Ambrosiaster's Bible the verse read "death reigned from Adam to Moses over those who sinned after the manner of Adam's transgression." To Ambrosiaster, the version he was reading made sense of the situation in the period between Adam and Moses, when people lived under the law of nature but without the law given to Moses. As he explains, death reigned over those who neglected God the creator, the one revealed to them in nature, and instead worshiped crea-

29. *In Rom.* 5:12.2a rec. β, γ (CSEL 81.1:164–65; trans. de Bruyn, 96–97, modified): "ideo dixit in quo, cum de muliere loquatur, quia non ad speciem retulit, sed ad genus."

30. *In Rom.* 5:12.3 (CSEL 81.1:164–65; trans. de Bruyn, 97): "manifestum {itaque} est in Adam omnes peccasse {quasi in massa}. ipse enim per peccatum corruptus quos |generauit {genuit}|, omnes nati sunt sub peccato. ex eo igitur cuncti peccatores, quia ex ipso sumus omnes."

31. *In Rom.* 9:21.1 (CSEL 81.1:326–29); *In 1 Cor.* 15:39 (CSEL 81.2:178–79).

tures, because their sin was like Adam's sin. Death did not reign over those who revered God but still transgressed some other aspect of natural law.[32]

Ambrosiaster is aware of the Greek version of the verse, and he observes that it indeed appears that death (created through Satan's jealousy) reigned over those who did not sin after the manner of Adam's transgression, since in fact all people die from Adam onward.[33] But he argues that the Latin translation he is using is based on older Greek manuscripts that were free of corruptions subsequently introduced by disruptive heretics:

> In response to this we cannot remain silent, since our codices derive from ancient Greek codices, which the simplicity of the times commends as being uncorrupted. But afterward many things were changed to fit with human understanding by disruptive heretics and by those tossed about questions, so that what seemed right to people was contained in the letter of the text. For this reason even the Greeks themselves have codices that vary.[34]

When Ambrosiaster revisits his comments, he is obliged to defend the translation he is using as well as his interpretation of it.[35] No doubt, one impetus for his extended remarks was Jerome's oblique criticism in *Epistula* (*Ep.*) 27, written to Marcella in 384, of Ambrosiaster's preference for his Latin translation.[36] However, equally important, if not more so, was Ambrosiaster's awareness, derived in part from biblical history,[37] that one could distinguish the extent to which people followed or abandoned the guidance of nature in the period between Adam and Moses. Some people continued to acknowledge and honor the Creator even though they transgressed other aspects of natural law.[38] It is instructive to observe what Ambrosiaster retains and what he alters when he makes this point:

---

32. *In Rom.* 5:14.2–3 (CSEL 81.1:170–73); cf. *In Rom.* 5:13.4 (CSEL 81.1:168–69).

33. *In Rom.* 5:14.4 (CSEL 81.1:172–75).

34. *In Rom.* 5:14.4–5 *rec. α* (CSEL 81.1:176–77; trans. de Bruyn, 104n97): "respondentes ad haec non tacemus, quia codices nostri ex graecis ueteribus originem habent, quos incorruptos simplicitas temporum probat. postea autem hereticis perturbantibus et quaestiones torquentibus multa inmutata sunt ad sensum humanum, ut hoc contineretur in litteris, quod homini uideretur. unde et ipsi graeci diuersos codices habent."

35. *In Rom.* 5:14.4a–5a *rec. β, γ* (CSEL 81.1:174–79).

36. Heinrich J. Vogels, "Ambrosiaster und Hieronymus," *RBén* 66 (1956): 14–19.

37. Cf. *In Rom.* 5:13.1–3 (CSEL 81.1:166–69).

38. Cf. *In Rom.* 5:13.4; 6:17–18.2 (CSEL 81.1:168–69, 204–7).

There were also people who sinned not by neglecting God, but against natural law. For if someone understood who God is <, whether by inherited tradition or natural judgment,> and revered him, attributing to no one else the honor of his name and his majesty|—if this person sinned, he sinned against the law, because he denied it. Therefore, death did not reign in these people; rather, those in whom death reigned, they abused the Lord himself. {—if this person sinned (since it is impossible not to sin), he sinned under God, not against God, whom he perceived to be judge. Therefore, death did not reign in such people; rather, as I have said, death reigned in those who served the devil under the appearance of idols.}|[39]

When revising this comment for the first time (*recensio* β), Ambrosiaster accepts that after the fall it is impossible for people not to sin. Still, prior to the law of Moses, those who acknowledged and revered God the creator are in a different category than those who worshiped idols; the latter are under the reign of death, the former not. When revising this comment a second time (*recensio* γ), Ambrosiaster introduces a further remark acknowledging that people are influenced by the teachings or practices of their kin ("inherited tradition" [*ex traduce*]) and that people retain a natural ability to discern what is just and true ("natural judgment" [*iudicio naturali*]).

Ambrosiaster frequently refers to his interpretation of verse 14 in his comments on the remainder of Romans 5, both in the first version of his commentary and in later revisions.[40] One final example illustrates how explanatory increments like the one just cited above, introducing the notion of generational influences, are still embedded within the prevailing soteriological narrative. Romans 5:20— "Now, the law slipped in such that trespass abounded"[41]—could be read to suggest that the law operated by stealth and is in fact responsible for increased

---

39. *In Rom.* 5:14.3 (CSEL 81.1:170–73; trans. de Bruyn, 101, with nn. 86–87): "fuerunt <etiam> qui peccauerunt non praeterito deo, sed in lege naturali. qui enim intellexit <siue ex traduce siue iudicio naturali> et ueneratus est deum, nulli honorificentiam nominis ac maiestatis eius inpertiens, |si peccauit, in lege peccauit, quia denegabat. ideo que in istos mors non regnauit, in eos autem in quos regnauit, ipso domino abusi sunt {si peccauit—quia inpossibile est non peccare,—sub deo peccauit, non in deum, quem iudicem sensit. ideo que in huiusmodi mors non regnauit,<sed> in hos autem, sicut dixi, regnauit, qui sub specie idolorum seruierunt diabolo}|."

40. Cf. *In Rom.* 5:15.1; 5:16.1; 5:17.2; 5:19.1a *rec.* β, γ (CSEL 81.1:178–81, 182–83, 184–85).

41. *In Rom.* 5:20 (CSEL 81.1:184–85): "lex autem subintrauit, ut abundaret delictum."

transgression. When he revises his initial comment on this verse, Ambrosiaster substantially expands his remarks to explain that, although the law of Moses was given to revive people's natural capacity for righteous behavior, people still tended to sin, as they had prior to the law, to the point that sin became habitual and sinning increased rather than diminished.[42] But Ambrosiaster again sets this history within his larger soteriological narrative, explaining that the devil actively incited unlawful behavior so that the law would result in people being punished rather than turning to God; the forgiveness Christ offers renders the devil's stratagems futile.[43]

Dying to Sin and Living for God

The Christian participates in Christ's victory over the devil through baptism. As Ambrosiaster says when he explains what Paul means by "dying to sin" (Rom. 6:2), "When the grace of God came upon us through Christ and the spiritual bath [i.e., baptism] regenerated us through faith, we began to live for God and to be dead to sin, who is the devil."[44] Ambrosiaster repeatedly states that those who have been baptized should no longer sin.[45] And although he places the onus on believers to renounce a base life and cultivate a holy one, he also states that God will help them by the presence of his Holy Spirit.[46]

In the course of his comments Ambrosiaster explains how a person is tempted to sin and how a person can resist such temptation. It is instructive to observe how Ambrosiaster moves from Paul's figurative language to his own reasoned explanation, which becomes clearer as he revises his comments. For example, to explain what Paul means by "the body of sin" at Rom. 6:6, Ambrosiaster initially states that it refers to the entirety of one's prior sins, "destroyed by the cross of Christ; for on the cross the author of sin, who is the devil, was destroyed."[47] When Ambrosiaster revises this comment, he shifts the focus from what Christ

---

42. *In Rom.* 5:20.2a–e *rec.* β, γ (CSEL 81.1:184–87).

43. *In Rom.* 5:20.4a *rec.* β, γ (CSEL 81.1:186–89).

44. *In Rom.* 6:2 (CSEL 81.1:190–91; trans. de Bruyn, 111): "superueniente |autem {enim} <ergo>| gratia dei per Christum et |nos per fidem <per fidem nos>| lauacro spiritali regenerante coepimus uiuere deo, mortui autem esse peccato, qui est diabolus."

45. *In Rom.* 6:1.1; 6:3; 6:4.2; 6:6 (CSEL 81.1:188–95).

46. *In Rom.* 6:13.3–4 (CSEL 81.1:200–201).

47. *In Rom.* 6:6 *rec.* α (CSEL 81.1:194; trans. de Bruyn, 114n22): "omnia enim peccata

accomplished with his death to what the Christian should accomplish "through a good life and a catholic faith."[48] He expands on what this means in his comment on Rom. 6:8, where he combines Paul's language about the body with Paul's language about the flesh:

> But the flesh{—that is, the body—}is crucified only if its cravings are trampled underfoot. These cravings are produced by the sin that remains in the flesh on account of the initial transgression of the first human being. The devil is crucified in the flesh; it is he who deceives by means of the flesh. {Thus, the flesh is sometimes understood to mean the world—that is, the elements—and sometimes the body of a human being or, more precisely, the soul that pursues corporeal faults.}[49]

By differentiating several meanings of the word "flesh" and by explaining that it can also mean the disposition of the soul toward corporeal desires, Ambrosiaster, via these additional remarks, adopts a more recognizable form of psychology that locates the decision-making power of the person in the soul, as he will explain in more detail when commenting on Rom. 7 and 8. (Ambrosiaster reads Rom. 7:7–24 as describing the condition of humankind under the law prior to being rescued and forgiven through Christ, and Rom. 7:25–8:17 as describing the condition and expectations of Christians who have been rescued and forgiven.)

AMBROSIASTER AND ROMANS 7

Paul's account of the workings of "sin" in Rom. 7 becomes an occasion for Ambrosiaster to explain in more detail how the devil works within those who are

---

corpus uocat quod destructum dicit cruce Christi; in cruce enim auctor peccati destructus est, qui est diabolus."

48. *In Rom.* 6:6 *rec.* β, γ (CSEL 81.1:194–95; trans. de Bruyn, 114): "omnia enim peccata simul corpus appellat, quod destrui dicit per bonam uitam et fidem catholicam."

49. *In Rom.* 6:8.1–1a (CSEL 81.1:196–97; trans. de Bruyn, 114, with nn. 25–26): "caro uero {id est corpus} sic crucifigitur, si desideria eius calcentur, quae manente in ea peccato creantur ex praeuaricatione primi hominis coepta. in carne enim diabolus crucifigitur; ipse |est enim {enim est} <est enim>| qui fallit |in carne {per carnem}|. {caro enim <ergo> aliquando mundus, |id est <hoc est>| elementa, aliquando uero corpus hominis intellegitur, uel ipsa anima sequens corporea uitia.}"

under his dominion to incite them to sin and thus subvert the purpose of the law.[50] When he revises his comments on the chapter, Ambrosiaster does not fundamentally alter his understanding of the situation of humankind under the law. He does, however, add significant explanatory details.

Initially Ambrosiaster explains the expression "sold under sin" at Rom. 7:14 as follows: "This is what it means to be found under sin: to derive one's origin from Adam, who was the first to sin, and to become subject to sin by one's own transgression. Adam sold himself first, and as a result all his descendants are subject to sin."[51] When he revisits this comment, his additional remarks describe how humankind becomes subject to sin through a combination of inherited tradition and personal transgression and why God's forgiveness and protection are needed to escape that servitude:

> For this reason, one is not strong enough to keep the commandments of the law unless one is fortified by divine reinforcements. This is why the apostle says: "The law is spiritual, but I am fleshly, sold under sin" (Rom. 7:14). That is: the law is strong and just and blameless, but humankind is weak and in subjection because of one's ancestor's and one's own transgression, such that one is unable to use one's ability in regard to obeying the law. Therefore, one should take refuge in God's mercy in order to escape the severity of the law and, once one has been freed from the burden of transgressions, to resist the enemy from then on with God's protection.[52]

When he first comments on verse 14, Ambrosiaster already holds that the body, now corrupted, is subject to the devil, here personified as "sin": "For what does it mean to be subject to sin, but to have a body that is corrupted, by

---

50. *In Rom.* 7:8.1–2; 7:11.1–1a; 7:13.2–2a; 7:14.4, 4a, 5; 7:17–18.1–2; 7:20 (CSEL 81.1:222–25, 228–31, 234–39, 238–41).

51. *In Rom.* 7:14.2–3 *rec.* α (CSEL 81.1:232; trans. de Bruyn, 134, with nn. 66, 68, and 69): "ueniri sub peccato hoc est ex Adam, qui prior peccauit, originem trahere et proprio delicto subiectum fieri peccato. Adam enim uendidit se primus ac per hoc omne semen eius subiectum est peccato."

52. *In Rom.* 7:14.3a *rec.* β (CSEL 81.1:232–34; trans. de Bruyn, 134): "quamobrem infirmum esse hominem ad praecepta legis seruanda, nisi diuinis auxiliis muniatur. hinc est unde ait: lex spiritalis est, ego autem carnalis sum, uenumdatus sub peccato. hoc est: lex firma est et iusta et caret culpa, homo autem fragilis est et paterno uel proprio subiugatus delicto, ut potestate sui uti non possit circa obaudientiam legis. ideo est ad dei misericordiam confugiendum, ut seueritatem legis effugiat et exoneratus delictis de cetero deo fauente inimico resistat."

which sin prevails."[53] When he revises this comment, Ambrosiaster locates the responsibility for this vulnerability in the weakness of the soul: "For what does it mean to be subject to sin, but to have a body that is corrupted through the weakness of the soul, by which sin insinuates itself and drives a person like a prisoner to transgressions, so that he does its [i.e., sin's] will?"[54] In his comment on Rom. 7:18, Ambrosiaster suggests that physical and moral corruptibility are somehow linked:

He does not say{—as it seems to some people—}that the flesh is evil, but rather that what dwells in the flesh is not good but is sin. How does sin dwell in the flesh, since it is not a substance but a transgression {of the good}? Since the body of the first human being was corrupted through sin such that it became subject to decomposition, the corruption of sin remained in the body on account of the nature of the offense, maintaining the force of the divine sentence {handed down to Adam}. This is the sign |of the law of the devil {of the devil}|, at whose instigation |Adam {he}| sinned.[55]

Although Ambrosiaster here rejects the view that the body itself is evil, he nevertheless regards sensorial experiences, now under the influence of the devil, as the medium by which the devil incites the soul to sin.

When he comments on Rom. 7:22, Ambrosiaster explains why the devil does not dominate the soul in the way that he dominates the body. Although the transgression of the first human beings was an act of the soul, not the body, it corrupted the body rather than the soul. This corrupted body is now transmitted from parents to children—with the exception of Christ's body, which,

53. *In Rom.* 7:14.4 *rec.* α (CSEL 81.1:234; trans. de Bruyn, 134n70): "quid est enim subiectum esse peccato, nisi corpus habere corruptum, cui praeualet peccatum?"

54. *In Rom.* 7:14.4 *rec.* β (CSEL 81.1:234; trans. de Bruyn, 134): "quid est enim subiectum esse peccato, nisi corpus habere uitio animae corruptum, cui se inserat peccatum et inpellat hominem quasi captiuum delictis, ut faciat uoluntatem eius?"

55. *In Rom.* 7:18.1 (CSEL 81.1:236–39; trans. de Bruyn, 135–36, with nn. 79–82): "non dicit {sicut quibusdam uidetur} carnem malam, sed quod habitat in carne, non esse bonum, sed esse peccatum. quomodo inhabitat in carne peccatum, cum non sit substantia, sed praeuaricatio {boni}? quoniam primi hominis corpus corruptum est |a peccatum {per peccatum}|, ut |possit dissolui <esset solubile>|, ipsa peccati corruptio per condicionem offensionis manet in corpore, robur tenens diuinae sententiae {datae in Adam}, |quod signum est legis diaboli {quod est signum diaboli}|, cuius instinctu peccauit |Adam {---}|."

having been formed in the womb of a virgin and purified by the Holy Spirit, was like the body of Adam before he sinned.[56] The soul is given once the body is formed:[57]

> For sin dwells not in the soul but in the flesh, |which originates from sin, and all flesh exists by transmission {because the flesh originates from the sin of the flesh, and all flesh is sinful through transmission}|. For if the soul existed by transmission as well as the flesh, sin would also dwell in the soul, because the soul of Adam sinned rather than the body. But the sin of the soul corrupted the body. Therefore, sin dwells in the flesh as if at the doorway of the soul, so that it does not let the soul go where it wishes. If sin in fact did dwell in the soul, the self would never recognize itself. But as it stands, it recognizes itself and delights in the law of God.[58]

When Ambrosiaster revises this comment a second time, he is more explicit about the moral capacity that the soul retains: "Sin is not allowed to dwell in the soul on account of the free choice of the will [*arbitrium liberum uoluntatis*]."[59] For that reason, Ambrosiaster argues elsewhere, one cannot attribute one's sinful behavior to fate or destiny.[60]

Much of this is reiterated in Ambrosiaster's long comment on Rom. 7:24–25, where he explains the new situation of those who are rescued by Christ and enabled to resist the devil. Initially—to focus on what has changed—Ambrosiaster concludes his remarks as follows: "The soul, now free by the grace of God, recalled to good habits, and helped by the Spirit, is able to reject evil suggestions. The flesh is susceptible to faults because it is not able to discern and has been

---

56. Cf. *In Rom.* 8:3.1–3 (CSEL 81.1:254–55).

57. Cf. *Qu.* 23 (CSEL 50:49–51).

58. *In Rom.* 7:22 rec. α, β (CSEL 81.1:240; trans. de Bruyn, 137–38, with nn. 95 and 98): "quia non in animo habitat peccatum, sed in carne, |quae {quia}| est ex origine {carnis} peccati, et per traducem |omnis caro fit {fit omnis caro peccati}|. si enim anima de traduce esset et ipsa, et in ipsa habitaret, quia anima magis Adae peccauit quam corpus; sed peccatum animae corrupit corpus. in carne ergo habitat peccatum quasi ad ianuas animae, ut non illam permittat ire quo uult. in anima autem si habitaret, numquam se cognosceret homo. nunc autem cognoscit se et delectatur lege dei."

59. *In Rom.* 7:22 rec. γ (CSEL 81.1:241; trans. de Bruyn, 137): "in animo autem non permittitur habitare propter arbitrium liberum uoluntatis."

60. *Qu.* 115.29–30 (SC 512:180).

corrupted."[61] Ambrosiaster expands his remarks considerably when he revises this comment. He begins by saying:

> The soul, now free and recalled to good habits, is able to reject evil suggestions with the help of the Holy Spirit. The authority by which it dares to resist the enemy has been restored to it; one who is no longer submissive can in no way be entrapped against his will. But the flesh lacks the faculty of judgment and is incapable of discernment; it is, in fact, brute nature. Therefore, it is unable to block the entrance to the enemy so that when he approaches, he may not come in and persuade the soul of the wrong things.[62]

He then explains why Christians are still beset by sinful tendencies, which will end only in the life to come, when their current mortal and corruptible corporeal existence will be transformed into an immortal and incorruptible corporeal existence.[63] He continues immediately in his comments on Rom. 8:2, however, to declare that the devil's sinful suggestions will not harm Christians—at least, will not result in their being condemned to the "second death"—provided that they fight those suggestions, mindful of the help of God.[64]

AUGUSTINE AND THE ASCENT TOWARD GOD

Readers familiar with Augustine's thought will have noted similarities between Ambrosiaster's and Augustine's views of the predicament and salvation of humankind, as well as some points of evident difference.[65] Before turning to Au-

---

61. *In Rom.* 7:24–25.5 *rec.* α (CSEL 81.1:246–48; trans. de Bruyn, 141n119): "iam enim liber animus gratia dei et in consuetudinem bonam reuocatus et adiutus per spiritum potest malas suggestiones spernere. caro enim, quia discernere non potest et est corrupta, recipit uitia."

62. *In Rom.* 7:24–25.5 *rec.* β (CSEL 81.1:246–48; trans. de Bruyn, 141): "iam enim liber animus et in consuetudinem bonam reuocatus sancto spiritu adiuuante malas suggestiones potest spernere. reddita est enim illi auctoritas, qua audeat resistere inimico; qui enim iam non est obnoxius, minime poterit indagari inuitus. caro autem, quia iudicium non habet neque capax est discernendi—est enim bruta natura—, non potest inimico aditum claudere, ne ueniens introeat atque animo contraria suadeat."

63. *In Rom.* 7:24–25.5a–b (CSEL 81.1:248).

64. *In Rom.* 8:2.1 (CSEL 81.1:250–51).

65. The extent to which Ambrosiaster's views concur with Augustine's is a subject of recurring discussion. See, e.g., Josef Jäntsch, "Führt der Ambrosiaster zu Augustinus oder

gustine's reading of Romans in the years after his ordination, we should begin by noting that Augustine accepted the account, so prominent in Ambrosiaster's comments on Romans, of how the devil gained and then lost his dominion over humankind.[66] Within Augustine's oeuvre, the explanation makes its first appearance in the third book of *De libero arbitrio* (*lib. arb.*), which Augustine wrote between 391 and 395 CE.[67] All the elements mentioned in various passages by Ambrosiaster are succinctly and precisely relayed there. The methodical exposition and balanced cadences, in keeping with Augustine's training as a philosopher and with his skill as a rhetorician, nicely illustrate how Augustine was able to assimilate and refine points that are narrated more diffusely in Ambrosiaster's comments:

> The Word of God, God's only Son, assuming human nature, brought the devil, whom he has always had and will have under his own laws, under subjection to humankind. He extorted nothing from him by violence but overcame him by the law of justice. For the devil, having deceived the woman, and by her having caused her husband to fall, claimed the entire offspring of the first human being as subject to the law of death inasmuch as it was sinful. This he did with a malicious desire to do harm, but at the same time with absolute right, so long as his power prevailed, that is, until he slew the just one, in whom he could point out nothing worthy of death. Not only was he [i.e., the just one] slain without fault, but he was also born without lust. And to lust, the devil had subjugated his captives, so that he might keep possession of all born of them, as fruits of his own tree, through a wicked desire to hold them, but also by a just right of possession. Most justly, therefore, is the devil compelled to give up those who believe in him whom he unjustly slew. In that they suffer temporal death, they pay what they owe. In that they live eternally, they live

---

Pelagius?," *Scholastik* 15 (1934): 92–99; Eugene TeSelle, *Augustine the Theologian* (London: Burns & Oates, 1970), 156–60, 165–67, 177–79; A. C. de Veer, "Saint Augustin et l'Ambrosiaster," BA 23:817–24; and Valero, "Pecar en Adan," 187–91.

66. Jean Rivière, *Le dogme de la rédemption chez saint Augustin* (Paris: Gabalda, 1933), 128–29, and Jean Rivière, "Le 'droit' du démon sur les pécheurs avant saint Augustin," *Recherches de théologie ancienne et médiévale* 3 (1931): 113–39.

67. For approximate dates of Augustine's early works, unless otherwise indicated, I follow Allan D. Fitzgerald, *AttA*, xliii–xlix. Cf. Roger Gryson, *Répertoire général des auteurs ecclésiastiques latins de l'antiquité et du moyen âge*, vol. 1, *Introduction. Répertoire des auteurs: A–H* (Freiburg: Herder, 2007), 207–71.

in him who paid on their behalf what he did not owe. But those whom the
devil has persuaded to persist in unbelief, he is justly allowed to keep as his
companions in eternal damnation. So, humankind was not snatched from the
devil by force, seeing that the devil had taken it captive not by force but by
persuasion. And humankind, which was justly brought so low as to serve him
to whose evil persuasion it had consented, was justly set free by him to whose
good persuasion it consented, because humankind sinned less in consenting
than the devil sinned in persuading it to sin.[68]

But this is not the prevailing narrative of Augustine's early works. As is well
known, in these works Augustine is preoccupied with his spiritual and intellectual pursuit of ways to return, or ascend, to God. There has been a lively debate
in recent years about the extent to which that early pursuit was already informed
by ideas that are central to Augustine's later works, particularly the conviction
that after the fall everyone's will is so weakened and hindered that only God
can enable a person to seek him and to continue loving him. (The literature related to this discussion, which I will not summarize here, includes an important
early study by Patout Burns.)[69] In Augustine's early works one finds, in Carol

68. *Lib. arb.* 3.10.31 (CCSL 29:293–94; ET Augustine, *Earlier Writings*, trans. J. H. S.
Burleigh, Library of Christian Classics [London: SCM; Philadelphia: Westminster, 1953],
190, modified): "atque uerbum dei unicus dei filius diabolum, quem semper sub legibus suis
habuit et habebit, homine indutus etiam homini subiugauit, nihil ei extorquens uiolento
dominatu sed superans eum lege iustitiae, ut, quoniam femina decepta et deiecto per fem-
inam uiro omnem prolem primi hominis tamquam peccatricem legibus mortis, malitiosa
quidem nocendi cupiditate sed tamen iure aequissimo, uindicabat, tam diu potestas eius
ualeret donec interficeret iustum, in quo nihil dignum morte posset ostendere, non solum
quia sine crimine occisus est sed etiam quia sine libidine natus, cui subiugauerat ille quos
ceperat, ut quicquid inde nasceretur tamquam suae arboris fructus praua quidem habendi
cupiditate sed tamen non iniquo possidendi iure retineret. iustissime itaque dimittere cogitur
credentes in eum quem iniustissime occidit, ut et quod temporaliter moriuntur debitum
exsoluant et quod semper uiuunt in illo uiuant qui pro eis quod non debebat exsoluit, quibus
autem infidelitatis perseuerantiam persuasisset iuste se cum haberet in perpetua damnatione
consortes. ita factum est ut neque diabolo per uim eriperetur homo quem nec ipse ui sed
persuasione ceperat, et qui iuste plus humiliatus est ut seruiret cui ad malum consenserat,
iuste per eum cui ad bonum consensit liberaretur, quia minus iste in consentiendo quam ille
in male suadendo peccauerat."
69. See, e.g., Athanase Sage, "Péché originel: Naissance d'un dogme," *REAug* 13 (1967):
211–48; J. Patout Burns, *The Development of Augustine's Doctrine of Operative Grace* (Paris:
Études Augustiniennes, 1980), 7–51; Paul Rigby, *Original Sin in Augustine's "Confessions"*

Harrison's words, an "emphasis on leaving behind the created, temporal, mutable realm, on turning within oneself, on ascending to God through reason, on avoiding the snares of the senses and the body and seeking higher, spiritual reality."[70] Augustine explores several routes for this ascent in his early works: through a study of the seven liberal disciplines, through an investigation of the seven grades of the soul, through a progression from being to living to understanding. Brian Dobell has argued that in treatises written between 387–388 and 391 CE, Augustine was working through problems he encountered in attempting to ascend toward God by the exercise of disciplined thought.[71] By the end of this period, Augustine had come to recognize that the mind was unable to hold on to its vision of God because it was inevitably distracted by the force of habits developed under the influence of a corruptible body.[72] Augustine was not yet fully cognizant of the implications of this recognition for his understanding of what might be required for the will to abandon false and detrimental objects of desire.[73] It is at this point that his study of Paul's Letter to the Romans comes into play. A record of that study is preserved in a series of works Augustine wrote between 394 and 398 (at the latest):[74] *Expositio quarundam propositionum ex epistula apostoli ad Romanos* (*exp. prop. Rm.*) and *Epistulae ad Romanos inchoata expositio* (*ep. Rm. inch.*), composed in 394–395; *De diuersis quaestionibus octoginta tribus* (*diu. qu.*) 66–68, which probably dates from the same period as the afore-

---

(Ottawa: University of Ottawa Press, 1987), 1–28; Pierre-Marie Hombert, *Gloria gratiae: Se glorifier en Dieu, principe et fin de la théologie augustinienne de la grâce* (Paris: Études Augustiniennes, 1996), 35–129; Volker H. Drecoll, *Die Enstehung der Gnadenlehre Augustins* (Tübingen: Mohr Siebeck, 1999); and Carol Harrison, *Rethinking Augustine's Early Theology: An Argument for Continuity* (Oxford: Oxford University Press, 2006). For overviews, with full bibliography, see Volker H. Drecoll, "Gratia," *AugLex* 3:193–201; Mathijs Lamberigts, "Peccatum originale," *AugLex* 4:599–604; and Anthony Dupont, Gratia *in Augustine's "Sermones ad Populum" during the Pelagian Controversy: Do Different Contexts Furnish Different Insights?*, BSCH 59 (Leiden: Brill, 2013), 69–74, 95–106, 203–6, 444–54.

70. Harrison, *Rethinking Augustine's Early Theology*, 40.

71. Brian Dobell, *Augustine's Intellectual Conversion: The Journey from Platonism to Christianity* (Cambridge: Cambridge University Press, 2009), 138–98.

72. Dobell, *Augustine's Intellectual Conversion*, 191–98.

73. For a lucid and incisive exposition, see John M. Rist, *Augustine: Ancient Thought Baptized* (Cambridge: Cambridge University Press, 1994), 173–88.

74. For a close reading of these works—along with ample bibliography—see Drecoll, *Die Enstehung*, 144–250.

mentioned works;[75] and *Ad Simplicianum* (*Simpl.*), composed in the first years of Augustine's episcopate (i.e., 396–398).

From Individual Ascent to Individual History

Through his reading of Romans, Augustine abandons the reasoned interior ascent toward God for a journey through time toward God. Whereas the former is often pursued in seven stages, the later unfolds in four: prior to the law, under the law, under grace, and in peace. As Augustine explains in *De diuersis quaestionibus octoginta tribus 66*:

> From this we understand that there are four phases even in a single person [*etiam in uno homine*] and, when they have been experienced in sequence, eternal life will be attained. For inasmuch as it was necessary and just that, after our nature fell into sin and the spiritual blessedness which is signified by the term "paradise" was lost, we should be born as animals and fleshly beings, there is a first period that is before the law, a second that is under the law, a third that is under grace, and a fourth that is in peace. The period before the law occurs when we do not know what sin is and pursue fleshly desires. The period under the law occurs when we are forbidden to sin and still we commit sin, having been overcome by the habit of it, because faith does not yet help us. The third period occurs when we believe utterly in our liberator and attribute nothing to our own merits but, loving his mercy, are no longer overcome by the pleasure of wicked habits when they strive to lead us to sin, yet we still allow them to disturb us even though we do not give in to them. The fourth period occurs when there is nothing whatsoever in a person that resists the spirit, but all things, harmoniously joined and linked together, preserve the unity of the person in an enduring peace, which will happen when the mortal body has been restored to life, this corruptible thing has put on incorruptibility and this mortal thing has put on immortality.[76]

75. See David L. Mosher's introduction to Augustine, *Eighty-Three Different Questions*, trans. David L. Mosher, FC 70 (Washington, DC: Catholic University of America Press, 1982), 18–19, which includes references to prior literature.

76. *Diu. qu.* 66.3 (CCSL 44A:154–55; trans. Ramsey, *Responses to Miscellaneous Questions*, WSA I/12, 105–6, modified): "ex quo comprehendimus quattuor esse differentias etiam in uno homine, quibus gradatim peractis in uita aeterna manebitur. quia enim oportebat atque id

However, Augustine's rendering of these four periods, derived from Paul, is different from Ambrosiaster's. Augustine presents the periods as a common personal history, a spiritual progression that can be observed "even in a single person" (*etiam in uno homine*).[77] There are no allusions to the recurring efforts of the devil over time to subvert God's action to rescue humankind, to which Ambrosiaster repeatedly refers.[78] Part of the reason for this approach is the first-person narrative that Paul adopts in Rom. 7:7–25, where, as Augustine explains in *Ad Simplicianum*, Paul presents himself as a person living under the law.[79] But a more fundamental reason for this approach is Augustine's longstanding preoccupation with the individual's ascent toward God.

THE PROBLEM OF THE WILL

Both the philosophical inquiries Augustine had taken in pursuing a reasoned ascent and his failure to achieve an enduring vision of God because of the allurements of embodied existence predisposed him, in ways that Ambrosiaster probably never would have been, to explore the predicament of a misdirected will. In book 6 of *De musica* (*mus.*), which was emended after its original composition in or after 388 CE,[80] Augustine explains how the soul, in attending to the bodily sensations that impinge on it, encounters resistance when it does not satisfy needs arising from

---

iustum erat, ut posteaquam natura nostra peccauit, amissa beatitudine spiritali, quae paradisi nomine significatur, animales carnales que nasceremur, prima est actio ante legem, secunda sub lege, tertia sub gratia, quarta in pace. ante legem actio est, cum peccatum ignoramus et sequimur carnales concupiscentias. sub lege est actio, cum iam prohibemur a peccato, et tamen eius consuetudine uicti peccamus, quoniam nos nondum adiuuat fides. tertia actio est, quando iam plenissime credimus liberatori nostro, nec meritis nostris aliquid tribuimus, sed eius misericordiam diligendo iam non uincimur delectatione consuetudinis malae, cum ad peccatum nos ducere nititur, sed tamen adhuc eam interpellantem patimur, quamuis ei non tradamur. quarta est actio, cum omnino nihil est in homine quod resistat spiritui, sed omnia sibimet concorditer iuncta et conexa unum aliquid firma pace custodiunt, quod fiet mortali corpore uiuificato, cum corruptibile hoc induerit incorruptionem, et mortale hoc induerit immortalitatem." Cf. *exp. prop. Rm.* 12.1–13 (CSEL 84:6–9).

77. Drecoll, *Die Enstehung*, 150–51, 356.

78. *In Rom.* 7:8.2; 7:11.1; 7:13.2 (CSEL 81.1:224–25, 228–29, 228–31).

79. *Simpl.* 1.1.1 (CCSL 44:8).

80. For details about this emended version, including its nature and date, see Martin Jacobsson, "Introduction," in CSEL 102:1–10.

those sensations. If in satisfying those needs the soul diverts its attention from God and becomes preoccupied with lesser things, it becomes difficult for the soul to avoid being ruled by—rather than to rule over—bodily desires.[81] As Augustine explains in De sermone domini in monte (s. dom. m.), written between 393 and 395, the soul is not responsible for the suggestions it experiences fleetingly from bodily sensations or memories of past pleasures. The soul sins when it consents to those suggestions, and sins further when this consent is acted on. Over time consent and act can become habitual, leading the soul to implore for help using the words of Rom. 7:24–25a: "Wretched person that I am! Who will set me free from the body of this death? The grace of God through Jesus Christ our Lord!"[82] The delusions and disappointments the soul experiences as a result of its misdirected desires are both a consequence and a punishment of its sins, as is, more importantly, the difficulty it encounters when it tries to overcome the desires for pleasure, excelling, and entertainment, as Augustine had observed earlier in De uera religione (uera rel.), written in 390–391.[83] In De libero arbitrio, book 3, completed by the time Augustine was commenting on Romans, Augustine has arrived at a conceptual shorthand to summarize the condition in which the soul finds itself as a punishment for prior sin: ignorance (an inability to recognize what is right) and difficulty (an inability to do what is right even when one wishes to do it).[84]

Augustine does not resort to this conceptual shorthand in his several explanations of the human predicament as he understood it to be described by Paul in Romans. In fact, ignorance recedes from view, except insofar as it describes the condition of those who, prior to the giving of the Mosaic law, did not know they were sinning. But difficulty—the influence that disordered desires, originating in bodily sensations, come to have over the soul—looms large, associated with Paul's description of "the flesh."[85] Augustine's assessment of the difficulty humankind experiences is slightly but significantly different from Ambrosiaster's. Ambrosiaster observes that "under the law" people recognize what is good and

---

81. Mus. 6.5.9–14 (CSEL 102:200–204).

82. S. dom. m. 1.12.34–36 (CCSL 35:36–39). On a subtle but important shift in Augustine's citation of Rom. 7:25 at this time, see William Babcock, "Augustine's Interpretation of Romans (A.D. 394–396)," AugStud 10 (1979): 60–61.

83. Vera rel. 20.38–40 and 38.69–70 (CCSL 32:210–12 and 232–33); cf. Drecoll, Die Enstehung, 111.

84. Lib. arb. 3.18.52 and 3.22.64 (CCSL 29:305–6 and 312–13).

85. Exp. prop. Rm. 12.10 and 38.1–7 (CSEL 84:8 and 19–20); diu. qu. 66.5–6 (CCSL 44A:155–62); as well as Simpl. 1.1.7 and 1.1.11 (CCSL 44:13 and 15–16).

may even wish to do it, but they are overwhelmed by the habit of sinning such that they are unable to fulfill that wish.[86] Augustine states that "under the law" people recognize that what they do is evil and that, by implication, they do not really want to do what they do; but, overwhelmed by the habit of sinning originating in the desires of "the flesh," they cannot truly wish to do what is right.[87] For Ambrosiaster, the soul "under the law" retains the capacity to desire to do good, even if in fact it cannot do good because of the domination of "the flesh," a domination eventually overcome by the grace of God through Christ.[88] For Augustine, the capacity to desire to do good and, by implication, not to consent to the desires of "the flesh"—that is, not to consent to sinful suggestions—belongs only to a person "under grace" and that only because of the "help of the Liberator." But Augustine has yet to work through the implications of this view.

JUSTICE, GRACE, AND MERIT

As is well known, two questions put to Augustine by Simplicianus, Augustine's mentor while he resided in Milan and Ambrose's successor as bishop of that city, impelled him to reflect further on how, for someone who cannot wish to do what is right, it could be possible to wish to change that disposition. When Augustine answered Simplicianus's first question, on the interpretation of Rom. 7:7–25, he held that "under the law" one still retained a capacity at least to turn in supplication to God, whose grace can enable one to fulfill the law.[89] When Augustine answered Simplicianus's second question, on the interpretation of Rom. 9:10–29, he concluded that, in the process of saving sinful humankind, God's mercy always precedes and effects any human response: people are saved not because of any initiative on their part but because God called them in a way that was suited to them, so that they were moved, understood, and followed his calling.[90]

The change in Augustine's thought can be observed in his handling of the example of Jacob and Esau at Rom. 9:10–16, where Paul argues that God chose Jacob over Esau before they were born or had done anything good or bad, and

86. *In Rom.* 7:18.4 (CSEL 81.1:238–39).

87. *Exp. prop. Rm.* 12.3 and 12 (CSEL 84:7–8); *diu. qu.* 66.5 (CCSL 44A:158); and *Simpl.* 1.1.11 (CCSL 44:15–16).

88. *In Rom.* 7:22 and 7:24–25.5 (CSEL 81.1:240–41 and 246–49).

89. *Simpl.* 1.1.14 (CCSL 44:18).

90. *Simpl.* 1.2.12 (CCSL 44:36–37).

that in doing so God was not unjust. The passage was problematic because the seeming arbitrariness of God's election was an affront to common notions of justice. When he first dealt with the passage, Augustine, like Ambrosiaster, resolved the problem by basing God's election on God's foreknowledge: God foreknows who will believe and elects them on that basis.[91] There can be no election without merit, Augustine asserted. But God cannot elect on the basis of works, since Paul explicitly excludes this possibility. Augustine reasoned, therefore, that God must elect on the basis of faith, foreknowing who would believe in him and thus be worthy of receiving the Holy Spirit, who by instilling the right love in the heart enables the believer to do good: "If [the sinner] follows God's call of his own free will [*libero arbitrio*], he will merit also the Holy Spirit, through whom he can do good works. And remaining in the Holy Spirit—no less also by free will—he will also merit life eternal, which cannot be marred by any flaw."[92]

Augustine abandons this explanation when he revisits the problem in his reply to Simplicianus. Paul, he argues, wants to exclude election based on works. Since God could have foreknown the works that issue from faith as well as the faith from which works issue, a distinction between foreknowledge based on faith and foreknowledge based on works is specious.[93] Election, therefore, cannot be based on foreknowledge of any form of human volition, whether in believing or in acting rightly; it must reside entirely in the will of God, as Paul testifies when he says, "It does not depend on the one who wills or the one who runs, but on God who has mercy" (Rom. 9:16)—a verse that Augustine will later cite with frequency in sermons and in his anti-Pelagian writings. To the rhetorical question posed by Paul about injustice on God's part (Rom. 9:14), Augustine supplies an explanation based on his understanding of the consequences of Adam's sin: since the entire human race shares in the penalty for that sin, they are all justly condemned and have no grounds for complaint if God should mercifully remit the debt of a few.[94]

---

91. *Exp. prop. Rm.* 52.1–15, esp. 5–11 (CSEL 84:33–35).

92. *Exp. prop. Rm.* 52.15 (CSEL 84:35; ET Paula Fredriksen Landes, trans., *Augustine on Romans: Propositions from the Epistle to the Romans, Unfinished Commentary on the Epistle to the Romans* [Chico, CA: Scholars Press, 1982], 33): "quod si uocatus uocantem secutus fuerit, quod est iam in libero arbitrio, merebitur et spiritum sanctum per quem bona possit operari, in quo permanens—quod nihilominus est in libero arbitrio—merebitur etiam uitam aeternam, quae nulla possit labe corrumpi."

93. *Simpl.* 1.2.5 (CCSL 44:29–30).

94. *Simpl.* 1.2.16 (CCSL 44:41–42).

In wrapping up his explanation of Rom. 9:10–29, Augustine explains with a new clarity the problem that leaves humankind wholly at the mercy of God. He asks, "Who has it in his power for his mind to be touched by such a manifestation as would move his will to faith? Who embraces in his heart something that does not attract him? Who has it in his power either to come into contact with what can attract him or to be attracted once he has come into contact?"[95] These questions are particularly acute if one recalls that the mass of humankind to which they apply is habitually accustomed to delight in the wrong things:[96] "The fleshly desire that results from the punishment for sin has, because of the original guilt, cast abiding confusion into everything, and now it presides over the whole human race as one complete lump."[97] As Augustine says, "The free choice of the will [*liberum uoluntatis arbitrium*] counts for a great deal, to be sure. But what does it count for in those who have been sold under sin"[98]—to those who are now ruled by their weakness for the desires of "the flesh"? Augustine concludes, therefore, that we would not be able to will or to run (in the words of Rom. 9:16) unless God moves or incites us:[99] "The upshot, then, is that wills are chosen. But the will itself, unless it comes into contact with something that attracts and beckons the soul, can by no means be moved. But that it may come into contact with this is not in a person's power."[100]

This realization—regardless of how one situates it in relation to Augustine's prior thinking—is purchased at a steep price. It obliges Augustine to accept that many will not be saved because they were never called by God in such a way that they would respond positively. This outcome, along with later developments that emerge in Augustine's anti-Pelagian writings, has proved to be among the more

---

95. *Simpl.* 1.2.21 (CCSL 44:53–54; trans. Ramsey, WSA I/12, 205): "quis habet in potestate tali uiso attingi mentem suam, quo eius uoluntas moueatur ad fidem? quis autem animo amplectitur aliquid quod eum non delectat? aut quis habet in potestate, ut uel occurrat quod eum delectare possit, uel delectet cum occurrerit?"

96. Rist, *Augustine*, 175–85.

97. *Simpl.* 1.2.20 (CCSL 44:51–52; trans. Ramsey, WSA I/12, 204): "sed concupiscentia carnalis de peccati poena iam regnans uniuersum genus humanum tamquam totam et unam consparsionem originali reatu in omnia permanente confuderat."

98. *Simpl.* 1.2.21 (CCSL 44:53; trans. Ramsey, WSA I/12, 205): "liberum uoluntatis arbitrium plurimum ualet, immo uero est quidem, sed in uenundatis sub peccato quid ualet?"

99. *Simpl.* 1.2.21 (CCSL 44:54).

100. *Simpl.* 1.2.22 (CCSL 44:55; trans. Ramsey, WSA I/12, 206): "restat ergo ut uoluntates eligantur. sed uoluntas ipsa, nisi aliquid occurrerit quod delectet atque inuitet animum, moueri nullo modo potest. hoc autem ut occurrat, non est in hominis potestate."

problematic aspects of Augustine's thinking.[101] In fact, Ambrosiaster's interpretation of Rom. 9 illustrates why it would have been difficult for others to accept Augustine's interpretation.

AMBROSIASTER AS AUGUSTINE'S FOIL

Like Augustine, Ambrosiaster insists that God is both good and just; these qualities cannot be called into question.[102] He agrees that human beings "are all from one and the same lump in terms of substance and are all sinners."[103] He accepts that few will in fact be saved from the multitude of humanity.[104] He insists that God's judgment of individual human beings, to be just, must be based on each individual's merits, since, as he asserts repeatedly, God shows no partiality.[105] For that reason he maintains that God's eventual condemnation of all who in the course of their lives do not heed the warnings or the call of God must be based on God's foreknowledge that they would be unwilling to change their ways, even after repeatedly being warned or called.[106] Not only is Pharaoh, whom Paul discusses, an example of this, but so are Saul and David, whose histories Ambrosiaster compares in order to defend God's justice in remarks he introduces when he revises his comments on Rom. 9.[107] (Here again, Ambrosiaster draws on the evidence of history as he understands it.)

In short, Ambrosiaster's understanding of justice leads him to the conclusion Augustine adopts in *Expositio quarundam propositionum ex epistula apostoli ad Romanos* but moves away from in *De diuersis quaestionibus octoginta tribus* 68 and finally abandons in *Ad Simplicianum*. In those latter two works, Augustine's preoccupation with the mutual exclusiveness of divine grace and human merits

101. See, e.g., Rist, *Augustine*, 266–89 and 307–13, as well as Gerald Bonner, *Freedom and Necessity: St. Augustine's Teaching on Divine Power and Human Freedom* (Washington, DC: Catholic University of America Press, 2007).

102. *In Rom.* 9:18–19.2 (CSEL 81.1:326–27).

103. *In Rom.* 9:21.1 (CSEL 81.1:326–29; trans. de Bruyn, 184): "omnes ex una atque eadem massa simus in substantia et cuncti peccatores."

104. *In Rom.* 9:27.2 (CSEL 81.1:332–33).

105. *In Rom.* 9:11–13.1, 5 (CSEL 81.1:312–17).

106. *In Rom.* 9:14; 9:22; and 9:23.2 (CSEL 81.1:318–19 and 328–31).

107. *In Rom.* 9:16.2a–2b *rec.* β, γ (CSEL 81.1:320–23).

dominates his interpretation of Romans. Still, even Augustine finds it difficult to abandon the conventional notion of justice based on merits. Thus, in *De diuersis quaestionibus octoginta tribus* 68 he reasons that since God cannot be unjust in showing mercy to some but hardening others,

> this springs from most hidden merits, because even though sinners themselves form a single mass on account of the universal sin, there is nonetheless a degree of diversity among them. There is something, then, that is already present in [some] sinners, by which they have been made worthy of righteousness even though they have not yet been made righteous, and in the same way something is already present in other sinners that makes them worthy of punishment.[108]

When people either heed or do not heed God's call, they are exercising their will. But those who heed God's call must attribute their salvation to God, since they would not have come if God had not called them, whereas those who do not heed God's call have only themselves to blame, since they neglected to come after having been called in free will (*in libera uoluntate*). God does not call the latter in such a way that they would heed the call because they did not possess some antecedent merit that would render them deserving of such a call.[109]

The precariousness of this position becomes apparent when it is compared with that taken by Augustine in *Ad Simplicianum* 1.2. The reason God has mercy on some and not on others, Augustine continues to argue, cannot be known; it lies in a divine justice inaccessible to human comprehension. But to defend God against accusations of arbitrariness, Augustine now appeals not to some hidden merit in each individual's past, much less to God's foreknowledge of each individual's merits in the future, but to the solidarity of all humankind in Adam's sin, which renders all deserving of punishment. Just as in human dealings it is within a creditor's prerogative whether to forgive a debt, so too, since all human beings are deserving of punishment because they all participate in the sin of Adam, there is no injustice if God foregoes punishment of some but exacts it of others.

---

108. *Diu. qu.* 68.4 (CCSL 44A:180; trans. Ramsey, WSA I/12, 119): "uenit enim de occultissimis meritis, quia et ipsi peccatores cum propter generale peccatum unam massam fecerint, non tamen nulla est inter illos diuersitas. praecedit ergo aliquid in peccatoribus, quo quamuis nondum sint iustificati, digni efficiantur iustificatione; et item praecedit in aliis peccatoribus, quo digni sint obtunsione."

109. *Diu. qu.* 68.5 (CCSL 44A:181).

Justice is still based on merit, but because humankind is "a kind of mass of sin" (*una quaedam massa peccati*) issuing from the penalty for Adam's transgression and the consequent diffusion of fleshly desires in all his descendants, all people in fact merit punishment.[110]

This line of reasoning is foreign to Ambrosiaster. According to his reading of Romans, even if all human beings are born into a condition that inclines them to sin, they retain the capacity to resist the inclination to sin, at least in intention if not in action.[111] Thus, whereas Augustine concludes that the reason that "God has mercy on whomever he wills, and he hardens the heart of whomever he wills" (Rom. 9:18) lies in "a form of equity which is most secret and far removed from human understanding,"[112] Ambrosiaster, reading the verse as a rhetorical objection, not as the view of the apostle, appeals to a sense of justice that is very much in keeping with human understanding. The apostle, he says, "replies categorically that justice is nevertheless preserved on account of [God's] foreknowledge" of each person's conduct, as he has repeatedly explained.[113]

Conclusion

One can observe a certain logic in both Ambrosiaster's and Augustine's explanations of the human predicament, grounded, for each of them, in the foundational narratives they espouse. But Augustine is more of a philosopher than Ambrosiaster, and his manner of thinking is more syllogistic and deductive. Over the course of his episcopate, those qualities will lead Augustine to derive conclusions from biblical myths and Christian rituals (as well as his own struggles with desire) that Ambrosiaster did not contemplate: that, as a result of their solidarity in Adam, all human beings bear the guilt of the original sin and constitute a "mass of perdition";[114] that infants who die without having been baptized "for the remission

---

110. *Simpl.* 1.2.16 (CCSL 44:41–42).

111. See nn. 86 and 88 *supra*.

112. *Simpl.* 1.2.16 (CCSL 44:42): "eorum autem non miseretur, quibus misericordiam non esse praebendam aequitate occultissima et ab humanis sensibus remotissima iudicat."

113. *In Rom.* 9:18–19.1 (CSEL 81.1:324–25; trans. de Bruyn, 183): "cui quidem ex auctoritate respondit, seruata tamen iustitia, ex supra memorate praescientia." Cf. *In Rom.* 9:11–13.1, 5; 9:14; 9:15.1 (CSEL 81.1:313–14, 316–19).

114. Paula Fredriksen, "Massa," *AttA*, 545–47, and Gregor Wurst, "Massa, massa damnata," *AugLex* 3:1196–99. In Ambrosiaster's usage, unlike Augustine's, *massa* is not coupled with *peccati, perditionis, damnata*, or similar modifiers.

of sins" will therefore be punished, albeit leniently;[115] that because reason is submerged by desire in sexual intercourse after the fall (a quintessential instance of the misdirection of the soul), it is unavoidably corrupting, even within marriage.[116] These aspects of Augustine's thought are not the whole story, but they are telling episodes. Ambrosiaster's collective narrative—the ransom of humankind from the dominion of the devil—eventually fell out of fashion. Augustine's more personal narrative—the (re)orientation of human desire toward enduring fulfillment—continues to fascinate. The two writers offer a choice, at key points, between conventional wisdom and reasoned inquiry. Would Augustine's reasoning in *Ad Simplicianum* 1.2 have persuaded Ambrosiaster, had the latter lived long enough to read it? I am doubtful. Ambrosiaster would have resisted, I suspect, what to him would have seemed to be an unprecedented innovation, just as, on another plane, he had resisted adopting a new Latin version of the scriptures based on the Greek text. Ironically, it is to that same conservative disposition that we owe the textual link forever associating him with Augustine: the "*in quo*" of Rom. 5:12.

115. Lamberigts, "Peccatum originale," *AugLex* 4:608. Ambrosiaster's view of the fate of unbaptized infants is slightly, but significantly, different. In one version of *Qu.* 81.2 (PL 35:2275), he states that although infants, as souls freshly born in a body, are innocent, they must receive the sign of the cross in baptism so as not to be held by the second death: "infantes autem propterea baptizantur, cum sint innocentes, ut anima rudis nata in corpore, signum habeat mortis euictae, ne possit ab ea teneri."

116. Rist, *Augustine*, 321–27. For Ambrosiaster's more neutral view of sexual relations after the fall, see David G. Hunter, *Marriage, Celibacy, and Heresy in Ancient Christianity: The Jovinianist Controversy* (Oxford: Oxford University Press, 2007), 159–69.

Chapter 15

Augustine's *Enchiridion* 26.100 and the Ninth-Century Predestination Debate

Brian Matz

Introduction

During the middle part of the ninth century, a controversy over predestination spread throughout Gaul. It began with a debate between a monk named Gottschalk and his abbot, Rabanus Maurus. It eventually grew to include more than a dozen writers and was the subject of no less than eight synods. Were it not for the intervention of the king of Gaul, Charles the Bald, the matter might not have outlived its initial participants. Noteworthy in the debate is the fact that the teachings of Augustine are acknowledged to be critical to the position of all its participants. Everyone quotes Augustine. Everyone seems quite clear that Augustine's teaching on predestination outweighs that of any other source. Elsewhere, I have surveyed the use of Augustine in the four principal contributors to the ninth-century debate.[1] In what follows, I expand on a point insufficiently explored there: the hermeneutical function in the writings of the ninth-century authors of a phrase Augustine used in several of his writings. Actually, there are a few different versions of the phrase: "predestined to punishment," "predestined to judgment," and "predestined to death." While these different versions are found in several of Augustine's writings, the version of it found in *Enchiridion* (*ench.*) 26.100—that is, *praedestinatio ad poenam*—was more frequently cited than the others in the ninth-century texts. At least one of our authors thought it was the interpretive key to every other text of

---

1. This was a two-part article. B. Matz, "Augustine in the Predestination Controversy of the Ninth Century," *AugStud* 46 (2015): 155–84 and *AugStud* 47 (2016): 17–40.

Augustine. Thus, while acknowledging that our authors were aware of the range of this phrase in Augustine's texts, the focus here will be on *Enchiridion* 26.100. Specifically, this chapter examines the hermeneutical function of *Enchiridion* 26.100 in the three writers of the ninth century who cited it: Gottschalk, John Scotus Eriugena, and Florus of Lyons. Their differing appropriations of *Enchiridion* 26.100 reveals the existence of an unbridgeable ninth-century chasm.

This chapter benefits from the recent interest among scholars in the literary and material cultural remains of this ninth-century debate. This is especially true of the reception of Augustine in the debate. In 2010, Victor Genke and Francis Gumerlock published a thorough review of the scholarship to that point and a translation of some of the key texts of the controversy.[2] During the mid 2010s, a project based in Paris traced the transmission, copying, and movement of manuscripts, especially Augustinian manuscripts, around monastic and ecclesiastical libraries. It revealed the widespread interest in Augustine and the access monks at the wealthier monasteries had to his texts.[3] In 2017 alone, three studies were published that locate the ninth-century writers in their social, ecclesiastical, and political contexts. Matthew Gillis examined Gottschalk's social networks and concluded that he was as much a victim of ecclesiastical power grabs as he was a product of the best of Carolingian literary culture.[4] Warren Pezé examined the intricate literary and social networks that Gottschalk cultivated during the 820s–840s CE, which facilitated his own (and, for that matter, his opponents') literary productivity during the years of his imprisonment. Pezé's study further reveals the attempts made to falsify and to correct patristic texts in order to buttress the arguments of one or another writer.[5] Andrew Romig's study situates Gottschalk's story in light of ideals of (Christian) masculinity—in particular, their manifestations of *caritas*—during the Carolingian era, setting him beside portraits of, among others, Martin of Tours, the memory of whom extended deep into Carolingian psyche, Paulinus of Aquileia, and the emperor Louis the

2. Victor Genke and Francis X. Gumerlock, *Gottschalk and a Medieval Predestination Controversy: Texts Translated from the Latin*, Medieval Philosophical Texts in Translation 47 (Milwaukee: Marquette University Press, 2010).

3. Pierre Chambert-Protat et al., *La controverse Carolingienne sur la prédestination: Histoire, textes, manuscrits*, Haut Moyen Âge 32 (Turnhout: Brepols, 2018).

4. Matthew Gillis, *Heresy and Dissent in the Carolingian Empire: The Case of Gottschalk of Orbais* (Oxford: Oxford University Press, 2017).

5. Warren Pezé, *Le virus de l'erreur: La controverse carolingienne sur la double prédestination; Essai d'histoire sociale*, Haut Moyen Âge 26 (Turnhout: Brepols, 2017).

Pious.[6] Finally, and nearer to the subject of this chapter, in 2016 two articles by
Jenny Smith analyzed the reception of Augustine in the ninth-century controversy.[7] Smith argued that Augustine's ambiguity on the subject of predestination
obliged ninth-century writers to seek out other church fathers as interpretive
partners. Like Smith's work, this chapter also examines the difficulty the ninth-
century writers had in appropriating Augustine's ambiguous language around
predestination to death, to judgment, and to punishment.

THE CONTROVERSY

To summarize briefly the controversy, a little before 840 CE, Gottschalk, a monk
at the monastery in Orbais and, before that, at the monastery in Fulda, sought ordination in order to justify leaving Orbais to serve as a "missionary." Enjoying for
several years the support of Eberhard, a nobleman in Frioul, Gottschalk preached
and taught on the subject of predestination. By May 840, news of Gottschalk's
teaching aroused the frustration of his former abbot, Rabanus Maurus of Fulda,
who wrote a letter to the bishop of Verona, attaching to it the first of many treatises
to be written on predestination as part of this ninth-century controversy. Yet, for
a complex set of reasons, the adjudication of Gottschalk's case would have to wait
until 848.[8] At that time, Rabanus takes up the Gottschalk matter again and writes
a letter to his supporter, Eberhard. One might wonder why Rabanus could not
ignore Gottschalk. After all, he had long ago associated himself with a different
monastery within a different diocese. While certainty is impossible, it is likely
because Gottschalk had won a rather public court case against Rabanus nearly two
decades earlier. Rabanus was compelled to release Gottschalk from monastic vows
and to allow him to relocate to another region of the Carolingian realm, an outcome that surely piqued the interest of other aggrieved monks in the region.[9]

---

6. Andrew Romig, *Be a Perfect Man: Christian Masculinity and the Carolingian Aristocracy*,
Middle Ages Series (Philadelphia: University of Pennsylvania Press, 2017). Gottschalk is the
principal subject of chap. 4.

7. Jenny Smith, "The Rebellious Monk Gottschalk of Orbais: Defining Heresy in a Me-
dieval Debate on Predestination," *Eras* 17 (2016): 1–24; Smith, "'As If Augustine Had Said':
Textual Interpretation and Augustinian Ambiguity in a Medieval Debate on Predestination,"
Past Imperfect 19 (2016): https://doi.org/10.21971/P7H300.

8. Genke and Gumerlock, *Gottschalk*, 28–29.

9. Genke and Gumerlock, *Gottschalk*, 15–16.

Regardless, in this letter to Eberhard, Rabanus states succinctly his problem with what he understood to be Gottschalk's teaching:

Gottschalk, who stays in your home, who teaches that the predestination of God binds [*constringat*] all people such that even if someone would want to be saved and would struggle for this by the correct faith and good works in order to come to eternal life by the grace of God, that person would labor in vain and for nothing, if he or she has not been predestined to life, as if God, who is the author of our salvation and not of our perdition, forces a human being to perish [*cogat hominem interire*] by his predestination.[10]

This kind of teaching has obvious pastoral ramifications. If Gottschalk had, in fact, taught such things, it would be a wonder that he was allowed to preach and to teach so freely. Little wonder, then, that Gottschalk, now invited to appear before Rabanus at a council in Mainz, appeared without delay. As will be discussed *infra*, this letter did not accurately reflect his teaching.

Yet Rabanus was not to be outsmarted this time. Now the archbishop of Mainz, Rabanus ensured the trial proceeded to its predetermined conclusion. Gottschalk was dutifully condemned and flogged as a heretic and then sent to Rheims for a second trial, since he had been ordained in that diocese. Hincmar, the archbishop of Rheims, convened a synod at Quierzy in early 849, and there, too, the outcome of the second trial was predetermined. By mid-849, Gottschalk was imprisoned at the monastery in Hautvilliers, where he would remain until his death in 868.

However, much to Hincmar's consternation, it was only after Gottschalk was imprisoned that the controversy really exploded. Rather than obey the order to perpetual silence, Gottschalk wrote prodigiously during his imprisonment.[11] His

---

10. Rabanus Maurus, *Ep. ad Heberardum comitem* (PL 112:1554; trans. is my own): "Gotescalcus, apud uos manere, qui dogmatizat quod praedestinatio dei omnem hominem ita constringat, ut etiamsi quis uelit saluus fieri, et pro hoc fide recta atque bonis operibus certet, ut ad uitam aeternam per dei gratiam ueniat, frustra et incassum laboret, si non est praedestinatus ad uitam, quasi deus praedestinatione sua cogat hominem interire, qui auctor est salutis nostrae, non perditionis."

11. Romig, *Be a Perfect Man*, 125–28. Prof. Romig also wrote of Gottschalk's prodigious output while at Hautvilliers in an unpublished 2014 paper titled "Prison and Predestination: The 'Jailhouse' Correspondence of Gottschalk of Orbais." I thank Prof. Romig for sharing a copy of this paper with me.

associates at monasteries he previously had visited—for example, Ratramnus of Corbie—wrote treatises in support of his position. Some writers, especially those associated with Lyons, were frustrated with Hincmar for ecclesiastical-political reasons unrelated to Gottschalk's teaching and used this as an opportunity to challenge Hincmar's own understanding of predestinarian theology. Hincmar appealed for help from the court theologian, John Scotus Eriugena, but, for reasons discussed later in this chapter, Hincmar also found his contribution to be problematic. After the convening of synods in Paris, Quierzy (again), Valence, Langres, Savonnieres, and Tusey during the 850s and 860s, Hincmar and the other participants turned to the king, Charles the Bald, who imposed the following, uneasy resolution on the controversy: by virtue of God's predestination, resistible grace is given only to some. Those to whom it is not given may be said to have been predestined to punishment.[12]

ENCHIRIDION 26.100 AND ITS LATER RECEPTION

The ninth-century authors were not the first to identify the importance of *Enchiridion* 26.100 for a debate over predestination. In fact, it is unlikely that they even looked up the text since it had already been incorporated into florilegia of Augustine's thought on predestination. Thus, following a brief exposition of the text itself, it will be helpful to summarize the reception of *Enchiridion* 26.100 in the centuries after Augustine. Augustine originally wrote,

> These are the great works of the Lord, sought out according to all his purposes, and sought out so wisely that when creatures, both angels and humans, had sinned, that is, had done not what he willed but what they willed, the creator fulfilled what he willed by means of that very will of the creature by which what was against his will was done, making good use even of evil creatures as befits the one who is supremely good, for the damnation of those whom he had justly predestined to punishment and for the salvation of those whom he had mercifully predestined to grace.[13]

12. This was decided at the Synod of Tusey (860). Cf. P. R. McKeon, "The Carolingian Councils of Savonnières (859) and Tusey (860) and Their Background: A Study in the Ecclesiastical and Political History of the Ninth Century," *RBén* 84 (1974): 75–110.

13. *Ench.* 26.100 (CCSL 46:103; trans. Harbert, *On Christian Belief*, WSA I/8, 331): "haec sunt magna opera domini, exquisita in omnes uoluntates eius, et tam sapienter exquisita ut

This "little book" (*enchiridion*) was written to a certain Laurence in order that he might know "what we should seek above all, what we should chiefly avoid . . . , to what extent reason comes to the support of religion, what lies outside the scope of reason and belongs to faith alone, what should be held first and last, what the whole body of doctrine amounts to, and what is a sure and suitable foundation of Catholic faith."[14] In other words, what Augustine says in 26.100 should point us to how a Christian ought to think about God. Indeed, the wider literary context of 26.100 concerns the resurrection and God's subsequent judgment (chaps. 23–29). Its narrower literary context concerns God's will in giving grace to save some (chaps. 25–27). And its immediate context, chapter 26, argues the will of God is unwavering and accomplished through both the good and evil actions that humans will to do. Taken together, these contexts suggest that the point of *Enchiridion* 26.100 is less about predestination than it is about the power of God to will to save some. This is made all the clearer by the fact that Augustine mentions predestination nowhere else in 26.100's wider literary context. It is mentioned only here, and this suggests that it serves merely as a foil to illuminate what the will of God can accomplish.

However, perhaps unsurprisingly, once the text was lifted from its literary context and inserted into digests and florilegia, its meaning changed. In the late fifth or early sixth century, this passage was included in a collection of quotes from Augustine's writings on predestination prepared by someone associated with the Scythian monastic community led by John Maxentius.[15] While the compiler copied almost exactly the relevant text from *Enchiridion* 26.100, the passage is now no longer about the power of God's will; rather, it is about two kinds of predestination.[16] Later in the sixth century, Fulgentius of Ruspe incorporated

---

cum angelica et humana creatura peccasset, id est, non quod ille sed quod uoluit ipsa fecisset, etiam per eandem creaturae uoluntatem qua factum est quod creator noluit, impleret ipse quod uoluit, bene utens et malis tanquam summe bonus, ad eorum damnationem quos iuste praedestinauit ad poenam, et ad eorum salutem quos benigne praedestinauit ad gratiam."

14. *Ench.* 1.4 (CCSL 46:49–50; trans. Harbert, WSA I/8, 274): "id est quid sequendum maxime, quid . . . sit fugiendum, in quantum ratio pro religione contendat, uel quid in ratione cum fides sit sola non ueniat, quid primum quid ultimum teneatur, quae totius definitionis summa sit, quod certum proprium que fidei catholicae fundamentum."

15. On John Maxentius, his community, and their interest in Augustine's theology of predestination, see Matthew Pereira, "From Augustine to the Scythian Monks: Social Memory and the Doctrine of Predestination," *StPatr* 54 (2012): 1–13.

16. (Ps.-)John Maxentius, *Capitula S. Augustini* 18 (CCSL 85A:268–69). The compiler makes one change to Augustine's text. He changes the verb *uoluit*, which appears in a sub-

an allusion to this text when he explained the phrase *praedestinatio ad poenam* in his letter to Monimus. Fulgentius's use of the phrase here is particularly important because it is what will be read by both Gottschalk and Eriugena, as well as nearly every other contributor to the ninth-century debate. Fulgentius recognized the potential for misinterpreting phrases like this in Augustine's writings, so, after bringing this passage into dialogue with other texts by Augustine, he argued *praedestinatio ad poenam* does not mean *praedestinatio ad culpam*:[17]

> Because God is compelled by no necessity to promise something against his will, he is not impeded by any obstacle or adversity so that he ends by doing less than he promised or by doing it later. Accordingly, he was able, as he willed, to predestine certain ones to glory, certain others to punishment. But those he predestined to glory, he predestined to justice. But those he predestined to punishment, he did not predestine to guilt. A sin could be from God's predestination if it were possible for anyone to sin justly. But no one sins justly, although God justly permits him to sin.[18]

Fulgentius's concern about misinterpretation was not limited to North Africa. At a council held in the city of Orange in 529 CE to dedicate a new church building, the metropolitan, Caesarius of Arles, asked its attendees to sign a statement in support of Augustinian theology on grace and predestination. However, in the summary statement appended to the canons of the council, one finds, "We not only do not believe that any are foreordained to evil [*praedestinatio ad malum*]

---

ordinate clause, to *uoluisset* in order to match the perfect subjunctive verb, *fecisset*, in the main clause.

17. Fulgentius's argument, which quite closely follows Augustine's arguments in *ench.* 26–27—esp. 27.103—is the subject of Francis X. Gumerlock, *Fulgentius of Ruspe on the Saving Will of God: The Development of a Sixth-Century African Bishop's Interpretation of 1 Timothy 2:4 During the Semi-Pelagian Controversy* (New York: Mellen, 2009).

18. Fulgentius of Ruspe, *Ad Monimum libri tres* 1.13 (CCSL 91:13; ET Fulgentius, *Selected Works*, trans. Robert B. Eno, FC 95 [Washington, DC: Catholic University of America Press, 1997], 204): "quia ergo deus nulla necessitate compellitur ut aliquid nolens promittat, nullius utique aduersitatis impeditur obstaculo, quo id quod promisit, aut minus quam uult, aut tardius faciat. proinde potuit, sicut uoluit, praedestinare quosdam ad gloriam, quosdam ad poenam. sed quos praedestinauit ad gloriam, praedestinauit ad iustitiam. quos autem praedestinauit ad poenam, non praedestinauit ad culpam. posset enim peccatum aliquod ex praedestinatione dei esse, si posset aliquis hominum iuste peccare." At 1.7 and 1.23 of *Ad Monimum* Fulgentius discusses his concern that these two matters ought not to be confused.

by the power of God, but even state with utter abhorrence that if there are those who want to believe so evil a thing, they are anathema."[19] This is the only place in the canons where the word "predestination" is used. Caesarius was concerned that the term not be misused to blame God for any person's unfortunate eternal destination. As with Fulgentius, whatever *praedestinatio ad poenam* suggests about God's will and action, it cannot include the actual sins of a person.

Enchiridion 26.100 again surfaces in another digest of Augustine's writings, this one by an anonymous compiler from either the sixth or the seventh century.[20] Its title suggests a concern to counter Christian appropriation of erroneous, seductive, and cunning pagan philosophies. Our text is cited in the second of its five disputations, a disputation on the mortality and eternal disposition of souls. It appears near the end of this section, one in which Augustine is pitched against a Stoic in a discussion of the justice of God. It is argued that God's justice is not contravened by the damnation of the reprobate or by their having been predestined to this punishment. The compiler does not evidence any particular interest either in Augustine's teaching on God's will in the wider literary context of *Enchiridion* or in the concern either of Fulgentius or of Caesarius to clarify the meaning of Augustine's teaching.

The text next appears in the ninth century in the writings of Gottschalk, Eriugena, and Florus of Lyons. Their use of the text will be analyzed *infra*. Setting them aside for the moment, one next encounters this text in writers of the twelfth and thirteenth centuries, such as Peter Abelard, Peter Lombard, and Thomas Aquinas. Peter Abelard quoted the passage in full in *Sic et Non* Q. 29, in which he asks whether predestination is only in the good or in both the good and the reprobate.[21] Abelard incorporates texts from Augustine, Fulgentius, Prosper, Ambrose, and Isidore, but nearly all of these are texts he must have found in the ninth-century writer Ratramnus of Corbie, since the latter's text uniquely

---

19. Second Council of Orange (SC 353:172; trans. Ross Mackenzie in John H. Leith, ed., *Creeds of the Churches: A Reader in Christian Doctrine from the Bible to the Present*, 3rd ed. [Louisville: John Knox, 1982], 44).

20. *Anonymi Contra philosophos uel Altercationes christianae philosophiae contra erroneas et seductiles paganorum philosophorum uersutias*, Disputatio 2 (CCSL 58A:105–6 [cf. lines 981–97]).

21. Peter Abelard, *Sic et Non*, Q. 29, S. 6–12 (*Sic et Non: A Critical Edition*, ed. Blanche B. Boyer and Richard McKeon [Chicago: University of Chicago Press, 1977], 172–74; ET Priscilla Throop, trans., *Yes and No: The Complete English Translation of Peter Abelard's "Sic et Non,"* 2nd ed. [Charlotte, VT: MedievalMS, 2008], 88–90).

includes the Ambrose quotations.[22] The only text in the list not found in Ratramnus is *Enchiridion* 26.100, but if he had access to Ratramnus, he also likely had access either to Gottschalk or to Eriugena, and either writer would have helped him recognize the importance of this additional text.[23] In any case, Abelard identified in the quotes from these patristic and early medieval authors a problem with which Gottschalk and Eriugena also had wrestled. That is, Abelard exposed differences in how the church fathers spoke about predestination, including even differences within Augustine's own writings. For example, Abelard's first quotation is *De praedestinatione sanctorum* (*praed. sanct.*) 10.19, in which it seems clear that predestination is only concerned with grace for the elect. Yet, in citing *In Iohannis euangelium tractatus* (*Io. eu. tr.*) 48.4 and 6 and *Enchiridion* 26.100, Abelard is able to document that Augustine taught that predestination concerns also the reprobate in those other texts. It is clear that, by relying for his material on ninth-century authors, which functioned for him as digests of these patristic authors, Abelard joined the growing list of those who appropriated *Enchiridion* 26.100 into a context foreign to that in and for which it was originally written.

In Peter Lombard and Thomas Aquinas, citation of *Enchiridion* 26.100 makes it clear that it was again being read in light of its original context. This is unsurprising, since Peter Lombard was well acquainted with *Enchiridion*, having quoted extensively from it throughout his *Sententiae*.[24] In fact, Peter quotes from our text in his *Sententiae* 1.47, and Thomas Aquinas includes it in his commentary on Lombard.[25] Unique among the authors and compilers who incorporated our passage, Peter Lombard includes additional material from the wider context of *Enchiridion*, which allows him to focus on Augustine's wider concern about the will of God rather than on the narrower subject of predestination. Indeed, after quoting from *Enchiridion* 25–26, he writes, "With these words, evidently it is demonstrated that the eternal will of God always is fulfilled from the works of human beings, even if human beings do those things that are contrary to the will

22. Cf. Timothy Roberts, "A Translation and Critical Edition of Ratramnus of Corbie's 'De predestinatione Dei'" (PhD diss., University of Missouri, 1977).

23. The ordering of Abelard's citations of Augustine follows that of Gottschalk rather than Eriugena, although the same citations occur in both ninth-century authors.

24. As noted by Harbert, WSA I/8, 271, Lombard cites it at least eighty times.

25. Peter Lombard, *Sententiae* 1.47.1 (Ignatius Brady, ed., *Magistri Petri Lombardi: Sententiae in IV libris distinctae*, 3rd ed., Spicilegium Bonaventurianum t. 4 pt. 2 [Grottaferrata: Editiones Collegii S. Bonaventurae ad Claras Aquas, 1971], 321–22). Thomas Aquinas, *Comm. in Sententiarum* I.47 Art. 4 (R. P. Mandonnet, ed., *S. Thomae Aquinatis: Scriptum super libros sententiarum* [Paris: Lethielleux, 1929], 1063–64).

of God."[26] He never discusses the predestination language in the text. To Peter— as well as to Thomas Aquinas who follows him in this regard—*Enchiridion* 26 is about the power of God to bring about his ultimate will through both the good and the evil that humans do.

ENCHIRIDION 26.100 IN GOTTSCHALK OF ORBAIS

With this understanding of the different ways in which *Enchiridion* 26.100 was appropriated into the works of later compilers and authors, our focus now shifts to the texts of the ninth century, beginning with Gottschalk. *Enchiridion* 26.100 is cited in two of his texts, his longer and shorter confessions. The shorter one dates to either during or shortly after his trial at the Synod of Quierzy; the longer to soon after his confinement at Hautvilliers.[27]

The *Confessio breuior* (*C. breu.*) has only the outlines of Gottschalk's thinking about predestination and only a handful of references to or brief quotations from earlier church authorities—for example, Augustine, Gregory the Great, Fulgentius, and Isidore. It may well have been written in response to a request by Hincmar, which Prudentius of Troyes encouraged Hincmar to make to Gottschalk.[28] The *Confessio prolixior* (*C. pro.*) is eight times the length of *Confessio breuior*. It includes extensive lists of biblical and patristic prooftexts for Gottschalk's position. It was surely written by someone with access to both a library and materials for text production, things that Gottschalk would have had once imprisoned at the monastery at Hautvilliers. It was only after the brief statement of his position was rejected and he was imprisoned that the need for a longer explanatory text would have become clear.

In both *Confessio breuior* and *Confessio prolixior*, Gottschalk taught a predestination that is *gemina id est bipartita*.[29] This is further explained in the first sentence of *Confessio breuior*:

26. Peter Lombard, *Sententiae* I.47.1 (Brady, *Magistri Petri Lombardi: Sententiae*, 322; trans. is my own): "his uerbis euidenter monstratur quod uoluntas dei aeterna semper impletur de homine, etiam si faciat homo contra dei uoluntatem."

27. A brief summary of the arguments for the different dates can be found in Genke and Gumerlock, *Gottschalk*, 71.

28. Prudentius of Troyes, *Epistola ad Hincmarum et Pardulum* (PL 115:971–1010).

29. Gottschalk, *C. pro.*, in C. Lambot, *Oeuvres théologiques et grammaticales de Godescalc d'Orbais* (Leuven: Spicilegium Sacrum Lovaniense Bureaux, 1945), 67. Here Gottschalk is interpreting a quote from Isidore of Seville's *Sententiae* 2.6.1 (PL 83:606; trans. is my own):

I believe and confess that the omnipotent and immutable God has gratuitously foreknown and predestined [*praedestinasse*] the holy angels and elect human beings to eternal life [*ad gloriam*], and that he equally predestined [*praedestinasse*] the devil himself... and also [all] reprobate human beings ... to rightly eternal death [*in mortem merito sempiternam*], on account of their own future, most certainly foreknown evil merits [*mala merita*], through his most righteous judgment.[30]

Gottschalk holds to a kind of double predestination: a *praedestinasse ad gloriam* and a *praedestinasse in mortem merito sempiternam*. This double predestination also is linked inextricably to God's foreknowledge.[31] Furthermore, the predestination of the elect to eternal life is a gratuitous gift, but the predestination of the reprobate to eternal death is the result of the reprobate's own evil merits (*mala merita*). This is not the double predestination with which Gottschalk was accused—namely, the type that claimed that God decided in advance to make the reprobate be reprobate.[32] Gottschalk's addition of *merita* to *mala* should have let him off the hook from this charge. It would be better to say that Gottschalk

---

"Predestination is double, either of the elect to rest or the reprobate to death" ("gemina est praedestinatio siue electorum ad requiem siue reproborum ad mortem").

The problem with Gottschalk relying on Isidore is that Isidore did not read double predestination through the framework of Augustine, who wrote of it principally in terms of preparation of the elect. Instead, Isidore read double predestination through the lens of Gregory the Great's *Moralia in Iob*, which thinks of predestination in terms of God's providence. The potential for misunderstanding here is great, as one discovers in Prudentius of Troyes, *Contra Iohannem Scotum*. After viewing predestination through the lens of Job 38:33—as did Gregory—Prudentius argues that it is entirely within God's predestination that "one is born in the error of unbelief and dies in that error; another, born into the correctness of the Catholic faith, ends his life in the correctness of the Catholic faith. On the other hand, one brought forth in the womb of a Catholic mother near the end of his life is devoured in the abyss of error. But another who is born in perfidy, and with the milk of his mother drinks the virus of error, ends his life in Catholic piety" (PL 115:1028; trans. is my own). Of course, it is Eriugena who is in view here as one who drank the "virus of error."

30. Lambot, *Oeuvres*, 51; trans. Genke and Gumerlock, *Gottschalk*, 71.

31. Cf. Lambot, *Oeuvres*, 52, lines 7–9. Gottschalk's linking of double predestination to foreknowledge exposed him, arguably, to a charge of Pelagianism. To his credit, he recognized the problem and so clarified his meaning in C. pro. There he argues that foreknowledge and predestination are simultaneous works of God and that the terms' interchangeability is to be understood by *metalepticos* (Lambot, *Oeuvres*, 64, line 14).

32. Despite Gottschalk's protests to the contrary, Hincmar continued to insist, as he

taught a single predestination with two effects.[33] God predestined to save gratu-itously some (i.e., the elect) despite their sin, and this results in two effects, the receipt of eternal life for those elect and damnation for the reprobate who are left, unredeemed, in their sinful state.

Considering the legitimate pastoral concerns raised by a theology of double predestination (which, again, Gottschalk did not actually teach), it should be noted that Gottschalk, too, appreciated the pastoral dimension to his teaching. He began his *Confessio prolixior* with an analysis of the world and its people, ac-knowledging the obvious fact that some of them are followers of God and many others are not. Even among those who were baptized as children and perhaps still attend Mass, not all of them are committed believers. He concluded from this that God had given grace only to some and had left the others in their state of damnation. This position would shape part of the compromise enforced on all the parties by the king at the Synod of Tusey.[34] Still, it would not satisfy Hincmar or lead to Gottschalk's release from prison.[35]

Enchiridion 26.100 is cited in *Confessio breuior* as one among its seventeen short quotations, thirteen of which are from Augustine. Of the remaining four, two are from Fulgentius and there is one each from Gregory the Great and Isidore of Seville. The majority of the citations, eleven of the seventeen, point to the singular problem Gottschalk had with his opponents: his claim that there ex-

---

did in *Ep. ad Egilonem* 2, that Gottschalk's teaching removed the merit of damnation from the reprobate.

33. Again, Gottschalk thought his own language in the *C. breu.* could be misconstrued on this point (cf. Lambot, *Oeuvres*, 52, lines 3–5, and esp. his *et ipsum* language in line 5) even though he quoted Isidore of Seville's *Sententiae* on twofold predestination (Lambot, *Oeu-vres*, 54, lines 15–16). Still, in the *C. pro.* Gottschalk clarifies that this means predestination is still only one thing and that it is the effects of that predestination that are double (Lambot, *Oeuvres*, 67, lines 2–10).

34. Cf. *supra*. See also J. D. Mansi, *Sacrorum conciliorum nova amplissima collectio*, vol. 15, *Ab anno DCCCLV usque ad anno DCCCLXVIII incl.* (Venice: Apud Antoniumzatta, 1770), 563–71.

35. Hincmar continued to insist that God's grace was extended to all persons even if only some chose to cooperate with it. He wished that Gottschalk had said God gives grace to all who are baptized, thus implying hope for everyone of a blessed afterlife. Still, Hincmar even-tually signed on to the positions articulated at the Synod of Tusey, which agreed with this part of Gottschalk's teaching. Besides, as noted *supra*, Gottschalk had engendered ill will through a series of (mis)steps: (1) he angered his abbot, Rabanus Maurus, by prevailing against him in a lawsuit; (2) he was a wandering preacher, something that just was not tolerated among the regular clergy; (3) he had gotten himself ordained by a subsequently disgraced bishop; and (4) he had—at least according to Hincmar—an incorrigible demeanor.

ist two predestinations. The citation of *Enchiridion* 26.100 is situated near the end of the Augustine quotations, which document Augustine's repeated references to a predestination to eternal death (*Io. eu. tr.* 43.13; *De ciuitate dei* [*ciu.*] 22.24.5), a predestination to punishment or to eternal punishment (*Io. eu. tr.* 48.4, 6; *De perfectione iustitiae hominis* [*perf. iust.*] 13.31), a predestination to perdition (*In Io. eu. tr.* 107.7), or a predestination to punishment (*ench.* 26.100). Here, *Enchiridion* 26.100 is not particularly prominent; it is merely one of many places where Augustine used language reminiscent of a kind of double predestination.

However, in *Confessio prolixior* this text takes on greater prominence. As he did in *Confessio breuior*, Gottschalk situates this text within a network of other Augustinian quotations.[36] He includes nearly all the same texts as before and adds to them a few new ones drawn from *De ciuitate dei*. Yet, whereas the other Augustine texts are quoted without explanation, Gottschalk pauses after his quotation of *Enchiridion* 26.100 to reflect on its importance for his wider argument. He writes,

> Likewise, in the *Enchiridion on Faith, Hope and Love*, which as an elderly man, with God wonderfully and uniquely helping him, he wrote and published with very keen insight, very experienced genius, very pure eloquence, and a very lucid style, he says: "To the damnation of those whom he has justly predestined to punishment." Likewise, in the same book he says: "They are also called the sons of hell, not born of it, but prepared for it, just as sons of the kingdom are prepared for the kingdom" (*ench.* 12). What clearer is asked for? What more sufficient? He says, "Just as the sons of the kingdom are prepared for a kingdom," so also the sons of hell have been prepared for it, which is absolutely nothing other than predestined. Surely, if such a great author as he had not perceived that all these things above and the many others were entirely true and in agreement with the catholic faith in every respect, he would in no way have left them uncorrected, but rather, when he had reexamined his books, in very carefully reviewing them, he would have made every effort to correct them. Nor would he have spoken on this to the people so frequently, both fearlessly and intrepidly, so willingly, openly, and freely, so faithfully, confidently, and joyfully, without servile fear and covered with your luminous love, and with your authority, if he had known that there was some danger in them.[37]

36. Gillis, *Heresy and Dissent*, 125–27, argues this allowed Gottschalk to pivot, in the next section of *C. pro.*, to styling himself as a new Augustine.

37. Gottschalk, *C. pro.* (Lambot, *Oeuvres*, 65, lines 2–19; trans. Genke and Gumerlock, *Gottschalk*, 83): "item in Enchiridion quod senex de fide spe et charitate sensu subtilissimo, ingenio exercitatissimo, eloquio quoque purissimo styloque luculentissimo mirabiliter sibi

Here, Gottschalk's use of *Enchiridion* 26.100 reveals a particularly important feature of his position. Gottschalk read the language of "predestination" that is found in *Enchiridion* 26.100 into Augustine's discussion of "preparation" from *Enchiridion* 12.39. He treats the terms as synonyms, even though Augustine used different words. Indeed, while Augustine defines predestination as God preparing good works for his elect in two other texts where he uses both words,[38] his language of preparation nevertheless suggests God's providential care and ordering of the world's affairs. To Gottschalk's opponents, this was part of his problem. Prioritizing predestination over preparation could lead one to think that absolutely everything that ever would happen was planned by God in advance to occur. Once God predestines his works, all that remains is for him to prepare for those works to be carried out. There is no room for God to maneuver in a person's life in light of her or his own actions. Understandably, this caused Gottschalk's opponents to question his repeated claims that the reprobate are predestined to punishment on account of the merits of their own sin.[39]

ENCHIRIDION 26.100 IN ERIUGENA

Eriugena's entry into this debate came at the request of Hincmar, who, after 850 CE, grew frustrated that the controversy not only had not gone away but, in fact,

ac singulariter, deo fauente, conscripsit et edidit: ad eorum inquit damnationem quos iuste praedestinauit ad poenam. item in eodem dicuntur etiam filii gehennae non ex illa nati sed in illam praeparati, sicut filii regni praeparantur in regnum. quid quaeritur euidentius? quid sufficientius? sicut inquit filii regni praeparantur in regnum, sic etiam filii gehennae in illam sunt praeparati, quod omnino nihil est aliud quam praedestinati. nempe haec omnia et aloia insuper plura si tantus auctor iste ueracissima et catholicae fidei per omnia congruentissima non esse perspexisset, nullatenus incorrecta relinqueret sed ea potius, quando libros suos diligentissime retractando recensuit, corrigere studuisset, nec inde prorsus tam frequenter ad populum impauide simul et intrepide, licenter libenter ac libere, fidenter ac fiducialiter ac gaudenter, seruili postposito timore luminosoque tui perfusus amore tua auctoritate locutus fuisset, si quid itidem periculi inesse cognouisset."

38. Cf. *praed. sanct.* 19 (PL 44:988–89) and *perseu.* 14.35 (PL 45:1014). The latter reads: "haec est praedestinatio sanctorum, nihil aliud: praescientia scilicet, et praeparatio beneficiorum dei, quibus certissime liberantur, quicumque liberantur."

39. Indeed, this is the point at which Ratramnus of Corbie, in *De praedestinatione Dei* 1, sought to rescue Gottschalk from himself. Predestination is not the overarching term for God's activity. Rather, as Ratramnus points out, in Augustine's teaching it is God's ordering of the world's affairs and his "inclining" (*inclinauit*) people to act in ways that are in accord with that ordering. Cf. Roberts, "Ratramnus of Corbie's 'De predestinatione Dei,'" 79.

had intensified once Gottschalk was imprisoned. Eriugena responded to Hincmar's request with *De diuina praedestinatione liber* (*De diu. praed.*).[40] Now, on the one hand, Eriugena agreed with Hincmar and others opposed to Gottschalk's position that Gottschalk had misinterpreted Augustine.[41] On the other hand, Eriugena approached the subject in an entirely different way compared to that taken by Gottschalk and, for that matter, to that taken by everyone else in the debate.[42] As noted earlier, Gottschalk began with an analysis of the world and its people, some of whom are followers of God and many of whom are not, and he concluded from this that God had given grace to some and had left others in their state of damnation. By contrast, Eriugena began with an analysis of who and what God is—an eternal being and a unity—and concluded that it is difficult to speak of God predestining anything at all. Yet, even if one wished to say, from a temporal, human perspective, that God predestines, then the only things God could predestine are the works God could do, which are good works.[43] In the case of humanity's salvation, God could be said to predestine the giving of grace to some (yes, only to some) in order that their wills are given aid to follow God.[44] In no individual's case, however, could God be said to predestine evil, since evil, which Eriugena defines as a privation of the good, does not actually exist.

With his different starting point to the debate, Eriugena can then turn to the texts of Augustine raised by Gottschalk.[45] Perhaps surprisingly, Eriugena admits that Augustine did, in fact, write in a contrary manner to his own about predestination: "The holy father Aurelius Augustine was indeed a most prolific author of Christian eloquence . . . and a most noble instructor in the literal and transferred use of language. . . . Yet, at different times in the course of his writings he is found to have said that God predestined the wicked to perdition or punishments."[46] If Augustine was supposed to be an unquestionable authority, it

---

40. The critical edition is CCCM 50, edited by Goulven Madec. For an English translation, see John Scottus Eriugena, *Treatise on Divine Predestination*, trans. Mary Brennan, Notre Dame Texts in Medieval Culture 5 (Notre Dame, IN: University of Notre Dame Press, 1998).

41. *De diu. praed.* 11.2 (CCCM 50:68).

42. Indeed, Eriugena's novel approach to the subject of predestination led nearly everyone, including Hincmar, to turn against him. The Lyons school (i.e., Florus, Remigius, and Pardulus) and Prudentius of Troyes both took the opportunity to compose multiple treatises critical of Eriugena.

43. *De diu. praed.* 9.1–10.2 (CCCM 50:55–63).

44. *De diu. praed.* 3.7 (CCCM 50:25).

45. *De diu. praed.* 11.4–12.6 (CCCM 50:69–76).

46. *De diu. praed.* 11.4 (CCCM 50:69; trans. Brennan, *Treatise on Divine Predestination*, 73–74): "quoniam uero sanctus pater Aurelius Augustinus eloquentiae christianae copiosis-

would seem that Eriugena had just handed Gottschalk the victory. Yet Eriugena goes on to argue that there may be another way to read Augustine, particularly *Enchiridion* 26.100, and that this different way frees Augustine from the narrow interpretations of Gottschalk.

The central text is *De diuina praedestinatione liber* 11–12. In chapter 11 Eriugena identifies thirteen quotations from Augustine that he acknowledges are problematic, ten of which he has lifted from Gottschalk's *Confessio prolixior*.[47] In chapter 12 Eriugena acknowledges that the most important of them all is *Enchiridion* 26.100. In fact, it is so important that Eriugena will continue to discuss it in each of the next six chapters of his text as he works out an interpretation of it in light of his own ideas.

According to Eriugena, two features of *Enchiridion* 26.100 aid in the interpretation of every other Augustine text, particularly those where Augustine uses the language of predestination to punishment, to judgment, or to death. The first feature is that *Enchiridion* 26.100 says both that some people are predestined to punishment and that others are predestined to grace. The second feature is the passage's claim that the works of the Lord are always oriented toward the good, a claim that includes the idea that God's judgment on sin is a good because it restores justice.[48] Taken together, these features allow Eriugena to assert two types of predestination. There is a type of predestination that leads to the good end of grace, and another type of predestination that leads to the good end of justice.

Thus, when Augustine says things like "predestined to punishment," he does not really mean "predestined" at all—at least not in the same way he means "predestined" in phrases such as "predestined to grace."[49] As noted earlier, Eriugena believed God can predestine only his own works, which are good things; more specifically, he believed that Augustine taught that God only predestines gifts. Eternal punishment, hell, damnation, torment—none of these are gifts. Thus, none of them are, properly speaking, things God predestines. They are, however, things God does. God does punish sin; God just does not predestine that he will

---

simus auctor . . . propriae translatae que locutionis . . . nobilissimus doctor, aliquotiens in suorum librorum serie inuenitur dixisse deum praedestinasse impios ad interitum seu poenas."

47. Note, however, that Eriugena did not respond to most of the Augustine quotes found in Gottschalk's *C. pro.* E.g., he did not include any of the *en. Ps.* citations or the *ep.* 186 citation, each of which concern scripture's language about God's having prepared an eternal punishment for the devil and his angels.

48. Cf. *De diu. praed.* 12.4 (CCCM 50:74).

49. *De diu. praed.* 12.4 (CCCM 50:74–76).

do so.[50] When Augustine writes "predestined to punishment," he is using the word "predestined" in a metaphorical sense *a contrario*.[51] That is to say, Augustine uses "predestined" in his phrase "predestined to punishment" not because it has something to do with predestination but in order to make clear he is speaking of something opposite to that which concerns the elect. This is the major contribution of Eriugena to the interpretation of Augustine in this debate. To Eriugena, Augustine uses "predestination" in multiple senses. He uses "predestined" metaphorically *a similitudine* to the divine nature when he writes of the elect, those who are predestined to grace. But he uses "predestined" metaphorically *a contrario* to the divine nature when he writes of those predestined to punishment.

Putting everything in *De diuina praedestinatione liber* 11.4–12.6 together with his earlier linguistic investigation, then, one discovers the following features of Eriugena's reception of Augustine. First, Augustine often uses language that can be misleading, such as phrases like "predestined to punishment." Second, one must pay attention to the distinction Augustine himself draws between foreknowledge and predestination. He distinguishes between what God can foreknow (including both individuals' sins and what God does in response to sins) and what God can predestine. *Enchiridion* 26.100 attests to this, which is why, to Eriugena, it is the interpretive key from within Augustine's own writings. Third, that interpretive key confirms one should read Augustine's use of "predestination" as applying only to the good works of God. Yet, fourth, one must admit Augustine was less careful in his language than a single-predestinarian like Eriugena might wish. Correcting this requires the application of linguistic tools to discern the different meanings Augustine applied to the word "predestined." As a metaphorical term, as Eriugena argues in chapter 3, predestined can mean one thing when speaking *a similitudine* but quite another thing when speaking *a contrario* to the divine nature. In the final analysis, although God cannot be

50. *De diu. praed.* 12.5 (CCCM 50:76–77).

51. *De diu. praed.* 10.2, 12.2, 12.5 (CCCM 50:62–63, 74, 77). Cf. Guy-H. Allard, "Jean Scot et la logique des propositions contraires," in *From Athens to Chartres: Neoplatonism and Medieval Thought; Studies in Honor of Edouard Jeauneau*, ed. Haijo Jan Westra (Leiden: Brill, 1992), 181–93; Monika Michalowska, "Grammar and Theology in Eriugena's Philosophy," *Philotheos* 7 (2007): 272–78, esp. 276–77; and Dominic J. O'Meara, "The Problem of Speaking about God in John Scottus Eriugena," in *Carolingian Essays: Andrew W. Mellon Lectures in Early Christian Studies*, ed. Uta-Renate Blumenthal (Washington, DC: Catholic University of America Press, 1983), 151–67, esp. 159–65.

properly said to predestine anything at all, Eriugena nevertheless acknowledges God can be *metaphorically* said to predestine that grace will be given to some.

ENCHIRIDION 26.100 IN FLORUS OF LYONS

Florus entered the ninth-century debate after reading Eriugena. A deacon in Lyons, he likely was deputized to write what his bishop, Remigius, did not want to say, which was that Hincmar shamefully confused the debate by having invited into it the "insane" arguments of Eriugena, since Hincmar is the one who had requested Eriugena's contribution.[52] Still, Florus's entry into the controversy was not due to any newfound love for Gottschalk. Like others, Florus was unsupportive of the position that God predestines the reprobate to be reprobate, which he initially thought was Gottschalk's position. Indeed, Amolo wrote a letter to Gottschalk begging him to rethink this idea.[53] Eventually, Florus would come to understand Gottschalk's position better and end up supporting it, but not without clarifying his own view that double predestination did not mean predestination of the reprobate to sin.[54]

Florus quotes *Enchiridion* 26.100 in one text, and he alludes to it in his critique of Eriugena's teaching in a second text.[55] The quotation that concerns us here is located in *Libellus de tribus epistolis*.[56] Although he calls Gottschalk

52. Florus calls "insane" the idea of Eriugena that predestination is to be understood metaphorically. In *Libellus aduersus Iohannem Scottum* (PL 119:178; trans. is my own) Florus writes, "[Eriugena's] proposition, as he has it, 'predestination to punishment is to be understood always from contrariety,' pertains to that insanity concerning which we said enough above, that he wishes we might understand predestination to be not-predestination" ("eius propositio, quae ita se habet: praedestinatos ad poenam a contrario semper intelligi, ad illam insaniam pertinet, de qua diximus, qua uult, ut intellegamus praedistinatos, id est non praedistinatos").

53. Amolo of Lyons, *Ep. ad Gothescalcum* (PL 116:84–96).

54. In *Libellus de tenenda immobiliter scripturae sanctae ueritate*, Florus writes, "But what [God] predestined to glory, [God] predestined to justice. But what [God] predestined to punishment, [God] did not predestine to sin" (trans. is my own; cf. CCCM 260:450: "sed quos praedestinauit ad gloriam, praedestinauit ad iustitiam. quos autem praedestinauit ad poenam, non praedestinauit ad culpam").

55. Cf. n. 51 *supra*.

56. Florus, *Libellus de tribus epistolis* 1 (CCCM 260:317–417). The quotation is located within a network of patristic citations including Gelasius, Beda, and Augustine.

"that miserable monk" (*miserabilis illius monachi*) earlier in the text,[57] Florus nevertheless deems it necessary to defend him since his teaching about predestination accords, in Florus's view, with patristic and scriptural evidence. Here Florus writes,

> Again, in the book *Enchiridion*, which he wrote to Laurence, an archdeacon of the church of Rome, concerning similar things it is said in one place, "When angels," he says, "and human creatures had sinned . . . [*Ench.* 26.100 continues] . . . whom he had mercifully predestined to grace." We have placed in two books this small part from the most blessed preface of the doctor [i.e., Gottschalk],[58] which he had written not only truthfully and in a Catholic way, but also revised diligently and faithfully, and evidently acknowledged that he gathered diligently in his revised books. At this moment, his [Gottschalk's] authorities concerning this teaching—that is, concerning divine predestination in both parts, namely of the elect to glory and of the reprobate to punishment—are scorned publicly and despised by some, it seems, because he himself piously and humbly caught [errors] and corrected them in certain of his own writings, yet they [i.e., his critics] perhaps presume licentiously to be able to catch him, where he has re-examined them. What he has done for the example of humility, they themselves have usurped and not been ashamed to swell with presumption.
>
> They acknowledge this [teaching of double predestination] from even these books, since this word of divine predestination is placed in part of the reprobate, since truly and rightly they are called by the divine judgment of predestination certainly not to sin but to punishment, not to evil works, which they themselves desire to do, but to evil, which in eternal punishment the reluctant will suffer.[59]

57. Florus, *Libellus de tribus epistolis* 1 (CCCM 260:320).

58. By "two books" Florus is referring also to his citation of this text later in the same work (CCCM 260:368).

59. Florus, *Libellus in tribus epistolis* 1 (CCCM 260:336; trans. is my own): "item in libro enchyridion, quem ad Laurentium ecclesiae Romanae archidiaconum scripsit, de eadem re ita loquitur: cum angelica, inquit, et humana creatura peccasset . . . [quote of *ench.* 26.100 continues] . . . quos benigne praedestinauit ad gratiam. haec pauca ex praefati beatissimi doctoris duobus libris posuimus, quos eum non solum catholice et ueridice scripsisse, sed etiam diligenter et fideliter retractasse, qui libros retractationum eius attentius legit, euidenter agnoscit. ut quia iam eius auctoritas de hac re, id est de diuina in utramque partem praedestinatione et electorum uidelicet ad gloriam et reproborum ad poenam, a nonnullis publice contemnitur et conculcatur, ita ut, quia se ipse in quibusdam scriptis suis pie atque humiliter reprehendit

It is noteworthy that this is not a direct quotation from Gottschalk's work. Indeed, Gottschalk includes only the last sentence of what Florus has here. This is true also in *Confessio prolixior*, so Florus must have looked up the text elsewhere to get the full citation. This is important, because Florus claims Gottschalk would have removed or corrected the Augustine quote if, upon later examination, he deemed it unsupportive of his cause. To Florus, Gottschalk correctly retained the citation in *Confessio prolixior* because, as Florus himself double-checked, it does, in fact, support a teaching of double predestination. The fact that Florus did not realize that the wider context of Augustine's text does not emphasize predestination but rather the will of God might suggest he did not refer to the *Enchiridion* itself but instead to a digest of the work that provided the fuller quotation.

Finally, Florus acknowledges what Gottschalk seemed incapable of explicitly acknowledging—that is, that *Enchiridion* 26.100 should not be construed as God's having caused the reprobate to sin or to do evil. Florus says, rather, that the text confirms that this second predestination is *ad poenam* and *ad malum*. The use of *ad malum* is particularly surprising. It was precisely this phrase, predestination *ad malum*, that was declared anathema at the Council of Orange, a detail that Florus certainly knew. It suggests that he defined *malum* in a way different from everyone else since not even Gottschalk used the phrase in the way Florus does here. To Florus, *malum* was not equivalent to *culpam*; instead, it ought to be equated with *poenam*.

Conclusion

In 421/422 CE Augustine composed *Enchiridion*, and in chapter 26 of that work he taught his reader about the power of God to will to save some. That God predestines certain things is a teaching that served to illuminate what the will of God can accomplish. Augustine wrote here what he had written in other places—that is, that God predestines some people *ad poenam*. As a result, *Enchiridion* 26.100

---

et corrigit, putent se, ubi eis uisum fuerit, licenter eum posse reprehendere. et quod ille fecit ad exemplum humilitatis, ipsi usurpare non erubescant ad tumorem praesumptionis. ex his saltim libris agnoscant, quia hoc uerbum diuinae praedistinationis in parte reproborum positum, quia uerissime et rectissime diuino iudicio praedestinati dicuntur non ad culpam utique, sed ad poenam, nec ad malum opus, quod ipsi uolentes agunt, sed ad malum, quod in aeternis suppliciis inuiti patientur."

would soon cease to be known as a text about the will of God. Instead, in the hands of composers of florilegia of Augustine's writings in the centuries that followed, *Enchiridion* 26.100 would come to be known as a text supporting double predestination, a situation that would not be corrected until readers like Peter Lombard returned to the *Enchiridion* and read it directly. This change in the meaning of the text facilitated three functions for the text among participants in the ninth-century debate over predestination. To Gottschalk, *Enchiridion* 26.100 facilitated his reading of the language of predestination into Augustine's language of preparation, even though he seemingly remained ignorant of the fact that Augustine did not use the term "preparation" for the reprobate but only for the elect. To Eriugena, *Enchiridion* 26.100 revealed the metaphorical nature of predestination, which is to say that it is not something God actually does. Finally, to Florus, like other supporters of Gottschalk who were uncomfortable with his seeming inability to avoid being misunderstood, *Enchiridion* 26.100 reminded everyone that Augustine should not be read as teaching predestination of the reprobate to sin, or even the predestination of them to be reprobate. That is something the reprobate have always willed for themselves.

Bibliography

Abelard, Peter. *Sic et Non: A Critical Edition*. Edited by Blanche B. Boyer and Richard McKeon. Chicago: University of Chicago Press, 1977.

"Acta S. Vincentii Martyris, Archidiaconi Caesaugustani, Qui Passus est Valentiae in Hispania, et Relatio Translationis Eiusdem." Analecta Bollandiana 1 (1882): 259–78.

Adam, Karl. *Die Eucharistielehre des hl. Augustin*. Paderborn: Ferdinand Schöningh, 1908.

Addey, Crystal. *Divination and Theurgy in Neoplatonism: Oracles of the Gods*. Burlington, VT: Ashgate, 2014.

Albrecht, Michael von. *A History of Roman Literature from Livius Andronicus to Boethius*. Rev. ed. Translated by Frances and Kevin Newman. Leiden: Brill, 1997.

Alexander, James. "Donatism." In *The Early Christian World*, edited by Philip F. Esler, 2:978–1000. New York: Routledge, 2000.

———. "The Donatist Case at the Conference of Carthage of A.D. 411." PhD diss., St. Andrews University, 1970.

Allard, Guy-H. "Jean Scot et la logique des propositions contraires." In *From Athens to Chartres: Neoplatonism and Medieval Thought; Studies in Honor of Edouard Jeauneau*, edited by Haijo Jan Westra, 181–93. Leiden: Brill, 1992.

Allenbach, J., et al., eds. *Biblia Patristica: Index des citations et allusions bibliques dans la littérature patristique*. Vol. 3, *Origène*. Paris: CNRS, 1980.

Altaner, Berthold. "Altlateinische Übersetzungen von Basiliusschriften." In Glockmann, *Kleine patristische Schriften*, 409–15.

———. "Augustinus und Basilius der Große." In Glockmann, *Kleine patristische Schriften*, 267–76.

———. "Augustinus und die griechische Sprache." In Glockmann, *Kleine patristische Schriften*, 129–53.

———. "Augustinus und Gregor von Nazianz, Gregor von Nyssa." In Glockmann, *Kleine patristische Schriften*, 277–85.

———. "Augustinus und Origenes." In Glockmann, *Kleine patristische Schriften*, 224–52.

———. "Eustathius, der lateinische Übersetzer der Hexaemeron-Homilien Basilius des Großen." In Glockmann, *Kleine patristische Schriften*, 437–47.

Ambrose. *Ambroise de Milan: Des Sacraments; Des Mystères*. Edited and translated by Dom Bernard Botte, OSB. SC 25. Paris: Cerf, 1950.

———. *St. Ambrose: Selected Works and Letters*. In vol. 10 of *The Nicene and Post-Nicene Fathers*, Series 2. Edited by Philip Schaff and Henry Wace. 1890–1900. 14 vols. Reprint, Peabody, MA: Hendrickson, 1995.

———. *Theological and Dogmatic Works*. Translated by Roy J. Deferrari. FC 44. Washington, DC: Catholic University of America Press, 1963.

Ambrosiater. *Ambrosiaster's Commentary on the Pauline Epistles: Romans*. Translated by Theodore S. de Bruyn, with an introduction by Theodore S. de Bruyn, Stephen A. Cooper, and David G. Hunter. Edited by Andrew Cain. WGRW 41. Atlanta: SBL Press, 2017.

Amidon, Philip R. *The Church History of Rufinus of Aquileia: Books 10 and 11*. Oxford: Oxford University Press, 1997.

Andreicut, Gavril. "The Church's Unity and Authority: Augustine's Effort to Convert the Donatists." PhD diss., Marquette University, 2010.

Angus, S. *The Sources of the First Ten Books of Augustine's "De civitate Dei."* Princeton: Princeton University Press, 1906.

Augustine. *Answer to the Pelagians II*. Translated by Roland J. Teske. Edited by John E. Rotelle. WSA I/24. Hyde Park, NY: New City, 1998.

———. *Answer to the Pelagians III*. Translated by Roland J. Teske. Edited by John E. Rotelle. WSA I/25. Hyde Park, NY: New City, 1999.

———. *Answer to the Pelagians IV*. Translated by Roland J. Teske. Edited by John E. Rotelle. WSA I/26. Hyde Park, NY: New City, 1999.

———. *Arianism and Other Heresies*. Translated by Roland J. Teske. Edited by John E. Rotelle. WSA I/18. Hyde Park, NY: New City, 1995.

———. *The City of God (Books 1–10)*. Translated by William Babcock. Edited by Boniface Ramsey. WSA I/6. Hyde Park, NY: New City, 2012.

———. *The City of God (Books 11–22)*. Translated by William Babcock. Edited by Boniface Ramsey. WSA I/6. Hyde Park, NY: New City, 2013.

———. *City of God*. Vol. 7, *Books 21–22*. Translated by William M. Green. LCL 417. Cambridge, MA: Harvard University Press, 1972.

———. *Concerning the City of God against the Pagans*. Translated by Henry Bettenson. London: Penguin, 2003.

———. *The Confessions*. Translated by Maria Boulding. Edited by David Vincent Meconi. Ignatius Critical Editions. San Francisco: Ignatius, 2012.

———. *The Confessions*. Translated by Maria Boulding. Edited by John E. Rotelle. WSA I/1. Hyde Park, NY: New City, 1997.

———. *Confessions*. Translated by Henry Chadwick. Oxford: Oxford University Press, 1991.

———. *Confessions*. Translated by Sarah Ruden. New York: Modern Library, 2017.

———. *De Doctrina Christiana*. Edited and translated by R. P. H. Green. OECT. Oxford: Clarendon, 2004.

———. *Earlier Writings*. Translated by J. H. S. Burleigh. Library of Christian Classics. London: SCM; Philadelphia: Westminster, 1953.

———. *Eighty-Three Different Questions*. Translated by David L. Mosher. FC 70. Washington, DC: Catholic University of America Press, 1982.

———. *Expositions of the Psalms 121–150*. Translated by Maria Boulding. Edited by Boniface Ramsey. WSA III/20. Hyde Park, NY: New City, 2004.

———. *The Happy Life; Answers to Skeptics; Divine Providence and the Problem of Evil; Soliloquies*. Translated by Ludwig Schopp, Denis J. Kavanagh, Robert P. Russell, and Thomas F. Gilligan. FC 5. Washington, DC: Catholic University of America Press, 2010.

———. *Homilies on the First Epistle of John*. Translated by Boniface Ramsey. Edited by Daniel E. Doyle and Thomas Martin. WSA I/14. Hyde Park, NY: New City, 2008.

———. *Letters 1–99*. Translated by Roland J. Teske. Edited by Boniface Ramsey. WSA II/1. Hyde Park, NY: New City, 2001.

———. *Letters 100–155*. Translated by Roland J. Teske. Edited by Boniface Ramsey. WSA II/2. Hyde Park, NY: New City, 2003.

———. *Miscellanea Agostiniana*. Edited by Germain Morin and Antonio Casamassa. 2 vols. Rome: Tipografia Poliglotta Vaticana, 1930–1931.

———. *New Testament I and II*. Translated by Kim Paffenroth, Roland J. Teske, and Michael Campbell. Edited by Boniface Ramsey. WSA I/15–16. Hyde Park, NY: New City, 2014.

———. *Newly Discovered Sermons*. Translated by Edmund Hill. Edited by John E. Rotelle. WSA III/11. Hyde Park, NY: New City, 1997.

———. *On Christian Belief*. Translated by Edmund Hill, Ray Kearney, Michael G.

Campbell, and Bruce Harbert. Edited by Boniface Ramsey. WSA I/8. Hyde Park, NY: New City, 2005.

———. *On the Holy Trinity; Doctrinal Treatises; Moral Treatises.* In vol. 3 of *The Nicene and Post-Nicene Fathers*, Series 1. Edited by Philip Schaff. 1886–1889. 14 vols. Reprint, Peabody, MA: Hendrickson, 1995.

———. *Responses to Miscellaneous Questions.* Translated by Boniface Ramsey. Edited by Raymond Canning. WSA I/12. Hyde Park, NY: New City, 2008.

———. *Sermons 51–94.* Translated by Edmund Hill. Edited by John E. Rotelle. WSA III/3. H Hyde Park, NY: New City, 1991.

———. *Sermons 94A–147A.* Translated by Edmund Hill. Edited by John E. Rotelle. WSA III/4. Hyde Park, NY: New City, 1992.

———. *Sermons 230–272B.* Translated by Edmund Hill. Edited by John E. Rotelle. WSA III/7. Hyde Park, NY: New City, 1993.

———. *Sermons 273–305A.* Translated by Edmund Hill. Edited by John E. Rotelle. WSA III/8. Hyde Park, NY: New City, 1994.

———. *Sermons 306–340A.* Translated by Edmund Hill. Edited by John E. Rotelle. WSA III/9. Hyde Park, NY: New City, 1994.

———. *The Soliloquies of St. Augustine.* Translated by Rose E. Cleveland. Boston: Little, Brown, 1910.

———. *Teaching Christianity.* Translated by Edmund Hill. Edited by John E. Rotelle. WSA I/11. Hyde Park, NY: New City, 1996.

Babcock, William. "Augustine's Interpretation of Romans (A. D. 394–396)." *AugStud* 10 (1979): 60–61.

Bardy, Gustave. "Saint Augustin et Tertullien." *L'année théologique augustinienne* 13 (1953): 145–50.

Barnes, Jonathan. "*Anima Christiana.*" In *Body and Soul in Ancient Philosophy*, edited by D. Frede and B. Reis, 447–64. Berlin: de Gruyter, 2009.

Barnes, Timothy David. "The Beginnings of Donatism." *JTS*, n.s., 26 (1975): 13–22.

———. *Early Christian Hagiography and Roman History.* Tria Corda 5. Tübingen: Mohr Siebeck, 2010.

———. *Early Christian Hagiography and Roman History.* 2nd ed. Tübingen: Mohr Siebeck, 2016.

———. *Tertullian: A Historical and Literary Study.* Rev. ed. Oxford: Clarendon, 1985.

Barreteau-Revel, Cécile. "Faire l'unité dans l'église d'Afrique du Nord: La réintegration des donatistes à la transition des IVe et Ve siècles." In *Les Pères de l'Église et les dissidents: Dissidence, exclusion, et réintegration dans les communautés chrétiennes des six premiers siècles*, edited by Pascal-Grégoire Delage, 223–59. La Rochelle: Caritas Patrum, 2010.

Basil the Great. *On Fasting and Feasts*. Translated by Susan R. Holman and Mark Del-Cogliano. Popular Patristics Series 50. Yonkers, NY: St Vladimir's Seminary Press, 2013.

Bass, Alden. "Scripture in Optatus of Milevis." In *The Bible in Christian North Africa, Part I: Commencement to the "Confessiones" of Augustine (ca. 180 to 400 CE)*, edited by Jonathan Yates and Anthony Dupont, 189–212. Handbooks of the Bible and Its Reception 4.1. Berlin: de Gruyter, 2020.

Bastiaensen, Antoon A. R. "Augustin commentateur de saint Paul et l'Ambrosiaster." *Sacris Erudiri* 36 (1996): 37–65.

———. "Augustin et les prédécesseurs latins chrétiens." In den Boeft and van Oort, *Augustiniana Traiectina*, 25–57.

———. "Augustin et ses prédécesseurs latins chrétiens." In den Boeft and van Oort, *Augustiniana Traiectina*, 25–57.

———. "Augustine's Pauline Exegesis and Ambrosiaster." In Van Fleteren and Schnaubelt, *Augustine*, 33–54.

Bavel, Tarsicius J. van. "The Influence of Cicero's Ideal of Friendship on Augustine." In den Boeft and van Oort, *Augustiniana Traiectina*, 59–72

Baxter, J. H. "Ambrosiaster cited as 'Ambrose' in 405." *JTS* 24 (1922–1923): 187.

Beatrice, Pier Franco. "*Quosdam Platonicorum Libros.*" *VC* 43 (1989): 248–81.

———. "The Treasure of the Egyptians." *StPatr* 39 (2006): 159–83.

Benjamins, H. S. *Eingeordnete Freiheit: Freiheit und Vorsehung bei Origenes*. Leiden: Brill, 1994.

Bennett, Camille. "The Conversion of Vergil: The *Aeneid* in Augustine's *Confessions.*" *REAug* 34 (1988): 48–54.

Bernardi, Jean. *La prédication des pères cappadociens*. Paris: Presses universitaires de France, 1968.

Bernoulli, Carl A., ed. *Hieronymus und Gennadius: De viris illustribus*. SAQ 11. Leipzig: Mohr, 1895.

Beyenka, Barbara. "The Names of St. Ambrose in the Works of St. Augustine." *AugStud* 5 (1974): 19–28.

———. "St. Augustine and the Hymns of St. Ambrose." *American Benedictine Review* 8 (1957): 121–32.

Bidez, J. *Vie de Porphyre*. Gand: Van Goethem, 1913.

Bishop, W. C. "The African Rite." *JTS* 13 (1912): 250–70.

Bochet, Isabelle. "Interprétation scripturaire et compréhension de soi: Du *De doctrina christiana* aux *Confessiones* de Saint Augustin." In *Comprendre et interpreter: Le paradigm herméneutique de la raison*, edited by Jean Greisch, 21–50. Paris: Beauchêsne, 1993.

———. *"Le firmament de l'Écriture": L'herméneutique augustinienne.* Paris: Études Augustiniennes, 2004.

———. "The Role of Scripture in Augustine's Controversy with Porphyry." *AugStud* 41, no. 1 (2010): 7–52.

Boeft, J. den, and J. van Oort, eds. *Augustiniana Traiectina: Communications présentées au Colloque International d'Utrecht 13–14 novembre 1986.* Paris: Études Augustiniennes, 1987.

Boersma, Gerald P. *Augustine's Early Theology of Image: A Study in the Development of Pro-Nicene Theology.* Oxford: Oxford University Press, 2016.

Bonner, Gerald. *"Dic Christi Veritas Ubi Nunc Habitas:* Ideas of Schism and Heresy in Post-Nicene Age." In Klingshirn and Vessey, *Limits of Ancient Christianity,* 63–79.

———. *Freedom and Necessity: St. Augustine's Teaching on Divine Power and Human Freedom.* Washington, DC: Catholic University of America Press, 2007.

———. "Rufinus of Syria and African Pelagianism." *AugStud* 1 (1970): 31–47.

Boodts, Shari, and Dupont, Anthony. "Augustine of Hippo." In *Preaching in the Patristic Era: Sermons, Preachers, and Audiences in the Latin West,* edited by Anthony Dupont, Shari Boodts, Gert Partoens, and Johan Leemans, 177–97. New History of the Sermon 6. Leiden: Brill, 2018.

Bouhot, Jean-Paul. "La lecture liturgique des Epîtres Catholiques d'après les sermons d'Augustin." In *La lecture liturgique des Épîtres Catholiques dans l'Église ancienne,* edited by Christian-Bernard Amphoux and Jean-Paul Bouhot, 269–81. Lausanne: Zèbre, 1996.

Bowlin, John R. "Augustine on Justifying Coercion." *Annual of the Society of Christian Ethics* 17 (1997): 49–70.

Bradshaw, Paul F. *The Search for the Origins of Christian Worship: Sources and Methods for the Study of Early Liturgy.* London: SPCK, 2002.

Bradshaw, Paul F., and Lawrence A. Hoffman. *The Making of Jewish and Christian Worship.* Two Liturgical Traditions 1. Notre Dame, IN: University of Notre Dame Press, 1991.

Brady, Ignatius, ed. *Magistri Petri Lombardi: Sententiae in IV libris distinctae.* 3rd ed. Spicilegium Bonaventurianum t. 4 pt. 2. Grottaferrata: Editiones Collegii S. Bonaventurae ad Claras Aquas, 1971.

Bremmer, Jan N., and Marco Formisano, eds. *Perpetua's Passions: Multidisciplinary Approaches to the "Passio Perpetuae et Felicitatis."* Oxford: Oxford University Press, 2012.

Brown, Peter. *Augustine of Hippo: A Biography.* Berkeley: University of California Press, 1967.

———. *Augustine of Hippo: A Biography.* New ed. Berkeley: University of California Press, 2000.

———. *The Body and Society: Men, Women, and Sexual Renunciation in Early Christianity.* New York: Columbia University Press, 1988.

———. "Religious Coercion in the Later Roman Empire: The Case of North Africa." *History* 48 (1963): 283–305.

Browne, Stephen Howard. "Michael Leff and the Return of the Rhetorical Text." *Rhetoric & Public Affairs* 13, no. 4 (2010): 679–88.

Bruyn, Theodore S. de. "The Transmission and Editions of the Commentary." In Ambrosiater, *Ambrosiaster's Commentary,* xxxi–lv.

Bruyn, Theodore S. de, Stephen A. Cooper, David G. Hunter. "Polemical Aspects of the Commentary." In Ambrosiater, *Ambrosiaster's Commentary,* xcvii–cxiii.

Burns, J. Patout, Jr. "Action in Suárez." *New Scholasticism* 38 (1964): 453–72.

———. "Ambrose Preaching to Augustine: The Shaping of Faith," in *Augustine: Second Founder of the Faith,* edited by Joseph C. Schnaubelt and Frederick van Fleteren, 373–86. New York: Lang, 1990.

———. "Appropriating Augustine Appropriating Cyprian." *AugStud* 36 (2005): 113–30.

———. "Augustine's Ecclesial Mysticism." In *The Wiley-Blackwell Companion to Christian Mysticism,* edited by Julia A. Lamm, 202–15. London: Wiley-Blackwell, 2013.

———. "Christ and the Holy Spirit in Augustine's Theology of Baptism." In *Augustine: From Rhetor to Theologian,* edited by Joanne McWilliam, 161–71. Waterloo, ON: Wilfrid Laurier University Press, 1992.

———. *Cyprian the Bishop.* New York: Routledge, 2002.

———. *The Development of Augustine's Doctrine of Operative Grace.* Paris: Études Augustiniennes, 1980.

———. "Establishing Unity in Diversity." *Perspectives in Religious Studies* 32 (2005): 381–99.

———. "Maréchal's Approach to the Existence of God." *New Scholasticism* 43 (1968): 72–90.

———. "Spiritual Dynamism in Maréchal." *The Thomist* 32 (1968): 528–39.

———, ed. *Theological Anthropology.* Sources of Early Christian Thought. Philadelphia: Fortress, 1981.

Burns, J. Patout, and Gerald M. Fagin. *The Holy Spirit.* Message of the Fathers of the Church 3. Wilmington, DE: Glazier, 1984. Reprint, Eugene, OR: Wipf & Stock, 2002.

Burns, J. Patout, Jr., and Robin M. Jensen. *Christianity in Roman Africa: The Development of Its Practices and Beliefs*. Grand Rapids: Eerdmans, 2014.

Burton, Philip. "The Vocabulary of the Liberal Arts in Augustine's *Confessions*." In Pollmann and Vessey, *Augustine and the Disciplines*, 141–64.

Butler, Rex C. *The New Prophecy and "New Visions": Evidence of Montanism in the Passion of Perpetua and Felicitas*. PatrMS 18. Washington, DC: Catholic University of America Press, 2006.

Byers, Sarah. "Augustine and the Cognitive Cause of the Stoic Preliminary Passions." *Journal of the History of Philosophy* 41, no. 4 (2003): 433–48.

Callahan, John F. "Basil of Caesarea: A New Source for St. Augustine's Theory of Time." *Harvard Studies in Classical Philology* 63 (1958): 437–54.

Cameron, Alan. *The Last Pagans of Rome*. Oxford: Oxford University Press, 2011.

Cameron, Michael. *Christ Meets Me Everywhere: Augustine's Early Figurative Exegesis*. Studies in Historical Theology. New York: Oxford University Press, 2012.

Cavadini, John C. "Ambrose and Augustine *de bono mortis*." In Klingshirn and Vessey, *Limits of Ancient Christianity*, 232–49.

———. "Eucharistic Exegesis in Augustine's *Confessions*." In *Visioning Augustine*, 184–210. Oxford: Wiley-Blackwell, 2019.

Cecconi, Giovanni A. "Elemosina e propaganda. Un analisi della 'Macariana persecutio.'" *REAug* 31 (1990): 42–66.

Chadwick, Henry. *The Sentences of Sextus*. Texts and Studies 5. Cambridge: Cambridge University Press, 1959.

Chambert-Protat, Pierre, Jérémy Delmulle, Warren Pezé, and Jeremy Thompson. *La controverse Carolingienne sur la prédestination: Histoire, textes, manuscrits*. Haut Moyen Âge 32. Turnhout: Brepols, 2018.

Chase, Michael. "'*Omne Corpus Fugiendum*?' Augustine and Porphyry on the Body and the Post-mortem Destiny of the Soul." Χώρα 2 (2004): 37–58.

Chevalier, Jean. *Saint Augustin et la pensée grecque: Les relations trinitaires*. Collectanea Friburgensia 33. Fribourg: Librairie de l'Universite, 1940.

Chronister, Andrew C. "Doctor Traditionum: Augustine and Appeals to Tradition in the Pelagian Controversy." PhD diss., St. Louis University, 2016.

Cicero. *De Senectute, De Amicitia, De Divinatione*. Translated by William Armistead Falconer. LCL 154. Cambridge, MA: Harvard University Press, 1964.

———. *Letters to Atticus*. Vol. 3. Edited and translated by D. R. Shackleton Bailey. LCL 97. Cambridge, MA: Harvard University Press, 1999.

———. *On Ends*. Translated by H. Rackham. LCL 40. Cambridge, MA: Harvard University Press, 1914.

—————. *Tusculan Disputations*. Translated by J. E. King. LCL 141. Cambridge, MA: Harvard University Press, 1927.

Ciccolini, Laetitia. "*Tertullianus magister*: Tertullien lu par Cyprien de Carthage." In Lagouanère and Fialon, *Tertullianus Afer*, 141–66.

Cipriani, Nello. "Agostino lettore dei commentari paolini di Mario Vittorino." *Augustinianum* 38 (1998): 413–28.

—————. "Augustine and the Writings of Marius Victorinus." In *Marius Victorinus: Pagan Rhetor, Platonist Philosopher, and Christian Theologian*, edited by Stephen Cooper and Václav Němec. Writings from the Greco-Roman World, Supplement. Atlanta: SBL Press, forthcoming.

—————. "La presenza di Mario Vittorino nella riflessione trinitaria di Agostino." *Augustinianum* 42 (2002): 261–313.

—————. "La retractatio Agostiniana sulla processione-generazione dello Spirito Santo (*Trin.* V.12.13)." *Augustinianum* 37 (1997): 431–39.

—————. "L'autore dei testi pseudobasiliani riportati nel *c. Iul.* (1.16–17) e la polemica agostiniana de Giuliano d'Eclano." In *Congresso internazionale su s. Agostino nel XVI centenario della conversione: Atti*, 1:439–49. Rome: Institutum Patristicum Augustinianum, 1987.

—————. "Le fonti cristiane della dottrina trinitaria nel primi dialoghi di S. Agostino." *Augustinianum* 34 (1994): 253–312.

—————. "Le fonti patristiche e filosofiche del De Trinitate di S. Agostino." *Augustinianum* 55 (2015): 427–60.

—————. "Un'altra traccia dell'Ambrosiaster in Agostino (*De pecc. mer. remiss.* II, 36, 58–59)." *Augustinianum* 24 (1984): 515–25.

Clark, C. U. *Ammiani Marcellini rerum gestarum libri qui supersunt*. Berlin: Weidmann, 1910.

Clark, Elizabeth A. *The Origenist Controversy: The Cultural Construction of an Early Christian Debate*. Princeton: Princeton University Press, 1992.

Clark, Gillian. "*Acerrimus inimicus*? Porphyry and the *City of God*." In *Le Traité de Porphyre Contre les Chrétiens*, edited by Sébastian Morlet, 395–406. Paris: Études Augustiniennes, 2011.

—————. "Augustine's Porphyry and the Universal Way of Salvation." In Karamanolis and Sheppard, *Studies on Porphyry*, 127–40.

—————. "In Praise of the Wax Candle: Augustine the Poet and Late Latin Literature." In Elsner and Hernández Lobato, *Poetics of Late Latin Literature*, 424–46.

—————. *Monica: An Ordinary Saint*. Oxford: Oxford University Press, 2015.

Cocchini, Francesco. *Agostino, Commento alla Lettera ai Galati*. Bologna: Dehoniane, 2012.

Cochrane, Charles Norris. *Christianity and Classical Culture: A Study of Thought and Action from Augustus to Augustine*. New York: Oxford University Press, 1940.

Cole, Spencer. *Cicero and the Rise of Deification at Rome*. Cambridge: Cambridge University Press, 2013.

Colish, Marcia L. *Ambrose's Patriarchs: Ethics for the Common Man*. Notre Dame, IN: University of Notre Dame Press, 2005.

Comeau M. "Sur la transmission des sermons de Saint Augustin." *Revue des études latines* 10 (1932): 408–22.

Congar, Yves. "L'interpretation de Mat., XVI, 18." BA 28:716–17.

———. "Optat de Milev." BA 28:721–22.

Conybeare, Catherine. *The Irrational Augustine*. Oxford: Oxford University Press, 2006.

Cooper, John M. *Pursuits of Wisdom: Six Ways of Life in Ancient Philosophy from Socrates to Plotinus*. Princeton: Princeton University Press, 2012.

Cooper, Stephen A. *Marius Victorinus' Commentary on Galatians: Introduction, Translation, and Notes*. OECS. Oxford: Oxford University Press, 2005.

Copeland, Rita. *Rhetoric, Hermeneutics, and Translation in the Middle Ages: Academic Traditions and Vernacular Texts*. Cambridge: Cambridge University Press, 1991.

Courcelle, Pierre. *Late Latin Writers and Their Greek Sources*. Translated by Harry Wedeck. Cambridge, MA: Harvard University Press, 1969.

———. *Les Confessions de Saint Augustin dans la tradition littéraire: Antecédénts et posterité*. Paris: Études Augustiniennes, 1963.

———. "Les exégèses chrétiennes de la quatrième églogue." *Revue des études anciennes* 59 (1957): 249–319.

———. *Recherches sur les Confessions de Saint Augustin*. Paris: de Boccard, 1950.

Crespin, Rémi. *Ministère et Sainteté: Pastorale du clergé et solution de la crise donastiste dans la vie et la doctrine de saint Augustin*. Paris: Études Augustiniennes, 1965.

Cuscito, Giuseppe. *Inscriptiones Christianae Italiae XVI: Mediolanum III*. Bari: Edipuglia, 2016.

Cyprian. *De Lapsis and De Ecclesiae Catholicae Unitate*. Translated by Maurice Bévenot. Oxford: Clarendon, 1971.

———. *The Letters of St. Cyprian of Carthage*. Translated by Graeme W. Clarke. Vol. 1. ACW 43. New York: Newman, 1984.

Daley, Brian. "The Giant's Twin Substances: Ambrose and the Christology of Augustine's *Contra sermonem Arrianorum*." In *Augustine: Presbyter Factus Sum*, edited by Joseph T. Lienhard, Earl C. Muller, and Roland J. Teske, 477–95. New York: Lang, 1993.

Dalvit, Matteo. "The Catholic Construction of Donatist Key Figures: A Critical Reading of Augustine and Optatus." In Dupont, Gaumer, and Lamberigts, *Uniquely African Controversy*, 237–49.

Daly, Cahal B. *Tertullian the Puritan and His Influence*. Dublin: Four Courts, 1993.

Daugherty, Bradley. "The Bishops of North Africa: Rethinking Practice and Belief in Late Antiquity." PhD diss., Vanderbilt University, 2015.

Dekkers, Eligius, ed. *Clavis Patrum Latinorum*. 2nd ed. Steenbrugis: Abbatia Sancti Petri, 1961.

Di Santo, Emanuele. *L'Apologetica dell'Ambrosiaster: Cristiani, pagani e giudei nella Roma tardoantica*. Rome: Istituto Patristico Augustinianum, 2008.

Dobell, Brian. *Augustine's Intellectual Conversion: The Journey from Platonism to Christianity*. Cambridge: Cambridge University Press, 2009.

Doignon, Jean. "La 'praxis' de l'admonitio dans les dialogues de Cassiciacum de St. Augustin." *Vetera Christianorum* 23 (1986): 21–37.

———. "'L'esprit souffle où il veut' (*Jean* III, 8) dans la plus ancienne tradition patristique latine." *Revue des sciences philosophiques et théologiques* 62 (1978): 356–57.

———. "'Nous bons hommes de foi': Cyprien, Lactance, Victorin, Optat, Hilaire (*De doctr. Christ.* 2,40,61)." *Latomus* 22 (1963): 795–805.

Dolbeau, François. *Vingt-six sermons au peuple d'Afrique*. 2nd ed. Collection des études augustiniennes, Série antiquité 147. Paris: Études Augustiniennes, 2009.

Doyle, Daniel E. "Introduction to Augustine's Preaching." In Augustine, *Essential Sermons*, edited by Daniel E. Doyle, translated by Edmund Hill, 21–22. WSA III. Hyde Park, NY: New City, 2007.

———. "Spread throughout the World: Hints on Augustine's Understanding of Petrine Ministry." *JECS* 13, no. 2 (2005): 233–46.

Drecoll, Volker H. *Die Enstehung der Gnadenlehre Augustins*. Tübingen: Mohr Siebeck, 1999.

Drewery, Benjamin. *Origen and the Doctrine of Grace*. London: Epworth, 1960.

Drobner, Hubertus R. "The Chronology of Augustine's *Sermones ad populum*." *AugStud* 31 (2000): 211–18; 34 (2003): 49–66; 35 (2004): 43–53.

———. "The Transmission of Augustine's Sermons: A Critical Assessment." In *Tractatio Scripturarum: Ministerium Sermonis*, vol. 2, *Philological, Exegetical, Rhetorical and Theological Studies on Augustine's Sermons*, edited by Anthony Dupont, Gert Partoens, and Mathijs Lamberigts, 97–116. IPM 65. Turnhout: Brepols, 2013.

Dubreucq, Eric. "La chair, la grâce et l'esprit: Métempsycose et résurrection de Porphyre à Saint Augustin." *Archives de Philosophie* 60, no. 1 (1997): 25–45.

Duchesne, Louis. "Le dossier du Donatisme." *Mélanges de l'école française de Rome* 10 (1890): 589–650.

Dulaey, Martine. "L'apprentissage de l'exégèse biblique par Augustin, Première partie: Dans les années 386–389." *REAug* 48 (2002): 267–95.

———. "L'apprentissage de l'exégèse biblique par Augustin (2): Années 390–392." *REAug* 49 (2003): 43–84.

———. "L'apprentissage de l'exégèse biblique par Augustin (3): Années 393–394." *REAug* 51 (2005): 21–65.

Dunkle, Brian "'Made Worthy of the Holy Spirit': A Hymn of Ambrose in Augustine's *Nature and Grace*." *AugStud* 50, no. 1 (2019): 1–12.

Dunn, Geoffrey D. "The Elements of Ascetical Widowhood: Augustine's *De bono viduitatis* and *Epistula* 130." In *Prayer and Spirituality in the Early Church*, vol. 4, *The Spiritual Life*, edited by Wendy Mayer, Pauline Allen, and Lawrence Cross, 247–56. Strathfield: St Pauls Publications, 2006.

———. "Heresy and Schism in Cyprian of Carthage." *JTS* 55 (2004): 551–74.

———. "Optatus and Parmenian on the Authority of Cyprian." In Dupont, Gaumer, and Lamberigts, *Uniquely African Controversy*, 179–96.

———. "The Reception of the Martyrdom of Cyprian of Carthage in Early Christian Literature." In *Martyrdom and Persecution in Late Antique Christianity: Festschrift Boudewijn Dehandschutter*, edited by J. Leemans, 65–86. BETL 241. Leuven: Peeters, 2010.

———. *Tertullian*. ECF. London: Routledge, 2004.

———. "Tertullian." In Esler, *Early Christian World*, 959–75.

Dupont, Anthony. *Gratia in Augustine's "Sermones ad Populum" during the Pelagian Controversy: Do Different Contexts Furnish Different Insights?* BSCH 59. Leiden: Brill, 2013.

———. "Imitatio Christi, Imitatio Stephani: Augustine's Thinking on Martyrdom; The Case Study of Augustine's Sermons on the Protomartyr Stephanus." *Augustiniana* 56 (2006): 29–61.

———. *Preacher of Grace: A Critical Reappraisal of Augustine's Doctrine of Grace in His "Sermones ad Populum" on Liturgical Feasts and During the Donatist Controversy.* SHCT 177. Leiden: Brill, 2014.

Dupont, Anthony, Matthew Gaumer, and Mathijs Lamberigts, eds. *The Uniquely African Controversy: Interdisciplinary Studies on Donatist Christianity.* Leuven: Peeters 2015.

Duval, Yvette. "Sur la genèse des *libelli miraculorum.*" *REAug* 52 (2006): 97–112.

Edwards, Mark. "Augustine and His Christian Predecessors." In Vessey, *Companion to Augustine,* 215–26.

———. "Porphyry and the Christians." In Karamanolis and Sheppard, *Studies on Porphyry,* 111–26.

Elsner, Jaś, and Jesús Hernández Lobato, eds. *The Poetics of Late Latin Literature.* Oxford Studies in Late Antiquity. New York: Oxford University Press, 2017.

Ennabli, Liliane. *Carthage: Une métropole chrétienne du IVᵉ à la fin du VIIᵉ siècle.* Études d'Antiquités africaines. Paris: CNRS, 1997.

Eno, Robert. "The Significance of the Lists of Roman Bishops in the Anti-Donatist Polemic." *VC* 47 (1993): 158–69.

———. "Some Nuances of Donatist Ecclesiology." *REAug* 18 (1972): 46–50.

———. "The Work of Optatus as a Turning Point in the African Ecclesiology." *The Thomist* 37 (1973): 668–85.

Eriugena, John Scottus. *Treatise on Divine Predestination.* Translated by Mary Brennan. Notre Dame Texts in Medieval Culture 5. Notre Dame, IN: University of Notre Dame Press, 1998.

Esler, Philip F. *The Early Christian World.* 2nd ed. London: Routledge, 2017.

Eusebius. *Ecclesiastical History.* Vol. 1, *Books 1–5.* Translated by Kirsopp Lake. LCL 153. Cambridge, MA: Harvard University Press, 1926.

Evans, Ernest. *Tertullian's Treatise against Praxeas: The Text Edited, with an Introduction, Translation, and Commentary.* London: SPCK, 1948.

———. *Tertullian's Treatise on the Incarnation: The Text Edited with an Introduction, Translation, and Commentary.* London: SPCK, 1956.

Eyl, Jennifer. "Optatus's Account of Lucilla in *Against the Donatists,* or, Women Are Good to Undermine With." In *A Most Reliable Witness: Essays in Honor of Ross Shepard Kraemer,* edited by Susan Ashbrook Harvey, Nathaniel DesRosiers, Shira L. Lander, Jacqueline Z. Pastis, and Daniel Ullucci, 155–64. Brown Judaic Studies 358. Atlanta: SBL Press, 2015.

Farrell, Joseph. "The Canonization of Perpetua." In Bremmer and Formisano, *Perpetua's Passions,* 300–320.

Fedwick, Paul Jonathan. *Bibliotheca Basiliana Vniversalis* II/2. Turnhout: Brepols, 1996.

———. "The Translations of the Works of Basil before 1400." In *Basil of Caesarea: Christian, Humanist, Ascetic; A Sixteen-Hundredth Anniversary Symposium,* edited by Paul Jonathan Fedwick, 439–512. Toronto: Pontifical Institute of Mediaeval Studies, 1981.

Ferrari, Leo C. "From Pagan Literature to the Pages of the Holy Scriptures: Augustine's

Confessiones as Exemplary Propaedeutic." In *Kerygma und Logos: Festschrift für C. Andresen*, edited by A. M. Ritter, 173–82. Göttingen: Vandenhoeck & Ruprecht, 1979.

Ferwerda, Rein. "Plotinus' Presence in Augustine." In den Boeft and van Oort, *Augustiniana Traiectina*, 107–18.

Finn, Douglas. "Holy Spirit and Church in the Early Augustine." *Augustiniana* 64 (2014): 153–85.

Fitzgerald, Allan D., ed. *Augustine through the Ages: An Encyclopedia*. Grand Rapids: Eerdmans, 1999.

Fladerer, Ludwig. *Augustinus als Exeget: Zu seinen Kommentaren des Galaterbriefes und der Genesis*. Vienna: Österreichische Akademie der Wissenschaften, 2010.

Fleming, Julia. "The Helpful Lie: The Moral Reasoning of Augustine and John Cassian." PhD diss., The Catholic University of America, 1993.

Ford, J. Massingberd. "Was Montanism a Jewish Christian Heresy?" *Journal of Ecclesiastical History* 17 (1966): 145–58.

Frassinetti, Paolo. "Le Confessioni agostiniane e un inno di Mario Vittorino." *Giornale italiano di filologia* 2 (1949): 50–59.

Fredriksen (Landes), Paula, trans. *Augustine on Romans: Propositions from the Epistle to the Romans, Unfinished Commentary on the Epistle to the Romans*. Chico, CA: Scholars Press, 1982.

———. "Massa." *AttA*, 545–47.

Frend, W. H. C. *The Donatist Church: A Movement of Protest in Roman North Africa*. Oxford: Oxford University Press, 2000.

Fulgentius. *Selected Works*. Translated by Robert B. Eno. FC 95. Washington, DC: Catholic University of America Press, 1997.

Fuller, J. M. "Tertullianus." In *A Dictionary of Early Christian Biography and Literature*, edited by H. Wace and W. C. Piercy, 940–53. London: Murray, 1911.

Fürst, Alfons. *Von Origenes und Hieronymus zu Augustinus: Studien zur antiken Theologiegeschichte*. Berlin: de Gruyter, 2011.

Gaddis, Michael. *There Is No Crime for Those Who Have Christ: Religious Violence in the Christian Roman Empire*. Berkeley: University of California Press, 2005.

Gamber, Klaus. "Ordo Missae Africanae: Der nordafrikanische Messritus zur Zeit des hl. Augustinus." *Römische Quartalschrift für christliche Altertumskunde und für Kirchengeschichte* 64 (1969): 139–53.

Gasparro, Giulia Sfameni. "Agostino di fronte alla 'eterodossia' di Origene." In *Origene e la tradizione origeniana in Occidente: Letture storico-religiose*, 123–50. Rome: Libreria Ateneo Salesiano, 1998.

Gasti, Fabio. *La letteratura tardolatina: Un profilo storico (secoli III–VII d.C.)*. Rome: Carocci, 2020.

Gaumer, Matthew Alan. *Augustine's Cyprian: Authority in Roman Africa*. Leiden: Brill, 2016.

———. "Dealing with the Donatist Church: Augustine of Hippo's Nuanced Claim to the Authority of Cyprian of Carthage." In *Cyprian of Carthage: Studies in His Life, Language, and Thought*, edited by Henk Bakker, Paul van Geest, and Hans van Loon, 181–201. LAHR 3. Leuven: Peeters, 2010.

Geerard, Maurice, ed. *Clavis Patrum Graecorum*. 5 vols. Turnhout: Brepols, 1974–1987.

Geiger, P. Godhard. *C. Marius Victorinus Afer, ein neuplatonischer Philosoph*. Beilage zum Jahres-Berichte der Studien-Anstalt Metten. Landshut: Thomann, 1888.

Genke, Victor, and Francis X. Gumerlock. *Gottschalk and a Medieval Predestination Controversy: Texts Translated from the Latin*. Medieval Philosophical Texts in Translation 47. Milwaukee: Marquette University Press, 2010.

Gerson, Lloyd P. *Platonism and Naturalism: The Possibility of Philosophy*. Ithaca, NY: Cornell University Press, 2020.

Gillis, Matthew Bryan. *Heresy and Dissent in the Carolingian Empire: The Case of Gottschalk of Orbais*. Oxford: Oxford University Press, 2017.

Girardet, Klaus Martin. "Konstantin d. Gr. und das Keichskonzil von Arles (314): Historisches Problem und methodologische Aspekte." In *Oecumenica et Patristica: Festschrift für Wilhelm Schneemelcher zum 75. Geburtstag*, edited by Damaskinos Papendreou, Wolfgang Bienert, and Knut Schäferdiek, 151–74. Stuttgart: Kohlhammer, 1989.

Glockmann, Günter, ed. *Kleine patristische Schriften*. TUGAL 83. Berlin: Akademie, 1967.

Gonzalez, Eliezer. "Anthropologies of Continuity: The Body and Soul in Tertullian, Perpetua, and Early Christianity." *JECS* 21 (2013): 479–502

———. *The Fate of the Dead in Early Third Century North African Christianity: Passion of Perpetua and Felicitas and Tertullian*. Studien und Texte zu Antike und Christentum 83. Tübingen: Mohr Siebeck, 2014.

Gore, Charles. "Victorinus Afer." In *A Dictionary of Christian Biography, Literature, Sects and Doctrines*, edited by Henry Wace and William Smith, 4:1129–38. London: Murray, 1887.

Graver, Margaret. *Cicero on the Emotions: Tusculan Disputations 3 and 4*. Chicago: University of Chicago Press, 2002.

Gray, John. *Seven Types of Atheism*. New York: Farrar, Straus and Giroux, 2018.

Greschat, K. "Theologische Traditionen Nordafrikas vor Augustin (Tertullian, Cyprian)." In *Augustin Handbuch*, edited by Volker Drecoll, 92–98. Tübingen: Mohr Siebeck, 2007.

Griffin, C. W., and Paulsen, D. L. "Augustine and the Corporeality of God." *HTR* 95 (2002): 97–118

Gronewoller, Brian. "God the Author: Augustine's Early Incorporation of the Rhetorical Concept of *oeconomia* into His Scriptural Hermeneutic." *AugStud* 47 (2016): 65–77.

Grossi, Vittorino. "Sant' Ambrogio e sant' Agostino: Per una rilettura dei loro rapporti." In *Nec timeo mori: Atti del congresso internazionale di studi ambrosiani nel XVI centenario della more di sant' Ambrogio: Milano, 4–11 Aprile 1997*, edited by Luigi Pizzolato and Marco Rizzi, 405–62. Milan: Vita e Penserio, 1998.

Gryson, Roger. *Répertoire général des auteurs ecclésiastiques latins de l'antiquité et du moyen âge*. Vol. 1, *Introduction. Répertoire des auteurs: A–H*. Freiburg: Herder, 2007.

Gumerlock, Francis X. *Fulgentius of Ruspe on the Saving Will of God: The Development of a Sixth-Century African Bishop's Interpretation of 1 Timothy 2:4 During the Semi-Pelagian Controversy*. New York: Mellen, 2009.

Hadot, Pierre. "L'entretien d'Origène avec Héraclide et le commentaire de Saint Ambroise sur l'Évangile de Saint Luc." In *Études de patristique et d'histoire des concepts*, 171–98. Paris: Les Belles Lettres, 2010.

———. "L'image de la Trinité dans l'âme chez Victorinus et chez saint Augustin." *StPatr* 6 (1962): 409–42.

———. *Marius Victorinus: Recherches sur sa vie et ses œuvres*. Paris: Études Augustiniennes, 1971.

———. *Porphyre et Victorinus*. 2 vols. Paris: Études Augustiniennes, 1968.

———. "Une source de l'*Apologia David* d'Ambroise: Les commentaires de Didyme de d'Origène sur le psaume 50." In *Études de patristique et d'histoire des concepts*, 199–224. Paris: Les Belles Lettres, 2010.

Hagendahl, Harald. *Augustine and the Latin Classics*. Stockholm: Almqvist & Wiksell, 1967.

———. *Latin Fathers and the Classics*. Göteborg: Almqvist & Wiksell, 1958.

Hammond Bammel, Caroline P. "Augustine, Origen and the Exegesis of Saint Paul." In *Tradition and Exegesis in Early Christian Writers*, 342–68. Aldershot, UK: Variorum, 1995.

Harl, Marguerite, Gilles Dorival, and Alain Le Boulluec, ed. and trans. *Origene, Traité sur les principes (Peri Archôn)*. Paris: Études Augustiniennes, 1976.

Harmless, William. *Augustine and the Catechumenate*. Collegeville, MN: Liturgical Press, 1995.

Harnack, Adolf. *History of Dogma*. Translated by Neil Buchanan. 7 vols. Boston: Little, Brown, 1988.

Harrison, Carol. *The Art of Listening in the Early Church*. Oxford: Oxford University Press, 2013.

———. *Rethinking Augustine's Early Theology: An Argument for Continuity*. Oxford: Oxford University Press, 2006.

Hawkins, Peter S. *Dante's Testaments: Essays in Scriptural Imagination*. Stanford, CA: Stanford University Press, 1999.

Heffernan, Thomas J. *The Passion of Perpetua and Felicity*. Oxford: Oxford University Press, 2012.

Heidl, György. *Origen's Influence on the Young Augustine: A Chapter of the History of Origenism*. Piscataway, NJ: Gorgias Press, 2003.

Hennings, Ralph. *Der Briefwechsel zwischen Augustinus und Hieronymus*. Leiden: Brill, 1993.

Henry, Paul. "The *Adversus Arium* of Marius Victorinus, the First Systematic Exposition of the Doctrine of the Trinity." *JTS* 1 (1950): 42–55.

———. "Augustine and Plotinus." *JTS* 38 (1937): 1–23.

Herdt, Jennifer. *Putting on Virtue: The Legacy of the Splendid Vices*. Chicago: University of Chicago Press, 2008.

Hermanowicz, Erika T. *Possidius of Calama: A Study of the North African Episcopate in the Age of Augustine*. Oxford: Oxford University Press, 2008.

Hilary of Poitiers. *St. Hilary of Poitiers, John of Damascus*. In vol. 9 of *The Nicene and Post-Nicene Fathers*, Series 2. Edited by Philip Schaff and Henry Wace. 1890–1900. 14 vols. Reprint, Peabody, MA: Hendrickson, 1995.

Hill, Edmund. *Being Human: A Biblical Perspective*. Introducing Catholic Theology. London: Geoffrey Chapman, 1984.

Hinard, François. *Les Proscriptions de la Rome republicaine*. Collection de l'École française de Rome 83. Rome: École française de Rome, 1985.

Hombert, Pierre-Marie. *Gloria gratiae: Se glorifier en Dieu, principe et fin de la théologie augustinienne de la grâce*. Paris: Études Augustiniennes, 1996.

———. *Nouvelles recherches de chronologie augustinienne*. Paris: Études Augustiniennes, 2000.

Hoondert, P. M. "Les sermons de saint Augustin pour le jour de la Pentecôte." *Augustiniana* 46 (1996): 291–310.

Hoover, Jesse A. *The Donatist Church in an Apocalyptic Age*. Oxford: Oxford University Press, 2018.

Höschele, Regina. "From Ecloga the Mime to Vergil's *Eclogues* as Mimes: *Ein Gedankenspiel*." *Vergilius* 59 (2013): 37–60.

Hunter, David G. "The Author, Date, and Provenance." In Ambrosiaster, *Ambrosiaster's Commentary*, xxiii–xxix.

―――. *Marriage, Celibacy, and Heresy in Ancient Christianity: The Jovinianist Controversy*. Oxford: Oxford University Press, 2007.

Hušek, Vít. "*Duplex gratia*: Ambrosiaster and the Two Aspects of His Soteriology." In *Für uns und für unser Heil: Soteriologie in Ost und West*, edited by Theresia Hainthaler, Franz Mali, Gregor Emmenegger, and Manté Lenkaityté Ostermann, 151–60. Innsbruck: Tyrolia, 2014.

Image, Isabella. *The Human Condition in Hilary of Poitiers: The Will and Original Sin between Origen and Augustine*. Oxford: Oxford University Press, 2017.

Jackson, Pamela. "Ambrose of Milan as Mystagogue." *AugStud* 20 (1989): 93–107.

Jäntsch, Josef. "Führt der Ambrosiaster zu Augustinus oder Pelagius?" *Scholastik* 15 (1934): 92–99.

Jensen, Robin Margaret, and J. Patout Burns. "The Eucharistic Liturgy in Hippo's Basilica Major at the Time of Augustine." *AttA*, 335–38.

Jerome. *Commentary on Galatians*. Translated by Andrew Cain. FC 121. Washington, DC: Catholic University of America Press, 2010.

Jewett, Robert, with Roy D. Kotansky. *Romans: A Commentary*. Minneapolis: Fortress, 2007.

Johnson, Lawrence J. *Worship in the Early Church: An Anthology of Historical Sources*. Vol. 2. Collegeville, MN: Liturgical Press, 2009.

Johnson, William A. *Readers and Reading Culture in the High Roman Empire: A Study of Elite Communities*. New York: Oxford University Press, 2010.

―――. "Toward a Sociology of Reading in Classical Antiquity." *American Journal of Philology* 121 (2000): 593–627.

Jones, A. H. M., J. R. Martindale, and J. Morris, eds. *The Prosopography of the Later Roman Empire*, vol. 1, *A.D. 260–395*. Cambridge: Cambridge University Press, 1971.

Kannengiesser, Charles. "The Interrupted *De doctrina christiana*." In *De doctrina christiana: A Classic of Western Culture*, edited by Duane W. H. Arnold and Pamela Bright, 3–13. Notre Dame, IN: University of Notre Dame Press, 1995.

Kannengiesser, Charles, and Pamela Bright. *A Conflict of Christian Hermeneutics in Roman Africa: Tyconius and Augustine*. Berkeley: Center for Hermeneutical Studies, 1989.

Kantzer Komline, Han-luen. "From Building Blocks to Blueprints: Augustine's Reception of Ambrose's *Commentary on Luke*." *StPatr* 85 (2017): 153–66.

Karamanolis, George, and Anne Sheppard, eds. *Studies on Porphyry*. London: Institute of Classical Studies, 2007.

Karig, Werner. "Des C. Marius Victorinus Kommentare zu den paulinischen Briefen." Inaugural diss., University of Marburg, 1924.

Kaster, Robert. *Guardians of Language: The Grammarian and Society in Late Antiquity.* Berkeley: University of California Press, 1988.

Kaufman, Peter I. "Donatism Revisited: Moderates and Militants in Late Antique North Africa." *JLA* 2 (2009): 131–42.

Kaufmann, Helen. "Intertextuality in Late Latin Poetry." In Elsner and Hernández Lobato, *Poetics of Late Latin Literature*, 149–75.

Kelly, J. N. D. *Jerome: His Life, Writings, and Controversies.* London: Duckworth, 1975.

Kenney, John Peter. *Contemplation and Classical Christianity: A Study in Augustine.* Oxford: Oxford University Press, 2013.

———. "Faith and Reason." In *The Cambridge Companion to Augustine*, edited by Eleonore Stump and David Meconi, 275–91. Cambridge: Cambridge University Press, 2014.

———. *The Mysticism of Saint Augustine: Rereading the "Confessions."* New York: Routledge, 2005.

Kenyon, Eric. *Augustine and the Dialogue.* Cambridge: Cambridge University Press, 2018.

King, Peter. "Augustine's Anti-Platonist Ascents." In *Augustine's "Confessions": Philosophy in Autobiography*, edited by William E. Mann, 6–27. Oxford: Oxford University Press, 2014.

Kitzler, Petr. "*Ex uno homine tota haec animarum redundantia*: Ursprung, Entstehung und Weitergabe der individuellen Seele nach Tertullian." *VC* 64 (2010): 353–38.

———. *From "Passio Perpetuae" to "Acta Perpetuae": Recontextualizing a Martyr Story in the Literature of the Early Church.* Arbeiten zur Kirchengeschichte 127. Berlin: de Gruyter, 2015.

———. "*Nihil enim anima si non corpus*: Tertullian und die Körperlichkeit der Seele." *WS* 122 (2009): 145–69.

———. "Tertullian's Concept of the Soul and His Corporealistic Ontology." In Lagouanère and Fialon, *Tertullianus Afer*, 43–62.

Klingshirn, William, and Mark Vessey. *The Limits of Ancient Christianity: Essays on Late Antique Thought and Culture in Honor of R. A. Markus.* Ann Arbor: University of Michigan Press, 1999.

Klöckener, Martin. "Die Bedeutung der neu entdeckten Augustinus-Predigten (Sermones Dolbeau) für die liturgiegeschichtliche Forschung." In *Augustin Prédi-*

cateur (395–411): *Actes du Colloque International de Chantilly* (5–7 septembre 1996), edited by Goulven Madec, 129–70. Paris: Études Augustiniennes, 1998.

Koch, H. "La sopravvivenza di Cipriano nell'antica letteratura cristiana: Cipriano ed Ottato." *Ricerche Religiose* 7 (1931): 321–35.

Koffmane, Gustavus. *De Mario Victorino philosopho christiano*. Breslau: Lindner, 1880.

Kotzé, Annemaré. *Augustine's "Confessiones": Communicative Purpose and Audience*. Leiden: Brill, 2004.

———. "The Puzzle of the Last Four Books of *Confessiones*: An Illegitimate Issue?" *VC* 60 (2006): 65–79.

La Bonnardière, Anne-Marie. *Recherches de chronologie augustinienne*. Paris: Études Augustiniennes, 1965.

Labrousse, Mirielle. "Le baptême des hérétiques d'après Cyprien, Optat et Augustin: influences et divergences." *REAug* 42 (1996): 223–42.

———. *Optat de Milève: Traité contre les Donatistes*. SC 412–13. Paris: Cerf, 1996.

———. "Optat de Milève (Saint)." In *Dictionnaire de Spiritualité*, 11:824–30. Paris: Beauchesne, 1982.

Lacger, Louis de. "Saint Vincent de Saragosse." *Revue d'histoire de l'Église de France* 13, no. 60 (1927): 307–58.

Lagouanère, Jérôme. "Augustine, lecteur critique du *De anima* de Tertullien." In Lagouanère and Fialon, *Tertullianus Afer*, 231–58.

Lagouanère, Jérôme, and Sabine Fialon. *Tertullianus Afer: Tertullien et la littérature chrétienne d'Afrique*. IPM 70. Turnhout: Brepols, 2015.

Lamberigts, Mathijs. "Augustine as Translator of Greek Texts: An Example." In *Philohistôr: Miscellanea in honorem Caroli Laga septuagenarii*, edited by A. Schoors and P. Van Deun, 151–61. Leuven: Peeters, 1994.

———. "Augustine's Use of Tradition in the Controversy with Julian of Eclanum." *Augustiniana* 60, no. 1–2 (2010): 11–61.

———. "Julian of Aeclanum: A Plea for a Good Creator." *Augustiniana* 38, no. 1/4 (1988): 5–25.

Lamberton, Richard. *Homer the Theologian: Neoplatonist Allegorical Reading and the Growth of the Epic Tradition*. Berkeley: University of California Press, 1986.

Lambot, C. "Les sermons de Saint Augustin pour les fêtes de Paques: tradition manuscrite." In *Mélanges en l'honneur de Monseigneur Michel Andrieu*, 263–78. Revue des Sciences Religieuses, Volume Hors Série. Strasbourg: Palais Universitaire, 1956.

———. *Oeuvres théologiques et grammaticales de Godescalc d'Orbais*. Leuven: Spicilegium Sacrum Lovaniense Bureaux, 1945.

Lamirande, É. "Vanité et orguiel des Donatistes." BA 32:735–36.

Lancel, Serge. *St. Augustine.* Translated by Antonia Neville. London: SCM, 2002.

Lane Fox, Robin. *Augustine: Conversions to Confessions.* New York: Basic Books, 2015.

Lapointe, Guy. *La célébration des martyrs en Afrique d'après les sermons de saint Augustin.* Montreal: Communauté chrétienne, 1972.

Law, Vivien. "St. Augustine's *De grammatica*: Lost or Found?" *RechAug* 19 (1984): 155–83.

Lazewski, Wojciech. "La Sentenza Agostiniana Martyrem Facit Non Poena Sed Causa." PhD diss., Pontificia Universitas Lateranensis, 1987.

Leal, Jerónimo. *La antropología de Tertuliano: Estudio de los tratados polémicos de los años 207–212 d.C.* SEAug 76. Rome: Institutum Patristicum Augustinianum, 2001.

———. "La salvación en el tratado *de anima* de Tertuliano." In *Pagani e cristiani alla ricerca della salvessa (secoli I–III): XXXIV Incontro di studiosi dell'antichità cristiana, Roma, 5–7 maggio 2005,* 505–11. SEAug 96. Rome: Institutum Patristicum Augustinianum, 2006.

Leeming, Bernard. "Augustine, Ambrosiaster and the *massa perditionis.*" *Gregorianum* 11 (1930): 58–91.

Leff, Michael. "Cicero's *Pro Murena* and the Strong Case for Rhetoric." *Rhetoric & Public Affairs* 1, no. 1 (1998): 61–88.

———. "Decorum and Rhetorical Interpretation: The Latin Humanistic Tradition and Contemporary Critical Theory." In de Velasco, Campbell, and Henry, *Rethinking Rhetorical Theory,* 163–84.

———. "Hermeneutical Rhetoric." In *Rhetoric and Hermeneutics in Our Time: A Reader,* edited by Walter Jost and Michael J. Hyde, 196–214. New Haven: Yale University Press, 1997.

Leith, John H., ed. *Creeds of the Churches: A Reader in Christian Doctrine from the Bible to the Present.* 3rd ed. Louisville: John Knox, 1982.

Levine, Lee I. *The Ancient Synagogue: The First Thousand Years.* 2nd ed. New Haven: Yale University Press, 2005.

Lewis, Charlton T., and Charles Short. *A Latin Dictionary.* Oxford: Clarendon, 1879.

Lienhard, Joseph T. "Augustine of Hippo, Basil of Caesarea, and Gregory Nazianzen." In *Orthodox Readings of Augustine,* edited by George E. Demacopoulos and Aristotle Papanikolaou, 81–99. Crestwood, NY: St Vladimir's Seminary Press, 2008.

Lim, Richard. "Augustine, the Grammarians, and the Cultural Authority of Vergil." In Rees, *Romane Memento,* 112–27.

Lof, L. J. van der. "De Invloed van Marius Victorinus Rhetor op Augustinus." *Nederlands Theologisch Tijdschrift* 5 (1950–1951): 287–307.

———. "The Plebs of the Psychici: Are the Psychici of De Monogamia Fellow-Catholics of Tertullian?" In *Eulogia: Mélanges offerts à Antoon A. R. Bastiaensen à l'occasion de son soixante-cinquième anniversaire*, edited by G. J. Bartelink, A. Hilhorst, and C. H. Kneepkens, 353–63. Steenbrugge: Abbey of St Peter, 1991.

Lohse, B. "Augustins Wandlung in seiner Beurteilung des Staates." *StPatr* 6 (1962): 470–75.

Lonergan, Bernard. *Grace and Freedom: Operative Grace in the Thought of St. Thomas Aquinas*. Edited by J. Patout Burns. New York: Herder, 1971.

Lössl, Josef. *Julian von Aeclanum: Studien zu seinem Leben, seinem Werk, seiner Lehre und ihre Überlieferung*. Brill: Leiden, 2001.

———. "Sallust in Julian of Aeclanum." *VC* 56 (2004): 179–202.

Lunn-Rockliffe, Sophie. *Ambrosiaster's Political Theology*. Oxford: Oxford University Press, 2007.

MacCormack, Sabine. "Classical Influences on Augustine." *AttA*, 206–13.

———. *The Shadows of Poetry: Vergil in the Mind of Augustine*. Berkeley: University of California Press, 1998.

MacCulloch, Diarmaid. *Silence: A Christian History*. New York: Penguin, 2013.

Madec, Goulven. *Lectures Augustiniennes*. Paris: Études Augustiniennes, 2001.

———. *Saint Ambroise et la Philosophie*. Paris: Études Augustiniennes, 1974.

Mandouze, André. "Optatus." In *Prosopographie chrétienne du Bas-Empire: 1, Prosopographie de l'Afrique chrétienne (303–533)*, 795–97. Paris: CNRS, 1982.

Mandonnet, R. P., ed. *S. Thomae Aquinatis: Scriptum super libros sententiarum*. Paris: Lethielleux, 1929.

Mansi, J. D. *Sacrorum conciliorum nova amplissima collectio*. Vol. 15, *Ab anno DCCCLV usque ad anno DCCCLXVIII incl*. Venice: Apud Antoniumzatta, 1770.

Marchese, Simone. *Dante and Augustine: Linguistics, Poetics, Hermeneutics*. Toronto: University of Toronto Press, 2011.

Margerie, Bertrand de. "Does Augustine's Moses Stand for Multiplicity in Unity?" In *An Introduction to the History of Exegesis*, vol. 3, *Saint Augustine*, translated by Pierre Fontnouvelle, 47–88. Petersham, MA: Saint Bede's, 1983.

———. "La doctrine de Saint Augustin sur l'Esprit-Saint comme communion et source de communion." *Augustinianum* 12 (1972): 107–19.

Margoni-Kögler, Michael. *Die Perikopen im Gottesdienst bei Augustinus: Ein Beitrag zur Erforschung der liturgischen Schriftlesung in der frühen Kirche*. Vienna: Österreichischen Akademie der Wissenschaften, 2010.

———. "North African Liturgical Readings: The Augustinian Legacy and Some Western Parallels." In *Liturgies in East and West: Ecumenical Relevance of Early*

Liturgical Development; Acts of the International Symposium Vindobonense I, Vienna, November 17–20, 2007, edited by Hans-Jürgen Feulner, 261–74. Österreichische Studien zur Liturgiewissenschaft und Sakramententheologie 6. Zürich: LIT, 2013.

Mariotti, Italo. *Marii Victorinii Ars grammatica, introduzione, testo critico e commento*. Florence: Felice Le Monnier, 1976.

Markschies, Christoph. "Ambrosius und Origenes: Bemerkungen zur exegetischen Hermeneutik zweier Kirchenväter." In *Origenes und sein Erbe: Gesammelte Studien*, 195–222. TUGAL 160. Berlin: de Gruyter, 2007.

———. *Gottes Körper: Jüdische, christliche und pagane Gottesvorstellungen in der Antike*. Munich: Beck, 2016.

———. "The *Passio Perpetuae et Felicitatis* and Montanism?" In Bremmer and Formisano, *Perpetua's Passions*, 286–87.

Markus, R. A. *Saeculum: History and Society in the Theology of St. Augustine*. Cambridge: Cambridge University Press, 1970.

Marone, P. "'Et modo Deo placuit quod passos vos esse dicitis': Ottato e la violenza in nome di Dio." In *Cristianesimo e violenza: Gli autori cristiani di fronte a testi biblici "scomodi"; XLIV Incontro di Studiosi dell'Antichità Cristiana, Roma 5–7 maggio 2016*. Rome: Institutum Patristicum Augustinianum, 2018.

Marrou, Henri-Irénée. *Saint Augustin et la fin de la culture antique*. Paris: de Boccard, 1938. Reissued with a *Retractatio* in 1949.

———. *Saint Augustin et la fin de la culture antique*. 4th ed. (with *Retractatio*). Bibliothèque des écoles françaises d'Athènes et de Rome 145. Paris: de Boccard, 1958.

Marti, Heinrich. *Rufin von Aquileia De ieiunio I, II: Zwei Predigten uber das Fasten nach Basileios von Kaisareia. Ausgabe mit Einleitung, Ubersetzung und Anmerkungen*. VCSup 6. Leiden: Brill, 1989.

———. "Rufinus' Translation of St. Basil's Sermon on Fasting." *StPatr* 16, no. 2 (1985): 418–22.

Martin, Dale B. *The Corinthian Body*. New Haven: Yale University Press, 1995.

Martin, Thomas F. "Augustine's *Confessiones* as Pedagogy: Exercises in Transformation." In *Augustine and Liberal Education*, edited by Kim Paffenroth and Kevin L. Hughes, 25–51. Aldershot, UK: Ashgate, 2000.

Martini, Coelestinus. *Ambrosiaster: De auctore, operibus, theologia*. Rome: Athenaeum Antonianum, 1944.

Mastrangelo, Marc. *The Roman Self in Late Antiquity: Prudentius and the Poetics of the Soul*. Baltimore: Johns Hopkins University Press, 2008.

Mattei, Paul. "La place du *De monogamia* dans l'évolution théologique et spirituelle de Tertullien." *StPatr* 18 (1989): 319–28.

Matthews, John. *The Roman Empire of Ammianus*. Baltimore: Johns Hopkins University Press, 1989.

———. *Western Aristocracies and Imperial Court: AD 364–425*. Oxford: Clarendon, 1975.

Matz, B. "Augustine in the Predestination Controversy of the Ninth Century. Part I: The Double Predestinarians Gottschalk of Orbais and Ratramus of Corbie." *AugStud* 46, no. 2 (2015): 155–84.

———. "Augustine in the Predestination Controversy of the Ninth Century. Part II: The Single Predestinarians John Scotus Eriugena and Hincmar of Rheims." *AugStud* 47, no.1 (2016): 17–40.

Mayer, Cornelius, et al., ed. *Augustinus-Lexikon*. 5 vols. Basle: Schwabe, 1986–.

Mayer, Wendy, and Pauline Allen. *John Chrysostom*. ECF. London: Routledge, 2000.

Mazzucco, Clementina. *Ottato di Milevi in un secolo di studi: Problemi e prospettive*. Bologna: Pátron Editrice, 1993.

McGill, Scott. *Virgil Recomposed: The Mythological and Secular Centos in Antiquity*. Oxford: Oxford University Press, 2005.

McGowan, Andrew B. *Ancient Christian Worship: Early Church Practices in Social, Historical, and Theological Perspective*. Grand Rapids: Baker Academic, 2014.

McKeon, P. R. "The Carolingian Councils of Savonnières (859) and Tusey (860) and Their Background: A Study in the Ecclesiastical and Political History of the Ninth Century." *RBén* 84 (1974): 75–110.

McLynn, Neil B. *Ambrose of Milan: Church and Court in a Christian Capital*. Berkeley: University of California Press, 1994.

Merdinger, Jane. "Roman North Africa." In *Early Christianity in Contexts: An Exploration across Cultures and Continents*, edited by William Tabbernee, 223–60. Grand Rapids: Baker Academic, 2014.

———. *Rome and the African Church in the Time of Augustine*. New Haven: Yale University Press, 1997.

Metzger, Michael D. "Marius Victorinus and the Substantive Infinitive." *Eranos* 72 (1974): 65–70.

Michalowska, Monika. "Grammar and Theology in Eriugena's Philosophy." *Philotheos* 7 (2007): 272–78.

Miles, Richard, ed. *The Donatist Schism: Controversy and Contexts*. Liverpool: Liverpool University Press, 2016.

Monaci Castagno, Adele. *Origene dizionario: La cultura, il pensiero, le opere*. Rome: Città Nuova, 2000.

Monceaux, Paul. *Histoire littéraire de l'Afrique chrétienne depuis les origines jusqu'à l'invasion arabe.* 7 vols. Paris: Leroux, 1901–1923. Reprint, Brussels: Culture et Civilisation, 1963.

Moreschini, Claudio, and Chiara O. Tommasi, ed. and trans. *Opere teologiche di Mario Vittorino.* Turin: Unione Tipografica-Editrice Torinese, 2007.

Moss, Candida R. *Ancient Christian Martyrdom: Diverse Practices, Theologies, and Traditions.* New Haven: Yale University Press, 2012.

———. *The Other Christs: Imitating Jesus in Ancient Christian Ideologies of Martyrdom.* New York: Oxford University Press, 2010.

Mullen, Roderic L. *The Expansion of Christianity: A Gazetteer of Its First Three Centuries.* VCSup 69. Leiden: Brill, 2004.

Müller, Gerhard Anselm. *Formen und Funktionen der Vergilzitate bei Augustin von Hippo.* Paderborn: Ferdinand Schöningh, 2003.

Musurillo, Herbert, ed. and trans. *The Acts of the Christian Martyrs.* Oxford: Clarendon, 1972.

Mynors, R. A. B. *P. Vergili Maronis Opera.* Oxford: Clarendon, 1969.

Napier, Daniel Austin. *En Route to the Confessions: The Roots and Development of Augustine's Philosophical Anthropology.* LAHR 6. Leuven: Peeters, 2013.

Nussbaum, Martha. *Upheavals of Thought: The Intelligence of Emotions.* Cambridge: Cambridge University Press, 2001.

O'Connell, Robert J. *The Origin of the Soul in St. Augustine's Later Works.* New York: Fordham University Press, 1987.

———. *St. Augustine's Early Theory of Man, A.D. 386–391.* Cambridge, MA: Harvard University Press, 1968.

O'Daly, Gerard. *Augustine's City of God: A Reader's Guide.* Oxford: Clarendon, 1999.

O'Donnell, James J. *Augustine: A New Biography.* New York: HarperCollins, 2005.

———, ed. *Augustine: Confessions.* 3 vols. Oxford: Clarendon; New York: Oxford University Press, 1992.

———. "Augustine's Classical Reading." *RechAug* 15 (1980): 144–75.

Ogilvie, R. M. *Titi Livi Ab urbe condita.* Oxford Classical Texts. Oxford: Clarendon, 1974.

Ollier, Jacques. *Firmamentum narrat: La théorie augustinienne des "Confessiones."* Paris: Collège des Bernardins, 2011.

O'Meara, Dominic J. "The Problem of Speaking about God in John Scottus Eriugena." In *Carolingian Essays: Andrew W. Mellon Lectures in Early Christian Studies,* edited by Uta-Renate Blumenthal, 151–67. Washington, DC: Catholic University of America Press, 1983.

O'Meara, John J. "Porphyry's *Philosophy from Oracles* in Eusebius' *Praeparatio Evangelica* and Augustine's *Dialogues* of Cassiciacum." *RechAug* 6 (1969): 103–39.

Optatus. *Against the Donatists*. Translated and edited by Mark Edwards. TTH 27. Liverpool: Liverpool University Press, 1997.

———. *The Work of St. Optatus*. Translated by O. R. Vassall-Phillips. London: Longmans, Green, 1917.

Origen. *Die neuen Psalmenhomilien: Eine kritische Edition des Codex Monacensis Graecus 314*. Edited by Lorenzo Perrone, Marina Molin Pradel, Emanuela Prinzivalli, and Antonio Cacciari. Berlin: de Gruyter, 2015.

———. *Homilies on the Psalms: Codex Monacensis Graecus 314*. Translated by Joseph W. Trigg. FC 141. Washington, DC: Catholic University of America Press, 2020.

Osborn, Eric. *Tertullian: First Theologian of the West*. Cambridge: Cambridge University Press, 1997.

Pace, Nicola. *Ricerche sulla traduzione di Rufino del "De principiis" di Origene*. Florence: La Nuova Italia Editrice, 1990.

Pacioni, Virgilio. "Liberal Arts." *AttA*, 492–94.

Page, Christopher. *The Christian West and Its Singers: The First Thousand Years*. New Haven: Yale University Press, 2010.

Paulinus. *The Poems of Paulinus of Nola*. Translated by P. G. Walsh. ACW 40. New York: Newman, 1975.

Paulsen, D. L. "Early Christian Belief in a Corporeal Deity: Origen and Augustine as Reluctant Witnesses." *HTR* 83, no. 2 (1990): 105–16.

Peper, B. "The Development of *Mater Ecclesia* in North African Ecclesiology." PhD diss., Vanderbilt University, 2011.

Pépin, Jean. *Théologie cosmique et théologie chrétienne*. Paris: Presses Universitaires de France, 1964.

Pereira, Matthew. "From Augustine to the Scythian Monks: Social Memory and the Doctrine of Predestination." *StPatr* 54 (2012): 1–13.

Perler, Othmar, and Jean-Louis Maier. *Les voyages de Saint Augustin*. Collection des Études Augustiniennes, Série Antiquité 36. Paris: Études Augustiniennes, 1969.

Perrone, Lorenzo. *La preghiera secondo Origene: L'impossibilità donata*. Brescia: Morcelliana, 2012.

Petrey, Taylor G. "Semen Stains: Seminal Procreation and the Patrilineal Genealogy of Salvation in Tertullian." *JECS* 22 (2014): 343–72.

Pezé, Warren. *Le virus de l'erreur: La controverse carolingienne sur la double prédestination; Essai d'histoire sociale*. Haut Moyen Âge 26. Turnhout: Brepols, 2017.

Pietri, Charles, and Luce Pietri. *Prosopographie chrétienne du Bas-Empire: 2, Prosopog-*

raphie de l'Italie chrétienne (313–604). 2 vols. Rome: École française de Rome, 1999–2000.

Pincherle, Alberto. *La formazione teologica di Sant'Agostino.* Rome: Edizioni Italiane, 1947.

Pizzolato Luigi F. "Il *modus* nel primo Agostino." In *La langue latine, langue de la philosophie: Actes du colloque de Rome (17–19 mai 1990),* 245–51. Publications de l'École française de Rome 161. Rome: École française de Rome, 1992.

Plato. *Timaeus. Critias. Cleitophon. Menexenus. Epistles.* Translated by R. G. Bury. LCL 234. Cambridge, MA: Harvard University Press, 1929.

Plotinus. *Enneads.* Vol. 5. Translated by A. H. Armstrong. LCL 444. Cambridge, MA: Harvard University Press, 1984.

———. *Enneads.* Vol. 6. Translated by A. H. Armstrong. LCL 468. Cambridge, MA: Harvard University Press, 1988.

———. *Plotini Opera.* 3 vols. Edited by Paul Henry and Hans-Rudolf Schwyzer. Oxford: Oxford University Press, 1964–1982.

Ployd, Adam. "*Non poena sed causa*: Augustine's Anti-Donatist Rhetoric of Martyrdom." *AugStud* 49, no. 1 (2018): 25–44.

Plumer, Eric. *Augustine's Commentary on Galatians: Introduction, Text, Translation, and Notes.* OECS. Oxford: Oxford University Press, 2003.

———. "The Influence of Marius Victorinus on Augustine's Commentary on Galatians." *StPatr* 33 (1997): 221–28.

Plutarch. *Lives.* Vol. 8, *Sertorius and Eumenes. Phocion and Cato the Younger.* Translated by Bernadotte Perrin. LCL 100. Cambridge, MA: Harvard University Press, 1919.

Pollastri, Alessandra. *Ambrosiaster: Commento alla Lettera ai Romani; Aspetti cristologici.* Collana di testi storici 7. L'Aquila: Japadre, 1977.

Pollmann, Karla, and Mark Vessey, eds. *Augustine and the Disciplines: From Cassiciacum to "Confessions."* Oxford: Oxford University Press, 2005.

Poque, Suzanne. "Les lectures liturgiques de l'octave pascale à Hippone d'après les Traités de S. Augustin sur la première épître de S. Jean." *RBén* 74 (1964): 217–41.

———, ed. *Sermons pour la Pâque.* SC 116. Paris: Cerf, 1966.

Powell, Douglas. "Tertullianists and Cataphrygians." *VC* 29 (1975): 33–54

Pucci, Joseph. *Augustine's Virgilian Retreat: Reading the* Auctores *at Cassiciacum.* Toronto: Pontifical Institute of Mediaeval Studies, 2014.

Quodvultdeus. *Quodvultdeus of Carthage: The Creedal Homilies; Conversion in Fifth-Century North Africa.* Translated by Thomas Macy Finn. ACW 60. New York: Newman, 2004.

Rader, William. *The Church and Racial Hostility: A History of Interpretation of Ephesians 2:11–22.* Beiträge zur Geschichte der biblischen Exegese 20. Tübingen: Mohr Siebeck, 1978.

Rankin, David. *Tertullian and the Church.* Cambridge: Cambridge University Press, 1995.

Raspanti, Giacomo. "Il peccato di Adamo e la grazia di Cristo nella storia dell'umanità: Rilettura del commento di Ambrosiaster a *Rom.* 5, 12–21." *Augustinianum* 48, no. 2 (2008): 435–79.

Ravvin, Norman. *A House of Words: Jewish Writing, Identity, and Memory.* Montreal: McGill-Queen's University Press, 1997.

Rebillard, Éric. "Augustine in Controversy with the Donatists before 411." In Miles, *Donatist Schism,* 297–316.

———, ed. *Greek and Latin Narratives about the Ancient Martyrs.* Oxford: Oxford University Press, 2017.

———. "A New Style of Argument in Christian Polemic: Augustine and the Use of Patristic Citations." *JECS* 8 (2000): 559–78.

Rees, Roger. *Romane Memento: Vergil in the Fourth Century.* London: Duckworth, 2004.

Richardson, Ernest Cushing, ed. *Hieronymus: Liber de uiris inlustribus; Gennadius: Liber de uiris inlustribus.* Texte und Untersuchungen 84. Leipzig: Hinrichs, 1896.

Ricoeur, Paul. "Life: A Story in Search of a Narrator." Translated by J. N. Kraay and A. J. Scholten. In *A Ricoeur Reader: Reflection and Imagination,* edited by M. J. Valdés, 425–37. Toronto: University of Toronto Press, 1991.

Rigby, Paul. *Original Sin in Augustine's "Confessions."* Ottawa: University of Ottawa Press, 1987.

Ring, Thomas G. *Aurelius Augustinus, Schriften gegen die Pelagianer, Prologomena.* Band 2, *Die Auslegung des Briefes an die Galater, Die angefangene Auslegung des Briefe an die Römer, Über dreiundachtsig verschiedene Fragen.* Würzburg: Augustinus-Verlag, 1997.

Rist, John M. *Augustine: Ancient Thought Baptized.* Cambridge: Cambridge University Press, 1994.

Rivière, Jean. *Le dogme de la rédemption chez saint Augustin.* Paris: Gabalda, 1933.

———. "Le 'droit' du démon sur les pécheurs avant saint Augustin." *Recherches de théologie ancienne et médiévale* 3 (1931): 113–39.

Roberts, Timothy. "A Translation and Critical Edition of Ratramnus of Corbie's 'De praedestinatione Dei.'" PhD diss., University of Missouri, 1977.

Roetzer, P. Wunibald. *Die heiligen Augustinus Schriften als liturgie-geschichtliche Quelle: Eine liturgie-geschichtliche Studie.* Munich: Hueber, 1930.

Romig, Andrew. *Be a Perfect Man: Christian Masculinity and the Carolingian Aristocracy.* Middle Ages Series. Philadelphia: University of Pennsylvania Press, 2017.

Roy, Otto du. *L'intelligence de la foi en la Trinité selon saint Augustin: Génèse de sa théologie trinitaire jusqu'en 391.* Paris: Études Augustiniennes, 1966.

Rufinus of Aquileia. *History of the Church.* Translated by Philip R. Amidon. FC 133. Washington, DC: Catholic University of America Press, 2016.

Runia, David. *Philo in Early Christian Literature: A Survey.* Assen: Van Gorcum, 1993.

Sadowski, Sydney. "A Critical Look and Evaluation of Augustine's *De haeresibus.*" *Augustinianum* 55 (2015): 461–78.

Sage, Athanase. "Péché originel: Naissance d'un dogme." *REAug* 13 (1967): 211–48.

Sagi-Bunič, T. "Controversia de Baptismate inter Parmenianum et S. Optatum Milevitanum." *Laurentianum* 3 (1962): 167–209.

Salisbury, Joyce E. *Perpetua's Passion: The Death and Memory of a Young Roman Woman.* New York: Routledge, 1997.

Salzman, Michele Renee, ed. *The Letters of Symmachus: Book 1.* Translated by Michele Renee Salzman and Michael Roberts. Atlanta: Society of Biblical Literature, 2011.

Satterlee, Craig Alan. *Ambrose of Milan's Method of Mystagogical Preaching.* Collegeville, MN: Liturgical Press, 2002.

Saxer, Victor, ed. *Saint Augustin: L'année liturgique; Sermons choisis.* Paris: Desclée de Brouwer, 1980.

Schiller, Isabella, Dorothea Weber, and Clemens Weidmann. "Sechs neue Augustinuspredigten: Teil 1 mit Edition dreier Sermones." *WS* 121 (2008): 227–84.

Schmid, Reinhold. *Marius Victorinus Rhetor und seine Beziehungen zu Augustin.* Kiel: Uebermuth, 1895.

Schrama, Martijn. "*Prima Lectio Quae Recitata Est*: The Liturgical Pericope in Light of Saint Augustine's Sermons." *Augustiniana* 45, no. 1–2 (1995): 141–75.

Shanzer, Danuta. "Augustine and the Latin Classics." In Vessey, *Companion to Augustine,* 161–74.

———. "Augustine's Disciplines: *Silent diutius Musae Varronis?*" In Pollmann and Vessey, *Augustine and the Disciplines,* 69–112.

Shaw, Brent D. "The Passion of Perpetua." *Past and Present* 139 (1993): 33–45.

———. *Sacred Violence: African Christians and Sectarian Hatred in the Age of Augustine.* Cambridge: Cambridge University Press, 2011.

Sigismund-Nielsen, Hanne. "Vibia Perpetua—an Indecent Woman." In Bremmer and Formisano, *Perpetua's Passions*, 103–17.

Simonetti, Manlio. *Gregorio di Elvira: La fede*. Turin: Società Editrice Internazionale, 1975.

Simonis, Walter. *Ecclesia visibilis et invisibilis: Untersuchungen zur Ekklesiologie und Sakramentenlehre in der afrikanischen Tradition von Cyprian bis Augustinus*. Frankfurt: Knecht, 1970.

Smith, Andrew. "Did Porphyry Reject the Transmigration of Human Souls into Animals?" *Rheinisches Museum für Philologie* 127, no. 3/4 (1984): 276–84.

———. "Philosophical Objections to Christianity on the Eve of the Great Persecution." In *The Great Persecution*, edited by D. Vincent Twomey and Mark Humphries, 33–48. Dublin: Four Courts, 2009.

———. "Porphyrian Studies since 1913." In *Aufstieg und Niedergang der römischen Welt*. Part 2, *Principat*, edited by H. Temporini and W. Haase, 36.2:719–73. New York: de Gruyter, 1987.

———. *Porphyrius: Fragmenta*. Leipzig: Teubner, 1993.

———. "Porphyry and the 'Platonic Theology.'" In *Proclus et la Théologie Platonicienne*, edited by Carlos Steel and Alain Philippe Segonds, 177–88. Leuven: Leuven University Press, 2000.

———. *Porphyry's Place in the Neoplatonic Tradition: A Study in Post-Plotinian Neoplatonism*. The Hague: Martinus Nijhoff, 1974.

Smith, J. Warren. "Justification and Merit before the Pelagian Controversy: The Case of Ambrose of Milan." *Pro Ecclesia* 16, no. 2 (2007): 195–217.

Smith, Jenny. "'As If Augustine Had Said': Textual Interpretation and Augustinian Ambiguity in a Medieval Debate on Predestination." *Past Imperfect* 19 (2016): https://doi.org/10.21971/P7H300.

———. "The Rebellious Monk Gottschalk of Orbais: Defining Heresy in a Medieval Debate on Predestination." *Eras* 17 (2016): 1–24.

Smith, William, ed. *A Dictionary of Greek and Roman Antiquities*. London: Murray, 1875.

Solignac, A. "Loci Sacrae Scripturae," BA 14:667–79.

Sorabji, Richard. *Emotion and Peace of Mind: From Stoic Agitation to Christian Temptation*. Oxford: Oxford University Press, 2000.

Souter, Alexander. *The Earliest Latin Commentaries on the Epistles of St. Paul*. Oxford: Clarendon, 1927.

Stendahl, Krister. "The Apostle Paul and the Introspective Conscience of the West." *HTR* 56 (1963): 199–215.

Stewart-Sykes, Alistair. *From Prophecy to Preaching: A Search for the Origins of the Christian Homily.* VCSup 59. Leiden: Brill, 2001.

Stock, Brian. *Augustine the Reader: Meditation, Self-Knowledge, and the Ethics of Interpretation.* Cambridge, MA: Belknap, 1996.

Strousma, Guy. *The End of Sacrifice: Religious Transformations in Late Antiquity.* Chicago: University of Chicago Press, 2008.

Strutwolf, Holger. *Gnosis als System: Zur Rezeption der valentinianischen Gnosis bei Origenes.* Göttingen: Vandenhoeck & Ruprecht, 1993.

Studer, Basil. "Augustine and the Pauline Theology of Hope." In *Paul and the Legacies of Paul,* edited by William S. Babcock, 201–21. Dallas: Southern Methodist University Press, 1990.

Suetonius. *C. Suetoni Tranquilli Opera.* Edited by M. Ihm. Leipzig: Teubner, 1908.

Tabbernee, William. *Fake Prophecy and Polluted Sacraments: Ecclesiastical and Imperial Reactions to Montanism.* VCSup 84. Leiden: Brill, 2007.

———. "Montanism and the Cult of the Martyrs in Roman North Africa: Reassessing the Literary and Epigraphic Evidence." In *Text and the Material World*: *Essays in Honour of Graeme Clarke,* edited by Elizabeth Minchin and Heather Jackson, 299–313. Studies in Mediterranean Archaeology and Literature 185. Uppsala: Astrom Editions, 2017.

———. *Montanist Inscriptions and Testimonia: Epigraphic Sources Illustrating the History of Montanism.* PatrMS 16. Macon, GA: Mercer University Press, 1997.

———. "'Our Trophies Are Better Than Your Trophies': The Appeal to Tombs and Reliquaries in Montanist-Orthodox Relations." *StPatr* 31 (1997): 206–17.

———. *Prophets and Gravestones: An Imaginative History of Montanists and Other Early Christians.* Peabody, MA: Hendrickson, 2009.

———. "Scillitan Martyrs." In *The New Westminster Dictionary of Church History,* edited by Robert Benedetto and James O. Duke, 1:598. Louisville: Westminster John Knox, 2008.

Taisne, Anne-Marie. "Salluste chez saint Augustin (Cité de Dieu, I-V)." In *Présence de Salluste,* edited by Rémy Poignault, 119–28. Tours: Centre de Recherches A. Piganiol, 1997.

Tertullian. *Tertullian, Apologetic Works, and Minucius Felix, "Ocavius."* Translated by Rudolph Arbesmann, Sister Emily Joseph Daly, and Edwin A. Quain. FC 10. Washington, DC: Catholic University of America Press, 2008.

———. *Treatises on Marriage and Remarriage: To His Wife; An Exhortation to Chastity; Monogamy.* Translated by William P. Le Saint. ACW 13. New York: Newman, 1951.

TeSelle, Eugene. *Augustine the Theologian*. London: Burns & Oates, 1970.

Teske, Roland J. "*Haeresibus, De*." *AttA*, 412–13.

Testard, Maurice. *Saint Augustin et Cicéron*. I: *Cicéron dans la formation et dans l'oeuvre de Saint Augustin*. Paris: Études Augustiniennes, 1958.

———. *Saint Augustin et Cicéron*. II: *Répertoire des Textes*. Paris: Études Augustiniennes, 1958.

Thomas, Richard. *Why Bob Dylan Matters*. New York: HarperCollins, 2017.

Throop, Priscilla, trans. *Yes and No: The Complete English Translation of Peter Abelard's "Sic et Non."* 2nd ed. Charlotte, VT: MedievalMS, 2008.

Tilley, Maureen, ed. *Donatist Martyr Stories*. TTH 24. Liverpool: Liverpool University Press, 1997.

———. "The Passion of Perpetua and Felicity." In *Searching the Scriptures: A Feminist Commentary*, edited by Elisabeth Schüssler Fiorenza, 2:829–58. New York: Crossroad, 1994.

———. "When Schism Becomes Heresy in Late Antiquity: Developing Doctrinal Deviance in the Wounded Body of Christ." *JECS* 15 (2007): 1–21.

Tommasi, Chiara O. "Tripotens in unalitate spiritus: Mario Vittorino e la gnosi." *Koinōnia* 20 (1996): 52–75.

Torró, Joaquín Pascual. *Gregorio de Elvira: La fede*. Fuentes Patrísticas 11. Madrid: Ciudad Nueva, 1998.

Treuer, David. *The Heartbeat of Wounded Knee: Native America from 1890 to the Present*. New York: Riverhead, 2019.

Trevett, Christine. "Montanism." In Esler, *Early Christian World*, 867–83.

———. *Montanism: Gender, Authority and the New Prophecy*. Cambridge: Cambridge University Press, 1996.

Trigg, Joseph W. "Divine Deception and the Truthfulness of Scripture." In *Origen of Alexandria: His World and His Legacy*, edited by Charles Kannengiesser and William L. Peterson, 147–64. Notre Dame, IN: University of Notre Dame Press, 1988.

Trout, Dennis. "Augustine at Cassiciacum: *Otium honestum* and the Social Dimensions of Conversion." *VC* 42 (1988): 132–46.

———. *Paulinus of Nola: Life, Letters, and Poems*. Berkeley: University of California Press, 1999.

———. "Re-textualizing Lucretia: Cultural Subversion in the *City of God*." *JECS* 2 (1994): 53–70.

Valero, Juan B. "Pecar en Adan segun Ambrosiaster." *Estudios eclesiásticos* 65 (1990): 147–91.

Van Fleteren, Frederick. "Principles of Augustine's Hermenutic: An Overview." In Van Fleteren and Schnaubelt, *Augustine*, 1–32.

Van Fleteren, Frederick, and Joseph C. Schnaubelt, eds. *Augustine: Biblical Exegete.* ColAug 4. New York: Lang, 2001.

Vannier, Marie-Anne. *"Creatio," "Conversio," "Formatio" chez S. Augustin.* Paradosis 31. Fribourg: Éditions Universitaires, 1991.

Van Reyn, Geert. "Hippo's Got Talent: Augustine's *Psalmus contra partem Donati* as a Pop(ular) Song." In Dupont, Gaumer, and Lamberigts, *Uniquely African Controversy*, 251–68.

Van Slyke, Daniel. *Quodvultdeus of Carthage: The Apocalyptic Theology of a Roman African in Exile.* Early Christian Studies 5. Strathfield, NSW: St Pauls Publications, 2003.

Veer, A. C. de. "Saint Augustin et l'Ambrosiaster." BA 23:817–24.

Velasco, Antonio de, John Angus Campbell, and David Henry, eds. *Rethinking Rhetorical Theory, Criticism, and Pedagogy: The Living Art of Michael C. Leff.* East Lansing: Michigan State University Press, 2016.

Verbraken, P. "Les sermons CCXV et LVI de Saint Augustin." *RBén* 68 (1958): 5–40.

Vessey, Mark, ed. *A Companion to Augustine.* Hoboken, NJ: Wiley-Blackwell, 2012.

———. "The Demise of the Christian Writer and the Remaking of 'Late Antiquity': From H.-I. Marrou's *Saint Augustin* (1938) to Peter Brown's *Holy Man* (1983)." *JECS* 6 (1998): 377–411.

———. "Introduction." In Pollmann and Vessey, *Augustine and the Disciplines*, 1–21.

Victorinus, Marius. *Commentari alle Epistole di Paolo agli Efesini, ai Galati, ai Filippesi.* Edited and translated by Franco Gori. Corona Patrum 8. Turin: Società Editrice Internazionale, 1981.

———. *Theological Treatises on the Trinity.* Translated by Mary T. Clark. FC 69. Washington, DC: Catholic University of America, 1981.

Virgil. *Eclogues. Georgics. Aeneid: Books 1–6.* Translated by H. Rushton Fairclough. Revised by G. P. Goold. LCL 63. Cambridge, MA: Harvard University Press, 1916.

Vitturi, Luigi. *La fraternità ecclesiale in Ottato di Milevi: "La dote della sposa."* Padova: Edizioni Messaggero, 2015.

Vogels, Heinrich J. "Ambrosiaster und Hieronymus." *RBén* 66 (1956): 14–19.

Vranić, Vasilije. "Augustine and the Donatist Claims to Cyprianic Ecclesiological Legacy." *Philotheos* 7 (2007): 232–40.

Waszink, J. H. *Quinti Septimi Florentis Tertulliani De Anima.* Rev. ed. VCSup 100. Leiden: Brill, 2010.

Webb, Melanie. "'On Lucretia who slew herself': Rape and Consolation in Augustine's *De civitate dei*." *AugStud* 44, no. 1 (2013): 37–58.

Weiskotten, H. T., ed. and trans. *Sancti Augustini Vita scripta a Possidio Episcopo*. Oxford: Oxford University Press, 1919.

West, Rebecca. *St. Augustine*. New York: Appleton, 1933.

Wetzel, James. "Augustine: Prodigal Heart." In *The Oxford Handbook of Religion and Emotion*, edited by John Corrigan, 349–63. Oxford: Oxford University Press, 2008.

Wilhite, David E. "Identity, Psychology, and the *Psychici*: Tertullian's 'Bishop of Bishops.'" *Interdisciplinary Journal of Research on Religion* 5 (2009): 1–26.

———. "Perpetua of History in Recent Questions." *JECS* 25 (2017): 307–19.

———. *Tertullian the African: An Anthropological Reading of Tertullian's Context and Identities*. Millennium Studies 14. Berlin: de Gruyter, 2007.

———. "True Church or True Basilica? The Song of Songs and Parmenian's Ecclesiology Revisited." *JECS* 22 (2014): 399–436.

Wilken, Robert Louis. *The Christians as the Romans Saw Them*. 2nd ed. New Haven: Yale University Press, 2003.

Williams, Megan Hale. *The Monk and the Book: Jerome and the Making of Christian Scholarship*. Chicago: University of Chicago Press, 2006.

Williams, Rowan. "Origen: Between Orthodoxy and Heresy." In *Origeniana Septima: Origenes in den Auseindersetsetzungen des 4. Jahrhunderts*, edited by W. A. Bienert and U. Kühneweg, 3–14. Leuven: Leuven University Press, 1999.

———. *The Wound of Knowledge*. Eugene, OR: Wipf & Stock, 2000.

Willis, Geoffrey G. *Saint Augustine and the Donatist Controversy*. London: SPCK, 1950.

———. *St Augustine's Lectionary*. London: SPCK, 1962.

Wills, Garry. *Font of Life: Ambrose, Augustine and the Mystery of Baptism*. Oxford: Oxford University Press, 2012.

———. "Vergil and St. Augustine." In *A Companion to Vergil's Aeneid and Its Tradition*, edited by Joseph Farrell and Michael C. J. Putnam, 123–32. Malden, MA: Wiley-Blackwell, 2010.

Wilmart, André. "Les tractatus sur le cantique attribués à Grégoire d'Elvire." *Bulletin de littérature ecclésiastique* 8 (1906): 233–99.

Wiśniewski, Robert. "Lucilla and the Bone: Remarks on an Early Testimony to the Cult of Relics." *JLA* 4 (2011): 157–61.

Wolff, Gustavus. *Porphyrii de philosophia ex oraculis haurienda*. Hildesheim: Olms, 1962.

Wolterstorff, Nicholas. "Augustine's Rejection of Eudaimonism." In *Augustine's "City of God": A Critical Guide*, edited by James Wetzel, 149–66. Cambridge: Cambridge University Press, 2012.

———. *Justice: Rights and Wrongs*. Princeton: Princeton University Press, 2008.

Woods, Marjorie Curry. *Weeping for Dido: The Classics in the Medieval Classroom*. Princeton: Princeton University Press, 2019.

Wright, Brian J. *Communal Reading in the Time of Jesus: A Window into Early Christian Reading Practices*. Minneapolis: Augsburg Fortress, 2017.

Yates, Jonathan P. "Augustine's Appropriation of Cyprian the Martyr-Bishop against the Pelagians." In *More Than a Memory: The Discourse of Martyrdom and the Construction of Christian Identity in the History of Christianity*, edited by Johan Leemans with Jürgen Mettepenningen, 119–35. Leuven: Peeters, 2005.

———. "The Use of the Bible in the North African Martyriological Polemics in Late Antiquity." In *Martyrdom and Persecution in Late Antique Christianity: Festschrift Boudewijn Dehandschutter*, edited by Johan Leemans, 393–419. BETL 241. Leuven: Peeters, 2010.

Yudin, Victor. "Porphyry against the Resurrection in Augustine." *StPatr* 50 (2011): 301–7.

Zarefsky, David. *Lincoln, Douglas, and Slavery in the Crucible of Debate*. Chicago: University of Chicago Press, 1990.

Ziolkowski, Jan M., and Michael C. J. Putnam. *The Virgilian Tradition: The First Fifteen Hundred Years*. New Haven: Yale University Press, 2008.

Zocca, Elena. "Tertullien et le donatisme: quelques remarques." In Lagouanère and Fialon, *Tertullianus Afer*, 63–104.

Zwinggi, Anton. "Die fortlaufende Schriftlesung im Gottesdienst bei Augustinus." *Archiv für Liturgiewissenschaft* 12 (1970): 85–129.

———. "Die Perikopenordnungen der Osterwoche in Hippo und die Chronologie der Predigten des hl. Augustinus." *Augustiniana* 20 (1970): 5–34.

Editors and Contributors

The Editors

David G. Hunter is the Margaret O'Brien Flatley Professor of Catholic Theology at Boston College. He has published numerous articles and several books, including the *Oxford Handbook of Early Christian Studies* (Oxford University Press, 2008) and *Marriage, Celibacy, and Heresy in Ancient Christianity: The Jovinianist Controversy* (Oxford University Press, 2007). He is past president of the North American Patristics Society and associate editor of the society's *Journal of Early Christian Studies*. Hunter is a general editor of the forthcoming *Brill Encyclopedia of Early Christianity* and editorial director of The Fathers of the Church translation series; he also serves on the board of several scholarly journals and book series.

Jonathan P. Yates is a professor of historical theology at Villanova University. He earned his PhD and STD in historical theology from the Katholieke Universiteit Leuven. He served as editor of *Augustinian Studies* for ten years. His research specialty is ancient Latin Christianity with a focus on how ancient North African Christianity understood and applied its sacred texts both theologically and within its day-to-day practice. Jonathan has published numerous peer-reviewed articles, book chapters, and edited volumes. Along with Anthony Dupont, he is currently serving as coeditor for a two-volume handbook titled *The Reception and Interpretation of the Bible in Christian North Africa* (de Gruyter). Volume 1 was published in 2020; volume 2 will appear in 2022.

The Contributors

Alden Bass is an assistant professor of theology and Bible at Oklahoma Christian University. He earned an MTS at Vanderbilt and a PhD in historical theology at Saint Louis University. He has written on biblical exegesis in the African church as well as late ancient African sermons. He is currently coediting *The Donatist Controversy*, vol. 2 (Works of Saint Augustine).

Michael Cameron is professor of historical theology at the University of Portland, Oregon. He is the author of *Christ Meets Me Everywhere: Augustine's Early Figurative Exegesis* (Oxford University Press, 2012), *The Essential Expositions of the Psalms by Saint Augustine* (New City, 2015), and a number of essays and reference articles. Michael was editor for late antique and early medieval Latin Christianity for volumes 1–16 of *The Encyclopedia of the Bible and Its Reception* (de Gruyter, 2009–) and is an associate editor of *Augustinian Studies* and the *Augustinus-Lexikon*. He is currently working on a book about the function of scripture in Augustine's *Confessions*.

John C. Cavadini is professor of theology at the University of Notre Dame, where he also serves as McGrath-Cavadini Director of the McGrath Institute for Church Life. He teaches, studies, and publishes in the area of patristic theology and its early medieval reception. He has served a five-year term on the International Theological Commission (appointed by Pope Benedict XVI) and in 2018 received the Monika K. Hellwig Award from the Association of Catholic Colleges and Universities for Outstanding Contributions to Catholic Intellectual Life.

Thomas Clemmons, assistant professor of Latin patristics and church history at the Catholic University of America, completed a master's degree in theology at Vanderbilt University, a master's degree in classics and early Christian studies at the University of Notre Dame, and a PhD from the University of Notre Dame in the history of Christianity. His research focuses on Augustine, especially his early writings, Augustine's reception, Manichaeism, and Christianity in North Africa.

Stephen Andrew Cooper received his MA in religion and PhD in the history of Christianity at Union Theological Seminary and Columbia University. Since 1993 he has taught as professor of religious studies at Franklin & Marshall College. He is the author of *Metaphysics and Morals in Marius Victorinus' Commentary* *on the Letter to the Ephesians* (Lang, 1995), *Augustine for Armchair Theologians* (Westminster John Knox, 2002), and *Marius Victorinus's Commentary on Paul's Letter to the Galatians* (Oxford University Press, 2005), and is coauthor with Theodore S. de Bruyn and David G. Hunter of *Ambrosiaster's Commentary on the Pauline Epistles: Romans* (SBL Press, 2017), with a second volume forthcoming. A volume of essays on Marius Victorinus, coedited with Václav Němec, will be published by SBL Press.

Theodore de Bruyn is professor of religious studies in the Department of Classics and Religious Studies at the University of Ottawa. He has published annotated English translations of the commentaries on Paul's Letter to the Romans by Ambrosiaster and Pelagius. He has studied aspects of the production of amulets in an increasingly Christian environment in late antique Egypt, leading to the publication of *Making Amulets Christian: Artefacts, Scribes, and Contexts* (Oxford University Press, 2017). He is currently investigating individual identity formation among Christians in Gaza in the sixth century as expressed in the correspondence of two monastic spiritual advisors, Barsanuphius and John.

Mark DelCogliano is associate professor of theology at the University of St. Thomas in St. Paul, Minnesota. From 2002 to 2004 he studied with Patout Burns at Vanderbilt University Divinity School. His research focuses on patristic doctrinal debates, theological developments, and scriptural exegesis in early and late antique Christianity. He recently edited *The Cambridge Edition of Early Christian Writings*, volumes 3 and 4, anthologies of christological texts from the first to the eighth century CE (Cambridge University Press, 2021).

Geoffrey D. Dunn is a fellow of the Australian Humanities Academy, an associate professor at the John Paul II Catholic University of Lublin, Poland, and an honorary research associate in the Department of Ancient and Modern Languages and Culture, University of Pretoria, South Africa. In 2019 he was Thomas F. Martin St. Augustine Fellow at Villanova University. His research interests cover Roman North Africa (Tertullian, Cyprian, Optatus, Augustine) and fifth-century Roman bishops, with numerous authored and edited books and more than 140 book chapters and journal articles.

John Peter Kenney is professor emeritus of religious studies at Saint Michael's College. He was previously professor of religion and humanities at Reed College and then dean of the College at Saint Michael's. He is the author of *Mystical*

Monotheism: A Study in Ancient Platonic Theology (Brown University Press, 1991), *The Mysticism of Saint Augustine: Rereading the "Confessions"* (Routledge, 2005), *Contemplation and Classical Christianity: A Study in Augustine* (Oxford University Press, 2013), and *On God, the Soul, Evil, and the Rise of Christianity* (Bloomsbury, 2018), and coeditor of *Christian Platonism: A History* (Cambridge University Press, 2021).

Brian Matz is the CSJ Endowed Chair and Professor of the History of Christianity at Fontbonne University in Saint Louis, Missouri. He earned a PhD in patristics from Saint Louis University in 2005 and a PhD in ethics from Katholieke Universiteit Leuven in 2009. His research interests include Cappadocian theology, early Christian social ethics, and the reception of patristic literature in the Carolingian era. He is the author or editor of six books, including *Patristic Social Thought and Catholic Social Thought* (University of Notre Dame Press, 2014), *Grace for Grace* (Catholic University of America Press, 2014), and *Gregory of Nazianzus* (Baker Academic, 2016). He is currently preparing a volume on Matthew 13–18 for the Novum Testamentum Patristicum series.

Andrew McGowan is dean of the Berkeley Divinity School at Yale and McFaddin Professor of Anglican Studies at Yale Divinity School. His scholarly work focuses on the life of early Christian communities, with particular focus on food, meals, and ritual, as well as on contemporary Anglicanism. His books include *Ascetic Eucharists* (Oxford University Press, 1999), *Ancient Christian Worship* (Baker Academic, 2014), and *Ancient and Modern* (Wipf & Stock, 2015). He is currently working on how early Christian and other ancient Mediterranean groups used, changed, and created notions of sacrifice.

William Tabbernee was president and Stephen J. England Distinguished Professor of the History of Christianity at Phillips Theological Seminary in Tulsa, Oklahoma, until his retirement. Most recently he has taught in the Department of Religious Studies of the University of Oklahoma. He is a fellow of the Melbourne College of Divinity and a past president of the North American Patristics Society. His scholarship focuses on the history, archaeology, and epigraphy of Christianity in Asia Minor and North Africa. His latest publication is *Early Christianity in Contexts: An Exploration across Cultures and Continents* (Baker Academic, 2014).

Joseph W. Trigg received his doctorate in 1978 from the University of Chicago Divinity School, where he studied under Robert M. Grant. He is now retired and living in Louisville, Kentucky, after serving as pastor of Episcopal churches in Kentucky, Virginia, and Maryland. He has written extensively on Origen and early biblical interpretation, including the article on Origen in *Augustine through the Ages* (Eerdmans, 1999). He recently translated the newly discovered *Homilies on the Psalms* by Origen for The Fathers of the Church (Catholic University of America Press, 2020) and is currently working with Patout Burns on a new edition of *Theological Anthropology* (Fortress, forthcoming).

Dennis Trout is professor of ancient Mediterranean studies at the University of Missouri–Columbia. He received his PhD from Duke University and taught at Tufts University before relocating to Missouri. He is the author of *Paulinus of Nola: Life, Letters, and Poems* (University of California Press, 1999), *Damasus of Rome: The Epigraphic Poetry* (Oxford University Press, 2015), and coauthor with Virginia Burrus and Marco Conti of *The Lives of Saint Constantina* (Oxford University Press, 2020). He remains at work on *Monumental Verse*, a study of the epigraphic poetry of late ancient Rome.

James Wetzel holds the Augustinian Chair in the Thought of Saint Augustine at Villanova, where he also teaches philosophy and directs the Augustinian Institute. He is broadly interested in the late antique transmission of Platonism, especially in Plotinus and Augustine, and in the implications of this tradition for philosophical conceptions of body, soul, and spirit. More simply, his focus has been on the persistence of spirit in an imperfect world. His major publications include *Augustine and the Limits of Virtue* (Cambridge University Press, 1992), *Augustine: A Guide for the Perplexed* (Continuum, 2010), and *Parting Knowledge: Essays after Augustine* (Cascade, 2013).

441

Index of Authors

Index of Subjects

Index of Scripture
and Other Ancient Sources

148	51, 52	241.4–5	175n	280–82	41
159.1	95	241.5–6	169n	280.1	79, 79n, 96
159.8	95	241.7	153n, 169n, 170n	280.4	96
159A.6	94	241.8	170n	280.6	93
159A.11	79	242	170–72, 174	281	79
169.15	95	242.1–3	171n	281.1	96
176.1	36	242.5	171n	281.2	96
185	47	242A.1	171n	282	79, 81n
189	47n	242A.3	170n	282.2	79n
195	47	247	50–51	282auct.6(3)	97n
196.A	47	252	48n	283augm.	73–74
197–98A	47	252.5	114n	283augm.1	74n, 94
198.9	95	257	51	283augm.2–3	73
198.12	95	258	52	283augm.3	73n, 94
198.46	95	259	52	283augm.4	74n, 94, 98n
205–7	47	259.2	115n	284	85
218–18C	49	260	51	284.2	85n
223A	49n	260D	52	284.3	94
225	50	260E	52	284.6	85n, 94n
226	50	272	50n	285.1	94
227.1	38	272B	52	286	44
229.5	84n	272B.2	75	286.2	87, 96
229.6	84n	273	41	286.4–5	90n
229.8–10	84n	273.1	93	286.7	94
229A.3	34	273.2	75n	295–99C	88
229H.3	94	273.3	41n	295.8	95
229J.3	95	273.6	96	299A.1	94
232	48, 49, 50–51	273.7	95	299A.7	93
235	50–51	274–77A	41	299D	78
235.1	51	275.1–2	96	299D.5	94
239	50–51	276	40	299E	78
240	167–68	276.1	93	299E.1	96
240–42	153, 167–72, 173	276.6	76n	299E.2	78
240.1	167n	277	40, 50, 73n	299F	78
240.4–5	168n	277A	40	299F.4	94n
241	162n, 168–70, 175	277A.2	94	300–301A	41
241.1–3	168n	280	79	300.1–3	88

300.6	41, 88	315.1	38, 74	359B.5	82
302	41n	317.1	92	359B.12	94
302–5	89	317.6	92	359B.13	76n
302.1	41n	318.1–2	92n	359B.15	96
302.7	94	318.2	94	359B.17	95
302.8	89n	319	44	359B.20	76n
302.12	95	320–24	44	359B.23	94
303	42n	321–24	92	362	87
305A	42n, 82, 89	322	44	370	46, 47
305A.2	96	323.4	92	378	52
306	87	325	86	380.8	88
306.2	95	325.1	86, 94n	382.3	39
306A	87	325.2	95	394	79
306B	87	326	86	394.1	94
306C	87	326.1	86n	397.4	94
306C.1	87	327.1	95		
306E	87	327.2	95		

Soliloquies (sol.)

1.3	304n
2.14.26	296n
2.15.29	222n

Basil

Homilia de ieiunio I
269–70, 275

3–4	262n

Homilia exhortatoria ad sanctum baptisma 267, 269–70, 279–80

2	262n, 267n

Cyprian

De catholicae ecclesiae unitate

5	107n

308A	82
309	82, 84
309.1	84n
310	81, 82
311	82
311.1	83n
311.6	82n
312	82
313A	82
313B	82
313C	82
313D	82
313D.1	39n
313E	82
313E.1	83n
313E.2	83n
313E.5	83, 94
313E.7	83, 84
313F	82
313G.3	82, 86, 87, 96n

328.2	94
328.8	94
335.1	94
335.2	95
335A.3	95
335B.5	84n
335D.3	94
335E	87
335H.2	95
341	35
345.7	94
348A.1	84n
348A.8	84n
348A.9	84n
348A.13	84n
351.11	94n
352	36
354.5	87
356.10	86
359B.4–8	94